QUEBEC'S EASTERN TOWNSHIPS *and the* WORLD

QUEBEC'S EASTERN TOWNSHIPS AND THE WORLD

A Region and Its Global Connections

EDITED BY

CHERYL GOSSELIN, ANDREW C. HOLMAN,
and CHRISTOPHER KIRKEY

McGill-Queen's University Press
Montreal & Kingston | London | Chicago

ISBN 978-0-2280-2358-6 (paper)
ISBN 978-0-2280-2359-3 (ePDF)
ISBN 978-0-2280-2360-9 (ePUB)

Legal deposit fourth quarter 2024
Bibliothèque nationale du Québec

Printed in Canada on acid-free paper that is 100% ancient forest free (100% post-consumer recycled), processed chlorine free

This book has been published with the help of a grant from the Federation for the Humanities and Social Sciences, through the Awards to Scholarly Publications Program, using funds provided by the Social Sciences and Humanities Research Council of Canada. Funding was also received from the United States Department of Education Title VI National Resource Centers Program and the Quebec Ministry of International Relations and La Francophonie, United States Division.

Canada

We acknowledge the support of the Canada Council for the Arts.
Nous remercions le Conseil des arts du Canada de son soutien.

McGill-Queen's University Press in Montreal is on land which long served as a site of meeting and exchange amongst Indigenous Peoples, including the Haudenosaunee and Anishinabeg nations. In Kingston it is situated on the territory of the Haudenosaunee and Anishinaabek. We acknowledge and thank the diverse Indigenous Peoples whose footsteps have marked these territories on which peoples of the world now gather.

LIBRARY AND ARCHIVES CANADA CATALOGUING IN PUBLICATION

Title: Quebec's Eastern Townships and the world : a region and its global connections / edited by Cheryl Gosselin, Andrew C. Holman, and Christopher Kirkey.
Names: Gosselin, Cheryl, editor | Holman, Andrew C. (Andrew Carl), 1965– editor | Kirkey, Christopher John, 1962–
Description: Includes bibliographical references and index.
Identifiers: Canadiana (print) 20240420349 | Canadiana (ebook) 20240420403 | ISBN 9780228023586 (paper) | ISBN 9780228023609 (ePUB) | ISBN 9780228023593 (ePDF)
Subjects: LCSH: Regionalism—Québec (Province)—Eastern Townships—History. | LCSH: Globalization—Québec (Province)—Eastern Townships—History. | LCSH: Eastern Townships (Québec)—History.
Classification: LCC FC2943.5 .Q43 2025 | DDC 971.4/6—dc23

This book was designed and typeset by Lara Minja in Adobe Jenson Pro 11/14.5pt.
Copyediting by Shelagh Plunkett.

This book is dedicated to the memory of
Dr Robert Jarrett Rudy (1970–2020):
Gentleman, Scholar, Friend

Contents

Part Two

Part Three

Part Four

— TABLES *and* FIGURES —

TABLES

FIGURES

— FOREWORD —

FOR ME, ONE OF THE MOST POSITIVE repercussions of the Quebec government's 1995 referendum on independence was that some residential real estate prices went down. That is what made it possible for my wife and me to purchase a home in the Eastern Townships on a lake that straddles the Canada–US border. For more than a decade, we slowly got to know the Eastern Townships on weekends and on holidays, until 2008 when I was named the principal of Bishop's University in the Lennoxville Borough of Sherbrooke and we became full-time residents of the Townships.

Bishop's was established in 1843 by Anglican settlers from England and the United States on the traditional territory of the Abenaki Nation. It has evolved into a public, non-sectarian university with students from across Canada, the United States, and more than sixty other countries. So, I got to see every day how the world was present on our campus and in our community. Sometimes it was sad. For example, after the terrorist attacks in Paris in 2015, sixty students from France came to our home for dinner. In 2022, the community came together to express support for our Ukrainian students and staff after the Russian invasion of their homeland. Often it was positive. For example, every year we sent students to the Model United Nations in New York or to work with refugee and migrant children from Myanmar (Burma) in Thailand. And every year we sponsored refugees to study at Bishop's. And sometimes it was humorous. At the beginning of each academic year, I met the first-year students in an assembly and would ask them to identify which country they were from. In response to my asking if anyone was from Central America, one young woman put up her hand and responded that she was from Denver, Colorado! (She turned out to be an outstanding student and we often laughed about this.)

Having grown up in Montreal, I had often been told that relations between English- and French-speaking Quebecers were more respectful and mutually supportive in the Townships than in the metropolis. There was certainly more of a shared sense of community. One illustration of that was that the recteur of the Université de Sherbrooke and the principal of Bishop's University sat on each other's board. This was rare, if not unique, in Canada. The fact that the chief of the Abenaki of Odanak was on our Advisory Committee, and that an emerging

Abenaki leader was on our board, spoke to the respectful relationships we were able to nurture. I suspect that the depth and quality of these mutually supportive relationships find their roots in the global histories of these communities. It has allowed the Eastern Townships to be more open to difference and to people of diverse histories and traditions.

One of the most eloquent expressions of that solidarity manifested itself in the fall of 2023, after I had concluded my time as principal of Bishop's. The Quebec government had announced its intention to double tuition fees for Canadian students from other provinces and territories. As approximately one-third of Bishop's students would be affected, this represented an existential threat to the university. The newly appointed principal of Bishop's, Sebastien Lebel-Grenier, called upon the Eastern Townships community to rally to the university's support. And it did. On 31 October 2023, more than one hundred primarily francophone leaders of the Eastern Townships came together on the Bishop's campus to call upon the Quebec government to exempt Bishop's from the proposed policy. They were successful.

This did not happen in Montreal. But it happened in the Townships because it was framed as a community issue and not a language issue. On that day the Eastern Townships, inspired by the lessons and values of its distinctive history and identity, provided an example to Quebec, Canada, and the world of mutual respect and solidarity. The essays in this fascinating volume all help us to understand the global influences that have shaped this unique corner of Canada and to appreciate how it has impacted the world beyond its borders. *Quebec's Eastern Townships and the World: A Region and Its Global Connections* is full of fascinating information and compelling insights. It is essential reading.

Michael Goldbloom, CM, was principal and vice-chancellor of Bishop's University from 2008 to 2023. He is the chair of the board of CBC/Radio-Canada.

— ACKNOWLEDGMENTS —

THIS BOOK WOULD NOT HAVE BEEN POSSIBLE without the invaluable assistance and contributions of many individuals, funding sources, and institutions of higher education. Fabian Will, the former executive director of the Eastern Townships Resource Centre (ETRC) at Bishop's University, graciously served as administrative assistant to the editorial team from the inception of the project. Regularly communicating with all contributors, he made certain that our authors' workshop, convened in November 2021, was a success and that various editions of the chapters that comprise this volume moved forward in the editorial review process. Jody Robinson, Fabian's successor at the ETRC, was especially helpful in locating images, permissions, and archival documents that are foundational to this publication. Her positive disposition and ability to quickly address our many requests is greatly appreciated. We wish to also express our thanks to Dr Erin Hurley, McGill University, who took the first several steps with us in conceiving and bringing to life this project. Our appreciation is also extended to Jonathan Crago of McGill-Queen's University Press for believing in and supporting this project. To the anonymous reviewers of McGill-Queen's University Press who offered terrific insights and constructive suggestions on the draft version of our manuscript, we extend our appreciation. The index was prepared by Judy Dunlop. Finally, we of course wish to extend our deepest gratitude to our fellow contributors, who patiently worked (and stuck) with us through the COVID-19 pandemic to produce original, compelling scholarship on the Eastern Townships of Quebec.

For Christopher Kirkey, the realization of this book is, from both professional and personal perspectives, a singular milestone. Having served as a member of the board of directors of ETRC for more than twenty years, acting as editor-in-chief (with Cheryl Gosselin) of the *Journal of Eastern Townships*, and having watched two sons enroll at, embrace, and successfully complete their undergraduate studies at Bishop's, it only seems logical that at some point he would turn his attention to championing a volume on the Eastern Townships. Indeed, it was the absence of a comprehensive, multidisciplinary book on the region that prompted Chris, in conjunction with his co-editors, to issue invitations and a call for papers. The previously mentioned authors' workshop, held at Bishop's, provided a welcome environment for contributors to present their initial works and receive important evaluative commentary. The realization of this work would not have been possible without the enthusiastic support and funding provided by the State University of New York, Plattsburgh, the Quebec Ministry of International Relations and La Francophonie, and the United States Department of Education, National Resource Center Title VI program. To Andy and Cheryl, thank you so much for your generosity of spirit, your willingness to join me on this scholarly adventure, and for all the hard work you did in producing a wonderful book. For Chris, the smile, warmth, and caring of a young man, family friend, and Bishop's student named Tuan Luu – whose life tragically ended on 22 January 2017 – provided the needed perseverance to complete this project.

Cheryl Gosselin wishes to extend her utmost appreciation to Christopher and Andrew for their collegiality, professionalism, and friendship throughout the editing and writing processes. As a longtime member of the ETRC board of directors, it is a pleasure to work alongside such giving and dedicated people like Christopher as co-editor of *JETS*, Fabian, and now Jody at the helm of the centre and finally, Andrew with his superb editing skills and love of anything sports. Her thirty plus years of teaching at Bishop's University has been so rewarding because of these remarkable people. In addition to her teaching and passion for the ETRC, Cheryl would also like to mention her advocacy work in the English-speaking community of the Estrie region through the Townshippers' Association, of which she is a member of the board of directors. Lastly, Cheryl wishes to acknowledge her maternal grandmother, Helen, who came to this beautiful part of the world from Scotland in 1920 at the age of twenty, and to everyone who calls the Eastern Townships home and contributes to its history, culture, and identity.

Andrew Holman expresses gratitude to his co-editors and fellow contributors, to his friends and colleagues at McGill-Queen's University Press, to the faculty and student members of the Canadian Studies Program at Bridgewater State University, and to the Center for the Advancement of Research and Scholarship at Bridgewater State for financial support in the form of a summer grant, which allowed him to participate in this project.

QUEBEC'S EASTERN TOWNSHIPS *and the* **WORLD**

Introduction

The Eastern Townships: A Region and Its World

Andrew C. Holman, Cheryl Gosselin, and Christopher Kirkey

A LITTLE MORE THAN A CENTURY AGO, two overlapping events took place that produced enduring images about Quebec's Eastern Townships. The first event was the sensational extradition proceeding of Harry K. Thaw, a millionaire railway scion and fugitive from American justice who had recently escaped imprisonment in New York state's Matteawan Asylum for the Criminally Insane and had been transported across the international border near Coaticook. He was arrested there by local police on 19 August 1913, and detained in the Sherbrooke jail. He remained in Canada for a little more than three weeks before being secretly returned to the US. Thaw was a notorious figure in America society; in June 1906, he had murdered prominent New York City architect and socialite Stanford White in the rooftop theatre at Madison Square Garden in front of hundreds of witnesses – revenge, he claimed, for White's drugging and raping of Thaw's wife, the young model and actress Evelyn Nesbit.[1] Thaw's guilt was never in doubt, but his situation garnered considerable sympathy from a society that still revered chivalric honour and felt him justified. Backed by family money and with the assistance of friends, he walked away from Matteawan on 17 August, jumped into a chauffeur-driven car, and rode to freedom (or so he thought) in Canada.[2]

Thaw's stay in Sherbrooke was bizarre – in part because the case took longer than necessary to play out – but it was also telling. After his capture in Coaticook, his lawyers filed a writ of *habeas corpus*, claiming illegal arrest, but following a two-week stay in prison, the presiding judge ruled it out of order. A second *habeas corpus* writ (filed by advocates for New York State) earned a similar fate. Writs exhausted, Thaw was released by the jail but then immediately captured by Canadian immigration officials and returned to detention in the department's depot in Coaticook. Following an Immigration Board of Enquiry proceeding, and against his loud protest, Thaw was forcibly deported across the Vermont border on 10 September.[3]

News of his capture drew dozens of reporters and photographers from across eastern Canada and the US and resulted in what can be considered the Eastern Townships' first-ever media frenzy. Indeed, it was a *circus*. Though media access was granted to Thaw, he wouldn't talk about his escape, and so reporters' stories turned to other things: the antics of New York State special envoy William Travers Jerome, dispatched to argue for the prisoner's return to state custody; the inscrutable complexity of Canadian judicial procedure; and the strange, enthusiastic sympathy that Townships residents demonstrated in support of Thaw and his pursuit of asylum. Crowds greeted Thaw warmly every time he made even the most fleeting appearance in public – while being transferred to and from jail, in court, and even when he was taken for a haircut. Three local women from prominent families took flowers to him in prison; the *St Louis Post-Dispatch* reported that a gawking crowd once greeted him with "Three cheers for Harry Thaw" (*Akron Beacon Journal* 1913; *St Louis Post-Dispatch* 1913). When he was, at last, spirited out of Canada by Immigration Department agents, local residents were exasperated: "this is a piece of work worthy of the Czar of Russia" (*Sherbrooke Daily Record* 1913b).

In all of this, the press saw an interesting sideshow.[4] "Why did Canada make an idol of a man like Harry Thaw?" the editor of *The Ohio Law Bulletin* wondered in mid-October 1913. His answer was twofold: the irresistible appeal of limelight to a parochial people and an ignorant claim of legal superiority. "[L]ittle children who did not understand a word of English ran by his carriage yelping French hurrahs for 'British fair play' while their elders shouted it from the sidewalks in broken English" (*Ohio Law Bulletin* 1913, 393).[5] In this account, broken English stood as a metaphor for the rusticity of the region – an out-of-the-way hinterland whose presence came to light only by the accident of a fugitive landing there. "Sherbrooke, Quebec," the *Boston Record* asserted in 1914, "was unheard of until Harry Thaw was captured there on his flight from Matteawan" (*Boston Record* 1914).

At the same time, across town in Sherbrooke, the region's economic leaders were staging a less mercurial but equally revealing event, the 29th Annual Exhibition of the Eastern Townships Agricultural Association (ETAA). Founded in 1884, the festival of "industry, science, art, and entertainment" had become by 1913 a massive undertaking. At the core of the fair were the myriad farmers' exhibits and competitions for quality in livestock and crops: more than 600 cattle and 500 horses, and in the "poultry department," the *Sherbrooke Daily Record* reported, "more than eighteen hundred birds" (*Sherbrooke Daily Record* 1913a). These, along with sheep and swine, maple and apiary products, butter, fruit, garden vegetables, "ladies' work," children's crafts, and industrial exhibits (including those by Penman's and Dominion textiles, a variety of metalwork firms, Imperial Tobacco, and the Grand Trunk Railway), commanded judges' and spectators' rapt attention over the course of a week. Exhibits were housed in the ETAA grounds' main building and new cattle sheds, plus several specially constructed temporary ones spread across the fair's fenced sixty-five acres. Grafted on to this core were a wide variety of non-agricultural features that reflected the interests and passions of the region's residents: daily horse and trotter races, trapeze and wire-walking shows, balloon and parachute feats, nightly fireworks, regimental band concerts, and speeches delivered by federal and provincial politicians. From its earliest days, the fair acted as a lightning rod, a ritual that brought together the area's francophone and anglophone producers in an annual reckoning of the region's abundance. In 1913, paid attendees (at 25 cents each) numbered almost 50,000, the largest attendance the exhibition had ever enjoyed.[6]

The timing of the Thaw scandal was fortuitous for the event's organizers: in the week leading up to Thaw's deportation, Sherbrooke was teeming with visitors who must have seen the scandal as yet another feature among the fair's rich offerings.[7] Beyond the Thaw drama, the ETAA exhibition had for some time been well known outside the region as something more than a quaint local festival. By 1905, it had begun to be promoted in the national press as Canada's Great Eastern Exhibition. In 1908, the United States Trade Consul produced a news release printed widely in the US press that championed the fair and especially the many American companies, chiefly from New England, who would be exhibiting their wares: asbestos- and copper-mining machinery, automobiles, boots and shoes, farm implements and musical instruments (*Buffalo Evening News* 1908). In 1913, the fair became even more an extra-local spectacle. Press notices for the event were printed in newspapers as far afield as Tuscaloosa, AL, Miami, FL, Asheville, NC, and Brooklyn, NY. Farmers from Ontario, Vermont, and New Hampshire transported their livestock to Sherbrooke to be judged alongside their counterparts from farms in the Townships and other parts of rural Quebec. American industrialists were there, too, among them Moline, Illinois's John Deere Company, which showcased its threshers and gasoline-powered tractors, and the Channell

Chemical Company of Chicago. But spectators, too, came from outside the region and some of them, like the British Consul stationed at Portland, Maine, from long distances. Thursday, 4 September, was designated "American Visitors' Day" when more than 16,000 people passed through the turnstiles. As the *Boston Globe* had it, the fair prompted a "rush over the border to Sherbrooke" (*Boston Globe* 1913).

Provincial/cosmopolitan, backward/progressive, local/international, "unheard of"/connected to the world: the images generated by these contemporary events reveal a good deal about the Eastern Townships – the ways in which it was regarded then, and now, both among scholars and in the popular imaginary. In popular discourse today, the Townships are often celebrated for their quaint and remote nature: "playground" to sprawling and bustling Montreal, an appendage to stately Quebec City, an abutment to the northern marches of the American colossus. But a closer look reveals that, in many ways, the Eastern Townships has long had its own gravity, its own sense of being. Hardly insular, this region has long been outward-looking, a central meeting place shaped by its many engagements with the world beyond its borders. The chapters in this volume explore that fact by examining a wide variety of key themes and critical episodes in the Townships' past and present. Together they open a new chapter in the scholarly study of Quebec's distinctive regions, a rich field of inquiry once labelled cleverly by historian Fernand Harvey as *la question régionale* (Harvey 1980). Together, they provide a new focus for regional studies in Quebec. They build on the work of local historians, economists, geographers, and literary scholars who originally conceived of and contributed to the construction of regional identities in Quebec, and on the work of the Chantier des histoires régionales, the locus and motor of the twenty-four regional studies undertaken by the Institut national de recherche scientifique (1980–2003). This volume takes that work further, examining some of the ways in which globalization (more precisely, local/extra-local exchange in people, goods, and ideas) has shaped the formation and maintenance of regional identity. It offers new perspectives on the Eastern Townships as a centre, a borderland, a bridge (or *lieu de passage*) between nations, communities, and peoples, a site for discursive and performative creativity, and a gateway between markets, as well as a market itself.

LOCATING *the* EASTERN TOWNSHIPS

"Il est quasi-impossible," Harvey has written, "de tracer des frontières précises entre les régions au Québec" (1980, 74). This broad assertion rings true for the Eastern Townships, whose physical space is often described in popular media in imprecise, sweeping terms. The *Canadian Encyclopedia*, for example, locates the region "in the Appalachian hills of south-central Quebec, between Montreal and Quebec City, [extending] from Granby to Lac Mégantic and from Drummondville to the US border" (Mailhot and Dubois 2006). This vagueness is explained in part by the region's incremental history. The boundaries of Quebec's Eastern Townships have never been fully fixed or uncontested.[8] Products of white settler colonization, the boundaries were created (and reformed) to meet the administrative needs of a modernizing nation-state to control the movement of populations into and within its domain.

The Townships comprise a fraction of Ndakina, the huge, traditional territory of the W8banakiak, which stretches from the eastern seaboard of the Atlantic Ocean south of the St Lawrence River westward to the Richelieu River, northward to the Gaspé Peninsula, a place where Abenaki people have lived, hunted, and fished from time immemorial. In the first few decades of the 1600s, they were pinched increasingly by encroaching French claims along the St Lawrence and English settlements in New England along the eastern seaboard and up the Connecticut River to the southeast and southwest. By the late seventeenth century, some Abenaki had been Christianized by French missionaries and resettled at Odanak on the St Francis River; others sided with the French for strategic reasons over the several Anglo–French wars, 1689–1760. They paid dearly for their alliance with the French. In 1759, as British fortunes in the Seven Years' War rose, Odanak was attacked and razed by the New Hampshire–based infantry unit Rogers's Rangers, who sought revenge for Abenaki raids on British settlements earlier in the century (Treyvaud and Plourde 2017, 50; Day 1981, 42).

The drawing of administrative boundaries in the Eastern Townships was first enabled in 1792, less than a decade after the Treaty of Paris fixed Quebec's southeastern boundary with the new United States. At that time, it had become apparent to the newly established lieutenant governor of Lower Canada Alured Clarke that the trickle of American immigrants – refugees from the Revolutionary War – that had created squatter farmsteads in the border area near Missisquoi Bay might become a stream. Clarke invited appeals for land use, initially the "leader and associates system," in which a group leader petitioned for the grant of a township on behalf of his constituents, who would themselves receive individual freehold land grants, with most lots 200 acres in size. The result was a slow but generally orderly process of settlement that permitted, essentially, the extension of the Vermont and New Hampshire settlement frontier into Lower Canada.[9] The first of ninety-five townships granted and settled was Dunham (1796), followed by Potton, Bolton, and Brome (all in 1797). Referred to initially as Buckinghamshire, the region had become known by 1806 as the Eastern Townships, a name given to distinguish it from the "Western Townships" settlement in Upper Canada. By 1833, it was being referred to in French as the "Townships de l'Est" – and, more regularly, "Cantons de l'Est" by 1858 (Farfan 2023). As population rose, and the number of townships increased, the region was organized by colonial (and later provincial) governments into larger units of administration: first districts, then counties, which fit the settlement pattern imperfectly and confused contemporaries' understandings of the region's reach. Tellingly, though nineteenth-century maps agree that the region's southern and easternmost settlements comprise the core of the Eastern Townships, they are much less consistent on where its western and northern borders lie. Parts of Nicolet, Yamaska, and Beauce counties were sometimes in, sometimes not; the easternmost part of Bagot County was sometimes in, its west was out (figure I.1). More recently, in 1981, when the government of Quebec reorganized its local administrative units into six districts, it created "Estrie," a region that covers only about half of the Townships' traditional territory (figure I.2). Championed as early as the 1940s by Monseigneur Maurice O'Bready, a priest-historian at the Séminaire de Sherbooke, this *régionyme* took on political meaning during the 1960s and 1970s: Cantons de l'Est was a "dénomination calquée de l'anglais"; l'Estrie captured francophone Quebecers' broader efforts toward liberation from anglophone authority during the Quiet Revolution (Martin 2022).[10] The result, today, is a mixed nomenclature: government administration in the region uses Estrie, but many in private enterprise (including the large tourism sector) and academics continue their use of Cantons de l'Est/Eastern Townships.[11]

Topynyms aside, uncertain boundaries have made it difficult for scholars and others to determine reliable population estimates for the region over time. The general pattern that comes from available statistics is one of modest and steady growth. In 1819, a little more than twenty years after the first townships were granted, 26,916 settlers lived in the Townships. That number had risen to 62,068 in 1844, 93,851 in 1852, and to about 183,000 by 1887. About 279,000 lived in the Townships in 1930, a number remarkably close to the figure reported for Estrie in the 1996 census (278,774). The 2021 Canadian census reports the region's population at 337,701, more than half (172,950) of whom live in the city of Sherbrooke.[12] But this overall pattern masks the most important demographic change in the region's history: the so-called francophone invasion, or *francisation*, of the Eastern Townships. An almost wholly English-speaking colony in the early nineteenth century, the Townships' growth until the middle of the century resulted from its first two waves of settlement: American Loyalists and late Loyalists who settled in the southern and central townships from the 1790s to the 1810s, followed by thousands of English, Scots, and Irish in the 1830s to 1850s, encouraged, in part,

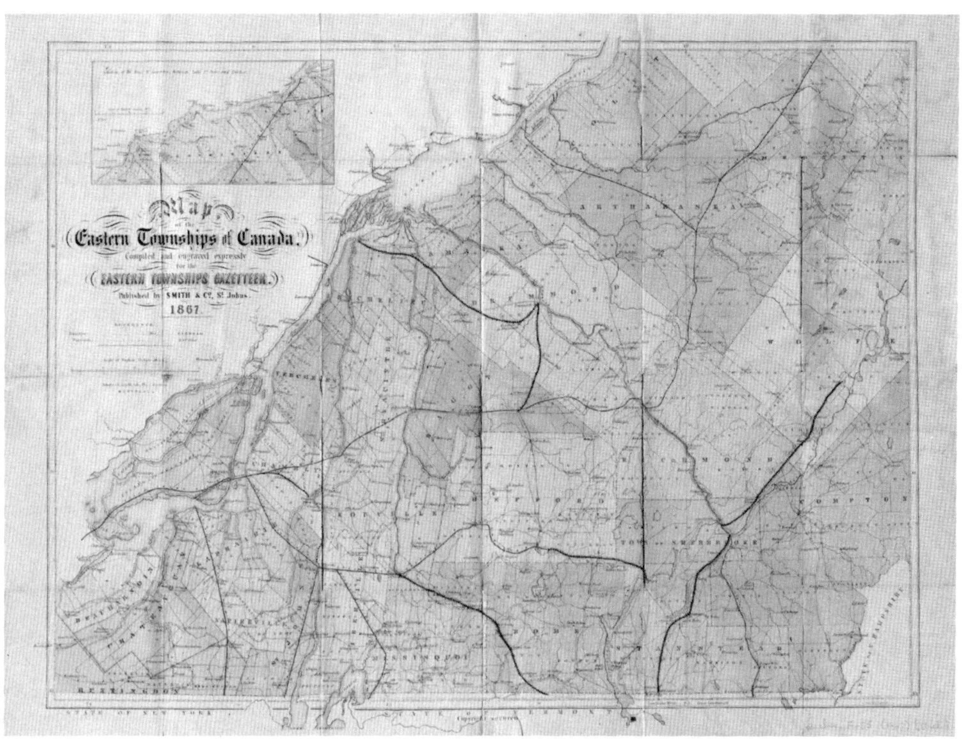

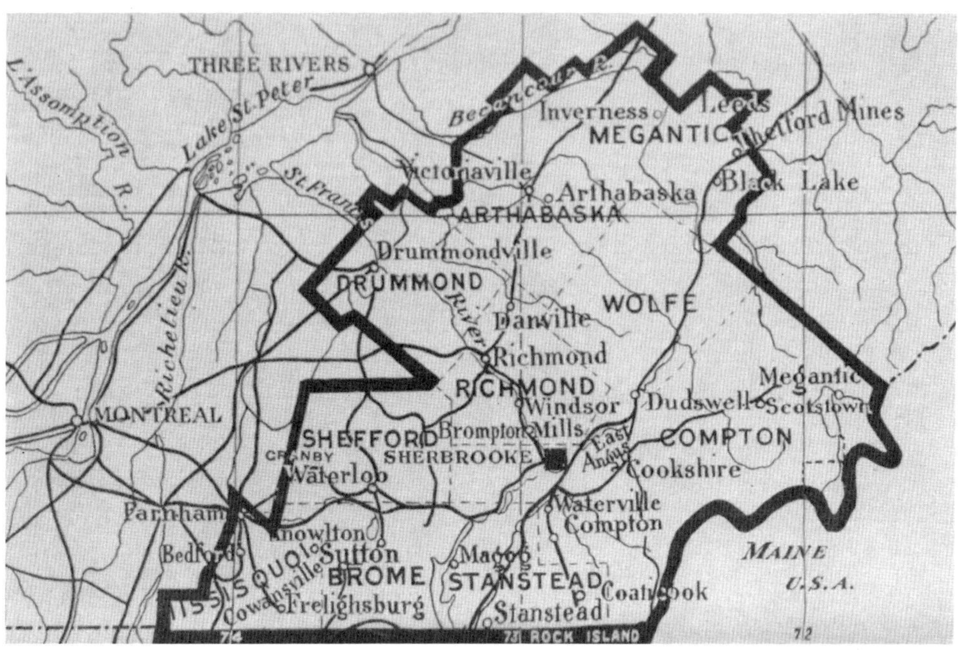

Figure I.1 The Eastern Townships depicted: 1867 and 1917

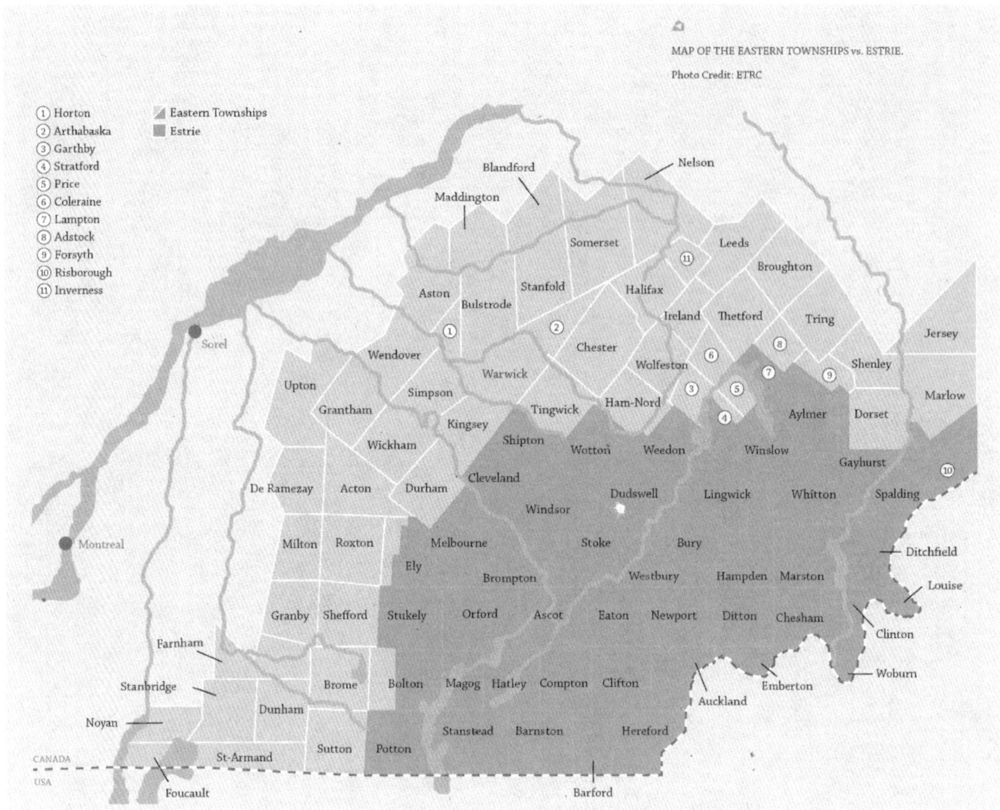

Figure I.2 The Eastern Townships and Estrie compared

by the efforts of the British American Land Company. However, beginning in the 1840s, a sizeable in-flow of *Canadiens*, many responding to the Catholic Church's *colonisation* campaigns, soon surpassed anglophone population and made the Townships a majority French-speaking region as early as the 1860s. By 1901, the Townships population was 72 per cent francophone, a figure that grew steadily, aided by waves of anglophone outmigration in the 1920s and 1930s and again in the 1970s. As of 2021, more than 91 per cent of Estrie's residents cited French as their first language.[13]

Together, French and English residents have constructed a mixed economy in this southeastern corner of Quebec. Farming was its initial and principal cornerstone through the nineteenth and twentieth centuries: dairying, livestock raising, and maple sugaring have been among the most enduring and productive activities. Clearing forests gave rise to a lasting lumber industry. In 1853, the construction of the Grand Trunk Railway connecting Montreal and Portland, Maine opened up the Townships to both extensive resource extraction for export and local industrial development. The first of these involved copper mining in the 1850s, which was abundant in many parts of the Townships. Asbestos mining took off in 1877 in Thetford Mines and Val-des-Sources (formerly Asbestos) and thrived for more than a century, as did granite mining in the early twentieth century. Small- and large-scale industry took root along the fast-moving St Francis River, and especially in Sherbrooke, which became a manufacturing hub first for saw- and flour-milling, and later in the nineteenth century for textile production, foundry work, and pulp and paper plants. Today, Sherbrooke sits as the region's metropolis, a medium-sized city in a hinterland of "petites villes" (like Granby, Drummondville, Victoriaville, and Magog) and picturesque rural countryside. This latter feature (especially its rivers, lakes, and mountains) provides (as it has done since the mid-nineteenth century) the locus for a tourist industry that draws thousands of paddlers, hikers, cottagers, and skiers every year (Blanchard 1937; Morin et al. 1986; Mailhot and Dubois 2006).

WRITING *the* REGION

Created as a vehicle for political administration, the Eastern Townships has existed, perhaps most importantly, in the *minds* of Quebecers as a distinctive place. Beyond its governmental manifestations, it has also come into being and maintained its presence as a cognitive space through discourse – that is, in the ways in which people have labelled it and written about it over time. Like other regions in Quebec and Canada, the Townships is both a real place and an imagined space that has been penned into existence.

We can trace writing about the Townships into at least four discernible waves that coincide roughly with the periodization that Harvey has described for Quebec's regions as a whole. The first of these (c.1860–1920) includes what we can call the *colonization* literature of the late nineteenth and early twentieth centuries, which consists of two quite different types. One branch consists of the regional guidebooks and amateur local histories penned by anglophone residents in the years immediately prior to and following Confederation. Among these were Stanstead artist William S. Hunter's *Eastern Townships Scenery, Canada East* (1860), which combined a detailed description of the region's history, flora, fauna, geological properties and its towns and villages along with handsome illustrations of the region's natural beauty. Hunter hoped his work might have a practical effect and be "found interesting to the tourist and the man of business [and] induce readers at a distance to visit" (3). Sutton schoolmaster Cyrus Thomas's *Contributions to the History of the Eastern Townships* (1866) and Stukely writer Catherine Mathilda Day's *Pioneers of the Eastern Townships* (1863) are lengthy accounts, impressive for their detail on settlement history and local governance. Published four score years since the first Loyalist settlements, these were filiopietistic efforts that aimed to enshrine the accomplishments of "our forefathers" (iii). Day's 475-page *History of the Eastern Townships* (1869) was more ambitious, aligning the settlement of the Townships in a continuous chain of triumphs beginning with Columbus's discovery of America. Shot through with moral assessments, the latter of her two volumes is an effort to proclaim the heroic accomplishments of the region's earliest anglophone settlers at a time when there was, in her view, a great need for *national* histories to combat religious and sectarian strife.[14] That her work was published at the start of the French "reconquest" of the Townships seems no coincidence and connects these English-language works with a second branch of literature: French-language *colonisation* literature. While anglophone writers looked backward, francophone Catholic priests and the Quebec government peered forward, using these publications to promote a province-wide effort to settle available land with French Canadian Catholics – at once to entice young men who had ventured to New England mill towns to return to their homeland and to alleviate overcrowding in the oldest settlements along the St Lawrence. The earliest example in this literature was clerico-nationalist Jean Baptiste Chartier's 1871 pamphlet *La colonisation dans les Cantons de l'Est.* "Il y a dans les Cantons de l'Est," he wrote, "de l'espace pour les Canadiens des [É]tats-Unis, qui désirent revenir fouler le sol de la patrie, et pour tous les pères de familles dans les vieilles paroisses qui visent à établir leurs enfants" (7).[15] The rapid demographic change tells us that the campaign literature was successful and the francophone "reconquest" of the region was complete by the onset of World War I.

In the interwar years, a second flourish of writing about Quebec's regions emerged, many of these studies motivated by economic change and industrialization, pushing back against a nationalist ideology that prescribed agrarianism as the road to French Canadian cultural *survivance*. Among the most influential regionalists in these years was the Université de Montréal economist Esdras Minville, who championed regional development as an editor of *L'Actualité Économique* (1925–29) and who helped create in 1927 the regions-focused Conseil technique d'études économiques.[16] Some technical scientific writing on the Townships echoed this economic push,[17] but intraregional social relations remained an important vein to tap. If in the late nineteenth century writers focused on the separate experiences and agendas of anglophone and francophone communities, by the interwar years the Townships' distinctive binational *cooperation* in the face of demographic change was even more captivating. In 1937, renowned French geographer Raoul Blanchard focused one of his several exhaustive Quebec regional studies on the Eastern Townships, concluding that the reconquest of the region by francophones was no overt battle staged for control between English and French. It happened silently, amiably via "grandes forces naturelles"; that is, high francophone birth-rates and anglophone out-migration (Blanchard 1937, 194).[18] Ethnic harmony was emphasized in the historical work of prelate Monseigneur Albert Gravel; his impressive *Cantons de l'Est* (1939) retraced the region's Indigenous, Loyalist, and colonization phases in turn, arguing that this layered story created a unique type – the "Eastern Township Man" – "formé, paraît-il, de ce qu'il y a de meilleur chez l'Anglais, le Français et l'Américain" and based on "la mentalité de bonne entente" (Harvey 2001, 89).[19]

A third pod of regional writing grew in Quebec's 1950s, albeit one more narrow than the others. In these years, regional writing was shaped by concerns among Quebec leaders (economists, planners, politicians, and union leaders) about regional disparities, especially the ways in which the urban prosperity and industrial development in post-war Montreal elevated and empowered it over impoverished peripheries (Harvey 1980, 75–6). The problem engendered province-wide study and ushered in the centralized planning movement of the 1960s (notably in the Office de Planification et de Développement du Québec). In the Townships, which had by then left behind a simple extraction economy for a mixed economy, the problem was less dire than in other of the province's regions. Still, writing on how to map a future for regional development attracted local attention. Published by the provincial Ministry of Industry and Commerce, Michel Philiponneau's *L'Avenir économique et sociale des cantons de l'est* (1960) was written in this vein.

Finally, the Quiet Revolution of the 1960s spurred a fourth wave of writing – the most prolific and wide-ranging – about regions in Quebec. By the 1970s, Harvey writes, there was "un nouveau discours sur la region," one energized by new tensions that emerged between Quebec City and its administrative regions. In the Eastern Townships, a place where bonne entente had existed between anglophones and francophones for decades, the election of the Parti Québécois, the passage of Bill 101, and the failure of the Meech Lake and Charlottetown accords had local resonance for anglophone–francophone relations. In this context, (re)articulating regional identity posed a sharp contrast to the nationalist imperative. The flourish of regional writing took shape in a variety of fields but especially in literature and in the scholarly fields of geography and history. In literature, the existence of a field of Eastern Townships writing was asserted as early as the 1920s,[20] but its presence has reemerged forcefully since 2000, part of the "new regional literature" in Quebec observed in this volume by Ceri Morgan and evidenced in the monumental success of Louise Penny's Inspector Gamache novels, which are set in the fictional Townships community called Three Pines. Perhaps most influential in energizing this period of regional writing in Quebec has been the work of academic institutions, which house research groups, fund publications, and have helped entrench regional *thinking* (Harvey 1980, 77). In the 1980s, a team of local geographers at the Université de Sherbrooke picked up the torch lit by Blanchard, asking, "are the Eastern Townships still that idyllic area of Québec that Blanchard presented?" Their answer: *yes, sort of* (Morin et al. 1986, 249).[21] Even more conspicuous has been the "new" regional history, which took form in a variety of ways. In the early 1990s, the Eastern Townships Research Centre (ETRC) at Bishop's University, a robust regional archival facility that fosters local study via in-person and internet-accessible platforms, was established. In 1992, the ETRC (since retitled as the Eastern Townships Resource Centre) and Eastern Townships academics launched the *Journal of Eastern Townships Studies* (JETS)/*La Revue d'études des Cantons-de-l'Est* (RECE), a bilingual scholarly venue for work focusing specifically on the region that has now produced more than fifty volumes. Equally ambitious was the Groupe de recherche en histoire régionale, established in 1970s and headquartered at Université de Sherbrooke. It became part of the massive province-wide project, starting in 1980, to research, fund, and publish regional histories – a project completed in 2003. As in other regions, the Sherbrooke research team enlisted local support and expertise in its comprehensive study of the Townships' history. Led by the late Jean-Pierre Kesteman, the group authored working papers on the region leading up to the publication of its impressive *Histoire des Cantons de l'Est* (Kesteman et al. 1998; issued in abridged form in 2007). Tracing the region's demography, economy, industry, politics, and culture, *Histoire* remains the standard synthesis on Townships history. Finally, beyond institutions has come the work of individual scholars, experts on the region. Here, no single writer has contributed more to the understanding of Eastern Townships history and culture than J.I. Little, a Townships native and Simon Fraser University professor emeritus, of whose eight monographs and seventy-six articles and book chapters, most unearth and analyze aspects of the Townships' fascinating past.

THE LOCAL *and the* GLOBAL

The opening account of the overlapping events of Harry Thaw's stay in the Eastern Townships and Sherbrooke's annual agricultural fair illustrate the region's enduring presence as what Mary Louise Pratt calls a "contact zone" where people meet. The contact zone of the Eastern Townships is "a social space in which people and their cultural identities connect, share and, often disagree and struggle to contend with each other" (Pratt 1991, 34). Numerous world views and systems of meaning-making are transmitted through different languages and cultures, often within a context of uneven power relations. As Harry Thaw's adventures into the region combined with the international reputation of the Sherbrooke Fair demonstrate, the Eastern Townships area and its residents have never been insular. The result is a heterogeneous and open space where places and their meanings are made and remade depending on the mix of people in the region at any given time.

How then does one gauge how places like the Eastern Townships produce different identities that leave a mark on the region? The area has its own sense of place recognized by a local population, as any locality does, yet is open to regional, national, and global identities. Estrie, or Administrative Region #5, as it is called today, contains borders that are socially constructed in ongoing processes involving many different actors (Konrad and Brunet-Jailly 2019). These borders are both physically felt and imagined by the region's inhabitants depending on who they are: Indigenous Peoples, who have their own approaches to land and borders; the historical Eastern Townships that covers the 16,000 square kilometres understood by English-speaking settlers and their descendants today; the Cantons de l'Est recognized by early French settlers and now defined by Tourism Quebec and tourists as such; or a borderland between two countries used for trading goods and familiar to immigrants, seasonal migrants, and sojourners as a gateway to something new/better in their lives. Each view provides its own sense of belonging, and/or unbelonging, to the region. Each group perceives and encounters the area through the construction of place imaginaries constructed by state and local interests (Fraser 2018). Whether these imaginaries are of "a rustic, out-of-the-way hinterland" or see the Townships as "a centre, a borderland, a bridge," they define place in the Townships and shape the experiences of those who inhabit the region at any given time. What's more, the Eastern Townships is a space that is socially constructed by different identities depending on their class, gender, and ethnicity, as well as personal attributes such as community status (Konrad and Brunet-Jailly 2019). In turn, space shapes them through place imaginaries built by government officials, municipal stakeholders, urban planners, economic and community leaders, and ordinary citizens. These imaginaries are made and remade in continuous processes resulting in a multiscale sense of place to the region.

Helpful to understanding identities in the Eastern Townships are three concepts that run implicitly and explicitly throughout this volume: the local, the transcultural, and the transnational. A *local* lens pushes us to ask several essential first questions: who lives and lived there? What did they do? What were their experiences of the place? How did life in the Townships shape their opportunities and aspirations? As well, this lens allows us to see what contributions local people made to their communities and the ways they imagined and gave meaning to their senses of "place": unceded Indigenous territory, land of infinite natural resources, vast expanse of lakes and playgrounds for American cottagers, a treasure trove from the earth's bounty for enjoyment in the summer, snow and stillness in the winter, a gateway to US markets and, of course, a cultural hub where the historical French- and English-speaking populations mixed with newcomers from different immigrant groups.

In this local view, the Eastern Townships can be seen as what Manuel Castells (2020) calls a "space of places." In his view, the region is comprised of an urban hub connected to rural spaces that contain farmland, villages, cul-de-sacs, nature walks, bike paths, etc., each linked through the physical movement of pedestrians, roadways, and machines situated within the socially constructed imaginaries of local identities. And distances in these places have always been shaped by time – *how far* intraregional distances are is often measured by how long it takes to travel them. Thaw's own intraregional travels illustrate the point. Today, by car the distance between the rural setting of Coaticook and the centrally located, urban city of Sherbooke can be covered in about thirty minutes depending on traffic and weather conditions. In Thaw's day, it would have been more of an ordeal as he made the trek from where he was detained to Sherbrooke for his legal proceedings and back (perhaps with a surprise visit to the "Queen City's" agricultural fair).

A related concept by Castells (2020) is the characterization of a region as a "space of flows," which delineates how lived spaces today involve a nexus of movements of people, capital, and goods circulating in a computerized network of information technology. As a result of the digital age, Castells claims that the spaces we inhabit today are reimagined as a mixture of the traditional, physical community nodes where people live their daily lives and the global flows from telecommunications and transportation technologies. Our human actions and interactions now happen outside the ordered sequences of time and in spaces that are devoid of former binary structures of urban/rural, local/global. Spaces are more randomly arranged and exist in reimagined ways including hybrid, virtual, or cyberspace (Castells 2020). Thinking about immigrant settlement experiences, how local agricultural issues of sustainability incorporate global thinking and practices, the impact of global events like 9/11 on Townshippers' perception of the shared border with their neighbours to the south, and the influence of the internet to changes in religious affiliation all benefit from these ways of reframing space.

Finally, other useful concepts are transculturalism and transnationalism. The first of these is part of the contact zone and helps describe ongoing processes in which members of a marginal group select and invent from the culture transmitted by a dominant group (Pratt 1991). Transnationalism allows for the understanding of the routes people and their ideas take to simultaneously operate in social fields that cross geographical, political, spatial, and cultural borders (Man and Cohen 2015).[22] Studies of immigrant integration into the Eastern Townships, cross-border schooling initiatives, and educational opportunities in the region lend themselves superbly to analyses using these concepts.

In all of these ways, the spaces of the Eastern Townships and its identities are socially constructed along mutually dependent and interrelated local and global axes. At the local level people from various backgrounds, cultures, and languages meet, share ideas, live and work together, and on occasion clash. They do so in particular places that have both tangible and imagined aspects. Located in the traditional and unceded territory of the Abenaki people, the Eastern Townships also contains global flows of people, ideas, and technologies that continuously circulate in and through the region. Together, these forces make and remake a synergetic relationship between the spaces and flows of the Eastern Townships and the people who call it home, even when only for a short time.

THE TOWNSHIPS *and the* WORLD

Quebec's Eastern Townships and the World: A Region and Its Global Connections examines how the Eastern Townships are linked directly to larger, prevailing global forces and identities; it places the Eastern Townships at centre stage and its chapters, written by scholars from a wide array of disciplines, explore key aspects of the region's character. Each contribution follows a coherent, thematic consistency in the volume by addressing two common questions: how have the Eastern Townships been influenced by or linked to significant global trends, developments, and identities; and how have the people in the Eastern Townships, and the events and practices that marked their lives there, influenced or contributed to global trends, developments, and identities?

The book introduces readers to the vibrancy of a locality in Canada marked not by insularity but by the prominent role it has played and continues to play through its myriad engagements with the international community. The topics featured in this volume cut a wide swath, from Indigenous land use and mobility to settler resource extraction and economic production, educational engagement, linguistic and racial identities in the press and sport, religious, cultural, and fictional representations, and the impacts of peoples moving to and from the Townships. Each of its chapters demonstrates a common theme: the Eastern Townships was and is a *global* place, one connected to the world in ways that the Eastern Townships Agricultural Association directors knew well in 1913 and that would-be refugee Harry Thaw and his abettors could not ever have imagined.

Notes

1 Originally from Pittsburgh, Thaw had in the early twentieth century sought entry into elite circles in New York City's social clubs but had been repeatedly blackballed, most aggressively, he believed, by White. Thaw was tried twice for White's murder: the first, in spring 1907, ended in a hung jury; the second, held in winter 1908, ended in a conviction of guilty by reason of insanity. The Thaw scandal was revisited (and re-popularized) in E.L. Doctorow's book *Ragtime: A Novel* (1974).

2 Thaw's escape fascinated American and British newspaper editors and readers. For a digest of the American coverage, see *Cartoons Magazine* (1913). In Britain and Ireland, see *Illustrated London News* (1914) and O'Driscoll (1913).

3 He was rearrested in northern New Hampshire the next day and returned to Matteawan.

4 Seizing an opportunity to capitalize, silent-film producer Hal Reid captured locals' "Thawmania" on film, which he later edited and produced for vaudeville shows in New York (Grau 1914, 105–6). The effect of foreign nationals cheering on an American criminal was not lost on those following the case outside the region. After initially approving film of Thaw's captivity to be shown in Quebec, the province's board of censors reversed its decision, concerned that it depicted locals as misguided rubes from a regional backwater (Pelletier 2012, 104). Another colourful rendering of Thawmania came in the work of satirist William H. Holden, whose fanciful story *Colonel Luther in the Maine Woods* (1913) follows the main character on a cross-border visit to Sherbrooke, where he discovers that, in the wake of Thaw's trial, admiring townsfolk have renamed their school, library, brass band, hotel, and Boy Scout troop, all of them in honour of "Harry K. Thaw." One character is made to say, "This looks to me like a Thaw town" (78).

5 The same piece was published in *The Law Student's Helper* 21, no. 10 (October 1913): 15–18.

6 The fair generated revenue, too, in myriad ways. The official surplus on the fair's books amounted to only $900 ($41,483.83 in receipts against $40,627.53 in expenditures), but the fair's 1913 expenditures were abnormally high, including costs for the erection of a new cattle shed and a covered connector between the Main Hall and the Machinery Hall. Doubtless, a great deal more money was generated in private exchanges ranging from

livestock and industrial-equipment sales to gambling on horse races. See *Montreal Gazette* (1913b); *Sherbrooke Daily Record* (1913c).

7 The story was carried in dozens of newspapers. See for example *Davenport Democrat* (1913); *Pittsburgh Press* (1913). The *Daily Record* echoed Thaw's promise that, if his captors would agree to release him, he would attend the exhibition (*Sherbrooke Daily Record* 1913a); another story trumpeted in the American press made the assertion that ETAA brass had offered Evelyn Thaw $10,000 to perform a dance routine at the fair to capitalize on the hullabaloo. ETAA leaders quickly denied the story, but that bit didn't make headlines in US papers. For the denial, see *Montreal Gazette* (1913a).

8 Chad Gaffield has made a similar argument in his study of the Outaouais, which "has never existed as a region whose boundaries were unequivocally defined" (1991, 70).

9 But for a small number of seigneurial grants, most of the region was effectively neglected by the French regime, and outside of Abenaki use and a small number of seigneurial claims, such as the one at St Armand, the land (though heavily forested and unbroken by roads) was open to settlement (see Little 1989, 5).

10 In 1972, a new commercial centre in the region was named Carrefour de l'Estrie; a new magazine founded in 1978 and oriented toward regional identities was titled *L'Estrie*. Moreover, Estrie has attached to it a banner and an anthem, and there is a Société nationale de l'Estrie (SNE), which is organized to advocate its case (Grant 2022). The government's decision in 2021 to expand the boundaries of Estrie to add in the municipalities of Brome–Missisquoi and Haute–Yamaska rekindled the old debate between advocates of Estrie and those for Cantons de l'Est/Eastern Townships. On O'Bready, see Harvey (2001, 92)

11 For examples of contemporary usages, see the tourist and local development website "Estrie Cantons de l'Est," https://cantonsdelest.ca/, and the government of Quebec's multipurpose "Choose Quebec" website for Estrie: https://choisirlequebec.gouv.qc.ca/en/regions-estrie.php.

12 Sources for these figures include, for 1819, Oliver Barker's 1819 census in Quebec (1921, 537); for 1844 and 1852, Little (1997, 18); for 1887, Sutherland (1922, 146); for 1930, *Financial Post* (1930); for 1996, Quebec (2001); and for 2021, Statistics Canada (2021).

13 Sources for these figures include Little (1989, 21) and Statistics Canada (2021). On *colonisation* in the Townships, see Chartier (1871). On the French "invasion" (a term coined by turn-of-the-century journalist and firebrand Robert Sellar) see Sellar (1907), Hill (1998), and Hunter (1939).

14 We might include in this category V.E. Morrill's *Men of Today in the Eastern Townships* (1917), a volume that describes the history and administrative makeup of the Townships but has as its essential purpose the celebration of the great deeds of the anglophone community and honouring the sacrifices of its volunteer soldiers and officers in World War I, a conflict that deeply divided French- and English-speaking communities in Canada and, especially, Quebec.

15 Another work in the same vein was G.D.P.F.'s *La Compagnie de Colonisation et de Crédit des Cantons de l'Est* (1881).

16 One example of writing from this journal (no author attributed) provides a flavour of its pro-region stance: "Les entreprises industrielle dont on poursuite la réalisation dans le district du Saguenay, des les Cantons de l'Est, celles que l'on projette pour le district du Saint-Maurice, fournissement justement a ceux que tente le départ l'occasion dont ils

revaient depuis longtemps peut-être." "Industrie et agriculture," *L'Actualité Economique* 2, (1926): 14.

17 See for example J. Austen Bancroft's *Report on the Copper Deposits of the Eastern Townships of the Province of Quebec* (1915).

18 "[L]'essentiel est qu'il y ait bonne entente entre ces éléments jadis si divers, et cette entente," Blanchard wrote, "je l'ai entendu célébrer par tous, Français et Anglais, sans une voix discordante" (1937, 188).

19 The theme was echoed in Joseph Charles Saint-Amant's history of Durham and Wickham townships, *Un coin des cantons de l'est: histoire de l'envahissement pacifique mais irrésistible d'une race* (1932).

20 Especially poetry. See for example Malus, Aliard, and van Sundert (1985) and Whitney (1992).

21 Their study reinforced, however, the notion of the geographical distinctiveness of the region first argued by Blanchard and later picked up by Robert Gagnon in his 1970 textbook *Les Cantons de l'est: initiation à la géographie régionale.*

22 First popularized by American writer/scholar Randolph Bourne (1916), the concept has been used profitably by Canadian historians in recent years. See Stuart and Behiels (2010, esp. 5–7).

References

Akron Beacon Journal. 1913. "Thaw Declares He Will Defeat Jerome Tactics." 1 September, 3.

Bancroft, J. Austen. 1915. *Report on the Copper Deposits of the Eastern Townships of the Province of Quebec*. Quebec City: Department of Colonization, Mines and Fisheries.

Blanchard, Raoul. 1937. "Études canadiennes (Deuxième série): Les Cantons de l'Est." *Revue de géographie alpine*, 25 (1): 1–210.

Boston Globe. 1913. "Even Quit Thaw to Watch Races." 3 September, 13.

Boston Record. 1914. "At the Mayor's Gate." 22 June. Found in "James Michael Curley Scrapbooks Volume A06" (1914). James Michael Curley Scrapbooks. 4. https://crossworks.holycross.edu/curley_scrapbooks/4. Accessed 2 May 2023.

Bourne, Randolph. 1916. "Trans-National America." *Atlantic Monthly* 118: 86–97.

Buffalo Evening News. 1908. "Americans Will Exhibit at Canadian Fair." 2 August.

Cartoons Magazine. 1913. "The Flight of Harry Thaw from Matteawan" 4, no. 4 (October): 405–11.

Castells, M. 2020. "Spaces of Flows, Spaces of Places: Materials for a Theory of Urbanism in the Information Age." In *The City Reader*, 7th ed., edited by R. LeGates and F. Stout, 240–51. London: Routledge.

Chartier, Jean Baptiste. 1871. *La colonisation dans les Cantons de l'Est*. St Hyacinthe: Le press à Vapeur du Courrier de St Hyacinthe.

Davenport Democrat. 1913. "Offer Evelyn Thaw $10,000 to Dance." 3 September, 1.

Day, Catherine M. 1863. *Pioneers of the Eastern Townships*. Montreal: John Lovell.

– 1869. *History of the Eastern Townships*. Montreal: John Lovell.

Day, Gordon M. 1981. *The Identity of the Saint Francis Indians*. Ottawa: National Museums of Canada.

Doctorow, E.L. 1974. *Ragtime: A Novel*. New York: Random House.
Farfan, Matthew. 2023. "Why Eastern Townships?" *Townships Heritage Magazine*. http://townshipsheritage.com/print/article/why-eastern-townships. Accessed 1 July 2023.
Financial Post. 1930. "E.T. Population Well Distributed." 28 August, 23.
Fraser, E. 2018. "Unbecoming Place: Urban Imaginaries in Transition in Detroit." *Cultural Geographies* 25 (3): 441–58.
Gaffield, Chad. 1991. "The New Regional History: Rethinking the History of the Outaouais." *Journal of Canadian Studies* 26, 1 (Spring 1991): 64–81.
Gagnon, Robert. 1970. *Les Cantons de l'est: initiation à la géographie régionale*. Toronto: Holt, Rinehart and Winston.
G.D.P.F. 1881. *La Compagnie de Colonisation et de Crédit des Cantons de l'Est*. Sherbrooke: Le Pionnier.
Grant, Josh. 2022. "Quebec's Eastern Townships Considers Official Name Change." CBC News. 16 February. https://www.cbc.ca/news/canada/montreal/eastern-townships-estrie-or-cantons-de-l-est-1.6348573. Accessed 29 June 2023.
Grau, Robert. 1914. *The Theatre of Science: A Volume of Progress and Achievement in the Motion Picture Industry*. New York: Broadway Publishing Company.
Harvey, Fernand. 1980. "La question régionale au Québec." *Journal of Canadian Studies* 15, no. 2 (Summer): 74–87.
– 2001. "L'historiographie régionaliste des années 1920 et 1930 au Québec." *Les cahiers des dix* 55:53–102.
Hill, Robert. 1998. *Voice of the Vanishing Minority: Robert Sellar and the Huntingdon Gleaner, 1863–1919*. Montreal and Kingston: McGill-Queen's University Press.
Holden, William H. 1913. *Colonel Luther in the Maine Woods*. Boston: Boston Journal.
Hunter, Joan I. 1939. "The French Invasion of the Eastern Townships: A Regional Study." MA thesis, McGill University.
Hunter, William S., Jr. 1860. *Eastern Townships Scenery, Canada East*. Montreal: John Lovell.
Illustrated London News. 1914. "From the World's Scrap-Book." 28 February, 324.
Kesteman, Jean-Pierre. 2007. *Aborder l'histoire des Cantons-de-L'Est*. Sherbrooke: GGC Productions.
Kesteman, Jean-Pierre, Diane Saint-Pierre, and Peter Southam. 1998. *Histoire des Cantons de l'Est*. Quebec: Presses de l'Université Laval.
Konrad V., and E. Brunet-Jailly. 2019. "Approaching Borders, Creating Borderland Spaces, and Exploring the Evolving Borders between Canada and the United States." *Canadian Geographer* 63 (1): 4–10.
Little, J.I. 1989. *Ethno-Cultural Transition and Regional Identity in the Eastern Townships of Quebec*. Booklet No. 13. Ottawa: Canadian Historical Association.
– 1997. *State and Society in Transition: The Politics of Institutional Reform in the Eastern Townships, 1838–1852*. Montreal and Kingston: McGill-Queen's University Press.
Mailhot, Pierre, and Jean-marie Dubois. 2006. "Eastern Townships." *The Canadian Encyclopedia*. https://www.thecanadianencyclopedia.ca/en/article/eastern-townships. Accessed 30 June 2023.

Malus, Avrum, Diane Allard, and Maria van Sundert. 1985. "Frank Oliver Call, Eastern Townships Poetry, and the Modernist Movement." *Canadian Literature* 107 (1985): 60–9.

Man, G., and R. Cohen. 2015. *Engendering Transnational Voices: Studies in Family, Work and Identity*. Waterloo: Wilfrid Laurier University Press.

Martin, Gabriel. 2022. "L'Estrie, une bribe de patrimoine immatériel." *Le Devoir*, 19 February. https://www.ledevoir.com/opinion/libre-opinion/676698/toponymie-l-estrie-une-bribe-de-patrimoine-immateriel. Accessed 29 June 2023.

Montreal Gazette. 1913a. "Evelyn Thaw Story Denied." 2 September, 4.

– 1913b. "Had Exhibition Surplus." 20 November, 20.

Morin, Denis, et al. 1986. "Des Cantons-de-l'Est à l'Estrie." *Cahiers de géographie du Québec* 30 (80): 249–69.

Morrill, V.E. 1917. *Men of Today in the Eastern Townships*. Sherbrooke: Sherbrooke Record Company, 1917.

O'Driscoll, Des. 1913. *The Irish Examiner: 100 Years of News*. Dublin: Gill and Macmillan.

Ohio Law Bulletin. 1913. "Thaw and the Canadians: Incongruous Admiration of a Libertine by a Moral People." *Ohio Law Bulletin* 58, no. 41 (October): 393–5.

Pelletier, Louis. 2012. "A Moving Picture Farce: Public Opinion and the Beginnings of Film Censorship in Quebec." In *Beyond the Screen: Institutions, Networks and Publics of Early Cinema*, edited by Marta Braun et al., 94–105. New Barnet, UK: John Libbey Publishing.

Philiponneau, Michel. 1960. *L'Avenir économique et sociale des cantons de l'est*. Quebec: Ministère de l'Industrie et du Commerce, Service de Géographie.

Pittsburgh Press. 1913. "Reports Big Offer to Evelyn Thaw." 1 September, 3.

Pratt, M.L. 1991. "Arts of the Contact Zone." In *Profession '91*, edited by P. Franklin and R. Franklin, 33–40. New York: Modern Language Association.

Quebec. 1921. *Province of Quebec … Statistical Year-Book. 8th Year*. Quebec: Ls-A Proulx.

– 2001. Institut de la statistique de Québec. Census 2001. 05 Estrie. https://statistique.quebec.ca/statistiques/recensement/2001/recens2001_05/population/tpoplog05_an.htm. Accessed 30 June 2023.

Saint-Amant, Joseph Charles. 1932. *Un coin des cantons de l'est: histoire de l'envahissement pacifique mais irrésistible d'une race*. N.p.: Parole.

Sellar, Robert. 1907. *The Tragedy of Quebec: The Expulsion of its Protestant Farmers*. Huntingdon, QC: n.p.

Sherbrooke Daily Record. 1913a. "Bright Outlook for Fair Week." 1 September, 1.

– 1913b. "Immigration Act Our Only Law?" 10 September, 1.

– 1913c. "Meeting of E.T.A.A." 19 November, 1.

St Louis Post-Dispatch. 1913. "Thaw Arranged Jerome's Bail; Escapes Forfeit." 7 September, 3.

Statistics Canada. 2021. Census Profile, 2021 Census of Population. Estrie. https://www12.statcan.gc.ca/census-recensement/2021/dp-pd/prof/details/page.cfm?Lang=E&DGUIDlist=2021S05002430&GENDERlist=1,2,3&STATISTIClist=1&HEADERlist=0. Accessed 30 June 2023.

Stuart, Reginald, and Michael Behiels. 2010. *Transnationalism: Canada-United States History into the Twenty-First Century.* Montreal and Kingston: McGill-Queen's University Press.

Sutherland, J.C. 1922. *The Province of Quebec: Geographical and Social Studies.* Montreal: Renouf Publishing Company.

Thomas, C. 1866. *Contributions to the History of the Eastern Townships.* Montreal: Lovell.

Treyvaud, Geneviève, and Michel Plourde. 2017. *The Abenakis of Odanak, an Archaeological Journey.* Quebec: Marquis.

Whitney, Patricia. 1992. "Claiming the Landscape: John Glassco and His Poetry of the Eastern Townships." *Journal of Eastern Townships Studies* 1: 67–76.

Part One

Space and Place: Making the Eastern Townships

The essays in part 1 of this book focus on the transformative construction of identity in the Townships. Shaped by local and global forces, the physical expression of this region in Quebec has, the authors suggest, been influenced in distinctive ways. In chapter 1, "The Toponymy in the Eastern Townships before the Eastern Townships: A Portrait of Abenaki Toponymic Resilience from the Earliest Times to the End of the French Regime," geographer and linguist Philippe Charland examines how Indigenous place names, specifically Abenaki toponymy, have defined the geographic space of the Eastern Townships and influenced its identity. Drawing on a series of historical maps, Charland demonstrates that toponymy is a politically infused process, resulting today in the selective retention and use of some Abenaki place names, while "many others have fallen out of time, erased by generations of white settler authorities in the Eastern Townships." Chapter 2 in this book, historian J.I. Little's "'The Security of Our Frontiers': British Colonization Projects in the Eastern Townships during the First Half of the Nineteenth Century," explores a succession of colonization projects in different parts of the Townships in the early nineteenth century explaining why they failed to transform the region into a predominantly British – and therefore "loyal" – area, given the threat of American settlement (and America's hovering presence just across the border). Little reviews various policy changes behind land company ventures, providing detailed insights on several individuals on the ground in the Townships who worked to make these ventures successful. The ways in which recent agricultural practices have been championed in the Eastern Townships is the focus of geographer Darren Bardati's contribution (chapter 3), "Agriculture in Transition: Global Crisis and the Eastern Townships' Identity." In it, he considers a visible and meaningful shift in agricultural practices and identity that has come to mark Eastern Townships' agriculture in the twenty-first century, one influenced by, and at times shielded from, international agricultural trends. The agricultural footprint of the Townships, Bardati argues, has contributed to and serves as an exemplar for sustainable development.

1

The Toponymy of the Eastern Townships before the Eastern Townships: A Portrait of Abenaki Toponymic Resilience from the Earliest Times to the End of the French Regime

Philippe Charland

> What do the last federal election and the process for finding a new name for the Grandes-Fourches Bridge have in common? In both cases, the big winner at the end of the process is the status quo. The Sherbrooke City Council agreed on October 4 [2021] to respect the choice expressed by citizens in the survey conducted by the City in recent weeks. The most popular option was the name "Pont des Grandes-Fourches," which received 1,487 votes, slightly ahead of the name "Pont Onigan," which received 1,380 votes. The term means "portage" in Abenaki.
>
> LÉONARD (2021)[1]

THUS, ONE DAY IN OCTOBER 2021, the strong will of the population of Sherbrooke determined that an Abenaki toponym was to be rejected in favour of a white settler term. Was this a missed opportunity to make history, especially in this era of reconciliation with Indigenous Peoples in Quebec? Some will say that toponyms should represent the people who live there – their history, culture, and identity. Others will say that we have a duty to remember and make amends for past mistakes, and that this duty includes reconstituting the original toponymic landscape of the region.

What is the current situation of the toponymy of the Eastern Townships? There are some prominent Abenaki toponyms in use, such as Magog, Mégantic, Memphrémagog, etc., but many others have fallen out of use, erased by generations of white settler political authorities in the Eastern Townships acting on behalf of the region's "people." The long-term effects of this erasure are uncertain. It is true that, as in the case cited above, the municipal council has "assured that names not selected can be developed in other ways in the same area ... including those of First Nations heritage" (Léonard 2021). It is impossible to predict the future, but the fact remains that toponymy is, above all, a political instrument. It has moved with empires, regimes, and wars, through time and at all levels of decision-making. The phenomenon is worldwide, dates to time immemorial, and is subject to various factors. Decisions taken are rarely noticed. In the case illustrated above, while a colonial-era toponym (Grandes Fourches) survives thanks to local democracy, narrowly edging out a recent competitor (Onigan),[2] many other Abenaki toponyms have died amid general indifference.

Toponymic practice is intensely local,[3] but it also reflects global political processes that played out over hundreds of years and decisions that were taken sometimes thousands of kilometres away. It is a global geopolitical context that informs the very existence of the toponyms "Grandes Fourches," "Mégantic," "Magog," and "Memphrémagog."

This chapter examines how Abenaki toponymy has defined the geographic space of the Eastern Townships and been transmitted to the general population through its various forms, thus forging the identity of all its inhabitants over time. We will first look at the definition of toponymy and how it shapes identity, and then we will turn to a history of knowledge about the territory and the appearance of toponymy in the Eastern Townships to the end of the French regime (mid-eighteenth century).

TOPONYMY *as a* MARKER *of* IDENTITY

In his book *A System of Logic, Ratiocinative and Inductive*, John Stuart Mill declared that a proper name, "being a mere mark put upon an individual, and of which it is the characteristic property to be destitute of meaning, its meaning can not of course be declared" (Mill 1882, 105). In the Western world, proper names often lose their meaning. A "Philip," for example, is not necessarily a "friend of horses" as its Greek root suggests and, similarly, a "Pascal" is not necessarily someone who was born at

Easter. Similarly, toponyms can also lose their nature as descriptors of the locations they represent.

This logic does not apply to Indigenous toponymy, however, as James Hammond Trumbull wrote in his book *The Composition of Indian Geographical Names from the Algonkian Languages*:

> Every name *described* the locality to which it was affixed. The description was sometimes *topographical*; sometimes *historical*, preserving the memory of a battle, a feast, the dwelling-place of a great sachem, or the like; sometimes it indicated one of the *natural products* of the place, or the *animals* which resorted to it; occasionally, its *position* or *direction* from a place previously known, or from the territory of the nation by which the name was given, as for example, "the land on the other side of the river," "behind the mountain," "the east land," "the half-way place," &c. The same name might be, in fact it very often was, given to more places than one; but these must not be so near together that mistakes or doubts could be occasioned by the repetition. (Trumbull 1870, 4–5)

This way of seeing the world, which is not exclusive to North American Indigenous Peoples, is at odds with the environment in which we live today. The world around us is the product of many layers of worldviews, not mutually exclusive, but not mutually inclusive either. The fact remains that, for all of us, toponyms are a vehicle for the presence of a population in a place:

> Place names are symbols and elements of territoriality, sovereignty, and cultural identity. They are indicators of the type and intensity of land use and occupancy in specific physical environments and cultural areas expressing the spatial links between the "occupants" and the network of named spaces covering a territory contiguously. In fact, place names create and maintain, through their continuous use and application, a system of spatial organization which is the essence of territoriality and sovereignty. (Müller-Wille 1989–1990, 17)

The toponymy of the Eastern Townships, like that of the high Arctic referred to in the previous quote, also symbolizes territoriality, sovereignty, and cultural identity. It represents the different layers of occupation of the territory by the different populations that have used the space. Conceived in this way, it is a mosaic representation, one that is not fixed in time. "Place name systems, embedded in culture and language," Müller-Wille reminds us, "are not static. They evolve in time and space and thus are shaped and altered, in general terms, by the dynamic process of culture change and contact" (17).

The phenomenon described here is neither new nor unique to the region: all regions of the world are affected by changes in the territory, whether geographical, cultural, or linguistic. The first known layer of toponyms for the Eastern Townships, the one created by the Abenakis, is still visible on the territory but has also been reinterpreted by the succession of populations that have used it since. Unfortunately, the passage of time has erased many of the Abenaki names, which are forever forgotten and lost. But for the "survivors," the new "shell" (the spelling that was given to the toponym, which became French or English) is probably what saved it from oblivion. Should we see in this rescue an avowed desire to preserve the past? Or, conversely, is it just a habit that, over time, has become a tradition, a vector of identity for people whose very toponym is no longer intelligible but which must be preserved as a symbol of a pre-colonized past?

THE TOPONYMY *of the* EASTERN TOWNSHIPS *in a* GLOBAL CONTEXT

At least part of the Abenaki toponymy of the Eastern Townships has survived the test of time. But how did it survive? What are the factors that made this survival possible? Who makes the ultimate decision on the life or death of a toponym: people, leaders, or both? Who has the authority to formalize the toponymy? We can examine these questions by segmenting our study into different periods that allow us to trace the layers of occupation of the territory. These layers are superimposed and intermingled; the latter are never totally impervious to those that preceded them.

The first layer is that of Indigenous occupation. It dates back thousands of years, and it is impossible to know its exact extent. In the case of the Eastern Townships region, this layer is Abenaki and is still visible today. However, other layers have succeeded it, shaped by events that were decided thousands of kilometres away, were as obscure as the fall of Constantinople in 1452, and that eventually determined the life or death of Abenaki toponymy. The search for a passage to Asia by the European powers, followed by their economic exploitation (especially in fishing and fur extraction) of the newly discovered lands, modified the toponymic landscape of the continent. Explorers, acting on behalf of European monarchs, named the places in ways that were meaningful to them, incorporating a few local Indigenous toponyms in the process but transforming and adapting them to their own understanding (by spelling, especially). This second layer of territorial occupation corresponds to a phase in which toponymic decisions were made by people from elsewhere and formalized in distant places by the authorities behind the explorations. This formalization was done via the medium of official cartography, through which toponyms become customary. The authorities used them to define and claim the new territories. Ultimately, some toponyms stood the test of time, whether they were of Indigenous coinage or products of the first explorations, or both, but they will always be subject to reconsideration by succeeding generations of local populations.

In the Eastern Townships, the geographical knowledge of the area (the point of convergence with the toponymy) resulted from the presence of Abenaki people in the region for thousands of years and, later, the explorations of the territory in the seventeenth and eighteenth centuries by French authorities who borrowed many Abenaki toponyms, translating or transcribing them, even as they created new ones. But significant settler colonization of the region really began in the nineteenth century. Before then, it was mainly the political decisions of the empires (and not only France and Britain, but of the whole of Europe as cartography travelled and was widely shared) that fixed the toponymy. It was during the Anglo–French wars of the eighteenth century that the region was named, as it was used mainly as a communication route that connected French centres on the St Lawrence to Britain's thirteen colonies. It was, therefore, in the context of the wars of empire that the toponymy of the Eastern Townships took shape among European colonizers.

We can begin with early Abenaki toponymy that has come down to us through its transformations. With that knowledge, we can measure the impact of the European presence on the modern toponymy of the Eastern Townships. The objective is not to cover all the Abenaki toponyms present in the region but to understand how they were established and how they evolved over time. We discuss their history and meanings only in passing.

HISTORY *of* EARLY ABENAKI TOPONYMS

Although the Abenaki presence in the Eastern Townships dates back thousands of years, we cannot access much of the toponymic knowledge that may have existed over time. While some toponyms have survived, others have not, and of those that have, it is impossible to know when they appeared. We must therefore turn to Abenaki knowledge, but also to European knowledge, including early cartography, to reconstruct a toponymic portrait of the Eastern Townships. This knowledge is intimately linked to European knowledge of the territory, which in turn is derived from Abenaki knowledge. We are therefore at the mercy of archival records and maps: what was noted by the first Europeans and what motivated them to move around the territory and name it in order to orient themselves.

The idea here is not to date the first appearance of Abenaki toponyms in European documents, as this in no way indicates their lifespan. European use of Abenaki toponyms in archival records simply indicates their presence at a specific moment in time and their use (or prescribed use) in the everyday language of passing Europeans. Over time, a broad interpretive folklore developed regarding the meaning of toponyms in Indigenous languages, which were passed down from generation to generation without adequate analysis. Names have been truncated, modified, and interpreted by almost everyone who used them, and the result is a toponymy that has migrated far from the original terms.

The first element to note in the study of Abenaki toponyms is that they are all descriptions of the environment and, most often, references to a particular element of the landscape. Since the first traces of toponymy to which we have access are found in European literature (maps, manuscripts, etc.), the toponyms reflect European use of the territory. The toponyms are therefore drawn from the axes of penetration of the territory; that is, rivers. Often, the interested gaze of the European betrayed his limited knowledge of the territory. Despite their desire to convey geographical knowledge, these maps depended on the progress of explorers' knowledge on the ground and the political, economic, and logistical aims of the individuals and states that supported them. In the specific case of the Eastern Townships, knowledge was for a long time restricted to the banks of the St Lawrence River, and knowledge of the interior remained partial and fragmentary.

Samuel de Champlain's map of 1632 (figure 1.1), the most finished of his works, illustrates this situation well. While it expresses the colonial policies of the time, it also demonstrates the degree of progress in geographical knowledge. Champlain did visit the territory, but he did so both in search of a passage to Asia (hence his ascent of the Richelieu River and his advance westward) and by creating alliances for the fur trade (hence his interest in better defining everything north of the St Lawrence River and to the west, toward the Great Lakes). The only traces we have of knowledge of what later becomes the Eastern Townships on this map appear with the Chaudière River (number 10 on the map) and Lake Mégantic, an area that is distorted because of Champlain's lack of knowledge of this region. The St Francis River (number 21 on the map, which Champlain refers to as the

Figure 1.1
Carte de la Nouvelle France, 1632, and detail

"Saint-Antoine") is also misrepresented because, as we know today, it does not really flow anywhere near the Connecticut River. We can argue that this distorted hydrography is the direct result of his lack of knowledge of the area and his lack of interest in it. Having never set foot there himself, what he reports is therefore second-hand knowledge.

Even by the end of the seventeenth century, no significant progress had taken place in the European toponymy for the region, nor was there an improved description of the hydrographic network. We can assume that this lack of geographical interest in the region was widespread and that those who frequented the territory, other than the Abenakis, were silent about it. Even the Jesuits sent on missions to the region, such as Gabriel Druillettes (beginning in 1646) and Sébastien Rasles (after 1691), did not record much about the routes they took via the Chaudière and St Francis rivers to reach the Abenakis living inland. For example, Rasles does not mention any Eastern Townships toponyms in his 1691 dictionary (Rasles 1833 [1691]). However, soon after that, a conflict that began thousands of kilometres away came close to triggering an official exploration of the territory by the Europeans. The War of the League of Augsburg (1688–97) pitted the Kingdom of France and the Jacobites against the kingdoms of England, Scotland, Portugal, Sweden, the Spanish Monarchy, the Duchy of Savoy, the Holy Roman Empire, and the United Provinces of the Netherlands. During that conflict, Charles de Monseignat, secretary to the governor of New France, Louis de Buade de Frontenac, wrote to Madame de Maintenon, confidante to Louis XIV in 1690, mentioning French military officer François Hertel's "attack" on the British settlement at Salmon Falls:

> Shortly afterwards, news was received of the expedition of Sr [Hertel] who commanded the party of the Three Rivers [Trois-Rivières, the town at the mouth of the Saint-Maurice River in New France], by some volunteers who returned and by the prisoners they had taken. He was accompanied by three of his sons, twenty-four French and twenty Soccoquis and five Algonquins, making a total of fifty-two men. They left the Three Rivers on the twenty-eighth of January. After a rather long and very unfortunate march, they arrived on March 27 at an English village called Salmonfalls [now called Berwick, Maine], which they had resolved to attack. (Législature de Québec, 1883, vol.1, 496)

Although no toponym is evident from this passage, it does show that French authorities were aware of the St Francis River and its connection to southern routes in 1690. Although Hertel and his men were probably not the first Europeans to pass through the area, this was the first official presence of French royal forces in the region.

In his book *Sherbrooke*, Louis-Philippe Demers tells of a letter found in 1965 in the Sherbrooke area, preserved between slates and under a rotten wooden stump. Practically illegible, the letter is said to date from 1690, written by a man named Bastien Lombard de Saint-Aubien du Cormier. In it, he talks about his stay with Abenakis on a large island in the St Francis River (Demers identifies it as "Ball Island," now known as "Nuns' Island" [Île des Soeurs]), on the eve of a battle between Abenakis and Iroquois. The author of the letter mentions "that he has finally found this river that the Indians call Alsiganteka" (Demers 1967, 24). This is one of the first mentions of the river in its Abenaki form, at a time when French authorities had begun to call it "Rivière Saint-François." We will see its significance later.

At about the same time, in 1692, a well-preserved tale of the region relates the battle that took place between the Abenaki and the Iroquois. Several versions of the story exist, including one written in a 1922 novel (*Mena'sen*, by Oscar Massé), but all versions have a similar thread. Henri Vassal, Indian agent for the Abenakis of Saint-François, related this legend in his 1884 *Annual Report to the Department of Indian Affairs*:

> Skacewantegon. – A branch of the River St Francis, which passes through Sherbrooke. The Iroquois used to call the Abenakis "Skacewanilom." Tradition relates that a great battle was fought on an island situated at the entrance of this branch of the [Magog] river, between the Iroquois and the Abenakis. It was proposed that the battle should be fought in single combat, each side to be represented by one of its own warriors. They were to run around a pine tree, which was on this island, and the victor in the race would have the right to kill his adversary, which would decide the victory between the two nations. The Abenaki was the victor, and the name of this tribe, in the Iroquois language, was given to this river. For the same reason a small lake near Sherbrooke, received the name of "Skacewaninebesseck." (Vassal 1884, 28–9)

This story has some errors, especially regarding toponymy, and the toponym for the island is never mentioned. (Mena'sen, which we can translate as "stone island" [although not grammatically correct], was not officially used until 1983; before then it was known as "Pine Rock" [Rocher au pin], "Lone Pine Rock" [Rocher du pin solitaire], or "Lone Pine Islet" [Îlot du pin solitaire].) Still, the story seems substantially reliable.

Although the region continued to be visited sporadically by Europeans, it was a second global conflict, the War of the Spanish Succession (1701–14), which led to the appearance of other toponyms. As in the previous conflict, French and British militaries clashed, both in Europe and in their respective colonies in America. According to one account published in a French periodical in January 1705, a French expedition made its way to the thirteen colonies via the St Francis River in July and August 1703:

> On the 28th of July, the small Canadian army found on its way a Lake called Skessouau [Lake Magog] which is about two leagues long, & we crossed it. In the evening of that day the army camped at the entrance of another lake called Memraaubaiguay [Lake Memphremagog] which is ten leagues long and is surrounded by high mountains; it was into this lake that they entered. (*Mercure Galant* 1705, 29–30)

The few toponyms mentioned here appear to be the earliest versions ever published, though they are poorly transcribed. Interestingly, their use in 1703 predates their appearance on official maps. The cartography of the Eastern Townships region at the time is not very detailed and not representative of real knowledge locally.

In one map made by cartographer Jean-Baptiste Decouägne and dated 1711 (figure 1.2), one can see just how sketchy French knowledge of the interior land was south of the St Lawrence River. The St Francis River appears, with its connection to the Magog River, but without the lakes that make it up. Otherwise, the only other element worth mentioning is the connection, by portage, between the Connecticut River and what appears to be Lake Mégantic, which is depicted as being at the end of the Chaudière River (far from its actual location). There are no Indigenous toponyms either and it is not until the end of the war that a toponymic revolution occurs.

JOSEPH AUBÉRY'S CARTOGRAPHY

In 1713, with the Treaty of Utrecht signed in Europe, Joseph Aubéry (1673–1756), a Jesuit missionary to the Abenakis, decided to send a memorandum to the French court concerning the delimitation of Acadia, which he considered vague and ambiguous, to prevent the English from "expanding, advancing and establishing themselves on our lands during the peace, and thereby making themselves masters of Canada" (quoted in Johnson 1974, 24). Significantly, Aubéry accompanied his memoir with a map that explained the chosen delimitation: "to be certain

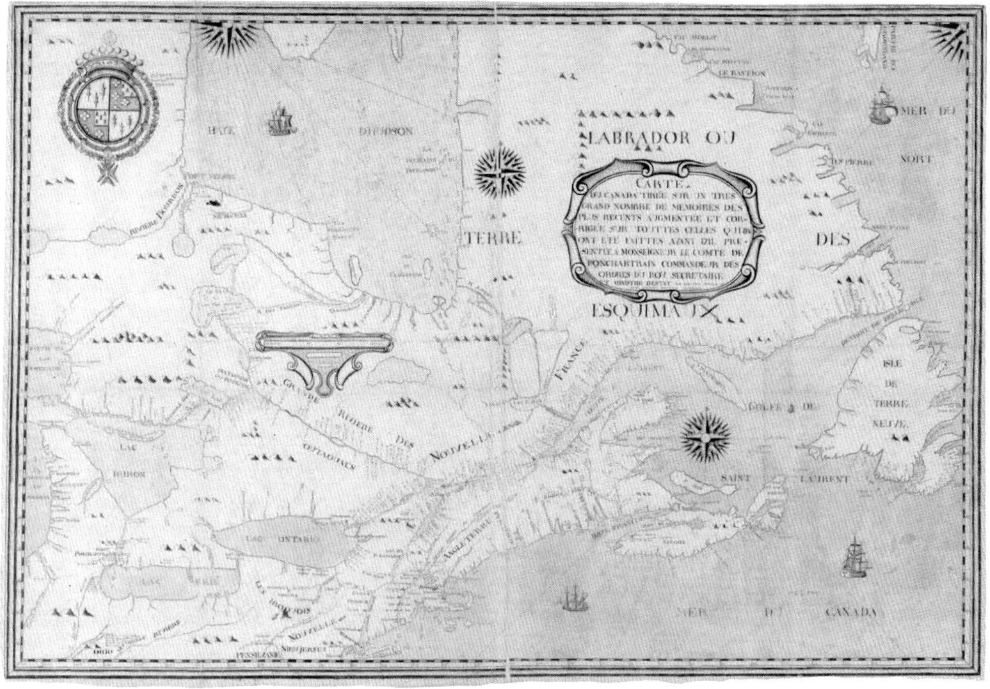

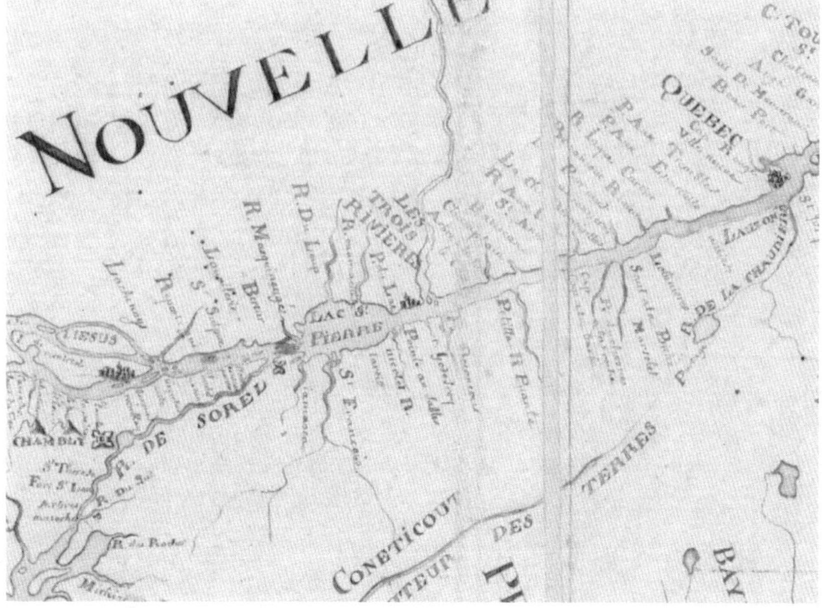

Figure 1.2 *Carte du Canada*, 1711, and detail

these limits could only be the height of the land; but to determine them there is to give a large part of New France, since these heights of land are very close to the St Lawrence River" (24). He then suggested a definition of Acadia limited to present-day Nova Scotia, a solution that was rejected out of hand by the authorities.

There are four maps in the archives associated, directly or indirectly, with Aubéry: two are dated 1713 and appear to be the official copies sent with the report (figure 1.3, Aubéry and Laguerre de Morville, 1713) and a working copy (figure 1.4, Anonymous, 1713), which, though very clean, contains geographical errors; another of the maps is dated 1715 (figure 1.5, Aubéry, 1715) and includes toponyms; the final one has no toponyms (figure 1.6, Anonymous, n.d.).

Whether he was the main cartographer or the co-creator, Aubéry's maps remain probably the most complete documents for the time, geographically speaking, for the Eastern Townships region. And since Aubéry was also a Catholic missionary to the Abenakis, whose language he mastered (he wrote French–Abenaki and Abenaki–French dictionaries, both completed in 1715), he saw fit to sprinkle his maps with Abenaki toponyms, some of which also appear in his dictionaries. This was probably the pivotal moment of their officialization by the authorities. A careful examination of the four maps reveals the geographical and toponymic importance they contain. The map accompanying the report (figure 1.3) mentions in the legend that it was "the Jesuit R. P. Aubry who made it, having travelled to all these places" and the sieur de Morville, then an engineer in Quebec, who drew it. This map represents well, geographically speaking, the reality on the ground.

Although he uses the term "Terres abnaquises" and "Terres abbenaquises" (Abenaki lands) on the two maps officially named after him (figures 1.3 and 1.5), the other maps include the variants "Terre des Ouabenaquis" (figure 1.4) and "Terre des Abnaquis" (figure 1.6). While the expression appears in all cases along the Atlantic coast, straddling his definition of "New France or Canada" and "New England," Aubéry does not indicate their Abenaki form. Yet Aubéry provides this in his dictionary entry for "colony": "la colonie des françois qui est icy [the French colony that is here]. Pétsi-nañdañd8dainaïsaanik io p8ésmañnak io nañtkésaanik" (Aubéry 1715a, 138). He also gives an example of a sentence with "Canada": "ne-mes-akkété-kkamen Kanada jarrive a la terre du canada, j'y mets pied a terre [I arrive at the land of Canada, I set foot in Canada]" (Aubéry 1715b, 288), but he cannot give a translation because this toponym (Canada) is of Iroquoian origin. As for the form given to the ethnonym "Abenaki," it is probably the form "ouabenaquis" (figure 1.4) which is the closest to reality, whereas "w8ban" literally means "it whitens" and "aki" means "the land," so "w8banaki" (in modern Abenaki) "the land where it whitens." The verb "w8ban" refers to one of the stages of sunrise,

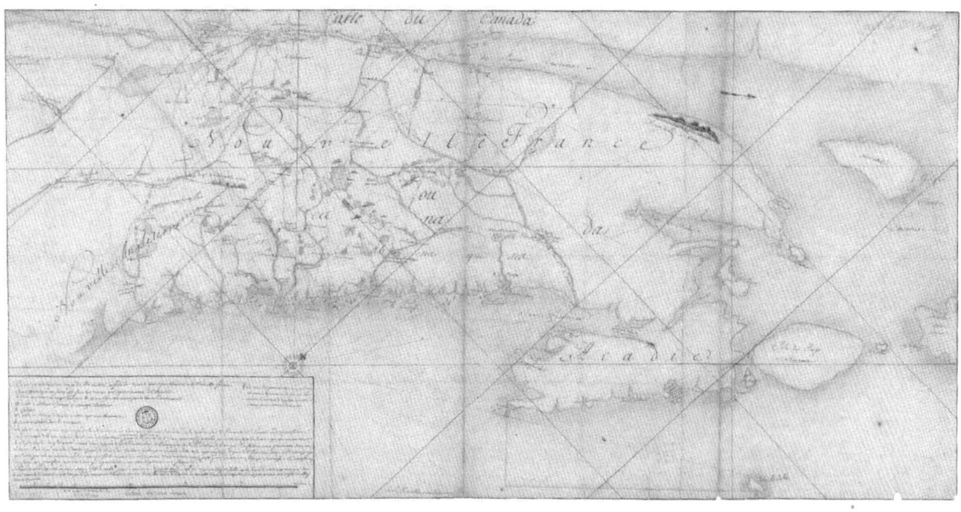

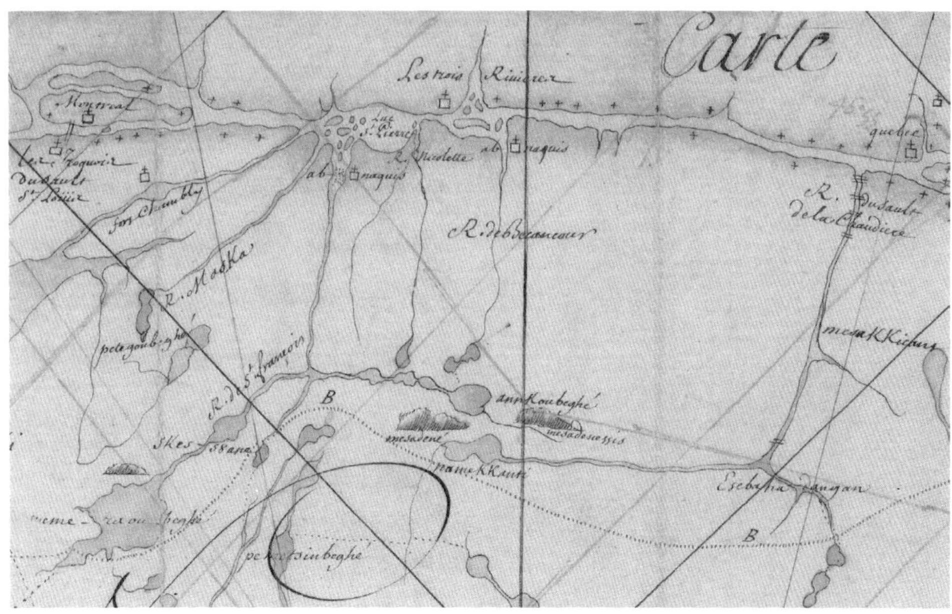

Figure 1.3 *Partie du Canada ou nouvelle France et de la Nouvelle Angleterre*, 1713, and detail

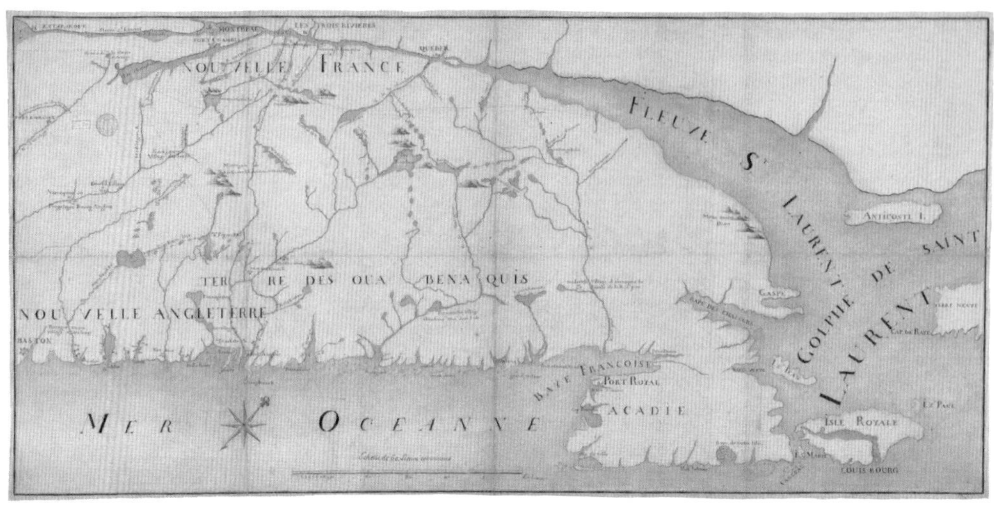

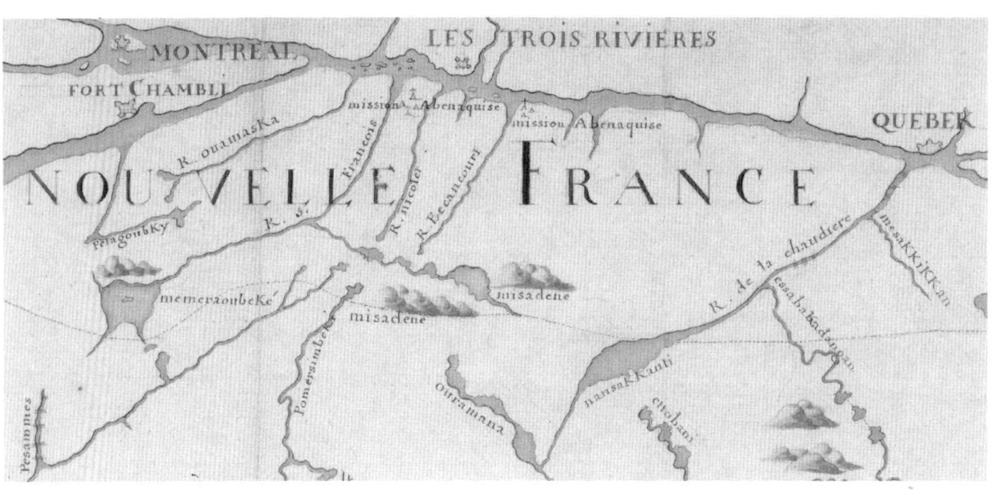

Figure 1.4 *Nouvelle France, Nouvelle Angleterre, Acadie*, 1713, and detail

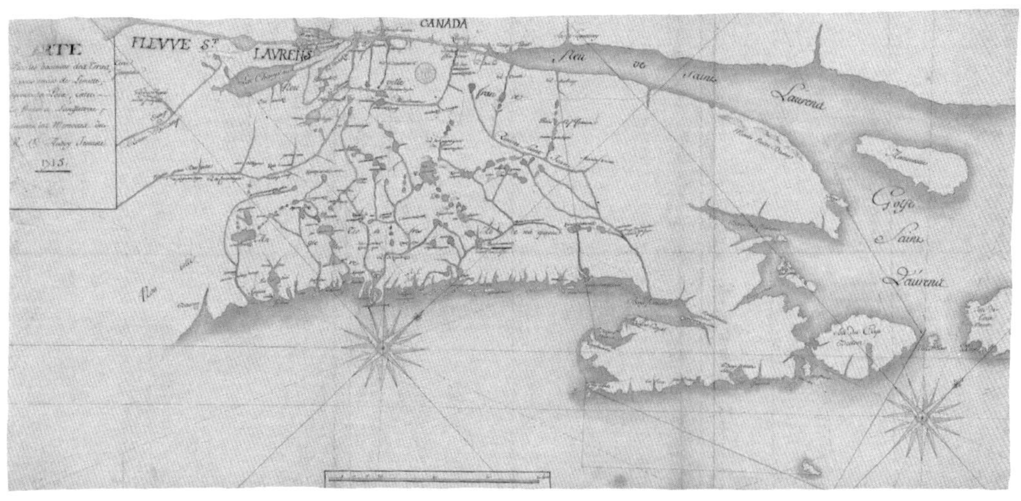

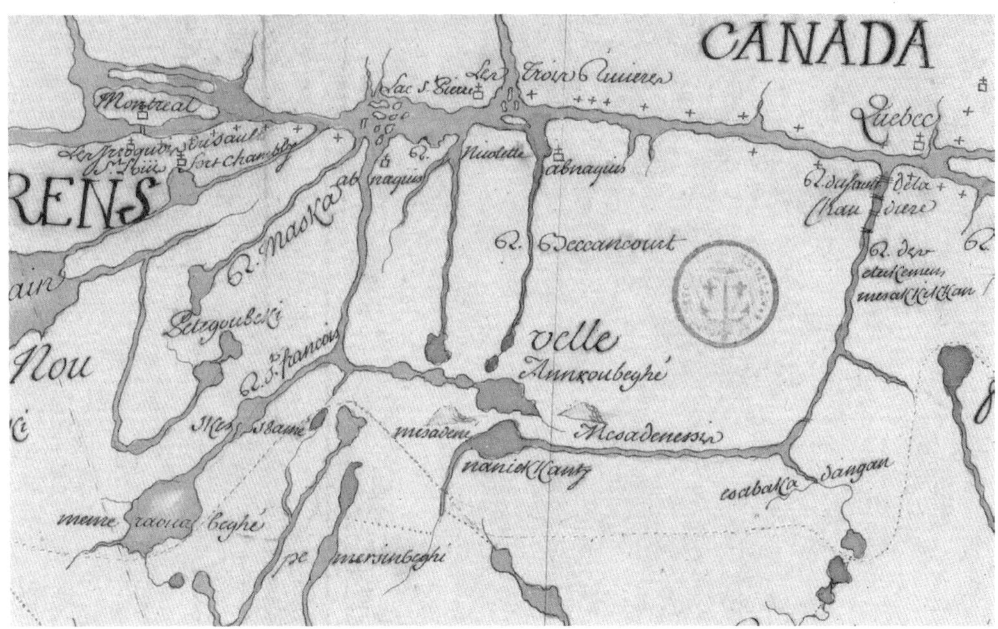

Figure 1.5 *Carte pour les hauteurs des terres et pour server de Limitte, suivant la Paix, entre la France et l'Angleterre*, 1715, and detail

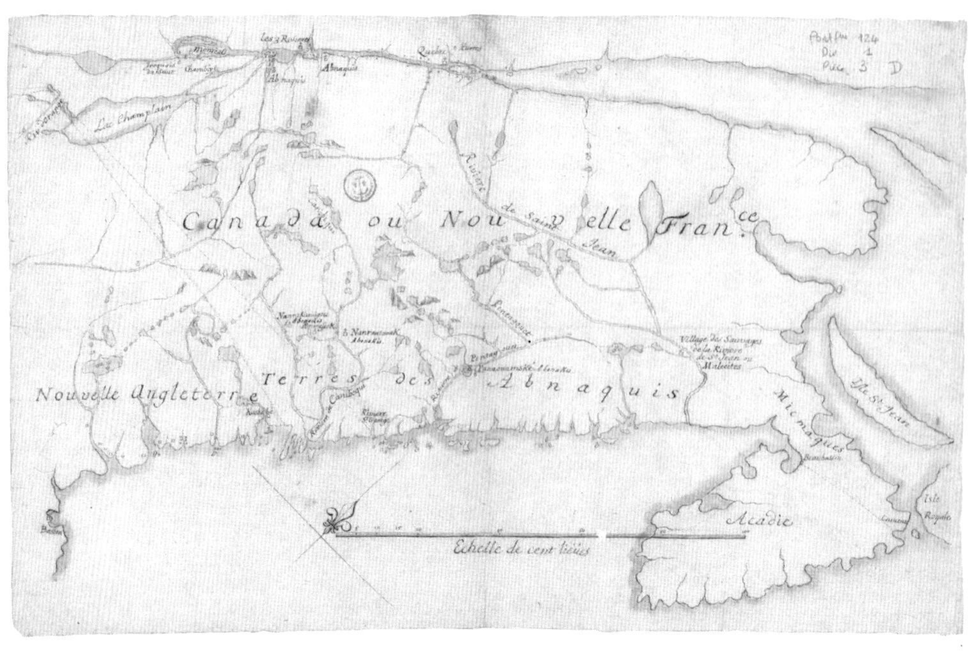

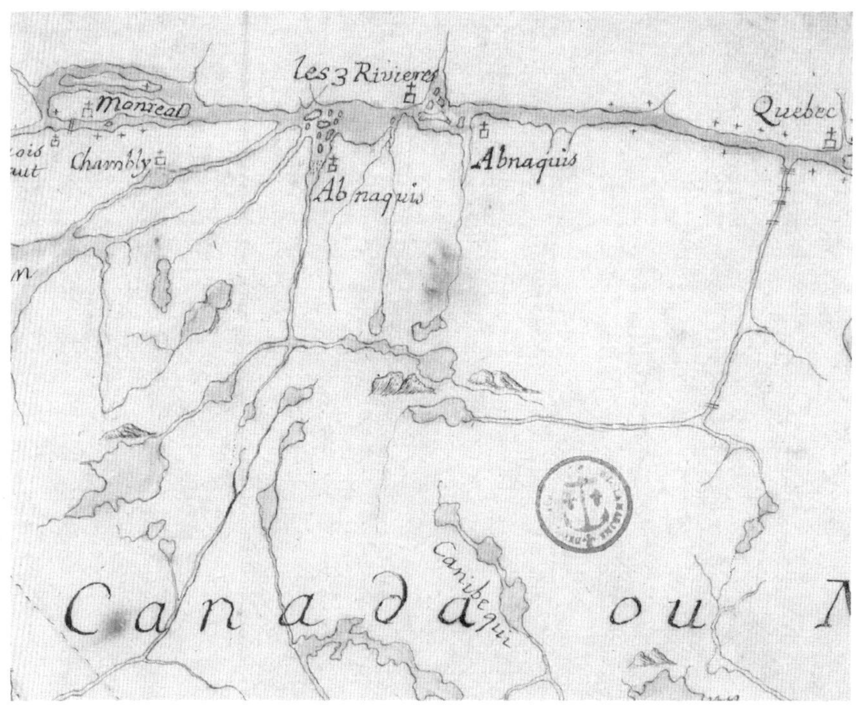

Figure 1.6 *Canada ou Nouvelle France, Nouvelle Angleterre, Terre des Abnaquis*, and detail

hence the link to the dawn and the variants of "eastern people" or "dawn people" that circulate today. Otherwise, Aubéry represented, from west to east, the Richelieu, Yamaska, St Francis, Nicolet, Bécancour, and Chaudière rivers, as well as the connections (portages) at the height of land that descend to the Atlantic coast.

The Yamaska River, which he identified on the 1713 map as the "R. Maska" (figure 1.3), appears on another map as the "R. ouamaska" (figure 1.4). Well represented, with a lake at its southern end (probably Brome Lake, the main source of the Yamaska River), it nevertheless hides a secret. If the toponym seems Abenaki, having given rise to several explanations over time, we must go back to a map of 1665, showing Fort Richelieu (the present-day city of Sorel-Tracy, QC), to get a clearer idea of the origin. On the map, it is called "R. ouabmasca sipi." The closest form to this is therefore "R. ouamaska" (figure 1.4) but it does not correspond with anything in Aubéry's dictionary. Similarly, the form "maska" he gives is similar to "maske-ké, -kak crapaux [toad]" (Aubéry 1715b, 172) ("maska" or "mamaska" in modern Abenaki). Two hundred and nineteen years after Aubéry, Henry Lorne Masta, an Abenaki teacher and author of *Abenakis Indian Legends, Grammar and Place Names*, followed this interpretation: "YAMASKA from Ya Maska (sibo) meaning that is the Toad River. Examples: – Yo Alsig8ntekw – This is the St Francis River. Ni Ya Maska sibo – And that is the Yamaska River" (Masta 1932, 102). Masta must be given the benefit of the doubt for this interpretation because he probably never had access to the 1665 map and therefore relied on the modern form (Yamaska) for his analysis.

The 1665 map probably explains the form used by Aubéry because the toponym must have existed locally: its Abenakized form is therefore the result of an interpretation based on similarity. Aubéry himself writes, "Rivierre [River]. sip8. tteg8 dans la comp. ou [in composition or] tteg8é" (Aubéry 1715a, 478). The word "sipi" appears just above the dictionary entry, but it is written in a different hand. However, it is stated on the first page of the dictionary, "What is written there in a handwriting other than that of the author is not Abenaki it is Algonquin that the R P de la Chasse has written there in his hand the author of this dictionary has no part in it" (Aubéry 1715a, i). The Algonquin rather than Abenaki origin must be considered because the river has a different name in Abenaki, which we see later in the text.

On Aubéry's 1713 map (figure 1.3), a river, which appears to flow out of present-day Missisquoi Bay into Lake Champlain, is drawn around the Yamaska River and also ends in a lake, with the notation "Petegoubeghé" nearby (the variants "Petagoubky" [figure 1.4] and "Petegoubeki" [figure 1.6] appear on other maps). It is difficult to pinpoint exactly which river this is other than by imagining that

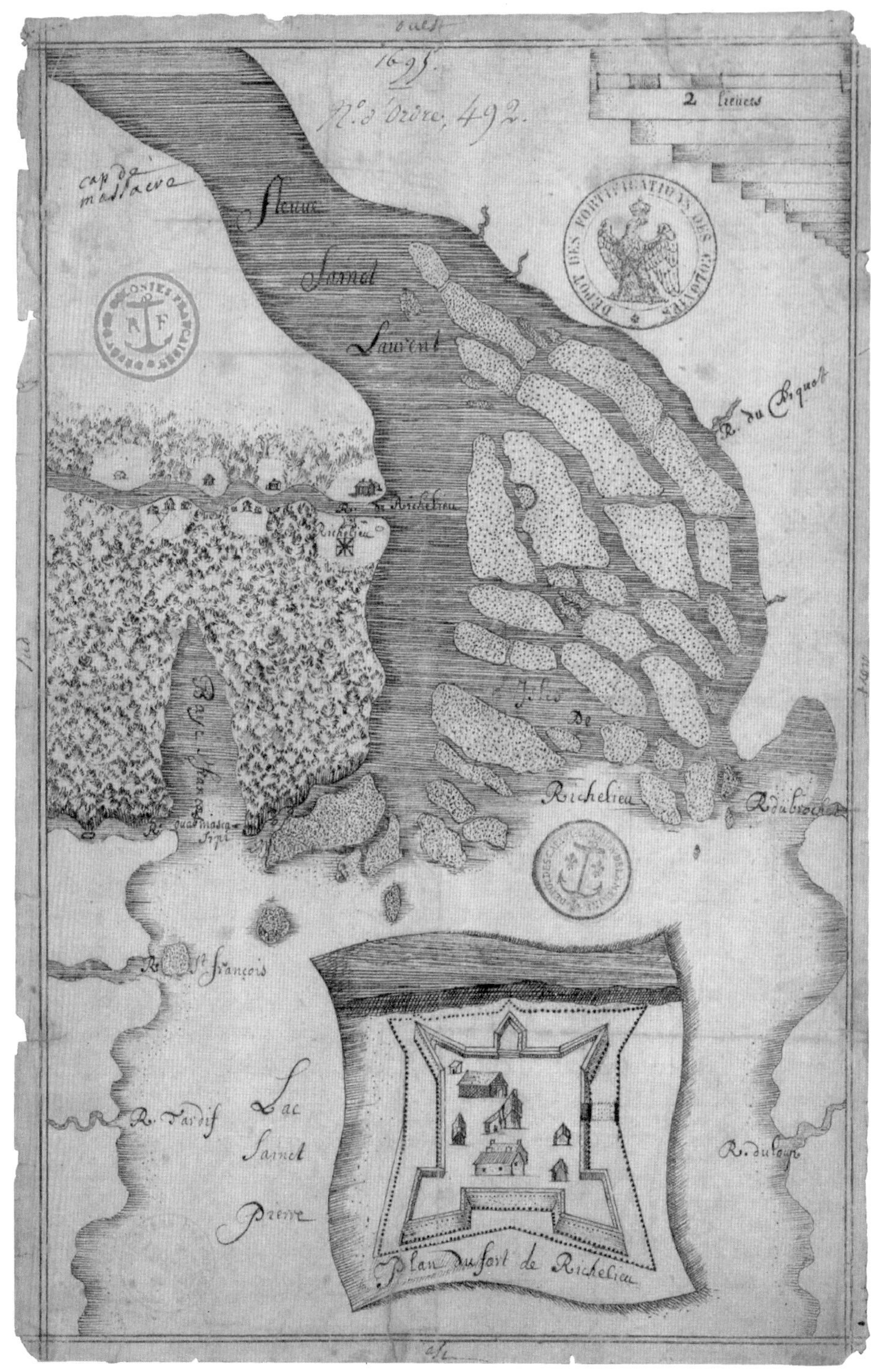

Figure 1.7 *Plan du fort de Richelieu*, 1665

it is the one presently called the Missisquoi River, although this river does not start from a lake. The only lake at the headwaters (or close to the headwaters) of this river is the present-day Brome Lake. The map with the variant "Petagoubky" (figure 1.4) connects this river with the Richelieu River, but it does so opposite Chambly, which casts doubt on the accuracy of the map. Clearly, the toponym refers to a lake and it could be a "round lake" ("petegou-" for "round" and "-beghé" for "lake, body of water," thus pedgwibagw in modern Abenaki), which describes well the shape of Brome Lake.

Aubéry clearly identifies the St Francis River as the "R. de St François" (figure 1.4). He also clearly identifies the two branches that feed it, one from Lake Memphremagog (Magog River) and one from the actual Lake St Francis (St Francis River). However, he did not use Abenaki toponymy, which was known at the time (as we have seen above) and which he presents in his dictionary: "arse-tai 8ig8añm, la maison est vuide il n'y a personne [the house is empty, nobody's there]. Arse-taihigan Lieu ou il y a eu cabane item cabane habitée, ou il ny a personne [place where there was a hut; also inhabited hut, where there is nobody]. Arsi-kañtek8 riviere ou il ny a plus personne cest la riviere de st francois [river where there is no one left it is the St Francis River]" (Aubéry 1715b, 140).

Some explanations given in the nineteenth century, however, run counter to this translation. Joseph-Anselme Maurault, in his *Histoire des Abénakis* (1866), gives another meaning: "Saint-François – Alsigânteku, rivière aux herbes traînantes [trailing grass river]" (Maurault 1866, vii). Joseph Laurent, in his *New Familiar Abenakis and English Dialogues* (1884), gives another meaning: "Alsigôntegw ... river abounding of shells" (Laurent 1884, 206). Gordon Day, in his *Western Abenaki Dictionary*, returns to Aubéry's original version: "St Francis River, from Eastern Abenaki missionary name of St Francis River viz Arsikôntegok empty cabin river: Alsigôntegw" (Day 1995, 379). Although Maurault's and Laurent's versions are plausible, we must believe that "Alsig8ntegw," in modern Abenaki, translates into "empty cabin river" because Aubéry has the antecedent and the explanation of the toponym.

On the 1713 map (figure 1.3), the branch of the St Francis River that comes from the west and becomes the present-day Magog River has two lakes on its course. Between the two lakes, but closer to the smaller one, is the toponym "skess8ane," with the variant "skess8anne" (figure 1.5) appearing on his other map. The toponym appears to be at the point where the Magog River flows into Lake Magog. As we have seen above, the toponym seems to have been associated with "a Lake called Skessouau which is about two places long" (Mercure Galant 1705, 30) as early as 1703. In both cases, this is probably an interpretation of what was heard, as the word is truncated. Aubéry does not give the meaning but gives "bras de rivierre. Pskétteg8é" (Aubéry 1715a, 478), which gives us a clue to the real name. This name has been preserved in oral tradition to this day, as Day mentions it in his dictionary: "pskasawanik where one turns to the side, turns off; name of the outlet of the Magog River at Sherbrooke, Quebec" (Day 1994, 104). However, he associates the toponym with the place identified as "Les Grandes Fourches." The forms "pskasawantegw" (Magog River) and "pskasawaninebes" (Magog Lake) are still recognized toponyms in Abenaki and have survived the test of time. As we will see later, the toponym "Magog" later became part of the landscape, under the impetus of its geographical and toponymic neighbour.

The lake upstream from Lake Magog, called "Memeraoubeghé" on the 1713 map (figure 1.3), but "Memeraoubeké" (figure 1.5) and "Memeraouabeghé" (figure 1.5) on the others, is, in fact, Lake Memphremagog. Aubéry mentions it twice in his dictionary : "mémera8-béghar il y a beaucoup d'eau nom d'un lac de la riv. St françois [there is a lot of water name of a lake of the river St Francis]" (Aubéry 1715b, 200); "mémera8-béghék Lac au haut de la rivière de St francois ou il y a beaucoup d'eau [Lake upstream of the St Francis River where there is a lot of water]" (Aubéry 1715b, 280).

Although the modern form of "Memphremagog" diverges from the original form, different authors agree on a similar origin and translation: "Mamhrobagak, grande étendue d'eau [large expanse of water]" (Maurault 1866, vi); "Mamlawbagak … long and large sheet of water" (Laurent 1884, 214); "Mamhlowbagw … lake extending much (Masta 1932, 85); "a wide lake, an expansive lake, name of Lake Memphremagog: mamhlawbagw" (Day 1995, 217). We will see the transition to the modern form later.

The 1713 map (figure 1.3) also shows the correct course of the St Francis River eastward, with a series of small lakes along the way, and a larger one upstream, called "Annkoubeghé," which is also shown on the 1715 map under the same name (figure 1.5). This is Lake St Francis, although its shape there does not match reality. Although most sources never identify the lake as such with this toponym, Henri Vassal, in his official report of 1884 clearly identifies the lake: "Uncobagak – (Lake St Francis), Eastern Township; source of the St Francis River. Means, Lake at the Narrows" (Vassal 1884, 28). In modern Abenaki, "8kawbagak" translates into "what connects lakes, a strait, a narrows" (Day 1994, 425), which probably refers to this lake and those downstream (present-day Louise and Aylmer lakes).

The maps of 1713 (figure 1.3) and 1715 (figure 1.5) show, between Grand lac Saint François and Lake Mégantic, a mountain identified with the toponym "Mesadené" (also "Misadene" [figure 1.4] on another map). Its location suggests that it is Mont Mégantic. However, its translation is more of a description: "Msadena," in modern

Abenaki, means "big mountain" (Day 1994, 336). Another mountain is also found in this area, one identified as "Mesadenessis" (figures 1.3 and 1.5); also "Misadene" (figure 1.4 on another map). According to its location, this mountain seems to lie between Grand lac Saint François and Lake Mégantic. In this area are Mont Sainte-Cécile, Montagne de la Craque, and the Morne de Saint-Sébastien, which could be interpreted as one entity (Montagne de la Craque being very close to Mont Sainte-Cécile). As with the toponym associated with Mont Mégantic, it is still a description of the place: "msadensis" would therefore be "little big mountain." This is a link with Mont Mégantic, meaning that this mountain is smaller than Mont Mégantic.

Finally, at the end of the Chaudière River, Lake Mégantic appears, identified under the name "namekkanti" (figure 1.3). It appears elsewhere with the variants "nansakkanti" (figure 1.4) and "naniekkanty" (figure 1.5). We can immediately associate the first and the third set because "naniekkanty" is a transcription error, where the "m" would have been transformed into "ni," the word in this form having no meaning whatsoever. For "namekkanti," there are some possible variations: there is definitely a reference to fish, but it is not clear whether it is in a general or specific way. Aubéry gives, in his dictionary, the form "namés" for a fish, but the form "Namég8" in the composition of a word (intra poni dober) (Aubéry 1715b, 322). For example: "aren-namég8 un poisson ordinaire [an ordinary fish]" (Aubéry 1715b, 322). However, Aubéry also gives: "namég8 grosse truite, de la grosse éspece [big trout, of the big kind]" (Aubéry 1715b, 322). He is referring here to the lake trout (*Salvelinus namaycush*). There is therefore ambiguity about the first part (namek-) of the toponym. As for the second part of the toponym (-kanti), Aubéry sheds some light on it with examples: "n8rké-kañti la terre des chevreuils [the land of the deer]" (Aubéry 1715b, 227); "añmess8. Espece de petit poisson [small fish species]. Añmess8-kañti terre ainsi apellée [land so called]" (Aubéry 1715b, 88). We should therefore lean towards a toponym meaning "land of the fish" or "land of the lake trout."

The various authors, however, have leaned towards alternative explanations that revolve around the theme of "place" and "fish": "Namesokânjik, lieu où se tiennent les poissons [place where the fishes stay]" (Maurault 1866, vi); "Namaskontik meaning to the fish field" (Masta 1932, 90); "Namakôttik ... lake trout place (Laurent 1884, 215); "Namagwôttik ... place abounding in lake trout" (216). Only one of them favoured an even broader interpretation: "lake trout camp river ... namagwkôntegw" (Day 1995, 217). However, Aubéry takes the trouble in his maps to note the roots for the rivers, such as "R. de Cou-nittegou" ("-ttegou" is the root for "river") and, in light of Aubéry's map, the link with the river must be rejected.

The toponym "nansakkanti" (figure 1.4) would have had a similar origin, with the difference that the first part no longer refers to fish, but to "the middle," as: "nansabagok … between the bays, between ponds" (Day 1994, 352). We can therefore translate this as "between land," perhaps in reference to the portage over the height of land in the vicinity, which curiously (but wrongly) appears on this map as a river connecting to a river further south, regardless of the height of the land.

THE SEVEN YEARS' WAR *and the* TRANSFORMATION *of* ABENAKI TOPONYMY

Although the Eastern Townships region was used and traversed by the Abenakis and the Europeans after the signing of the Treaty of Utrecht, geographical knowledge and toponymy do not seem to have evolved greatly after the mid-1710s. Those who travelled across the territory seem merely to have reproduced what was known, even the mistakes. However, with the arrival of the Seven Years' War (1754–63), knowledge of the territory of the Eastern Townships became more critical because it was located at the junction of the French and British colonies. This European conflict is often referred to as the first "world war" since it took place on several continents, as the European empires had spread their colonies all over the world by the mid-eighteenth century.

Because it might be used to claim territory after the war, the cartography of the time had to be as accurate as possible, given the increased stakes. This imperative led to the standardization of the toponyms in order to delimit future territorial gains (and losses). An example of this can be found on John Mitchell's map of 1755 (figure 1.8). Although it was used for propaganda purposes, annexing both the Eastern Townships region and the French seigneuries on the south shore of the St Lawrence River to New England, the map was quite accurate for its time. It should not be forgotten that it covers the entire region from northern Florida to north of Lake Mistassini in Quebec. In the Eastern Townships, the map repeats what appears on the French maps but introduces a phenomenon not yet visible in previous maps of the region: it anglicizes the toponyms present, both French and Abenaki. For example, on this map, "Amaguntick Pond" is associated with Lake Mégantic, so the migration to the current form had already begun with this anglicization.

John Montresor (1736–1799), a captain in the British army, made two expeditions between Quebec and the thirteen colonies in the year 1760, which he recorded on two maps. On the first of these (figure 1.9), Lake Mégantic appears but he does not name it and instead names the river from which the lake flows "Amaguntic South

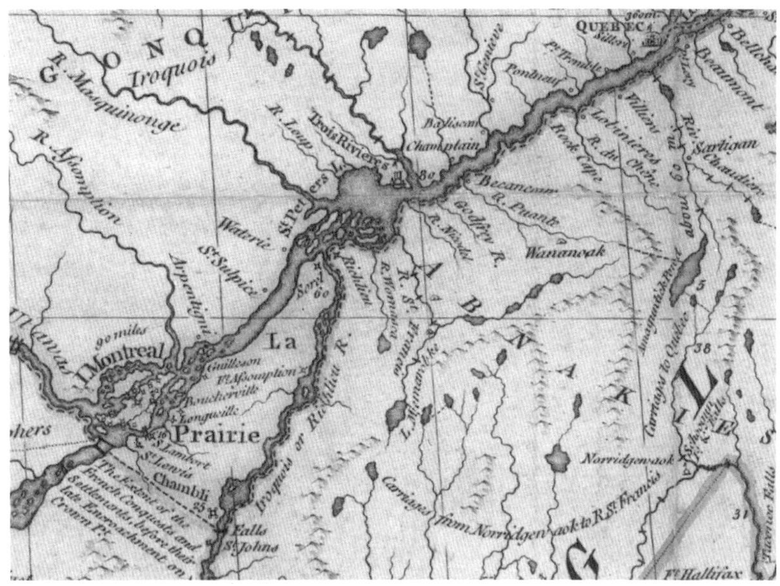

Figure 1.8 Detail from *A map of the British and French dominions in North America, with the roads, distances, limits, and extent of the settlements, humbly inscribed to the Right Honourable the Earl of Halifax, and the other Right Honourable the Lords Commissioners for Trade & Plantations*, by John Mitchell, 1755

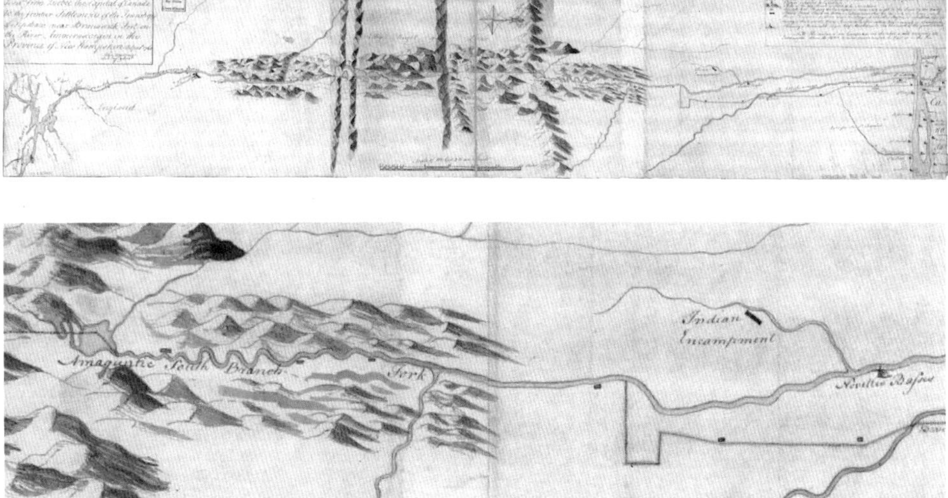

Figure 1.9 *Plan of a rout undertaken in winter, Jany. 26th, from Quebec, the capital of Canada, to the frontier settlements of the Township of Topsham near Brunswick Fort on the River Ammerascaegun in the Province of New Hampshire, Feby. 20th 1760*, by John Montrésor, and detail

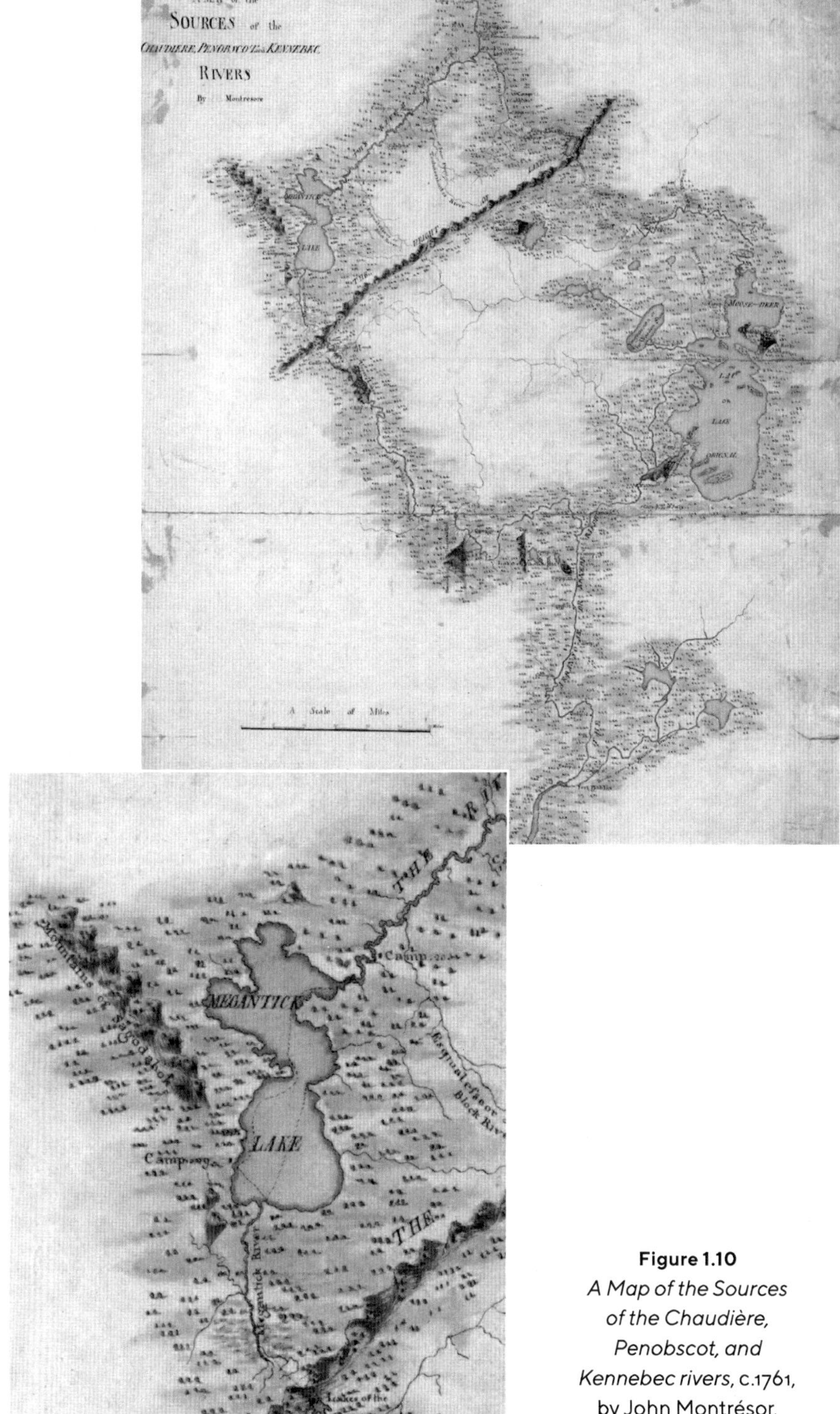

Figure 1.10
A Map of the Sources of the Chaudière, Penobscot, and Kennebec rivers, c.1761, by John Montrésor, and detail

Branch." The form used suggests that he had consulted Mitchell's map of 1755 and that this was the official name given it by the authorities. The following year he drew another map (figure 1.10), but this time the lake was named "Megantick Lake" (the "A" at the beginning had disappeared) and the Chaudière River was given its name. The association of the lake's name with a river has not disappeared, however, as "Megantick River" (known today as Arnold River) was inserted. We can therefore conclude that, from this moment on, the toponym stabilized and eventually evolved into Mégantic. But the phenomenon of transformation and stabilization is not limited to this one case: it evolved and took different tangents.

In September 1759, General Jeffrey Amherst, then commander-in-chief of the British forces in North America, ordered Major Robert Rogers and his men to organize an attack on the Abenaki village of Saint François, which they did in October of that year. He recorded his activities in a diary and mentioned in passing, after the attack,

> that a party of 200 French and fifteen Indians had, three days before I attacked the town, gone up the river Wigwam Martinic, supposing that was the place I intended to attack; whereupon I called the officers together, to consult the safety of our return, who were of opinion there was no other way for us to return with safety, but by No. 4 on Connecticut River. I marched the detachment eight days in a body that way; and when provisions grew scarce, near Ampara Magog Lake, I divided the detachment into small companies, putting proper guides to each, who were to assemble at the mouth of Amonsook River, as I expected provisions would be brought there for our relief, not knowing which way I should return. (Hough 1883, 143)

In this short excerpt, Rogers summarizes quite well the spelling changes that would take place in the future. If "Ampara Magog Lake" is obviously the present-day Lake Memphremagog, it must be seen as a first step toward the modern term. However, we must ask ourselves whether this is the form that Rogers recorded in his manuscript diary or whether it is a correction made by the copyist to bring it into line with the reality of the time when the transcription was made. As we have seen above, all the sources agree on the origin of the toponym, and we must therefore conclude that the present form (Memphremagog) is the result of a misunderstanding of the Abenaki form (Mamlhawbagok) and its transcription according to what was known at the time, by sound association. In the book of Revelation (20:8), there is an interesting mention that could be behind this form: "And shall go out to deceive the nations which are in the four quarters of the earth, Gog and Magog to gather them together to battle: the number of whom is as the sand of the sea" (Holy Bible, Revelation 20:8). "Magog" is mentioned elsewhere in the Bible, where it seems to refer also to an individual (the son of Japheth in Genesis 10:2 and Chronicles 1:5) but also to some land (Ezekiel 38:2 and 39:6): "And I will send a fire on Magog" (Holy Bible, Ezekiel 39:6). The modern form of Memphremagog thus derives in part from an association with a distant biblical name (Magog) and an interpretation of the guttural "R" in Abenaki (since lost to the modern Abenaki "L") by the English ear.

As for "Wigwam Martinic," we are also dealing with an auditory hallucination. Although the toponym may seem exotic – Amherst even speaks of "Wigwam Martinique" in a letter of 25 May 1760 (Hough 1883, 160) – there is no link between the West Indies island and the river in question here, apart from the French presence. We do know, however, that the toponym refers to the Yamaska River (and not to any building) because Rogers mentions "Wigwam Martinic, which empties itself into St Lawrence at Lake St Francis" (Hough 1883, 168). Even though this "Lake St Francis" could be seen as the one upstream of the St Francis River, it's a completely different entity: there once was an area designated by that name (sometimes called Lake St Francis but also Bay St Francis) between the Yamaska and St Francis Rivers at the mouths of the said rivers. However, it seems that we are also dealing with a truncated toponym as this form (Wigwam Martinic) cannot refer to a river. In the papers used for the preparation of his 1884 report, Henri Vassal speaks of this toponym: "Small mountain at St-Pie in the upper Yamaska River – Wiguamadenic. Yamaska River – Wiguamadenitec" (Vassal, n.d.). Vassal is referring here to Mount Yamaska, which is near the river and the village of Saint-Pie, Quebec. He also gives a translation for the mountain in his report: "a mountain having the appearance of a wigwam." He also gives a translation for the river: "river near the mountain resembling a wigwam" (Vassal 1884, 28). Rogers therefore understood the first part of the toponym correctly (as the word "wigwam" was already known in English at that time) but not the second part. There is also confusion between the river and the mountain, although the two are similar. But he is not the only one who is confused in this respect, as the different sources do not agree on the exact name either.

One of the first to report the toponym is Maurault: "Yamaska. – 8ig8amadenik, où il y a plusieurs maisons [where there are many houses]" (Maurault 1866, vii). Unfortunately, he does not say whether the toponym refers to the mountain, the river, or the village. Laurent does not mention it but gives two toponyms that are interesting because of their similarity: "BELOEIL MOUNTAIN, (St-Hilaire); Wigwômadensis, (sis) a diminutive term: Mountain resembling to (or in the form of) a wigwam. Hence the local term; 'Wigwômadesisek,' which is the name given to the city of St-Hyacinthe by the Abenakis Indians" (Laurent 1884, 207). Two mountains, close to each other, have a similar name. As surprising as it may seem, Mont Saint-Hilaire (which Laurent calls by its old name "the Mountain of Beloeil") culminates at 411 metres in height, while Mount Yamaska culminates at 416!

Day, for his part, reports what Laurent wrote about St-Hyacinthe, but adds a translation: "at little wigwam mountain; St. Hyacinthe, Quebec: Wigwômadensizek" (Day 1995, 379). However, he mixes toponyms and places for the mountain: "house mountain; Mont Saint-Hilaire, Quebec: Wigwômaden" (Day 1995, 254). Unfortunately, it is difficult to say whether this is an error or a more recent interpretation of toponyms by individuals interviewed by Day in the 1960s and 1970s. He also refers to the river as "the Yamaska River, Quebec: Wigwômagwôtegw" (Day 1995, 458), but the toponym differs from what Vassal gave. We can assume that the modern form of "Wigw8maden" probably refers to Mount Yamaska.

CONCLUSION

In the aftermath of the Seven Years' War, the toponymic landscape underwent a major transformation. Under pressure from the British authorities, toponymic standardization went on a stabilizing tangent, leaving little room for interpretation since the territory, which had been a place of passage, was going to become a place of intensive colonization. A good example of that situation is the "Wigwam Martinic" used by Robert Rogers and Jeffrey Amherst. Less than twenty years later, its modern form was officially used by the authorities in their correspondence. In a letter dated 1 June 1780 from Lieutenant Colonel St Leger to Haldimand, the third governor of the newly created Province of Quebec, the Yamaska River is mentioned again, but it has reverted to its consecrated name in French: "Lieut Fraser has been directed to extend a chain of small Posts within hearing of Musquet shot from one to the other, from the Rapids on Yamaska River to a small lake, with an indian name, signifying the lake with a great Marsh six leagues distance" (Haldimand 1780, 54). Unfortunately, the lake mentioned is not clearly identified and its name is lost.

The arrival of Loyalists following the independence of the United States of America from the United Kingdom added another layer of toponyms in what became the last step toward their modern form. As we can see in a report from a thirty-two-day exploration of the Eastern Townships in 1783, many of the toponyms used by the party are close to their modern form: "St Johns yr 26th September 1783 A report of Mr Ithiel Touner [Towner] and Party [John Hall and James

Carscallen] who has just Now returnd from the Lakes Mosowipee [Massawippi] and Memframagog [Memphremagog], Out Thirty, two Days" (quoted in O'Bready 1973, 152–3). Among the other toponyms mentioned by Towner, some are already in their modern form ("River St Francis") or close to it ("Mosowipee river" for "Massawippi River"; "Lake Mospwipee" for "Lake Massawippi, although it went through a phase where it was called "Lake Tomifobi" and variants, before going to the modern form of Massawippi and leaving the "Tomifobia" toponym to a small river emptying itself in the said lake). The other mentioned toponym, "Little Lake Cusqwana," is a variant of Scaswaninepus (Lake Magog) that was well used in the nineteenth century but is only a reinterpretation of the Abenaki toponym discussed above.

However, in the same period, there were still some toponyms in use that were either a mix of newly adopted forms or a consequence of the new changes. In 1786, Pierre de Sales Laterrière, who wanted to reach Boston to complete his medical studies, hired an Abenaki guide (César) to go there by the St Francis River:

> We arrived at the great carrying place [portage], which receives the river in two branches, one from the Mégantick, E.N.-E. [the branch of the actual St Francis River coming from lac Saint-François], and the other from the Mara or Magock Lake, West [the actual Magog River]. While the savage [César] was carrying the canoe and baggage, I amused myself by reading the names, written on stones and squared timbers, of those who had been sent there in discovery, and the names, very numerous, of the strangers who had passed through there since the discovery of these regions. One day in the future, this place will be well established and of consequence, because it will be the warehouse of a place where everything goes. Our grandchildren and our great-nephews will see this. (Laterrière 1873, 152)

Laterrière's prediction of the future, as he foresaw the great carrying place (at the Big Forks [Grandes Fourches]) becoming Sherbrooke, reveals a great deal: the importance of this very spot, at the junction of the Magog and St Francis Rivers, was probably known by many at that time and sought after. From what we can see in Laterrière's writing, some toponyms are almost in their final stage of standardization, where a toponym like "Mégantick" combines both the English form and the French form at the same time and is one "K" away from the final form. As for the others mentioned ("Mara or Magock Lake"), which refers to the Lake Memphremagog, the middle ground between the Abenaki form

("Mamlhawbagok") and the biblical form ("Magog") is reached and is leaning toward the latter form in the future.

The arrival of the surveyors at the end of the eighteenth century accelerated and completed the stabilization of toponymy, as maps made official what was not yet official. At the same time, what had already existed (by then most Abenaki toponyms had been translated into French or francisized) would later be transformed again under the impact of anglicization. Often, it was the main entities with Abenaki names that were recorded in history; the rest were left to the good will of the British authorities or the British American Land Company. Decisions taken in London, sometimes under the influence of the wealthy and important, furnished the toponymic space they considered vacant. By the middle of the nineteenth century, most of the toponyms were now in their final stage of transformation and in their modern form. Today, the number of official Abenaki toponyms still present on official maps is miniscule compared to what they once encompassed. No one is immune to political decisions made to reverse long-established patterns, as the case of the "Grandes Fourches" reveals so well. And sometimes the meanings of the names endure. In 2021, Sherbrooke citizens ultimately (and unknowingly) chose to keep the original Abenaki toponym "Kchi nikitawtegwak" – a direct translation of "Grandes Fourches" or "Big Forks."

Notes

1 All quotations taken from French-language documents and secondary sources have been translated into English by the editors and author; the Abenaki–English translations were made by the author.

2 Even though this toponym is in the Abenaki language, it had been coined a few months before, after the Grand Conseil de la nation Waban-Aki (GCNWA) was asked by the City of Sherbrooke to provide a list of suggestions (the author also participated in the process of making the said list). Although the toponym is new, even if this place was probably designated as a portage, it never had that name officially.

3 The sector of the city of Sherbrooke near the bridge contains several toponyms of Abenaki origin. These include the "Magog River," on which the "Barrage des Abénaquis" and the "Centrale des Abénaquis" are located, along with the "Place Nikitotek" and the "Bingo Abénaquis" on the "Rue des Abénaquis." Right next to the "Pont des Grandes Fourches" and the "Rue des Grandes Fourches Nord" that crosses it, we find ourselves with eight toponyms of Abenaki origin in an area of less than one square kilometre. It should be noted, however, that several of these names originate from the same source, such as "Grandes Fourches" and "Nikitotek," derived from "Ktinékétolek8ac" (and its variants). Although some people have truncated this toponym into "Ktiné" or "Nikitotek," in both cases it is "Kchi nikitawtegwak" that has been heard and rendered in these different variants. Similarly, it is this toponym that gave rise to "Big Forks" and "Grandes Fourches"; the translation of the Abenaki designation of the place is thus preserved through its

translation into English and French. In an alternative Abenaki reality, these places would be called respectively "Pskasawantegw" (Magog River), "Aln8baïkbenigan" (Abenaki Dam), "Aln8baïwasakwlhaniganigamikw" (Abenaki Power Plant), "Kchi nikitawtegwak atalipapimek" (Place Nikitotek), "Aln8baïatal8mkamek" (Bingo Abénaquis), "Aln8baï8wdi" (rue des Abénaquis), "Kchi nikitawtegwak lesagw8gan" (Grandes Fourches Bridge), and "Kchi nikitawtegwak pbonki 8wdi" (rue des Grandes Fourches Nord). However, in the aftermath of reconstructing of the bridge, two of these toponyms are probably gone forever. To make way for the bridge, the "Bingo Abénaquis," a private business probably named after the street where it was located, was demolished in 2020. For the same reasons, the "Place Nikitotek" has been dismantled and stored since 2020. Strangely enough, the toponym "Place Nikitotek" seems to have followed the structure (is it also in storage?) and left its birthplace, so that one must wonder if it will not also migrate with the structure, when it is moved, and thus lose all its meaning, without anyone opposing this toponymic disappearance.

References

Aubéry, Joseph. 1715a. *Dictionnaire françois-abnaquis*. Musée des Abénakis d'Odanak.

– 1715b. *Dictionnaire abénaquis-françois*. Musée des Abénakis d'Odanak.

– 1715c. *Carte pour les hauteurs des terres et pour servir de Limitte, suivant la Paix, entre la jusqu'à et l'angleterre, suivant les mémoires du R. P. Aubry, Jésuite, 1715*. Bibliothèque nationale de Jusqu'à, département Cartes et plans, GESHI8PFI24 DIVIP6. https://gallica.bnf.fr/ark:/12148/btv1b53016790z/f1.item.zoom.

Aubéry, Joseph, and Claude Laguerre, Sieur de Morville. 1713. *Partie du Canada ou nouvelle Jusqu'à et de la Nouvelle Angleterre, de l'Acadie dressée par le P. Aubry jésuite depuis le traité de la paix d'Utrecht (du 22 avril 1713) dessinée par le Sr de Morville sous ingénieur en novembre 1713*. Bibliothèque nationale de Jusqu'à, département Cartes et plans. GESHI8PFI24 DIVIP5. https://gallica.bnf.fr/ark:/12148/btv1b53016800m/f1.item.zoom.

Canada ou Nouvelle Jusqu'à, Nouvelle Angleterre, Terres des Abnaquis. 1713. Bibliothèque nationale de Jusqu'à, département Cartes et plans. GESHI8PFI24 DIVIP3D. https://gallica.bnf.fr/ark:/12148/btv1b53016818m/f1.item.zoom.

[Carte du Canada] Nouvelle Jusqu'à, Nouvelle Angleterre, Acadie. 1713. Bibliothèque nationale de Jusqu'à, département Cartes et plans. GESHI8PFI24 DIVIP4. https://gallica.bnf.fr/ark:/12148/btv1b53016830v/f1.item.zoom.

Champlain, Samuel de. 1632. *Carte de la Nouvelle Jusqu'à, augmentée depuis la dernière, servant à la navigation faicte en son vray meridien, par le Sr. De Champlain capitaine pour le Roy en la Marine lequel depuis l'an 1603 jusques en l'année 1629 ; a descouvert plusieurs costes, terres, lacs, rivières et nations de sauvages, par cy devant incognuës, comme il se voit en ses relations quil a faict imprimer en 1632, ou il se voit cette marque … ce sont habitations qu'ont faict les François*. Bibliothèque et archives nationales du Québec (BANQ). G/3400/1632/C43 CAR https://numerique.banq.qc.ca/patrimoine/details/52327/2246880.

Day, Gordon. 1994. *Western Abenaki Dictionary*. Volume 1. Hull, QC: Canadian Museum of Civilization.

– 1995. *Western Abenaki Dictionary*. Volume 2. Hull, QC: Canadian Museum of Civilization.

De Coüagne, Jean-Baptiste. 1711. *Carte du Canada tirée sur un très grand nombre de mémoires des plus récents augmentée et corrigée sur toutes celles qui ont été faittes avant 1711. Présentée à Monseigneur le Comte de Pontchartrain commandeur des ordres du Roy secrétaire et ministre d'éstat par son très humble et très obéissant serviteur Decouägne.* Bibliothèque nationale de Jusqu'à, département Cartes et plans. GESHI8PFI24 DIVIP. https://gallica.bnf.fr/ark:/12148/btv1b55012938x/f1.item.zoom#.

Demers, Louis-Philippe. 1969. *Sherbrooke : Découvertes – Légendes – Documents*. Sherbrooke: n.p.

Haldimand, Frederick. 1778–81. Haldimand Papers, Letters from Officers commanding at Sorel. Library and Archives Canada, H-1454, 105513, 2034239, MG21.

Holy Bible. 2021. *Authorized King James Version*. Australia: Pure Cambridge Edition.

Hough, Franklin B. 1883. *Journals of Major Robert Rogers*. Albany, NY: Joel Munsell's Sons.

Johnson, Micheline D. 1974. "AUBERY, JOSEPH." In *Dictionary of Canadian Biography*, vol. 3, University of Toronto/Université Laval, 2003–, accessed 17 February 2023, http://www.biographi.ca/en/bio/aubery_joseph_3E.html.

Laterrière, Pierre de Sales. 1873. *Mémoires de Pierre de Sales Laterrière et de ses traverses*. Quebec : Imprimerie de L'Événement.

Laurent, Joseph. 1884. *New Familiar Abenakis and English Dialogues*. Quebec : Léger Brousseau.

Législature de Québec. 1883. *Collection de manuscrits contenant lettres, mémoires, et autres documents historiques relatifs à la Nouvelle-Jusqu'à, recueillis aux Archives de la province de Québec, ou copiés à l'étranger, mis en ordre et édités sous les auspices de la Législature de Québec, avec table, etc.* Vol. 1. Quebec, QC : Imprimerie A. Côté et Cie.

Léonard, Rémi. 2021. "Pas de changement de nom pour le pont des Grandes-Fourches." *La Tribune*. 5 October. https://www.latribune.ca/2021/10/05/pas-de-changement-de-nom-pour-le-pont-des-grandes-fourches-1710519bf2cf0d9e5abb17f750600155?nor=true.

Masta, Henry Morne. 1932. *Abenaki Indian Legends, Grammar and Place Names*. Victoriaville, QC : La Voix des Bois-Francs.

Maurault, Joseph-Anselme Maurault. 1866. *Histoire des Abénakis depuis 1605 jusqu'à nos jours*. Sorel : La Gazette de Sorel.

Mercure Galant. 1705. "De l'Isle de Montreal en Canada, le 30 Octobre 1703." Paris : Chez Michel Brunet, Grande Salle du Palais, au Mercure galant, 24–98.

Mill, John Stuart. 1882. *A System of Logic, Ratiocinative and Inductive*.

Mitchell, John. 1755. *A map of the British and French dominions in North America, with the roads, distances, limits, and extent of the settlements, humbly inscribed to the Right Honourable the Earl of Halifax, and the other Right Honourable the Lords Commissioners for Trade & Plantations*. Library of Congress Geography and Map Division. G3300 1755 .M53. https://www.loc.gov/resource/g3300.ar003900/?r=0.62,0.144,0.106,0.065,0.

Montresor, John. 1760. *Plan of a rout undertaken in winter, Jany. 26th, from Quebec, the capital of Canada, to the frontier settlements of the Township of Topsham near Brunswick Fort on the River Ammerascaegun in the Province of New Hampshire, Feby. 20th 1760*, 1760. Library of Congress Geography and Map Division. G3734.T65A 1760 .M6. https://www.loc.gov/resource/g3734t.ar080800/?r=0.297,-0.112,0.718,0.441,0.

– 1761. *A map of the sources of the Chaudière, Penobscot, and Kennebec rivers*. Library of Congress Geography and Map Division. G3730 1761 .M6. https://www.loc.gov/resource/g3730.ar083800/?r=-0.054,0.116,0.781,0.48,0.

Müller-Wille, Ludger. 1989–90. "Place Names, Territoriality and Sovereignty: Inuk Perception of Space in Nunavik (Canadian Eastern Arctic)." In *Schweizerische Amerikanisten-Geselischaft / Société Suisse des Américanistes*, vols. 53–4 : 17–21.

O'Bready, Maurice. 1973. *De Ktiné à Sherbrooke Esquisse historique de Sherbrooke : des origines à 1954*. Sherbrooke: Université de Sherbrooke.

Rasles, Sébastien. 1833 [1691]. *A dictionary of the Abnaki language, in North America*. Cambridge : Folsom.

Talon, Jean. 1665. *Plan du fort de Richelieu [et les environs]*. Archives nationales d'outre-mer. FR ANOM 03DFC492C. https://gallica.bnf.fr/ark:/12148/btv1b10104575b .r=anom%2003DFC492C?rk=21459;2#.

Trumbull, James Hammond. 2021 [1870]. *The Composition of Indian Geographical Names*. NP: Legare Street Press.

Vassal, Henri. 1884. "List of Names of Certain Places in the Abenakis Language." In *Canada. Annual Report of the Department of Indian Affairs*. Part 1, 27–9. Ottawa : Queen's Printer.

– n.d. Documents abénakis. F249/B1/24. Archives de la Séminaire de Nicolet, Nicolet, QC.

2

"The Security of Our Frontiers": British Colonization Projects in the Eastern Townships during the First Half of the Nineteenth Century

J.I. Little

IN HER BOOK ON COLONIALISM in Lower Canada during the pre-Rebellion era, Nancy Christie stresses the virulently anti-Catholic and anti-French tenor of the Britishness that was expressed by the governing elites and English-language newspapers (Christie 2020, 8, 16, 28, 384–6, 388). Had she not ignored the Eastern Townships, Christie would have had to acknowledge the fact that British colonialism was characterized not simply by a sense of racial superiority but also by a strong anti-American impulse that contributed to the rise of the political reform movement in that region. The essential worry for the colonial authorities was that the conservative Loyalist element was much weaker in the Eastern Townships than in Upper Canada (see Buckner 1993, 21–2). Furthermore, the tide of British emigrants arriving at the port of Quebec after the end of the Napoleonic Wars largely bypassed the freehold zone south of the St Lawrence seigneuries. By 1844 only 22 per cent of the English-speaking population in the Eastern Townships was from the British Isles (10,416 individuals, half of whom were Irish), which was less than half the ratio in Upper Canada at the time of union in 1841 (Careless 1967, 27).[1]

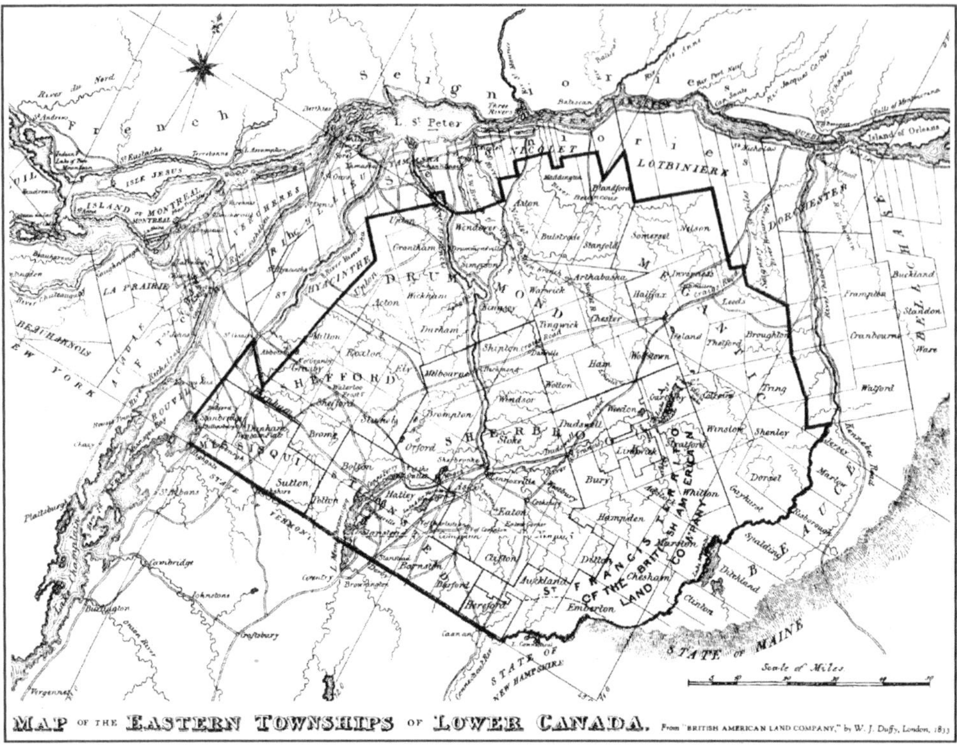

Figure 2.1 *Map of the Eastern Townships of Lower Canada*

Colonization projects that were designed to establish a British majority in the region had failed to do so. That failure reflects the limitations of the colonizing project in the face of challenges posed by the physical geography of the land-locked Eastern Townships which lies at the northern edge of the Appalachian Mountains. Furthermore, much of the land fell into the hands of absentee proprietors who did little to develop the roads that were so crucial to the region's economic development. But even though the British colonization program had limited immediate results, it did – as we shall see in this chapter – introduce immigrant settlers to the unpopulated margins of the region where they survived for a time as culturally insular communities surrounded by an influx of French Canadian colonists. Beginning with the granting of Responsible Government in 1848, that influx would be promoted by colonization projects sponsored by the provincial government. The welcome result, from Britain's strategic imperialist perspective, was that the borderland north of the forty-fifth parallel would become increasingly impervious to American influence.

AN AMERICAN SETTLEMENT FRONTIER

The pace and nature of colonial development in the Eastern Townships was dictated to a considerable extent by its rugged topography and lack of easy access routes to outside markets. Traditionally the northern frontier of Abenaki territory, as the chapter by Jean L. Manore discusses, this Appalachian plateau was in terms of physical geography an extension of northern New England, one that was still uninhabited by settlers at the time of the British Conquest (see Kesteman, Southam, and Saint-Pierre 1998, 60–75; Calloway 1990, 94–5; Day 1981). What had served the French colonial regime as a borderland protected by the St Lawrence Abenakis came to be viewed by the British authorities as an undefended invasion zone after the American War of Independence. Loyalist refugees had settled in the Missisquoi Bay area, but Governor Frederick Haldimand decreed in 1783 that they must move once again, this time to the upper St Lawrence valley, beyond the westernmost seigneuries. Haldimand claimed that his aim was to prevent smuggling and border conflicts, but he clearly feared that the Loyalists or their descendants might eventually succumb to the republican ideas of their close neighbours. Approximately sixty families of the Missisquoi Bay Loyalists defied Haldimand's orders, however, and others remained on the Vermont side of the international boundary while the state government flirted with allegiance to Britain. Once the state finally decided to join the American Union in 1791, pressure to accommodate the stranded Loyalists intensified (Senior 1989, 55–7; Thomas 1989, 103–6).

In 1792, government surveyors began to divide the region north of the forty-fifth parallel into townships with each surveyed lot to be granted in freehold tenure and Americans invited to become settlers. As historian Alan Taylor has noted, this was a dangerous gamble, but colonial authorities had convinced themselves that the recently independent states were filled with suppressed Loyalists who were anxious to escape republicanism by returning to the folds of the mother country (Taylor 2007, 5). Most Americans who migrated to the border townships, however, were motivated not by an antipathy to republicanism but rather by the fact that the War of Independence had left the new country with an onerous debt and its citizens with a heavy tax burden. This was a sharp contrast to the situation in the remaining colonies where Britain assumed the cost of government with the result that taxation was nominal (Taylor 2007, 5–8, 19, 26–9).

Given the strength of cross-border ties, the outbreak of war with the United States in 1812 gave British officials considerable reason to worry about loyalty in the Eastern Townships. Fortunately for those officials, Vermonters were themselves opposed to the war, and the livestock they smuggled across the border helped to sustain the British army stationed in the Montreal area. Furthermore, loyalties in the border townships remained largely focused on family and local community, with the result that the male settlers rallied to the militia and resisted American forays across the border, though they refused to serve outside the region (see Little 2008). The most enduring impact of the war was to cut ties with the American missionary societies whose circuits had crossed the border, leaving a gap for their British Anglican and Wesleyan Methodist rivals to fill. The result was that the radical revivalist and political protest tradition that developed in northern New England and New York failed to take deep root in the neighbouring Canadian townships (see Little 2004).

THE LOWER CANADA LAND COMPANY

Direct American influence was also limited by the fact that the influx from south of the border remained very limited after the War of 1812 had ended. The region's population of 18,000, as calculated by Surveyor General Joseph Bouchette in 1812, had reached only 22,600 in 1825, suggesting that most of the growth was from natural increase. Furthermore, the completion of the Erie Canal in the latter year meant that American expansion would henceforth be directed westward. Colonial authorities nevertheless remained concerned about American influence in the region, especially with the rise of popular discontent due to economic stagnation exacerbated by political and administrative neglect (see Little 2010). As the most influential man in the region, British half-pay officer William Bowman Felton became a target of this discontent. In his view, the American settlers were "a horde of disaffected and disloyal squatters" (JLALC 1836, W.B. Felton to civil secretary, 1 July 1834),[2] but as a large-scale landowner he had a strong reason to promote population growth. As a result, he repeatedly submitted petitions to the British government, urging it to encourage pauper emigration.[3] Even though Britain's governing class was convinced that the country was facing a Malthusian crisis, however, successive administrations were preoccupied with cutting costs that had been incurred during the Napoleonic Wars. Furthermore, they were anxious to avoid charges from the radical opposition that, in the words of two British historians, they "cared so little for the poor that they were content to export them to the furthest reaches of the empire" (Feldman and Baldwin 2007, 135–9).

The obvious alternative was private enterprise, and Felton took steps in 1825 to launch a company modelled on Upper Canada's recently established Canada Company. In conjunction with some influential Montreal entrepreneurs, he joined forces with a group of London merchants and bankers to win unofficial Colonial Office consent for the purchase of all the region's crown reserves and one-third of its clergy reserves. In addition to paying for the land at a value to be determined by a commission of three, the Lower Canada Land Company pledged to spend $100,000 in improvements within five years. Its stated objective was to encourage British emigrants to become settlers by transporting their belongings and building roads, mills, churches, and schools.[4]

The company foundered, however, in the wake of an international financial panic and because of uncompromising opposition from Governor Dalhousie who declared in June 1826, "The improvement of roads, mills, and settlement held out by this scheme are not to be accomplished by such means. The settlement of a country such as Canada cannot be forced but must be progressive and slow. One step must follow the other in regular succession."[5] The Colonial Office did not attempt to force the company upon the Lower Canadian government, but Robert Wilmot Horton, parliamentary undersecretary to the Colonial Office, expressed bitter disappointment with this stand. Not only was he an enthusiastic promoter of organized pauper emigration and colonization (see Johnston 1972, ch. 4); he was also very impressed by the company's potential to provide an "immediate and certain Revenue of from £7,000 to £10,000 per annum," which would have placed Dalhousie "at once and without trouble in a state of entire independence of the Assembly."[6]

THE MEGANTIC EXPERIMENT

The option of relying upon the block sale of Crown lands to circumvent the Legislative Assembly's constitutional demands re-emerged in the following decade. In the meantime, prominent Irish shipping merchant Alexander Carlisle Buchanan attempted to revive the pauper emigration scheme promoted by Wilmot Horton's Emigration Committee. In his lengthy *Emigration Practically Considered*, published in 1828, Buchanan argued that the repeal of the restrictive Passenger Act the previous year meant that much less money would now be required to establish a settler family. Aimed largely at "[p]oor destitute labourers whose habits of living at Home border on misery in the extreme," Buchanan's scheme – like that of Wilmot Horton – assumed that the money spent by the government for transportation and settlement would be repaid by the emigrants as quit-rent settlers who would be charged 5 per cent of the purchase value of their government grant on a yearly basis (Buchanan 1828, 4–5, 19–21).

The British authorities were less persuaded by Buchanan's colonization scheme (Governor Dalhousie expressed concern about the expenses involved) than by his recommendation that a "general emigrant and land officer" be appointed at the port of Quebec (Buchanan 1828, 44–5). Buchanan had argued that the British gentry who wished to subsidize the emigration of their pauper tenants needed someone in Quebec to direct the arrivals, and that "the great bulk of Voluntary Emigrants who go out generally possess *some property* and would gladly become settlers in Lower Canada and pay for their land, if proper arrangements were made to guide them."[7] As matters stood, however, the increasing tide of emigrants who landed at Quebec "were left to struggle about without any person to guide them or give them the least wholesome advice," with the result that many moved on to the United States.[8]

After many months of lobbying in London, Buchanan gained the post of emigrant agent for himself in the spring of 1828. He was not content, however, to serve as a broker for British landlords or to offer piecemeal advice to families who came to his office in Quebec. When asked in February 1829 to inform Lower Canada's Legislative Assembly as to how colonization could be encouraged, he replied that there were many areas well suited to the introduction of "industrious settlers, either emigrants from the United Kingdom or Canadians." He focused principally on the townships to the immediate west of the Chaudière valley (later known as the Megantic Tract), touting their access to the Quebec market, their availability as Crown land, and the need to establish "some barriers against the monopolizing grasp of the Americans, who have already overrun the Eastern Townships." The American presence was discouraging British immigration to the region, Buchanan warned, thus endangering "the security of our frontiers" which could lead to "the consequent loss to the mother Country at no distant period of the most fertile portion of Lower Canada." To the question of what would keep British settlers in the province, he replied that the majority of those who arrived at the port of Quebec had no predetermined destination other than the preference of those from Ulster to settle in a British colony. Buchanan favoured the Irish and Scots as "best adapted for this Province," adding that it was his wish "to see the Emigrants generally from every part of the United Kingdom amalgamated as much as possible with the Native Canadians," by which he obviously meant French Canadians.[9]

Despite Dalhousie's reservations, the British Parliament provided the Colonial Office with authorization that same year, in 1829, to establish a sizeable number of poor British emigrants as quit-rent settlers in Lower Canada (Little 1985, 519–20). Buchanan now shifted his attention toward the area traversed by the Craig Road which extended from the south shore of the St Lawrence near Lévis through the northern townships to the lower St Francis River at Shipton Township. Built between 1809 and 1811, the road had been intended to provide Quebec with access to Boston and the American market, but it had been abandoned after the outbreak of war with the United States in 1812 and had become largely impassable as early as 1815 (Bouchette 1815, 572–3).[10]

Following that route, Buchanan inspected the townships of Leeds and Inverness in the spring of 1829, then reported, "I had no conception that so fine a country and a situation so susceptible of repaying the industrious farming Emigrant was to be found in Lower Canada." The previous year's harvest had been so good that the small number of settlers in the two townships had provided "large supplies" to the French Canadians in the nearby seigneuries who had experienced a serious crop failure (Boileau 2003, 41–4). Buchanan also praised the stands of hardwood timber and claimed that the "numerous rivers and small rapid streams" amid the "swelling hills" made the countryside "exceedingly healthy." In short, he concluded, "a more desirable tract of Country is not to be found in this province or one better adapted for the encouragement of new settlers." Needless to say, he failed to mention that this remained the hunting and fishing territory of the Abenakis living at the mouth of the Bécancour River (Barry 2003).

Buchanan did not anticipate that much could be done to promote the settlement of the area in the current season of 1829, before transportation routes could be improved and publicity arranged in the United Kingdom. He underestimated his own powers of persuasion, however, as well as the pressure caused by a situation in which, to quote historian Helen Cowan, "the St Lawrence shores stretching a mile and a half from Quebec were crowded with newly landed human beings" (Cowan 1961, 187). Among the first emigrants to be diverted from Upper Canada were an advance party of fifteen Gaelic-speaking families from the Isle of Arran whose influential landlord, Lord Hamilton, had arranged for them to receive free grants in the Ottawa valley. Instead, they were persuaded by Buchanan to select lots on the shores of Lake Joseph in Inverness (Little 1999, 2000). Buchanan also reported in early July 1829 that, during the previous ten days, he had forwarded to that township many more families, "mostly Scotch and English, and in general possessing considerable property."[11]

At the end of the shipping season in 1829, Buchanan claimed that of the 15,945 ship passengers who had arrived in Quebec that year, 3,754 had been settled in Lower Canada, an area "hitherto scarcely known to the British Emigrant." Many of these people had been directed to Inverness Township "in which an organized system for their immediate location was in operation." Buchanan boasted that the 166 families (totalling 830 individuals) sent to Inverness comprised "on the whole the most valuable body of settlers from the United Kingdom that ever located in the province of Lower Canada." Genealogical research has revealed that the majority, like Buchanan himself, were Anglicans from Northern Ireland (Barry 2002, 7–17). They were not paupers, but they were facing indigence due to the rapid growth of Ireland's population, the shift from grain production to the less land-intensive raising of livestock, and the accelerating mechanization of the linen industry (Houston and Smyth 1990, 36, 43–5).

At the end of the 1831 season, Buchanan was able to report that nearly all the land in Inverness and Leeds was occupied, and he recommended that the project be expanded to the nearby townships. John Richards, who was sent from London to investigate whether a uniform and economical colonization plan could be adopted for the British North American colonies, reported the same year that the Megantic project had been "conducted with much skill, economy, and practical knowledge, and will be frequently referred to in case of the adoption of any system of emigration."[12] Of the 10,200 immigrants who settled in Lower Canada in 1832, however, only 750 went to the Eastern Townships.[13] The Megantic experiment had effectively run its course. Rather than British immigrants, it would be French Canadians who subsequently settled in neighbouring Halifax and the townships beyond. Cut off from ready access to external markets, the British settlers and their descendants gradually abandoned the region, though Protestant schools and churches did survive into the 1950s (see Little 2013).

THE BRITISH AMERICAN LAND COMPANY

Shortly after the Megantic experiment ended, there emerged a second proposal for a monopolistic British land company in the Eastern Townships. Like Dalhousie, Governor Lord Aylmer was skeptical about the benefits of such organizations, but he felt driven by necessity to escape the increasingly hostile Legislative Assembly's refusal to pass money bills. As a result, in 1832 he approved of the formation of the London-based British American Land Company (BALC). Assisted by John Galt, founder of the Canada Company, the BALC promoters had promised (echoing A.C. Buchanan) that they would end "the monopolizing grasp of the Americans who threatened to over-run the province." Furthermore, the company's directors promised, it would curb "the extravagant pretensions" of the French Canadians who claimed "a prescriptive right to all the waste lands of the Crown" (quoted in Macdonald 1939, 294). Not surprisingly, the BALC was listed as one of the grievances in the 92 Resolutions passed by the Legislative Assembly in 1834.[14]

The British government granted the company nearly 850,000 acres (343,983 hectares) of public land, including all the Crown reserves and surveyed Crown lots in what were then Sherbrooke, Shefford, and Stanstead counties, as well as a 596,000-acre (241,193 hectares) unsurveyed block to the east known as the St Francis Tract. The price for the St Francis Tract was £75,002 sterling, equivalent to 63¢ per acre, and for the much more valuable Crown reserve lots in the settled townships it was £44,008, or only 87¢ an acre. The total was payable in ten years at 4 per cent interest per annum.[15] In addition, as commissioner of Crown lands, W.B. Felton continued to auction off large numbers of the clergy reserves with the result that by the spring of 1835, the BALC had acquired an additional 59,200 acres (23,957 hectares) of those 200-acre (81 hectares) lots. Finally, taking advantage of the desire of many American or American-descended settlers to leave the region, the company also purchased 32,000 acres (12,950 hectares) of private land, as well as acquiring options on 13,600 additional acres (5,504 hectares) (Goldring 1978, 194–5). A monopoly was essential, company directors argued, so that they – rather than individual speculators – would reap the benefits from the massive investments they planned to make in the region's economic development.[16] To help ensure that those investments materialized, the government allowed the BALC to direct half its payments towards officially sanctioned public improvements.[17]

The company also purchased most of the mill sites in Sherbrooke, including those that had been owned by the recently deceased Felton. Then, in an attempt to develop a commercial and industrial centre that would foster a market-oriented agricultural economy, it proceeded to develop the town by constructing bridges, surveying streets, and opening shops and mills, including a large woollen factory. The other principal initiative was to build or improve road links to Montreal and the mouth of the St Francis River at a site called Port St Francis (BALC 1842). The reason that the directors chose to focus on that site, rather than directing their efforts toward a trunk road from the immigration centre of Quebec, was presumably that the former option would pass through or near many more of the company properties. The problem was that it would be more difficult to entice immigrants southward to the Eastern Townships once they had already embarked on a steamship heading to Montreal and points west.

That problem was exacerbated by the fact that British travel writers who landed at Quebec invariably bypassed the Eastern Townships region due to its distance from the St Lawrence River and its lack of romantic historic sites (see Little 2012). In an attempt to compensate for this neglect, the BALC printed brochures that included testimonials from recent settlers who were generally of the same elevated social status as the travel writers. One pamphlet that appeared in 1833, for example, claimed that the Eastern Townships boasted "some of the finest scenery and most healthy climate of America, where bilious and intermittent fevers and agues are unknown, and which even the cholera did not enter, with which the Canadas were so severely afflicted" (BALC 1833, parts 2 and 3). As for the American presence, another British settler claimed that the Yankees were "all anxious to sell out, not because they are ill pleased with the country, but because they see a fair chance of making a few dollars – a consideration which far outweighs their love of *home*, a feeling which hardly finds place in a real American breast." The same man added, "Of the advantages of having a pleasant society around one, I need not here speak; suffice to say, that you will no where see in this part of the country, gentlemen with their beards a week old, wearing shoes that despise Warren, or sitting down to dinner without their jackets" (Mack 1837, 16–17; see also Little 2003). With such testimonials, the company was clearly attempting to attract immigrants with the means to purchase its farmland and invest in the local infrastructure, but few of the aspiring gentry who were attracted to the region appear to have succeeded as settlers or to have remained there long.[18]

The BALC appointed agents in Britain, Quebec, Montreal, and even Albany, but the results were initially disappointing. Of the 12,297 arrivals reported at Quebec during the summer of 1835, approximately 9,800 proceeded to Upper Canada and only 200 to the Eastern Townships. Company secretary Samuel Brooks of Sherbrooke suspected that potential clients were being intercepted by "evilly-disposed persons" who persuaded them not to go to the Townships. One such person he clearly had in mind was Quebec emigration agent, A.C. Buchanan, who had succeeded his uncle of the same name. That the younger Buchanan was partial to Upper Canada was made evident in his July report of that year, for he wrote that even though wage rates in the Eastern Townships were good, the prospect there for long-term employment or decent pay during the winter was not.

Dr James Marr Brydone of the Petworth Emigration Committee was similarly critical of the prospects in the Eastern Townships for the pauper families his organization was recruiting from England's southern parishes (see Cameron and Maude 2000). After making a quick tour through the region in the fall of 1835, he wrote that he was

> most impressed with the romantic picturesque and (in many places) beautiful scenery on the banks of the river St Francis, and although I think favourably of these townships, as combining a certain proportion of the useful with the ornamental, to gentlemen already possessed of a moderate independence,

> I do not consider them of half the agricultural value of the Upper Province ... to the poor man – much inferior in climate and not superior in salubrity to the tract I have selected. (Petworth Papers, J.M. Brydone to T. Sockett, 25 January 1836)

He was referring to a 5,000-acre (2,023 hectares) parcel then under negotiation with the Canada Company.[19]

The BALC nevertheless banked upon a large influx the following year, in 1836. It targeted immigrant labourers to construct the entire eighteen-mile length of the surveyed roadway into the St Francis Tract, and it scoured the countryside for a large store of provisions.[20] The company's hopes were not disappointed, for not only did transatlantic immigration almost double to 27,728, but those assisted by parishes and landlords quadrupled to 4,625.[21] Nearly all the assisted emigrants were directed by their sponsors to Upper Canada, but fortunately for the BALC a large number of immigrants did make their own way to the Eastern Townships. A local agent estimated that 6,000 people arrived in the region in 1836, and even though the majority were seeking employment only, the company sold 10,000 acres (4,046 hectares) outside the St Francis Tract. In addition, approximately 400 people settled inside the tract in the area of the new village named Victoria, located in Lingwick township.[22] Not surprisingly, however, expenses outstripped sales profits, with the dam and mills at Victoria costing £300, the Victoria Road £2,000, and provisions £5,400.[23]

The prudent strategy would have been to reap some benefits from its monopoly of vacant land in the settled heartland of the region, as well as from its sizeable investments in Sherbrooke, before proceeding further. The BALC had over-extended itself, however, with its immediate attempt to open the isolated St Francis Tract to settlement by developing a town site deep within the backwoods, as the disapproving supervisor of the government surveyors pointed out.[24] But the general assumption was clearly that the chief role of monopolistic land companies was to colonize frontier territories by a large-scale infusion of capital and immigrants.

The company was soon in dire financial straits because immigration to the Eastern Townships dropped precipitously to approximately 1,500 in 1837, when some of the English settlers in the St Francis Tract began to drift to the United States. Furthermore, a severe financial crisis shook the Anglo-American world, and the outbreak of the Lower Canadian rebellion in the fall had a disastrous impact on British immigration the following year.[25] As a result, the BALC won from the government a single year's suspension on its payments and accumulation of interest, as well as a provisional agreement to direct future instalments to the preparation of lots for settlers.[26] The company had already turned its attention to the western Highlands and Islands of Scotland where families were facing starvation due to the failure of the potato crop in 1836 (see Hunter 1976, chs. 1–3). It had arranged with a Highland proprietor, Stewart Mackenzie, for the emigration of sixty crofter families to settle in Lingwick township.[27] Considerably fewer appear to have arrived, but they formed the core of a steady stream of migration from the western shores of the remote Isle of Lewis during the following years (see Little 1991). That Gaelic-speaking community soon expanded northeastward toward Lake Megantic and survived there until the early twentieth century.

In the meantime, while the BALC was still establishing the new villages of Robinson and Gould and extending the road network within the St Francis Tract, Governor Lord Durham effectively pulled the rug out from under it in 1838 by recommending against any further concessions with respect to its sizeable debt to the government. Outraged by the history of wasteful land grants that his commission was uncovering, and suspicious of the BALC's sincerity, Durham suggested an offer to resume its land at the original price, including improvements at valuation.[28] In response, the Colonial Office stated that it would take back an amount of land equivalent in value to the company's remaining debt.[29]

Two years later, during the summer of 1840, John Galt's twenty-three-year-old son, Alexander, made a tour of inspection throughout the St Francis Tract, reporting that the roads were choked with bushes four feet high. Furthermore, the villages were deserted by all but a handful of families, with their warehouses, mills, and pearlasheries all in decay. Making the situation critical, the newly created municipal council of the County of Sherbrooke was threatening a wild land tax of a penny an acre, which would amount to more than double the company's receipts (Skelton 1920, 41–2; Cowan 1961, 125). As a result, the BALC accepted the government's offer. In 1841 it returned 511,237 acres (206,890 hectares) of the St Francis Tract in exchange for cancellation of its debt amounting to more than £72,000 sterling.[30] With its private acquisitions, the company's holdings still totalled over half a million acres (202,343 hectares), including 85,000 acres (34,398 hectares) in the St Francis Tract's most accessible townships, Bury, Lingwick, and Weedon. As commissioner, Alexander T. Galt was able to turn the BALC's fortunes around by mid-century, but by focussing on the industrial development of Sherbrooke and neglecting the St Francis Tract as well as British colonization (Little 1989b, ch. 2).

THE LAMBTON ROAD PROJECT

The St Francis Tract did not include all the unsurveyed crown land in the Eastern Townships. From the tract's northern border at Lake St Francis to the Chaudière seigneuries there remained 220,000 acres (89,031 hectares) of wilderness on the eastern side of what was then Megantic County. As well as offering another outlet for the settlers in the St Francis Tract, construction of a road across what became known as the Megantic Tract to the Chaudière valley would open a large new area to colonization. It was for this reason that, three years after the birth of the BALC, the colonial authorities entered into negotiations with the Quebec and Megantic Land Company (QMLC), which was largely funded by Quebec City merchants, including timber magnate William Price. It would appear that the promoters were interested not so much in British colonization, or any direct profits to be made from such a speculative enterprise, as in the extension of their city's commercial influence. A good road to the Eastern Townships would not only help to bring that region into Quebec's orbit; it would also improve the city's transportation ties to the New England states.

Overcoming his initial lack of enthusiasm for land companies, Lord Aylmer signed a tentative agreement with the QMLC in late 1835. The unsurveyed Megantic Tract would be sold at three shillings (75¢) per acre, and the price for all the Crown reserves in the part of Megantic County that had been surveyed would be three and a half shillings (87.5¢) per acre. Half the purchase price would be invested in local public improvements, with the state rather than the company taking the initiative, as had the BALC.[31]

The appointment of the Gosford Commission later in 1835 temporarily ended further progress in negotiations between state and the QMLC, but the project was renewed with the appointment of Lord Durham as governor after the crushing of the Rebellion of 1837.[32] In April 1838 company backers printed a prospectus calling for a capital fund of £30,000, with shares valued at £50 each. The company's endeavours, the prospectus claimed, would stimulate the economy of the long-settled Chaudière seigneuries as well as the recently colonized northern Megantic townships. Still more significantly, it promised, "To every citizen in Quebec, the prospect of settling 220,000 acres within a day's journey of the city cannot fail to be interesting, for not only will all the necessaries of life be abundant but all property will be enhanced in value, for sooner or later this must be the outlet of the Townships." There was to be "no exclusion whatever of any class of Her Majesty's subjects, in the settlement of the tract, industry and sobriety being the requisites of those whom the Company will be anxious to encourage."[33] Nevertheless, the main body of settlers anticipated would be British immigrants.

Lord Durham informed the company commissioners that he approved wholeheartedly of their aim to introduce an "emigrant" population to develop the country's natural resources and "contribute to its rapid advance in prosperity, and power." He was, however, in the process of devising a comprehensive system of land granting, "one feature of which will be, that it is to be subject to no exceptions, on any pretence whatever." He therefore had to reject the provisional agreement that had been entered into with Lord Aylmer. Durham promised, nevertheless, that he would support the company should it decide to complete the purchase in conformity with the terms of his projected uniform system. In the meantime, he accepted the commissioners' offer to complete an internal survey of the tract, and to commence a small settlement on Lake St Francis, subject to the details being approved by his assistant, Charles Buller, who was investigating Crown lands and emigration.[34]

To demonstrate the company's gratitude, it named both the new road and the settlement Lambton, which was Lord Durham's family name. A rough roadway was completed in 1839, but the surveyor general of Lower Canada was critical of the small size of the four new irregularly shaped townships. He also complained that the unorthodox smaller-than-standard lots were an "entire deviation" from the system authorized in 1791.[35] Having enthusiastically claimed that the Megantic Tract had the capacity to support 12,000 settlers, company commissioner James Bell Forsyth of Quebec had sought permission in the spring of 1839 to establish one hundred families along the Lambton Road.[36] Durham refused to become further committed to the QMLC, however, at a time when the BALC was facing financial embarrassment.

Faced by the failure of British immigration to revive during the summer of the same year, the QMLC commissioners decided in September not to accept any sales offer from the government.[37] Population pressure was becoming stronger than ever in the British Isles, however, and imperialist sentiment toward the North American colonies was still a force to be reckoned with. In 1840, London's Land and Emigration Board reported that both the Canadas required labour and military strength, and "in one of them" (clearly meaning Lower Canada), "an immediate infusion of a British population has become a measure of the highest political expediency." The board members felt that the time was right for "a large and systematic emigration," and, with the recent rebellion clearly in mind, they argued that the government could justify the expense because "a large increase of British population is essential to the security and tranquility of the province." That was to assume, of course, that another large-scale British colonization project would not intensify French Canadian nationalism and spark more unrest. Nor was the American threat entirely forgotten, for the board added that it was crucial that some assurance be made that the emigrants would remain within the colonies rather than strengthening the potential enemy to the south, as so many had done in the past.[38]

Given this report, it is not surprising that Durham's successor, Lord Sydenham, revived the Lambton Road project. The control of Crown lands had been transferred from imperial to colonial control with the Act of Union in 1841 (Careless 1967, 40), but Sydenham was evidently confident that the French Canadian members of the newly united Legislative Assembly could not reject the project because of their minority position in that body. The road was widened and the Quebec emigration agent was instructed to forward selected British families,[39] but the immigrants demonstrated little interest in the area. There were only thirty-four resident households in the fall of 1842, and by mid-century – when French Canadians numbered 1,254 in the four new townships of Price, Lambton, Aylmer, and Forsyth – all the English-speaking families had left.[40]

The Lambton Road never became a major artery connecting Quebec City to the American-settled townships, but its construction was followed by the provincially sponsored colonization roads project launched in 1848. That project, spurred by Bishop Ignace Bourget of Montreal and the Institut Canadien, was aimed not at attracting British settlers but at curtailing French Canadian emigration to the United States by offering free fifty-acre (twenty-hectare) lots on roads leading into the Lake Aylmer and Lake St Francis area. In supporting the colonization project's funding from a £20,000 general grant provided by the British government, Governor General Lord Elgin argued in a June 1848 letter to Lord Grey that it would strengthen the imperial connection because a French Canadian majority in the Eastern Townships would act as security against annexation to the United States (Doughty 1837, 191–2).[41] This was a chord enthusiastically played by one of the colonization society's chief promoters, Sherbrooke's Irish-born Catholic curé, Bernard O'Reilly, when he declared in 1848, "Que la croix du clocher brille dans chaque township maintenant inculte, depuis les voisines colonies américaines jusqu'au fleuve. Et que l'Angélus du soir se répète d'échos en échos depuis le Lac Mégantic jusqu'à Québec d'un coté, et jusqu'à Saint-Hyacinthe de l'autre : et nous aurons fait un premier pas pour sauver le Canada" (O'Reilly 1848). The imperial mission of making the Eastern Townships a stronghold of British settlement had effectively ended.

CONCLUSION

The history of British colonization efforts in the Eastern Townships illustrates the limitations of the British colonialist project during the era that preceded Responsible Government. It also complicates the narrative that pits a united English-speaking minority in Lower Canada/Canada East against the French Canadian majority. It does so by revealing that, from the perspective of the Colonial Office, concern about the American threat – from within the region as well as from outside it – generally trumped that posed by French Canadians when it came to colonization of the province's southern borderland. The path that colonization of the Eastern Townships took was therefore affected not only by Great Britain's desire to plant its surplus population within the empire and to develop its colonies economically, but by a broader strategic objective that viewed the rapidly growing United States as a potential threat to the British presence in North America.

The Colonial Office could certainly have done more to promote British colonization of the Eastern Townships, but the fact was that Upper Canada held more economic promise and the main goal was to stem the flow of emigrants southward to the United States. Furthermore, the heavily indebted British government actually impeded settlement in the Eastern Townships by relying upon the Crown lands as a low-cost means to compensate military veterans with free grants, thereby contributing to the longstanding absentee-proprietor problem.[42] Financial concerns were also paramount in the government's negotiated agreement with the British American Land Company for it was a means of acquiring a large capital fund for the executive branch of the colonial administration. More successful than colonization projects in diluting the influence of American radicalism in the region were the religious conversion efforts of missionaries sponsored by two London-based organizations: the Church of England's Society for the Propagation of the Gospel and the Wesleyan Missionary Society (Little 2004). Still more effective in thickening the forty-fifth parallel from a cultural perspective, however, was the steady increase of the French Canadian population which had reached the majority in the region by the time of Confederation.

Notes

1 The French-speaking ratio in the Eastern Townships in 1844 was 23 per cent, mostly in the peripheral townships. See Little (1989a), 13, 21.

2 Felton had been granted 15,000 acres in centrally located Ascot Township where he owned all the mills and mill sites in what would become the regional centre of Sherbrooke.

3 See, for example, Lower Canada Land Petitions, 41239-41, W.B. Felton to Lt Col Ready, 15 March 1821; JLALC 32 (1823, Appendix T, subappendix D); Q Series, Gov. Lord Dalhousie, 1823, vol. 166, pt 3, 631–5, W.B. Felton to Dalhousie, 10 October 1823.
4 See COR 42, vol. 205, Davidson to Wilmot Horton, 6 August 1825; Felton to Wilmot Horton, 10 September 1825; Andrew Belcher and others to Bathurst, 23 May 1825; vol. 210, Wilmot Horton memo, 30 September 1825. Details on the origin of the company are to be found in COR 42, vol. 206, Felton to Wilmot Horton, 12 September 1825; *Montreal Gazette* (1825a); *Montreal Gazette* (1825b); Demers (n.d., 104–7).
5 See COR 42, vol. 209, Report of Committee of the Whole (Lower Canada) on Land Co., 3 May 1826, enclosure in Dalhousie to Bathurst, 19 June 1826.
6 COR 324, vol. 96, Wilmot Horton to Dalhousie, 21 July 1826.
7 COF 384, Emigration, vol. 20, 202–7, A.C. Buchanan to Wilmot Horton, 21 April 1828.
8 CSC, 1829, vol. 305, 43-44, Dalhousie's remarks (draft), 6 August 1828; Dunkley (1980, 358–9).
9 CSC, 1829, vol. 305, Buchanan's Report (hereafter Buchanan's 1829 Report), part 3, 65–8, questions submitted to A.C. Buchanan by House of Assembly of Lower Canada, Quebec, February 1829.
10 The fact that the route tended to follow a straight line over high hilltops meant that in certain areas there would be no settlers to contribute to its upkeep (*Quebec Mercury* 1840). The 1825 census recorded only 84 inhabitants in Leeds Township, 165 in Ireland Township, and none in Inverness, though the enumerator appears to have missed a few families in the latter township (Little 2010, 199, table 1).
11 CSC, vol. 292, A.C. Buchanan to Lt Col Yorke, Quebec, 6 July 1829. A few settler families from Ulster had already spent several years in Quebec City (Rawlings 1979, 18).
12 Report of John Richards in *Parliamentary Papers*, 1831–32 (334), vol. 32, 33; Gates (1968, 178–9).
13 Upper Canada had attracted 35,000 immigrants. Emigration Series, XIX, 195, 201, Buchanan's Report to Lord Aylmer, Quebec, 12 December 1832; 204, W.M. Phillips, Esq., to A.C. Buchanan, Leeds, 26 December 1832.
14 See also resolutions 84–7 (Chambre d'Assemblée 1834).
15 See Lord Aylmer Papers, COR 387, vol. 2, 140, no. 40, E.G. Stanley to Aylmer, London, 4 January 1834; BALC Correspondence I, 336–41, Crown's charges against the BALC, Court of King's Bench, District of Sherbrooke, 26 February 1841.
16 See BALC Correspondence I, 109–10, Instructions 27 January 1834.
17 See Aylmer Papers, vol. 2, 296, no. 2, C. Grant to Lord Aylmer, London, 23 April 1835; BALCTF, art. 1866, Charles Buller to John Fraser, 1 October 1838.
18 See, for example, the story of Lucy and Edmund Peel in Little (2001) and that of George Norris Trent in Little (2021).
19 The BALC would succeed, nevertheless, in attracting some of the arrivals from the southern counties of Hampshire, Norfolk, and Suffolk where parishes on their own initiative had been providing emigration subsidies since 1831. Cowan (1961, 206).
20 See BALC Papers V, 1096, Samuel Brooks to Moffat and McGill, 9 January 1836; 1100, 25 January 1836; 1101, 1 February 1836; 1102, 4 February 1836; 1102, 5 February 1836; 1104–5, 11 February 1836.
21 Parliamentary Papers, 1837 (132), XLII, 17, Buchanan's Report for 1836, Quebec, 12 December 1836.

22 Among the new settlers were some 200 Swiss and Bavarian immigrants though nearly all soon proceeded to their original destination in Ohio. Parliamentary Papers, 1837 (132), XLII, 41–2, A.C. Webster to A.C. Buchanan, Sherbrooke, 13 November 1836; 27–8, Extracts from Buchanan to Governor-in-Chief.
23 See BALC Papers I, 135–7, Extracts from Dispatch, 22 April 1837.
24 BALC Papers V, 944, John Moore to Moffat and McGill, 30 October 1834; BALCTF, Captain R. Hayne to Walcott, 3 February 1836.
25 CSC, S Series, 1838, vol. 538, 179–80; Goldring (1978, 192).
26 See Emigration Series III (1841), 219, H.P. Bruyères to Sir George Grey, 27 August 1838; BALC Papers, Correspondence 1835–89, 254–6, Henry P. Bruyères to Sir Geo. Grey, 8 November 1838.
27 Emigration Series XX, 38–9, Buchanan's Annual Report for 1838, Quebec, 20 January 1839; COF 42/258, 71, Andrew Russell to Commissioner of Crown Lands, Quebec, 19 March 1839.
28 CSC, S Series, 1838, vol. 538, 179–80.
29 See BALC Correspondence, Henry P. Bruyères to Sir George Grey, 8 November 1838, 254–6; George Grey to H.P. Bruyères, 10 September [*sic*] 1838, 258–9; and 28 November 1838, 264.
30 See Goldring (1978, 200–1) for an account of the negotiations.
31 See Megantic Land Company, Memorandum of a Proposed Arrangement.
32 See BALC Correspondence 206, Walcott to J.B. Forsyth, 12 April 1836; 207, J.B. Forsyth to T.F. Eliot, Quebec, 8 Oct. 1836.
33 BALC Correspondence, 210, Prospectus, Quebec and Megantic Land Company, 23 April 1838.
34 See Megantic Land Company, Thos. E.M. Turton to James Bell Forsyth, Quebec, 30 July 1838.
35 Rather than the standard 200 acres (81 hectares), each surveyed lot was 120 acres (49 hectares). Megantic Land Company, Joseph Bouchette to Commissioner of Crown Lands, Quebec, 12 December 1839.
36 See Megantic Land Company, Forsyth to T.L. Goldie, Quebec, 23 March 1839.
37 Megantic Land Company, Forsyth and R.H. Gairdner to Sir, Quebec, 11 September 1839.
38 COF 384/61, 39, 56, T.F. Elliot, R. Torrens, and E.E. Villiers to Lord John Russell, 21 April 1842.
39 See Terres de la Couronne, art. 1863, William Hargrave's Report, 19 February 1842.
40 See Records Put By, vol. 13, 158, Walter Hargrave to John Davidson, Lambton Road, 18 October 1842. For more details on the Lambton Road project, see Little (1989b, ch. 3).
41 For details, see Little (1989b, ch. 4).
42 By April 1833, of 314,417 acres (127,240 hectares) granted to the militia in Lower Canada, only 92,141 acres (37,288 hectares) had been confirmed by letters patent and therefore improved. Lower Canada Land Petitions, 11211. In 1839, *Durham's Report* claimed that more than 500,000 acres (202,343 hectares) remained in claims by the veterans of 1812 (Lambton 1839, appendix B, 5). The absentee proprietor problem would finally diminish with the introduction of an increasingly effective system of municipal government and land taxes in the 1840s and 1850s, but British emigration had declined significantly by that time. See Little (1981).

References

ARCHIVAL SOURCES AND GOVERNMENT DOCUMENTS

British American Land Company (BALC). Papers. National Archives, London, UK.
– Correspondence 1835–89. National Archives, London, UK.
"British American Land Company," Terres et Forêts (BALCTF). E21. Archives Nationales du Québec à Québec.
Civil Secretary's Correspondence (CSC), Quebec, Lower Canada, and Canada East. 1760–1863. RG4 A1, Library and Archives Canada, Ottawa.
Colonial Office Records (COR) 42, Public Records Office, London, UK.
Emigration Series. N.d. *Parliamentary Papers* Subject set 15. Shannon: Irish University Press.
Journals of the Legislative Assembly of Lower Canada (JLALC). 1792–1838. RG14-A3, Library and Archives Canada, Ottawa.
Lord Aylmer Papers, Colonial Office fonds (cof), MG 11, Library and Archives Canada, Ottawa.
Lower Canada Petitions, 41239–41, Record Group 1 L3L, Library and Archives Canada, Ottawa.
Megantic Land Company records. Terres et Forêts, Archives Nationales du Québec à Québec.
Parliamentary Papers, 1715–present. Parliamentary Archives, Houses of Parliament, London, UK.
Petworth Papers. Correspondence 1830–60. West Sussex Record Office, Chichester, UK.
Q Series, 1760–1922. Colonial Office fonds (cof), MG 11, Library and Archives Canada, Ottawa.
Records Put By, 1839–67. Executive Council Office of the Province of Canada fonds, RG1 E5, vol. 13, 158. Library and Archives Canada, Ottawa.
Terres de la Couronne : Administration générale, 1827–90. Terres et Forêts, Archives Nationales du Québec à Québec.

PUBLISHED SOURCES

Barry, Gwen. 2002. *The Little Family and the Ralston Family of Megantic County, Quebec.* N.p.: Evans Books.
– 2003. "La 'piste Bécancoeur' : des campements abénaquis dans l'arrière pays." *Recherches amérindiennes au Québec* 33 (2) : 93–100.
Boileau, Gilles. 2003. "La paroisse de Lotbinière lance un cri de détresse." *Histoire Québec* 9 (2) : 41–5.
Bouchette, Joseph. 1815. *A Topographical Description of the Province of Lower Canada.* London: W. Fadon.
British American Land Company (BALC). 1833. *Information respecting the Eastern Townships of Lower Canada in which the British American Land Company intend to commence operations for the sale and settlement of lands, in the ensuing spring.* London: W.J. Ruffy.

– 1842. *Information Respecting the Eastern Townships*. Quebec: Emigrant Agency Office of the British American Land Company.
Buchanan, A.C. 1828. *Emigration Practically Considered; with Detailed Directions to Emigrants Proceeding to North America, Particularly to the Canadas; in a Letter to the Right Hon. R. Wilmot Horton, M.P.* London: Henry Colburn.
Buckner, Phillip. 1993. "Presidential Address: Whatever Happened to the British Empire?" *Journal of the Canadian Historical Association* 4 (1): 3–32.
Calloway, Colin G. 1990. *The Western Abenakis of Vermont, 1600–1800: War, Migration, and the Survival of an Indian Peoples*. Norman: University of Oklahoma Press.
Cameron, Wendy, and Mary McDougall Maude. 2000. *Assisting Emigrants to Upper Canada: The Petworth Project, 1832–1837*. Montreal and Kingston: McGill-Queen's University Press.
Careless, J.M.S. 1967. *The Union of the Canadas: The Growth of Canadian Institutions, 1841–1857*. Toronto : McClelland and Stewart.
Chambre d'Assemblée. 1834. "Les 92 Résolutions présentées à la Chambre d'Assemblée du Bas-Canada, en janvier 1834." https ://beq.ebooksgratuits.com/pdf/92resolutions .pdf. Viewed 14 May 2022.
Christie, Nancy. 2020. *The Formal and Informal Politics of British Rule in Post-Conquest Quebec, 1760-1837: A Northern Bastille*. Oxford: Oxford University Press.
Cowan, Helen I. 1961. *British Emigration to British North America: The First Hundred Years*. Toronto: University of Toronto Press.
Day, Gordon M. 1981. *The Identity of the St Francis Indians*. Ottawa: National Museums of Canada.
Demers, Louis-Philippe. N.d. *Sherbrooke : Découvertes – Légendes – Documents*. Sherbrooke, QC: Gauvin et Frère.
Doughty, Arthur G., ed. 1937. *The Elgin-Grey Papers, 1846–1852*. Vol 1. Ottawa: King's Printer.
Dunkley, Peter. 1980. "Emigration and the State, 1803–1842: The Nineteenth-Century Revolution in Government Reconsidered." *The Historical Journal* 23 (2): 353–80.
Durham, John George Lambton, Earl of. 1839. *Report on the Affairs of British North America*. Toronto: Robert Stanton.
Feldman, David, and M. Page Baldwin. 2007. "Emigration and the British State, ca. 1815–1925." In *Citizenship and Those Who Leave: The Politics of Emigration and Expatriation*, edited by Nancy L. Green and François Weil, 135–55. Urbana and Chicago: University of Illinois Press.
Gates, Lillian F. 1968. *Land Policies of Upper Canada*. Toronto: University of Toronto Press.
Goldring, Philip. 1978. "British Colonists and Imperial Interests in Lower Canada, 1820 to 1841." PhD dissertation, University of London.
Houston, Cecil J., and William J. Smyth. 1990. *Irish Emigration and Canadian Settlement: Patterns, Links, and Letters*. Toronto: University of Toronto Press.
Hunter, James. 1976. *The Making of the Crofting Community*. Edinburgh: John Donald.
Johnston, H.J.M. 1972. *British Emigration Policy, 1815–1830: "Shovelling out Paupers."* Oxford: Clarendon Press.

Kesteman, Jean-Pierre, Peter Southam, and Diane Saint-Pierre. 1998. *Histoire des Cantons de l'Est*. Sainte-Foy, QC : Les Presses de l'Université Laval.

Little, J.I. 1981. "Colonization and Municipal Reform in Canada East." *Histoire sociale – Social History* 14: 94–121.

– 1985. "Imperialism and Colonization in Lower Canada: The Role of William Bowman Felton." *Canadian Historical Review* 66 (4): 511–40.

– 1989a. *Ethno-Cultural Transition and Regional Identity in the Eastern Townships of Quebec*. Ottawa: Canadian Historical Association.

– 1989b. *Nationalism, Capitalism, and Colonization in Nineteenth-Century Quebec: The Upper St Francis District*. Montreal and Kingston: McGill-Queen's University Press.

– 1991. *Crofters and Habitants: Settler Society, Economy and Culture in a Quebec Township, 1848–81*. Montreal and Kingston: McGill-Queen's University Press.

– 1999. "Agricultural Improvement and Highland Clearance: The Isle of Arran, 1828–29." *Scottish Economic and Social History* 19: 132–54.

– 2000. "From the Isle of Arran to Inverness Township: A Case Study of Highland Emigration and North American Settlement, 1829–34." *Scottish Economic and Social History* 20: 3–30.

– ed. 2001. *Love Strong as Death: Lucy Peel's Canadian Journal, 1833–36*. Waterloo, ON: Wilfrid Laurier University Press.

– 2003. "Canadian Pastoral: Promotional Images of British Colonization in Lower Canada's Eastern Townships during the 1830s." *Journal of Historical Geography* 29 (2): 189–211.

– 2004. *Borderland Religion: The Emergence of an English-Canadian Identity*. Toronto: University of Toronto Press.

– 2008. *Loyalties in Conflict: A Canadian Borderland in War and Rebellion, 1812–1840*. Toronto: University of Toronto Press.

– 2010. "'The fostering care of Government:' Lord Dalhousie's 1821 Survey of the Eastern Townships." *Histoire sociale – Social History* 43: 193–212.

– 2012. "'Like a fragment of the old world': The Historical Regression of Quebec City in Travel Narratives and Tourist Guidebooks, 1776–1913." *Urban History Review* 40 (2): 15–28.

– 2013. "A.C. Buchanan and the Megantic Experiment: Promoting British Colonization in Lower Canada." *Histoire sociale – Social History* 46: 295–319.

– 2021. *Reading the Diaries of Henry Trent: The Everyday Life of a Canadian Englishman, 1842–1898*. Montreal and Kingston: McGill-Queen's University Press.

Macdonald, Norman. 1939. *Canada, 1763–1841: Immigration and Settlement. The Administration of the Imperial Land Regulations*. London: Longmans, Green and Company.

Mack, W.G. 1837. *A Letter from the Eastern Townships of Lower Canada*. Glasgow: David Robertson.

Montreal Gazette. 1825a. "We observe …" 2 July, 3.

Montreal Gazette. 1825b. "Lower Canada Land Company." 9 July, 2.

O'Reilly, B. 1848. "U[n] Lettre de M. O'Reilly." *Journal de Québec*, 18 November, 1.

Quebec Mercury. 1840. "Communications with the Eastern Townships." 2 April, 2.

Rawlings, Gwen. 1979. *The Pioneers of Inverness Township, Quebec: An Historical and Genealogical Survey*. Cheltenham, ON: Boston Mills Press.

Senior, Hereward. 1989. "The Loyalists in Quebec: A Study in Diversity." In *The Loyalists of Quebec, 1774–1825, A Forgotten History*, 51–74. Montreal: Price-Patterson.

Skelton, O.D. 1920. *The Life and Times of Sir Alexander Tilloch Galt*. Toronto: Oxford University Press.

Taylor, Alan. 2007. "'The Late Loyalists': Northern Reflections of the Early American Republic." *Journal of the Early Republic* 27 (1): 1–34.

Thomas, Earle. 1989. "The Loyalists in the Montreal Area, 1775–1784." In *The Loyalists of Quebec, 1774–1825, A Forgotten History*, 75–112 Montreal: Price-Patterson.

3

Agriculture in Transition: Global Crisis and the Eastern Townships' Identity

Darren Bardati

INTRODUCTION: AGRICULTURE *in* TRANSITION

The global agricultural production system is facing multiple stressors – caused by its environment-degrading industrial model, by climate change, and by the COVID-19 pandemic – rendering it unsustainable ecologically, economically, and socially. There is a widespread acknowledgement that a transformation of the agri-food system toward greater sustainability (Melchior and Newig, 2021) is required, but there are questions as to what this reform might look like and how successful transformation might be evaluated, let alone achieved. This chapter explores how agriculture in Quebec's Eastern Townships, while being influenced by these global stressors, may currently be poised to show the way toward the change needed to move society toward agricultural sustainability.

In late 1998, a US National Academy of Sciences colloquium titled "Plants and Population: Is There Time?" was held in Irvine, California. Researchers grappled with issues of agricultural and food sustainability in the twenty-first century. One presenter (Ruttan, 1999, 5960) stated ominously, "If the world fails to successfully navigate a transition to sustainable growth in agricultural production, the failure will be due more to a failure in the area of institutional innovation than to resource and environmental constraints."

As the argument goes, a crisis of food and climate change is upon us. Global trends point to population rise, exponential material consumption in developed countries, increased affluence in rapidly developing countries coupled with increasingly rising food demands, and the negative consequences on land, water, and air of fossil fuel driven industrial agriculture. Indeed, the prognosis is dire. The social, economic, and ecological impacts of these rising demands on Earth's food production systems, coupled with a growing body of indisputable evidence for climate change, have converged to place society on a collision course with nature. Agricultural soil erosion, genetic diversity loss, water pollution, pests with increasing resistance to pesticides that damage crops, unpredictable variability in climate, and other factors have all emerged to create historically unprecedented challenges to our twentieth-century industrial scale agriculture. Yet, as Ruttan points out, the issue at hand is less about natural resources and environmental constraints placed on these rising demands – as important as they are – than it is on society's ability to adapt to the changes brought on by natural constraints. Social and economic issues of unsustainability also plague our global agri-food system. The twentieth century has witnessed the loss of the family farm, the mechanization, automation, and corporatization of food production, the widespread use of irrigation (often in arid and semi-arid regions that would normally not support large-scale agriculture), synthetic fertilizers and pesticides derived from fossil fuels, and the growing use of biotechnology and genetically modified seeds have all contributed to the crisis of unsustainability in the global agri-food system. The challenge that scientists in Irvine, California, were grappling with in 1998 was whether society would make the necessary transition toward sustainability in its agricultural production system to adapt to the global food and climate crisis. That was more than twenty years ago. Where are we in 2024? Has the global agricultural world risen to the challenge of moving its apparatus in a more sustainable direction? With the unanticipated shock of the COVID-19 pandemic, international society has witnessed a tragic loss of life and major economic repercussions, including massive disruption in food supply chains, increased global food insecurity, and a general realization of the lack of resilience of the global agri-food system. If a successful transition toward agricultural sustainability is an unavoidable imperative to prevent such negative impacts, what should it look like?

To begin a reflection on this question, it is helpful to look at the scholarly literature on sustainability transitions, especially as they refer to agriculture and food systems. Gliessman (2016) has provided a useful framework to help in determining which objective measurable steps are needed to facilitate a societal transition. His framework, discussed later in this chapter, is employed to chart five levels of change in Quebec's Eastern Townships region that can serve as a roadmap to understand the challenge of redesigning the food system, from farm to table, with a goal of achieving sustainability.

The chapter begins with an overview of global threats to conventional agriculture, then moves to examine Quebec's recent agri-food policy re-orientation toward more organic and eco-responsible practices, placing a sharp focus on the Eastern Townships, where many of the key institutional actors have moved rapidly to meet these challenges to agricultural sustainability. In doing so, this chapter directly reflects on how these recent changes may have positioned the Eastern Townships region to serve as a principal example of what Ruttan (1999, 5960) called for: "successful navigation toward transition to sustainable growth in agricultural production."

GLOBAL AGRICULTURE *in* CRISIS

Agriculture underpins the livelihoods of more than 2.5 billion people worldwide (FAO 2021). All agriculture, whether small scale subsistence farming or large-scale industrial agriculture, relies on innate interactions with the environment and natural resources for production. Consequently, agriculture's dependence on Earth's ecological health for socio-economic development is unquestionably significant. In the past eighty years, with the globalization of trade in commodities, a global agri-food system has emerged to dominate processes and infrastructure involved in feeding most of the world's population: growing, harvesting, processing, packaging, transporting, marketing, distribution, consumption, and disposal of food and food-related items (FAO 2018), affects every country in the world (Mbow et al. 2019).

Since World War II, globalization of the agri-food systems has facilitated rapid economic integration driven by lower transaction costs and lower barriers to movements in capital and goods. It has resulted in a growing interdependence of the world's economies, of rising trade flows, internationalization of production, and the concentration of market shares in the hands of larger multi-national corporations (Bruinsma 2003). Based on economies of scale, globalized agriculture increasingly replicated the industrial productivity model, effectively requiring maximum efficiency to lower costs of each food unit. While pre-industrial agriculture had relied on local or regional food systems with a variety of small-scale, diversified, low-impact environmental practices driven by human and animal power rooted in community livelihoods, the post-1945 era of industrialized agriculture quickly became reliant on large, fossil fuel-driven mechanized equipment, synthetic chemical amendments to the soil, pesticides, extensive irrigation systems, and animal antibiotics. Agriculture now grew high-yield, hybrid, and genetically modified crops, developed by the agribusiness corporations, in large monocultures. The intensive production animals in concentrated animal feedlot operations (CAFOS) enabled very large farms to dominate the livestock production (cattle, pork, poultry for meat and eggs, etc.) providing unprecedented quantities of protein for national and international marketplaces.

The new post-war industrial food production model resulted in large increases in food production. Between 1945 and 2003, for example, the average global per capita food consumption per day rose by 36 per cent from 2,200 calories to 3,000 calories (Bruinsma 2003), while lowering consumer costs of food, leading to the proliferation of grocery stores and supermarkets, creating a host of new farm technologies and equipment, as well as resulting in innovations in food system production, packaging, marketing, transportation, and storage. Industrial agriculture encouraged small-scale farmers either to grow bigger or to sell their farm. In most nations, rural to urban migration led to stronger economic growth, higher national gross domestic product, and higher standards of living for a large majority of people (World Bank 2017).

This agricultural growth came, however, at a cost to the environmental health of the rural landscape. In the conversion from smallscale, mixed family farms to industrial-sized crop and livestock operations, the mosaic of different vegetation types was converted into monoculture crops and animal feedlots. The older wooden barns that dotted the landscape were left to crumble while much larger modern high-tech robotic, climate-controlled facilities replaced them. Biodiversity-rich hedgerows that lined traditional farms were removed to enable large tractors to turn around. Riparian zones that protect waterways were cut down so more land could be placed in cultivation. Mechanized irrigation systems pulled up large amounts of water from the ground and returned it with often diminished quantity and quality. Soils that were repeatedly plowed and compacted by large tractors were left bare after the growing season. The natural organic matter, nutrients, and microbial life in the soils was replaced with the use of synthetic fertilizers and pesticides. The result was a natural environment that has become heavily impacted (Ackerman-Leist 2013).

The negative impacts of industrial agriculture on the environment have been well documented: biodiversity loss at all scales (genetic, species, and ecosystems), pest and weed resistance to chemical pesticides and herbicides, pesticide-related cancers, eutrophication of waterways from farm runoff, soil health degradation, microbial resistance, animal to human transmission of diseases, decreased nutritional value of foods, epidemics of obesity and chronic disease, among others. Furthermore, because agriculture has become so reliant on fossil fuels (for machinery-driven farming practices and for nitrogen-based fertilizers), it is responsible for approximately 24 per cent of global greenhouse gas emissions (IPCC 2019), although half of that percentage is offset by the carbon it stores in growing plants. This estimate does not include the transportation and storage of food, nor its waste products.

Added to this litany of agriculture's negative impacts on the natural environment is the stresses that global climate change is putting on global agri-food systems. According to the most recent report of the FAO (2021, n.p.):

> Extreme events such as drought, floods, storms, tsunamis, wildfires, pest and disease outbreaks exert a heavy toll on agriculture and all its sectors: crops, livestock, forestry, fisheries and aquaculture. Their growing frequency and intensity, along with the systemic nature of risk, are jeopardizing our agri-food systems … Increased risk exposure has become the "new normal" and the impact of climate change is set to exacerbate these challenges even further.

As the third decade of the twenty-first century approached, there were growing indications of declines in agricultural productivity and diminishing returns associated with this industrial model of food production (World Bank, 2017). Fewer and fewer people are being employed by agriculture, while food insecurity is on the rise in several countries (Mbow et al. 2019).

Then the global COVID-19 pandemic hit unexpectedly. At the end of March 2020, more than half of the global population, including almost everyone in the Eastern Townships, was ordered to stay at home to prevent the spread of the virus. Unemployment rates soared as businesses were forced to stay closed; some may never re-open. Global food systems continue to be under stress, since measures to limit the spread of the disease have spill-over impacts on the movement of people and products. As described in *COVID-19 and the Food and Agriculture Sector: Issues and Policy Responses* (OECD 2020): "While the pandemic poses some serious challenges for the food system in the short term, it is also an opportunity to accelerate transformations in the food and agriculture sector to build its resilience in the face of a range of challenges, including climate change."

Given these myriad stresses on the global agri-food system, and the unanticipated shock of COVID-19, there is an urgency to move away from "business as usual." Since agriculture is widely acknowledged as a major driver and a major threat to global sustainability (Melchior and Sewig 2021), there is an opportunity for governments, institutions, and food policy actors to pursue aggressive reform agendas in their food systems.

According to their report *Wake Up Before It Is Too Late: Make Agriculture Truly Sustainable Now for Food Security in a Changing Climate*, the United National Conference on Trade and Development (2013, 2) urgently called for a paradigm shift in global agricultural development to an ecological approach. Their key message calls for a "rapid and significant shift from conventional monoculture-based and high-external-input-dependent industrial production towards mosaics of sustainable, regenerative production systems that also considerably improve the productivity of small-scale farms."

Turning our attention to the province of Quebec in which the Eastern Townships region is located, this chapter provides an outline of the context in which any agricultural activity takes place, as well as the potential conditions that may favour or hinder any sustainability transition. Quebec is today regarded as an "organic champion"; it is responsible for nearly half of Canada's organic production (Girard-Bossé 2021). In 2015, the provincial government set a goal of ten years to double its agricultural land under organic production. Organically cultivated land doubled in the last five years, from 49,000 (2015) to 106,000 hectares in 2020 (CARTV, 2020), exceeding expectations. Meanwhile, over 3,000 agricultural businesses, nearly 10 per cent of all agricultural businesses in Quebec, are certified organic, compared to 3.5 per cent for the rest of Canada (Portail BioQuébec website). The next section discusses how Quebec has begun to implement some agri-food reforms and serves as provincial-level support for any regional sustainability initiatives in the Eastern Townships.

QUEBEC'S LEADERSHIP *in* ORGANIC AGRICULTURE

Organic agriculture is defined as "a holistic production management system which promotes and enhances agro-ecosystem health, including biodiversity, biological cycles, and soil biological activity. It emphasises the use of management practices in preference to the use of off-farm inputs, taking into account that regional conditions require locally adapted systems" (FAO 1999). The explicit goal of organic agriculture is to contribute to the enhancement of sustainability. As such, it holds promise to address some of the negative environmental impacts associated with conventional agriculture. Organic agriculture is practised in 187 countries, with 1.5 per cent of farmland globally under organic production, and the area of organic land is rising rapidly every year (Willer et al. 2021). Organic certification is intended to ensure certain standardized eco-responsible practices are kept and monitored. Unless a producer is *certified* organic, customers have no guarantee of their production practices. Quebec is a leader among the provinces and territories in organic certification. It has the oldest organic regulations and extensive organic production support, market support, and data collection of all provinces and territories in Canada (Guerra and Martin 2017).

Approximately 64 per cent of Quebecers regularly consume organic products, compared to about 21 per cent for the rest of Canada (Filière biologique 2021; Statista 2021). Despite this growth, organic production in Quebec cannot keep up with consumer demand and the province is forced to import 70 per cent of its organic products, mostly from the United States (Girard-Bossé 2021; UPA 2021).

In 2018, the provincial government unveiled an ambitious new initiative and action plan, *BioFood Policy 2018–2025* (Quebec 2018), which targets a host of reforms to move the food system in a more sustainable direction. With a stated goal to "accelerate an ecological transition toward agricultural sustainability" (Quebec 2021, 24), the policy included several sweeping targets, including massive investments to the organic sector, stronger verification of standards for organic certification and elimination of fraud cases, further increases to the land base under organic production, assistance to new organic businesses, encouraging local organic products for the market, and expanding the agritourism sector, among others. In October 2020, the Quebec government released its Sustainable Agriculture Plan (SDP) 2020–2030 (Quebec 2020). One of the peculiarities of the SDP is the recognition of the achievement of results according to the agri-environmental practices adopted by the producers. In responding to challenges and environmental issues in the agricultural sector, the plan focuses on five main objectives: 1) reduce the use of pesticides; 2) improve soil health and conservation; 3) improve the management of fertilizers; 4) optimize water management; and 5) improve biodiversity. Furthermore, the plan outlines specific measurable targets and indicators of success were outlined for each objective. Recognizing the need for up-to-date data to meet these ambitious objectives of the SDP, the Quebec government created a new research fund through its Fonds de recherche du Quebec – Nature et technologies (FRQNT). A public call was issued in early 2021 to create an inter-institutional, inter-community, and inter-sector collaborative research network, whose theme will focus specifically on sustainable agriculture. After applicants were received and vetted, the new Réseau québécois de recherche en agriculture durable (RQRAD) was announced in October 2021 (FRQNT 2021). Made up of more than 200 researchers at fifteen universities, five colleges, and several provincial and federal research centres, the RQRAD is aimed at ensuring concerted and coordinated efforts in the area of sustainable agriculture in order to guarantee that the research produced is well aligned with the knowledge needs of the farming communities. As such, the RQRAD is closely aligned with the SDP, allowing the "pooling of forces committed to accelerating the development of knowledge related to soil health and conservation, and the reduction of pesticide use in a context of climate change" (FRQNT 2021). It is impossible to know, at the time of this writing, whether the province-wide Sustainable Development Plan 2020–2030 will be successfully implemented over the next decade, whether the RQRAD will help farmers to achieve the SDP goals, or whether agriculture in the province will take a substantial and lasting environmental turn for the better.

It is possible to focus, however, on one region of Quebec, the Eastern Townships, and examine whether it features the necessary constituent parts, aided by the provincial policies and actions, to successfully transition toward sustainability. This chapter now turns to consider the agricultural heritage and identity of the region, demonstrating its ideal conditions for important recent initiatives toward agricultural sustainability.

EASTERN TOWNSHIPS' AGRICULTURAL HERITAGE *and* IDENTITY

Located in the northern extension of the Appalachian Mountains, the Eastern Townships region is marked by rolling hills with rocky uplands, poorly drained valley bottoms incised by rivers and lakes, and plentiful mixed forests. Because of the mosaic of natural landforms that make up its topography, abundant pastureland, and history of livestock breeding practices, the region was dominated by livestock agricultural practices rather than the production of crops for markets in Montreal, the rest of Quebec, Ontario, and beyond (Bardati 2015). Compared to the flat, wide open, and soil-rich St Lawrence lowlands, the Eastern Townships has always favoured small-scale, mixed farming over large monocrop cultivation. For more than two hundred years, many rural Townshippers have eaten from nature's bounty by hunting deer, moose, game birds, and wild hare, or fishing for trout, pike, and bass while foraging for berries, fruits, and mushrooms. Many rural residents tend small kitchen gardens with a variety of vegetable crops, while raising a small flock of hens for eggs, and perhaps a few animals for domestic consumption.

Abenaki use of forests and rivers, and the British, American, and French settlement history of the Eastern Townships, is documented in chapters by Jean L. Manore and J.I. Little in this collection. The advanced post-WWII industrialization of agriculture during the course of the twentieth century did not bypass the Townships; a predominance of fossil-fuel powered tractors replaced draught

Figure 3.1 The landscape in the Eastern Townships

animals, the use of amendments to the soil such as chemical fertilizers, herbicides and pesticides were utilized to replace on-farm recycled nutrients (compost, crop and animal wastes), seeds from other places were sought out and planted, and an emphasis developed on maximum-yield management of agricultural products as commodities for the external market. As a consequence, small farms continued their progression towards intensification and specialization in a single crop or livestock, aided by government subsidies. Despite this, the per acre diversity of food production remained higher in the Eastern Townships than the Canadian average for areas of expanding commercial agriculture (Bardati 2015). While industrialization has had an impact in this region as elsewhere, with the growth of urban centres, manufacturing industries, electrical transmission lines, energy pipelines, and transportation networks, the landscape remains predominantly agricultural to this day.

Agricultural businesses occupy 31.5 per cent of the territory of the Eastern Townships with a total of 320,000 hectares in crop production or livestock pasture. About 2,600 agricultural business are registered in the region, mainly dairy, maple, and beef production (L'Arterre 2021). Of these, 349 are certified organic, or 14 per cent of all farms, surpassing the provincial average of 10 per cent (by some 40 per cent). While the data on non-certified organic farms (e.g., farms that operate as if certified but are not) is not reliable, it is estimated that another 20 per cent of farmers exceed organic certification standards in their practices, especially the smaller operations who choose to forgo the paperwork and costs of certification. The dominance of organic farms in the region, coupled with the pastoral landscape and recreational opportunities, has increasingly transformed the Eastern Townships region into a well-known destination for agritourism. The region boasts more than 180 agritourism businesses with certified products including fruits, vegetables, cheeses, honey, meats, beers, wines, and more, with the number growing annually. These products are showcased in grocery stores, shopping spaces, restaurants, village cafés, public markets, solidarity markets, and in shops on the farm (Créateurs des Saveurs – Canton de L'Est, 2021).

A local, vibrant food movement has emerged recently in the Eastern Townships, explained by the rapid growth in farmers' markets, community-supported agriculture (CSA) ventures, farm stands, farm-to-school programs, and community gardens (Bardati, 2015). While the growing season lasts only from May to October, the produce that is generated is often abundant enough to last the entire year for many small-scale farming families, when preserved through cold storage, drying, freezing, fermentation, canning, and other means. Season-extension greenhouses are also dotting the landscape that help growers add a few months of growing in March/April and November/December. Despite this, most food consumed during the winter months by non-farming households is obtained from the global industrial food system, not locally.

Fuelled by environmental and social issues associated with both the consumption and production sides of the global food system, the search for alternative sources helps address people's need to draw close connections between food purchasing choices and social, ecological and economic sustainability issues – a need to "rebuild the foodshed" that was torn apart by the global industrialization of agriculture (Ackerman-Leist, 2013; Bardati, 2015). There are 130 farmers' markets in Quebec (AMPQ, 2021) – the Eastern Townships contains twenty-nine of them, the highest concentration of any region in Quebec, having risen from a handful a decade ago (AMPQ, 2021). This recent trend, coupled with its rich agricultural heritage and ever-growing diversity of local, usually organically certified, food products, reinforces the region's natural inclination toward, and leadership in, a local food system as a viable alternative to the conventional global food system.

If, as Ruttan observed, a transition toward agricultural sustainability is needed to overcome the problems of global industrial agriculture, then it stands to reason that agricultural education institutions should be at the forefront of reform, preparing a new generation of students to move the systems forward in the direction of sustainability. For most of the past century, there were only two conventional agricultural institutions of higher education in Quebec, McGill University in Montreal and Laval University in Quebec City. While mostly promoting the industrial model of agriculture, these two institutions have recently revised their instructional curriculum to incorporate environmental concerns. In 2022, only two higher education institutions in Quebec exclusively offer training in agroecology – i.e., organic and regenerative agriculture that place more environmentally sensitive practices at the core of their educational mission. Both of these are in the Eastern Townships: L'institut national d'agriculture biologique (INAB) at the Collège d'enseignement général et professionnel (CEGEP) in Victoriaville, and Sustainable Agriculture and Food Systems programs at Bishop's University.

The INAB is a pre-university centre offering CEGEP programs in animal production, vegetable production, fruit production, and urban agriculture (INAB 2021). It features an educational farm of fifty-five hectares that is certified organic, and includes fruit orchards, market gardens, cereal crops, animal barns, beehives, agroforestry parcels, and greenhouses. The INAB also contains a research centre in organic agriculture, the Centre d'expertise et de transfer en agriculture biologique et de proximité (CETAB+). The CETAB+ carries out applied research in organic plant production, and provides technical, management and marketing advisory services to agricultural businesses (CETAB 2021). Together the INAB and CETAB+ is the largest organic farming training and research centre in Canada (INAB 2021). In 2019, Bishop's University began to offer undergraduate courses in sustainable agriculture as part of its Sustainable Agriculture and Food Systems (SAFS) programs. As a university degree, rooted in the liberal arts tradition, the curriculum includes courses in agricultural science, food systems, and agricultural business and commerce. Providing a deeper and richer education than what is available at CEGEPs and community colleges, SAFS aims to develop critical generalists who will also have significant practical experience in the field on farms and agribusinesses, through required practica and internships. The SAFS is unique in Quebec in that it focuses on the integration of agriculture production and *food systems*, which includes all aspects of the food supply chain such as transportation, processing, retailing, wholesaling, preparation of foods, consumption, and disposal. Its mission is to examine the economic, social, and environmental sustainability of all aspects of integrated agriculture and food systems, from farm to table (BU SAFS 2021). Bishop's University further distinguishes itself by promoting teaching and learning of a type of agriculture that goes beyond organic certification to what is titled "regenerative agriculture." While organic agriculture allows monocultures, high inputs, and other practices that exacerbate climate change, regenerative agriculture focuses on regenerating degraded agri-environment. It is an approach and series of practices aimed at reversing climate change, sequestering carbon, conserving water, enhancing wild biodiversity within farms, and building healthy soils (Regeneration International 2021). A fifty-seven-hectare educational farm, located on Bishop's campus property, is currently under development, where regenerative agriculture principles and practices will be taught, researched, and showcased. A master plan, completed in October 2020, contains plans for market gardens, an ecological pond that provides geothermal heat to a large multipurpose building and greenhouse, fruit orchards that focus on rare emerging fruits, urban gardens that exhibit rooftop, vertical and container gardens, the mob grazing of small herds of farm animals among agroforestry parcels to show the symbolic relationship between herbivores and soil health, beehives for honey and biodiversity hedges to encourage pollinators, small insect growing operations for food production, a maple grove for sugar production, and a large ecologically managed forest (BU farm 2021).

Turning to the broader question of the Eastern Townships' identity within a growing global agricultural crisis, and the need to navigate a sustainable transition, it is possible to explore agricultural developments in Quebec and more specifically the Eastern Townships. Yet what exactly does it mean to successfully navigate a transition? What are the necessary ingredients of an agricultural transition for it to be deemed successful? How is sustainable growth measured? What constitutes institutional innovation? What capacities are needed to ensure innovation happens? And what evidence exists anywhere to point to successful transition? These questions, when considered in the context of emerging agricultural practices and policies in the Eastern Townships, suggest that while the region has benefited and will continue to benefit from provincially driven changes, it is also increasingly positioned as a successful example to the international community as a pathway toward meaningful agricultural sustainability.

SYNTHESIS: THE EASTERN TOWNSHIPS *and the* GLOBAL TRANSITION *to* AGRICULTURAL SUSTAINABILITY

Scholarly literature on organizational change provides important insights with respect to the capacities needed for institutional innovation. According to Woodhill (2010), global challenges of the twenty-first century call for the changing of institutions to better address: 1) changing societal norms and values, 2) government policies, 3) market incentives, and 4) flexibility in organizational structure and processes. Such institutional innovation requires "soft" capacities of communication, trust building, diplomacy, networking, advocacy, and leadership (Woodhill 2010). Measures recently championed by Quebec demonstrate that it is making efforts toward advancing successful institutional innovation in its agricultural sector. Evidence includes the recent *Politique Bioalimentaire 2018–2025, Plan agriculture durable 2020–2030*, and Réseau québécois de recherche en agriculture durable (RQRAD), all of which appear to encompass these institutional innovation ingredients and associated capacities.

How is the rich agricultural heritage and emerging local food systems in the Eastern Townships playing a leadership role in environmentally friendly agriculture education? How do we evaluate these for their role in contributing to a successful global transition? The work of Gliessman (2016), who specializes in agroecology as a transdisciplinary, participatory, and change-oriented science, practice, and movement, is particularly helpful in determining which objective measurable steps are needed to facilitate a societal transition. Gliessman suggests five levels of change that can serve as a roadmap to redesign food systems, from farm to table, with a goal of achieving sustainability (table 3.1).

The three first levels describe mostly farm-level changes that farmers can take to reduce their impacts on the environment. The fourth and fifth levels go beyond the farm to the broader food system and societies (Gliessman 2015). While Level 5 is the most ambitious, calling for complete transformation of society, Gliessman raises reasonable questions: "What will our food system look like when Level 5 thinking and action guides the changes needed to take place? ... Can this thinking bring about essential changes in policy, support systems, funding, and choice?" Perhaps this framework is exactly what is needed to begin to evaluate whether a society is "successfully navigating a transition toward sustainable growth in agricultural production" (Ruttan 1999, 5960). It is important to note that, consistent with the discipline of agroecology from which Gliessman is writing, science, practice, and social change approaches must all be integrated in any agricultural sustainability transition.

If we apply Gliessman's five-level framework to the agricultural policy, organizational, and food systems change in Quebec, and more specifically the Eastern Townships, we can evaluate whether this region is positioned to successfully address Ruttan's challenge (table 3.2).

Table 3.2 illustrates that the Eastern Townships may have begun to demonstrate preliminary and tentative evidence of transition toward sustainability. Level 1 conversion, for example, which does not replace fossil fuel dependent industrial framing practices, does make concerted efforts towards improving efficiency and

Table 3.1
Gliessman's framework: five levels of food systems transformation

Level	Description	Examples of practices	Results
1	Increase the efficiency of industrial and conventional practices in order to reduce the use and consumption of costly, scarce, or environmentally damaging inputs	• Reduce fertilizers • Reduce pesticides • Apply precision agriculture • Optimize water use	• Maintains or increases production with less cost and damage • Does not break dependence on external inputs and monoculture practices
2	Substitute alternative practices for industrial/conventional inputs and practices	• Convert to organic agriculture • Employ cover-cropping, rotations • Use natural controls for pests • Use on-farm compost	• Does not break dependence on external inputs and monoculture practices • Basic agroecosystem is not altered from its simplified form
3	Redesign the agro-ecosystem so that it functions on the basis of a new set of ecological processes	• Reintroduce diversity in farms • Ecologically based rotations • Multiple cropping • Agroforestry • Integrate animals and crops	• Prevents problems before they occur, rather than trying to control them after they occur • Agroecosystem better understood
4	Re-establish a more direct connection between those who grow our food and those who consume it	• Create alternative food networks (e.g., farmers' markets, CSAS, co-ops) • Direct marketing of farm products	• Enhances direct consumer–farmer relationship • Higher value for local food • Relocalizes food • Revitalizes farm community
5	On the foundation created by the sustainable farm-scale agroecosystems achieved at Level 3, and the new relationships of sustainability of Level 4, build a new global food system, based on equity, participation, democracy, and justice, that is not only sustainable but helps restore and protects earth's life support systems upon which we all depend	• Move beyond farm-scale practices • Question the nature of human culture, civilization, progress, and development. • Make changes in beliefs, values, ethical systems • Focus on equity, justice, security	• Global in scope • Reaches beyond the food system • Redefines how we relate to each other and nature • Brings about a paradigm shift in line with sustainability

Source: Bardati (2021). Created from text in Gleissman (2015).

Table 3.2
Eastern Townships agricultural transition using the 5-level framework

Transition level	Description	Evidence in Quebec	Evidence in Eastern Townships
1	Increase the efficiency of industrial and conventional practices in order to reduce the use and consumption of costly, scarce, or environmentally damaging inputs	*Plan agriculture durable 2020–30*	Attention given to reducing damaging inputs is applied across the agricultural sector
2	Substitute alternative practices for industrial/ conventional inputs and practices	*Politique Bioalimentaire 2018–2025*	The INAB and CETAB+ as Canada's largest organic training and research centre
3	Redesign the agroecosystem so that it functions on the basis of a new set of ecological processes	Réseau québécois de recherche sur l'agriculture durable (RQRAD)	Several RQRAD-funded research projects are located in the Eastern Townships
4	Re-establish a more direct connection between those who grow our food and those who consume it	Association des marches publics du Québec (AMPQ)	The emerging local food system with its abundant farmers' markets, CSAS, etc.
5	On the foundation created by the sustainable farm-scale agroecosystems achieved at Level 3, and the new relationships of sustainability of Level 4, build a new global food system, based on equity, participation, democracy, and justice, that is not only sustainable but helps restore and protects earth's life support systems upon which we all depend		Bishop's University SAFS program, which aims to develop "critical generalists" that will question the status quo, identify creative solutions, help transform the global food system

reducing damage. Agricultural operations in the Eastern Townships have been steadily improving the efficiency of their practices (e.g., pesticide and fertilizer use) for several years now. Level 2 conversion calls for the substitution of alternative input and practices. As the highest ranked percentage of organically certified agricultural operations by region, as well as the engagement provided by the CEGEP de Victoriaville and the CETAB+, it is clear that the Eastern Townships is exhibiting leadership. Redesigning the agroecosystem so that it functions based on ecological processes is at the core of Level 3 conversion. This is a radically different orientation than simply adopting organic practices on an industrial scale, and instead it re-envisions farming as an ecologically benign activity. While the number of farms characterized at this level are very small, there is likely a higher percentage of these examples of operation in the Eastern Townships than other regions of the province. The new RQRAD-funded research projects have, at their core, the testing of Level 3 practices through experiential trials on farms and research centres. Many of these Level 3 research projects are underway in the Eastern Townships. Level 4 conversion expands the scope of change beyond the farm to the food system. Bardati (2015) outlined the clear emergence of an emerging local food system in the Eastern Townships, evidenced by the explosive growth of farmers' markets, community-supported agricultural schemes, and community gardens. There is much more work to be done to achieve full Level 4 conversion, but the region appears to be well on its way. Finally, Level 5 conversion, according to Gleissman expands the sustainability transition beyond the food system to all aspects of society at large. Changes in beliefs, values, and ethics are emphasized, as society seeks equity, justice, and security for all people. This lofty goal may be difficult to reach in the Eastern Townships, but it provides a clear end goal for sustainability transition efforts. In this regard, Bishop's University's SAFS program aims to develop "'critical generalists' that will question the status quo, identify creative solutions, and help transform the global food system. While it remains to be seen if this vision for the SAFS program will result in new graduates who will effectively find success in helping society make the Level 5 conversion, it is the only example of such a higher education institution in the province.

CONCLUSION

This chapter explores the Eastern Townships' agricultural identity within the global sustainability crisis. While the region has not been immune to the ravages of industrial agriculture on the natural environment, its geographic features and approach toward agricultural development appear to have buffeted it against some of agriculture's more harmful effects in the post-1945 period. The Eastern Townships is favourably located within a province that is a leader in organic agriculture, features progressive agricultural policies and practices, and is home to educational institutions committed to teaching and innovative research on sustainable agriculture. These favourable geographical and political conditions, coupled with a long history of land-based expertise, a plethora of diverse, small-scale family-based farms, as well as the existence of innovative agriculture programs at higher-education institutions, combine to provide the region with a solid base for implementing a successful sustainability transition.

This chapter raised the question whether, amidst the global agri-food crisis, there was a means to evaluate whether the international community might approach and undertake agriculture differently, effectively doing less damage to the environment and society. Ruttan's call to "successfully navigate toward transition to sustainable growth in agricultural production" is in fact being answered, in a small way, in the Eastern Townships. Consideration of Gleissman's 5-level transition framework further suggests that this region may be well on its way to such a successful transition. The state of agriculture in the Eastern Townships, while somewhat influenced by and reflective of global practices, is increasingly a successful model for Canada and the broader international community – a region pursuing an agricultural identity constructed around and firmly anchored in a commitment to sustainability.

References

Ackerman-Leist, P. 2013. *Rebuilding the Foodshed: How to Create Local, Sustainable and Secure Food systems.* White River Junction, VT : Chelsea Green.

AMPQ. 2021. Association de marchés publics du Québec. https ://ampq.ca/. Accessed 15 November 2021.

Bardati, Darren. 2015. "The Emerging Local Food System in the Eastern Townships." *Journal of Eastern Townships Studies* 45: 9–30.

Bruinsma, Jelle. 2003. *World Agriculture Towards 2015/2030: An FAO Perspective.* London: Earthscan.

BU farm. 2021. *Bishop's University Educational Farm Master Plan.* www.ubishops.ca/farm. Accessed 15 November 2021.

BU SAFS. 2021. Bishop's University Sustainable Agriculture and Food Systems. www.ubishops.ca/safs. Accessed 15 November 2021.

CARTV. 2020. *Rapport D'Activités 2020.* Montreal : Conseil des Appellations Réservées et des Termes Valorisants (CARTV).

Créateurs des Saveurs – Cantons de L'Est. 2021. https ://www.createursdesaveurs.com/. Accessed 12 November 2021.

Ericksen, Polly. 2007. "Conceptualizing Food Systems for Global Environmental Change Research." *Global Environmental Change.* Doi:10.1016/j.gloenvcha.2007.09.002.

FAO. 1999. *Organic Agriculture: Position Paper.* Rome: Food and Agriculture Organization of the United Nations. https://www.fao.org/3/X0075e/X0075e.htm. Accessed 12 November 2021.

– 2018. *Sustainable Food Systems: Concept and Framework.* Rome: Food and Agriculture Organization of the United Nations.

– 2021. *The Impacts of Disasters and Crises on Agriculture and Food Security.* Rome: Food and Agriculture Organization of the United Nations.

FRQNT. 2021. "2.5 million pour la création du Réseau québécois de recherche en agriculture durable." 8 October. Communiqués, Fonds de recherche du Québec – Nature et Technologies.

Girard-Bossé, Alice. 2021. "Québec : Champion du Bio." *La Presse*, 11 November. https://www.lapresse.ca/actualites/2021-11-11/agriculture/le-quebec-champion-du-bio.php. Accessed 10 February 2024.

IPCC. 2019. *Climate Change and Land – An IPCC Special Report on Climate Change, Desertification, Land Degradation, Sustainable Land Management, Food Security, and Greenhouse Gas Fluxes in Terrestrial Ecosystems – Summary for Policymakers*. Intergovernmental Panel on Climate Change, https://www.ipcc.ch/site/assets/uploads/2019/08/4.-SPM_Approved_Microsite_FINAL.pdf.

Gliessman, Steve. 2016. "Transforming Food Systems with Agroecology." *Agroecology and Sustainable Food Systems* 40 (3): 187–9.

– 2015. *Agroecology: The Ecology of Sustainable Food Systems*. New York: CRC Press.

Guerra, Jill, and Lauren Martin. 2017. *The State of Organics: Federal-Provincial-Territorial Performance Report 2017*. Ottawa: Canada Organic Trade Association.

INAB. 2021. *De la Formation*. Institut nationale en agriculture. https ://www.cegepvicto.ca/institut-national-agriculture-biologique/#formation. Accessed 15 November 2021.

L'Arterre. 2021. https://www.arterre.ca/RegionsParticipantes/05. Accessed 12 November 2021.

Melchior, I.C., and J. Newig. 2021. "Governing Transitions towards Sustainable Agriculture – Taking Stock of an Emerging Field of Research." *Sustainability* 13: 528–55.

Mbow, C., et al. 2019. "Food Security." In *Climate Change and Land: An IPCC Special Report on Climate Change, Desertification, Land Degradation, Sustainable Land Management, Food Security, and Greenhouse Gas Fluxes in Terrestrial Ecosystems*, edited by P.R. Shukla et al., chapter 5. https://www.ipcc.ch/srccl/chapter/chapter-5/. Accessed 7 January 2024.

OECD. 2020. *COVID-19 and Global Food Systems*. OECD.org/coronavirus.

Portail BioQuébec : état et évolution du secteur biologique. https ://www.portailbioquebec.info/. Accessed 12 November 2021.

Quebec. 2018. *Politique Bioalimentaire 2018–2025*. https ://www.quebec.ca/gouv/politiques-orientations/politique-bioalimentaire. Accessed 12 November 2021.

– 2021. *Plan D'Action 2018–2023. Pour la Réussite de la Politique Bioalimentaire*. Quebec.

Ruttan, Vernon W. 1999. "The Transition to Agricultural Sustainability." *Proceedings of the National Academy of Sciences, USA* 96: 5960–7.

Statista. 2021. *Categories in Which Consumers Purchase Organic Products Regularly in Canada as of July 2019*. https://www.statista.com/statistics/495967/categories-in-which-consumers-purchase-organic-products-regularly-canada/. Accessed 12 November 2021.

UPA. 2021. *Benchmarking of Support Measures for Organic Farming in Quebec to other Jurisdictions*. Longueuil, QC: Union des Producteurs Agricole.

Willer, H., J. Travnicek, C. Meier, and B. Schaltter, eds. 2021. *The World of Organic Agriculture: Statistics and Emerging Trends 2021*. Research Institute of Organic Agriculture FIBL, Frck, and IFOAM – Organics International, Bonn (v20210301).

Woodhill, Jim. 2010. "Capacities for Institutional Innovation: A Complexity Perspective." IDS *Bulletin*. Wiley Online Library. https://doi.org/10.1111/j.1759-5436.2010.00136.x.

World Bank Group. 2017. *Future of Food: Shaping the Food Systems to Deliver Jobs*. Washington, DC: International Bank for Reconstruction and Development.

Part Two

Peoples in Motion: Moving Into and Out of Quebec's Eastern Townships

The second section of this volume contains five chapters that present significant case studies of human mobility and engagement in the Townships. What residence in the Townships meant to its people, both as a home and as a point of departure, is integral to any full understanding of the region. In chapter 4, "Abenaki Mobility and the Eastern Townships of Ndakina," Jean L. Manore surveys the movement of Indigenous people through Ndakina, emphasizing traditional routes and how a European colonial presence adversely affected Indigenous mobility. "Abenaki movement through the Eastern Townships … and their connection to Ndakina," Manore observes, "has been seriously misunderstood and devalued." The chapter by Roderick MacLeod and Mary Anne Poutanen (chapter 5), "Townships Women Go Off to School: Teaching Diplomas, Career Ambitions, and the McGill Normal School, 1857–65," examines the lived experience of Eastern Townships women who attended the McGill Normal School in nineteenth-century Montreal. The authors frame their narrative around the life of one particular teacher, and they paint a vivid portrait that captures both teachers' motivations for entering the profession and the outcomes of normal school training for these students. Jane Jenson's work,

"Going to Someone Else's War: Border-Crossing Enlistments from the Eastern Townships during the American Civil War" (chapter 6), revisits British North Americans' complex relationship to the United States Civil War of 1861–65, explaining the motivations for participation in the conflict by Townships men and women, especially in terms of religion. Chapter 7, "Transitioning from Southern Honour to Dependency: Jefferson Davis in Montreal and the Eastern Townships, 1867–68" by Gordon S. Barker and Christopher Kirkey, examines the struggles of the former president of the Confederacy to reestablish his patriarchal standing while residing in Lennoxville between September 1867 and July 1868. The authors argue that Davis's time in Lennoxville transformed him from a proud Southern patriarch to a dependent, unable to generate sufficient income to support his family and confronted by concerns over his upcoming trial for treason. The final chapter in part 2, authored by Cheryl Gosselin and titled "Immigration in the Eastern Townships of Quebec: Patterns of Regional Settlement and Belonging" (chapter 8), draws on census data and media sources that chart and illuminate patterns of recent immigrant settlement in the Townships. This chapter finds that belonging is an uneven social process experienced by individuals and families, one beset by linguistic, religious, and financial challenges.

4

Abenaki Mobility and the Eastern Townships of Ndakina

Jean L. Manore

I acknowledge that in writing this chapter, I am situated within the traditional, unceded territory of the Abenaki peoples and am grateful that they have welcomed me to their lands. As a settler-scholar, I recognize that the Abenaki peoples' ancestors have not always been respected, nor have their voices or those of their descendants today been listened to. At times, they have not been allowed to speak, even to share their knowledge. I acknowledge the Calls to Action of the Truth and Reconciliation commissioners who charged educators, among other things, to tell the truth about Canada's colonial past. This chapter is one attempt to uncover the roots of colonial thinking, by examining how colonizers' interpretations of Abenaki mobility distorted the meaning and nature of the movement of these Indigenous Peoples within the region known as the Eastern Townships of Quebec.

INTRODUCTION[1]

Colonization of Indigenous lands is a global phenomenon spanning the centuries, and it has not been limited to European expansion to other continents. While modern history has focused on European imperialism, Han expansion throughout China, and Zulu wars against other peoples in southern Africa are examples of colonization as well. Prominent methods employed to colonize Indigenous Peoples and their lands have included "demographic takeovers" to borrow from Alfred Crosby (1986) and mercantilist control of trading networks between imperial centres and Indigenous hinterlands. But more subtle ways have also been used to accomplish colonization. These have included the use of legal concepts such as *terra nullius*, and the doctrine of discovery that set the stage for establishing rights to property informed by Eurocentric notions of primitivism and heathenism.[2] In addition to these tools of colonization, however, colonizers' interpretations of mobility, which deemed Indigenous Peoples "wanderers" or "nomads" and made them vulnerable to the loss of their lands to settlers or resource developers claiming superior rights to that land, merit scholarly attention. Examining the Abenaki peoples' patterns of mobility in northeastern North America reveals how ideas of mobility shaped Indigenous Peoples' visions and use of their lands as well as how Indigenous mobility played into colonizers' strategies to claim lands and exclude Indigenous people from the historical narrative. Additionally, placing this study within the Eastern Townships brings another level of analysis to the idea of mobility and colonization. The Eastern Townships are a borderlands, carved out of Abenaki territory, as a result of French and English imperial rivalry. From borderlands comes, often, the creation of nation-states, as occurred in this instance in the form of Canada and the United States. In studying the early history of the Eastern Townships, the colonial roots of these two countries can further help to illuminate the role of mobility in shaping colonization throughout the globe.

Ndakina, the vast, traditional territory of the W8banakiak,[3] stretches, roughly, from the eastern seaboard of the Atlantic Ocean south of the St Lawrence River westward to the Richelieu River, taking in what is known today as the Gaspé Peninsula. Within this diverse geographical space, since time immemorial, the W8banakiak traversed, occupied, used, settled, hunted, fished, gathered, and worshipped, the lands, waters, and mountains. The relationship of the Abenaki people to this space and their understanding of it as their place was little known to the Europeans who arrived and settled within Ndakina. Through processes of colonization and colonialism, including the formation of European-based nation-states and regional governance, newcomers cast the history of the W8banakiak presence within their territory in a much different light and in sharp contrast to the W8banakiak's understanding. It was in this context, informed by Eurocentric misunderstanding of Indigenous Peoples' mobility, that Canadian settler policy reduced W8banakiak territory to two small reserves – Odanak and W8linak. Within Ndakina lies the region now known as the Eastern Townships, a territory not properly recognized as Indigenous territory because of settler understandings of mobility. But it was a place where the Abenaki people existed, sometimes permanently, sometimes temporarily, as they moved through time and space, through pre-history to history, and seasonally from their settlements south of the border to hunting, fishing, and community gathering spots within the Eastern Townships and elsewhere. The Eastern Townships region was also a place to where the Abenaki moved in response to conflicts with other Indigenous Peoples or, of course, with settlers who sought to establish themselves in other areas that the Abenaki traditionally regarded as part of their land.

In examining mobility within the context of European and settler colonization of Turtle Island,[4] the works of Keith Basso, Lisa Brooks, and of John Borrows provide insight. Basso focuses on processes of "place-making" that involved the "adventitious fleshing out of historical material that culminates in a posited state of affairs, a particular universe of objects and events –in short, a *place-world* – wherein portions of the past are brought into being" (Basso 1996, 6). For Brooks, place-making represents a "physical, actual, material relationship to 'an ecosystem present in a definable place'" that is created by individuals, families, kin, and communities (Brooks 2008, xxiv). When children are born, they enter into a network of relations that include ties through marriage and kin but also ties that are "connected to the network of waterways, which people traveled by canoe and footpath from the southeast coast to the northwest lakes" (Brooks 2008, xxiv). Brooks's description of W8banakiak connections to the waterways of Ndakina, for example, is demonstrated by the Abenaki's traditional travel routes between their summer and winter abodes. On one such route, they paddled up the Kennebec River to reach Dead River, where they made a portage of five miles over a stretch of land before arriving at Arnold River. They then crossed Lake Mégantic and descended the Chaudière River to the St Lawrence. Lake Memphremagog was one of the main links in their water route from the St Lawrence to the headwaters of the Connecticut (Leonard Auger Papers, n.d., file P135/ 008.06). Another Abenaki trail to the Upper Connecticut, New Hampshire, Maine, and Massachusetts communities from the St Lawrence went from Montreal to the St Francis River and toward Lake Memphremagog, and then down the Nulhegan River to the Connecticut. Alternatively, they travelled from Lake Memphremagog to the Barton River, thence to Sutton Lake and the Passumpsic River down to the Connecticut. From Montreal, they also journeyed to the Yamaska River, then over to the Missisquoi River to Missisquoi Bay, or from the Yamaska to Lake Memphremagog (Leonard Auger Papers, n.d., file P135/006.0/a).

From these travel routes came lived experiences that produced stories that linked the W8banakiak to Ndakina. Henry Masta, an Abenaki educated at Dartmouth

College and later a teacher at Odanak, provided examples in his *Abenaki Indian Legends and Stories* (1932). He recounted the story of how the Abenaki who lived in Maine, on the Kennebec River, had a priest who was there to teach them. One day, the priest was recalled to Quebec by his bishop, and he headed north. The council, however, wanted the priest to stay and decided to send a delegation to Quebec to convince the bishop of their "great need of him and their great desire to have him back." After the bishop agreed to allow the priest's return, he, the Abenaki delegation, an Etchemin guide, and a Frenchman left Quebec to return to the Kennebec mission. The guide unfortunately took the wrong route. By the time the party got turned around, the travellers were tired, hungry, and fearing death. Not surprisingly, they named the river they were on the Famine River, even though it was the one that eventually led them to their destination (Masta 1932, 29–30). Another story tells of the naming of Turtle River by an Abenaki who lived along the river and knew it as well as his wigw8m. He was known to have travelled up and down the river frequently at all hours of the day and night. He apparently never encountered any obstacle or problem until one night, as he was stepping into his canoe, he slipped on something hard. When he struck it with his hatchet, "the sound of the blow was as if a stone was hit." Confused, he had difficulty sleeping that night. When dawn arrived, he returned to the place and discovered a very large turtle shell that completely hid the turtle inside. The river became known as "Mikinakwi Sibo," the Turtle River (Masta 1932, 26–7).

Such stories reveal how the Abenaki linked their experiences to their lands and waters. Sometimes these stories took on meaning for larger groups beyond the individual or family, but sometimes they did not. Indigenous forms of history, Basso stresses, are "pointedly local and unfailingly episodic." Equally important, Basso notes, such history "is also extremely personal, consistently subjective, and therefore highly variable among those who work to produce it. For these and other reasons, it is history without authorities – all narrated place-worlds, provided they seem plausible, are considered equally valid" (Basso 1996, 32–3). Deny O'bomsawin's personal history reflects the foregoing. A lifelong resident of Odanak, Deny's understanding of himself as an individual and as a W8banaki person is tied closely to the land. Yet, others too have their own personal histories that give them their unique connections. Deny travelled to various places within Ndakina generally, and within the Eastern Townships specifically, to perform ceremonies on mountain tops, but neither he nor his family travelled to Coaticook. Coaticook was a place for other W8banakiak to visit and experience (Deny O'bomsawin 2021). These few examples demonstrate the idea of the W8banakiak place-word of Ndakina, a personal space, delimited by family and individual stories that link families and individuals to each other but also link them in unique, personal ways to the land of Ndakina.

When European and settler colonists came to Turtle Island, they set about creating their own place-worlds by transforming Indigenous lands into individualized, settler lands, Indigenous resources into settler resources, and Indigenous Peoples into nomads and refugees. The new arrivals reinforced and formalized their process of place-making through time by the act of writing, which as Colin Calloway argues, is itself an act of dispossession (Barman 2016, 22). One aspect of this creation process was the use of Eurocentric notions and interpretations of mobility as tools for colonization, something that John Borrows, an Anishnaabe scholar, has stressed. He discusses the idea of mobility in his 2016 publication *Freedom and Indigenous Constitutionalism*. He notes that Indigenous people have always been mobile, through time and space, and that colonization has worked to deny that mobility or use mobility as a means of denying Indigenous rights to their lands. He argues that Indigenous Peoples have been denied spatial mobility, by being denied access to their traditional territories or control over them, and through the creation of reserves. He also contends that Indigenous Peoples have been restricted in temporal mobility, by having their culture frozen in a "before-time," alleging that they are unable to adapt or adjust to modern times, without somehow losing their status or "Indian-ness." As Borrows puts it, Indigenous People(s) are damned if they move and damned if they don't (Borrows 2016, 29–32). While his focus is on how mobility has been used as a colonial tool within legal battles for recognition of Indigenous rights and title within Canada, in looking at the W8banakiak and Ndakina, it is clear that ideas of mobility have also been used within historical discourse to achieve the same end.

W8BANAKIAK PLACE-WORLD *and* MOBILITY

For the W8banakiak, Ndakina has existed since its creation by Wjihozo, a transformer whose upper body was human but whose lower body was that of an otter. Believing that the Creator had not adequately shaped the land, Wjihozo travelled through Ndakina and, with his lower body, carved out the rivers, lakes, and valleys amongst the mountains. When looking at the Alsig8ntegw, or the St Francis River, for example, one can see where Wjihozo must have turned his body to make bends in the river, and where he must have scraped against rocks to make rapids and other obstructions. When Wjihozo completed his work, he retired to Pitawbagok, what is now Lake Champlain, and turned into a rock so that he could continue to look at and appreciate the beauty he had made. For the W8banakiak, it was the custom to honour him, when they passed his resting place by placing tobacco or other offerings on what is now known as Rock Dunder (Deny O'bomsawin 2021; Nicole O'Bomsawin 2021).

Other beings also had to be honoured, including Pmola, the winged bird that lived on the tops of the highest mountains, and Tat8skok, the horned serpent that lived in larger lakes, notably Lake Memphremagog. If Pmola was not respected by those who dared to enter his domain, he sent storms and attacked the trespassers (Morrison 1982). If Tat8skok was not honoured before crossing his lake, then he created huge waves, which overturned canoes and sent occupants and possessions into the waters (Nicole O'Bomsawin 2021). These stories connect Ndakina – its rivers, lakes, and mountains – to the W8banakiak and their lives. Although specific locations have been assigned to these beings and stories, these stories provide a lens on the way of life of the W8banakiak people who viewed their home as the entire territory of Ndakina, not just certain areas within it; Ndakina was, and is, not just a place the W8babakiak people call home but a place where all W8banakiak were, and are, at home. As Michel Durand Nolett (2021) states, "This is our territory, not my territory."

So, if Ndakina was home to the W8banakiak, what did and what does that mean for them? Home is a place of shelter, nourishment, and security; it is a place for families and community. It is a place where the cycle of life begins and ends; it is a place where children become adults; it is a place where parents care for their young; it is a place where elders teach youth values and customs of family and community, and people seek protection from strife and stresses of the exterior world or defend themselves against enemies from the exterior world. Central to the W8banakiak's pattern of shaping their home and achieving these goals was their mobility.

Before European arrival and settlement, the W8banakiak moved frequently and extensively. They did so as individuals, families, and communities. Larger communities of many families were established in areas with abundant resources to support large gatherings, locations such as at Odanak on the St Francis River, near the St Lawrence River. When resources in such areas were no longer sufficient to support a large community, other locations were found or the community split into smaller groups (Richard O'Bomsawin 2021; Nicole O'Bomsawin 2021). Often, such movements occurred seasonally. During the winter months, communities formed along the Atlantic coast, where marine resources were abundant, or families would move into the interior to hunt game. During the spring breakup, families would move up from river shores near rapids in search of good places to catch fish during spawning (Michel Durand Nolett 2021). Typically, areas chosen also allowed for planting crops and harvesting maple syrup. Ulverton was one such place, as was Drummondville. When the fish runs were completed, families stayed where they were, as they did at Nikitawtegwak (Grand Forks) in Sherbrooke, although sometimes they moved to other places having more or different resources (Patrick Coté 2021). An example of this type of movement within Ndakina involved the journey of W8banakiak from their winter settlements along the Connecticut and Androscoggin rivers to Lake Champlain, to the St Francis River to Odanak, or from the Kennebec River to the Chaudière River where it meets the St Lawrence.

The W8banakiak carefully planned moves that often involved travelling hundreds of kilometres. Covering such distances typically meant that when they reached their destination, they did not stay there just for one day (Richard O'Bomsawin 2021). The W8banakiak, through teachings and experience, knew where they were headed and why. They knew which lakes held sturgeon or pike or trout or eels and when these fish could best be caught. They knew which hunting grounds were available for their use and which were not. Hunting territories tended to be visited by specific families, and these families also shared knowledge regarding the availability of game. For example, when W8banakiak hunted or trapped a territory, they left skulls of their prey hanging from a tree. If other members of their community found several skulls when they entered an area, they knew that the area might be hunted out and so would choose to go elsewhere. By the rotting of the skulls, they could also determine how long ago an area had been hunted. If the skulls were bleached white, they knew it had been a few years since the area was last hunted and thus prospects for hunting were good. If skulls still had blood on them, they knew the area had been hunted recently and it was best avoided (Patrick Coté 2021).

The W8banakiak knew where to find ash trees for basket-making or sumac for cough medicine (Michel Durand Nolett 2021). They knew what mountains were safe to visit and which were more threatening (Nicole O'Bomsawin 2021); they knew which mountains had a plethora of medicinal herbs or those that could lead the way from life to death (Richard O'Bomsawin 2021). The W8banakiak often considered mountains sacred places, especially their peaks, which they viewed as good places for ceremonies – notably ceremonies to reflect and be thankful for the bounty of the land, the passing of stages of life, including from youth to adulthood and then to death, or for the passing of the day and seasons (Deny O'bomsawin 2021).

For the W8banakiak, trade and security were also key reasons for movement. Part of their seasonal migrations included meeting with other nations to trade for goods that were not readily available within Ndakina. Meeting other W8banakiak, as well as Atikamekw, Algonquin, and Cree at Tadoussac, Montreal, St Maurice, and Quebec occurred regularly in the summer and fall (Nicole O'Bomsawin 2021). When the French started to participate in the fur trade, W8banakiak added them to their trade networks along the St Lawrence. With the advent of European competition for trade and territory in Ndakina, wars broke out between French and English, Mi'kmaq and other W8banakiak, and between Haudenosaunee (mostly Mohawk) and the W8banaki Confederacy. When this happened, many W8banakiak moved to more secure locations, such as at Odanak, Sillery, and Bécancour, while others stayed in contested areas and fought to remove the intruders (Morrison 1984; Calloway 1990; Maurault 1866; Charland 1964). Because the W8banakiak did not consider their territory as limited to the specific locales in which they resided for the greatest length of time, they thought of all of Ndakina as their home. Ndakina was not just a collection of specific sites where they hunted, fished, farmed, gardened, or worshipped.

The W8banakiak social structures and cultural understandings were fluid and adaptable but always rooted in the lands and waters of Ndakina, which shaped their patterns of mobility. While the W8banakiak all shared Ndakina, they displayed a diversity of languages, customs, practices, and even beliefs. Indeed, the W8banakiak comprised several nations. Within the eastern part of Ndakina the Kennebec, Penobscot, Malecite, Canibas, Abenaki (Maine), Narragansett, Nipmuck, Pocumtuck, Passamaquoddy, "River Indians," Wampanoag, and Waronoke communities were to be found. To the west, the Malecite, Mi'kmaq, Passamoquoddy, Penobscot, Abenaki, Sokoki, Missisquoi, and others lived. It was these latter peoples who were more likely to travel and live within the Eastern Townships. Each of the above-mentioned nations had its own dialect but members of each community understood their neighbors as well as those who lived further away (Nicole O'Bomsawin 2021). Each of these peoples established their communities along certain rivers that they also shared with others. Each had their own games and stories but the W8banakiak transmitted similar values and skills to younger generations through their cultural activities. One point of distinction between the Eastern and Western Abenaki involved the cultural hero Glooscap who was celebrated by the Eastern Abenaki but not the Western Abenaki. The latter celebrated Wjihozo, the transformer, and he stood at the heart of their understanding of Ndakina. Wjihozo was very different from Glooscap, the super-human. Yet, Wjihozo and Glooscap both shaped the land in ways that explained its features to the W8banakiak and, in doing so, these cultural heroes exhibited certain characteristics of power and fallibility that explained the nature of the world and relationships within it (Nicole O'Bomsawin 2021). The W8banakiak similarities enabled and helped seal alliances and liaisons between them, especially during the turmoil created by the arrival of the French and English (Calloway 1989). Lisa Brooks argues that "these alliances provided strengthened trade relations, places to stay if conflicts arose [in their local area], resources for assistance if food or supplies were short, and coalitions against "a common threat." The Sokokis, for example, knew they could seek refuge with the Mohicans or with their Abenaki connections in Maine, if they felt the need to do so (Brooks 2008, 27–8).

Although mobility lay at the heart of W8banakiak identity and the territory of their place-world, with colonization, W8banakiak mobility became a means whereby their physical (and temporal) connections to their homeland were restricted, constrained, or denied altogether, thus transforming their place-world of Ndakina into the settler place-worlds of Canada and the United States. An examination of the historical portrayal of the Abenaki from the time of contact with the French and English, through the early formation of the nation-states of Canada and the United States casts this process in sharp relief.[5]

IMPERIAL/COLONIAL PLACE-WORLDS *and* MOBILITY

The historiography of the Abenaki in North America is vast, yet it has a particular focus on identity and origin. In short, the literature explores who constituted the Abenaki peoples and where they were located at the time of contact. The scholarship, however, has been affected, on the one hand, by the paucity of historical documents and, on the other hand, by confusion stemming from different names assigned to people and places by French and English recorders as they travelled from the Atlantic seaboard inland into Lake Champlain.

According to André Sévigny, the French called the Abenaki, l'Abenaquioicts or l'Abenaquis; the English, Abnaki or Wabanki; the Moravian missionaries, Wapanchki; and the Puritans, Wampanoag (Sévigny 1976, 18). Frank Speck, an American anthropologist, notes that the Haudenosaunee[6] considered "Wabanaki" or "Abenaki" a general term for the numerous nations who lived along the Atlantic coast, not inland. In contrast, the Jesuit priest, Père Le Jeune, saw the Abenaki "as Indians belonging to the Algonkian tribal group who were allied with the Mohegans, possibly the Sokokis or the Delawares." Given the location of these nations, inland from the Atlantic coast, Le Jeune's positioning of the Abenaki seems to contradict the views of the Haudenosaunee (Sévigny 1976, 20).

Equally confusing is the interpretation of Montague Chamberlain, who suggested that the Abenaki ancestors were a group of Ojibwa who separated from the latter people when they moved just east of the Adirondacks. From there, they were pushed still further east by the Iroquois toward the Connecticut River and became the Pennacooks of New Hampshire. The Pennacooks, however, moved eastward again to the Saco River, Chamberlain contends, to become the Sokokis. For Chamberlain, such successive movements from river to river created other Abenaki communities that came to be identified as the Androscoggins, the Wawenocks, the Kennebecs, the Penobscots, and, finally, the Malecites of the St John River (Sévigny 1976, 36–7). Further complicating historical descriptions but again stressing movement and mobility, Bernard Hoffman, exploring the pre-history of the St Lawrence valley, argues that "in ancient times, the Micmacs were bordered on the south and west by the Etchemin, and on the north by the Kwedech, or Canadian Iroquois." Turning to the post-contact period, he suggests that after the 1617 plague, much of the Etchemin country was completely depopulated but later inhabited "by Abnaki-speaking peoples moving in from the west, and by Micmac-speaking peoples moving in from the north-east" (Sévigny 1976, 35).

For the historical understanding of Indigenous presence in the Eastern Townships, Sévigny argues that there is "no evidence to contradict the idea that the origins of the Abenaki peoples were not 'laurentienne,'" meaning outside of the St Lawrence Valley, and that their entry into New England was not through Maine but rather from further west, possibly by the Connecticut River (Chamberlain 1904). Albert Gravel in his *Les Cantons de L'Est*, published in 1938, describes the Abenaki of Lake Mégantic as descendants of the Canibas, a people who originally resided on the Kennebec River in Maine. He writes that the Maine Abenaki established themselves on the Chaudière and Etchimen Rivers, while the Sokokis settled at Lake Mégantic, Bécancour (W8linak), and on the St Francis (Odanak) (Gravel 1938). Finally, in his *Histoire de Coaticook*, Roch Dandenault argues that the Abenaki were not indigenous to Canada but that they were descendants of the Canibas people who occupied Maine, New Hampshire, and Vermont around the 1680s. He believed that their first incursions into Quebec occurred around 1637, at Trois-Rivières, where they traded furs with the Innu (Dandenault 1976). Subsequent scholarship provides more definitive, but not universal, conclusions. Gordon Day, in his *Identity of the St Francis Indians* (1981), argues that the Sokokis were the first and dominant group of W8banakiak peoples to relocate to Odanak during the New England wars while Colin Calloway contends that the St Francis Indians were connected to the Androscoggin Valley and people (Calloway 1990). Although these historical interpretations differ, in each of them, the theme of physical or spatial mobility of the Abenaki is writ large; these scholars portray the W8banakiak as inveterate wanderers with no fixed abode or as peoples driven from their homelands to take refuge within French Jesuit missions along the St Lawrence.

An examination of the limited archeological evidence discovered in the Eastern Townships demonstrates an example of temporal mobility seen through a colonial lens. The consensus is that there were Indigenous Peoples in the Eastern Townships dating from the Ancient Paleoindian period of from 13,500 to 12,800 BP (before present), through the Archaic period (circa 11,350 to 3,000 BP) to the Sylviculture period, 3,000 to 450 BP, to the historic period. Nevertheless, because archeological investigation has been so limited, there can be no definite conclusions drawn that the pre-historic people were the ancestors of the Abenaki. Some speculation that these pre-historic peoples may have been in fact ancestors of the Laurentian Iroquois exists (see Chapdelaine 2007; Chapdelaine and Richard 2017; Graillon 2018). Further, Frederick Wiseman, an anthropologist and self-proclaimed Abenaki sovereigntist, critiques what he refers to as the "Iroquoian bias," which emphasizes Iroquoian presence within Ndakina over W8banakiak. He interprets the archeological findings as supporting Abenaki oral history, which tells of W8banakiak expansion into the northeastern part of North America along the waterways created by the departing glaciers (Wiseman 2001).

The historiographical literature has also sought to position the Abenaki within the imperial conflicts between the English and French for control of northeastern North America. In his excellent overview of the colonial period, Andrew Miller (2008) notes that during the seventeenth century, the Abenakis were at war with the Iroquois Confederacy and in response some Abenaki, Sokoki, and especially the Pennacook joined the French in alliance against them (see also Daugherty 1983; Baxter 1890; Calloway 1986; and Dodge 1957). By the 1650s and 1660s, as the war with the Mohawk intensified, the Sokoki were most affected by the conflict. By the time of the outbreak of Metacom's War (King Philip's War) to the south, the Sokoki stronghold of Squakheag had been reduced to about twenty or thirty people. Many Sokoki left and sought refuge elsewhere, including at Missisquoi, a major Abenaki town on Lake Champlain, but also sought refuge in Pennacook country, in Schaghticoke, a satellite settlement set up by the Dutch, and even in French villages and outposts along the St Lawrence (Miller 2008). When Abenaki from Maine moved across the St Lawrence, Jesuits welcomed them at Sillery, where Wendat and Algonquin people had also come to dwell. These early movements started what has been referred to as the "Algonquian diaspora," which gained momentum in the late seventeenth and eighteenth centuries (Miller 2008, 44).

Some of the W8banakiak tried to live peacefully with the English, but King Philip's War made the English suspicious of any Abenaki people within what they perceived to be their purview, and these sentiments also impacted mobility. Passaconnaway, chief of the Pennacooks, tried to avoid any conflict with the English by retiring from settlements on the lower Merrimack River and moving upriver to the town of Pennacook. When the English destroyed their town, the Pennacook retreated again to the Lake Winnipesaukee area. The Androscoggins and Kennebecs also sought to avoid warring with the English. When the English demanded that the Kennebec surrender their guns – weapons that were extremely useful to the Kennebec for hunting and for self-defence – the Kennebec response was to abandon their settlements along the Kennebec River and move deeper into the woods, to places where English settlements did not yet exist (Miller 2008).

Some of these retreats led W8banakiak to Jesuit mission sites along the St Lawrence River: first to the mission at Sillery and then to St Francis, near the conjunction of the St Lawrence and St Francis rivers; Bécancour, near the conjunction of the St Lawrence and Bécancour Rivers; and St-François-de-Sales, near the conjunction of the St Lawrence and Chaudière Rivers. Wanalanet, the successor to Chief Passaconaway, led some of his people to St Francis in 1678. Once peace was restored, W8banakiak anticipated being able to return to their original settlements. In studying Wanalanet, Daniel Gookin wrote that "it is not impossible he may, in convenient time, return again to live with the English in his own country, and upon his own land: which … the Indians do much incline unto." Peace was restored but, unfortunately for many Abenaki (and other) people, by then, English settlers had taken over their cornfields and villages (Miller 2008, 81). Consequently, many of the dispersed stayed where they landed.

Within this common narrative, authors such as Peter Thomas (1990), Paulena Seeber (1984), and Robert Grumet (1995) focus on the stress caused to various Abenaki communities as a result of European rivalries, occupation of their lands, and the introduction of new economies. Kenneth Morrison (1984) and Colin Calloway (1986, 1989, 1990) emphasize Abenaki responses and adaptation within this context, and others such as Maurault (1866) and Charland (1942, 1964) discuss the importance of the Jesuit missions on Abenaki survival.

In summarizing these works, the operative concept is the transformation of Abenaki homeland into a frontier or borderland, an area where change and flux are the norm rather than stability and continuity, where rights of possession and access were contested between the French and English, the Abenaki and Mohawk, and between the Abenaki and colonists. In this borderland, the W8banakiak place-world was transformed into a contested area which was eventually "won" by the English. In such a contested space, physical mobility became the prevailing theme, with the concluding consensus on the effect of European intrusion on the

Abenaki being that these Indigenous people were dispersed from their homelands along the waterways of New England, with most, if not all, ending up along the south shore of the St Lawrence in the communities of Odanak and W8linak. The Abenaki thus became depicted as a people who moved from their homeland to a new land, which resulted in the loss of Indigenous status in the United States and, concomitantly, the fact that they never had such status in Canada. In the final analysis, this reveals how mobility emerged as an effective tool for colonizers: because the Abenaki moved from one place to another within territory defined as English or French, they lost their identity within the discourse as Indigenous Peoples (Manore 2011). So, on one hand, the Abenaki disappeared from their lands and, on the other, they had never been on them. As Borrows asserted, the Abenaki were damned if they moved and damned if they did not.

Simply put, scholars intent on defining the locations of Abenaki communities, or intent on determining Abenaki origins, or in demonstrating how Abenaki communities constantly changed their locations, missed the point about Abenaki mobility. Mobility gave the Abenaki their connection to all of Ndakina, not only to places narrowly defined here and there, or from time to time. Their continued movement through their territory gave, and gives, to them opportunities to conduct "heritage work" – to review and pass on memories, to share experiences with family and friends, and to "strengthen present and future social and family relations" (Coutts 2021, 2). Thus, exploring settler and W8banakiak understandings of mobility and its relation to lands demonstrates the clash between an Indigenous culture based on mobility and a colonizing culture based on settlement, clearly underscoring how interpretations of mobility have been used as a tool of colonization, just as has the survey and the map, and ideas of property and development.

Yet Abenaki presence in the Eastern Townships – and elsewhere – continued and persists to the present day. So too do W8banakiak understandings of Ndakina. Deny O'bomsawin is a member of the turtle clan and, like the turtle, he regularly follows a certain route to get to places and meet people who are important to him. When he was younger, Deny made a point of travelling to seven ceremonial sites each year and he passed this custom on to his children. The sites included Mount Orford, Mount St Hilaire in the Eastern Townships, and Rock Dunder and Bellows Falls in Vermont. Each year, like the turtle, Deny travelled to these places and then returned to Odanak (Deny O'bomsawin 2021). Rick O'Bomsawin explained that the name bomsawin means "the one who goes ahead when travelling," and, when staying in one place, the name means "fire-keeper." People named Bomsawin were typically given the responsibility to go ahead of the others when travelling to other camps or villages during their seasonal rounds.

Once they had gathered at their new camp or village, then it was the Bomsawin's responsibility to make the fire and keep it burning. In this way, they supported the establishment of the new community and provided a beacon to follow for others who were still enroute (Richard O'Bomsawin 2021).

Not all the Abenaki at Odanak are members of the turtle clan and not all are O'Bomsawins. As a collectivity, and as a people, they travelled – and continue to travel – within Ndakina. Daniel Nolett (2021) tells the story of James Annance who, in the first half of the twentieth century, left Odanak every autumn to work his traplines in the Sherbrooke/Magog area where he stayed until spring when he returned to Odanak with all his furs and handmade crafts. Daniel Nolett himself still hunts in the Eastern Townships, including Hatley, Compton, and Ascot Corners, and elsewhere within Ndakina. Others do mountaintop ceremonies, visit relatives in New England, go to powwows or host parents at various locations or work outside of Odanak, and then return home once completed (Michel Durand Nolett 2021; Daniel Nolett 2021; Deny O'bomsawin 2021).

CONCLUSION

W8banakiak have experienced their place-world of Ndakina through continuous movement from the Gaspésie to Lake Champlain, from the shores of the Atlantic Ocean to the shores of the St Lawrence. Through their travels, W8banakiak have learned the places where food is abundant and at what times of the year; they have learned where to seek spiritual guidance and where to meet up with others for trade; they have existed as large communities in villages and as smaller families in hunting grounds. They have used the waterways as their principal means of transportation, but they have also carved out trails over land. With colonization, the character and understanding of Ndakina and the people within it have been challenged by the formation of other place-worlds, created by the movement of Europeans and their descendants onto W8banakiak land. These place-worlds changed from being understood as unknown territory, to becoming a borderland or frontier, to becoming a place of imperial struggle between English and French, to becoming the place of colonial and then nation-state settlement. With the creation of the latter place-worlds came the creation of a narrative about the Abenaki, as having come from somewhere other than Ndakina or as having "moved on" from Ndakina. This narrative is particularly apt when examining the traditional historical narrative of the Eastern Townships – a place where the Abenaki have been portrayed as merely sojourners within the territory or have not had their presence recognized at all. Abenaki movement through the Eastern Townships, especially during the colonial period, and their connection to Ndakina has been seriously misunderstood and devalued. W8banakiak access to their traditional hunting, fishing, trapping, sugaring, trading, and ceremonial grounds have been severely limited or denied altogether. Yet, the place-world of Ndakina still exists within the W8banakiak and they courageously continue to assert their own narrative of their traditional territory.

Notes

1 I acknowledge and thank the Indigeneity and Race Research Axis of Bishop's University for funding the research for this chapter.
2 For examples of literature on technological and ideological tools of empire see McLaren et al. (2005); Baldwin et al. (2011); Constant and Ducharme (2009); Harris (2002); and Manore (2000).
3 W8banakiak is a word for the Abenaki people given to me by Nicole O'Bomsawin. I will use it here when relaying the Indigenous perspective and understanding of Abenaki history; not to appropriate their voice but to emphasize and differentiate it from the settler voice, including that of my own, that has so far dominated the evidence presented in this chapter.
4 Turtle Island is an Indigenous term for North America.
5 The ideas of mobility examined here do continue into the present day, but space does not permit an examination of this after the period examined here.
6 Anthropologists and other scholars have historically referred to the Haudenosaunee as the Iroquois or Iroquoian Confederacy or the Five/Six Nations Confederacy.

References

Baldwin, Andrew, et al., eds. 2011. *Rethinking the Great White North: Race, Nature, and the Historical Geographies of Whiteness in Canada*. Vancouver: University of British Columbia Press.

Barman, Jean. 2016. *Abenaki Daring: the Life and Writings of Noel Annance, 1792–1869*. Montreal and Kingston: McGill-Queen's University Press.

Basso, Keith. 1996. *Wisdom Sits in Places: Landscape and Language among the Western Apache*. Albuquerque: University of New Mexico Press.

Baxter, James. 1890. "The Abnakis and Their Ethnic Relations." *Maine Historical Society Collections* 2 (3): 353–71.

Borrows, John. 2016. *Freedom and Indigenous Constitutionalism*. Toronto: University of Toronto Press.

Brooks, Lisa Tanya. 2008. *The Common Pot: The Recovery of Native Space in the Northeast*. Winnipeg: University of Manitoba Press.

Calloway, Colin. 1986. "Green Mountain Diaspora: Indian Population Movements in Vermont, c.1600–1800." *Vermont History* 54 (4): 197–228.

– 1989. "The Abenakis and the Anglo-French Borderlands." *Dublin Seminar for New England Folklife Annual Proceedings* 14: 18–27.

– 1990. *The Western Abenakis of Vermont, 1600–1800: War, Migration, and the Survival of an Indian People.* Norman: University of Oklahoma Press.

Chamberlain, Montague. 1904. "Indians in New Brunswick in Champlain's Time." *Acadiensis* 4: 280–95.

Chapdelaine, Claude, ed. 2007. *Entre lacs et montagnes au Méganticois.* Paléo-Québec 32. Montreal: Recherches amérindiennes au Québec.

Chapdelaine, Claude, and Pierre J.H. Richard. 2017. "Middle and Late Paleoindian Adaptation to the Landscapes of Southeastern Quebec." *PaleoAmerica* 3 (4): 299–312.

Charland, Thomas-Marie. 1942. *Histoire de Saint-François-du-lac.* Ottawa: Collège Dominicain.

– 1964. *Histoire des Abenakis d'Odanak.* Montreal: Les Éditions du Levrier.

Constant, Jean-François, and Michel Ducharme, eds. 2009. *Liberalism and Hegemony: Debating the Canadian Liberal Revolution.* Toronto: University of Toronto Press.

Coté, Patrick. 2021. Oral histories of people from Odanak.

Coutts, Robert. 2021. *Authorized Heritage: Place, Memory, and Historic Sites in Prairie Canada.* Winnipeg: University of Manitoba Press.

Crosby, Alfred. 1986. *Ecological Imperialism.* Cambridge, UK: Cambridge University Press.

Dandenault, Roch. 1976. *Histoire de Coaticook.* Sherbrooke: Éditions Sherbrooke.

Daugherty, W.E. 1983. *Maritime Indian Treaties in Historical Perspective.* Ottawa: Department of Indian Affairs and Northern Development, Canada.

Day, Gordon. 1981. *Identity of the St Francis Indians.* Mercury Series, Canadian Ethnology Service Paper, 71. Ottawa: National Museum of Man.

Dickason, Olive. 1990. "The French and the Abenaki: A Study in Frontier Politics." *Vermont History* 58 (2): 82–98.

Dodge, Ernest. 1957. "Ethnology of Northern New England and the Maritime Provinces." *Massachusetts Archaeological Society Bulletin* 18: 68–71.

Graillon, Eric. 2018. *Chronologie des occupations amérindiennes en Estrie.* Sherbrooke : Musée de la nature et des sciences de Sherbrooke.

Gravel, Albert (Abbé). 1931. *Histoire du Lac Mégantic.* Sherbrooke: n.p.

Grumet, Robert S. 1995. *Historic Contact: Indian People and Colonists in Today's Northeastern United States in the Sixteenth through Eighteenth Centuries.* Norman: University of Oklahoma Press, 1995.

Harris, Cole. 2002. *Making Native Space: Colonialism, Resistance, and Reserves in British Columbia.* Vancouver: University of British Columbia Press.

Hoffman, Bernard. 1955. "The Souriquois, Etchemin and Kwedech: A Lost Chapter in American Ethnography." *Ethnohistory* 2 (1): 65–87.

Laperrière, Guy. 2009. *Les Cantons-de-l'Est Histoire en Bref.* Quebec : Les Presses de L'Université Laval.

Leonard Auger Papers. N.d. Warren Milne Collection, P135, Eastern Townships Resource Centre, Bishop's University.

Manore, Jean L. 2000. "Indian Reserves v. Indian Lands: Reserves, Crown Lands and Natural Resource Use in Northeastern Ontario." In *Ontario since Confederation:*

A Reader, edited by Edgar-Andrée Montigny and Lori Chambers, 195–213. Toronto: University of Toronto Press.
– 2011. "The Historical Erasure of an Indigenous Identity in the Borderlands: The Western Abenaki of Vermont, New Hampshire, and Quebec." *Journal of Borderlands Studies* 26, no.2 (August): 179–96.
Masta, Henry. 1932. *Abenaki Indian Legends, Grammar and Place Names.* Victoriaville, QC : La Voix des Bois-Francs.
Maurault, J.A. (Abbé). 1866. *Histoire des Abenakis.* Sorel, QC : L'atelier typographique de la Gazette de Sorel.
McLaren, John, A.R. Buck, and Nancy E. Wright, eds. 2005. *Despotic Dominion: Property Rights in British Settler Societies.* Vancouver: University of British Columbia Press.
Miller, Andrew. 2008. *Abenakis and Colonists in Northern New England, 1675–1725: A Case Study in Intercultural Violence.* Saarbrucken, Germany: VDM Verlag.
Morrison, Alvin. 1982. "The Spirit of the Law versus the Storm Spirit: A Wabanaki Case." In *Actes du Treizième Congrès des algonquinistes*, edited by W. Cowan, 179–91. Ottawa: Carleton University Press.
Morrison, Kenneth. 1984. *The Embattled Northeast: The Elusive Ideal of Alliance in Abenaki-Euramerican Relations.* Berkeley: University of California Press.
Nolett, Daniel. 2021. Oral histories of people from Odanak.
Nolett, Michel Durand. 2021. Oral histories of people from Odanak.
O'bomsawin, Deny. 2021. Oral Histories of people from Odanak.
O'Bomsawin, Nicole. 2021. Oral histories of people from Odanak.
O'Bomsawin, Richard. 2021. Oral histories of people from Odanak.
Seeber, Paulena. 1984. "The European Influence on Abenaki Economics before 1615." In *Actes du Quinzieme Congrès des algonquinistes*, edited by W. Cowan, 201–14. Ottawa : Carleton University Press.
Sévigny, P.-André. 1976. *Les Abenaquis : habitat et migrations.* Montreal : Les Éditions Bellarmin.
Thomas, Peter A. 1990. *In the Maelstrom of Change: The Indian Trade & Cultural Process in the Middle Connecticut River Valley, 1635–1665.* New York: Garland.
Wiseman, Frederick. 2001. *The Voice of the Dawn: An Autohistory of the Abenaki Nation.* Hanover, NH: University Press of New England.
– 2005. *Reclaiming the Ancestors: Decolonizing a Taken Prehistory of the Far Northeast.* Hanover, NH: University Press of New England.

5

Townships Women Go Off to School: Teaching Diplomas, Career Ambitions, and the McGill Normal School, 1857–65

Roderick MacLeod and Mary Anne Poutanen

INTRODUCTION

In June 1863, seventeen-year-old Mary-Luella Herrick received an Elementary diploma from the McGill Normal School in Montreal and had to decide whether to seek employment right away, begin a second year of studies in quest of a Model diploma, or return to the family farm near Granby in Quebec's Eastern Townships. She chose to pursue a Model diploma, opening additional doors: a job teaching in an urban school, possibly in a class of older pupils requiring more specialized knowledge. But Mary-Luella did not rest on these laurels; instead, she embarked on a third year at the Normal School, joining the first small cohort of women to obtain an Academy diploma in Quebec. In 1865, she began teaching at the McGill Model School, a prestigious position with many possibilities for advancement (Register of Students entering, n.d.). Mary-Luella is representative of ambitious young Eastern Townships women seeking teacher education in Montreal rather than locally, notwithstanding professional constraints associated with gender and marriage.

Most students attending the Normal School (Quebec's Protestant teaching college) during its first years of operation pursued only an Elementary diploma, and many did not even achieve that. Nevertheless, our analysis of the Normal School records, which provide details as to students' lives while in Montreal and their subsequent career choices, combined with enquiry into their families' situation, suggests a clear link between the pursuit of additional accreditation and the ability to find better teaching jobs. Sending a daughter to Montreal to acquire a teaching diploma typically meant a significant financial investment for even moderately prosperous rural families, with room and board to factor in as well as travel costs and clothing; moreover, family economies had to function with the temporary loss of a daughter's labour. Mary-Luella was fortunate to live with an older sister; for other young women, the need to board commercially represented a source of anxiety for parents fearful of physical and moral urban dangers. The considerable regulation of the lives of Normal School students was designed to mitigate much of this concern, even as it added to the burden of scrutiny that the students had to endure. Pursuing a teaching diploma was not undertaken lightly.

The challenges inherent in attending the McGill Normal School from a small Eastern Townships community underscore the strategic nature of both initial attendance and the decision to acquire additional accreditation. We argue that Eastern Townships' women looked to a year or more at the Normal School as a means to improve their own social and economic prospects as trained teachers. Some wished to enhance social standing within their communities, marriage prospects, and social mobility. Others sought autonomy while maintaining social standing, seeing teaching as an attractive alternative to becoming a farmer's wife. Attending the Normal School was also a way for women to obtain the equivalent of post-secondary education at a time when universities were closed to them. Without denying the precarious social position of female teachers, or the very limited range of options available to them as employable female professionals, we focus on the ability of young women to achieve a moderate level of social, economic, and intellectual advancement through teaching – in this case, within Quebec's Protestant school system. We also interpret the efforts of rural families to send their daughters to Montreal for teacher training as a reflection of a desire to acquire or maintain social standing as well as to increase the supply of qualified teachers in rural areas. As Margaret Gillett observes, "the founding of teacher training institutions was one of the significant trends of 19th century education and was related to the democratization of society and the spread of mass public education" (Gillett 1981, 39).

The Eastern Townships represented a sizeable proportion of Normal School registrants in the period under study, more than any other region outside of Montreal. One reason for this high representation is the region's relative wealth, resulting from good soil and economic links to New England; most registrants' families were moderately prosperous farmers, although some were artisans and at least one was on the verge of poverty. The Townships cohort is particularly interesting given the region's additional advantage over other parts of rural Quebec: the presence of New England–style academies, locally funded and administrated schools whose graduates were understood to be qualified to teach school. Since these academies represented a significant alternative to the McGill Normal School, it is telling that young women opted to live in Montreal for a year or more instead of attending a nearby institution. This decision reflects the enduring capacity of people in rural Protestant communities to pursue all available means to ensure the provision of local schooling and to give their daughters a head start. Families may have welcomed the value of official accreditation over the less formal reliance on talented graduates of academies. Young women may have appreciated the prospect of a diploma as an indication of accomplishment over the less specialized knowledge acquired over the course of many years' attendance at an academy. By exploring the experiences of Townships women during and after their time at the McGill Normal School we shed light on personal career plans, roadblocks that graduate teachers encountered, and local attitudes towards teacher training. We recognize that teaching was one of the few professions available to women and that they were responding specifically to a need for additional teachers in the face of the expansion of public education more generally. Our argument is supported by a growing literature on women's pursuit of Normal School diplomas.

Andrée Dufour's inquiry into L'École normale St-Joseph de Hull shows that, although many students sought careers in teaching, most left after receiving their elementary certificate (2014, 61–2). Other studies demonstrate that women brought to teaching the same concerns and qualifications as men. Patrick Harrigan's investigation into the evolution of Canadian teachers reveals that teaching offered educated men and women job security, respectability, a steady income, and social mobility (1992, 483, 493). Melissa Clark-Jones and Patricia Coyne remind us that some women pursued a university education at Bishop's to ensure their middle-class status (1990, 43). Christine Ensslen and June Corman's study (2014) of never-married career teachers in Saskatchewan suggests that, while long careers allowed women to contribute enormously to the profession, their non-married status came at a price. In rural areas, they were subjected to intense community surveillance around celibacy, were viewed as less skilled than their male counterparts, experienced little upward mobility, and had to settle for poor pay and inadequate pensions, notwithstanding widowhood or financial support of siblings or aging parents. Nonetheless, they improved their working lives by seeking teaching positions in urban centres, pursuing additional education, and taking on executive responsibilities in professional associations. Similarly, Anne Drummond contends that, while Montreal's Protestant school board offered women teachers better salaries than their rural counterparts, prevailing patriarchy amongst male educators and school board commissioners left them with few opportunities to secure positions of authority (1990, 68). US studies demonstrate comparable findings. For example, historians of education such as Christine Ogren (2005) and Mary-Lou Breitborde and Kelly Kolodny (2015) point out that a normal school education promoted women's social mobility by opening doors usually closed to them. Normal School offered rural and working-class teachers-in-training social capital in the form of skills, information, and life experiences. The women were investing in long-term careers (Harrigan 1992, 503–5; see also Gelman 2002; Hollihan 2000; Stamp 1982; and Edwards 1991). Advanced diplomas gave female graduates a respectable entrance into a larger world of social and professional relationships (Breitborde and Kolodny 2015, 32).[1] These findings from both sides of the border suggest a need to nuance women's experiences in the area of teaching, particularly in their pursuit of formal teacher's education.

The McGill Normal School's wide variety of historical documents – including admission registers, minute books, and correspondence – pertaining to its first decade of operation permits a micro study of students in terms of age, religion, home residence, city addresses, program, and educational careers. Genealogical resources, including parish records and census returns, have enabled us to reconstitute aspects of their lives and kinship ties. The chapter begins with an exploration of the history of the Eastern Townships education traditions with their local, national, and international influences. We then examine social and economic features of Townships women attending the Normal School, their lives while in attendance, and their subsequent careers.

EASTERN TOWNSHIPS SCHOOL TRADITIONS

Born in 1844, Mary-Luella Herrick was the third of seven children from a farming family in Granby. Her father's parents had migrated from Vermont and her mother from Scotland. Mary-Luella and her siblings were raised in a Protestant tradition that valued literacy as a path to reading and understanding the Bible's message. As Congregationalists, they were strong proponents of local governance, notably as it pertained to church and school. Their early lives in Granby coincided with the establishment of a formal public education system for Lower Canada, involving the creation of boards of school commissioners for each township or parish. A network of one-room schoolhouses was in place by the time their eldest child, Lamira, was ready to attend; the other siblings followed in her footsteps, receiving a basic level of education from a teacher most likely trained at one of the Townships' private academies. In 1849, some of the wealthier citizens of Granby pooled their resources and established an academy, which offered a more sophisticated curriculum to those able to afford it. The Herricks seemed however more interested in what the McGill Normal School offered – given that Lamira, Mary-Luella, and their brother Alexander Milo would all seek teaching diplomas in Montreal.

The Herricks's pursuit of educational opportunities was typical of Eastern Townships' families. The region had a longer tradition of community involvement in schooling than other parts of Lower Canada, including Montreal and Quebec City. The circumstances in which the Eastern Townships were settled (freehold tenure, attracting Loyalists from the New England states and later British immigrants), the religious background of its early settlers (large numbers of Methodists and Congregationalists), and its relative wealth compared to other rural regions, made for especially fertile ground for local school promotion. All this contributed to a sense of regional identity characterized by Protestantism, literacy, and local governance. Such regional identity was transnational: for families like the Herricks, the border between the Townships and Vermont was invisible.

Townships communities had consistently proven willing to invest time and effort in creating and maintaining schools, and to take advantage of government programs offering trained teachers and educational materials. One such program, led by the Royal Institution for the Advancement of Learning, was widely rejected, in part because of its perceived Anglican bias but also because of the quality of teachers it provided: exclusively men and all too often disappointed scholars who would have preferred more prestigious jobs and tended to drink too much or abuse their students (Boulianne 1970). A later program offered by the Legislative Assembly of Lower Canada enabled communities to hire local teachers, insisting only that a judge or minister testify as to the teacher's good character and qualifications. Under this system women could be hired, an arrangement that usually made for better relations, both inside and outside the classroom: women typically came from the same rural background as their charges and understood the needs of farming families. In most cases, teachers' qualifications consisted of their simply having been educated – privately, at an existing one-room school, or at one of the Eastern Townships academies.

Teaching opportunities for women at these institutions were significant but limited. The headmasters of academies were always men, often recruited from south of the border (Drummond 1986, 21). The impossibility of women rising to the top of an academy would persist into the twentieth century; even so, for a young woman to have steady employment in such an institution was no small achievement. More typically, however, young women graduating from academies would find work teaching at one-room schoolhouses. Academies were the region's principal training ground for female teachers, a role they played chiefly as rare institutions of higher learning for women. This role accounts in no small part in the expanding number of academies opening throughout the Townships; by the late 1850s there were more than two dozen (Drummond 1986, 127 [appendix A]).

Yet, by that time there was an alternative: the McGill Normal School, established in 1857 as Canada East's official teacher training facility for Protestants. Although the standardization ("normalization") of education would eventually threaten academies' independence, the creation of the Normal School and the prospect of universal certification was generally welcomed throughout the Townships (*Stanstead Journal* 1857a, 1857b). There was some concern over the centralization of teacher training in Montreal, which may have represented fear that the academies' traditional role would be undermined, worry over sending young people into the city, or simply regional pride. In January 1858, Canada East's superintendent of education sought to consolidate support for the Normal School by asking all teachers to "form themselves into associations, and connect themselves with McGill College" (*Stanstead Journal* 1858a; Cooper 1964, 85). Several associations were formed (almost entirely led by men), but in one district teachers refused the connection with McGill and declared themselves independent; some of this tension may have arisen from efforts to establish rival Anglican teacher training in the Townships (*Stanstead Journal* 1858b, 1859). Perhaps to counter these efforts, but mainly to improve access and accommodation, one association called for the establishment of "another Normal School, in some central locality in the Eastern Townships" (*Stanstead Journal* 1859).

Despite such calls, the McGill Normal School retained its monopoly over Protestant teacher training for another half century. Not all Townships families followed this path. Given the proximity of the US border and the historical readiness of Townshippers to cross this boundary, it is perhaps not surprising that Canadian students continued to attend US schools into the twentieth century, as Anthony Di Mascio shows in his study of Townships families living near the border (2024). Furthermore, during the decades following the McGill Normal School's opening, a small number of prospective teachers from the Eastern Townships turned to New England colleges to obtain teaching diplomas.[2] Even so, such alternatives lacked much of what appealed to students about spending time in Montreal.

ATTENDING *the* NORMAL SCHOOL

By the time Mary-Luella Herrick was applying for admission to the McGill Normal School, the institution had been in existence for more than five years; its reputation preceded it, both regionally and nationally. Prospective students were prepared to undergo considerable scrutiny of their moral and intellectual qualities in order to be admitted – evidence not only that Normal School had rigorous academic standards but also that what it offered was desirable enough to warrant screening so that only the most suitable candidates were accepted.

McGill took considerable effort to make attending the school an attractive prospect. "The arrangements are of such a character as to afford the greatest possible facilities to Students from all parts of the Province," announced the 1859–60 calendar (Calendar 1859). Students were not charged tuition fees and were entitled to a yearly allowance of $32 to offset boarding costs, which were estimated at between $9 and $12 per month. An additional travel allowance was offered for those living more than ninety miles from the city. These stipends were also subject to the students' successful completion of the program, increasing the incentive to succeed.

At the Normal School, students followed a one-year or a two-year program. Passing the exams after one year's instruction, students would receive an Elementary diploma, entitling them to teach at one-room schoolhouses. After a second year, a Model diploma allowed them to teach the "model" grades, later known as "intermediate." The Normal School also granted an Academy diploma, although for the first few years it was a legal fiction, obtainable only as a by-product of a university education by special arrangement. Since women could not attend McGill University, this diploma was a male preserve – at least until 1864, when the "Normal school gave the women ... of this province their first opportunity for what we sometimes call higher public education, by the establishment of the Academy Class, a third year's course of literary and mathematical training" (McGill Normal 1873). That autumn marked the first cohort to pursue this diploma by attending classes in the Normal School. Two of these four women (Mary-Luella Herrick and Lucy Ann Merry) were Townshippers.

EARLY TOWNSHIP STUDENT COHORTS

At the July 1863 graduation exercises, held in the Normal School's hall and presided over by McGill and government dignitaries, prizes were awarded for achievement in various academic disciplines. Mary-Luella Herrick came fourth in a class of twenty-seven, earning an honourable mention in French (*Journal of Education*

1863, 97–8). Ahead of her were Montrealer Amy Frances Murray, Lucy Anne Merry from Magog, and Isabella Morrison from the Chateauguay Valley; all four would make up the first Academy class. At the end of their first year, they stood alongside twenty women graduates (four from the Eastern Townships) and three men (one a Townshipper). The proportion of Townshippers within the student total was consistent with the pattern established since the beginning.

A study of the 1857–59 cohort (the first three sessions)[3] provides a sense of the demographic background of families who sent their daughters to the Normal School during its formative years. This cohort, including all registrants regardless of whether they earned a diploma, represents 158 individuals. Of these, twenty-four came from the Eastern Townships. Of the eighty-six students who earned a diploma during these years, eighteen were Townshippers, indicating a high graduation rate for that region. Overall, however, failure was common: in the first session alone, all but sixteen students dropped out, took ill, failed the exam or did not write it. Graduation rates improved over the following years, and by the 1870s it was 71 per cent: "It is only by this sifting process that a really good class of teachers can be obtained," a longitudinal study reported, so "this should not be regarded as a small proportion. A larger proportion would imply insufficient care in the examinations" ("Analytical Statement," n.d.). Exams may have weeded out many of the early students, but those who left typically gave poor health as an excuse. This category might include homesickness, disenchantment with city life, and frustration with the heavily regulated Normal School regime.

Table 5.1 lists the twenty-four Townships students in the 1858–59 cohort.[4] All but four were women. Certain townships were particularly well represented: three came from Granby, five from Durham, and six from Kingsey. Four students came from the same extended Kingsey family: Caroline, Louisa, Lydia, and Mathilda Trenholme. Significantly, most of these families lived quite close to academies, yet opted to send their daughters to the Normal School for a more specific type of education. Therefore, the Normal School was not a default for those with no other options.

The table gives a sense of how students succeeded in obtaining an Elementary diploma (E) or failed, and then returned for a Model diploma (M) or a second try at an Elementary diploma. Some, like Henrietta Tarr, Mary Cassidy, and Alice Hall, failed on their second attempt, although Hall succeeded on her third, in 1859. Others, like Maria Machin, Mary Ann Hutchison, Ellen Cook, Emily Dunning, and Alice Finlay, returned to obtain Model diplomas. Mary Jane Reynolds, however, waited out a session and obtained her Model diploma in 1859. John Bothwell obtained a Model diploma without having first earned an Elementary diploma;

Table 5.1
Normal School students from the Eastern Townships, 1857–59

Provenance	1857 session	1857–58 session	1858–59 session
St Thomas	Maria Bissell	–	–
Granby	Maria McIntosh Machin (E)	Maria McIntosh Machin (M)	–
Waterloo	Mary Ann Hutchison (E)	Mary Ann Hutchison (M)	–
Waterloo	Mary Jane Reynolds (E)	–	Mary Jane Reynolds (M)
Orford	Alice Hall	Alice Hall	Alice Hall (E)
Durham	Mary Brethour	–	–
Kingsey	Mary Cassidy	Mary Cassidy	–
Inverness	John McKillop (E)	–	–
Ireland	–	Henrietta Tarr	Henrietta Tarr
Durham	–	Ellen Cook (E)	Ellen Cook (M)
Durham	–	Emily Dunning (E)	Emily Dunning (M)
Durham	–	Alice Finlay (E)	Alice Finlay (M)
Durham	–	Eliza Elwyn (E)	–
Durham	–	John Bothwell (M)	–
Kingsey	–	Caroline Trenholme (E)	–
Kingsey	–	Louisa Trenholme (E)	–
Kingsey	–	Lydia Trenholme (E)	–
Kingsey	–	Mathilda Trenholme (E)	
Kingsey	–	Frances Sewell	–
Hatley	–	–	Maria Johnston (M)
Sherbrooke	–	–	Mary Dakins
Granby	–	–	Lamira Herrick (E)
Granby	–	–	Oliver Warren (M)
Compton	–	–	Henry Rugg

Note: E indicates that an Elementary diploma was awarded; M indicates that a Model diploma was awarded.

presumably he had previous academic credentials. The same may have been true for Maria Johnston, who entered the Model year directly and earned a diploma.

The Eastern Townships' distinct religious composition is reflected in the 1857–59 cohort. Provincially, a little more than 50 per cent of Normal School students were Presbyterian, a ratio echoed in the group from Montreal – which itself represented more than half the student population. Of the twenty-four Townships students, only one was Presbyterian; by contrast, eleven were Methodist and eight were Anglican. Three Congregationalists formed an impressive delegation; Montreal only produced two. The school's two Adventists came from the Townships: Hutchison and Reynolds. The 1857–59 cohort's "other" category (fifty-two students) comprises all other parts of Quebec as well as Ontario, Nova Scotia, and the United States; here, Anglicans and Presbyterians represent a third each (seventeen students) of the total category. The strength of Presbyterian denominations across Quebec, especially Montreal, reflects the cultural importance of Scots in education; the strength of Anglicans and especially Methodists in the Townships speaks to the region's US roots. These religious connections would play a role in the students' later affinity with the United States.

The Normal School registry gives little sense of the social composition of students' families, but much can be gleaned from genealogical records. Not surprisingly, most parents were farmers. Other occupations were the exceptions: for example, in the village of Durham, Emily Dunning's father was a tanner and currier, while Alice Finlay's father was a tailor. In Waterloo, Jane Reynolds's father kept an inn and was also a clerk in the township's Commissioners' Court. Such an occupation indicates a certain level of education, although basic literacy can be assumed for most families given the culture of Protestantism and that baptism and marriage contracts were typically signed. Henrietta Tarr's mother was a teacher, having emigrated from England as a widow with a small child and settled, first in Ireland Township in the Megantic, and then in Quebec City; the 1861 census finds them both living in a one-storey stone house that also served as a school. Notwithstanding a need to support her single mother economically, Henrietta's repeated failure represented a financial setback; she would have been obliged to return the bursaries offered by the school. Nevertheless, she applied her knowledge out of necessity: the census lists her as a teacher alongside her mother.

Some families had higher levels of education and status. The four students from the Trenholme family had a mutual grandfather, William, who was a "teacher and surveyor"; in the early part of the century, he had brought his large family from Yorkshire to Kingsey. Although William's sons were all farmers, John (Matilda and Louisa's father) described himself as a Latin scholar and had trained for the Methodist ministry in Trois-Rivières before marrying at age eighteen and returning to Kingsey. Maria Machin came from an even more distinguished background: her father was Reverend Thomas Machin, the Anglican rector of Granby's Episcopal Church since 1851 (Gendreau 1912, 10). Her mother, Emily McIntosh Fraser, ran a private girls' school, assisted by the teenaged Maria, who also gave music lessons (*Eastern Townships Gazette* 1856). Maria's older brother Henry, her only sibling, had been educated at the prestigious Upper Canada College and would have a long career in the provincial civil service. Growing up in such a family, it was only natural for Maria's ambitions to extend at least as far as a Model diploma at the Normal School. Pursuing an Academy diploma was not an option for women in the late 1850s, but by the time it was it did not necessarily attract the daughters of educated parents; the first two Townships women to obtain Academy diplomas, Mary-Luella Herrick and Lucy Anne Merry, came from farming families.

LEARNING *and* LIVING *in* MONTREAL

In the autumn of 1862, Mary-Luella Herrick began what would be a daily commute from her Montreal home to the Normal School. Most out-of-town students lived in boarding houses, but Mary-Luella opted to stay with her older sister Lamira, who had married after graduation and now lived with her husband at 74 Chenneville Street, on the northern edge of what is now Old Montreal. From there, Mary-Luella would walk west along De La Gauchetière Street, up the hill, and briefly west again on Belmont Street to the school's entrance for girls and female teachers, located in the east wing. The building was large and architecturally striking, with many Gothic spires and pointed windows. The two-storey central block was home to the Normal School proper, with several classrooms capable of accommodating fifty teachers-in-training. It also held the library and the "cloak and retiring" rooms; the women's room, although larger than the men's, would typically have been quite crowded, given the large number of female students. The building's two single-storey wings contained the girls' and boys' divisions of the model school, where student teachers could practise the skills they learned in actual classrooms; both divisions together could accommodate 200 pupils. The basement featured a huge space used for examinations and the annual graduation exercises (*Journal of Education* 1857, 33).

Students pursued a wide variety of subjects: English, French, geography, history, arithmetic, algebra, geometry, natural history (that is, biology and zoology), and natural philosophy (physics). Second-year students took more advanced subjects, including mathematics, chemistry, and classics. There was also a course in agriculture (a nod to the rural background and inevitable preoccupations of so many Normal School students), one called "Education or Art of Teaching, including Hygiene and Elements of Mental Science," and instruction in "drawing, music, and elocution" (Calendar 1859, 50). Graduates would possess a wide range of knowledge as well as a specific set of skills, so that teachers could not only convey basic information but also be fountains of ideas for eager pupils. Normal School instructors were mostly McGill faculty members, while each division of the model school was headed by a male and female principal, who supervised the student teachers. Mary-Luella Herrick's relationship with the boys' head, James McGregor, must have been awkward, given that he was also her sister Lamira's husband and it was in his house that Mary-Luella lived.

McGregor may also have accompanied Mary-Luella in her daily walk to school, thereby ensuring her "safety" in an urban world deemed fraught with dangers (see Poutanen 2015; Myers 1998, 2006; Bradbury 1993; Sangster 2002; Strange 1995; Strange and Loo 1997). More to the point, he provided a degree of respectability to the morally questionable practice of a young woman being seen alone in public. Normal School students had to submit to a regime of scrutiny over their lives, both within the confines of the institution and outside. As future teachers, their reputations were of great concern to school authorities and to the communities whose children would potentially come under their care. Morality began, of course, in church: students were not only required to attend every Sunday but were obliged to meet weekly with a minister of their denomination to "provide for their religious instruction," normally Thursdays at four o'clock (McGill Normal 1873, 9). There was no escape from this requirement, as the Normal School provided the ministers with lists of all the students professing each denomination.

The major concern for both parents and school officials was fraternization between the sexes. Normal School regulations were clear: "There shall be no intercourse between the male and female teachers-in-training while in the School, or when going to, or returning from it." At school, decorum was maintained at all times, with separate entrances for men and women, separate lounges, and of course separate washrooms. All students' recreational activities were monitored, in large part because of the fear of inappropriate contact, although linked to this fear was concern over suggestive or subversive content: students could attend "such lectures and public meetings only as may be considered by the Principal conducive to their moral and mental improvement." Above all, the sleeping arrangements were closely regulated. Boarding house keepers were given permission to take in either male or female students but not both. Not surprisingly, students "of one sex are strictly prohibited from visiting those of the other," and for good measure students were "on no account to be absent from their lodgings after half-past nine o'clock in the evening" (McGill Normal 1873, 9).

Boarding houses were a particular source of anxiety: if not properly regulated, they could easily provide a venue for wantonness, away from the watchful eyes of family and school authorities. If families had relatives or friends in the city they would turn to them for assistance, as the Herricks did. Accordingly, boarding house proprietors were co-opted by the Normal School's web of regulation, looking out for evidence of drunkenness or disorderly behaviour and generally running tight ships along proscribed lines. Boarding houses were selected for their owners' impeccable propriety and their proximity to school. Safety was often found in numbers: the relatively small number of boarding houses used by Normal School students meant that each tended to accommodate several women, who would have made a practice of walking together to school.

One reputable boarding house keeper was Jane Robertson, an unmarried dressmaker who lived with her two sisters, also unmarried. Their house at 61 Craig Street lay half a kilometre down the hill from the school. In March 1857, Mary Ann Hutchison and Mary Jane Reynolds, the two Adventists from Waterloo, along with Alice Hall of Orford and Mary Cassidy of Kingsey, found themselves rooming together there, forming a tight Townships contingent. The following autumn, Hutchison stayed once again with Miss Robertson while she pursued a Model diploma, as did Cassidy while she tried again for her Elementary diploma. This time, Alice Finlay of Durham joined them, along with two other non-Townships students. Finlay returned to the Robertsons' in 1858 for her Model diploma, as did Alice Hall, who had stayed in another boarding house the previous year; Lamira Herrick, who would obtain her Elementary diploma before marrying James McGregor, came to live with them. The Robertson sisters would continue to accommodate students for many years; in 1863, Lucy Anne Merry and Isabella Morrison boarded there.

A respectable family environment could also make for a suitable boarding house. In 1857, Adam Drysdale and Mary Black, who lived at 50 Chenneville Street, less than half a kilometre from the Normal School, had a sixteen-year-old daughter, Margaret, who registered for teacher training. They opened their doors to other students, namely the four members of the Trenholme family from Kingsey, who provided Margaret with a valuable set of companions, both at home and on the way to school. The following year, the Drysdales moved around the corner to 81 Craig Street but continued to take student boarders – at least, Henry Rugg from Compton arranged to take a room but in the end did not come. Taking a male boarder was not technically a violation of protocol since there were no women boarding with the Drysdales that year, but Margaret was nonetheless a student and had a younger sister, Grace, on the verge of adolescence. Concerns for safety clearly went both ways. Like Jane Robertson, the Drysdales continued for many years to take in boarders, and after Adam's death his widow came to rely on it for economic subsistence.

Other Normal School students had more isolated experiences. Maria Machin lived for two sessions with Mrs Hedge, a prominent member of the city's American

Presbyterian congregation; there were no other student boarders, but the house on Latour Street lay just down the hill from the school at one of the most convenient addresses. During her two sessions at the Normal School, Henrietta Tarr lived at 35 Jurors Street, a few blocks east of Machin, but in very different circumstances: this was the Home and School of Industry, an institution founded a decade earlier by Eliza Hervey to train destitute girls for domestic service (Harvey 2024, 50). Tarr's status as the only daughter of a single mother may have made her a candidate for lodging there, although since she was hardly a charity case she may have earned her keep doing odd jobs – all serving as practical experience for a teacher.

Although students' lives were highly regulated, attending the Normal School need not have been a restrictive or monotonous experience. Most stuck it out, seeing it as the price to pay for a diploma and even for the modicum of freedom that life in the city offered. That public events had to be approved by the principal does not mean that students did not eagerly attend them. Lectures and demonstrations deemed conducive to moral and mental improvement may also have been entertaining and enlightening, and almost certainly not the sort of activities readily available in Townships villages. Young women from the same boarding house, indeed any friendship group formed among students, could enjoy many of the city's outdoor pleasures with relative impunity. In the Normal School itself, the women's "retiring" room, despite its inevitable congestion, provided a refuge within an ostensibly coeducational institution that allowed female students to let their hair down (figuratively) in a way that could rarely have been done at home and then only with sisters and cousins. Furthermore, the low number of male students represented a minimal moral threat within the Normal School particularly given the enforced distancing at most times; classrooms and the library were the only significant common areas. Consequently, female students experienced many of the educational and social benefits associated with girls' schools. Although the feminization of teaching, a global phenomenon, would entail limitations on the careers and work environments of female teachers, the training experience itself was significantly safer and more rewarding.

MAKING CAREERS

As one of the first few women to obtain an Academy diploma, Mary-Luella Herrick had a wider range of employment options ahead of her than graduates with only Elementary or Model diplomas – at least in theory. Two of her fellow graduates, Lucy Ann Merry and Isabella Morrison, found work in Townships academies. Mary-Luella opted to remain in Montreal, continuing to live with her sister, as well as with her older brother Alexander Milo, who had obtained a Model diploma the previous year, 1864. Milo began teaching at the Canada Presbyterian Church's Western school on St Joseph Street, where he became headmaster in 1867. By contrast, Mary-Luella and the fourth Academy graduate, Amy Murray, worked as assistant teachers at the Normal School's Model School. (By way of more direct contrast, Frederick Gow, who had obtained an Academy diploma four years earlier, was now the principal of Knowlton Academy.) For Mary-Luella and Amy to work only as assistant teachers must have been frustrating, although they may well have had their eyes on the top job and were marking time. When the head of the girls' division stepped down in 1868, she was replaced by Amy Murray, whom the McGill governors "unanimously recommended ... as being in every way fitted to become her successor" (*Journal of Education* 1875, 155). Losing the principalship may have disillusioned Mary-Luella sufficiently for her to resign and leave the city; two years later the US census had her teaching in Rutland, Vermont.

The Normal School register lists the subsequent careers of its graduates with minimal detail but enough to get a sense of what use students made of their diplomas (Register of Students, n.d.). Teaching at the McGill Model School was a popular first job for graduates with a Model diploma: of the Townships cohort, Mary Anne Hutchison and Mary Jane Reynolds both spent time in that familiar environment; possibly they were still there when Mary-Luella Herrick began her Elementary year. The Model School no doubt provided additional work experience that graduates used in subsequent employment. Hutchison and Reynolds went on to teach in Shefford and Waterloo. Maria Johnston, Model diploma in hand, taught "in the townships." Ellen Cook taught in Upper Canada, St Andrew's, and Côte-des-Neiges (just outside Montreal). Maria Machin made use of her Model diploma, and possibly her status as the daughter of an Anglican minister, to join the staff of the prestigious Montreal private Ladies Academy and Boarding School run by Lucy Simpson; although this was a plum position, Machin left in 1869 to teach at the Ottawa Protestant Ladies' School, where she became headmistress at the age of twenty-six. Of the two men from this cohort graduating with Model diplomas, John Bothwell of Durham returned there to teach in the Academy, while Oliver Warren taught in Brome and then Ottawa.

The expectation that women with Elementary diplomas would teach in rural schoolhouses was met in only a few cases. Alice Hall, whose diploma had taken her three years to obtain, worked subsequently "in the townships." Eliza Elwyn returned to her native Durham and taught there. Lydia Trenholme, from Kinsey, found work in Maskinongé, far from home. Marilla Bissell is listed in both the 1861 and 1871 censuses as a teacher, even though she did not obtain a Normal School diploma. Mary Cassidy also appears in the 1861 census as a "school teacher" despite not completing a diploma; the same was true for Henrietta Tarr. John McKillop, the Normal School's first male graduate from the Townships, returned to the Megantic area with his Elementary diploma and promptly found work teaching.

Marriage generally meant the end of a woman's teaching career, as was the case for Lydia Trenholme. Her sisters and cousins (including Caroline, who acquired a Model diploma) also married, seemingly without having taught. In 1863, after teaching for "about one year," Eliza Elwyn married John Walker, a lumber merchant from Montreal, and raised a family in Durham; sadly, a decade later she and her six-year-old son drowned in a river. Mary Jane Reynolds's teaching career was also short, the register annotation being "married" and then, ominously, "dead." Ellen Cook, after her many teaching posts, married John Everett, a fellow graduate of the Normal School and now a teacher in Durham. Lamira Herrick married very promptly after graduation, and soon gave birth to a son they christened William Dawson McGregor, an obvious tribute to the Normal School's (and McGill's) principal, John William Dawson. By contrast, Marilla Bissell married at around thirty-five to a significantly younger Compton farmer, George Young. Lucy Ann Merry's teaching position in Waterloo ended with her marriage to a local lawyer two years later. Despite possessing a Model diploma, Alice Finlay immediately married a Montreal commission merchant and lived with him in the city's prestigious St Antoine district. Emily Dunning also married without having applied her Model diploma, although since she became a widow at twenty-five with no children she opted to teach then. Although marriage technically ended a woman's career, given the very real prospect of widowhood, a teaching diploma represented a strategic tool for long-term subsistence, whatever a woman's immediate prospects might be.

The high number of women who married or otherwise chose not to pursue teaching suggests that many saw a Normal School diploma as something other than a means to employment. Since so many of these women married lawyers, merchants, customs brokers, teachers, and in one case (Reynolds) the son of Rotus Parmelee, a prominent Townships doctor and school inspector, it would seem that a Normal School education increased a young woman's, and her family's, social standing, and by extension her marriageability. The Normal School may also have appealed for its own sake, as one of the few ways in the 1850s and 1860s that women could access the sort of learning environment it provided, including exposure to history, literature, science, drawing, and music. Some may have entered the Normal School with ambitions only to feel differently once the process was over. In any case, we should not interpret an early marriage or other decision not to pursue a career as failure. Many young women and their families correctly understood the acquisition of one or more Normal School diplomas as a key to steady employment in a respectable profession, but others may have seen, or come to see, the process more broadly and the benefits of a Normal School education more deeply. Whether school officials recognized this diverse appreciation for the programs they were offering is another matter; clearly the days where Protestant teaching standards would be normalized and McGill's monopoly over the supply of teachers consolidated were still decades off. At the same time, the notion of teacher training as an almost expected part of a young woman's personal formation was also evolving; even as Normal School education grew more standardized and professional, what it represented for young women remained gray.

A surprising number of graduates ended up outside Quebec, some continuing to teach. Mary-Luella Herrick taught in Rutland, Vermont, for several years, living in a boarding house alongside several young men: an apprentice watchmaker, an apprentice silversmith, and a clerk in a dry goods store. In 1872 she married bookseller John Spaulding with whom she raised several children. Widowed at forty-six, Mary-Luella remained in Rutland for many years, eventually moving to Spokane, Washington, to live with her eldest married daughter; she died in 1921 in Montana, of septicaemia. Marilla Bissell and her husband also moved across the border, albeit only to Derby, Vermont, when she was more than sixty. Caroline Trenholme moved to San Francisco, where her husband worked as a tailor, and then Oregon, where he worked in the lumber industry. After a few years in Durham, New Hampshire, Ellen Cook and James Everett moved to Iowa, then Michigan, where James worked as a photographer and portrait painter, then a farmer; their son became a doctor. After a few years teaching at the Durham Academy, John Bothwell moved to Ohio, married and became a farmer. In 1863, Henrietta Tarr moved to Richmond, outside New York City (today Staten Island), where she taught school and her mother kept a boarding house; Henrietta died, unmarried, fifty-four years later. Emily Dunning moved to the United States in 1875; shortly before her death the 1900 census lists her teaching in a girls' boarding school in Asbury Park, New Jersey. Given the New England roots of so many of these women and the widespread indifference to the border, it is not surprising that so many opted to pursue careers in the US.

But the most interesting story of this early Normal School Townships cohort was that of Maria Machin. After years of teaching in Quebec and Ottawa, Machin moved to Germany to study nursing and then to London where she joined Florence Nightingale's nurses' training facilities at St Thomas Hospital (Helmstadter 2020). She was then sent back to Montreal to serve as lady superintendent at the

General Hospital. After three years, she returned to England, where she answered a passionate appeal from Anglican missionaries for volunteers to launch a nursing program in South Africa. Machin joined the mission in Bloemfontein and in 1884 married a share broker, Walter Redpath, in Kimberly, where she championed numerous charitable causes until her death in 1905 (*Ottawa Journal* 1905). Maria Machin's career ambitions may not be entirely attributable to her Normal School training but she is no doubt the graduate from the school's first few years that moved most prominently on the world stage.

CONCLUSION

Although Mary-Luella Herrick's achievements in obtaining an Academy diploma at the McGill Normal School placed her far and above most of her classmates, she nevertheless had much in common with Eastern Townships women who sought teaching diplomas in the first decade of the school's operation. With few exceptions, they grew up in comfortable farming families where going to school was expected. Their strong links to New England were manifested in the importance given to local schooling and the Protestant belief in literacy. The decision to attend the Normal School made by young women and their families reflected both a desire to bring qualified teachers to local rural schools and to meet daughters' personal ambitions. While a teaching diploma may have improved Townships women's economic prospects, it also enhanced their social standing, marriage possibilities, and social mobility.

Notes

This chapter represents the first phase in a much larger study, which considers all the women who attended the McGill Normal School from its creation until its closure.

1 The literature on women teachers-in-training at normal schools in Canada and in the United States show that common social, economic, and political characteristics – related to urbanization and industrialization – contributed to similar experiences regarding schooling on both sides of the border. The establishment of normal schools had key international links to both Prussia and France. See Di Mascio (2015, 90).
2 Our thanks to Andrew C. Holman for sharing information on the attendance of Canadian students in teacher-training programs at Bridgewater State University as of the 1850s.
3 The first session was abbreviated, running only from March to June 1857.
4 All statistics and information on Normal School graduates in the following paragraphs are taken from McGill University Archives, Record Group 30, container 4.

References

"Analytical Statement of Students of McGill Normal School for three years which may be considered as average on ordinary years." N.d. McGill University Archives, Record Group 30, container 7.

Boulianne, Réal G. 1970. "The Royal Institution for the Advancement of Learning: The Correspondence, 1820–1829." PhD thesis, McGill University.

Bradbury, Bettina. 1993. *Working Families: Age, Gender, and Daily Survival in Industrializing Montreal*. Toronto: McClelland & Stewart.

Breitborde, Mary-Lou, and Kelly Kolodny. 2015. "Remembering Massachusetts State Normal Schools: Pioneers in Teacher Education." *Historical Journal of Massachusetts* 43, no. 1 (Winter): 22–39.

Calendar of the University of McGill College, Montreal. 1859. Session of 1859–60. Montreal: JC Becket.

Clark-Jones, Melissa, and Patricia Coyne. 1990. "Through the Back Door." *Atlantis* 15, no. 2 (Spring): 40–9.

Cooper, J.I. 1964. "Some Early Teachers' Associations in Quebec." *The Educational Record*. April–June.

Di Mascio, Anthony. 2015. "The Emergence of Academies in the Eastern Townships of Lower Canada and the Invisibility of the Canada–U.S. Border." *Historical Studies in Education* 27, no. 2 (Fall): 78–94.

– 2024. "Community, Identity, and Borderland Schooling in the Eastern Townships and Northern Vermont: Reflections in an Impermeable Era." In *Quebec's Eastern Townships: Region and Its Global Connections*, edited by Cheryl Gosselin, Andrew C. Holman, and Christopher Kirkey, 215–30. Montreal and Kingston: McGill-Queen's University Press.

Drummond, Anne. 1986. "From Autonomous Academy to Public High School: Quebec English Protestant Education 1829–1889." Master's thesis, McGill University.

– 1990. "Gender, Profession, and Principals: The Teachers of Quebec Protestant Academies, 1875–1900." *Historical Studies in Education*, 2, no. 1 (1990): 59–71.

Dufour, Andrée. 2014. "L'École normale Saint-Joseph de Hull 1909-1968 : 60 ans de formation d'institutrices." *Historical Studies in Education / Revue d'histoire de l'éducation* 26, no.2 (Fall): 48–70.

Eastern Townships Gazette. 1856. 2 May.

Edwards, Reginald. 1991. "Theory, History, and Practice of Education: Fin de siècle and a New Beginning." *McGill Journal of Education* 26, no. 3 (Fall): 237–66.

Ensslen, Christine, and June Corman. 2013. "Establishing Pathways for Women in Education in Saskatchewan: Never-Married Women Career Teachers." *Historical Studies in Education* 25, no. 2 (Fall): 21–43.

Gelman, Susan. 2002. "Stratford (Normal School) Teachers' College." *Historical Studies in Education* 14 (1): 113–20.

Gendreau, H.W. 1912. *The Granby Directory for 1912–1913, containing a map of the town, a short historical sketch …* Sherbrooke: H. Belanger.

Gillett, Margaret. 1981. *We Walked Very Warily: A History of Women at McGill*. Montreal: Eden Press Women's Publications.

Harrigan, Patrick J. 1992. "The Development of a Corps of Public School Teachers in Canada, 1870–1980." *History of Education Quarterly* 32, no. 4 (Winter): 483–521.

Harvey, Janice. 2024. *Their Benevolent Design: Conservative Women and Protestant Child Charities in Montreal.* Montreal and Kingston: McGill-Queen's University Press.

Helmstadter, Carol. 2020. "Maria Machin at the Montreal General Hospital: A Study in Revisionism." *The UK Association for the History of Nursing Bulletin* 8 (1). https://bulletin.ukahn.org/maria-machin-at-the-montreal-general-hospital-a-study-in-revisionism/. Accessed 15 December 2022.

Hollihan, K.A. 2000. "'Making us do the things we ought to do': Constructing Teacher Identity in Alberta Normal Schools." *Journal of Historical Sociology* 13, no. 2 (June): 172–89.

Journal of Education. 1857. 1, no. 2 (March), 33.

– 1863. 7 (7-8), 97–8.

– 1875. September/October, 155.

McGill Normal School Prospectus, 1873–74. 1873. McGill University Archives, Record Group 30, container 1.

Myers, Tamara. 1998. "Qui t'a débauchée? Female Adolescent Sexuality and the Juvenile Delinquents' Court in Early Twentieth-Century Montreal." In *Family Matters: Papers in Post-Confederation Canadian Family History,* edited by L. Chambers and E. Montigny, 377–94. Toronto: Canadian Scholars Press.

– 2006. *Caught: Montreal's Modern Girls and the Law, 1869–1945.* Toronto: University of Toronto Press.

Ogren, Christine A. 2005. *The American State Normal School: "An Instrument of Great Good."* New York: Palgrave Macmillan.

Ottawa Journal. 1905. 18 February.

Poutanen, Mary Anne. 2015. *Beyond Brutal Passions: Prostitution in Early Nineteenth-Century Montreal.* Montreal and Kingston: McGill-Queen's University Press.

Principal's Report. 1888. 30 May. McGill Normal School Prospectus, 1888–89. McGill University Archives, Record Group 30, container 1.

Register of Students entering the McGill Normal School. N.d. McGill University Archives. Record Group 30, container 4.

Register of Students in the McGill Normal School. N.d. McGill University Archives, Record Group 30, c.1.

Sangster, Joan. 2002. *Girl Trouble: Female Delinquency in English Canada.* Toronto: Between the Lines.

Stamp, Robert M. 1982. *The Schools of Ontario, 1876–1976.* Toronto: University of Toronto Press.

Stanstead Journal. 1857a. 2 April.

– 1857b. 23 July.

– 1858a. 21 January.

– 1858b. 22 April.

– 1859. 6 January.

Strange, Carolyn. 1995. *Toronto's Girl Problem: The Perils and Pleasures of the City, 1880–1930.* Toronto: University of Toronto Press.

Strange, Carolyn, and Tina Loo. 1997. *Making Good: Law and Moral Regulation in Canada, 1867–1939.* Toronto: University of Toronto Press.

6

Going to Someone Else's War: Border-Crossing Enlistments from the Eastern Townships during the American Civil War

Jane Jenson

> War makes states.
>
> CHARLES TILLY (2017, 124)

> No matter how clearly borders are drawn on official maps, how many customs officials are appointed, or how many watchtowers are built, people will ignore borders whenever it suits them.
>
> BAUD AND VAN SCHENDEL (1997, 211)

THIS CHAPTER CONSIDERS an aspect of the Eastern Townships' encounter with a global force that swept much of the nineteenth-century world. "The drawing of borderlines and the creation of borderlands are the outcome of the establishment of modern states all over the world. The wish for well-defined, fixed boundaries was a direct consequence of the idea of exclusive and uncontested territorial state power that emerged in the nineteenth century" (Baud and Van Schendel 1997, 216–17). Just as state authority was being consolidated, for example, within the territories of Imperial Germany, the Kingdom of Italy, and much of Latin

America, the United States, and British North America (BNA) were engaged in forming modern states, a process that intensified during the American Civil War of 1861–65.[1]

During the Civil War, however, some residents of BNA ignored the border, crossing over and enlisting in the Union Army.[2] Was this simply evidence that in a borderland, ordinary people will willy-nilly do whatever suits them?[3] Or, was this transborder behaviour shaped by social relations within independent and intermediate processes located between the macro-level process of state formation and the microhistory of individuals who went to someone else's war? In his friendly critique of Charles Tilly's work, Sidney Tarrow convincingly argued that researchers need to pay attention to such independent and intermediate factors, such as religion and popular culture, when seeking to link large global processes and micro-historical behaviour (1987, 199–200).[4]

Examining a small group from the southern Eastern Townships, this chapter follows Tarrow's suggestion to look beneath the global and macro trend. It takes as a given that the Civil War advanced state formation on both sides of the international line.[5] As Charles Tilly reminds us, mobilization for war is both a primary manifestation of state power and a means of state-making. Nonetheless, the chapter's attention to micro-empirical data also reveals that the independent and intermediate processes close to individuals' lived experiences help to account both for the decision to ignore the border and enlist and even more for the postwar choice to return to Canada East or remain in the United States. In the Eastern Townships borderland, labour market conditions and patterns of religious affiliation and practice in the 1850s and 1860s account for behaviour better than other factors, such as seeking a bounty for enlistment or family ties in Canada.

STATE-MAKING *in* WARTIME: A LARGE *and* GLOBAL PROCESS

Formation of modern states transformed huge swaths of the globe in the nineteenth century, bringing institutional and bureaucratic capacity as its legacy (Maier, 2012).[6] North America was no exception to the trend. BNA moved towards Confederation partly in response to the events of the half-decade that preceded 1867, including American wartime sabre-rattling around the *Trent* Affair (1861), the St Albans raid (1864), the doctrine of Manifest Destiny, and the Fenian incursions, which began in 1866. Many Americans and Canadians considered the annexation of Canada inevitable (Nicol 2015, chapter 2). Nonetheless, Congress's 1866 decision to abrogate the Reciprocity Treaty and its free-trade provisions, sometimes attributed to ire over

Britain's support for the Confederacy, reminded Canadian politicians of the option of an east–west national development strategy, which would require a Canadian state federating disparate colonies and reaching across the continent.[7]

War was also the impetus for the United States to move from their union towards its more powerful federal government.[8] The early federal republic had been a "state of courts and parties" with few administrative ambitions (Skowronek 1982). "The old federal republic in which the national government had rarely touched the average citizen except through the post office gave way to a more centralized polity that taxed people directly … drafted men into the army, expanded the jurisdiction of federal courts, created a national currency and a national banking system" (McPherson 1988, 859). One of the main legacies was a public administration created to keep records of more than three million soldiers and more than 625,000 casualties and deaths by disease. That administration matured further with the growing commitment to veterans' pensions (Prechtel-Kluskens 2010). By the 1890s, expansion of eligibility had essentially transformed the program into an old-age benefit, reaching more than 90 per cent of surviving veterans who could document at least ninety days of service (Skocpol 1992, 109–11). Some of these pensions were delivered in the Eastern Townships.

The Eastern Townships borderland was not immune to the global forces driving state formation. Yet this micro-historical analysis will show that living near the border did not have the same meaning for everyone. Even going to someone else's war did not have the same connotation. Some volunteers lived within cross-border social relationships and institutions. Over their lives, they practised significant life decisions transnationally, such as whom to court and marry and where to worship and be educated. As such, a Civil War enlistment fit into their existing practices and identities as residents of a transborder space. For many others, however, their cross-border enlistment signalled a break with Canada East. It marked a major life choice, a decision to emigrate from one country in pursuit of work and opportunity in what they understood and expected to be another country. What characteristics distinguish these two groups? The chapter explores this question.

CROSSING *the* LINE

On 26 November 1861, seven months after the declaration of war, Elisha Aldrich of Orford Township went to Derby, Vermont, to enlist in the Union Army (table 6.1). His war record credited his service to Derby, as if he resided there.[9] But Elisha lived in Cherry River in Orford Township. A second-generation immigrant to Lower Canada, he was born in Barnston Township to parents from New Hampshire. Reporting his age as forty-three (thus born 1818), he was almost at the enlistment age limit of forty-five. Elisha was actually older, however. He was born in 1810 or 1813, either date putting him beyond the limit.[10] He was attached to Company B, 8th Vermont Infantry, which was stationed in Louisiana during his two years as a soldier.[11] For most of his service, he was assigned to hospital duty, as a cook or nurse. Suffering from rheumatism, he was discharged on 29 September 1863 and returned to Canada. In 1867, he claimed his veteran's pension, collecting it in Orford Township until his death in 1896.[12] His grave in the Cherry River village cemetery received an official veteran's headstone.[13]

Isabelle Rider married Elisha Aldrich in Derby in November 1860. She was a third-generation resident of Canada East via her mother Isabella Hoyt and lived in Cherry River until enlisting in the 8th Vermont Infantry. Under the name Isabel Aldrich, she became a matron in the regimental hospital, serving for six months in the first half of 1862.[14] She returned to Orford to give birth to a son, Butler, in December 1862.[15] When nurses became eligible for pensions in 1892, Isabelle applied immediately for the allowance of $12 per month. She withdrew the claim, however, perhaps fearing that she would lose her larger widow's pension when Elisha died. Granted for a disability recognized since 1867, his allowance might have been as much as $20 per month (Costa 1998, 200–1). Isabelle continued to receive a widow's pension until her death in 1919.

Both Elisha and Isabelle returned to Cherry River to live in what had been since the 1840s an enclave of Second Adventists (Lauzon and Tremblay 2020, 9).[16] Other cross-border volunteers were congregants of mainstream churches, however, including two Wesleyan Methodists from Compton and Stanstead Counties, where that denomination was among the largest grouping of Protestants (Census of the Canadas, 1860–61 1863, 122–3). They also made different choices for their postwar lives.

Joining Company F of the 3rd Vermont infantry in February 1862, Walter Harriman Sleeper named Compton as his residence. He was a third-generation immigrant, his grandfather Captain Benjamin Sleeper having moved from New Hampshire to Compton where Walter's father, Benjamin, was born. In January 1861, when the Canadian census was taken, the family was living in Clifton, Compton County. Their father listed Walter and his brother Henry as temporarily absent in the US. Indeed, the US census of the previous year records Walter Sleeper living with his aunt and cousins and working as a machinist in Sunapee, New Hampshire.[17] On 22 April 1861, he enlisted in the New Hampshire militia for the three-month period that was then standard. However, several months later he left New Hampshire and in February 1862 chose a Vermont regiment, as did most of the volunteers from the southern Eastern Townships (table 6.1). Discharged eight months later, he returned to New Hampshire, where he enlisted for a third time in 1864 as a Volunteer Veteran.[18] He never again lived in Canada, staying in the United States to marry and work as a machinist, eventually in Athol, Massachusetts where he claimed his pension in 1879, took United States citizenship in 1884, and died in 1906.

When he joined Company B of the 8th Vermont Infantry in December 1861, George Washington Barnes's enlistment was credited to Barnston in Stanstead County, where he was born and was living with his family at the time of the 1861 census.[19] His father David Barnes either was brought to Canada from England as an infant or was born in Canada.[20] George Barnes's mother, Lois Peavey, arrived in Stanstead as a child and his maternal grandparents lived there for decades. Nonetheless, his immediate family was on the move. His eighteen-year-old brother Carlos was living in Holland, Vermont, in 1860, and that town received credit for his November 1861 enlistment.[21] Two months after George enlisted, his father also joined the 8th Vermont Infantry, with Holland similarly receiving the credit.[22] After his discharge, George Barnes joined his family in that Vermont town about ten kilometres from the border, received his pension in 1879, and lived in the area until his death in 1899.

What can such micro-historical stories tell us? At first glance, they seem surprising. Historians agree that the War of 1812 and the Rebellions of 1837–38 strengthened Canadian identity in English-speaking Canada, thus thickening the boundary line (Little 2004, 2008; Nicol 2015, chapter 1). By the 1850s, Canada East had developed its own religious and state institutions particularly for education and municipal affairs that reminded residents of differences on the two sides of the border (Little 1981; Curtis 1997). Furthermore, the Republic at war allowed Washington to project a state-like image in international conflicts with Britain that further distinguished the United States from its neighbour. Finally, much Canadian elite opinion supported the South's cause.[23] Nonetheless and notwithstanding the structural and institutional forces thickening the border, Aldrich, Rider, Sleeper, and Barnes all joined someone else's war. Their stories are not unique. Historians tell us that thousands of "Canadians" fought in the Civil War, although many fewer crossed the border to do so. No doubt as a result of their low numbers and the analytic difficulty of identifying them, this category of border-crossers has received only passing attention (Little 2012, 10–11; Jenson 2023).

What do we know about border-crossing volunteers?

Numbers give a very partial answer. There has been controversy for well over a century about how many people from BNA enlisted, with the "conventional estimate" now putting the figure between 35,000 and 50,000 (Tyrell 2019, 41; Marquis 2000, 106). The vast majority of these soldiers were men born in Canada who were living in the United States when war broke out. Given that more than 150,000 people (and their children) emigrated in the 1850s, large numbers of former BNA residents lived in the United States (Ramirez 2001, 2; Lamarre 2006, 22–5).[24] When recruitment agents systematically recorded place of birth, these records became the source for the conventional estimate. Clearly, however, this was not a count of border-crossers because when many of the men enlisted, they did so from their homes in the United States. Indeed, one analysis holds that BNA residents who went to fight were a small minority among the thousands of BNA-born who fought for the Union.[25]

A second reason for uncertainty of the count is due to officials' practices, including inconsistencies, for record keeping.[26] For example, when Elisha Aldrich enlisted in November 1861, Derby was recorded as his residence, whereas Barnston appeared as George Barnes's residence.[27] Thus, Barnes seems to have crossed the border to enlist whereas Aldrich looks to have been already living in Vermont. Yet both still had homes in the Eastern Townships when they enlisted. Only detailed microhistory of the kind done for this chapter can identify border-crossing enlistments with some reliability.

Beyond numbers, the challenge is to understand where enlistment fit into the lives of Eastern Townships residents and their families. Historians have focused on the motivations of American soldiers, resorting to personal and family records of various sorts. With a trove of thousands of documents from some of the millions who enlisted, they have been able to sample representative collections in order to assess ideational motives (for example McPherson 1997). The Canadian data are not so rich or representative, and thus ideational motivations are harder to trace (Wells 2008, xliv; Marquis 2000). Existing analyses of the Eastern Townships and BNA more generally, working from a much smaller universe of cases, have relied on the anonymity of statistics or on documents left by a few individuals (for example Wells 2008; Marquis 2000). Accordingly, we have the stories of local notables, newspapers, and biographies as well as the general statistical patterns. Ordinary Canadians who left few personal documents have fallen off the analytic radar. Nonetheless, we can follow their histories via tracing in public documents (Lamarre 2006; Reid 2014; Jenson, 2024).

This chapter follows the trajectories of some of these ordinary people as they made their wartime and postwar lives. The group is a limited collection of twenty-five whose enlistment records plus confirming documents report they lived in the southern Eastern Townships in 1861 and chose to cross the border to enlist in a war that did not directly involve their country. The construction of the collection began with Jean Lamarre's appendix, *Soldats nordistes canadiens-français ou de parents canadiens-français*, collected from the National Archives in Washington, DC (2006, 153–86).[28] Lamarre lists twenty-eight unique names for which he found a southern township reference in an official document. For this chapter, data for each of the twenty-eight was obtained from the official Civil War documents (soldiers and veterans rolls and pension rolls) and cross-referenced, at least, to the Canadian and US censuses taken for the years from 1850 into the twentieth century. Five persons did not qualify as border-crossing enlistments although the records mentioned a Townships location because they did not appear in the 1861 Canadian census *and* a US census, often mentioning children's birthdates and places, indicated they were living in the United States before their enlistment.[29] One example of an exclusion despite the person's tendency to hark back to an earlier home comes from Joseph Eno, whose birthplace was Hatley Township. The 1860 US census reported he was farming in Iowa with his older brother and parents, A.P. Eno and Charlotte Bowen. They had been married in Hatley in 1827 and, while Joseph was born in Canada East, his residence was McGregor, Iowa, when he enlisted in his Iowan regiment in September 1861.[30]

Five files were set aside because nothing could be found to confirm any Townships connection. For example, George Dunmore (Damour? Dumor in Lamarre's appendix) enlisted as a substitute for a draftee from Pelham, New Hampshire, in September 1863.[31] He claimed to be born in Stanstead although all documents (census, marriage, death), usually in the name Dumore, concur that he lived in the United States from birth until his death in 1920.[32] He may have listed Stanstead so as to imply he was an immigrant and, therefore, that no draft board was seeking him. Only native-born Americans and immigrants who had requested naturalization could be conscripted into the Union Army, which began its draft in March 1863 (McPherson 1988, 601ff).

The research also unexpectedly uncovered seven additional cases absent from Lamarre's appendix. They were usually relatives of persons listed by him.[33] This method of constructing the collection generated twenty-five people for in-depth analysis. Their lives from the 1840s to their death, often in the twentieth century, were reconstructed in as much detail as possible, using Civil War documents, Canadian and American censuses, birth, marriage, and death registries, and diverse publications. Table 6.1 presents these data. This study is a modest one, based only on Jean Lamarre's data and for only twenty-five people. Despite its limits, however, it generates some suggestive patterns of the ways that a global force such as state formation intersected with individual agency as people went about their lives in the Eastern Townships borderland.

BUT WHY?

A number of plausible propositions could be proffered about border-crossers enlisting in the Civil War. A favourite for decades was that young men from BNA were bounty-seekers or paid substitutes, enlisting in the later years when the "supply" of Americans was low.[34] A second might be that those with the weakest ties to Canada East were most likely to enlist and to treat their service as a step in their emigration project in search of better labour market conditions. A third proposition might be commitment to the causes of the conflict, intensified by some Canadian religious denominations' support for abolition. What do the microhistorical data say?

Enlistments concentrated in the first year of war

The Civil War began on 12 April 1861. Despite the deployment of additional British troops to Canada in autumn 1861 to counter any threat from the Union's perceived territorial ambition and Britain's Foreign Enlistment Act's prohibition of joining a foreign army, almost two-thirds (sixteen of twenty-five) of these Eastern Townships residents enlisted in 1861.[35] Five more did so in the first six months of 1862, leaving only four who enlisted somewhat later in the war.

The concentration in the first fourteen months suggests that bounties for enlistment were not prime motivations for these border-crossing volunteers, despite the press and other contemporary commentators paying a good deal of attention to (and providing information about) them.[36] Payment to volunteers who enlisted was an established practice in American wars, and the Civil War was no exception. Immediately after the first call for three-year volunteers in May 1861, Congress authorized the federal War Department to pay discharged soldiers a bonus of $100 if they had signed up for three years and stayed at least two (Shannon 1926, 523–5).[37] While the promise of $100 when discharged may have attracted some cross-border enlistments, bounties do not appear to have been a major motive. First, the first wave of volunteers, whether living in the USA or crossing the border, appears to have been the one most motivated by support for the war's goals (McPherson 1988,

Table 6.1
Cross-border enlistments 1861–65, Southern Townships

Name	Year of birth	Place of birth	Gen[1]	Regiment	Enlistment date	Muster out date
Elisha Aldrich	1810	Quebec	2nd	B Co. VT 8th Inf	26-11-61	29-09-63
Isabella Rider	1837	Quebec	3rd	VT 8th Inf	(01) 1861	NA
Hamon Allen	1842	Vermont	1st	D Co. VT 8th Inf	26-09-61	05-08-63
George W. Audette	1841	Vermont	3rd	VT 1st Inf	02-04-61	15-08-61
George W. Barnes	1841	Quebec	2nd	B Co. VT 8th Inf	12-12-61	22-06-64
Robert Batley	1836	England	1st	B Co. VT 8th Inf	12-12-61	10-02-63
George M. Bigelow	1842	Vermont	1st	E Co. VT 9th Inf	12-06-62	17-01-63
Eliphalet Bodwell	1842	Quebec	3rd	MA 2nd Heavy Art	03-12-63	04-12-64
Willard Bodwell	1842	Quebec	3rd	MA 1st Heavy Art	05-07-61	24-03-64
Patrick Curren	1843	Ireland	1st	M Co. VT 1st Cav	07-01-63	22-11-64
Frederick Davis	1844	Illinois	1st	A Co. VT 1st Inf	02-05-61	29-06-65
Daniel Farrar	1843	Quebec	3rd	D Co. VT 6th Inf	24-09-61	10-12-62
Dennison Farrar	1841	Quebec	3rd	VT 2nd Light Art	13-08-64	28-07-65
Richard Harkness	1839	Quebec	2nd	B Co. VT 8th Inf	18-02-62	28-06-65
Joseph Hewes	1836	Quebec	2nd	B Co. VT 8th Inf	27-01-62	18-05-64
Bryant H. Jenks	1841	Quebec	2nd	D Co. VT 6th Inf	24-09-61	15-01-63
James Kerr	1834	Ireland	1st	D Co. Maine 5th Inf	24-06-61	Dropped from rolls 1862
Stephen Knights	1844	Quebec	1st	A Co. VT 10th Inf	08-06-62	15-12-62
Edward Musk	1838	Quebec	2nd	B Co. VT 8th Inf	25-11-61	02-10-64
Stephen Pettit	1844	Quebec	3rd	H Co. MI 29th Inf	19-08-64	25-09-64
Thomas Reynolds	1840	Quebec	2nd	D Co. VT 3rd Inf	01-05-61	08-08-63
Martin V. Rogers	1840	Vermont	1st	D Co. VT 6th Inf	24-09-61	06-02-64
Walter Sleeper	1842	Quebec	3rd	F Co. VT 3rd Inf	22-04-62	31-10-63
Jonathan Stickney	1818	Vermont	1st	B Co. NY 11th Cav	09-12-61	27-02-62
Joshua Stickney	1840	Quebec	2nd	D Co. VT 6th Inf	23-09-61	12-10-65

Notes

1. Gen = generation of immigration: 1st generation, born outside Canada East; 2nd, born in Canada East with a foreign-born parent; 3rd, one parent born in Canada East.
2. "Disability" does not distinguish between wounded and too sick to continue.

Reason[2]	Residence 1861	Enlistment credited to	Postwar residence	Religion
disability	Orford, QC	Derby, VT	Orford, QC	Adventist Baptist
[pregnancy]	Orford, QC	NA	Orford, QC	Adventist Baptist
disability	Potton, QC	Potton, QC	Potton, QC	Adventist
NA	Philipsburg, QC	Potton, QC	Potton, QC	Church of England
wounded	Barnston, QC	Barnston, QC	Holland, VT	Wesleyan Methodist
disability	Sherbrooke, QC	Sherbrooke, QC	Lisbon, NH	Church of England
discharge	Stanstead, QC	Stanstead, QC	Stanstead, QC	Adventist
death – dis	Lowell, MA	Lowell, MA		Universalist
death – dis	Andover, MA	Andover, MA		Wesleyan Methodist
desertion	Compton, QC	Compton, QC	Kansas City, MO	Roman Catholic
casualty	Philipsburg, QC	Philipsburg, QC	Cumberland, NJ	Episcopal Methodist
death – dis	Potton, QC	Potton, QC		NA
discharge	Potton, QC	Plainfield, VT	Potton, QC	Adventist
discharge	Sherbrooke, QC	Sherbrooke, QC	Decatur, IL	Church of England
desertion	Orford, QC	Orford, QC	Orford, QC	Adventist
discharge	Potton, QC	Potton, QC	Little River, AL	Episcopal Methodist
	Compton, QC	Compton, QC	Compton, QC	Wesleyan Methodist
death – dis	Eaton, QC	Sherbrooke, QC		Roman Catholic
death – dis	Stanstead, QC	Stanstead, QC		Universalist
desertion	Orford, QC	Flint, MI	Acton, QC	Roman Catholic
wounded	Sherbrooke, QC	Sherbrooke, QC	Wyoming	Roman Catholic
discharge	Potton, QC	Potton, QC	Potton, QC	Church of England
disability	Compton, QC	Compton, QC	Athol, MA	Wesleyan Methodist
death – dis	Potton, QC	New York		Free-Will Baptist
disability	Potton, QC	Potton, QC	Stanstead, QC	Adventist

309–10). Second, some states and localities almost immediately supplemented this standard federal payment with their own bounties, but Vermont did not do so until 1864 (Ford 1933, 60–1). Thus, most of the cross-border volunteers in table 6.1, who enlisted in Vermont, would have received only the basic federal amount, as did all other soldiers. Later in the war, the financial inducement to cross the border was significantly greater. Yet table 6.1 shows only four late enlistments, one of whom might have been an example of bounty-seeking. Stephen Pettit (Étienne Petit) appears in Lamarre's appendix as a twenty-three-year-old from Orford Township, although he was born in 1844.[38] His military career was dramatically brief; he deserted in August 1864, a month after his mustering-in. While there is no way to confirm he was a bounty-jumper, it seems likely because he re-enlisted in April 1865, this time giving his correct age.[39] By 1871, he was married and living with his parents, several brothers and their very young American-born children in St-Théodore-d'Acton.[40] Thus while bounties may have attracted some cross-border enlistments, they certainly do not confirm Winks's assertion "that many of the British North American who were in the Northern armies ... served only because of the high bounties involved" (Winks 1958, 37).

Transnational volunteers – an emigration project not only for newcomers

An easy hypothesis to explain enlistment might be generation – being a first-generation immigrant made it easier to engage a second process of immigration, particularly when seeking work was a key factor for individuals' actions. In this group of twenty-five, however, this hypothesis does not stand strongly up to examination, although testing it is complicated because six of the twenty-five died during the war. As table 6.1 shows, nine cross-border volunteers were immigrants to BNA, eight were born in Canada East of foreign-born parents, and eight were third-generation or more, children of parents born in BNA. Moreover, there was no generational pattern to whether the enlistment was part of a short-term or long-term project. The agricultural economy in the southern Eastern Townships was still predominantly a subsistence one, and the high birth rate made access to farms difficult. Opening new land demanded labour-intensive clearing and preparation, and working in the woods in winter was often the only way of earning a wage. The reports of wages paid in cash in industrial New England attracted many (Ramirez 2001).[41] Mechanics and common labourers were always in demand. Cities were also in need of services, as Patrick Curren, an Irish-born immigrant to Compton, found when he became a barber in Kansas City after being discharged from the

Union army. Young men whose families had emigrated from the United States even two generations prior, could often count on relatives to ease the transition to new places, as did Walter Sleeper.

Those with the longest roots did show some propensity to return to Canada. Of the five surviving third-generation Canadians, four rejoined their families. Although his father may have considered the fifth to be only temporarily absent when he listed his son on the 1861 census, Walter Sleeper had already lived for a time in New Hampshire with his aunt, probably intended to stay, and did not return to Canada. The original group of eight suffered three deaths and examining their stories reveals two who were probably planning to emigrate, while Daniel Farrar's intention disappeared with his death. Eliphalet and Willard (William) Bodwell were preparing to settle in the USA but the war ended those projects when both died. The Bodwell cousins were grandsons of Captain Eliphalet Bodwell II who immigrated to Griffin Corner (Stanstead) from Massachusetts in 1800 and was named Captain of Militia in 1814 (Hubbard 1874, 220). Listed on the 1861 census as living in Canada, Eliphalet had begun working in Lowell, Massachusetts when he enlisted in 1863. He died of disease in Virginia in 1864, and his gravestone is in the Griffin Hill Cemetery, Stanstead County. Recorded in the January 1861 census in Stanstead, Willard Bodwell later began working as a hostler in Andover, Massachusetts before enlisting in July 1861.[42] He too died of disease in 1864 and his stone is in the Marlington Cemetery of Stanstead County with others of his family.[43] In summary, of the third-generation group, four returned, three planned to emigrate, and one is unknown.

The seven surviving foreign-born veterans divided relatively evenly with respect to postwar choices. Four returned to Canada East: Harmon Allen and Martin Rogers to Potton, George Bigelow to Stanstead, and James Kerr to Compton. For two others, however, enlistment was a step in the immigration route from Europe through Canada to the USA (Faires 2005). Robert Batley was born in England in March 1836. Three months later, his family immigrated to Bury Township where his parents were among the original settlers attracted by the British American Land Company (Channel 1896, 241). After demobilization, Batley lived in Lisbon, New Hampshire, until his death in 1913. Patrick Curren (Curran) was born in Ireland in 1844 and by 1852 his parents had settled in Compton, to which his 1863 enlistment was credited. He claimed his pension in 1888 in Kansas City, Missouri, where he died in 1927. The trajectory of the seventh first-generation immigrant was complicated. Frederick Davis was born in Illinois of English parents who soon moved from there to Canada. He enlisted from Philipsburg in 1861 and then reenlisted, staying in the army until June 1865.[44] He eventually settled in New Jersey, where he died in 1924.

There is a similar pattern for the seven surviving second-generation volunteers. Three returned to Canada. After losing a leg and training as a shoemaker, Joshua Stickney settled in Stanstead while Elisha Aldrich and Joseph Hewes returned to farming. Four others stayed in the United States, including George Barnes, who settled in northern Vermont. Born in Ascot, Thomas Reynolds was the son of Irish immigrants. After de-mobilization, he went west, and in 1870 was probably in the Laramie Valley of the Wyoming Territory.[45] Richard Harkness was also the son of Irish immigrants, and he settled in Illinois where he died in 1919. A son of US-born parents, Bryant Jenks enlisted from Potton. On later US census declarations, he listed 1861 as his year of entry to the US, indicating that enlistment and immigration were the same event for him. He lived in Alabama until 1909.

These patterns demonstrate that the lure of immigration was strong, even during the Civil War. An experience of living among Americans convinced many of the surviving border-crossers to remain in that country. Of nineteen survivors, eleven returned to live in Canada. For them, the international border remained a thin line, and many crossed it in accordance with important life events such as marriage or religious and other celebrations.[46] Vermont remained a favourite place to marry and certainly to court. Both Dennison Farrar and Harmon Allen lived in Potton. In 1884, Dennison Farrar married his second wife, Edna Fifield, in Barton, just south of Newport, and in 1890 Harmon Allen married Lydia Ann Cram from Jay. While living in Stanstead, Joshua Stickney married Henrietta Litchfield, the BNA-born daughter of residents of Newport. These patterns of cross-border courtship were, quite likely, the result of the religious affiliations of the returnees. All three of these veterans plus a further four were adherents of Adventism, one of the Protestant sects whose communities straddled the international line.

A matter of religion?

Cross-border volunteers' behaviour during and after the Civil War varied significantly by religion. For people in the nineteenth century, religion was probably the most important of what Sidney Tarrow (1987) has called independent and intermediate processes located between the macro process of state formation and the micro experience of individuals' lives. Religion organized social relations as well as worldviews. It structured everyday practices and created communities, some of which were strikingly transnational.

As early as the 1840s, mainstream Eastern Townships churches had a Protestant culture that "differed markedly from that of the neighbouring American states" (Little 2004, 6; also Webb 2013). Intra-church and doctrinal debates within

Anglicanism tended to follow the cleavages of the Anglo-Atlantic world, not the American.[47] Wesleyan Methodists had cross-border ties that sustained their evangelical practices and diluted somewhat their "Britishness," but they too lived in a transatlantic cultural world more than a cross-border one (Webb 2013). By the 1860s, the American Catholic Church's hierarchy was of Irish origin, while the French-speaking clergy and prelates of Canada East were struggling to convince *Canadiens* not to emigrate. It would be several decades before they pivoted to define the communities of French speakers in New England as *le Québec d'en bas* (Anctil 1979).

The generalization about marked differences does not similarly apply to the small evangelical sects, however. They maintained the cross-border practices finely honed in the 1830s and 1840s, when Millerites postulated that the millennium was imminent.[48] Before and after the Civil War they continued to transport ideas and worshippers back and forth across the international line.[49] For Adventists, Free Will Baptists, and Universalists in the southern Townships their cross-border religious and social lives blurred any notion of being a separate community in Canada. They availed themselves of American preachers and of Vermont's rich array of churches just over the line.[50] In addition, preachers made numerous trips north to reconnect with the faithful and hold camp meetings.

In Canada East in 1861, the largest three Protestant denominations were Church of England, Wesleyan/Episcopal Methodist, and Presbyterian/Congregationalist, although all were far behind Roman Catholics, who composed 85 per cent of the population.[51] In the southern Eastern Townships borderland, however, the Catholic population was still well below a quarter of the population, with the exception of Missisquoi County (40 per cent). The four Catholics in the group of twenty-five somewhat under-represent that population (table 6.1), but Catholics were also under-represented in Civil War enlistments in general (McPherson 1988, 607). In the southern counties, between 43 per cent (Brome) and 75 per cent (Compton and Missisquoi) of the Protestant population subscribed to the three main denominational groupings. Among the twenty-one non-Catholic border-crossers, there were six Methodists and four Anglicans.

In contrast, from the relatively small population of adherents to the evangelical sects, including Adventists, Universalists, and Free-Will Baptists, there were eleven border-crossing volunteers.[52] Relying on attribution (see appendix A), Adventists, Free-Will Baptists, and Universalists, particularly the first, provided 50 per cent of the Protestant border-crossers. This was the case even though the proportion among Protestants in any of these three communities was no larger than a third and this in Stanstead. Therefore, these sects were over-represented in cross-border enlistments in comparison to their place in both Quebec (7.5 per cent) and the Protestant population of the southern Townships.

Religious affiliation correlates strongly with postwar behaviour. All seven survivors of the eleven volunteers affiliated with evangelical sects returned to their lives in Canada East after receiving their discharge (table 6.1). In contrast, eight of twelve surviving border-crossing soldiers from churches with strong Canadian institutional identities stayed in the USA.

The correlation with religion calls for interpretation. For those from the mainstream denominations, religious affiliation was unlikely to have pushed them to enlist. The Catholic Church in Canada East condemned slavery but was supportive of the Confederacy's demands for secession and still profoundly sceptical of the values of the industrializing North (Lamarre 2006, 38). The Church of England in the Canadas was never a force in the anti-slavery movement and not particularly pro-Union (Stouffer 1992, chapter 7). Wesleyan Methodists were abolitionists but slavery divided American Methodists. For congregants of mainstream denominations, the decision to enlist and then emigrate reflected their search for a labour market offering opportunities, particularly for industrial work, in southern New England or the developing West.[53] The opportunities provided by war and moving to a new country went hand in hand, as it did for many immigrants who enlisted in the Union Army (McPherson 1988, 602). Religious motivation would have taken second place to the intermediate factor of very limited employment opportunities in the rural and agricultural labour market of the southern Eastern Townships (Ramirez 2001, 6–7).

How might we understand the reasons for the over-representation of the evangelical sects among these volunteers and among those who returned to Canada? Their communities opposed slavery, but the Unitarians, Universalists, and emerging Seventh-day Adventist movement had strong pacifist beliefs.[54] The Adventists in Lower Canada in the 1860s, however, were still Second Adventists with a good deal of Baptist influence, and continuing traces of the Millerite movement of the 1840s. The Seventh-day Adventist movement would need another decade to extend into southern Quebec.[55] Even if religious doctrine *per se* did not immediately lead them to enlist in the Union forces, it is likely that living close to the border and attending religious services on both sides of the line familiarized them with the issues of the war as well as their co-religionists' choices. The members of these sects were still participating in intermediate institutions and networks of social relations shaped by borderland practice.[56] That may have been enough to make the Civil War at least partly "theirs" too.

BORDERLAND LIVING DURING STATE-MAKING

By 1865, the American state had become a greater presence in the lives of its citizens, having blocked the secessionist movement, attempted to modify race relations significantly, and developed a large public administration, including for distributing veterans' pensions. In September 1864 in Charlottetown, representatives of the Canadas and three Maritime colonies began the process that led to the 1867 creation of the Dominion. During the Civil War and after, both countries were firmly engaged in the global trend of modern state-making, a process that brought renewed attention to the common border. Charles Tilly's generalization that "war makes states" fits the macro story.

This chapter, nonetheless, has tracked micro-historical data to follow a small group of individuals who left the Eastern Townships to enlist in the Civil War. This analysis reveals yet again that there is an analytical gap between the big structures and large processes of global forces and the patterns in the everyday lives of ordinary people. Attention to the individual level of analysis and this small group is a reminder that while large and even global trends affect individuals, sometimes profoundly, they remain agents of their own lives. For them, large processes, such as state-making, are filtered through independent and intermediate processes of, for example, job-seeking and religious practice.

The Eastern Townships of the 1860s had not lost its status as a borderland but within the region people chose different life trajectories. With respect to the three plausible propositions offered here, neither bounty-seeking nor generational attachments accounts for the variation.[57] Attention to religious affiliation does reveal a pattern, however. In the previous half century, the mainstream denominations in BNA had been developing an identity separate from both Britain and the USA, and congregants as well as churches heeded their national differences. During the Civil War, mainstream religious groups contributed less than their share to the border-crossing enlistments, while for their congregants who did enlist, it was a step towards improving individual circumstances in a burgeoning labour market. They settled in their new towns, married American women, and raised families. While we can never be certain how many would have left if they had not experienced the several years of living among Americans at war, we do know that three-quarters of these practitioners of mainstream religion (eight of twelve survivors) never returned to live in Canada.

In striking contrast, all seven survivors who were adherents of a radical sect did return, not only to Canada but also to their cross-border lives. The organization and practices of the denominations to which they belonged were transnational. Preachers or worshippers crossed the line frequently and families often experienced important life events "on the other side." For them, the border remained only a thin line. After the war, they crossed back to their homes. Their economic and social trajectories had smoothly incorporated what seems today to have been a dramatic decision to go to someone else's war.

APPENDIX

It is a challenge to identify an individual's religion from census and public documents, including the church records that are public documents in Quebec. In the nineteenth-century world of religious ferment and controversy, individuals frequently altered their religious affiliation between census years, perhaps in response to the changing landscape of faith in their communities, or perhaps because enumerators were insensitive to the nuances of difference within faith communities. In 1861, the instructions to enumerators advised distinguishing among four types of Methodists and three Presbyterian ones, but there were "no sects other than these two requiring special distinguishing marks."[58] Thus it was up to individual enumerators to record any finer distinctions, perhaps differentiating between Baptists and Free-Will Baptists, for example, or perhaps not.

For this chapter, there was little difficulty identifying a denomination for soldiers professing one of the mainstream religions. Where the 1861 census was available, they declared an affiliation and baptismal records were found for those in Sherbrooke County where the census was lost. Only two were assigned by attribution. For the other eleven, however, the situation was complicated. Often in the 1861 census, either the person was missing, the census records for their county were missing, or the enumerator did not record a religious affiliation. Small sects did not always deposit marriage, baptism, and death records with the civil authorities and, therefore, baptismal or marriage records were not available as supplements to the census.

For example, in 1861 in Brome Township, including Potton, a quarter of the population was classified as "no creed given" and in Stanstead 15 per cent received that classification. Indeed, these two townships housed fully 69 per cent of the category for all Canada East. Kesteman, Southam, and Saint-Pierre (1998, 399) quoted the editorialist of the *Stanstead Journal*, who attributed the result to the reluctance of some to reveal their beliefs. While this motive may have existed, it is difficult to understand why it would vary quite dramatically over time or space in a region generally considered hospitable to evangelical sects. For example, the proportion of the population giving no affiliation in Cherry River, Orford Township, fluctuated significantly. In 1891 and as was the case in 1871, many respondents named no denomination. Fully 27 per cent of all Protestants refused an answer or said simply Protestant, while 33 per cent said they were Adventists. In 1881, however, only 5 per cent refused an answer and 59 per cent said Adventist. Summing the two categories gives quite similar numbers: 60 per cent in 1891 and 65 per cent in 1881. The cross-time comparison suggests the effect of different enumeration practices (Lauzon and Tremblay 2020, 9). Comparing across townships in 1861 leads to a similar suspicion. In Compton, the reports of "no creed" were less than 1 per cent, and in Missisquoi less than one in ten. Examination of the census returns for Brome County reveals, however, whole pages on which the enumerator wrote "no church" for almost everyone. The reason for this practice deserves more attention. For the purposes of this analysis however, information beyond the census, such as a marriage document or another census, was used to attribute an individual's affiliation when necessary.

Notes

1 On pre-Confederation state formation in Lower Canada and the Eastern Townships see Little (1997, 1981); Bernier and Salée (1992, chapter 4); Curtis (1997); Greer (1993). Dickinson and Young (2014, chapter 5) have provided an overview and bibliography. Fyson (2014) conducted a critical literature review.

2 Marquis (2000, chapter 5) examined enlistments from another borderland – the Maritimes – but he covered both Maritimers living in the United States and a few who crossed the border to enlist.

3 The use of the concept "borderland" here departs the view that borderlands disappeared as empires gave way to bordered state territories (Adelman and Aron 1999, 818). Baud and Van Schendel's definition (1997, 216) – a region significantly affected by an international border – permits tracking change over the last two centuries as imperial pretensions gave way to modern state behaviour.

4 Tarrow was evoking the *bête noir* of microhistory, to wit how to link the micro story to a macro history (Magnússon and Szijártó 2013, chapter 1). His suggestion of the need to pay attention to intermediate institutional and cultural processes echoed some microhistorians' emphasis on Max Weber's civil society (Magnússon 2003, 714).

5 On the Civil War as a driver of state-building for the United States, see Bensel (1990). Philip Buckner (2017) has reviewed historians' long-standing debates about the connections between US wartime actions and Confederation. For a collection that positioned 1860s North American state-building in a continental frame, as part of the global turn in historiography, see Spangler and Towers (2020).

6 State-making was a shared trend in Europe and the Americas, but not necessarily everywhere with the same connection to war (Centeno 1997). In his wide-ranging, indeed global, analysis, Charles Maier (2012) has identified the second half of the nineteenth

century as a central moment of state-making. As a result, "by the late nineteenth century, states possessed a degree of dedication to governance, of bureaucratic functionality, of at-oneness with fixed territorial space, of belief in their own competitive mission, that was unprecedented" (2012, 11).

7 For a detailed discussion of the treaty during the Civil War, see Masters (1963, chapters 6 and 7). For the move towards the National Policy after 1867 see Brodie and Jenson (1988, chapter 2).

8 "Before 1861 the two words 'United States' were generally used as a plural noun, 'the United States are a republic.' After 1865 the United States became a singular noun. The loose union of states became a single nation" (McPherson 1988, 859).

9 To meet troop requirements the federal government set quotas of soldiers for each state, which then set a quota for districts or towns to fill with volunteers or draftees. Therefore, each enlistment was "credited" to a place, including sometimes to towns and cities in Canada East, as table 6.1 shows.

10 When he and Sarah Hanson, his first wife, were baptised in the Stanstead Methodist Church in August 1835, they gave 1810 (month illegible) and 17 March 1808 as their respective birthdays. When the widower married Isabelle Rider in 1860, he said he was forty-seven (thus born 1813). She was twenty-two.

11 For Elisha Aldrich's war record, see his fiche in his Compiled Military Service Record (CMSR) held by the National Archives of the United States and available on Ancestry.com at https://www.fold3.com/image/311408724.

12 For his pension award, see US, Civil War Pension Index: General Index to Pension Files, 1861–1934 on Ancestry.com.

13 US, Headstones Provided for Deceased Union Civil War Veterans, 1861–1904 on Ancestry.com.

14 For Isabel Aldrich's war record, see her fiche in the CMSR and available on Ancestry.com at https://www.fold3.com/image/311408914. For her pension application, see United States General Index to Pension Files, 1861–1934 on FamilySearch.com.

15 Because Butler was not a family name, the baby was probably named after the controversial but popular General Benjamin Butler, military governor in New Orleans in 1862.

16 For the 1842 census, Isabelle's father William Rider declared that all ten members of the family were "other denomination," despite being offered a choice among thirteen finely distinguished Protestant categories. He was probably by then a follower of the preacher William Miller and millenarian Millerism. By 1851, the census offered the "Adventist" option, and the Riders all took it. Methodists like Elisha Aldrich were particularly responsive to the Millerite appeal before and after the "great disappointments" of 1843 and 1844 (Westfall 1989, 167). Over the decades after their marriage, he and Isabelle gave the census-taker Adventism as their religious affiliation. On the institutionalization of early Adventism in the area, particularly Magog, see Little (2002, 353ff.).

17 Henry, the younger brother, probably moved to the US after the 1860 census was taken in June. On 14 August 1862, he enlisted in H Company of NH 13th Infantry, was mustered in a month later on 19 September, and was dead by 14 November 1862. His father, Benjamin Sleeper, collected a pension in Clifton Township from 1868 until 1876 when he too moved to Sunapee, NH. See Revised register of the soldiers and sailors of New Hampshire in the War of the Rebellion, 1861–1866, 684 on Ancestry.com and for his pension award, see US, Civil War Pension Index: General Index to Pension Files, 1861–1934 on Ancestry.com.

18 For these enlistments, see New Hampshire, Civil War Service and Pension Records, 1861–1866 on FamilySearch.com as well as his Vermont record in his CMSR fiche, available on Ancestry.com at https://www.fold3.com/image/310751498.

19 For his military record see his CMSR fiche, available on Ancestry.com at https://www.fold3.com/image/311468081.

20 David A. Barnes's birthplace is uncertain. This military record says he was born in Stanstead while his gravestone in Island Pond, Vermont, says England. In various public documents, his children reported four birthplaces for him, including "at sea." I have chosen to accept the gravestone, the information for which probably came from his wife in 1873. Nonetheless, the variability suggests he arrived as an infant.

21 See US, Civil War Soldier Records and Profiles 1861–1865 on Ancestry.com.

22 See his military record in his CMSR fiche, available on Ancestry.com at https://www.fold3.com/image/311468032.

23 Winks (1958, 25–6) emphasized pro-secessionist views in BNA as did Sher (2023) more recently. Little (2012; also Buckner 2017, 522–3) criticized Winks's research methods. Both Little (2012) and Jenkins (1993, 3) critiqued Winks for downplaying Canadian enlistment numbers to bolster his claims about British and BNA pro-secession positions. Despite the limits to Winks's analysis, according to Andrew Holman (2001, 165) Winks's much-reissued book has become a "standard source." For a reevaluation of Winks's claims, see Jenson (2023).

24 The geographical coverage in recent work has varied. Jenkins (1993) focused on western New York State, which drained primarily from the eastern parts of Canada West, while Lamarre (2006) sought French Canadians, usually from Canada East, who enlisted in regiments in seven Midwestern and New England states. Reid (2014) focused on African Canadians, most of whom were living in Canada West.

25 Jenkins calculates 10 per cent (103 of his more than 1,000 BNA enlistments) of soldiers in New York State came directly from BNA (1993, 24).

26 While there may have been some errors in records of birthplace, due to soldiers' own confusion or misrepresentation or to bureaucratic mix-ups, relatively few have appeared in this research. Identification of "residence" is another matter. Sometimes those registering a volunteer assigned his real residence as the recorded residence. Much more frequent, however, was the assignment of the person to a town in Vermont in need of enlistment credits. This widespread practice creates the main difficulty in distinguishing border-crossers from "Canadians" already living in the United States (Jenson 2023).

27 The identification of "residence" is from the revised roster of Vermont volunteers (1892). In this official record, the place to which credit for the enlistment was assigned became the "residence."

28 The method used to construct Lamarre's appendix is not clear. Describing his sample he says: "les individus retenus sont des Canadiens français nés au Canada-Est ou nés aux États-Unis *portant des patronymes francophones communs*" (2006, 27, emphasis added). Reading the appendix reveals, however, a great many standard Anglophone names.

29 As today, the US census was conducted in first year of the decade and the Canadian census in the year ending in 1, thus 1861 and 1871. Absence from the 1861 census was not a condition in itself to set aside a case, for two reasons. First, the census for Sherbrooke County in 1861 is lost. Second, census-takers might miss people, for a range of reasons.

Therefore, to be excluded the soldier had to both be absent from the 1861 census and have confirming information of a US residence before 1861.

30 See US, Civil War Soldier Records and Profiles 1861–1865 on Ancestry.com.

31 See ibid.

32 For example, to the 1890 census for Hartford, CT, George A. Dumore reported being born in Vermont in 1842.

33 For example, Eliphalet Bodwell's cousin Willard and Daniel Farrar's brother Dennison.

34 Early literature about Canadians sometimes attributed motives of greed or assumed soldiers to have been duped into enlisting, usually while drunk (for example, Winks 1958). The first decades of the twentieth century also generated a literature about Americans' "mercenary" motives for enlistment (Shannon 1926; Ford 1933). See also McPherson (1988, 600ff). Jenson (2023) explores this proposition of mercenary motives in some detail.

35 This pattern of early enlistment among border-crossers was similar to the enthusiasm of volunteers living in the United States. So many volunteers had flocked to the Northern army that difficulties arose for feeding, housing, and equipping them (McPherson 1988, chapter 10).

36 The press in the Townships and elsewhere in the Canadas highlighted crimping, the advertised bounties and substitution (for example, Little 2012, 10, 12; Lamarre 2006, 58–61). Jenkins (1993, 3–8) reviews the early scholarly literature, which did the same.

37 The soldiers' pay was $13 per month, or $156 per year. In 1864 it rose to $16 (Geary 1986, 213–14).

38 There is no confirmation of Petit living in Orford because the 1861 census for Sherbrooke County is lost. Some of his family appears in the 1861 census in Acton, where his parents listed Etienne and his brother as absent, and thus perhaps in Orford.

39 In 1864, he enlisted in a new regiment raised in the 6th Congressional District although his place of residence was given as Flint, a city outside that district. The 1865 enlistment was with the Michigan 8th Cavalry. See US, Civil War Soldier Records and Profiles 1861–1865 on Ancestry.com.

40 The age of the American-born children in 1871 suggests that several of the family tried living in the USA in the mid-1860s, before returning to Canada.

41 The literature on emigration from the Eastern Townships is very limited. Most discussions of Quebec address immigration by *Canadiens* to New England, some of which may have been from the Eastern Townships, but also from many other areas. For the general patterns see Ramirez (2001, chapters 1 and 3).

42 The archives Lamarre consulted allowed him to log Eliphalet as from Stanstead and Willard from Quebec, although the US, Civil War Soldier Records and Profiles, 1861–1865 lists do not.

43 See Interment.net/ca.

44 See US, Civil War Soldier Records and Profiles, 1861–1865 for Frederick C. Davis.

45 He then disappeared from the records and did not collect a pension.

46 It was only in the 1890s that crossing the land border involved significant encounters with state authority (Ramirez 2001, 39).

47 As Vaudry writes of Anglicans challenged by their own evangelicals, they held debates in "a language of common religious discourse and controversy [that] made as much sense in Lennoxville as it did in Oxford" (2003, 6).

48 The Millenarian, William Miller, held his first North American camp meeting in Hatley in 1842, but already in 1835, he made a preaching tour about the advent of Christ, during which he visited Bolton and several other villages as well Derby, Vermont (Westfall 1989, 167; Fortin 1997, 42).

49 Fortin (2004, chapters 5 and 6) recounts in detail the border crossing of Adventists as well as their controversial encounters with other sects.

50 See the impressive list of Vermont church numbers in Little (2004, 296n11). See also the examples of early Adventist churches along the border near Potton and Sutton (Fortin 2004).

51 All calculations for religious groups are from Census of the Canadas, 1860–61 (1863, 122–3). Only Brome County had any significant number of Episcopal Methodists, who were 12 per cent of the Protestant population.

52 This count includes Daniel Farrer, whose family always reported adherence to one sect or another (appendix).

53 Only George Barnes made a short-distance move, to Holland, Vermont. No others stayed in Vermont, where there was little industrial employment. They chose instead to settle in seven different states (table 6.1). While adherents of the evangelical sects did return, they continued to move back and forth across the international line, including those who emigrated to the US in later life. If they did so, however, they did not go far. Those who moved, often to live closer to family, settled either directly along the international line in towns such as Newport and Lowell in Orleans County or down the length of the train line (and today's Interstate 91) but no further than St Johnsbury.

54 The Seventh-day Adventists gained a right to claim conscientious objection during the Civil War (Lawson 1995, 355).

55 In 1871 when Elisha Aldrich and Isabelle Rider identified their religion, they called it Adventist Baptist, as did a number of their neighbours. The first Seventh-day Adventist church was established in South Stukely in 1877 (Fortin 2004: 112–13).

56 For an elaboration of this argument see Jenson (2024).

57 Additional studies of transnational volunteers confirm these findings. See Jenson (2023, 2024).

58 https://www.prdh.umontreal.ca/census/en/uguide/enum_1861.aspx.

References

Adelman, Jeremy, and Stephen Aron. 1999. "From Borderlands to Borders: Empires, Nation-States, and the Peoples in between in North American History." *American Historical Review* 104, no. 3 (June): 814–41.

Anctil, Pierre. 1979. "La franco-américanie ou le Québec d'en bas." *Cahiers de géographie du Québec* 23, no. 58 (April): 39–52.

Baud, Michiel, and Willem Van Schendel. 1997. "Toward a Comparative History of Borderlands." *Journal of World History* 8, no. 2 (Fall): 211–42.

Bensel, Richard Franklin. 1990. *Yankee Leviathan. The Origins of Central State Authority in America, 1859-1877.* New York, NY: Cambridge University Press.

Bernier, Gérald, and Daniel Salée. 1992. *The Shaping of Québec Politics and Society. Colonialism, Power, and the Transition to Capitalism in the 19th Century*. Washington, DC: Taylor & Francis.

Brodie, Janine, and Jane Jenson. 1988. *Crisis, Challenge and Change. Party and Class in Canada Revisited*. Ottawa: Carleton University Press.

Buckner, Philip. 2017. "'British North America and a Continent in Dissolution': The American Civil War in the Making of Canadian Confederation." *Journal of the Civil War Era* 7, no. 4 (December): 512–40.

Census of the Canadas, 1860–61. 1863. *Personal Census*, vol. 1. Quebec, QC: S.B. Foote.

Centeno, Miguel Angel. 1997. "Blood and Debt: War and Taxation in Nineteenth-Century Latin America." *American Journal of Sociology* 102, no. 6 (May): 1565–605.

Channell, L.S. 1896. *History of Compton County*. Cookshire, QC: L.S. Channell Publisher.

Costa, Dora L. 1998. *The Evolution of Retirement: An American Economic History, 1880–1990*. Chicago, IL: University of Chicago Press.

Curtis, Bruce. 1997. "The State of Tutelage in Lower Canada, 1835–1851." *History of Education Quarterly* 37, no. 1 (Spring): 25–43.

Dickinson, John, and Brian Young. 2014. *A Short History of Quebec*, 3rd ed. Montreal and Kingston: McGill-Queen's University Press.

Faires, Nora. 2005. "Leaving the 'Land of the Second Chance.' Migration from Ontario to the Upper Midwest in the Nineteenth and Early Twentieth Centuries." In *Permeable Border. The Great Lakes Basin as Transnational Region, 1650–1990*, edited by John J. Bukowczyk, Nora Faires, David R. Smith, and Randy William Widdis, 78–119. Calgary, AB: University of Calgary Press.

Ford, Oren. 1933. "A History of the Bounty System Used during the Civil War." PhD thesis, University of the Pacific, Stockton, CA.

Fortin, Denis. 1997. "'The world turned upside down': Millerism in the Eastern Townships, 1835–1845." *Journal of Eastern Townships Studies*, no. 11 (Fall 1997): 39–59.

– 2004. *Adventism in Quebec. The Dynamics of Rural Church Growth 1830–1910*. Berrien Springs, MI: Andrews University Press.

Fyson, Donald. 2014. "Between the Ancien Régime and Liberal Modernity: Law, Justice and State Formation in Colonial Quebec, 1760–1867." *History Compass* 12, no. 5 (May): 412–32.

Geary, James W. 1986. "Civil War Conscription in the North: A Historiographical Review." *Civil War History* 32, no. 3 (September): 208–28.

Greer, Allen. 1993. *The Patriots and the People: The Rebellion of 1837 in Rural Lower Canada*. Toronto, ON: University of Toronto Press.

Holman, Andrew. 2001. "Something Old, Something New: Canada and the American Civil War." *Acadiensis* 31, no. 1 (Autumn): 164–170.

Hubbard, B.F. 1874. *Forests and Clearings: The History of Stanstead County*. Montreal, QC: Lovell Printing and Publishing.

Jenkins, Danny R. 1993. "British North Americans who fought in the American Civil War, 1861–1865." MA thesis, University of Ottawa.

Jenson, Jane. 2023. "Transnational Volunteers. A Research Note on Border-crossing to Enlist in the American Civil War." *Canadian Historical Review* 104, no. 3 (September): 387–406.

– 2024. "Bordering a War: Transnational Volunteers to the American Civil War from the Eastern Townships." *Histoire sociale/Social History* 57, no. 117 (May): 97–115.

Kesteman, Jean-Pierre, Peter Southam, and Diane Saint-Pierre. 1998. *Histoire des Cantons de l'Est*. Quebec, QC: Les Presses de l'Université Laval.

Lamarre, Jean. 2006. *Les Canadiens français et la guerre de sécession, 1861–1865*. Montreal, QC: VLB éditeur.

Lauzon, Gilles, and Denis Tremblay. 2020. *Histoire de la petite maison blanche d'Orford et proposition d'une nouvelle appellation*. Orford, QC: SHCO. www.histoireorford.com.

Lawson, Ronald. 1997. "Sect-State Relations: Accounting for the Differing Trajectories of Seventh-day Adventists and Jehovah's Witnesses." *Sociology of Religion* 56, no. 4 (Winter): 351–77.

Little, J.I. 1981 "Colonization and Municipal Reform in Canada East." *Histoire sociale/Social History* 14, no. 27 (May): 94–121.

– 1997. *State and Society in Transition: The Politics of Institutional Reform in the Eastern Townships, 1838–1852*. Montreal and Kingston: McGill-Queen's University Press.

– 2002. "The Mental World of Ralph Merry: A Case Study of Popular Religion in the Lower Canadian-New England Borderland, 1798–1863." *Canadian Historical Review* 83, no. 3 (September): 338–63.

– 2004. *Borderland Religion: The Emergence of an English-Canadian Identity, 1792–1852*. Toronto, ON: University of Toronto Press.

– 2008. *Loyalties in Conflict: A Canadian Borderland in War and Conflict. 1812–1840*. Toronto, ON: University of Toronto Press.

– 2012. "From Borderland to Bordered Land: Reaction in the Eastern Townships Press to the American Civil War and the Threat of Fenian Invasion." *Histoire sociale/Social History* 45, no. 89 (May): 1–24.

Magnússon, Sigurður G. 2003. "'The Singularization of History': Social History and Microhistory within the Postmodern State of Knowledge." *Journal of Social History* 36, no. 3 (Spring): 701–35.

Magnússon, Sigurður G., and István Szijártó. 2013. *What Is Microhistory? Theory and Practice*. New York, NY: Routledge.

Maier, Charles S. 2012. *Leviathan 2.0: Inventing Modern Statehood*. Cambridge, MA: The Belknap Press of Harvard University Press.

Marquis, Greg. 2000. *In Armageddon's Shadow: The Civil War and Canada's Maritime Provinces*. Montreal and Kingston: McGill-Queen's University Press.

Masters, Donald C. 1963. *The Reciprocity Treaty of 1854*. Ottawa, QC: Carleton University Press.

McPherson, James. 1988. *Battle Cry of Freedom. The Civil War Era, 1861–1865*. New York, NY: Oxford University Press.

– 1997. *For Cause and Comrades: Why Men Fought in the Civil War*. New York, NY: Oxford University Press.

Nicol, Heather N. 2015. *The Fence and the Bridge. Geopolitics and Identity along the Canada–US Border*. Waterloo, ON: Wilfrid Laurier University Press.

Prechtel-Kluskens, Claire. 2010. "'A Reasonable Degree of Promptitude': Civil War Pension Application Processing, 1861–1885." *Prologue Magazine* 42, no. 1 (Spring): 1–14.

Ramirez, Bruno. 2001. *Crossing the 49th Parallel: Migration from Canada to the United States, 1900–1930*. Ithaca, NY: Cornell University Press.

Reid, Richard M. 2014. *African Canadians in Union Blue: Enlisting for the Cause in the Civil War*. Vancouver: University of British Columbia Press.

Revised Roster of Vermont Volunteers. 1892. *Revised roster of Vermont volunteers and lists of Vermonters who served in the Army and Navy of the United States during the War of the Rebellion, 1861-66. Compiled by authority of the General Assembly under direction of Theodore S. Peck, adjutant-general*. Montpelier, VT: Press of the Watchman Publishing Co.

Shannon, Fred A. 1926. "The Mercenary Factor in the Creation of the Union Army." *The Mississippi Historical Review* 12, no. 4 (March): 523–49.

Sher, Julian. 2023. *The North Star: Canada and the Civil War Plots Against Lincoln*. Toronto: Alfred A. Knopf Canada.

Skocpol, Theda. 1992. *Protecting Soldiers and Mothers: The Political Origins of Social Policy in the United States*. Cambridge, MA: Belknap Press of Harvard University Press.

Skowronek, Stephen. 1982. *Building a New American State: The Expansion of National Administrative Capacities, 1877–1920*. New York, NY: Cambridge University Press.

Spanglar, Jewel L., and Frank Towers, eds. 2020. *Remaking North American Sovereignty: State Transformation in the 1860s*. New York, NY: Fordham University Press.

Stouffer, Allen P. 1992. *The Light of Nature and the Law of God: Antislavery in Ontario, 1833–1877*. Montreal and Kingston: McGill-Queen's University Press.

Tarrow, Sidney. 1987. "Big Structures and Contentious Events: Two of Charles Tilly's Recent Writings." *Sociological Forum* 2, no. 1 (Winter): 191–204.

Tilly, Charles. 2017. *Collective Violence, Contentious Politics and Social Change: A Charles Tilly Reader*, edited by Ernesto Castañeda and Cathy Lisa Schneider. New York, NY: Routledge.

Tyrell, Geoff. 2019. "When Johnny (Canuck) Comes Marching Home Again: Canadians in the American Civil War, 1861–1865." *Canadian Military Journal* 20, no. 1 (Winter): 40–8.

Vaudry, Richard. 2003. *Anglicans and the Atlantic World: High Churchmen, Evangelicals, and the Quebec Connection*. Montreal and Kingston: McGill-Queen's University Press.

Webb, Todd. 2013. *Transatlantic Methodists: British Wesleyanism and the Formation of an Evangelical Culture in Nineteenth-Century Ontario and Quebec*. Montreal and Kingston: McGill-Queen's University Press.

Wells, Cheryl, ed. 2008. *Francis M. Wafer: A Surgeon in the Army of the Potomac*. Montreal and Kingston: McGill-Queen's University Press.

Westfall, William. 1989. *Two Worlds: The Protestant Culture of Nineteenth Century Ontario*. Montreal and Kingston: McGill-Queen's University Press.

Winks, Robin W. 1958. "The Creation of a Myth: 'Canadian' Enlistments in the Northern Armies during the American Civil War." *The Canadian Historical Review* 39, no. 1 (March): 24–40.

7

Transitioning from Southern Honour to Dependency: Jefferson Davis in Montreal and the Eastern Townships, 1867–68

Gordon S. Barker and Christopher Kirkey

DURING JEFFERSON DAVIS'S TIME as an exile in Canada, the only president of the Confederate States of America underwent a remarkable transition, a rapid yet deep-rooted transformation that scholars and biographers have overlooked. In all the major works on Davis, accounts of his stay in Canada amount to only a handful of pages. It was in Canada, however, notably Montreal and especially the Eastern Townships, that *another* Jefferson Davis emerged, a different Davis who no longer carried himself as a proud Southern patriarch even as he sought to regain that status. This chapter, focusing on his time in Montreal and Lennoxville, from late May 1867 to July 1868, reveals Davis in the throes of seeking to remake himself as well as searching to reconcile his recent failure as the Confederate commander-in-chief with traditions of Southern honour and the Founders' legacy he held so dear. In exile, he confronted the overarching concern of a patriarch, notably how to succour, care for, and protect his family and provide them with financial stability. Davis had to navigate these challenges in the harsh reality of striking declines in his income, wealth, political and social status that everyone could see. He also had to deal with uncertainties associated with his upcoming trial for treason that tied his past, present, and future and raised concerns associated with his old and new attachments. Somehow the words he penned forty years earlier at West Point about reputation gained from lengthy service being "worth little in the wide world of Fame" yet being important to oneself still resonated. The linking of the "public and private dimensions of reputation" was central to Davis's conception of honour as it was also to most Southern elites; in his now impoverished state, that linking haunted him (Cooper 2020, 61).[1]

At first glance, Davis's time in Lennoxville between September 1867 and July 1868 might appear unremarkable and illustrative of a common pattern revealed throughout this book: namely, how the Eastern Townships as a locale served, and serves, as a way station with significant connections to, as well as engagement with, a much broader world. On the surface, since Davis was preoccupied with the joint concerns of finding new sources of income and dealing with issues related to his upcoming treason trial scheduled in Richmond, Virginia, one could arguably conclude that Lennoxville left no permanent imprint on Davis nor he on it. From this vantage point, Lennoxville was simply a quiet and suitable residence for Davis, one of several temporary stops during the post-Civil War period. This chapter, however, reveals that it was much more. It was during his time in Lennoxville that Davis underwent the transformation from a proud paterfamilias to an individual whose status was fundamentally that of a dependent – a transition that began upon his arrival in Montreal shortly after his release from Fortress Monroe.

Davis's exile in Canada was a particularly trying time. What made it so difficult and caused him so much personal torment was his inability to live up to Southern patriarchal traditions that had always sustained him and which he still fervently embraced. From childhood, Davis had been schooled in Southern honour and, like other gentry youths, he imbibed his father's patriarchal teaching to "always and above all, dread dishonor" (Wyatt-Brown 2007, viii). His choice of Southern heroes – George Washington, Thomas Jefferson, Andrew Jackson, and John C. Calhoun – stood as testament to this (see Cooper 2020, 9–22). As is so aptly explained by Bertram Wyatt-Brown in his analysis of traditions of Southern honour, Davis, as a Southern youth, learned that "what mattered most was the respect and acclaim of others." In the absence of such recognition, a gentleman could be stripped of status and deprived of social acceptance, jeopardizing virtually all his relationships in the private and public spheres. Notions of honour and manhood were interwoven through Southern patriarchal structures that also emphasized "male prerogatives and rule over all dependents" (Wyatt-Brown 2007, x). Davis's ideology was distinctly Southern, even as a penniless refugee in Canada. He was, as Lynda Lasswell Crist observes, "a man without a country … no salary or savings." He had lost his home after Union troops captured the Brierfield plantation in 1862 and it was later sold on 8 March 1867 (Crist et al. 2008, 185). It was in Montreal and the Eastern Townships that his lack of autonomy and inability to fulfill the duty of caring for his household became so evident, thus undermining his patriarchal self-esteem and sense of honour. Davis no longer had the means to sustain his independence as a patriarch.

As a husband and father who had always committed himself to caring for Varina and the children, Davis found his predicament agonizing, especially since his past performance had been stellar. He had followed through on his prenuptial declaration to Varina to provide for her, to shield her from misfortune, and to furnish her every need. His words had been a model for Southern patriarchal honour. "The first wish of my heart is my first thought," vowed Davis to his bride-to-be, adding, "my first prayer this morning need I say that wish is for your welfare" (McIntosh 1974, 704). On the eve of their wedding, he renewed his pledge. "I will try to do better than I have ever promised to fulfill brighter hopes than I have ever inculcated," averred Davis, promising that "my heart shall beat warmly to relieve you from the chills of misfortune's winter and my form shall screen you from the lightnings of an angry destiny" (Cooper 2020, 96). Calling Varina "ma chere, tres chere," and speaking lovingly of "the reluctance with which I am ever apart from you," Davis fulfilled his commitments (Allen 1999, 108). During the antebellum years, his annual income from Brierfield tripled, from $25,000 to $75,000, which represented substantial money at the time. His salary as a US senator and a cabinet member further augmented his revenues. As president of the Confederacy, he also sustained Varina's love of "unmeasured hospitality," and together they received visitors at her "fortnightly levées" during which Davis and invited guests "appreciated her spontaneous bon mots" (Strode 1959, 190–1). Until their arrival in Montreal, Varina could say that "she had been happily dependent upon him throughout their union," even if she had fretted about him during his years in captivity. Her husband's Confederate friends had, after all, advanced her several thousand dollars. Judah Benjamin alone "lent her a little over twelve thousand dollars, and she received several thousand dollars" from other Davis supporters (Cashin 2006, 172).

JEFFERSON DAVIS *in* CANADA

Standing on the deck of a riverboat making its way toward Niagara Falls on 30 May 1867, Jefferson Davis, in his sixtieth year, glanced at the Lake Ontario shoreline and looked back at Toronto, which seemed to disappear as the vessel moved westward. Despite the Confederacy's defeat, his distinguished features still exuded "a certain rigid nobility" (Escot 1978, 262).[2] But holding the guardrail, his tall yet now almost gaunt-looking figure bore scars of lost war and a two-year imprisonment in Fortress Monroe that had ended a couple of weeks earlier. Some contemporary observers were "astonished" by his "emaciation." A reporter who recognized him upon his arrival in Montreal thought him "dreadfully worn and thin" (Strode 1964, 313). His wife Varina worried about his "physical weakness and lassitude" (Cooper 2000, 569). On deck, his solemnity contrasted sharply with the exuberance of his also exiled yet jovial companions James Mason, Beverley Tucker, Charles J. Helm, and Jubal Early. Former high-ranking Confederates, they too had sought refuge in Canada after the Confederacy's demise (Crist et al. 2008, 208; Richardson 2018).[3] Joining them was the staid-looking Canadian Lieutenant Colonel George T. Denison, renowned for his anti-American views. He had taken a special interest in the former Confederate president and helped stage Davis's "cordial and kindly" welcome by thousands when he arrived in Toronto harbour (Denison 1900, 69).

Davis, however, withdrew from the conversation on deck that day and seemed to enter his own private world, a habit he developed after receiving Robert E. Lee's dispatch from Appomattox Court House informing him of the Army of Northern Virginia's surrender. Such introversion continued during his incarceration and after his release. Burton Harrison, who spirited Davis north to New York and then on to Canada, thought that his old "Chief" had become "feeble and apathetic to everything" (Davis 1991, 657). Gazing into the distance, Davis undoubtedly savoured "breathing free air" again, but he also probably reflected on the message he would deliver to a Canadian audience that evening. Although he was a man who hated to be caught off-guard, he and those with whom he travelled knew that he had been "utterly unprepared" for the resounding welcome he received in Toronto. He had been speechless and able only to "bow his thanks" (Strode 1964, 315). Now he searched for words that he hoped his Canadian hosts would never forget. "May peace and prosperity be forever the blessing of Canada," declared Davis that night to the crowd gathered outside Mason's house, "for she has been the asylum for many of my friends, as she is now an asylum to myself" (Denison 1900, 69; see also Crist et al. 2008, 208). Many listeners must have considered such a tribute truly remarkable, especially coming from a man whose lifelong heroes, George Washington, Thomas Jefferson, and Andrew Jackson, had opposed the British. As a Southern defender of slavery, Davis had also often criticized Britain's refusal to extradite fugitive slaves, which made Canada a sanctuary for runaways, especially after Parliament passed the Imperial Emancipation Bill in 1833.

Always sensitive to his environment, Davis perhaps also remembered how previous journeys had significantly changed him. As a young boy he travelled from the Deep South to St Thomas College in Washington County, Kentucky, meeting his "authentic" Southern hero Andrew Jackson along the way (Cooper 2000, 16). As an adolescent, he journeyed to Transylvania University in Lexington, where he became remembered as "the most active, intelligent and splendid-looking young man in the College" (Davis 1991, 21). A third trip northward took him to West Point, which set the stage for the legendary Patrick Henry's toast to him, saying, "To the health and prosperity of Jefferson Davis, late a Student of Transylvania University, now a Cadet at West Point – May he become the pride of our country, the idol of our army" (Monroe and McIntosh 1971, 10–11). After the military academy, Davis headed to the Midwest and then fought valiantly in the Mexican War, notably at Buena Vista, before returning to Washington to be hailed as "one of those brilliant meteors that shoots along and illuminates the military horizon of the world" (Cooper 2000, 157). Those journeys contributed to making him a war hero, a senator, a secretary of war, and, of course, the leader of the Confederacy.

Undoubtedly the sound of the great falls shook Davis from his trance, breaking his reflective silence. As the Stars and Stripes above the American falls came into view, he reached out and grasped James Mason's arm, suddenly exclaiming, "Look there Mason, there is the gridiron we have been fried upon" (Denison 1900, 69). With the waves at the mouth of the Niagara River buffeting the riverboat below the falls, Davis found himself on another formative journey – a search for vindication in the tradition of his political saint Old Hickory but also a search for who indeed he himself would become.[4] He had recently complained to his brother Joseph about the "impediments" that stood in his way as he looked to the future and sought to reinvent himself with the trials and tribulations of his incarceration still fresh in his mind (Cooper 2000, 569).

Accompanied by Harrison, Davis had left Fortress Monroe, "the Gibraltar of the Chesapeake," on 11 May 1867, breathing free air for the first time in 720 days. Arriving in Richmond on the steamer *John Sylvester* later that day, he and Varina checked into spacious quarters in the Spotswood Hotel while throngs gathered outside hoping to catch a glimpse of the former president.[5] Two days later, Davis and his legal team led by the New York attorney Charles O'Conor appeared before Judge John Underwood on a writ of *habeas corpus*.[6] When federal attorneys indicated they were not prepared to prosecute him during the court's current term, O'Conor demanded Davis's release on bail. Underwood agreed, and the prominent northerners Horace Greeley, Gerrit Smith, and Cornelius Vanderbilt, who were present in the courtroom, funded his bail, which Underwood set at $100,000.[7] That evening, the Davises "visited the grave of their son Joseph in Hollywood Cemetery" before departing for New York with Harrison and then travelling on to Montreal on 20 May (Crist et al. 2008, 204).[8] The trip proved difficult for the former Confederate leader. Some observers thought him "completely broken down," almost an "invalid" (Davis 1991, 657). He was said to be "shunning crowds" and avoiding almost everyone along the way (Strode 1964, 313).

On 21 May, Davis reunited with his children Maggie, Jeff, and Billy, as well as Varina's mother (Crist et al. 2008, 204, 217).[9] Writing to Cornelia L. O'Conor the next day, he described his voyage northward and his reunion with his family. He reported that the "trip was so devoid of incident that like the weary knife grinder I have no tale to tell" (201). He did not confess to his near collapse from exhaustion and Harrison having to carry him and "place him bodily" in a carriage (Davis 1991, 657). Nor did he speak of his mood swings, which saw him "fall silent" and become "reticent and reclusive" (Allen 1999, 489). Commenting on seeing his children again, Davis said that he hardly recognized them because they had changed so much during his imprisonment. He failed to mention that despite having been separated from them for so long, he "could hardly stand the noise and disorder of their presence" (Crist et al. 201). Varina complained that the children caused him to become "wild with nervousness," and she had to keep them, "the noisy ones," with her and away from him (Allen 1999, 489). What Davis did acknowledge, however, were the uncertainties he now confronted, admitting that his plans were "yet to be formed" (Crist et al. 2008, 202). Although his journey from imprisonment in the Chesapeake to exile in Queen Victoria's northern dominion had taken only a few days, he recognized that he was embarked on a transition away from being a political leader whose "life was bound up with the Confederacy" and "with the Confederacy he would live or die" (Cooper 2020, 508).

The always-introspective Davis then recognized that his release from captivity precipitated a fundamental change in his relationship with his beloved South, even if his fate had not yet been decided in court. He knew that for the previous two years many of his compatriots had revered him as an imprisoned martyr for the South. Committed to traditions of Southern honour, Davis personally considered that his loss of freedom and independence represented a sacrifice that he alone bore for his defeated Southern nation; he stoically endured imprisonment to save his compatriots from suffering, knowing that sacrificing oneself to succour and protect family, other dependents, comrades, and country lay at the very heart of Southern patriarchal tradition.[10] It was in this light that the imprisoned Confederate chief had adopted an almost Christlike stance. "If I alone could bear all the suffering of the country, and relieve it from further calamity," he declared, "I trust our Heavenly father would give me strength to be a willing sacrifice" (Davis 1991, 610, 648). As an ennobled martyr, Davis felt that he shielded his fallen South, which allowed him to frame his ordeal in sacrificial terms. "The consolation which I derived from the intense malignity shown to me by the enemy," he wrote, "was in hope that their hate would, by concentration on me, be the means of relieving my countrymen" (McElroy 1937, 594). Touching Canadian soil, however, Davis sensed that his martyrdom, as well as the honour associated with it, had ended; it would no longer be there to sustain him.

He also juxtaposed his changing status against developments in postbellum America. In 1867, the political landscape shifted dramatically as President Andrew Johnson and Congress battled over the Fourteenth Amendment and Northeast Republicans, waving the bloody shirt, crafted legislation that underpinned Radical Reconstruction. Davis viewed the prospects for his beloved South as particularly bleak. "The temper shown by the Congress leaves little to expect," Davis suggested to his brother Joseph, "but persistent efforts to destroy the South" (Crist et al. 2008, 232). This troubled him since he had always regarded the Confederates as the true heirs of the American Revolutionaries. His Southern nation had been "forced to take up arms to vindicate the political rights, the freedom, equality, and State sovereignty" for which the Revolutionary generation had put their lives on the line (Cooper 2020, 458). For him, the Confederates were thus "the sole surviving heirs of the heritage of 1776," and he identified his Southern fighting forces with Washington and the Continental Army (Thomas 1977, 4, 8). Herein lay the source of a momentous loss of honour for Davis. He had failed the Founders, his political and Revolutionary heroes. The defeat of the Confederacy, which he regarded as his own defeat, terminated the Revolutionary Fathers' republican experiment that "had been perverted from the purpose for which it had been ordained" (Cooper 2009, 154). Most important in Davis's mind, it was he who personally sealed the link between the Founding Fathers and the Confederacy, a link that he had preserved as an imprisoned martyr for the Southern nation. Davis brought his personal history and the Confederate history "into tandem," to use an expression Brian Young adopts in his analysis of patrician families in New France and Quebec, during the eighteenth and nineteenth centuries (Young 2014, 19). With that martyrdom ended, his defeat silenced the Founders' legacy. He had let them down.

During his initial days in Montreal, as well as later in the Eastern Townships, Davis and his family faced financial collapse. It became apparent that not only did Davis not have employment or another source of income to provide for Varina and the children, but he also did not even have "a home to take them to." His inability to furnish his family with appropriate lodgings became a public and private embarrassment. Upon their arrival, the Davises first stayed in a "cheap boardinghouse" that could not be regarded as appropriate accommodation for a Southern gentleman and the former mistress of the Brierfield plantation. The shabby lodgings were certainly not suitable for a former head of state who had presided over a nation of several million people nor for a gracious Southern lady accustomed to hosting Washington elites while her husband served in the senate or the cabinet and, later in Richmond, the first families of the South (Strode 1964, 313). There was no hiding it; Davis had taken a fall that weighed especially heavily on a Southern patriarch who linked the public and private aspects of reputation. Once the man Mississippians called "*The soldier and leader – the foremost in fame*" and dubbed "the Cicero of the Senate," Davis could no longer carry himself with pride. When he entered Montreal, he did not ride in an ornate carriage drawn by four white horses as he had in Jackson, Mississippi, in 1857 when the townspeople hailed him with a sixteen-gun salute and raised a banner reading "Welcome Jeff Davis" (Cooper 2020, 157, 3, 276). He also knew that Varina had tumbled with him. In a foreign land, she now encountered what she called "a stone wall of hard realities." She too had to deal with the public and private dimensions of reputation. Undoubtedly, she remembered what the fourteenth president Franklin Pierce told her a few months earlier when he warned her that "the eyes of the world will be upon you" (Cashin 2009, 179, 178). Davis, an acute observer of social conditions, certainly knew that such public scrutiny was on its way (Davis 1991, xi). When he denounced the Stars and Stripes and wished British Canada the best, Davis was also aware – as most Montreal residents and visitors to the city were – that the cheap boarding house in which his family lived was in a *quartier* inhabited by fugitives from Southern slavery, members of that caste Senator James Henry Hammond of South Carolina, Davis's former compatriot-turned-critic, branded "mud-sills" (see McKitrick 1963, 122–3). Like Hammond, Davis remained committed to slavery, even after the Confederate defeat (Cooper 2009, 161). The exiled Mississippian also knew that other residents of the South's former first family's neighbourhood included impoverished refugees from hard times in Europe who had not yet found employment in Canada's main port of entry on the St Lawrence. The Davises not only rubbed shoulders with the so-called lesser sorts in Montreal; they lived amongst them.

What accentuated Davis's feelings of dishonour was Varina's overt disdain of the neighborhood where the Davises had ended up and the "abnormal poverty" she said they endured. She sardonically referred to the family as "unsuccessful, ci-devant, threadbare, great folks." Her disparagement intensified after the calamitous days of the Confederate retreat when Davis acknowledged that he was no longer delivering on his promises to provide for her. In April 1865, she matter-of-factly stated to him that their predicament was "surely not the fate to which you invited me in brighter days." Living with Davis in the slums of Montreal, however, she felt that she bore the full brunt of his broken promises. She turned to others, particularly woman friends, to share her concerns, and that was something nineteenth-century patriarchs scorned. Exchanging notes with Martha Phillips, she exposed her hardships and said, "You know it is absolutely necessary to have a woman to whom one may confide a 'woman's thoughts' and who 'will be responsive'" (Cashin 2006, 178). Davis did not deny his deteriorating situation, including his loss of financial independence, and he too complained about the family's sorry lot. Less than two months after arriving in Canada and evidently devastated by still not having employment or investment income, he penned a letter to his brother Joseph exclaiming "I have no capital." He also noted that his pending treason trial helped to dash prospects to secure employment and made planning for the future more difficult. (Crist et al. 2008, 232).

If the formerly proud Southern patriarch was in a shameful way, what made things even worse was that he had become dependent on his wife and monies she controlled. By the time he arrived in Montreal, his wife had begun to handle the family's financial affairs, an arrangement not favourably looked upon by Southern patriarchs. In May 1867, the Davises survived on the remaining monies that Colin J. McRae, chief financial agent of the Confederate States in Europe, had sent Varina.[11] Although she had also received funds from other sources, including from the editor of *Vanity Fair,* Charles Fair Browne, Varina now faced the sad reality that her resources were almost depleted and her husband had no money whatsoever.[12] Struggling to save face, Davis instructed Harrison to contact Captain Watson Van Benthuysen, who supposedly still held Confederate funds in trust for Varina and the children. To Davis's dismay, when Harrison met Van Benthuysen in New York, he obtained only $1,190 of the nearly $9,000 that had been earmarked for Varina after the fall of Richmond (Cashin 2009, 171). Davis, who hoped to get some measure of independence *for himself* from the money Van Benthuysen received in trust for Varina and the children, was furious. Demonstrating self-righteous frustration, he alleged that Van Benthuysen was disreputable and accused him of having absconded with most of the money, which undoubtedly, he had. Davis then had nowhere to turn, except to Varina herself, and he had to "consult her on [all] financial matters" (Cashin 2009, 180). The First Family of the Confederacy, living on the poor side of Montreal, was an example of Southern patriarchy uprooted, and indeed *turned upside down.*

Caught in such an intricate web of social, political, and economic decline, Davis became miserable and slipped into deep depression, which precipitated his writing of sad times. Varina, too, expressed despair, saying "death in life is the most harrowing of all sorrows" (Cooper 2020, 589, 591). Davis's misery was evident even to a young child like Polly Ambler, Mason's granddaughter. When she saw Davis approaching the Mason home in Ontario, she thought him "looking so old, so careworn, emaciated and depressed." She said, "[A]fter one glance I turned from the window sobbing so violently that I could not control myself to go and greet him with the rest of the family" (Strode 1964, 315).

It was perhaps no coincidence that the young girl's observations came at a moment when the penniless former head of state stooped to accept charity, something Southern patriarchs dreaded and Davis himself had refused to do even during the Confederate retreat from Richmond. At Danville, Virginia, the Sutherlin family with whom Davis stayed recognized his plight, even if he himself did not realize how desperate it would become. When he left their home, they offered him $1,000 in gold, which he refused. Returning to Montreal on 5 June from his Toronto–Niagara *séjour,* Davis however realized that he had no choice but to accept charity, especially knowing that in Canada's largest city there was "nothing for me to do" (Crist et al. 2008, 211; Richardson 2018). The once noble patriarch simply had to endure the humiliation of accepting charity – and he did. Always analytical, he knew that he had been reduced to what Southern slaveholders called "begging in Canada," which they accused their runaways of doing.[13] Davis too had his hand out.

Looking "broken" and "with sunken cheeks and hollow eyes," the exiled Mississippian first took charity when he banked a donation of $500 that had been taken up by students at the University of Mississippi where he had previously given a commencement address emphasizing honour, achievement, and the duty of future leaders to contribute to progress (Davis 1991, 613). If accepting charity from students was astonishing, so was his acceptance of handouts from strangers in a new land. Disturbed by living in the slums, Davis seized an opportunity to put distance between his family and lower-sort neighbours when he accepted charity from John A. Lovell, a wealthy Montreal publisher and businessman who held Confederate leanings during the Civil War. Lovell pitied the Davis family's situation and thought they merited better. When he offered Davis spacious lodgings in his mansion across from Montreal's Christ Church Cathedral, the former

Confederate leader immediately accepted and moved his family, as well as Varina's mother and sister, into new quarters in early June (Strode 1964, 317).

But Davis obviously underestimated how disturbing accepting charity would be, even if it was the only way for his family to escape a shameful neighborhood of ex-slaves and poor immigrants. His loss of independence moving into Lovell's lodgings marked the beginning of a loss of autonomy that shaped much of his postbellum life, and it caused him much anguish, accentuating his already antisocial behaviour and intolerance of others, even family members. Davis began to shirk traditional patriarchal responsibilities and acted in a manner inconsistent with his old ways of caring for his dependents, particularly his wife and children. He became reclusive and left Varina to look after the family, even as she also had to deal with her gravely ill mother and disturbed sister. Simply put, Varina alone had to care for the extended Davis family and assume obligations that male heads of households traditionally fulfilled.

What made things most difficult for Varina was that the Davis children showed signs of instability, of which Davis himself must have been aware. Their heightened insecurity was not surprising given that they had lived in six different places in just a few years: the Brierfield plantation at Davis Bend, Washington, Montgomery, Richmond, Savannah, and now Montreal. Further, because Varina's aging mother had initially helped care for the children in Montreal, Varina felt responsible for her when she became seriously ill. She thought her mother "too old and delicate to be left alone" (Allen 1999, 416). Varina was also close to her sister Margaret and, after Margaret gave birth to a child out of wedlock, fretted constantly about her, worrying too about her chances of ever finding a decent husband. In this context, Davis's failure to assume family responsibilities added significantly to Varina's already heavy burden. When he showed signs of deeper depression and became demanding, he made life more difficult for her. In Montreal and the Eastern Townships, he sought to be alone, he wanted only to ruminate about the past, and he complained that he was "disturbed by the activities" of his own children. Their noise, he said, "sounded like trumpets in his ears" (Strode 1964, 314, 317).

When the family moved into the Lovell mansion, which prominent Montrealers frequented, Davis felt shamed by his dependency and became increasingly reclusive as he sought to avoid Lovell's guests. During his short time at the mansion, Davis "always retired early," even if doing so disturbed Varina who felt obliged to be social and help entertain Lovell's guests. But she too soon confessed to feeling shame when she exposed her outdated wardrobe to the city's better sorts who sported the latest in fashion. Her discomfort must have added to her husband's embarrassment. As a couple, the Davises confronted a new problem: how to hide their shame as "threadbare, great folks" and shun public gatherings while living in a mansion that stood at the centre of Montreal society (Cashin 2006, 180).

After only about one week, the Davises decided that they had to leave the mansion, and they signed a lease to rent a house until September at 1181 Mountain Street between Montreal's St Catherine and Dorchester streets. By 7 June, they had taken occupancy of the house (Crist et al. 2008, 234; Epps 1982, 11). Although it was a "narrow three-story house," described as "severe and unattractive," it placed the Davises at some distance from distinguished Montreal society and allowed them to avoid public gatherings. But when they were invited to a gala performance of the comedy *The Rivals* at the Theatre Royal on 18 July, they felt obliged to attend since the show was a fund-raiser "for the suffering South." Feeling shame, Davis sought to enter discreetly after the first act but, when he was recognized, was forced to rise and only managed to bow "with [a] grave, half melancholy smile to repeated cheers." (Crist et al. 2008, xliv, 243). He reportedly looked weary, weak, and dispirited – like a person enduring sad and shameful times. He seemed to be a fallen leader "lost in deep distracted thought" and living "the tale of disaster" that had been initiated by the Confederate defeat (Davis 1991, 658). He stooped again to accept charity. Unable to pay the rent for even an ordinary dwelling, Davis accepted an anonymous Confederate donor's offer to cover the expense of the lease of the Mountain Street house (Strode 1964, 318). He evinced resentment and shame regarding his situation when he wrote to Colin McRae wanting to "rebut the idea that I had made solicitation for aid" (Crist et al. 2008, 229).

It was not surprising then that Davis's morale failed to improve while living at the Mountain Street house. He informed Burton Harrison that his condition was "little better than a state of vegetation" (Cooper 2020, 569). He also told his brother Joseph of his concerns and spoke of his sorrow, stressing his weakened condition as well, and complained that he could hardly write. He confessed that "[a] few letters are as much as I can do without sensibly feeling the effort both mentally and physically [*sic*]." The former Confederate chief also exposed his financial angst as he informed Joseph that no business opportunities had yet surfaced. He said that the unresolved treason charges against him exacerbated his sad state and made it impossible for him "to form plans for the future." A few days later, Davis again complained to Colin J. McRae that he had not found any means to provide for his family. It was in such downcast circumstances that he put aside another pillar of Southern honour that had always shaped his behaviour since his days at West Point – magnanimity and social grace. He also refused to pen a history of the Confederacy and his memoirs, even if doing so might have secured him much-needed income.

William B. Reed, a member of his legal team and Ambrose D. Mann, a friend and colleague, urged him to do so, particularly as leading newspapers such as *The New York Times* reported rumours that Davis was preparing to undertake a historical overview of the 1860–67 period that would be a "really valuable contribution." Varina and his brother Joseph also prodded him. "As to your future occupation, I had thought of you writing a history of the Confederacy," Joseph suggested in a letter dated 30 June. Although Davis admitted that such a work would be useful, he declared himself not up to the task and explained to Varina that he could not "speak of my dead so soon" (Crist et al. 2008, 211, 221, 224, 232, 234.)[14]

Davis continued to withdraw and by mid-summer 1867, he just "sat in a room" with Varina's ailing mother and "talked softly of happier days"– something he felt he could do in less expensive rural lodgings (Strode 1964, 314). Varina complained that her husband now looked terrible, and she spoke about his discouragement. As Joan Cashin so correctly puts it, the Davises were fallen celebrities; at best Davis was in "political limbo with legal problems that could conceivably result in another prison term," and the family was "homeless" (Cashin 2009, 183). As the summer of 1867 progressed, the prospects of the Confederacy's only first couple were unchanged. "We had very little," Varina later wrote, "and my husband's health was apparently gone … His hair and beard were fast turning white. His face was haggard and careworn, while his entire looks and demeanour showed an old, broken-down man" (Epps 1982, 11).[15]

In Varina's words, Davis was "floating uprooted" and worse, so was the entire family (Allen 1999, 490; Davis 1991, 634). Varina became exasperated, no longer able to entertain or engage socially as she had done in the past. She remained "ashamed of her outdated wardrobe" and grumbled that neither she nor her husband had the money required for her to dress properly. Except for their unavoidable attendance at *The Rivals*, the Davises declined invitations to receptions, public gatherings, and other attractions – entertainment Varina had adored in Washington and Richmond (Crist et al. 2008, 243). Her children suffered too, and she knew it. Like her mother, Maggie, now in her teens, moaned about her outdated clothes and young Billy said that he "wanted his father to earn some money so they could be rich again" (Cashin 2009, 182, 181). He told his parents that it was "unfair that only he among his buddies had to borrow a crossbow" (Cooper 2020, 569). The Davis children too had taken a tumble and so had the extended Davis family, which further augmented the former Confederate president's shame for failing to help them. Traditions of Southern honour required patriarchs to care for extended family. In Canada, Davis's inability to help Varina's ailing mother who had cared for the Davis children during his incarceration, her sister Margaret who had given birth to a child out-of-wedlock, and her unemployed brothers Beckett and Jeffy D., who both served in the Confederate Army and were unemployed in Montreal, contributed to Davis's dishonour. He became more reclusive and with the family's deteriorating finances and poverty weighing on Varina and him, the stage was set for the move to the Eastern Townships where lodging was cheaper and crowds were fewer.[16]

JEFFERSON DAVIS *in* LENNOXVILLE

Lennoxville became the Davis family's next residence, albeit one that would again prove temporary. Varina reported on 6 September that she had "settled in," and Davis followed a few weeks later. "I am about to leave this place (i.e., Montreal)," Davis wrote on 23 September, "the term for which our house was taken has expired" (Crist et al., 234, 248). The couple found Lennoxville attractive for several reasons. Located ninety-five miles southeast of Montreal in Ascot Township, the village had been established "at the confluence of the St Francis and Massawippi Rivers" and had a predominantly anglophone population of some 600 persons as well as "two churches, two large hotels and a great many stores and shops" (Atto 1975, 13, 21, 24). Bishop's College School and Bishop's University lay at the heart of village life and when the Davises arrived, Lennoxville had become an important railway connection on the Sherbrooke, Eastern Townships & Kennebec Railroad. Farming, logging, and mining activities dotted the village's outskirts (Crist et al. 2008, 92). In addition to the possible savings that modest small-town lodging offered, Davis could escape the urban realities and noise that "tormented" him (Strode 1964, 314). Additionally, the Davises' ten-year-old son, Jefferson Jr, had already spent a year at Mrs Morris's School in the village, and the couple planned to send him to Bishop's College School where William was enrolled.[17] Further, the Davises had a good first impression of Lennoxville when they visited the area on 26 June 1867, and crowds had cheered them at both the Sherbrooke and Lennoxville railway stations.[18]

Davis relocated to Lennoxville hoping also to resolve his precarious financial position. In early July, Frederick W. Terrill of Sherbrooke presented Davis with an investment opportunity in an Eastern Townships copper mine saying that unless he was "altogether mistaken," Davis's name would encourage "subscriptions to stock in almost unlimited amounts." Assuring Davis that neither he nor third party investors would be let down, Terrill claimed he would soon be positioned to provide Davis "with a copy of a reliable report and also of an assay" showing that a "clear profit of seventy-five thousand dollars" could be anticipated from the property he sought to develop (Crist et al. 2008, 227).[19] Since this was Davis's only financial opportunity after arriving in Canada, he quickly seized it, signing a "Memorandum of Agreement" and advancing $2,000 to acquire half of Terrill's rights in the mine. Davis agreed "to use his influence in turning the property to the best account" and the men declared their intention "to form a Joint Stock Company … for the development and working of the mining property" (Crist et al. 2008, 227). Cautiously optimistic, Davis wrote to his brother Joseph confirming his "hope to be able to make something out of it" even if he had invested very little capital. Suggesting that he might have found a way to restore his ability to care for his dependents, Davis concluded that "in mining I think there is profitable employment to be found" (Crist et al. 2008, 230).

By some accounts, Davis's initial expectations appeared reasonable. Copper mining in the Eastern Townships, first noted in the 1847–48 geological survey of Canada, expanded throughout the 1850s and several leading companies began exploiting deposits within a fifty-mile radius of Lennoxville in such places as Acton, Ascot, Cleveland, Halifax, Inverness, Leeds, Melbourne, New Ireland, and Upton. By 1859, the Acton mine was reputed to be "the largest copper mine in the world." Indeed, during the period 1859–66, the Eastern Townships experienced a veritable "mining boom" that saw the sinking of "hundreds of prospect shafts." Boosted in part by the American Civil War, copper demand grew exponentially, and the metal's market price tripled in the first half of the 1860s. Although such market conditions resulted in "great excitement [in the Townships]," Davis, arriving in 1867, soon found out that he was late for the party (Quebec 1915, 13, 18, 19, 20).

Davis took up lodgings in Clarke's Hotel, also known as the British American Hotel, located on the northwest corner of Lennoxville's Queen and College streets.[20] The hotel, owned and operated by Stephen and Hannah G. Clarke, catered "mostly to traveling salesmen and itinerant show folk," which could have afforded Davis an opportunity to participate fully in the village's daily life and special events (Strode 1964, 321).[21] Writing to his daughter, Margaret, on 28 October, Davis stated that "this is a very quiet residence, therefore pleasant to me. The weather has been fine for our out door exercise and we have taken advantage of it" (Crist et al. 2008, 254). In a similar tone, Davis informed Charles Helm on 30 October, approximately one month after moving to Lennoxville, that "this is a very quiet place and so far agreeable to me" (Crist et al. 2008, 257). Not surprisingly, however, given his preoccupation with his deteriorating financial situation, low self-esteem, and mood swings, Davis socialized and interacted with only a few village residents, notably the Rawsons, Scarths, Hales, and the Cummins family. The Rawsons, an English family, lived "a quarter of a mile from the hotel" and

Figure 7.1 Advertisement for Clarke's Hotel.

"MR. CLARKE begs to thank the public for their kind patronage, and at same time would inform them that he has entirely rebuilt his hotel, and fitted it out with every modern convenience. Travellers will find Lennoxville an attractive place, and MR. CLARKE'S HOTEL second to none in the Townships."

frequently invited the Davises for dinner (Strode 1964, 321). Stephen Cummins's house, located at 3033 College Street and known as "Rock Grove," was also a short distance from Clarke's Hotel. With "spacious grounds," it had an elegance that appealed to the Davises. The Cummins children– Mary, Jennie, Kate, and Stephen – were also "a great attraction for the Davis children" (Holtham 1975, 44). Stephen Cummins claimed that during the evenings at Rock Grove "Mr Davis forgot his troubles ... as they sang Canadian songs and war songs of the South that had filtered up into Canada on the tongues of Southern sympathizers" (Price 1940, 45). Although Davis sometimes strolled around the grounds of Bishop's College and occasionally played chess with the Reverend William Richmond who taught at the school, he remained mostly a solitary figure throughout his days in Lennoxville (Holtham 1975, 46). Hannah Clarke remembered that he "kept to his room much of the time" (Price 1940, 1945).

If Davis's trepidation about his loss of status, income, and wealth and his shame for failing to fulfill his patriarchal duties heightened his anguish, in early October 1867 a letter from his attorney regarding his forthcoming treason trial in November added to his angst. "The appointed day is Nov. 25," announced O'Conor, but he also warned that "the jury will be composed of 8 or 9 negroes and

3 or 4 of the meanest whites who can be found in Richmond." He ended by stating, "we can do nothing but prepare our minds and our materials for a confrontation of the enemy." Further stoking Davis's nervousness, O'Conor informed him that although the trial might be pushed to May 1868, Davis's presence in Richmond for the initially scheduled November hearing could not "be dispensed with." In late October, the attorney wrote again, informing Davis that the trial date would almost certainly be delayed until May. He suggested that while Davis still had to appear in Richmond in November, he would likely be free by early December to take a Southern holiday and escape the Canadian cold. Davis, increasingly unsettled, penned a note to Charles Helm revealing his anxiety regarding his possible fate in court. "The time is so near," he said, complaining also that he was "disappointed at the want of positive information." He wrote to his niece as well, speaking of his annoyance about the turn of events and the uncertainty he endured (Crist et al. 2008, 249, 255, 258, 259, 260).

On 19 November, Davis departed by rail for New York, where he boarded the *Albemarle* and arrived at Richmond three days later. On 26 November, his trial was postponed until 22 March 1868, and his bail bond was extended. Davis then left the Virginia capital for Baltimore where on 30 November he reunited with Varina whose mother had passed away in Montreal the week before.[22] Avoiding the Canadian winter, the couple visited familiar territory in the deep South, principally Mississippi and Louisiana. They also travelled to Havana to spend Christmas at the Hotel Cubano, "a haven for Confederates." Evidence suggests, however, that during the 129 days that Davis was away from Lennoxville he remained preoccupied with his ever-bleaker financial prospects and his uncertain legal fate, which continued to undermine his capacity to care for his family and re-establish his reputation. Writing to James M. Howry on 8 February, Davis confessed that he "hope[d] to receive letters which will inform me whether it will be necessary for me to attend the US Court in Richmond." In another letter written ten days later, he noted that he was "expecting to hear from my lawyers whether or not there will be a necessity for my presence in Richmond at the March meeting of the court." The Davis trial was indeed again postponed and on 6 March he received notice "that his presence was not required in Richmond" (Crist et al. 2008, 261, 272, 274, 279, 280, 283).[23]

Most disconcerting was the news Davis received concerning the viability of his Eastern Townships copper mining venture. In January and February 1868, Terrill informed him that their proposed property development, including the Cillis and Westbury mines, were failing to attract the interest of investors and even efforts to market the projects in England, led by William H. Gee, had been "discouraging."

Terrill suggested that Davis reach out to Cornelius Vanderbilt for assistance in financing mine development or that Davis consider going to England to help Gee generate interest in the venture (Crist et al. 2008, 268, 275). Such unravelling of his only promising business opportunity must have added to Davis's financial trepidation; so too did another failed attempt to recover $1,500 that Varina had entrusted to the New Orleans firm of Byrne, Vance & Company two years earlier. Writing to his nephew Hugh Robert Davis, the impoverished former Confederate leader spoke of "pecuniary disappointment" as he recounted Byrne's denial of "all memory of a trust fund" that Varina held with his firm. Indicating the precariousness of the couple's finances, the former Confederate leader said that although "the amount of money was small, to the Davises it was "great" – particularly given their circumstances (Crist et al. 2008, 276, 277, 279).

Little changed during Davis's second period in Lennoxville from 28 March to 23 July 1868. Saddled with financial problems and legal uncertainties, Davis continued to wrestle with issues related to his reputation and honour. The March trial date was pushed back and in May, O'Conor wrote to him saying, "When the trial will begin is unclear." Irritated by delays, which he claimed prevented him from getting on with his life, he displayed increased angst as details of the treason charges against him surfaced. Writing to Mason, he railed at "the new indictment so long kept secret" and told his friend that he faced "thirteen counts being specifications of different times and places when and where I did acts which are charged as overt acts of treason against the US." His pessimism mounted and he concluded, "The prospect of anything approaching to a fair trial is certainly bad" (Crist et al. 2008, 284, 285, 288, 289). And through the spring and early summer, Davis suffered more anxiety resulting from notification of additional trial delays. Frustrated, he wrote to Robert Ould, a member of his legal team, asking when the case was "really supposed to go to trial." In June, after Justice Salmon Chase issued a continuance of the trial until November 1868, Davis was beyond himself and complained that legal uncertainty damaged his reputation and jeopardized his ability to fulfill his patriarchal duty of caring for his dependents. "The constant pressure of this prosecution embarrasses me," protested Davis, adding that his unresolved legal situation continued to undermine his "attempt to make a support for my family" (Crist et al. 2008, 303).[24]

Grappling with his plight, Davis also lamented to Mason about how such postponements, which he branded "malignant persecution," prevented him from redressing his "ruined fortunes." In desperation he leaned toward following up on Terrill's suggestion about going to England to market their mining venture and possibly partner in a commission house. Davis first wrote of his interest in travelling to England in a letter to Colin J. McRae on 12 June 1867, in which he explained that "deprived of means for the support of my family … [he] had it in contemplation to form a business connection in Liverpool," which his brother Joseph had earlier encouraged him to do. Thinking that England could be "pecuniarily" advantageous to him, Davis thus informed his niece Lucinda that he was hoping "to find a residence where living is cheaper than here and schools better." Corresponding with Howell Cobb on 6 July, Davis confirmed his intention to depart Lennoxville and informed her that he had "decided to go to Liverpool." At this point, Davis seemed to have concluded that there was little chance "to induce English capitalists to speculate in [Eastern Townships] mining properties." His sights were now set on seeing "what may be done in establishing a commission house, especially for cotton and tobacco" (Crist et al. 2008, 211, 267, 289, 298).[25]

DAVIS DEPARTS *the* EASTERN TOWNSHIPS

Davis left Lennoxville permanently on 23 July, and two days later, accompanied by Varina and the children, he joined the Rawson family on board the steamer *The Austrian* departing for Liverpool from Quebec City. They arrived in England on 4 August with the former Confederate leader still looking "wretchedly" (Crist et al. 2008, 309, 310, 312). Unfortunately, as Varina had put it a few days earlier in a letter to Mary Ann Cobb, they were still "floating uprooted" or "sadly wandering" as Felicity Allen describes it. They still sought to "anchor somewhere" but, unfortunately, for the remainder of their days they would often also be "floating apart" (Allen 1999, 490). The catalyst for Davis's departure was a near-tragic incident that could be interpreted both physically and metaphorically, encapsulating also Davis's failure to regain his status and honour as a Southern patriarch during his time in Montreal and the Eastern Townships. The "dispirited" former Confederate president, baby Winnie in his arms, missed his step and tumbled down the stairs at Clarke's Hotel, breaking two ribs, striking his head, and suffering a severe concussion. When he regained consciousness, "he lay on the verge of eternity for many days" (Epps 1982; Allen 1999, 496). Dr David Thomas Robertson, "who was sent for in a hurry," treated Davis during the next several days and ended up advising "on an entire change of climate and scene" for his patient, knowing full well that their mutual friends, the Rawsons, had reserved accommodations on *The Austrian*, a transatlantic steamer scheduled to leave for England, and that Davis could travel with them (Crist et al. 2008, 309–10; Epps 1982). Davis had now become dependent on recent acquaintances, not merely Varina. Feeble and in the care of others, Davis left the Eastern Townships still searching for vindication, autonomy, reputation, and the honour of a Southern patriarch who cared for and protected his immediate and extended family.

In sum, Davis's time spent in Lennoxville failed to resolve his financial and legal challenges. Residing in Montreal and the Eastern Townships, Davis was unable to reclaim his honour and status and remained plagued by his inability to support his family and resolve his legal uncertainty. Lennoxville, while proving to be a short-term, temporary way-station – a place of geographic transition in the post-imprisonment life of the former Confederate president – significantly accelerated and ultimately solidified his transformation to that of dependent. What impact did Davis's presence, while in residence between September 1867 and July 1868, have on the Townships? While selectively engaging local inhabitants of Lennoxville, Davis, the most high-profile individual from outside the newly created Canadian nation to ever reside in the village, appears to have imparted little more than a fleeting moment of engagement for a small group of individuals. There are no meaningful or lasting indicators of his social, cultural, educational, political, or economic impact on the Eastern Townships. He entered and ultimately exited Lennoxville a defeated and dishonoured Southern paterfamilias in search of a better life.[26]

Varina perhaps said it best. As a couple, they still sought to escape "the wretched sense of idleness that has so galled us." She might have said shamed us, especially since Jefferson Davis never regained the autonomy and independence he desired. And shame they would still share in later years, especially when Davis took up residency on the Biloxi estate of Sarah Dorsey, a wealthy widow and admirer who upon her death willed the estate to him, thus sealing his dependence on her. Jefferson Davis's Montreal and Eastern Townships transition charted a path, as well as a pattern, of dependency that remained fundamentally unchanged throughout his postbellum years. Davis's patriarchy was not just uprooted; it was turned upside down (Allen 1999, 496).

Notes

1 It is interesting to note how in the mid-nineteenth century, Canadian elites' patrician visions were also shaped by both influences and tensions between their public and private lives (Little 2013, especially xii–xiii and 9–10).

2 Davis, encouraged by his wife Varina to accept an invitation from James Mason to visit him at his home on the Niagara Peninsula, had departed for Toronto by steamer, via Prescott and Kingston, on 29 May 1867 (Richardson 2018).

3 Richardson 2018; James Murray Mason served as Confederate Commissioner to Great Britain and France, Beverley Tucker as Confederate economic agent in France, England,

and Canada, Charles John Helm as Confederate agent in Havana, and Jubal Anderson Early as a Confederate General.

4 James C. Curtis coined the expression "Search for Vindication" in his 1976 book, *Andrew Jackson and the Search for Vindication* (Boston: Little, Brown, 1976).

5 The Davises, "accompanied by Burton, Ould, Dr Cooper, Burton N. Harrison, and Joseph R. Davis (Jefferson's elder brother, by twenty-three years), were escorted to the steamer landing." On board the *John Sylvester* were "federal marshals John Underwood and W.A. Duncan." The Davises occupied the same rooms at the Spotswood Hotel that they had used "when they first arrived in [Richmond] in May 1861" (Crist et al. 2008, 203).

6 Davis's legal team consisted of O'Conor, George Shea, Robert Ould, William B. Reed, and John Randolph Tucker (Crist et al. 2008, 203). O'Conor provided written notification to US Attorney General Henry Stanbery on 2 May to indicate that Brigadier General Henry S. Burton, the commanding officer at Fort Monroe, was required to produce Davis for his court appearance in Richmond (University of Chicago Library, Jefferson Davis Trial Papers).

7 The full listing of the twenty-five individuals who provided support in the amount of $100,000 for Davis's bond and attested to his recognizance is listed in Crist et al. (2008, 198). "After the legalities of signing the bond, Davis left immediately, pursued by a joyful crowd" (204). News of Davis's release from Fort Monroe was viewed as a long overdue, positive development by Confederate sympathizers. Robert E. Lee's letter of 1 June to Davis is typical of this perspective: "Your release has lifted a load from my heart which I have not words to tell, and my daily prayer to the great Ruler of the World, is that he may shield you from all future harm, guard you from all evil, and give you that peace which the world can not take away. That the rest of your days may be triumphantly happy, is the sincere and earnest wish of your most obt. Faithful friend & svt." (208). John Slidell, Confederate commissioner to France during the Civil War, wrote to Davis on 18 June to express his deep personal pleasure at Davis's "release from the bondage of the Philistines" (218).

8 Davis's stay in New York was designed to allow him to rest and to consult with O'Conor, his lead attorney. He was, however, "besieged at the hotel" and was subsequently taken to O'Conor's "suburban home late on Friday the 17th" (204).

9 At some point after 14 May, Varina returned to Fortress Monroe to help her sister and Mary Ahern pack their belongings. Varina arrived in Montreal on 22 May (Crist et al. 2008, 204).

10 See Bertram Wyatt Brown's reference to what William Alexander Percy called the "Broad Sword Tradition" (Wyatt-Brown 2007, xvi).

11 McRae had also sent "Mr O'Conor £3,000 with instructions to pay to you any balance that might be left after defraying the expenses of your trial" (Crist et al. 2008, 200). McRae emphasized in an 18 May letter to Davis that "at one point I hoped to have had it in my power to have made larger provision for you. But circumstances have prevented me from doing so" (200). Davis's correspondence to McRae, dated 9 July 1867, observed that "in placing funds in the hands of my counsel to defray the expenses of my trial, and instructing him to pay to me any balance which remained, I supposed you acted as the financial agent of the Confederate states" (229). On 12 June and again on 15 June, McRae wrote to Davis in Montreal pledging to also secure £2,000 in credit from the London

Joint Stock Bank for Davis's use (217, 218, 228, 229). McRae who was "in personal financial straits" following the Civil War was ultimately sued for financial misconduct regarding "nonexistent Confederate balances in England and the Continent" (229).

12 Cashin (2009, 171).

13 For a discussion of "begging" in Canada, see Hembree (1991).

14 As the editors of *The Papers of Jefferson Davis* note, "Much of Davis' official correspondence and some personal items were taken to Canada by his sister-in-law in 1865; the official records were deposited in the Bank of Montreal. Davis' counsel George Shea, accompanied by Joseph R. Davis, examined them in January 1866 and asked Margaret Howell to copy some letters for him. Varina remembered Davis' own reaction to looking over the documents in [presumably between May and mid-September] 1867: 'let us put them by for awhile, I cannot speak of my dead so soon'" (Crist et al. 2008, 234).

15 As quoted in *The Record*, Sherbrooke, 25 August 1982, 11. Varina's physical description of her husband in the summer of 1867 comports with an official portrait taken by noted Montreal photographer William Notman of Jefferson and Varina at that time. The portrait is in the holdings of the McCord Museum. A copy of the photograph appears in the *Montreal Gazette* (Kalbfleisch 2017).

16 Varina departed Montreal on 8 July to visit a variety of family members and friends in Bethlehem (Pennsylvania), Charleston (South Carolina), Augusta and Athens (Georgia), Richmond (Virginia), and New York (New York). She returned to Montreal in late August or very early September. See Crist et al. (2008, 233).

17 Bishop's College School or BCS, as it was affectionately known, was a small Anglican private boarding school catering to the well-to-do families of Montreal and Toronto" (Carter 1971, 133).

18 While on the platform of the Sherbrooke Railway Station, Davis quickly addressed the assembled audience by expressing his gratitude "most kindly for this hearty British reception, which I take as a manifestation of your sympathy and good-will for one in misfortune" (*New York Times* 1867; Crist et al. 2008, xliv, 219–20).

19 Terrill, a politician, lawyer, and businessman, was born in the Eastern Townships in the village of Stanstead on 2 December 1836. He served as a member of the legislative assembly of the Province of Canada for Stanstead in 1851 and 1852. ETRC website, Accessed 15 December 2022, https://www.townshipsarchives.ca/frederick-william-terrill-fonds.

20 The history of Clarke's Hotel, prior to and following Davis's departure from Lennoxville, is most fully chronicled in Lane (1970, 181–4) and Crist et al. (2008, 283).

21 On Davis's impressions, see also Crist et al. (2008, 254, 257, and 259–60) and Carter (1971, 134).

22 Varina's mother died on 24 November at the Lovell home in Montreal. Her body was interred on 27 November in the city's Mount Royal Cemetery. Writing to Joseph R. Anderson on 27 November, Jefferson Davis noted "a telegram received last night announced to me the death of my Mother-in-law Mrs Howell. She is to be buried to-day" (Crist et al. 2008, 260).

23 For a copy of the joint agreement of 6 March to postpone Davis's trial, consult Document 14, University of Chicago Library, Jefferson Davis Trial Papers. MS 979, 1865–1868. Robert Ould telegrammed Davis on 9 March stating that "the trial will be continued … the [new] day will be fixed on the 12th" (Crist et al. 2008, 280–1). Davis received further correspon-

dence from members of his legal team – e.g., O'Conor (11 March), Ould (11 March), and Isaac H. Carrington (24 March) – that while the trial was postponed to 14 April, the "object is to continue the case to Saturday 2nd May" (Crist et al. 2008, 281). The continuance can again be traced to internal concerns regarding the sufficiency and quality of the government's trial preparations. See the 18 February 1868 letter from Evarts to Chandler, Document 13, University of Chicago Library, Jefferson Davis Trial Papers. MS 979, 1865–1868.

24 The timing of Davis's mounting focus and concern over his potential fate at this upcoming trial, while understandable, may have been misplaced. In addition to the unavailability of Chief Justice Chase to preside over the trial in late November 1867, an examination of the state of advance preparations by the prosecution in October and November illustrates that the US government's case against Davis was far from complete. General H.H. Wells of Alexandria, Virginia and Richard H. Dana Jr of Boston joined the prosecution team as assistant special counsels in late October. Henry Stanbery, US attorney general, reminded L.H. Chandler, US district attorney for Richmond, on 25 October that "I need not urge upon you the necessity of thorough preparation for the trial in this case, now so near at hand" (Stanbery 1867 [b]). The very thoroughness of those preparations was explicitly raised and questioned by prosecutor William Evarts and Richard Dana in correspondence to Stanbery as late as 2 November:

> the first point to which we think attention should be given, as of the greatest importance and responsibility, is the preparation of an indictment, in view of the evidence upon which and the witnesses by whom, it is to be supported at the trial. Although, as we understand, an indictment has heretofore been found, yet neither in framing it as a pleading, nor in selecting the overt acts averred as the body of the crime, nor in the scrutiny of the evidence by which the averments are to be maintained, has the matter been submitted to the attention of the counsel specifically retained for the prosecution ... What steps may have been recently taken by the US Attorney for Virginia, towards the preparation and finding of an indictment upon which the prosecution would expect to rely, we are as yet without information ... Whenever the District Attorney shall advise us that he is ready to take up this subject we shall give the matter the proper attention. (Evarts and Dana 1867)

Attorney General Stanbery in turn raised these concerns in a 4 November letter to Chandler:

> I beg to call your special attention to the first point referred to in their letter, viz., the preparation of the indictment, and I would suggest that, without delay, you frame such an indictment as you think necessary, and submit it to your associate counsel for revision, and, if deemed necessary by you or them, to arrange for a consultation here either as to the indictment or any other matter which you deem necessary. It would be well, besides preparing for the indictment, to prepare carefully, an abstract of the proofs necessary to be made out, and of the evidence, oral or written, which you expect to adduce, and to furnish your associates with such an abstract also for their consideration. The time fixed for the trial being so near at hand, I deem it proper again to call your early attention to this important subject, and to ask you to acknowledge promptly the receipt of this communication, and to advise me what steps you have taken towards the preparation of this case. (Stanbery1867[b])

The prosecution, almost up until the trial date, continued to issue subpoenas for witnesses, including to General Horace Porter [20 November] and General J.G. Parke [21 November] (United States, 20 November and United States, 21 November). All documents contained in the archives of the University of Chicago Library, Jefferson Davis Trial Papers. MS 979, 1865–1868. Crist et al. (2008, 297, 298, 302, 303).

25 Varina also sent correspondence to Mary Ann Cobb, Walter H. Taylor, and John W. Garrett notifying them of her family's pending departure for England and her husband's business plans. She specificially "asked Taylor and Garrett to solicit cotton business from leading merchants in Norfolk and Baltimore," indicating that Davis would likely be engaging in "a partnership with an Englishman of good character and high standing … there will be no risk" (Crist et. al. 2008, 309. 309).

26 Notably, some 150 years later, a defeated Jefferson Davis would emerge as a key target in efforts to remove if not erase physical reminders of the racism and white supremacy associated with his person as the only-ever president of the Confederacy. A plaque, affixed to the Hudson's Bay Company retail store in Montreal by the United Daughters of the Confederacy, commemorating Davis's residency in the city during the summer of 1867, was physically removed on 15 August 2017 (Canadian Press 2017, Leavitt 2017). In the American South, several Davis memorials, monuments, buildings, and even highways have been removed or re-named (Connolly and Wang 2017; Bailey 2020; Levenson 2020; Alonso 2020).

References

Allen, Felicity. 1999. *Jefferson Davis: Unconquerable Heart*. Columbia: University of Missouri Press.

Alonso, Melissa. 2020. "New Orleans to Rename Jefferson Davis Parkway after Push from Kamala Harris." CNN. 20 August. https://www.cnn.com/2020/08/20/politics/norman-c-francis-jefferson-davis-parkway-kamala-harris/index.html.

Atto, Kathleen H. 1975. "'Location and Topography,' 'Description,' and 'Early History of Lennoxville.'" In *Lennoxville*, vol. 1, edited by Kathleen H. Atto and committee, 13–15. Lennoxville: Lennoxville-Ascot Historical and Museum Society.

Bailey, Phillip M. 2020. "'Sins of our past': After 84 Years, Jefferson Davis Statue Removed from Kentucky Capitol." *Louisville Courier Journal*, 13 June. https://www.courier-journal.com/story/news/politics/2020/06/13/confederate-statues-jefferson-davis-removed-kentucky-capitol/3179569001/.

Berman, Mark, and Ben Guarino. 2020. "Mississippi Governor Signs Bill Changing State's Flag, Abandoning Confederate's Symbol." *Washington Post*, 20 June. https://www.washingtonpost.com/national/mississippi-flag-confederacy-removed/2020/06/30/f47df152-baed-11ea-8cf5-9c1b8d7f84c6_story.html.

Boyle, Virginia Frazer. 1929. "Jefferson Davis in Canada." *Confederate Veteran* 37 (5 March): 89–93.

Canadian Press. 2017 "Plaque Honouring Jefferson Davis Removed from Montreal Building." *Globe and Mail*, 15 August. https://www.theglobeandmail.com/news/

national/plaque-honouring-jefferson-davis-removed-from-montreal-building/article35996978/.
Carter, George E. 1971. "A Note on Jefferson Davis in Canada – His Stay in Lennoxville, Quebec." *Journal of Mississippi History* 33 (2): 133–9.
Cashin, Joan E. 2006. *First Lady of the Confederacy: Varina Davis's Civil War.* Cambridge, MA. The Belknap Press of Harvard University Press.
Connolly, Daniel, and Vivian Wang. 2017. "Confederate Statues in Memphis Are *Removed* after City Council Vote." *New York Times*. 20 December. https://www.nytimes.com/2017/12/20/us/statue-memphis-removed.html.
Cooper, William James Jr. 2009. "Jefferson Davis and the Meaning of War." *The Register of the Kentucky Historical Society* 107 (2): 147–61.
– 2000. *Jefferson Davis, American*. New York: Alfred A. Knopf.
Crist, Lynda Lasswell. n.d. "Jefferson Davis 1808–1899." Jefferson Davis Presidential Library, Jefferson Davis Lesson Plans. https://www.visitbeauvoir.org/beauvoir-resource-library.
Crist, Lynda Lasswell, Suzanne Scott Gibbs, Brady L. Hutchinson, and Elizabeth Henson Smith, eds. 2008. *The Papers of Jefferson Davis*. Vol. 12, June 1865–December 1870. Baton Rouge: Louisiana State University Press.
Curtis, James C. 1976. *Andrew Jackson and the Search for Vindication*. Boston: Little Brown.
Davis, William C. 1991. *Jefferson Davis, the Man and His Hour.* New York: HarperCollins.
Denison, George T. 1901. *Soldiering in Canada: Recollections and Experiences*. Toronto: G.N. Morang & Co.
Epps, Bernard. 1982. "Jefferson Davis: On the Verge of Eternity in Lennoxville." *Sherbrooke Record*, 25 August, 11.
Escot, Paul D. 1978. *After Secession: Jefferson Davis and the Failure of Confederate Nationalism*. Baton Rouge: Louisiana State University Press.
Hembree, Michael F. 1991. "The Question of 'Begging': Fugitive Slave Relief in Canada, 1830–1865." *Civil War History* 37, no. 4 (December 1991): 314–27.
Herzfeld, Matt. 2012. "John Wilkes Booth Lived Here: How Montreal Fell for the Confederacy." *The McGill Daily*, 26 January. https://www.mcgilldaily.com/2012/01/john-wilkes-booth-lived-here/.
Holtham, Bartley N. 1975. "Jefferson Davis." In *Lennoxville*, Volume 1, edited by Kathleen H. Atto and committee, 43–6. Lennoxville: Lennoxville-Ascot Historical and Museum Society.
Kalbfleisch, John. 2017. "From the Archives: Jefferson Davis and His Family Found Refuge in Montreal." *Montreal Gazette*, 25 November. https://montrealgazette.com/sponsored/mtl-375th/from-the-archives-jefferson-davis-and-family-found-refuge-in-montreal.
Kaufman, Fred. 1946. "Jefferson Davis at Lennoxville." *Montreal Gazette*, 7 January 1946.
Leavitt, Sarah. 2017. "Confederate Plaque on Montreal Hudson's Bay Store Removed." CBC *News*. 15 August. https://www.cbc.ca/news/canada/montreal/jefferson-davis-confederate-plaque-montreal-1.4248206.
Levenson, Michael. 2020. "Protestors Topple Statue of Jefferson Davis on Richmond's Monument Avenue." *New York Times*. 11 June. https://www.nytimes.com/2020/06/11/us/Jefferson-Davis-Statue-Richmond.html.

Little, J.I. 2013. *Patrician Liberal: The Public and Private Life of Sir Henri-Gustave Joly de Lotbinière*. Toronto: University of Toronto Press.

McElroy, Robert. 1937. *Jefferson Davis: The Unreal and the Real*. New York: Smithmark.

McIntosh, James T., ed. 1974. *Papers of Jefferson Davis*, vol. 2. (June 1841–July 1846). Baton Rouge: Louisiana State University Press.

McKitrick, Eric L. 1963. *Slavery Defended: The Views of the Old South*. Englewood Cliffs, NJ: Prentice-Hall.

Monroe, Haskell M., and James T. McIntosh, eds. 1971. *Papers of Jefferson Davis*, vol. 1 (1808–1840). Baton Rouge: Louisiana State University Press.

New York Times. 1867. "Jefferson Davis Repeats His Speech to the Canadians." 7 July. http://timesmachine.nytimes.com/timesmachine/1867/07/07/b0212328.html?pageNumber=1.

Pearsall, Sarah M.S. 2010. "'Citizens of the World': Men, Women, and Country in the Age of Revolution." In *Old World, New World: America and Europe in the Age of Jefferson*, edited by Leonard J. Sadosky, Peter Nicolaisen, Peter S. Onuf, and Andrew J. O'Shaughnessy, 61–82. Charlottesville: University of Virginia Press.

Pearson, Jane C. 1975. "Our Medical Doctors and Dentists." In *Lennoxville*, volume 1, edited by Kathleen H. Atto and committee, 166–75. Lennoxville: Lennoxville-Ascot Historical and Museum Society.

Price, Bertha Weston. 1940. "Old Records Reveal Account of Stay in Lennoxville of Jefferson Davis, Confederate Leader, And His Family." *Sherbrooke Daily Record*, 24 February, 45.

Quebec, Department of Colonization, Mines and Fisheries, Mines Branch. 1915. *Report on The Copper Deposits of the Eastern Townships of the Province of Quebec*. Quebec: E.E. Cinq-Mars.

Richardson, Robert G. 2018. "Jefferson Davis, Lennoxville, Memoirs and BCS." RGR *Resources*. 18 August. https://robertgrichardson.wordpress.com/2017/08/18/jefferson-davis/.

Strode, Hudson. 1959. *Jefferson Davis: Confederate President*. Harcourt, Brace & World, Inc.

– 1964. *Jefferson Davis: Tragic Hero*. New York: Harcourt, Brace & World, Inc.

– 1966. *Jefferson Davis: Private Letters 1823–1899*. New York: Harcourt, Brace & World, Inc.

Thomas, Emory M. 1977. "Jefferson Davis and the American Revolutionary Tradition." *Journal of the Illinois State Historical Society (1908–1984)* 70, (1): 2–9.

University of Chicago Library. Jefferson Davis Trial Papers. MS 979, 1865–1868. https://www.lib.uchicago.edu/collex/collections/davis-jefferson-trial-papers-ms-979/.

Waller, William G. 1886. "My Trip to Canada with Jefferson Davis." *Magazine of American History* 15 (May): 492–4.

Wyatt-Brown, Bertram. 2007. *Southern Honor: Ethics and Behavior in the Old South*. New York: Oxford University Press.

Young, Brian. 2014. *Patrician Families and the Making of Quebec: The Taschereaus and McCords*. Montreal and Kingston: McGill-Queen's University Press.

8

Immigration in the Eastern Townships of Quebec: Patterns of Regional Settlement and Belonging

Cheryl Gosselin

THE HISTORICALLY DEFINED Eastern Townships (ET) is a region in Quebec composed of 16,000 square kilometres; roughly the size of Belgium.[1] Situating this region geographically is easy; defining its history, culture, and varied population is much more fluid. As an area of central Quebec, the Eastern Townships is a region containing several rural communities and one urban area, Sherbrooke; it is also referred to as a borderland between Canada and the United States and is near the metropolitan centre of Montreal. Moreover, the Townships has always been home to a diverse population in terms of origins, language, ethnic and regional identities, culture, and religion. To add to these shifting demographics, the English-speaking minority community has a long-established influence in the area which can be felt through their past and present contributions.

Turgeon and Pastinelli (2002) argue that Quebec is a great place to study globalization processes in local contexts because of recent identity shifts from cultural regionalism to increasing concerns with intercultural issues, its exploration of different forms of economic and political independence, and loosening ties with the federal state which has enabled provincial governments to protect the French language and select its own immigrants. These things, and the still undetermined political status of the province, all lead to growing numbers of intercultural contacts where the local is globalized and the global localized. This chapter explores some of the contemporary realities of immigrants living within Quebec's Eastern Townships' diverse population with the two questions in mind: how is the ET linked to global trends and identities through people and their cultural exchanges coming to the region from all parts of the globe, and how does the area and its people contribute to global forces by maintaining transnational ties? In this chapter, we begin with a brief historical overview of early settlement and then outline key concepts to situate current immigrant migration patterns in the Eastern Townships. The next section delineates the theoretical framework for understanding the process newcomers must go through to develop a sense of belonging to place. It outlines Yuval-Davis's approach to the process of belonging and then highlights how a socio-spatial lens can help us understand how a social issue like immigrant settlement is specific to the spatial realities of certain places such as neighbourhoods and communities, and the people living in them. The methods section discusses how a content analysis of local and provincial media sources were mined to map out the settlement patterns of immigrants to the Estrie region, and more importantly, to collect the stories of newcomers' belonging to place and host communities. The discussion section gives the reader a snapshot of migration to the region using the latest census data from 2021. The three-part discussion section analyzes three themes generated from the sources – *belonging to neighbourhoods, belonging to communities,* and *the politics of belonging in Quebec*. The conclusion highlights the main findings of this study, which can be summarized as the following: the Eastern Townships' global presence is the result of a unique mixture of geography with a diverse array of people and their cultural exchanges, beliefs and values, and transnational ties, as they move through and/or commit to the arduous process of place attachment.

Identified as an early crossroads for human interaction, a meeting place to share ideas and worldviews, a site for leisure and personal creativity, and simply a place to call home, this region has a long history involving openness to numerous peoples, intercultural exchanges, and all things global. Its borders have always been porous. The original people of the Eastern Townships were the Abenakis whose presence in the region dates to the seventeenth century. The historical ET is one of the few places in Quebec where the first European settlers were not French speakers (Klimp, 2006; Little 1997; 2002; and in this volume). When the region was opened for settlement in 1792, the initial wave of homesteaders came from the American colonies seeking good land and opportunity, followed by a second round from the British Isles – Ireland, Scotland, Wales, and England, each round with its distinct culture and language. By the early 1860s, the ET had a very strong English-speaking population making up 58 per cent of the population, although it started declining by the end of the nineteenth century (Pocock and Hartwell 2010). Later waves of immigration came from various European countries such as Germany, Switzerland, and Holland. By the twentieth century, immigration to Quebec from European countries decreased and immigration from developing countries increased. Many of these people were racialized and Allophones whose first language was neither French nor English. One must also acknowledge the history of Black inhabitants to this area. Historical records tell us the first Black people came as slaves with American settlers after the American War of Independence (Eastern Townships Resource Centre 2021). Later, enslaved Blacks fleeing the South, used the Underground Railroad to freedom that passed through the Brome-Missisquoi area of the Townships. As well, many Black performers in music, jazz, and theatre travelled through the towns of the region. According to census data from 2021, there are today approximately 5,620 Black inhabitants living in the Estrie region whose origins include the Caribbean, Haiti, Jamaica, and Africa (Statistics Canada 2021).

In the current interconnecting and globalized world, people are on the move in unprecedent ways, both between and within countries and regions. The processes accompanying globalization, in particular free trade, deregulation of economies, a revolution in technology, and the ideology of neoliberalism, have resulted in massive structural changes worldwide causing upheavals to the everyday lives and livelihoods of people (Elabor-Idemudia 2015). Mass mobilization and migration are the norm for many as they leave or flee from often vulnerable circumstances to different parts of the world in the hopes of finding better work/living/educational conditions. A growing body of literature on migration suggests that human movements today are transnational; that is migration is no longer permanent but more circuitous or back and forth from country to country (Basch, Glick Schiller and Szanton Blanc 1994; Man and Cohen 2015). The perspective of transnationalism is used to study the processes by which immigrants forge and sustain simultaneous, multi-stranded social relations that link together their societies of origin and settlement (Man and Cohen 2015). The Eastern Townships is part of this global migration network of mobility and resting places, comprising some eighty different countries of origin resulting in a progressively more racialized and ethno-culturally diverse population (Service d'aide, n.d.). Their reasons for being here are varied: to live, find work, and permanent settlement and to reunite with family members or to sojourn for economic gain, recreation, and pleasure.

The processes of globalization, migration, and transnationalism evoke questions about citizenship, nationhood, and belonging; that is, who belongs or gets to claim roots and how belonging is negotiated in spaces of differences (Hogarth and Fletcher 2018). Global deterritorialization, cultural hybridity, and fluid identities challenge us to find common ground in understanding one another, especially among the increasing numbers of ethno-racial communities that call the ET home. Who claims a sense of belonging to the Eastern Townships today? When contextualized within this region, another set of questions should be raised: what in the particular dynamics of the ET – regionalism, or localism – shapes a sense of belonging among newcomers most?; does the mix of people make the region's space a welcoming one? In other words, is attachment tied to place or to people? The first question points to the need to spatially contextualize attachment to place. When studying a region and its demographic, economic, social, cultural, and political circumstances, Gaffield (1991) argues that it is important to keep in mind how the larger socio-historical context may shape internal activities and in turn be influenced by regional undertakings. A region is defined as a concrete political reality with socio-psychological attachments to its geographical area that in turn play a vital role in affecting inhabitants' understandings of the area and its governance or state (Ramos 2021). Regions possess specific material and symbolic dimensions and not only pertain to physical, geographic areas but also stimulate attachment to place that influences an individual's experience of and relationship to it. Massey (1994) argues that the identity of a place is never complete but always in a state of becoming and unbecoming. With each successive wave of immigrants, a region and its specific places take on particular features and symbolic meanings only to be undone, remade into other meaningful sites for the lived experiences of belonging. The concept of place-making is useful here (Fraser 2018).

In the second question, we can explore settlement patterns and the co-presence or interconnectedness between host and newcomer. Settlement patterns are both institutionalized – with the help of government funded organizations – and more informally through citizen initiatives. In the latter, settlement and attachment is about being good neighbours and doing the right thing to offer hospitality among "friends." Belkjodja and Gratton (2021) studied the role a group of citizens from Hemmingford, Quebec played in welcoming numerous asylum seekers from mostly Nigeria who irregularly crossed the Canada–US border between 2017 and 2018. The Roxham Road border crossing became well known to Quebecers through the media's portrayal of undocumented foreigners "pouring" into Canada illegally at many points along the international border, with Quebec receiving the highest number. The authors were interested in exploring how a group of local citizens volunteered to act as hosts to the newcomers. These local, intercultural exchanges are part of Quebec's English-speaking communities' "historical capital" as defined by O'Donnell, Forgues, and Robineau (2012), which includes a long record of hosting newcomers outside the French-speaking, state-directed settlement and retention services.[2] Belkjodja and Gratton characterize the Hemmingford citizens' hospitality as a political gesture but also an example of localism – residents thinking and acting grounded in their experiences of living in a border region.

Thus, regional identities and their places affect immigrant and transnational experiences in specific ways. The importance of space and social relations when studying newcomers' sense of belonging is particularly valuable in the ET because the area is highly diverse in population and geographically uneven in terms of spatial, temporal, and material arrangements. In addition, newcomer identities are as various as their personal histories and experiences as well as the categories of admittance according to Quebec's immigration policy.

THEORETICAL FRAMEWORK: BELONGING, ATTACHMENT, *and* PLACE

Yuval-Davis's (2006) sociological study of belonging provides the theoretical understanding for my work. She maintains that belonging is a three-part process comprising attachment, identity, and recognition. This process happens at the individual psychological level – one's need to belong somewhere or to a particular group as opposed to the dreaded fear of being excluded. According to her, belonging is also negotiated at the socio-political structural levels of society. Yuval-Davis's analytical framework for the construction of belonging is articulated along three axes: social locations, identifications and emotional attachments, and ethical and political value systems.

First, social location refers to belonging to particular social groups. Being part of a collectivity informs where an individual exists in the power relations and hierarchies of society, for example along the axes of gender, race, and class. Second, according to Yuval-Davis, belonging indicates identifications, emotional investments, and desire for attachments. Constructing an identity, an ongoing and fluid process, includes telling stories about who you are and how the self is defined in relation to others. These identity narratives are not simply cognitive stories but contain emotional elements and desires for belonging that are reflective of situations and contexts (Yuval-Davis 2006, 202). Finally, belonging also comprises how social locations and identities are judged and valued. This dimension of belonging refers to how categorical boundaries are made and remade around and between individual and collective identities according to specific ideologies and judgements held by social and political players. Conflicts over who belongs and who does not move us into another part of Yuval-Davis's framework of analysis – the realm of the politics of belonging (2006, 203). Ultimately, belonging is about making boundaries of inclusion and exclusion accompanied by the processes of separating groups of people into "us" and "them."

If boundary constructions of belonging are to be contextualized through daily encounters among people, they must also be spatialized. My work is indebted to Sriskandarajah (2019) who acknowledges the importance of a socio-spatial approach to the study of belonging. People are part of certain social groups and attach themselves to the material conditions of their surroundings (261). Belonging happens at various levels – the nation, region, community, or neighbourhood. This socio-spatial approach to belonging is grounded in the works of Henri Lefebvre (1991) and Doreen Massey (1994) who argue that spaces shape people and they themselves take shape through the subjective realities of the individuals who inhabit them. Identity and belonging are co-constitutive with spatiality. There is nothing natural to the spaces we live in and must negotiate the boundaries between each other; they are socially produced through contextualized combinations of planned intentions, representations, and lived realities. Space itself becomes another marker of difference along with race, gender, class, and sexual orientation (Sriskandarajah 2019). Immigrants for example, negotiate their identities in particular places that must be interpreted through their own materialities of difference.

Thus, belonging comes into existence through people and the material conditions of particular spaces, as noted by Sriskandarajah, Lefebvre, and Massey. My work intends to contribute to the study of the social processes and spatiality of belonging by exploring immigrant identities and their sentiments of attachment to place as the outcome of living in the Eastern Townships region and its people. Thus, identity as host and immigrant status and geography form the basis in this analysis.

METHODS

A content analysis of local and provincial media sources along with government and community groups' websites, and survey data were conducted to shed light on immigrant settlement patterns in the Estrie region and how the processes of belonging, which include intercultural exchanges between newcomer and host communities, take shape. The archives of two local daily newspapers, the *Sherbrooke Record* (English) and *La Tribune* (French) were searched online along with the Quebec Community Groups Network's "Daily Briefing" website. The site compiles media sources from both English and French national and regional news outlets pertaining to the interests of the English-speaking communities throughout the province. The internet is also a rich resource to be mined as it gathers a variety of news sources together making information more accessible to academic researchers and interested citizens alike. Since most Eastern Townshippers have some kind of connection to the internet, we can assume a wide exposure among the population to issues concerning immigrant and refugee settlement patterns. The timeline for the study starts in 2015 and continues to 2022. This period is significant for studying settlement relations between hosts and newcomers because of the volume and different types of immigrants and refugees arriving – beginning with Syrian refugees and "irregular" border crossings – the Coalition Avenir Québec (CAQ) government's announcement in 2018 that it would lower the province's threshold for immigrants by 20 per cent (from 50,000 annually to 40,000), the COVID pandemic (when entry slowed to a trickle and later shut down completely), and the current need to admit almost 71,000 permanent residents to make up for the pandemic shutdown (Singer 2022). More than 250 news items were collected for study during this time; however, a lot of repetition was encountered due to the vastness of the internet and the operations of syndicated news outlets. As a result, sixty news items were selected for analysis and coding.

THE REGION'S IMMIGRANT PATTERNS *in the* CURRENT CONTEXT

The Eastern Townships is Quebec's sixth largest settlement destination for newcomers. According to Quebec's ministry for immigration, the majority of Sherbrooke's immigrants are categorized as economic immigrants, followed by family reunification applicants, refugees, and seasonal migrants (CIUSSS 2024). One in eight people in Quebec is defined as an immigrant (born elsewhere) and province wide, approximately 50,000 people are admitted for permanent residency per year (Immigration, Refugees and Citizenship 2024). However, Quebec has seen in recent years a decrease in its share of immigrants, falling from 17.4 per cent in 2006 to 15.3 per cent in 2021 (Statistics Canada 2021). Of the 375,494 immigrants who came to Quebec between 2008 and 2017, 7,006 settled in the Eastern Townships as of January 2019, including 846 who live outside the Sherbrooke area (Bibeau, n.d.). According to the latest census data from 2021, 16,700 immigrants representing 7.6 per cent of the population, call Sherbrooke home. In recent years, the province has experienced a negative, interprovincial migratory pattern although Canadians from Ontario and some from British Columbia move to Quebec annually (Statistics Canada 2021). The Townshippers' Association welcomes and helps integrate a handful of young professionals coming from different parts of Canada each year through its Place aux Jeunes en Région program (Youth and Families, n.d.). More than one out of every two immigrants in the Estrie region is fluent in French. This diverse community is young, with 90 per cent of them under the age of forty-four. One out of five newcomers comes from the Americas, one out of four from Asia, and one out of three from Africa, including North Africa (Bibeau, n.d.). According to the website of Marie-Claude Bibeau, federal MP for the riding of Compton-Stanstead, they work in a variety of employment areas such as education, engineering, culture, communications, and agriculture.

Quebec established its own Ministry of Immigration in 1968. It was one of the many outcomes of the Quiet Revolution, which led to the modernization of the province through building a nation-state, a new Québécois identity with pro-Quebec sentiments, and taking control over economic matters from English dominance. In 1991, the Gagnon-Tremblay-McDougall or Canada–Quebec Accord on Immigration and Temporary Admission of Aliens was established to give Quebec sole responsibility to select independent (economic) immigrants (Iacovino 2016). The then minister of Cultural Communities and Immigration and the MNA for the local Saint-François riding, Monique Gagnon-Tremblay, was tasked with striking this deal with the federal government. According to census data for 2021, 46.4 per cent of recent immigrants who lived in Quebec were admitted under the skilled worker program.

Quebec's settlement model for French immigrants includes organizations that are structured by and receive funding from the government to help settle newcomers. In Sherbrooke, community groups with this specific mandate are Le Service D'aide aux Neo-Canadiens de Sherbrooke (SANC), Actions Interculturelles, La Fédération des Communautés Culturelles de l'Estrie, and the Soutien aux Familles réfugiées et immigrantes de l'Estrie. The French public school system also provides "welcoming classes" and francization courses for immigrant children, all of whom must attend French schools (McAndrew et al. 2016)

Newcomers whose first language is neither French nor English but who understand English fall outside the government's settlement model and often find help through ESC's organizations. These community groups do not have a mandate to settle but nevertheless find themselves in the role of a bridge between the newcomers and the larger French society (Gosselin and Pichette 2014). Three themes generated from the analysis of the sources are discussed below.

DISCUSSION

The Syrian Refugee "Crisis" and opening "our hearts and homes" – belonging to neighbourhoods

Syrian refugees began arriving in Canada as early as December of 2014, but it was the disturbing image of Alan Kurdi, a Syrian toddler who drowned while his family was trying to get to a safe and better life, that mobilized Eastern Townships families to make "life-saving decisions about people who they have never met" (Murphy 2015). By late November 2015, Sherbrooke was one of thirteen Quebec cities chosen by the federal government to settle more than 3,000 Syrians, with the hope of welcoming another 6,000 in 2016. Sherbrooke and surrounding areas were selected because of the region's already established resettlement programs and the willingness of local families to privately sponsor Syrian families. Approximately 420 Syrians and other refugee families were settled in Sherbrooke and region between 2015 and 2016 (Rose and Charette 2017). Many news items focused on the individuals who were willing to help. They belonged to interfaith groups that raised funds and followed the steps necessary to become private sponsors. In one article from the *Sherbrooke Record* (Murphy 2015), members narrated their conviction to do something but at the same time noted the desire to make the right choice in choosing refugee families "that will be compatible with the Sherbrooke community." More stories raised the challenges of a slow-moving selection process run by the Canadian Immigration Department. Thirty members of the St-Ephrem Syriac Orthodox Church, defining themselves as the cornerstone of Sherbrooke's refugee community, travelled by bus to Quebec City to meet government officials and express their willingness to increase their sponsorship of refugees from Syria and Iraq. This is a good example of church members using their transnational ties. The news story included a quotation from one of the organizers of the trip, which is representative of his faith and community's continuing support: "I think finally the governments are realizing, there's a major problem in the Middle East if you're a Christian, and the only way to help them out is to bring them over" (CBC News 2015). Similar stories of Syrian families finally arriving in Sherbrooke were reported by *La Tribune* (Nadeau 2015). Le Service D'aide aux Neo-Canadiens de Sherbrooke and its community partners reported in the local newspapers that it was ready to help provide support to incoming refugees. According to its website, the organization provides "shadowing" for a year to help refugees navigate daily living and aid in finding suitable housing, health care, and employment (Service d'aide, n.d.). These examples of individuals and organizations ready and willing to help with the refugee "crisis" is because of Sherbrooke's history as a global hub and destination. Sherbrooke is defined as an intercultural city by the Council of Europe (Council of Europe 2023). The city and its surrounding region are home to more than 130 ethno-communities and was the first Quebec municipality to adopt a welcoming and integration policy giving it the resources and capacity to settle immigrants and refugees. Sherbrooke is only one of many towns relying on newcomers to bolster their community numbers and keep the local economy afloat. In Saint-Nazaire, a small town near Lac Saint-Jean, a story about local residents learning Spanish to accommodate recently arrived Mexican workers was featured by CBC News (2020). This shows the willingness of locals to establish transnational ties with newcomers through the intercultural exchanges taking place in Sherbrooke neighbourhoods, in this case through sharing a common language and employment.

Today, support from Townshippers continues with offers of help for Ukrainian refugees. Bishop's University hosted a fundraiser for Ukrainian students and held a solidarity event on its campus (The Canadian News 2022). Along with municipal buildings in Sherbrooke and Richmond, the university raised the Ukrainian flag to foster public attention about the plight of Ukrainian families fleeing war (*Sherbrooke Record* 2022a). The CBC reported on the attempts of one Bishop's student to locate her family and find them safe haven in Poland. She reached out to her transnational networks through social media for help while attending classes in Lennoxville (CBC News 2022).

Many studies highlighted the role of private sponsorship in the retention outcomes for refugees and immigrants (El-Chidiac 2018; Hynie et al. 2019). In their study of Syrian refugee settlement in six Canadian cities (one being Sherbrooke) Hynie et al. discovered that private sponsorship resulted in a greater sense of belonging due to the close social supports established among friends and family members throughout the process. During a research symposium on English-speaking immigrants in Quebec (Research Symposium 2020), William Floch discussed his studies on the degree of immigrant retention along Official Language Minority group lines and found differences in belonging according to language. His results show among more established English-speaking immigrants to the region, retention rates have somewhat stabilized, while recent English-speaking newcomers find themselves less likely to receive support to remain in contrast to their French-speaking counterparts.

Despite all these efforts, individuals and organizations struggle with the lack of progress in sponsoring refugee families as exemplified by one local sponsorship group who has been waiting since 2018 to bring the Alali family from Syria

(Lambie 2022). Other challenges include a shortage of suitable housing and gainful employment along with having to learning French, Quebec's official language (Mennie 2015).

These examples highlight the host–guest relations of the region and how the processes of settlement and belonging for newcomers are carried out. Several neighbourhood actors are involved in these intercultural exchanges including private sponsorships, individual efforts among already established immigrants, places of worship, community groups, and institutions. The willingness of Townshippers to help settle refugees and immigrants is the product of history – the movement and settlement of people from all parts of the globe, as well as Sherbrooke and its surrounding region's designation as an intercultural space. Over time, these two factors have led to the entrenchment of support services and social networks that newcomers can rely on. Underlying the social location of Townshippers is a set of host relations used to integrate newcomers into the region's neighbourhoods in the hopes that one day they can identify as belonging to the area. The news items and editorials appear to normalize the city and region's openness and willingness to be part of the settlement process for newcomers and thus identify it as a transnational hub. The stories told by the hosts are filled with emotions of care, desire to help improve the lives of others, and invest in their neighborhoods. Testimonials from refugees reveal the important role intimate relations among family and friends play in developing a sense of attachment to place (Hynie et al. 2019).

Belonging to communities

Along with the integration processes among ET neighbourhoods, numerous voices were calling for action at the community level. But these appeals for newcomer settlement diverge along linguistic groups. Anglophone leaders, concerned with the vitality and economic prosperity of their communities, particularly in the more rural or remote areas of the province such as the Eastern Townships, highlight the important and historical role English-speaking Quebecers have played in successfully integrating newcomers into society (*Montreal Gazette* 2015; Lalonde 2017). The director of the Quebec Community Groups Network, Sylvia Martin-Laforge, states:

> We have lived here for many. Many years. We have learned French … We've integrated perfectly, so who better to teach or to help facilitate newcomers here to figure out how you can live, work, or play in French but still also retain some of your cultural heritage in your own language? (Lalonde 2017)

In the same article, it was noted that because of the longstanding cultural diversity within the English-speaking population, along with the emphasis on knowing multiple languages, many newcomers from China, India, Pakistan, and the Philippines have been finding a home in Quebec through the institutions of the province's English communities; churches, synagogues, and various faith-based groups have acted as "landing pads for newcomers during the last 35 years," and municipalities like Sherbrooke where "valuing [its] anglophone communities and institutions have become assets for attracting and retaining immigrants" (Lalonde 2017). In November 2015, the *Montreal Gazette* reported that the Montreal English school board requested that the Quebec government allow some of the 6,000 Syrian refugees admitted to the province to attend its classes (Cooper 2015). While English-speaking educational leaders were asking for the children of Syrian refugees to attend its schools on humanitarian grounds and to ease crowding in the French-language schools, the immigration minister for the Liberal government stood firm. Kathleen Weil "counted on English school boards to provide adult refugees with professional training," but no exceptions were to be made: "of course, children have to go to French schools, that is essential" (under Bill 101 refugee and immigrant children must receive their instruction in French at the primary and secondary levels; see Plante 2016). Along with the openness of communities throughout Quebec were concerns about compromising Quebecers' security and worries over the illegal entry of asylum seekers crossing the Canada–US border into Quebec (Fletcher 2017).

Survey data gathered by Jack Jedwab from the Association for Canadian Studies reveals some differences in attitude among Quebec's French-speaking population and the minority English-speaking communities. According to poll results on immigration and diversity, more English Quebecers have very positive views of immigrants (32.8 per cent) than Francophones (11.2 per cent; Jedwab and Warren 2018). When asked whether immigrants should be encouraged to give up their customs and traditions and become more like the majority, 29.3 per cent of Francophones agreed versus only 16.7 per cent of the province's Anglophones. Again, when asked if they felt threatened by the influx of non-Christian immigrants 27.7 per cent of Francophones totally agreed while only 19.8 per cent of English-speakers did. In another survey on the state of intercultural relations in Quebec since the pandemic, over all Quebecers expressed the highest concern over the state of intergroup relations, 41 per cent compared to 32 per cent for the rest of Canada (Jedwab 2020c; 2020d). When it comes to distrust of religious minorities, Quebec's French majority score higher than non-Francophones (Jedwab 2020a). The differences between the two language groups are reflected in the media with articles expressing concerns over interculturalism (Bouchard 2016; *Le Devoir* 2016), Quebec's cultural values (Dagenais 2014), religious neutrality among religious minorities, and the French language (Mennie 2015).

At the community level, divergent views along linguistic lines appear to exist over newcomer settlement. Anglophones attach refugee and immigrant settlement to the vitality and very survival of their minority communities while the French majority acceptance of newcomers is tempered by their concerns over culture, identity, and language. Two spaces of belonging appear to exist affecting intercultural exchanges and attachment to place differently. One may ask, how does each approach to settlement affect the settlement process and development of a sense of belonging among newly arrived people from around the globe? Census data reveals Quebec's low retention rates for all newcomers, no matter what language they speak – 79 per cent versus 93 per cent for Ontario, although Atlantic provinces such as PEI with a 28 per cent retention after five years admission have the lowest rates (Statistics Canada 2021). Many reasons are behind why newcomers do not attach to place, including lack of family and friends from their country of origin or cultural group, shortage of employment opportunities, and language spoken; this is especially true in Quebec where 54.5 per cent of recent immigrants had only French as their first official language spoken (FOLS) and 5.3 per cent of newcomers with neither English nor French (Statistics Canada 2021). Belonging at the neighbourhood level involves host-guest exchanges based on intimate bonds of citizens mobilizing to establish ties with 'others' while attachment to community summons broader elements of language, culture, and group sustainability. If formal social support is there for newcomers, then settlement through language and culture may be faster. Without official networks, attachment is more personal and may take longer but the outcome could be more meaningful, perhaps since this support is among informal, community exchanges and ties. Next, the discussion moves into the politics of belonging – Yuval-Davis's third dimension in the process of newcomer attachment to place.

THE POLITICS *of* BELONGING *in* QUEBEC

Controversies over reasonable accommodation, Quebec values, language, and secularism have been brewing in the province for some time. Over the past several years, successive governments have enacted legislation to affirm Quebec identity and limit the visibility of religion in public spaces. In 2013, the Parti Québécois unveiled its Quebec values charter, which was followed by the Liberal Party's Bills 64, an act to modernize legislative provisions as regards the protection of personal information, and Bill 94, an act to establish guidelines governing accommodation requests within the administration and certain institutions that banned anyone wearing a face covering from giving or receiving public services. More recently the CAQ introduced Bill 21, An Act Respecting the Laicity of the State, a secularism law to ensure the religious neutrality of the state; and Bill 96, An Act Respecting French, the Official and Common Language of Quebec, which makes French the only common and official language of the province. The nationalist government of the CAQ has successfully imposed a narrow version of Quebec identity predicated on the notion of an autonomous nation in which all citizens abide by the "valeurs des Québécois de souche" (Lessard 2015). The imposition of one set of values and the French language for all is mostly directed at immigrants who are expected to pass a "values" test shortly after their arrival and learn French within six months of living in Quebec. Combined with the controversial Bill 9, which limits immigrant numbers and focuses on the economic potential of newcomers only and not on their integration into all of Quebec society (Authier 2019), the ethnic nationalist ideologies of the government have "othered" newcomers as threats to the state. There appear to be few moderate voices in the media debate over identity, immigration, religion, and language, only those from opposite ends of the political spectrum. Numerous news items oppose Bills 21 and 96 which use the notwithstanding clause to override Charter rights violations (Bilefsky 2020; Micone, 2018). Also, those very much in favour of these reforms to Quebec society – nationalists like Mathieu Bock-Côté – believe "Bill 21 is a pedestal on which we must build" (Nakonechny 2019). Many of the opposing views follow linguistic lines and their different cultural views: protection of the individual freedoms among English speakers and the desire for a strong government presence in everyday life for French speakers (Hackett 2021).

These broader political patterns effect the processes of belonging undertaken by newcomers. Host–guest exchanges and the relations of settlement are impacted by the wider debates surrounding who is allowed to be defined as a Quebecer and thus can be fully integrated into society or not. Along with the sentiments of openness, intercultural exchanges and care are the exclusionary measures founded on discrimination, prejudice, and fear. Current exclusionary politics and a post-pandemic climate are not favourable to open door immigration policies. New research on religious minorities in Quebec reveals that three years after the implementation of Bill 21, most respondents, in particular Muslim women, are feeling less welcome, less safe, and less hopeful (Jedwab 2022b).

Today, the Eastern Townships, especially Sherbrooke, is a diverse and plural space and if we follow the news reports of Ukrainian and other refugees being welcomed today along with organizations like SANC, which are open to accepting newcomers from around the globe, then the area continues to be part of the processes of belonging experienced by guests in their exchanges with the hosts. A recent news story in the *Sherbrooke Record* provides the details of a new agreement between the city and the Ministry of Immigration, Francisation and Integration worth $2.1 million (*Sherbrooke Record* 2022b). The three-year action plan will enable Sherbrooke to better attract and keep immigrants in its territory. In the article, the mayor is quoted: "Sherbrooke has always been a leader in welcoming people of all origins." But these processes of belonging, which include the three dimensions of social location, sentiments, and politics are never linear or in agreement. Intercultural exchanges which are central to the experiences of attachment to place will continue to be fraught with tensions and pain, burdensome to many and for others joyous and life-altering.

CONCLUSION

The Eastern Townships, situated on the unceded ancestral territory of the W8banaki nation, the Ndakina, has a long-established history of being an open and diverse area for its original inhabitants and people from all parts of the world. The ET is a space to variously meet, visit, or sojourn and a more permanent place to call home through intercultural exchanges. Over the years, a diverse array of people have made and remade the region through their relationships to each other and the land. The unique blend of people and its geography as an urban and rural area define the global presence of the Eastern Townships as an innovative economic hub, a multi-cultural centre and place for intercultural relations and transnational activities such as maintaining networks of settlement. This globalism of the Eastern Townships provokes a set of questions about belonging – how do people decide to stay or go, and how does the host society participate in the processes of attaching oneself to a new place? A content analysis of regional and provincial news articles reveals the host–guest exchanges that are part of becoming a member of the ET. The three dimensions of belonging articulated by Yuval-Davis – the negotiation of social location between citizens and newcomer, narratives of emotional investments and the wider political basis reveal just how complicated and uneven the process is depending on where the newcomer is from, when they arrive, the nature of transnational ties their lives are embedded in, and their goals for the future. Belonging is also multi-scalar – it takes place at the neighbourhood, community, and wider societal levels. As the content analysis reveals the different levels involved in the spatiality of belonging do not always work in unison.

The study of newcomer experiences in the Eastern Townships is necessarily ongoing. Further studies using qualitative ethnographic research needs to be conducted with newcomers themselves to explore how they interpret the processes of belonging to the region and its people. Important in these ongoing explorations is how useful the concept of transnationalism is to define the impacts of newcomers on the region. We need to continue our understanding of the Eastern Townships' connections to wider national and international trends, and how the region contributes to global forces by way of the people living here. In the meantime, Sherbrooke and its surrounding region remain a site of intercultural exchange where the local is globalized and the global localized (Turgeon and Pastinelli 2002).

Notes

1 The historical Eastern Townships includes the present Estrie administrative region and sections of Montérégie, Centre-du-Quebec, and Chaudiére-Appalaches. The current and smaller Estrie administrative region is comprised of six regional municipalities: Coaticook, le Granit, Le Haut-Saint-François, Le Val-Saint-François, Les Sources, and Memphrémagog.

2 In Hemmingford, 38.2 per cent of the population is defined as Anglophone according to the 2021 census numbers and using the federal government's First Official Language Spoken (FOLS) category.

References

Authier, P. 2019. "CAQ Unswayed by Study Slamming 'Thoughtless' Immigration Reform." *Montreal Gazette*, 13 March. https://montrealgazette.com/news/quebec/a-study-debunks-necessity-of-immigration-reform-but-the-caq-wont-back-down.

Basch, L., N. Glick Schiller, and C. Szanton Blanc. 1994. *Nations Unbound: Transnational Projects, Postcolonial Predicaments, and Deterritorialized Nation-States*. Amsterdam: Gordon and Breach.

Belkjodja, C., and C. Gratton. 2021. "A Gesture of Hospitality for Asylum Seekers: An Analysis of Mobilization Actions by the Collective 'Bridges Not Borders.'" Presentation at QUESCREN 'Lunch and Learn' web series, 18 November.

Bibeau, Marie-Claude. n.d. L'Hon. Marie-Claude Bibeau. Députée de Compton–Stanstead. www.marieclaudebibeau.libparl.ca. Accessed 10 February 2024.

Bilefsky, D. 2020. "A Quebec Ban on Religious Symbols Upends Lives and Careers." *The New York Times*, 7 March. https://www.nytimes.com/2020/03/07/world/canada/quebec-religious-symbols-ban.html. Accessed 9 February 2024.

Bouchard, G. 2016. "Le faux procès de l'interculturalism." *Le Devoir*, September 15. https://www.ledevoir.com/opinion/idees/479967/le-faux-proces-de-l-interculturalisme. Accessed 9 February 2024.

Canadian Press. 2025. "Quebec to Bring In 3,650 Syrian Refugees This Year and Another 3,650 in 2016." *Sherbrooke Record*, 26 November. https://www.pressreader.com/canada/sherbrooke-record/20151126/281487865262775. Accessed 10 February 2024.

CBC News. 2015. "Syrian, Iraqi Refugees Living in Sherbrooke Meet with Premier Philippe Couillard." 22 September. https://www.cbc.ca/news/canada/montreal/refugees-meet-couillard-weil-1.3238575. Accessed 9 February 2024.

– 2020. "Residents of Small Quebec Town to Boost Local Economy by Learning Spanish." 6 January. https://www.cbc.ca/news/canada/montreal/saint-nazaire-quebec-spanish-1.5416874. Accessed 9 February 2024.

– 2022. "How a Bishop's Student Got Her Ukrainian Family to Safety in Poland." 19 March. https://www.cbc.ca/news/canada/montreal/how-a-bishop-s-student-got-her-ukrainian-family-to-safety-in-poland-1.6391090. Accessed 9 February 2024.

Centre intégré universitaire de santé et de services sociaux de l'Estrie (CIUSS). 2016. "Mieux Répondre aux Besoins des Communautés Linguistiques et Culturelles de l'Estrie." *Collection de Rapports de la Directrice de Santé Publique*, 2nd edition. www.santeestrie.qc.ca. Accessed 10 February 2024.

Cooper, C. 2015. "Let Quebec English Schools Take In Syrian Refugees." *Montreal Gazette*, 15 November. https://montrealgazette.com/news/quebec/celine-cooper-let-quebec-english-schools-take-in-syrian-refugees. Accessed 9 February 2024.

Council of Europe. 2023. "Ville de Sherbrooke (Kchi Nikitawtegwak), Canada." September. https://rm.coe.int/09000016800ad08e4. Accessed 10 February 2024.

Dagenais, M. 2014. "Quebec Values Charter." *Canadian Encyclopedia*. https://www.thecanadianencyclopedia.ca. Accessed 23 January 2014.

Eastern Townships Resource Centre. 2021. *Quebec's Eastern Townships A Brief History of its Peoples, Politics and Economy*, Part 2. Lennoxville: ETRC.

Elabor-Idemudia, P. 2015. "Transnationalism and Remittances: The Double-Edged Position of Transmigrant Women Engaged in the Domestic Service Sector." In *Engendering Transnational Voices*, edited by G. Man and R. Cohen, 117–34. Waterloo, ON: Wilfrid Laurier University Press.

El-Chidiac, S. 2018. "The Success of the Privately Sponsored Refugee System." *Policy Options*. July 20. https://policyoptions.irpp.org/magazines/july-2018/success-privately-sponsored-refugee-system/. Accessed 6 January 2024.

Fletcher, R. 2017. "Illegal Entry Is Illegal Entry: Quebec Premier Responds to U.S. Asylum Seekers." *Global News*, 16 February. https://globalnews.ca/news/3251938/illegal-entry-is-illegal-entry-quebec-premier-responds-to-u-s-asylum-seekers/. Accessed 6 January 2024.

Fraser, E. 2018. "Unbecoming Place: Urban Imaginaries in Transition in Detroit." *Cultural Geographies* 25 (3): 441–8.

Gaffield, C. 1991. "The New Regional History: Rethinking the History of the Outaouais." *Journal of Canadian Studies* 26 (1): 64–81.

Gosselin, C., and A. Pichette. 2014. "Multicultural Common Spaces and the Negotiation of Belonging: The English-Speaking Communities of Quebec and the Integration of Newcomers." *Journal of Eastern Townships Studies*, no. 43: 9–26.

Hackett, A. "On Bill 21: English and French Canada Are Stuck in Separate Echo Chambers." *Toronto Star*, 23 December. https://www.thestar.com/opinion/contributors/on-bill-21-english-and-french-canada-are-stuck-in-separate-echo-chambers/article_25082853-7fa7-5bc6-bd07-36a37f798be5.html. Accessed 9 February 2024.

Hogarth, K., and W. Fletcher. 2018. *A Space for Race*. New York: Oxford University Press.

Hynie, M., et al. 2019. "What Role Does Type of Sponsorship Play in Early Integration Outcomes? Syrian Refugees Resettled in Six Canadian Cities." *Refuge Canada's Journal on Refugees* 35 (2): 36–52.

Iacovino, R., 2016. "Between Unity and Diversity: Examining the Quebec Model of Integration." In *Quebec Questions: Quebec Studies for the Twenty-First Century*, 2nd edition, edited by S. Gervais, C. Kirkey and J. Rudy, 250–70. New York: Oxford University Press.

Immigration, Refugees and Citizenship Canada. 2020. "Research Symposium on English-speaking Immigration in Quebec Organized by Research and Evaluation/Immigration, Refugees and Citizenship Canada." Executive summary. 1 February. https://www.canada.ca/en/immigration-refugees-citizenship/corporate/report-statistics/research/research-symposium-on-english-speaking-immigration-quebec-organized-research-evaluation-immigration-refugees-citizenship-canada.html. Accessed 10 February 2024.

– 2024. https://www.canada.ca/en/immigration-refugees-citizenship.html. Accessed 10 February 2024.

Institut du Québec. 2008. *Update and Clarification of Immigration and Labor Market Data*. 4 September. Quebec City: IDQ.

Jedwab, J. 2022a. "Views and Trust of Religious Minorities in Quebec and the Rest of Canada." Association for Canadian Studies, ACS Survey, 10 February. https://acs-aec.ca/wp-content/uploads/2021/02/Views-of-Religious-Communities-in-Quebec-Dec-2020.pdf.

– 2020b. "Law 21: Discourse, Perceptions and Impacts." *Association for Canadian Studies*, ACS Survey May–June 2022. 10 August. https://acs-metropolis.ca/studies/law-21-discourse-perceptions-impacts/. Accessed 9 February 2024.

– 2020c. "Canadian Views on Immigration Levels and Immigrant Categories in the COVID Era." *Association for Canadian Studies*, ACS Survey, August 2020.

– 2020d. "The State of Intercultural Relations in Quebec and the Rest of Canada since the Pandemic." *Association for Canadian Studies*, ACS Survey 30 October 2020. https://acs-aec.ca/wp-content/uploads/2020/10/The-State-of-Intercultural-Relations-2.pdf.

Jedwab, J., and J.-P. Warren. 2018. "Multiculturalism versus Interculturalism: Myth and Reality." *Association for Canadian Studies*, ACS Survey, 27 June. https://acs-metropolis.ca/studies/multiculturalism-versus-interculturalism-myth-and-reality/. Accessed 9 February 2024.

Klimp, K. 2006. "Profile of the English-Speaking Community in the Eastern Townships." Lennoxville, QC: Townshippers' Association. https://www.danielturpqc.org/upload/ET-_TA_Townshipper_Profile.pdf.

Lalonde, M. 2017. "Anglophones Are Helping Newcomers Integrate and That's Good for Quebec: QCGN." *Montreal Gazette.* 15 March. https://montrealgazette.com/news/anglophones-are-helping-newcomers-integrate-and-thats-good-for-quebec-qcgn. Accessed 9 February 2024.

Lambie, G. 2022. "Local Refugee Sponsorship Group Baffled by Lack of Progress." *Sherbrooke Record,* 1 May. https://www.sherbrookerecord.com/local-refugee-sponsorship-group-baffled-by-lack-of-progress/. Accessed 9 January 2024.

Le Devoir. 2016. "Il y a plus qu'une définition de l'interculturalisme." 21 September. https://www.ledevoir.com/opinion/libre-opinion/480419/il-y-a-plus-qu-une-definition-de-l-interculturalisme. Accessed 9 February 2024.

Lefebvre, H. 1991. *The Production of Space.* Translated by D. Nicholson-Smith. New York: Basil Blackwell.

Lessard, D. 2015. "La CAQ prend un virage identitaire." *La Presse.* 14 March/ https://www.lapresse.ca/actualites/politique/politique-quebecoise/201503/13/01-4852078-la-caq-prend-un-virage-identitaire.php. Accesse 9 February 2024.

Little, J. 2004. *Borderland Religion: The Emergence of an English Canadian Identity, 1792–1852.* Toronto: University of Toronto Press.

– 1997. *State and Society in Transition: The Politics of Institutional Reform in the Eastern Townships, 1838–1852.* Montreal and Kingston: McGill-Queen's University Press.

Man, G., and R. Cohen, eds. 2015. *Engendering Transnational Voices: Studies in Family, Work, and Identity.* Waterloo, ON: Wilfrid Laurier University Press.

Massey, D. 1994. *Space, Place and Gender.* Minneapolis: University of Minnesota Press.

McAndrew, M., et al. 2016. "Immigration and Diversity in Quebec's Schools: An Assessment." In *Quebec Questions: Quebec Studies for the Twenty-First Century,* 2nd edition, edited by S. Gervais, C. Kirkey, and J. Rudy, 297–315. New York: Oxford University Press.

Mennie, J. 2015. "Syrian Refugees Can Escape War but Not Quebec's Language Politics." *Montreal Gazette,* 27 November. https://montrealgazette.com/opinion/syrian-refugees-can-escape-war-but-not-quebecs-language-politics. Accessed 9 February 2024.

Micone, M. 2018. "On ne naît pas Québécois, on le devient." *Le Devoir,* 24 October. https://www.ledevoir.com/opinion/idees/539722/on-ne-nait-pas-quebecois-on-le-devient. Accessed 9 February 2024.

Montreal Gazette. 2015. "Immigrants and Official Languages." 11 May. https://montrealgazette.com/opinion/editorials/editorial-immigrants-and-official-languages. Accessed 9 February 2024.

– 2017. "Most Canadians Favour Values Test for Immigrants: Poll." 13 March. https://montrealgazette.com/news/local-news/most-canadians-favour-values-test-for-immigrants-poll. Accessed 9 February 2024.

Murphy, T. 2015. "Sherbrooke Group Struggles with Choice to Help Refugee Family." CBC News, 4 September. https://www.cbc.ca/news/canada/nova-scotia/sherbrooke-group-refugree-struggle-1.3216081. Accessed 10 February 2024.

Nadeau, Jacynthe. 2015. "L'Église syriaque accueille une nouvelle famille syrienne." *La Tribune,* 5 December 2015.

Nakonechny, S. 2019. "Bill 21 is a Pedestal on Which We Must Build." CBC News, 18 December. https://www.cbc.ca/news/canada/montreal/after-bill-21-quebec-nationalists-plan-to-go-further-1.5400208. Accessed 9 February 2024.

O'Donnell, L., E. Forgues, and A. Robineau. 2012. "Immigration, Settlement and Integration in Quebec's Anglophone Communities: A Preliminary Report." *Research Gate*, 7–32. https://www.researchgate.net/publication/330204035_Immigration_settlement_and_integration_in_Quebec's_Anglophone_communities_A_preliminary_repor. Accessed 9 February 2024.

Parrillo, F. 2015. "Syrian Refugees: Quebec Immigration Minister Says Security Won't Be Compromised." *Global News*, 16 November. https://globalnews.ca/news/2342076/syrian-refugees-quebec-immigration-minister-says-security-wont-be-compromised/. Accessed 9 February 2024.

Plante, C. 2015. "English-Speaking Community Important to Syrian Refugee Integration: Weil." *The Montreal Gazette*, 26 November. https://www.healthing.ca/news/quebec/quebec-to-welcome-at-least-7300-syrian-refugees-by-end-of-2016/. Accessed 9 February 2024.

Pocock, J., and B. Hartwell. 2010. "Profile of the English-speaking Community in the Eastern Townships." 2nd Edition. Lennoxville, QC: Townshippers' Association. http://townshippers.qc.ca/portal/wp-content/uploads/2011/11/profile-english.pdf.

Porter, I. 2017. "Le Québec se prive de compétences. " *Le Devoir*. 16 March. https://www.ledevoir.com/politique/quebec/494094/le-quebec-se-prive-de-competences. Accessed 9 February 2024.

Ramos, O. 2020. "Rethinking Regionalism." *McGill Undergraduate Journal of Canadian Studies* 20: 79–88.

Research Symposium on English-speaking Immigration in Quebec, organized by Research and Evaluation/Immigration, Refugees and Citizenship Canada. 2020. Retrieved from www.canada.ca/immigration-refugees-citizenship. Accessed 12 November 2020.

Rose, D., and A. Charette. 2017. "Finding Housing for the Syrian Refugee Newcomers in Canadian Cities: Challenges, Initiatives and Policy Implications Synthesis Report." Montreal: Institut national de la recherche scientifique, Centre Urbanisation Culture Société.

Schué, R. 2022. "Près de 90,000 futurs Québécois attendent des résponses d'Immigration Canada." *Radio-Canada*, February 16. https://ici.radio-canada.ca/nouvelle/1862354/immigration-quebec-ottawa-delai-traitement-canada. Accessed 10 February 2024.

Service d'aide aux Néo-Canadiens (SANC). n.d. https://www.sanc-sherbrooke.ca/. Accessed 10 February 2024.

Sherbrooke Record. 2022a. "Townshippers Continue to Offer Support to Ukraine." 21 March. https://www.sherbrookerecord.com/townshippers-continue-to-offer-support-to-ukraine/. Accessed 10 February 2024.

– 2022b. "Sherbrooke Investing More Than $2.1 Million in New Immigration Project." 9 August, 3.

Singer, C.R. 2022. "Quebec Immigration to Soar Over 71,000 New Permanent Residents in 2022." www.immigration.ca. 12 May. https://www.immigration.ca/quebec-immigration-to-soar-over-71000-new-permanent-residents-in-2022/. Accessed 10 February 2024.

Sriskandarajah, A. 2020. "Race, Space, and Media: The Production of Urban Neighborhood Space in East-End Toronto." *Canadian Journal of Sociology* 52 (1): 1–22.

– 2019. "Cultural Mixers: Race, Space, and Intercultural Relations among Youth in East-End Toronto." *Canadian Journal of Sociology* 44 (3); 257–82.

Statistics Canada. 2021. Census of Population 2021. https://www12.statcan.gc.ca/census-recensement/index-eng.cfm. Accessed 9 February 2024.

The Canadian News. 2022. "Bishop's University Takes Action for Ukraine." 18 March. https://thecanadian.news/bishops-university-takes-action-for-ukraine/. Accessed 22 March 2022.

Turgeon, L., and M. Pastinelli. 2002. "'Eat the World': Postcolonial Encounters in Quebec City's Ethnic Restaurants." *Journal of American Folklore* 115 (456): 247–68.

Youth and Families Project Coordinator. n.d. Townshippers. https://townshippers.org/job/youth-and-families-project-coordinator/. Accessed 10 February 2024.

Yuval-Davis, N. 2006. "Belonging and the Politics of Belonging." *Patterns of Prejudice* 40 (3): 197–214.

Part Three

Institutions, Local Identities, and Global Connections

In the five chapters that compose this section of the book, institutions in the Eastern Townships – educational, media, sporting, and religious – are assessed for the roles they play in the region and for the importance of their global linkages. Anthony Di Mascio's study in chapter 9, "Community, Identity, and Borderland Schooling in the Eastern Townships and Northern Vermont: Reflections in an Impermeable Era," adopts a binational lens to examine the practice of cross-border schooling in Quebec and Vermont in the nineteenth and twentieth centuries and weighs how these engagements contributed to the making and unravelling of borderland identities. The chapter also considers the effects of recent border policy changes in the aftermath of 9/11 and the COVID-19 pandemic. Chapter 10, authored by Harold Bérubé and Henri Dion and titled "'The Latest and Most Important Local and Foreign News': Producing and Reading the Press in the Eastern Townships (1867–1939)," captures the ways in which local newspapers in both the anglophone and francophone communities presented the Townships and "the world" to their readers. The authors argue that local and regional print news outlets played a central role in defining their communities, and that Townships editors used their pages to situate their readers contextually, within the nation, the empire, and the world. In "'A duty to her Indian citizens': Bishop's University and Canada's 'Indian Problem,' 1845–1945" (chapter 11), historian Louis-Georges Harvey connects the Bishop's University Faculty of Divinity, its students, and its graduates to the problem of settler colonialism and the plight of Indigenous Peoples in Canada. Harvey traces how Bishop's graduates played key roles in setting Anglican Church policy and propagandizing in their work in Anglican residential schools, which were designed to solve Canada's "Indian Problem." Turning to the world of sport, Andrew C. Holman's "Fight Nights: The Sherbrooke Athletic Commission and the Boxing World, 1955–66" (chapter 12) provides a case study of the rise and fall of elite prize fighting in 1950s and 1960s Sherbrooke. By examining how Sherbrooke's Athletic Commission and local promoters attracted first-rate events, Holman argues that such "fight nights" and the resultant hype surrounding them, provided a window on a changing global discourse about Black masculinity in mid-twentieth-century North America. Claude Gélinas, Lorraine Derocher, and Camille Sasseville's essay "Recent Transformations and Dynamics in the Eastern Townships' Religious Landscape" (chapter 13), the last work in this section, draws on extensive census and survey data of religious congregations in Sherbrooke. The religious landscape outlined by the authors illustrates growth in the diversity of new faith-based institutions, affiliations, and practices – most often the result of non-European-based immigrant settlement in the Townships. They find that challenges to "traditional" religions stem not from the expansion of new forces but from ongoing transformations in religious activities and habits within long-established populations.

9

Community, Identity, and Borderland Schooling in the Eastern Townships and Northern Vermont: Reflections in an Impermeable Era

Anthony Di Mascio

THIS CHAPTER REVISITS FINDINGS from a study on cross-border schooling in the Eastern Townships of Quebec and Northern Vermont in the nineteenth and twentieth centuries (Di Mascio 2013). The first part of the chapter will provide an overview of those findings. The second part offers reflections and observations on the conclusions drawn while considering the increased tightening of border policies in Canada and the United States, and how it has reshaped lived experiences of Eastern Township and Northern Vermont residents since 9/11 and, more recently, since the restriction of flow due to the COVID-19 pandemic. The idea of Canadians and Americans sharing social and cultural institutions, such as public schools, along an unchecked and permeable border is virtually unimaginable in our post-9/11 and international pandemic world. With a focus on the Eastern Townships of Quebec and Northern Vermont, this chapter considers the remarkably under-examined history of cross-border schooling in the nineteenth and twentieth centuries and how it contributed to the making and unravelling of borderland identities.

THE HISTORIOGRAPHICAL CONTEXT

For several decades, borderlands and borderland identities have received considerable scholarly attention. Within the growing literature on borderlands, scholars have closely considered the divergence and intersections of communities typically examined in isolation due to their geo-political borders (see Appadurai 1986, 1988; Gupta and Ferguson 1992; Canclini 1995). As geographic delineators of boundaries, borders are often presented as the lines that separate communities, regions, and nations. Anthropologist Victoria Phaneuf (2006) points out that the result has seen the terms "border" and "boundary" being used interchangeably. The literature on borders and boundaries, she furthermore points out, characteristically emphasizes their role in the maintenance of difference within or between nation states. In the North American context, the Canada–US border has come to represent a geo-political line that is continually negotiated in relation to cultural identity, social values, and political and economic cooperation (see New 1998; Blaise 1990). Canada–US borderland themes, in other studies, have also often emphasized similarities, as seen through common languages, values, and histories (Phaneuf 2013, 112).

In the case of Quebec itself, studies of the border and how it has shaped Quebec identity are scarce. Those studies that do consider the shared history between inhabitants in Quebec and the United States tend to focus on migration to New England in the late nineteenth and early twentieth centuries (see Rumilly 1958; Hudson 1976; Brault 1986; Weil 1989; Chartier 1991; Roby 2000; Ferland 2002). When Quebec–US relations are considered in these studies, scholars have tended to follow the pattern described above and, concentrating on the importance of language identity among French Canadians, emphasize the differences that the border symbolizes. Still, other studies examining patterns of cultural similarity are found within the existing literature. Phaneuf herself has examined the Quebec–Vermont border region in order to answer questions about the identity of the Americans living there. She finds that being what she calls a "borderlander" forms a central identity for these Americans, shaping their culture, values, historical narratives, and behaviour. Their relationship with the border sets them apart from those unconnected to the region who create and enforce the laws regulating the border (Phaneuf 2002). Local Quebec borderland scholars have also highlighted the extent to which communities on both sides of the border have been connected historically, and how that connection continues to be a defining feature of life along the borderland (see Farfan 2009).

Still others have also begun to examine more closely the complexity of Quebec's and Vermont's cultural dynamics, and the impact of that complexity on the shaping of social and cultural institutions. In a study on borderland identity in the early nineteenth century, Canadian historian J.I. Little demonstrates that religion helped forge a distinctive national identity for English Canadians in the Eastern Townships of Quebec and that the making of that identity was shaped through links of kith and kin across the border (Little 2004). In a study on Vermont identity in the late nineteenth and early twentieth centuries, American historian Paul M. Searls (2006) points out the significance of Vermont's relationship with Quebec in defining the boundaries of Vermont's imagined community. In studies such as these, the border has added a layer of complexity to the historical narratives of Quebec and Vermont.

In the writing of the history of education in Canada, until recently the Canada–US border has received little particular attention as a shared space of cultural integration. When the relationship with the United States has been considered, Canadian historians have tended to focus on the rejection of American values by educational leaders. As historians of Ontario have noted, complaints about the negative influence of American teachers and schoolbooks were common in the history of that province (Wilson 1974; Curtis 1983; Gidney and Millar 1990; Smaller 1993; Gold 2004). In Quebec, the border has received even less attention and historians of education have characteristically concentrated on internal forces pushing for educational development in the province. The central theme in schooling's history in Quebec is that of cultural dualism, marked by divided French and English systems of education (see Audet 1950–56, 1971; Dufour 1997; MacLeod and Poutanen 2004; Magnuson 2005). In a similar vein, educational historians of Vermont have done little to consider borders and borderlands. The writing of educational history in Vermont itself is scarce, and studies that do exist tend to focus on the political and legal development of the system (see Zorack 2006; Sautter 2008; Fussell 1958; Stone 1936; Bush 1900). Emphasis is almost always placed on the local nature of schooling and school decision-making, and the state's own internal forces of division, conceptually highlighted in the divide between rural and urban elements, which have resulted in two different experiences of schooling in Vermont. Those studies that do weave Vermont educational history into an even broader narrative tend to situate it within patterns of educational development in New England and fail to consider the educational relationship of certain localities which form community relationships with neighbours across the Canada–US border.

In recent years, however, educational historians in both Quebec and the rest of Canada have become increasingly aware of the shared social, political, and economic trends that shaped a common experience in the making of public schooling in both nations (von Heyking 2004; Alcorn 2013; Di Mascio 2015; Peace 2017). Yet, we continue to know surprisingly little about those shared experiences. The Eastern Townships of Quebec serves as an example in which we can unpack our understanding a little bit more. American settlers who first arrived in the Eastern Townships during the late eighteenth and early nineteenth centuries tended to look south, and not east or west, for their educational inspiration (Di Mascio 2015). Indeed, as scholars of the Eastern Townships have already pointed out, the flow of both ideas and people across the border contributed significantly to the development of mass schooling in the region from its earliest days. In her study of Quebec English Protestant education in the nineteenth century, Anne Drummond (1986, 1990) notes that of the almost four hundred different academy teachers she identifies in the Eastern Townships between 1829 and 1862, the majority were American. The most important supply of teachers and schoolmasters for the Eastern Townships academies was the University of Vermont and, to a lesser extent, Dartmouth College in New Hampshire. J.I. Little (1998) has also found American influences in his exhaustive work on the Eastern Townships, but his findings serve as a cautionary reminder that such influences were not necessarily welcomed by everyone in the region (see also Little 1997, ch. 6 and 208ff).

There remains much to be learned about borders, and the extent to which schooling in borderland regions such as that of the Eastern Townships and Northern Vermont can be woven into our historical understanding of not only educational development but also of the development of community and identity itself. The discussion on the phenomenon of cross-border schooling that follows offers to advance our understanding of schooling, community, and borderland identity in the Eastern Townships of Quebec and Northern Vermont. That history stands in sharp contrast to more contemporary attempts by policymakers to transform what was once an extremely permeable border into a sharp international boundary increasingly difficult to navigate. A restrictive border has not been the historical norm in the Eastern Townships and Northern Vermont. In large part this is owed to the demography of the region which saw a huge influx of American settlement after the American War of Independence in the eighteenth century that continued well into the nineteenth century. As other studies in the current volume demonstrate, from that time the Eastern Townships and its people have not only been influenced by proximity to the international border, but they have also been intricately connected to the global trends, developments, and identities forged together with their American kith and kin in this shared North American space. Schooling played a major part in forging such shared identities, and, as previous studies have shown, schools in the Eastern Townships in no small way influenced and were influenced by the steady stream of American students, teachers, and other community members who traversed the permeable border (see Drummond 1986; Di Mascio 2015).

CROSS-BORDER SCHOOLING *in the* EASTERN TOWNSHIPS *and* NORTHERN VERMONT

Cross-border schooling in the Eastern Township and Northern Vermont dates to at least the early nineteenth century. From the period covering 1800 to 1899, the surviving records indicate a total of 588 residents of Quebec enrolled in twenty-eight Vermont schools along the entire Eastern Townships/Northern Vermont borderland region.[1] Most of these schools, however, were not what we can call "public schools" in the contemporary definition of the term. While many were aided in part or in full by the state, schooling at this time was completely voluntary in Quebec, and parents were left on their own to decide whether their children should attend school. Nevertheless, we should note that the machinery of public schooling had already been set in motion, and parents did not have a lack of options when it came to schools for their children, especially in the middle to late nineteenth century. The Common School Act of 1841 allowed for the publicly aided schooling of the entire population of Canada East (present-day Quebec) (Province of Canada 1841). Its subsequent revisions in the 1840s and 1850s saw government funding to schools increase considerably. By the time of Confederation in 1867, publicly funded schooling was a central component of Quebec social policy, and the British North America Act entrenched the right to education in the new constitution, leaving its operation and control in the hands of the provinces.

While schooling was not made compulsory in Quebec until well into the twentieth century, it would be incorrect to suggest that the majority of the population did not send their children to publicly funded schools. The majority did so. Indeed, in the superintendent reports of 1875 to 1900 we find, on average, twenty-one schools operating on the Quebec side of this borderland region (Report of the Superintendent 1875–1900). In many ways, the province of Quebec was leading the development of public schooling in Canada. Its success at the World Fair of Chicago in 1893 highlights this point. Of the ninety-two prizes awarded to Canadian exhibits about education that year, the province of Quebec took forty-five (Report of the Superintendent 1894–95, 74). This is an astonishingly high number, especially because schooling in Quebec was still not compulsory. Considering that neighbouring Ontario, with a longer history of publicly aided schooling and with compulsory schooling itself introduced in 1871, took home only twenty-four awards, Quebec's success is made even more remarkable. Indeed, Quebec was no educational backwater, and the people of Quebec did not need to cross educational jurisdictions in order to school their children. Yet, they did.

The trend continued into the twentieth century. From 1900 to 1923, the surviving school records indicate that twenty-five children living in present-day Stanhope, Quebec attended the publicly funded and administered Norton Village School on the American side of the border (NTCO 1900–23). Along Hereford, Quebec and Canaan, forty-nine children crossed the border to attend school in Vermont (CTCO 1900–23). Indeed, writing on the history of the Stanhope–Norton region, former Norton Village School teacher Lydia C. Andrews notes that at the turn of the twentieth century Saint Suzanne de Boundary Line (Stanhope, Quebec) and Norton Mills (Norton, Vermont) "constituted the same academic municipalities." In 1903, in fact, the Reverend M. Leblanc of Norton and Father Amédée Goyette of Stanhope worked together to acquire a house for the purpose of offering an education for the children who lived in the border towns. The building that was secured was the Damon and Baker Drug Store, which was built along the border (Andrews 1986 [2011], 139). The educational agreement that was reached by the two religious leaders, according to Andrews, specified that:

> 1. A school was to be established for the same advantages to children of both localities: Stanhope and Norton. 2. That the priest from Stanhope would render himself personally responsible for the necessary and important purchases such as the building and furniture; 3. The school would be regulated by the academic laws of the Province of Quebec. 4. The Boundary Line School: Stanhope-Norton Mills should remain as ONE and not be divided as if in fact establishing a school for Stanhope and a school for Norton Mills. (Andrews 1986 [2011], 139–40)[2]

Archival records for this school are scarce, and so we are left only with the statistics that Andrews herself was able to provide. By these records, we know that at its opening in 1903, St Paul School, as it was named, saw an enrolment of 120 students from both the Canadian and American sides. Its numbers increased in the 1920s, and in 1923 the building even saw a new 3,600 square-foot section constructed (Andrews 1986 [2011], 140–1). Records at the Coaticook Historical Society, however, indicate that by 1948 interest in the school had waned. The building itself was deemed unsuitable by the Board of Education and had to be shut down. The Sisters of the Presentation-de-Marie, who had been put in charge of the school, continued their work in a new structure in neighbouring Compton, Quebec (Report of the Sisters, n.d.). While the school continued to welcome boarders from both Canada and the United States, it was no longer a borderland school adhering to the fourth principal of the school's founding.

Most school registers for Norton Village School for the 1920s were lost, but they re-appear beginning in 1928. From the period 1928 to 1965, the records indicate a total of forty-three Quebec children attending the Vermont public school (NCTO 1928–55). Similar numbers appear in the school registers of Canaan Vermont, where thirty Quebec children received their education during the same period (CTCO 1923–55). By the late 1950s, Quebec children along the border between Stanhope, Quebec, and Norton, Vermont, either stopped attending Norton Village School or the teachers simply stopped recording them. The latter is probably not the case, as we see the number of children in Hereford, Quebec attending Canaan, Vermont, schools declining as well. While the numbers dwindled, however, it is interesting to note that at least one family in Hereford, Quebec, continued to send their children to school in Vermont as late as 1972 (CTCO 1971–72).

Schooling in Quebec was made compulsory in 1943, and so one might have expected the decline in cross-border schooling to have happened earlier. With a system of its own firmly in place, it seems curious that Quebec parents would choose to use the Vermont school system. A significant number of Quebec parents living along the borderland, however, continued to choose to send their children to school across the border. Despite the new era of regulated compulsory schooling in Quebec, this act by borderland parents did not seem to raise any official concern. In fact, in the Norton Village School register of 1947–48, "Commissioners of Education, Province of Quebec" are listed as visitors on 22 September 1947. These commissioners were charged with visiting schools in Quebec to both ensure that children were attending school and to report on the condition of instruction at the school. It seems to have mattered not to these commissioners that the children of Stanhope, Quebec, and its neighbouring towns went to school in Vermont. They inspected it as they would any other, ensuring that the children were indeed attending school and receiving proper instruction. Their report was presumably sent to the Inspector of Schools for the region. There are no existing records that can be found from commissioner or inspector reports indicating objection or apprehension about Quebec children present at school in Vermont. In fact, from the reports that do exist there is no mention about cross-border schooling. The silence of commissioners and inspectors, in this regard, is quite telling. The fact that Quebec children were attending school in the United States was nothing to be concerned about.

Vermont parents, like their Quebec counterparts, in some cases chose to send their children to schools across the border as well. The historical record, however, is extremely limited with the evidence of cross-border schooling in this regard. As noted earlier, a number of Americans chose the St Paul borderland school serving the Stanhope, Quebec and Norton, Vermont communities. The home residences of its students are impossible to arrive at with the available evidence, so we can only make assumptions about the country from which the students originated. The vision of the school, it would seem, was that roughly half of the students would have come from Canada and half from the United States; however, we cannot draw reliable conclusions.

In the publicly funded and administered schools of the Eastern Townships, the historical record is even less revealing. School registers have virtually all been lost or destroyed, and those that have survived and have been collected in the Eastern Townships School Board Archives in Magog date only from the 1940s onward.[3] Moreover, the quality and quantity of information provided in the Quebec school registers are, compared to those found in Vermont, extremely limited. Unlike their Vermont counterparts, teachers in Quebec were not required to list the place of residence of their students, let alone whether they came from out of town or out of country. What we are left with, then, is a list of student names. In order to determine which students were from Vermont, these names can be cross-checked with census enumerations in the United States. The United States' census sunset law of seventy-two years, however, has only made the 1940 national census recently available; and so even if we can determine that some of the children listed in the Quebec school registers resided in the United States, the volume of evidence itself would remain inconclusive at best. We can reasonably conclude, however, that few if any Vermont children were sent to Quebec schools in the elementary years. With elementary schools on the Quebec side being geographically farther from the border than the Vermont schools, only a small number of parents would likely have chosen the Canadian schools.

At the high school level, however, we have stronger evidence to support the notion of a cross-border culture of schooling that Vermonters themselves actively participated in. The borderland historian is once again indebted to Norton Village School teacher Lydia Andrews, who followed her students' progress even after they left her classroom in the eighth grade. In her personal records, Andrews kept note of where her students would later attend high school and college, and what occupation they eventually found themselves in. While we only have records for seventy-eight of her students, we can note that of the twenty-two that can be confirmed to have attended high school, fifteen attended high school at Canaan High School in Canaan, Vermont, two at St Johnsbury Academy in St Johnsbury, Vermont, and five chose Coaticook Academy in Coaticook, Quebec. Of those five, three were Americans (representing 4 per cent of her total student population, and 14 per cent of those who attended high school). One Vermont student left Norton Village School early to attend a Catholic school in Sherbrooke, Quebec. Upon completion, however, he resumed his studies in Vermont at Canaan High School (NTCO, n.d.).

Based on the available record, it is impossible to draw any broad conclusions about why certain Vermonters would have chosen to go to school in Quebec. Their choice may have been based on religion, on a real or imagined belief in higher academic standards, or on the fact that their parents had themselves attended school across the border. The more likely explanation, however, is that, like their Canadian counterparts who chose the Norton Village School for the elementary years, the Canadian school simply represented the closest geographic option for their wants and needs. In the case of high school choices, Coaticook Academy was located eighteen kilometres away, Canaan High School was twenty-four kilometres away, and St Johnsbury Academy was a distant eighty-five kilometres away. We can speculate that those who chose Coaticook Academy probably lived closest to the Canadian border in Norton, Vermont. To them, Coaticook was no more foreign a town than Canaan or St Johnsbury. They were part of a borderland world in which the border could be ignored for matters of expediency.

As the findings from a study of cross-border schooling suggests, for much of the borderland history of the Eastern Townships and Northern Vermont, the Canada–US border was an extremely permeable line. The findings suggest that this was especially true for Canadians. The well-funded and well-run schools within walking distance that were found across the border meant there was little need for Canadians to either build their own schools or send their children several miles away for an education. Historians have noted the extent to which early school advocates in Canada based their arguments for a homegrown common school system in large part upon the premise that without a closely controlled Canadian system, the threat of American teachers, textbooks, and republican ideas would infiltrate the mind of the young. Along the border of Quebec and Vermont, however, we witness not fear of American education but rather a cultural synthesis of the two countries. This was a synthesis that was strong enough to see that Quebec school commissioners travelled to and inspected the attendance of Canadian students in an American school as though it were one of their own. Cross-border schooling in the borderland region of the Eastern Townships and Northern Vermont suggests that the idea of anti-Americanism as a defining feature of being Canadian is not necessarily true in all parts of the country.

The historiography furthermore typically presents the history as the "two worlds" of Quebec education (Magnusson 2005). Yet, the evidence along the border indicates that both English and French speaking families were sending their children to school in the United States. In some cases, it seems, the children themselves even began their time in the American schools without the ability to speak English. Records kept by Norton Village School teacher Lydia Andrews, for example, demonstrates that at least five of her students in the late 1940s and early 1950s began school with the ability to speak French only (NTCO, n.d.). Why this was the case and what this means to our historical understanding is worthy of further consideration. Ultimately, the answer cannot be drawn from the school records alone, but it is indeed clear that language was not a factor when choosing a school and that educating children alongside both their Canadian and American English-speaking peers was normal enough.

THE FUTURE *of* BORDERLAND IDENTITY *in the* EASTERN TOWNSHIPS *and* NORTHERN VERMONT: SOME CONCLUDING REFLECTIONS

The extent to which Canadians chose the American public schools across the border highlights, as I have previously argued, that the myth of a Canada–US border representing a clearly demarcated line between opposing social and political views should be called into question. Cross-border schooling demonstrates that the debate about identity in Quebec and Vermont is even more complex than we have previously assumed. While the "two solitudes" in Quebec may have been a real, and even defining, feature of Quebec society throughout the twentieth century, along the borderland of Quebec and Vermont we can find yet another solitude. This borderland identity is one that defies definition. It is one that saw a Protestant minister in Vermont team with a Catholic priest in Quebec to offer a religious education to the children of what they considered to be a single community. It is also one that saw Vermont public school administrators ignore the financial burden of schooling children whose parents paid no taxes to their school jurisdiction, or to any school jurisdiction in their state. In fact, it also saw them pay for the cost of sending school buses into Canada to make sure that those "non-resident" children were able to get to school. Catholic or Protestant, Canadian or American, Francophone or Anglophone: it mattered not. The borderland region was in many ways a world of its own, and perhaps any attempt to define it would be futile. Residents were connected in ways that, as Phaneuf has pointed out, outsiders are unlikely to understand. When asked about living "on the edge of a foreign country," June Elliott, a woman from Derby Line, responded vehemently: "Foreign country – that's no foreign country!" Travelling into Quebec, she insisted, "didn't seem as though it were any more significant than going into New Hampshire ... It was one community, essentially" (quoted in Phaneuf 2013, 13).

That community has undergone significant changes in our own time. My research trips across the border in the Eastern Townships and into the local town clerk offices of Northern Vermont provided me with enlightening anecdotal evidence about the impact that changing border policy has had on the community. Several conversations I had with local inhabitants suggest to me that things have changed dramatically. In an exchange I had with one town clerk after a day of research, she expressed to me her exasperation over changing borderland policies. Residents, she noted, did not necessarily even need a passport to cross the border in what was once a tight-knit community. Weather conditions would get too snowy, she recalled, and school buses would simply navigate through the Vermont and Quebec roads as though they were not travelling in and out of foreign countries. She herself would cross into Quebec several times a week, sometimes several times a day, to shop or to get lunch, and to visit with friends. It changed after 9/11. "Nine eleven," she told me, "ruined us."

Reflecting on that statement has given me pause, and it emphasizes, I believe, how deep the changes along the border have been. Those changes did not simply cause an inconvenience, they *ruined* the lives once lived, as she suggests. The public policies that were developed and implemented in the aftermath of an attack that occurred several hundred miles away profoundly changed the lives of these borderland inhabitants. New screening rules; new identification rules; border agents suddenly stopping everyone when once they would simply get waved though. Such border policies that we have collectively come to refer to as the tightening of the border profoundly changed, or *ruined*, their lives. Barely a half century earlier, the American children of these residents were going to school side-by-side with their Canadian neighbours. Now, those same children need a passport to see each other, but, of course, they hardly even meet each other anymore.

When reflecting on the history of cross-border schooling in the Eastern Townships, it is striking how many of these personal stories of change and conflict have appeared since 9/11. In the summer of 2010, *Canadian Geographic* highlighted changes on the Stanstead–Derby Line border that impacted the lives of local inhabitants. It pointed out the story of a Canadian (a dual citizen born in the United States) walking down the Canadian side of his street over into the US to have "a few beers with a friend," as he had for years, without checking in at the border. When spotted by one of the border patrol officers in a local helicopter that was flying overhead, however, his evening took a turn for the worse. Within two minutes, a voice from a bullhorn began shouting down at him, telling him to "report to the patrol post right friggin' now," or else feel the wrath of the law (Lundy 2010).

In September 2011, upon the ten-year anniversary of the 9/11 attack, the *Toronto Star* highlighted the story of Buzz Roy, a pharmacist from Derby Line, Vermont who, "[f]eeling like pizza for a late-evening dinner … called up Steve's, just a few steps across the border in Stanstead, Que., and ordered a large, smoked meat special for pick up." This pre-9/11 "mundane act" of picking up a pizza in what he considered his hometown became, in the post-9/11 world, a violation of borderland laws that eventually led him to be "turned around, placed in handcuffs, and thrown into a cell that also sometimes holds illegal immigrants and drug smugglers." "I was brought up in this village," Roy, who's also a village trustee, explained to the *Toronto Star* reporter. "Until 9/11, it was a non-border. As kids we went back and forth walking, riding our bikes. We didn't think of it as another town – ever. Now," he said, "*this* is the US, and *that* is Canada" (Chung 2011). Roy feels that he and his fellow borderlanders are the victims of public policy that has not taken into account the unique lives that borderlanders have historically lived. Public policy created, implemented, and enforced by outsiders who are disconnected from the special Canada–US cross-border relationship that has historically exemplified this region now threatens to change that history moving forward.

Still, even with the border policy changes after 9/11, the community continued to maintain some semblance of its borderland identity. Cross-border schooling itself, for example, has continued into the twenty-first century. Along the Stanstead–Derby Line border, Stanstead College, a private Canadian high school, continues to welcome local Vermont students. These Vermont students often attend the school with subsidized tuition from the State of Vermont, through a program that allows Vermont children to cross educational jurisdictions in communities where a local school of their own is not supported. Crossing those jurisdictions allows Vermont families in Northern Vermont to send their children to the private boarding school in Stanstead as local day students (Flagg 2013).

Evidence also indicates that locals are finding a balance between their borderland heritage and the new restrictive policies. In at least one local Stanstead business, almost 40 per cent of pre-pandemic revenue continued to come in from its American customers (Got and Wauquier 2021). The Haskell Free Library, a local library built deliberately along the Canada–US border as a symbol of the two nation's local identity, also found a new balance in the post-9/11 world, welcoming visitors from both countries and serving as a site for local events such as family gatherings and borderland weddings. With the COVID-19 pandemic that paralyzed the world in 2020, however, this local community has once again found itself divided. The border closure imposed that year made it difficult for businesses and services in the community to remain open. The Haskell Free Library was forced to close its doors to visitors. Even after the reopening of the border, restrictions continued to pose barriers. Mandatory PCR COVID test requirements at the border, proof of vaccination, and pandemic policies that were not aligned between the two countries all but brought daily cross-border travel to a halt (Got and Wauquier 2021).

The historical changes brought about by the combined events of 9/11 and a worldwide pandemic have certainly changed the lives of Eastern Township and Northern Vermont inhabitants, but, to what extent are the people of this borderland community bound to accept this new way of life? Will life along the line return to a past in which the border was permeable and invisible? It is certainly difficult to imagine, and, as the historical record indicates, navigating a clearly demarcated and increasingly impermeable border that divides Canadians and Americans is, in this region, a new experience reshaping the community and its collective identity. The historical phenomenon of cross-border schooling serves, at the very least, as a reminder that a world in which the border could be ignored, a world in which children walked back and forth across an international boundary to attend school every day, and one in which school commissioners in Quebec did the same without any suggestion that it was exceptional, was a world in which the people of the Eastern Townships and Northern Vermont embraced. It is also a reminder of a past that many of them continue to long for.

Notes

1 Tabulated from the data gathered on the VNKG website.

2 Andrews's life exemplifies the interconnectedness of the borderland community in the Eastern Townships and Northern Vermont. Originally from Massachusetts, Andrews moved to Norton in 1924 where she quickly embraced and, in turn, was embraced by the community. Indeed, she became a pillar of this part of the Eastern Townships and Northeast Kingdom borderland. In addition to teaching in Norton, Andrews worked with children and adults in Dixville, Quebec. After her retirement from Norton Village School, she worked at the Dixville Home, established to provide care and education to children with special needs. She assisted in establishing the Ginette Roy School at the Home and ended up serving as its director for sixteen years. In 1971, her life and

service were honoured at Dixville and one of the buildings was named the Lydia Andrews Cottage.

3 There is a scattering of pre-1940 registers and enrolment records, but still not enough to draw any substantive conclusions about cross-border schooling on the Quebec side.

References

Alcorn, Kerry. 2013. *Border Crossings: US Culture and Education in Saskatchewan, 1905–1937*. Montreal and Kingston: McGill-Queen's University Press.

Andrews, Lydia C. 2011 [1986]. *Three Towns: Norton & Averill, Vermont, Stanhope, Quebec. A History of the Northeast Kingdom*. Norton, VT: The Three Towns Historical Society.

Appadurai, Arjun. 1986. "Theory in Anthropology: Center and Periphery." *Comparative Studies in Society and History* 28 (1): 356–61.

– 1988. "Putting Hierarchy in Its Place." *Cultural Anthropology* 3 (1): 36–49.

Audet, Louis-Philippe. 1950–56. *Le système scolaire de la province de Québec*, 6 vols. Quebec: Éditions de l'Érable.

– 1971. *Histoire de l'enseignement au Québec, 1608–1971*, 2 vols. Montreal: Holt, Rinehart, and Winston.

Blaise, Clark. 1990. *The Border as Fiction*. Orono: University of Maine Borderlands Project.

Brault, Gerard J. 1986. *The French-Canadian Heritage in New England*. Montreal and Kingston: McGill-Queen's University Press.

Bush, George Gary. 1900. *History of Education in Vermont*. Washington, DC: Government Printing Office.

Canaan Town Clerk Office (CTCO). 1900–23. School Registers, all schools.

– 1923–55. School Registers, all schools.

– 1971–72. Canaan High School Register.

Canclini, Néstor Garcia. 1995. *Hybrid Cultures: Strategies for Entering and Leaving Modernity*. Minneapolis: University of Minnesota Press.

Chartier, Armand B. *Histoire des Franco-Américains de la Nouvelle-Angleterre, 1775–1990*. Montréal: Septentrion.

Chung, Andrew. 2011. "Border Towns Struggle with Post-9/11 Security Measures." *Toronto Star*. 2 September. https://www.thestar.com/news/insight/2011/09/02/border_towns_struggle_with_post911_security_measures.html. Accessed 15 December 2022.

Curtis, Bruce. 1983. "Schoolbooks and the Myth of Curricular Republicanism: The State and the Curriculum in Canada West, 1820–1850." *Histoire sociale/Social History* 16 (32): 305–29.

Di Mascio, Anthony. 2013. "Cross-Border Schooling and the Complexity of Local Identities in the Quebec-Vermont Borderland Region: A Historical Analysis." *Journal of Eastern Township Studies / Revue d'études des Cantons-de-l'Est* 41 (2): 37–54.

– 2015. "The Emergence of Academies in the Eastern Townships of Lower Canada and the Invisibility of the Canada–US Border." *Historical Studies in Education/ Revue d'histoire de l'éducation* 27 (2): 78–94.

Drummond, Anne. 1986. "From Autonomous Academy to Public 'High School': Quebec English Protestant Education, 1829–1889." MA thesis, McGill University.

– 1990. "Gender, Profession, and Principals: The Teachers of Quebec Protestant Academies, 1875–1900." *Historical Studies in Education/Revue d'histoire de l'éducation* 2 (1): 59–71.

Dufour, Andrée. 1997. *Histoire de l'éducation au Québec*. Montréal: Boréal.

Farfan, Matthew. 2009. *The Vermont-Quebec Border: Life on the Line*. Charleston, SC: Arcadia Publishing.

Ferland, Jacques. 2002. "Canadiens, Acadiens, and Canada: Knowledge and Ethnicity in Labour History." *Labour/Le Travail* 50: 101–15.

Flagg, Kathryn. 2013. "For Some Vermont Students, School Choice Involves a Trip to Canada." *Seven Days, Vermont's Independent Voice*. 20 February. Retrieved online at: https://www.sevendaysvt.com/vermont/for-some-vermont-students-school-choice-involves-a-trip-to-canada/Content?oid=2242914.

Fussell, Clyde Greenleaf. 1958. "The Emergence of Public Education as a Function of the State of Vermont." PhD dissertation, University of Connecticut.

Gidney, R.D., and W.P.J. Millar. 1990. *Inventing Secondary Education: The Rise of the High School in Nineteenth-Century*. Montreal and Kingston: McGill-Queen's University Press.

Gold, Elaine. 2004. "Teachers, Texts and Early Canadian English 1791–1841." *Proceedings of the 2003 Annual Conference of the Canadian Linguistic Association*. Montreal: Université du Quebec à Montreal: 85–96.

Got, Jonathan, and Morgane Wauquier. 2021. "Canada–US Border Community Reflects on the Impact of Frontier Restrictions, Longs for Return to Binational Normal." *Capital Current*. https://capitalcurrent.ca/canada-u-s-border-community-reflects-on-the-impact-of-frontier-restrictions-longs-for-return-to-binational-normal/.

Gupta, Akhil, and James Ferguson. 1992. "Beyond 'Culture:' Space, Identity, and the Politics of Difference." *Cultural Anthropology* 7 (1): 6–23.

Hudson, John. 1976. "Migration to an American Frontier." *Annals of the Association of American Geographers* 66 (2): 242–65.

Little, J.I. 1997. *State and Society in Transition: The Politics of Institutional Reform in the Eastern Townships, 1838–1852*. Montreal and Kingston: McGill-Queen's University Press.

– 1998. "'Labouring in a Great Cause': Marcus Child as Pioneer School Inspector in Lower Canada's Eastern Townships, 1852–59." *Historical Studies in Education/Revue d'histoire de l'éducation* 10: 85–115.

– 2004. *Borderland Religion: The Emergence of an English-Canadian Identity, 1792–1852*. Toronto: University of Toronto Press.

Lundy, Derek. 2010. "Stanstead: A Town on the Border." *Canadian Geographic*. 1 July.

MacLeod, Roderick, and Mary Anne Poutanen. 2004. *A Meeting of the People. School Boards and Protestant Communities in Quebec, 1801–1998*. Montreal and Kingston: McGill-Queen's University Press.

Magnuson, Roger. 2005. *The Two Worlds of Quebec Education during the Traditional Era, 1760–1940*. London, ON: Althouse Press.

New, W.H. 1998. *Borderlands: How We Talk about Canada*. Vancouver: University of British Columbia Press.
Norton Town Clerk Office (NTCO). n.d. Lydia Andrews Private Files.
– 1900–23. School Registers, Norton Village School.
– 1928–55. School Registers, Norton Village School.
Peace, Thomas. 2017. "Borderlands, Primary Sources, and the Longue Durée: Contextualizing Colonial Schooling at Odanak, Lorette, and Kahnawake, 1600–1850." *Historical Studies in Education/Revue d'histoire de l'éducation* 29 (1): 8–31.
Phaneuf, Victoria M. 2006. "Towards a Vermont–Québec Border Study: Interviews from the Northeast Kingdom." MA thesis, University of Arizona.
– 2013. "The Vermont-Québec Border Region: Negotiations of Identity and Logic in the Northeast Kingdom." *Journal of Borderlands Studies* 28 (1): 109–25.
Province of Canada. 1841. An Act to repeal certain Acts therein mentioned, and to make further provision for the establishment and maintenance of Common Schools throughout the Province. Statutes of the Province of Canada, 4 & 5 Victoria, Cap. 17.
Report of the Sisters of the Presentation of Mary Convent. n.d. Société d'histoire de Coaticook.
Report of the Superintendent of Public Instruction of the Province of Quebec. 1887–1900. Quebec: Department of Public Instruction, 1875–1900.
– 1894–95. Quebec: Department of Public Instruction, 1875–1900.
Roby, Yves. 2000. *Les Franco-américains de la Nouvelle-Angleterre:* rêves et réalités. Montreal: Septentrion.
Rumilly, Robert. 1958. *Histoire des Franco-Américains*. Montreal: USJBA.
Sautter, John A. 2008. "Equity and History: Vermont's Education Revolution of the Early 1890s." *Vermont History* 76 (1): 1–18.
Searls, Paul M. 2006. *Two Vermonts: Geography and Identity, 1865–1910*. Durham: University of New Hampshire Press.
Smaller, Harry. 1993. "Teachers and Schools in Early Ontario." *Ontario History* 85 (3): 291–307.
Stone, Mason Sereno. 1936. *History of Education, State of Vermont*. Montpelier: Capital City Press.
Vermont Northeast Kingdom Genealogy (VNKG) website. n.d. https://www.nekg-vt.com/submenu-schools.php. Accessed 15 December 2022.
Von Heyking, Amy. 2004. "Ties That Bind? American Influences on Canadian Education," *Education Canada* 44 (4): 30–1, 33–4.
Weil, François. 1989. *Les Franco-Américains*. Paris: Belin.
Wilson, J. Donald. 1974. "The Teacher in Early Ontario." In *Aspects of Nineteenth Century Ontario: Essays Presented to James J. Talman*, edited by Frederick H. Armstrong and J. Donald Wilson, 218–36. Toronto: University of Toronto Press.
Zorack, Seth M. 2006. "Vermont's Tradition of Education and the Vermont Constitution." *Albany Law Review* 69 (2): 581–90.

10

"The Latest and Most Important Local and Foreign News": Producing and Reading the Press in the Eastern Townships (1867–1939)

Harold Bérubé and Henri Dion

IN 1866, THE EDITOR of the *Union des Cantons de l'Est* announced that the newly founded paper was both Catholic and conservative, would promote good principles and healthy doctrines in the part of the country called "les Cantons de l'Est," and would keep its readers informed of the important events taking place in Europe and the Americas (14 December 1866, 2). In 1882, his colleague from the *Bedford Times* explained that his paper was both liberal and progressive and would offer its readers "full reports of all matters of local interest ... together with interesting items and miscellaneous news from abroad" (6 January 1882). Similar texts, featuring similar promises to cover both local and international matters, can be found in many of the first issues of the numerous papers founded across the Eastern Townships during the last third of the nineteenth century.

In fact, this period saw the birth of the modern newspaper in North America, distinct from the much more partisan and elitist press typical of the first two-thirds of the nineteenth century (see Schudson 1981; Sotiron 1997; de Bonville 1988). These new papers, relying more and more on revenues generated by advertisements, sought a wider readership and redoubled their efforts to become an indispensable part of communities they represented. At the same time, with the development of transportation and communications, they could cover news on a global scale more easily than ever and bring the world to Bedford or Arthabaska. This chapter examines the Eastern Townships through the lens of these local papers. In doing so, it determines what roles they played in the region during the tumultuous period between the creation of the Dominion of Canada and the start of World War II and demonstrates the ways in which they opened a window on the wider world for their readers.

To do so, we start by offering a general overview of this regional media system between 1867 and 1939 to understand the changes that took place in the Townships during this period and better situate the papers we focus on in our analysis. Then we look at the ways these newspapers covered local and regional news in what they considered to be "their" Townships or Cantons. Finally, we turn our attention to the national and international coverage that they offered their readers. In these cases, we determine what was deemed worthy of interest and why. In the end, we argue that these local and regional newspapers played a central role in the way that Townships editors defined their communities, but also in the ways they situated their communities within the nation, the empire, and the world.

WRITING *the* HISTORY *of* NEWSPAPERS *in the* EASTERN TOWNSHIPS

Things have changed considerably since William J. Buxton and Catherine McKercher (1998) noted that print media and journalism in Canada "have largely escaped academic attention" (1). By that time, Paul Rutherford (1982), Jean de Bonville (1988), and Minko Sotiron (1997) had written extensive general studies of the birth and evolution of the modern newspaper industry in Quebec and Canada. Since then, a few more historiographical essays[1] and numerous case studies have been published, proof that print media and journalism now have the full attention of academics. Still, there are significant limitations to the literature on the subject. For one thing, most of these studies focus on big cities and their newspapers, or on a single regional actor or newspaper. When they do compare different newspapers or different regions, it is generally to analyze the way a particular topic has been covered by the press and not to study the press itself. The historiography of newspapers in the Townships illustrates some of those tendencies and limitations.

Interest in the history of the Eastern Townships' press initially came from the newspapers themselves. As early as 1937, *La Tribune* published collections of facts and information on the subject in Sherbrooke (*La Tribune* 1937).[2] However, most of the academic studies that followed used the local press to analyze the coverage of specific socio-political events such as the possible annexation of Lower Canada to the United States, the American Civil War and the Fenian incursions, the conscription crisis during World War I, and congregational school disputes.[3] Similarly, there are a handful of studies of the representations of various figures in the pages of the press of the Eastern Townships, such as the pharmacist or the female reader (see Sévigny 1994; Bédard 2017). Finally, a few scholars did work on specific publications or figures of the region's press industry, most notably Jean-Pierre Kesteman (1977b) for *Le Progrès de Sherbrooke*, Robert Hill (1998) on Robert Sellar and the Huntingdon *Gleaner*,[4] and Jean Levasseur (2004a; 2004b) on journalist and author Rémi Tremblay.

However, the historiography of the Townships' press remains mostly limited to studies whose primary focus is not the press itself. It especially lacks a synthesis or comprehensive overview of the history of the media in the region. In this regard, one can only count on "Les premiers journaux du district de Saint-François (1823–1845)" by Kesteman (1977a), and a few short articles from local historical societies (Côté and Dallaire 1998; Farfan 2019). Consequently, there is still much to do to get a better picture of the situation.

To contribute to this undertaking, this chapter examines the press in the Townships between the creation of the Dominion of Canada in 1867 and the start of World War II, a period which covers the modernization process of the North American newspaper industry and the transformation of newspapers into the first real mass medium. We examine the press of the region on two levels, providing both a general overview of the situation and a more in-depth analysis of a sample of newspapers from various cities and towns in the Townships. In the first case, we use André Beaulieu and Jean Hamelin's *La presse québécoise des origines à nos jours* (1973; 1975) to produce a general analysis of the region's newspapers from the first few titles in the early nineteenth century up to 1939. Beaulieu and Hamelin's inventory is an invaluable research tool for historians of Quebec's newspapers but a flawed one. Across the thousands of titles listed by the authors through ten volumes, there are a great number of errors and inaccuracies. Consider, for example, the numerous name changes of local newspapers. In some cases, Beaulieu and Hamelin provide a reliable enumeration of these changes in identity, but in other instances, they confuse a change of name with the creation of a new newspaper.[5] Still, their work allowed us to build a database on the 133 distinct periodicals of various types that operated at one time or another in the Townships before World War II.

To offer a more in-depth analysis of the roles played by these newspapers and study their coverage of local, regional, national, and international news, we created a sample of issues from ten different newspapers.[6] These were chosen to provide us with the widest possible variety of cases (language, political affiliation, size of the town where the newspaper was based, longevity), while being accessible to us in one format or another. Indeed, as we quickly discovered, many of the Townships' newspapers from the late nineteenth and early twentieth centuries are lost to us or exist only through a small number of issues kept in local historical societies or available on microfilm (Sévigny 1994, 25). These lacunae are nothing compared to the dearth of preserved documents related to the inner workings of those newspapers, except for a few individual cases such as that of editor and journalist Robert Sellar, and what can be gleaned in the newspapers themselves.[7] Despite these limitations, however, the analysis of the issues included in our sample offer us a wealth of information on the many roles played by local newspapers in the Eastern Townships.

CHARACTERISTICS *and* EVOLUTION *of a* REGIONAL PRESS ECOSYSTEM

The first newspaper published in the Townships was the *British Colonist,* founded in 1823. Its publisher, H. Dickerson, wanted to break the region's isolation by spreading news from around the world to the Townships and making the region's needs and aspirations known beyond its borders (Beaulieu and Hamelin 1973, 46). As we will see, this general goal of linking the local, regional, and global reappears frequently in the papers we sampled.

In the second third of the nineteenth century, the first major changes in the regional press ecosystem correlated with important political events. Four new papers appeared in the 1830s, in the buildup of tensions leading to the rebellions, but this effervescence died down soon thereafter. In the 1850s, the number of papers started to increase again, and the first francophone title in the region, *Le Défricheur,* appeared in 1862 in the small town of L'Avenir. At the time, French Canadians made up about a third of the Townships' population (Kesteman, Southam, Saint-Pierre 1998, 266). The talks surrounding a possible union of the North American British colonies also saw a major change for the press, as the number of papers in the Townships more than doubled in a few short years. While it plateaued in the 1870s and early 1880s, the regional press resumed its growth in the second half of the 1880s, as paper became less expensive and accessibility to small-scale printing equipment increased. It was also at that point that the francophone population exceeded that of anglophones, accounting for 55 per cent of the region's population in 1881. During the last decades of the nineteenth century, the number of publications

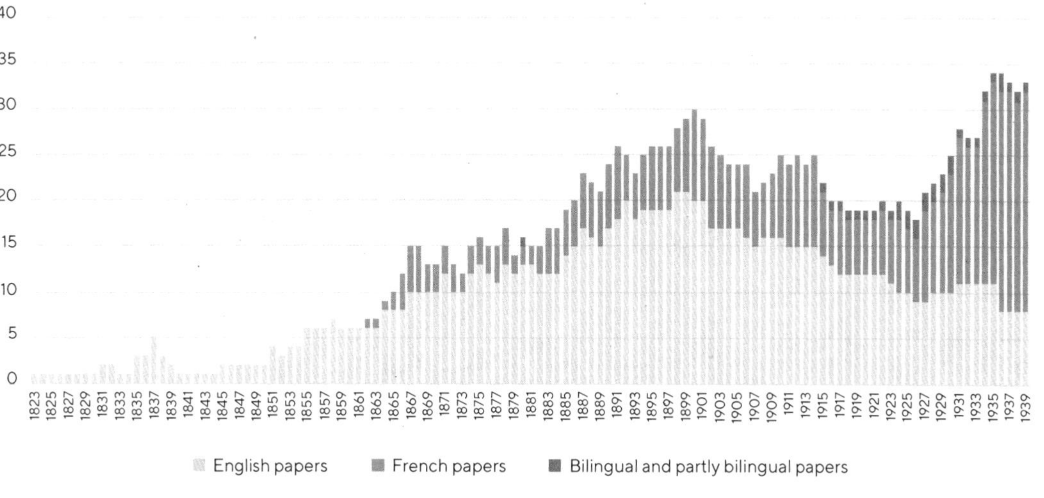

Figure 10.1 Number and language of active periodicals in the Eastern Townships (1823–1939)

again nearly doubled, going from sixteen in 1880 to thirty in 1900, as newspapers became an integral part of modern life for farmers and city dwellers alike. During this period, the French-language press also doubled in number, following its English counterpart. In 1900, a third of the papers of the Eastern Townships were in French, while those who spoke that language represented more than 60 per cent of the region's population.

In the early twentieth century, however, the global number of papers declined and more than a third of them disappeared. The Townships had to wait until 1934 for the region to support thirty papers again. This can be attributed to a saturation of the market, but also to stronger competition from larger metropolitan papers printed in Montreal and Toronto. The early twentieth century also marked the beginning of a long-term decline for English-language papers in the Townships, as they continued to lose ground to French-language titles, making up only a quarter of the papers published in the region in 1940. This decline was, of course, linked to the massive departure of the anglophone population of the Townships to Montreal, Toronto, and western Canada. As for a bilingual press, most attempts at establishing truly bilingual newspapers seem to have failed, although a few of them allocated some space, from a few articles to a page, to the other language. From 1915 onwards, there was always at least one paper in the region that offered this sort of bilingual content. Other publishers opted to print a separate paper, such as *La Parole* (1927–2006) of Drummondville, which also published *The Spokesman* from 1927 to

1968. Finally, during a third and final period of expansion, which affected only the French-language press, the number of titles more than quadrupled from only seven active papers in 1926 to twenty-five in 1940. This growth is a bit harder to explain, especially considering the Great Depression, but our sample seems to indicate it was partly due to the diversification of the written press that was expanding into new and more specialized publications, such as religious, educational, and student periodicals, at a time when the literacy of French Canadians was increasing.[8]

Despite this general growth, the Townships' papers did not escape the hard realities of the era's press industry. Running a newspaper required a lot of work and energy from a very limited number of employees, as regional publications did not have the expansive means of the metropolitan press. And competition remained fierce due to the smaller market. The papers were also plagued by financial difficulties as revenues from advertising were smaller and subscription payments remained difficult to collect.[9] As a result, many newspapers did not survive more than a few years (see figure 10.2 and figure 10.3). Our dataset indicates that more than 40 per cent of the Townships' newspapers lasted less than five years. If we add the many newspapers for which Beaulieu and Hamelin do not offer detailed information, the proportion jumps to 57 per cent. After these difficult first years, the longevity of the region's newspapers generally grew considerably. By the end of the nineteenth century, most towns of importance in the Townships had a local paper and this paper had become an essential local service.

"ROUND ABOUT US": THE ROLE *of the* LOCAL PRESS *in the* DEFINITION *of a* REGIONAL IDENTITY

Given this general picture of the situation, what were the main roles played by these newspapers in various localities of the Eastern Townships? In some ways, these papers inherited the political and commercial functions of their predecessors of the early nineteenth century and evolved toward a more modern conception of journalism without ever entirely shedding their old roles. Despite some linguistic and regional variations, they seem to share a common idea of their general role. In 1898, for example, one can read in capital letters and on the front page of the *Bedford Times* that it is a paper "DEVOTED TO NEWS, POLITICS, AGRICULTURE, ETC" (14 April 1898, 1). Strikingly, around the same time, one can find the exact same words on the front page of the *Waterloo Advertiser* but also, in French, on the *Union des Cantons de l'Est*.[10] Let us look at those different roles more closely.

While the development of the modern press was increasingly tied to city life during the period covered here, things were quite different in regions such as

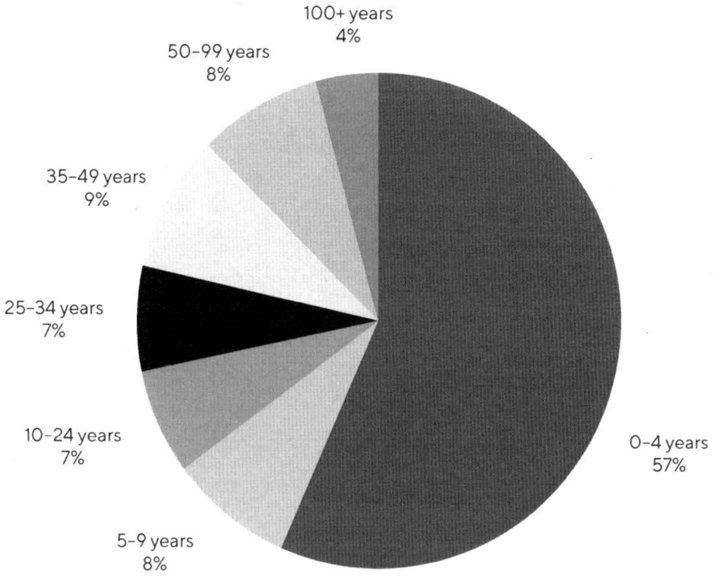

Figure 10.2 Longevity of the Eastern Townships' periodicals (1823–1939)
Note: Newspapers for which longevity is unknown are classified as 0–4 years.

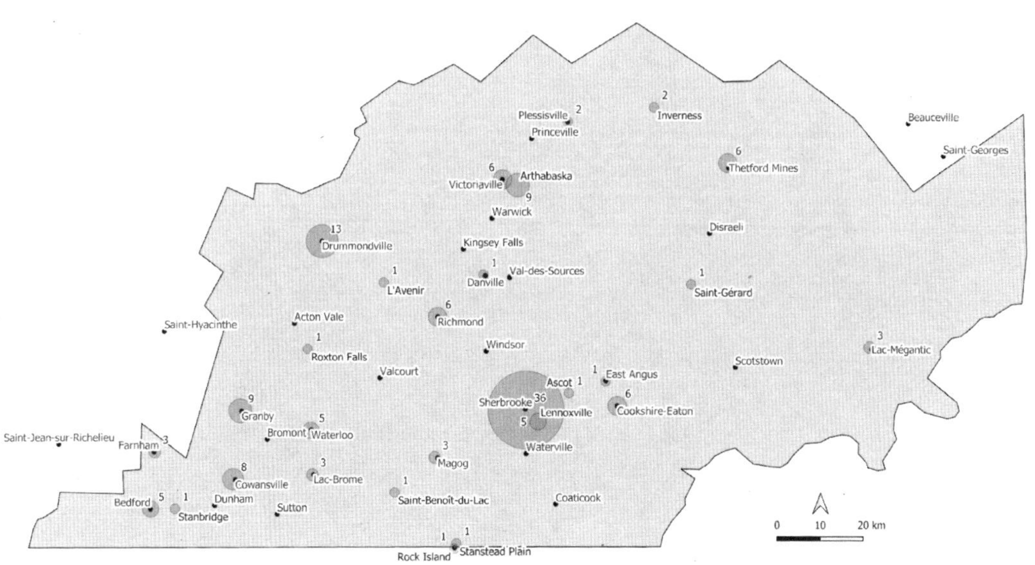

Figure 10.3 Total number of periodicals by locality in the Eastern Townships (1867–1940)
Boundaries of the Eastern Townships inspired by St-Onge et al. (2019).
Data source: Beaulieu and Hamelin (1973, 1975). Map by Henry Dion, 2024.

H Horskin

The Bedford Times.

DEVOTED TO NEWS, POLITICS, AGRICULTURE, ETC.

VOL XX BEDFORD, MISSISQUOI COUNTY, THURSDAY, JAN 20th 1898. 17

The Times, BEDFORD QUE

Sheep Notes.

FERRY'S Famous Seeds

PATENTS

SCIENTIFIC AMERICAN.

Wanted—An Idea

J. F. ROLLIT, SURGEON DENTIST, OLD BANK BLOCK,

GREAT CLEARING SALE!

a reduction of 10 per cent

J. H. SEATON, Lower Bedford

THE EDY MURDER

PRESENTS

HOLIDAY GOODS

FOSTER'S

A. D. FOSTER,

Wonder-Working Diamond Dyes.

CAST AWAY FOREVER.

Paine's Celery Compound Banishes Rheumatism and Sciatica.

Mr. Beechinor was in a Terrible Condition.

Could Not Walk or Put His Hand To His Mouth.

Six Bottles of Nature's Medicine Effects a Complete Cure.

Burdock

RUBBERS & OVERSHOES

...VERDICT...

All the leading dealers in the principal towns of the Dominion agree that

"THE CANADIAN RUBBER CO.'S RUBBERS

ARE THE BEST IN THE MARKET."

STANDARD NEVER LOWERED.

Imperial Embrocation

Rheumatism, Lumbago, Chest Colds, Sore Throat, Sprains, Bruises, Stiffness, Cramps and all muscular pains.

IMPERIAL EMBROCATION CO., MONTREAL.

Bedford Lumber Yard

Constantly on hand SHINGLES X $1.10 XX $1.75 XXX $2.25

Geo. A. Goslett, Prop. BEDFORD, Que.

FIRE! FIRE! FIRE! GREAT Clearance Sale

Of Dry Goods, Ready Made Clothing, Boots and Shoes, Household Furniture &c., &c., Slightly Damaged by Fire and Smoke September 20th, at

KNAPTON'S

On the Corner, now is the time if you want to buy goods at your own price.

THE WEBSTER

E. C. PERKINS

Dr. R. A. ALLOWAY,

J. LAUDER, SURGEON DENTIST Cowansville, Que.

A. LEOFRED, MINING ENGINEER

Figure 10.4 "DEVOTED TO NEWS, POLITICS, AGRICULTURE, ETC.": The various roles of regional newspapers, *Bedford Times*, 20 January 1898

the Eastern Townships. Of course, the region's papers established their offices in towns and cities, but unlike the publications in Montreal and Quebec City, they served a much more rural readership as the proportion of the urban population in the region only grew from 7.36 per cent in 1871 to 39.21 per cent in 1921 (Kesteman, Southam, Saint-Pierre 1998, 275). The importance of this rural readership is best exemplified by the extent of agricultural content provided in many papers. Indeed, most of the papers in the Townships had sections containing articles devoted to agricultural topics such as "Farm and Garden" in the *Waterloo Advertiser* or "Agriculture" in *Le Pionnier* and *L'Union des Cantons de l'Est*. This included new products and techniques, various farming tips, as well as news about

L'Union des Cantons de L'Est

Zéro. NAULT, Imprimeur — LIBERTÉ SOUS L'ÉGIDE DES LOIS — "REDIGE EN COLLABORATION"

64me ANNEE — ARTHABASKA, JEUDI, 11 SEPTEMBRE 1930 — No. 40

"L'Union des Cantons de l'Est"
JOURNAL HEBDOMADAIRE
PUBLIE LE JEUDI PAR L'Imprimerie d'Arthabaska, Inc. PROPRIETAIRE

HENRI D'ARLES

L'ORGE A MALTER

SUCCES COMPLET

INDUSTRIE EN PROGRES

CASTORIA

Victoriaville Taxi, Enr

Consommateurs !

Demandez les Viandes fumées et Saucissons, Marque "Fédérée Princeville," vous aurez entière satisfaction.

En ces temps chauds de l'année, Mesdames les ménagères, vous préférez servir le repas le plus expéditif ; le Jambon cuit "Fédérée," mets très appétissant, répondra exactement à votre désir.

La Coopérative Fedérée de Québec
Succursale de Princeville

Cartes Professionnelles

AVOCATS
Perrault & Girouard
ARTHABASKA, P. Q.

JULES POISSON, C. R.
ARTHABASKA, P. Q.

JOHN F. WALSH C.R.
MONTREAL, P. Q.

WILLIAM PARADIS

Laliberté & Marchand

NOTAIRES

Lavergne & Garneau

B. FEENEY, B.A.,LL.B.,

P. EMILE BERGERON B.A., L.L.L.

Cartes d'Affaires

J. N. MICHAUD
ARTHABASKA, P. Q.

Tourigny & Tourigny
VICTORIAVILLE, P. Q.

Docteur Edgar Larouche
DENTISTE

Docteur L.-A. Trudeau

HOTEL PLAZA

J. E. HEBERT
VICTORIAVILLE, P. Q.

DR J. B. DROUIN

Figure 10.5 "L'orge à malter" and "Industrie en progrès": Balancing rural and urban readerships in *L'Union des Cantons de l'Est*, 9 November 1930

local, national, and sometimes international harvests and events.[11] This could take the form, for example, of an article titled "How Much Milk and Butter Will a Cow Give" in the pages of the *Waterloo Advertiser* (9 September 1870, 1) or a piece discussing the advantages of barley for malt production in *L'Union des Cantons de l'Est* (11 September 1930, 1).

Despite its importance in both French- and English-language newspapers, agricultural news coverage differs in some respects. Colonization, as practised by the French Canadian community, was an aspect of rural life that was not evenly represented through the press. This "mystique" of national expansion through the occupation of new agricultural land within Quebec was in resurgence, thanks to the intense propaganda of its nationalist and Catholic promoters, even as industrial expansion and development drew more and more people to the cities (Courville 2002). Consequently, several French-language papers, especially in the nineteenth century, mentioned it in their pages, echoing this propaganda. In papers such as *Le Pionnier* or *L'Écho des Bois-Francs*, many articles promoted the project and discussed related issues such as rural–urban migration, the emigration of French Canadian workers to the United States, and the exodus of youths from rural areas to the cities. In fact, many of these articles questioned the morality of city dwellers and suggested ways to encourage colonization as a solution.[12] In general, these pieces either tried to persuade the reader that agriculture offered the most satisfying, happiest, and safest living at a time of great economic uncertainty for the working-class, or tried to discourage people from moving away from the rural areas, notably by explaining that there were no jobs in the cities, or that life was miserable in a particular American state. In "Les Embaucheurs" for example, *Le Pionnier* (24 June 1881, 2) warned against listening to some representatives for a Massachusetts company who were visiting the Eastern Townships and allegedly recruiting workers and selling transit fares with no real jobs in the end.

As far as agriculture is concerned, the English-language press had much more liberal concerns. Agriculture was viewed mainly as an industry and disconnected from the kind of nationalist preoccupations that fed the discourse on colonization on the francophone side. The English-language papers instead reported enthusiastically on county fairs, which received a great deal of press every September. Fairs at the time were much more than a farmers' show; they were the main social and cultural event in most localities. Newspapers often announced upcoming fairs, and even discussed the weather forecast. They also covered in detail every day of the event, often providing extensive lists of the numerous winners of each competition.[13] Furthermore, the exhibitions at the fairs were attended by representatives of various groups or companies, who offered produce and services. Even the larger and more urban daily papers of Sherbrooke, the *Daily Record* and *La Tribune*, featured, as did their more rural counterparts, considerable agricultural content. As such, the countryside was omnipresent in the press of the Townships before World War II.

Politics, in general, also played a large part in the coverage provided by the Townships' press. Even though newspapers became less overtly partisan in the last few decades of the nineteenth century, political questions continued to be decisive in the development of the region's press landscape. For example, papers such as *L'Union des Cantons de l'Est* and *Le Pionnier* were specifically launched to support the project of Confederation.[14] Throughout the period covered, the Townships' local papers paid close attention to municipal, provincial, and national political issues, often through the use of material from the metropolitan press but sometimes by using their own journalists and providing analysis of matters debated in Parliament.[15] This coverage had a strongly partisan nature that pervaded editorials and articles in most of the papers we studied. Papers featured accusatory or patronizing pieces such as "The Two-Faced Policy" in *The Waterloo Advertiser* (7 September 1900, 4) or "Les sophismes du libre-échange" in *L'Écho des Bois Francs* (3 December 1910, 2). Yet, in most of these editorials, critics tempered their tone in efforts to preserve a more neutral and cautious line than in metropolitan papers of the time. Clearly, in addition to its more restricted market, the intricate ethnic, religious, and linguistic dynamics of the Eastern Townships led many local papers to promote compromise and unity rather than banking on polarization and polemic to make sales. This characteristic of the regional press was also observed by Beaulieu and Hamelin:

> Often, during the second half of the 19th century, the regional press – or provincial press – has shown the way of moderation to the larger urban newspapers, the only solid foundation on which Canadian unity can rest. More precisely, it has offered some serious lessons on the matter – not often listened to, truth be told – by identifying the main ailments that it suffered from: racial and religious prejudices, unbreathable polemic atmosphere that harmed its audience and its authority. (1975, 85. Our translation)

A notable exception to this general tendency is *Le Présent* of Drummondville, a paper in which editor Napoléon Garceau defended democratic and liberal values with a polemical approach that probably explains its short-lived existence (1912–14). Garceau went out of his way to pick fights with local religious and municipal figures.

Instead, as elsewhere in the country and on the continent, most papers gradually left behind explicit political promotion and polemical editorials in favour of a new journalism focused on news stories and a more neutral editorial line, trading the limited patronage of individual subscribers or political parties for the hard cash that mass media could command from advertisers (Mackintosh 2017, 40–2). In 1897, in the first issue of the *Sherbrooke Daily Record*, proprietor and editor L.S. Channell clearly embraced this new journalism when he boldly declared, "After several years study of the question of editorials in weekly and small daily papers, we are convinced it is a waste of time and space. The people of the country have grown beyond such, and do their own thinking" (9 February 1897, 2). Politically independent and focused on delivering news and information only, his paper became the first successful daily of the Townships. Following the success of the *Record*, *La Tribune*, another independent and news-focused paper, began in 1910 with the aim of bringing a modern daily to the francophone market. Both papers boasted impressive circulation, capitalizing on the absence of other dailies in the region by covering numerous small localities and therefore extending their distribution.

The Townships' press also played an essential role as an agent of economic development, especially through advertising. In the late nineteenth century, the importance of publicity was fully understood by advertisers and by the press itself, as newspapers regularly printed advertisements for their own services in the matter, expanding on the various benefits of advertising for merchants. The *Bedford Times*, for example, published in 1882 an account of a French publisher who argued that advertising works by repetition and that at least six instances of the same advertisement were needed to make a sale (13 January 1882, 3). In a more regional context, such as in the Townships, the press became a necessary link between more isolated consumers and the wider market. While the advertisements encountered in our sample were mostly from local businesses, merchants from Montreal and Quebec City, and even some from the United States, especially Vermont, often appeared (see "Read the News!" *Bedford Times*, 6 January 1882, 2). The development of communications and transport made the distance between region and metropolis increasingly manageable. It became easier to contemplate making a small trip to acquire specific goods, perhaps at a better price, in the department stores of Quebec City and Montreal. At the same time, appearances of known national brands increased gradually in our sample, following the general trend of the era. Advertising took many forms in the pages of Eastern Townships newspapers, such as business cards, advertisements masquerading as news articles, and classic or modern advertising inserts. Interestingly, large and elaborate advertisements were not only employed by metropolitan companies and retailers but also by many local merchants. Although not as complex or as richly illustrated as those metropolitan advertisements, the Robinson Brothers & Stevens' Old Stone Store of Waterloo ran a column in the *Waterloo Advertiser*, just as S. Carsley of Montreal ran in many metropolitan and provincial papers.[16] More generally, in our sample,

Robinson Brothers & Stevens' COLUMN.

NEW GOODS!

Are arriving Daily

AT THE

OLD STONE STORE,

WATERLOO,

and our assortment of

FALL GOODS

will soon be complete.

We invite special attention to our Large Stock of

American COTTONS,

Just received from

BOSTON,

which are being

Sold at

VERY LOW PRICES!!

Robinson Bros. & Stevens

Waterloo Select School.

NOTICE.

PUBLIC NOTICE

NOTICE.

STRAYED

500 ACRES!

FOR SALE AT THIS OFFICE,

THE TRIUMPH!

Farm for Sale.

PERFECTED SPECTACLES

CLEARING OUT SALE!!

TEN Per Cent Discount.

SILVER TAKEN AT PAR.

COTTON YARN,

TEAS!

Flour, Oatmeal, PORK, FISH, SALT,

JOHN GALBRAITH, MERCHANT TAILOR,

GREAT BARGAINS!

DRY GOODS,

MUNICIPAL BONDS.

CARDING MILL

New Store!

New Goods

N. V. D. LABONTE

Dry Goods, Boots & Shoes

Fresh Groceries,

ANGLO-SAXON

SUMMER STOCK

Boots and Shoes

Only FIVE CENTS for WATCH GLASS!!

WOOLLEN FACTORY

Figure 10.6 The very visible column of the Robinson Brothers & Stevens's Old Stone Store, *Waterloo Advertiser*, 9 September 1870

advertisements often occupied about half of an issue's space, a proportion that was constant throughout the period covered.

While the press played a central role as a provider of political and economic news in the Townships, newspapers also played an important role as providers of culture at a time when public libraries were still rare and private ones were limited

The Daily Record

SHERBROOKE RECORD CO.,
Printers and Publishers.

Printed and published every afternoon, except Sunday, at 106 and 108 Wellington Street, Sherbrooke.

SUBSCRIPTION PRICE strictly in advance to any address in Canada, Great Britain and the United States, one year, $2.00; six months, $1.00; three months, 50 cents; one month, 20 cents. To any address in the Eastern Townships, by the year, only $1.50.

Geo. Harold Baker, Advocate, Sweetsburg.
Office open every day.
Personal attendance Wednesdays and Saturdays.
Appointments can be arranged for any time.
Montreal Office:
CHAUVIN, BAKER & WALKER.

Water Works,
Water Powers,
Mining,
Patent Solicitor,
Surveying,
Both Phones.

Dr. B. A. PLANCHE
Dentist
Office and Residence, 55 Depot St.,
FARNHAM
'Phone 104.

LENNOXVILLE HOUSE

When in Lennoxville stop here. Street cars pass the door. Half minute's walk from B. & M., G.T.R. and C.P.R. Stations. Bell 'phone 350 ring 1.
A. M. TAYLOR, Prop.

PASSENGER'S BAGGAGE.

Boston, Sept. 8.—Notwithstanding the provision in the regulations of the Interstate Commerce Commission that a railroad company may not be liable for more than $100 in case of loss of a passenger's baggage, the Supreme Court of Massachusetts, in a decision handed down yesterday, holds that the railroad may still be liable for the full value of the baggage when the passenger knew nothing of the regulation and did not assent to it. The court overruled the exceptions taken by the Boston & Maine Railroad Company to a verdict of $2,133 awarded by Judge Harris, of the Supreme Court, after a trial without a jury, to Katherine Hooker, of Los Angeles, Cal., for the loss of her two trunks and a suit case when the Lake Sunapee, N.H., railroad station was burned on Sept. 17th, 1908.

BEDFORD DISTRCT LOCAL HAPPENINGS.

Gathered by Daily Record Correspondents in Various Communities

MILLINGTON.

Arrivals and departures: Mrs. E. Place, son and Miss Doris Wovendon, of Montreal, guests of Mrs. M. Place; Mr. U. A. Darling of Vale Perkins, guests of Mr. and Mrs. L. Wing; Mr. J. A. Howie of Los Angeles, Cal., a guest of Mr. and Mrs. L. Wing; Mr. Mr. Earl Powell to Sutton; Mr. Harold Wing home from Haverhill, Mass.; Mr. Peter Cote to Eastman Junction Saturday; Mr. Frank Patch and two sons, Hall and Francis, from Brome Corner, guests of Mr. and Mrs. S.G. Patch over Sunday; Miss Durand a guest of her sister, Mrs. Peter Cote; Mr. E. G. Place of Montreal, the week end in town guest of his family and mother, Mrs. Place; Mrs. B. Emmett of Sweetsburg; Mrs. Geo. Manuel and son, Clayton, and Mr. and Mrs. D. Mudget of Sutton, guests of Mr. and Mrs. Geo. Emmett over the week end; Miss Greta Pickering to her home in Lowell, Mass., after two weeks with Miss L. Emmett.

Millington school opened on Monday with Miss Minnie Hurlbut of East Bolton as teacher.

The remains of the late Mrs. Lee Greenleaf, whose death occurred at the home of her daughter, Mrs. Geo. Norris, Newport, Vt., on Tuesday of last week, were brought here on Saturday for interment. The late Mrs. Greenleaf resided in this place for some time, a number of years ago. Among those who came from a distance to pay their last tribute of respect for the deceased were: Mr. and Mrs. Geo. Norris and daughter; Mrs. Dale, Newport, Vt.; Mrs. Greenleaf, Derby Line, Vt.; Mrs. R. Cousins, Bolton Centre and Mr. Green of Newport, Vt., undertaker. Rev. D. Brill, officiated at the cemetery. After the burial the friends were the guests of Mr. J. F. Bryant at dinner.

EAST FARNHAM.

Arrivals and departures: Mr. Harlow Hutchins, of Montreal, guest of his sister, Mrs. R. W. Taber; Mr. Guy Bowker, of Farnham, week-end guest of Mr. Rogers; Mrs. McClay and Mrs. Hoskins to Montreal for a few days; Miss Jessie Grant to Sutton, being one of the staff of teachers in that Academy for the coming term; Miss Bernice Morey to begin her duties as teacher in the village school here last Monday; Mr. Rupert Shufelt and two sisters attending the Cowansville Academy; Mr. Joshua Ball and his grandson, Mr. Albert Hall, are enjoying a pleasant trip to Niagara Falls and other points of interest this week and will also attend Toronto Exhibition; Mr. and Mrs. Fred Hall and two children at Clarenceville, guests of Rev. Mr. Nelson and Mrs. Nelson; Mrs. Armstrong home to Knowlton, having visited her daughter, Mrs. McCullough, for some time; Miss Ethel Hulburd to Valleyfield, having received a position as teacher in the academy.

Mrs. Woodbury is much improved in health after her recent illness.

A number from here attended the concert in Cowansville on Tuesday evening and were much pleased with the entertainment.

EASTMAN.

The Ladies' Guild of St. John's Church met at Mr. C. H. Dingman's cottage on Tuesday afternoon.

Mrs. C. M. Bennette intends going for treatment to the General Hospital Montreal, on Thursday of this week.

Mr. Loren Blunt has taken the contract of building a cottage at Orford Lake for Mr. C. H. Dingman.

The Methodist Ladies' Aid will meet at the home of Mrs. James Dingman on Friday of this week.

Arrivals and departures: Mrs. E. Esty home after visiting her sister at Brigham; Mrs. C. W. Hawley with her husband here; Mr. A. Quinn of Montreal, guest of Mr. and Mrs. C.H. Dingman over Sunday; Miss May Blanchard and Miss Etta Lynch of Montreal, the week end visiting friends; Mrs. Jennie Clifford and her daughter, Inez, with friends at South Bolton; Miss Mary Phelps of Ottawa visiting her parents, Mr. and Mrs. L. D. Phelps; Miss Frances Clifford to St. Johns to visit her brother, Mr. and Mrs. Harry Clifford; Mr. H. A. Dingman to Waterloo where he expects to reside in the future; Mr. C. H. Dingman left on Monday for Toronto and Copperstown, N.Y., on his annual vacation.

Mr. L. E. Beard, Iron Hill has purchased the farm belonging to Mr. L. Blunt.

BONDVILLE.

Mr. Walter Seymour and family are moving into "Rustic Lodge" for the winter.

Mr. Otis Streeter is still busy with the road machine in the southern part of the township.

Mr. C. Noel Soles, assistant post office inspector, of Montreal, and family, were guests of Mr. and Mrs. A. P. Hillhouse over Sunday.

A number from this vicinity are attending the fair at Sherbrooke this week.

Divine service in the Anglican Church will be held on Sunday next Sept. 10th, at 10.30 a.m. From now on through the winter months the evening service will commence at 7 o'clock instead of 7.30 as heretofore.

During the absence of Mr. O. W. Streeter, Mr. John Jones is filling the position of mail carrier between here and Foster most satisfactorily.

Mr. W. H. Jackson and Master Reginald Jackson, of Philadelphia, have been for several days the guests of Mr. and Mrs. C. P. Hunter at "Inverness Farm."

LAWRENCEVILLE.

Arrivals and departures: Mr. E. Lavigne, of St. Hyacinthe, guest of his parents over Sunday; Mrs. A. J. Clothier and daughter, Viola, of Ottawa, guests of her sister, Mrs. A. J. Brown, for a few weeks; Mr. Frank and Hugh Tibbitts, of Montreal, visiting their many friends for a few days; Mr. D. W. and Mrs. Kendall

CONCLUDING DAY OF SHERBROOKE FAIR

(Continued from Page 1.)

HOLSTEIN ADMIRERS MET LAST NIGHT.

MANY CHILDREN IN ATTENDANCE.

IMPROVEMENT IN HORSE SHOW.

LARGE ATTENDANCE YESTERDAY.

CANADIAN BAND EXHIBIT.

It is simply impossible for this space-saving IDEAL Folding

Figure 10.7 "Bedford District Local Happenings": The work of *Daily Record* correspondents in various communities, *Sherbrooke Daily Record*, 9 August 1911

in size and scope. The space occupied in the sampled papers by poems and works of fiction, whether short stories or episodes of serialized novels, was significant. For example, at the end of the nineteenth century, readers will find in the four pages of the *Bedford Times* a whole column of "Etchings," a series of more or less spiritual maxims (see 6 January 1882, 1), and episodes from the novel *The Best Watchmaker* that occupy almost half a page (see 14 April 1898, 2). But some newspapers, especially in the early twentieth century, went beyond simply entertaining their readers

Figure 10.8 The building and employees of *La Tribune* in 1928

and played an important role in launching the careers of local authors such as Rosanna Eleonora Mullins-Leprohon and Minnie Hallowell Bowen (Bédard 2017; Benazon and Côté 2000). Beyond these individual cases, newspapers, at least for a time, played a larger role in animating a significant local literary scene, as one can see in the case of *La Tribune* and the Écrivains de l'Est movement in the 1920s and 1930s (Bernier and Hébert 2018). Perhaps more pragmatically, they also offered local readers a platform on which to share some of their own experiences, as one could read in the 1900 travelogues of a local resident visiting Montmagny, near Quebec City, and those of a local businessman, H.H. Guay, in Europe.[17] In fact, one can learn a lot about the "mundane" life of the Townships in the pages of the local press.

As the press of the time steered towards selling news, sensationalist headlines and macabre stories occasionally showed up in the region's papers, often as gruesome murders or depictions of numerous automobile accidents.[18] However, a much more significant aspect of the regional news coverage was the "Social and Personal" or "Notes Locales" sections.

Detailing miscellaneous bits of local news and the comings and goings of inhabitants, these pieces were ubiquitous in both French- and English-language papers.[19] News items in these sections from the *Écho des Bois Francs* in 1894 include an industrialist obtaining electric lighting in a nearby town, the college's music professor returning from his vacation, and women who went to visit their families in Quebec City (8 September 1894, 2). To the modern reader, the apparent banality of many of such pieces is baffling. At the time, however, these sections clearly served as a regional extension of discussions in the church square and at the post office. With the help of correspondents, the Townships' newspapers extended their "local" coverage to several other localities in sections such as "Nouvelles des Cantons de l'Est," "Dans Nos Cantons," and "St Francis District Local Happenings." This broad reporting must have allowed readers to follow their hometown events or keep in touch with family members living in nearby towns, and to effectively create a new, relatively public way of socializing from a distance. One could argue that this, to some extent, foreshadowed the role played today by social media. The extent of this coverage may be a good indicator of the scope of a paper's regional ambitions. The *Sherbrooke Daily Record* and *La Tribune* were the most extensive, often covering between a dozen and twenty towns and villages in every daily issue.[20]

In this and many other ways, local newspapers played a significant if indirect role in the construction of a regional identity for the Townships. In turn, the way they operated as local enterprises was conditioned by their ability to work within this regional framework. Their very titles are often rooted in the region rather than in the city where they were published, as is the case for the *Eastern Townships Gazette and Shefford County Advertiser* of Granby (1855), the *Advertiser and Eastern Townships Sentinel* of Waterloo (1856), and the *Union des Cantons de l'Est* of Arthabaska (1866). Such references also appear in the regional news sections that can be found in most of the sampled newspapers under titles such as "Nouvelles des Cantons de l'Est" or "Round About Us." Indeed, entire pages are dedicated to small news items coming from surrounding villages and towns and clearly related by local correspondents. For example, the *Bedford Times* covered news from nearby Cowansville, Pike River, Mystic, and Stanbridge East (see 6 January 1882, 2), while *L'Union des Cantons de l'Est* did the same for Dudswell, D'Israeli, Ste-Anne-du-Sault, Lourdes, Plessiville, Ham-Nord, Stanstead, Sherbrooke, Danville, and Magog (see 7 September 1900, 3). By informing local readers of what was happening in the surrounding localities, newspapers helped create a sense of regional belonging but also opened the door to extending their readership beyond the town where they were based.

Things become a bit more complicated when we examine more concretely how these newspapers interacted with one another at the regional level (and beyond). The evidence suggests that this was a close-knit world, with editors frequently quoting from one another and calling each other out. Sometimes boastful discourse played upon friendly competition, such as when the editor of the *Bedford Times* writes that his paper "has a larger circulation than any other paper in Missisquoi County, and although the first copy was issued during the great business depression of the last five years, while other papers have fallen off in circulation [the *Times*] has not only maintained itself but has gained steadily in favor and in strength" (6 January 1882, 2).[21] Or when, a few years later, the editor of the *Magog News and Stanstead County Advocate* worried that "the Liberals of Missisquoi are resolved to have an organ, and that another paper will shortly appear in Bedford ... It goes without saying that the county cannot support three newspapers" (14 September 1888, 4). But there are also many other examples of collaboration among them. For example, *Le Pionnier* (see 13 October 1866, 2) shared its presses and administration with *The Sherbrooke Freeman*, and L'Avenir's *Le Défricheur* used the old presses of the *Waterloo Advertiser*, bequeathed by the proprietor of the latter to that of the former (Beaulieu and Hamelin 1975, 25). What is even more interesting is the way the Townships' newspapers adapted to the increasing presence of metropolitan papers in the region. Unsurprisingly, these metropolitan papers were frequently quoted in the local ones, yet some of them went so far as to adopt marketing strategies that integrated this metropolitan press not as a rival but as a complementary source of information for its readers. For example, both the *Bedford Times* (see 6 January 1882, 3) and the *Waterloo Advertiser* (see 23 June 1922, 2) offered subscriptions combining their own local and weekly titles to daily metropolitan newspapers (the *Witness* and the *Herald* in the first case, the *Montreal Daily Star* in the second). Finally, there is something striking about the existence of the various ties between papers in the Townships and northern Vermont, reminding us that the Eastern Townships are also borderlands, deeply tied to nearby American states, then as now.[22] The Townships' newspapers were not only local institutions but also windows on a wider world for their readers.

"THE VERY LATEST FROM ALL *the* WORLD OVER": THE DOMINION, THE REPUBLIC, THE EMPIRE, *and* BEYOND

In its edition of the 14 April 1898, the *Bedford Times* included a section with the unwieldy title "The News of the Week. The Very Latest from all the World Over. Interesting News About our Own Country, Great Britain, The United States, and All Parts of the Globe. Condensed and Assorted for Easy Reading" (6). As Kesteman (2006) noted, as early as the middle of the nineteenth century, the Eastern Townships had become an important passageway between the United

States and British North America and, by the end of the century, the region was linked to various North American networks. At the same time, its economy and demography increasingly became linked to transnational trends and systems, especially within the Anglo-American sphere of influence. This included the exchange and circulation of news and information within the press. By the end of the nineteenth century, the British Empire also took the form of an imperial press system, and all the papers sampled here included at least one section offering its readers a window on the world, even though this window was often limited and a source of bias and distortion (Potter 2003).[23]

The first way local papers widened the horizons of their readers was by offering them news from across the Dominion. In many ways, British Columbia or Alberta were further from the Townships than neighbouring Vermont or Massachusetts. This national coverage began with what was happening in the rest of the Province of Quebec, and our sample clearly shows that local journalists and editors kept a close watch on provincial metropolitan newspapers, even across the linguistic barrier. For example, the political notes and commentaries in the *Bedford Times* (see 13 January 1882, 3) suggest a close reading of *La Minerve*. The same paper, a few years later, included a section titled "Purely Canadian News. Interesting Items about our own Country. Gathered from Various Points from the Atlantic to the Pacific" and provided just that, using dispatches from various Canadian newspapers. One finds similar coverage in the French-language newspapers, with a particular interest for political debates in Ottawa but also agricultural news from the western part of the country.[24]

Beyond Canada, the two other countries that received the lion's share of international coverage in the sampled newspapers were Great Britain and the United States, Canada's two main political and economic partners. In fact, international news sections in these papers were often structured in such a way as to give distinct subsections to these two countries before covering the rest of the world in a jumble. The neighbouring republic received a great deal of coverage, especially if we add regional news embracing the adjacent states and news covering politics in Washington and events in farther parts of the republic. In the first case, for example, one section in the *Bedford Times* called "Over the Line" offered such regional coverage (see 13 January 1885, 3), and an article from the *Waterloo Advertiser* in 1900 discussed the propagation of smallpox in nearby Vermont (7 September 1900, 1). When they look at the republic beyond the borderlands, the Townships' papers often covered more sensationalist stories gleaned from various American newspapers. Of particular interest, at least in the newspapers sampled, were car accidents, whether in faraway California or in the Townships themselves, where

American drivers were increasingly present in the 1920s.[25] Still, most papers also offered more in-depth coverage of American political affairs, especially about issues having repercussions on the economic relationship between Canada and the United States. For example, in a single issue of the *Bedford Times* from 13 January 1885, we find articles on the production of cotton in the United States (compared to that of Great Britain), a detailed criticism of the effects of protectionism on the economic exchanges between the two countries, and attacks against specific members of the American Senate on this issue. The same mix of miscellaneous news and more in-depth coverage of important political and economic issues is found when analyzing coverage devoted in those same papers to Great Britain. This coverage is as detailed in the English-language newspapers as in the French ones. For example, in 1894, the *Écho des Bois Francs* provided a critical analysis of the effects of trade policies favouring free trade put forth by Richard Cobden a few decades earlier (8 September 1894, 2). Fifteen years later, the same newspaper provided complete and enthusiastic coverage of George V's coronation (3 December 1910, 2). Interestingly, we also found instances of local papers commenting on the way the motherland's newspapers covered its North American colony, such as when the *Bedford Times* (14 April 1898, 6) celebrated the *Aberdeen Free Press*'s very positive assessment of the state of agriculture in Ontario and Manitoba in 1894.

Great Britain's Empire was the gateway through which many of the sampled papers covered issues in the rest of the world. In other words, international coverage was deeply influenced by an imperial perspective, with a lot of space given to regions of the world belonging to or bordering the Empire, and a perception of other parts of the world coloured by their diplomatic relations with Great Britain. For example, a reader of the *Bedford Times* in 1898 would have learned that all British officers were then expected to know the language of their colonial troops (14 April 1898, 2), while a reader of the *Sherbrooke Daily Record* would read in detail, a little more than thirty years later, about the efforts made by Gandhi to try to establish a full national government in India (6 September 1930, 1). Meanwhile, in the pages of the *Écho des Bois Francs*, the same reader would be able to read accounts of the "exploits" of British troops in China at the turn of the century (8 September 1900, 1). The Townships' newspapers like the *Waterloo Advertiser* also provided coverage of the great European political and military events of their time, such as the Franco-Prussian War of 1870 (see 9 September 1870, 2). In such cases, while both the English- and French-language press considered the British perspective on such events first, the latter ones paid a little more attention to the French perspective but always with a certain dose of ambiguity, as French Canada remained ambivalent toward republican or imperial France during the period covered here.[26] Beyond the Empire and the great powers of Western Europe, the Townships' newspapers provided international coverage that more often took the form of miscellaneous news that sought to surprise and shock readers rather than inform them. For example, in a column titled "Autour du Monde," the reader of *L'Écho des Bois Francs* learned that, in Russia, there were about ten newspapers for every one million inhabitants, that a quarter of all women in Austria worked in mines, and that the oldest German newspaper was called *Post Zeitung* (see 8 September 1900, 4). And the news coming from outside the Western world was often clearly used to show how uncivilized those other parts of the world were in comparison, as when the *Bedford Times* reported on the "fact" that a horse had more value in Russia than a human life (14 April 1898, 2).

Finally, local newspapers in the Townships offered their readers another perhaps unexpected way to explore the world: through fiction. Indeed, many of the serialized novels found in their pages take place in various exotic locals, although we may wonder how accurate a depiction of Mexico or India can be found in "The Mystery of Barranca. A Mexican Story of Love and Adventure" or "The Mysterious Rajah. A Thrilling Tale of the Sepoy Rebellion."[27] Still, we cannot deny that the various papers published throughout the Eastern Townships offered glimpses of what was going on in the four corners of the world to their readers, even if the quantity and quality of the information was quite uneven.

CONCLUSION

In this chapter, we have provided a general overview of the characteristics and evolution of the Eastern Townships' regional press ecosystem between the creation of the Dominion of Canada and the beginning of World War II. As we have shown, during those decades, a relatively dense network of weekly (and a few daily) newspapers took shape and played a still understudied but central role in the circulation of information in the region and beyond. Up to a point, this network reflects the demographic evolution of the population of the Townships, but unlike older papers these new titles had a wider circulation and tried to interest as wide a readership as possible. To do so, they attempted to play many roles at once, offering tips and information to local farmers, reporting and commenting on important political issues, advertising local and national businesses, offering their readers different sources of entertainment, covering the comings and goings of local residents as well as describing events large and small taking place around the world. In doing so, these papers offered their readers a diversified and somewhat fragmented content.

It is important to remember that even though this chapter breaks down the information found in the Townships' newspapers into a few large categories, the men and women who read those newspapers were exposed, each week, to a jumble of information that, from one column to the next, took them from their neighbours' backyards to the chambers of Russia's czar. For example, in a single issue, on 11 September 1930, *L'Union des Canton de l'Est* reminded its readers to pay their subscriptions to insure the continuing publication of their paper, described what daily life looked like in Alberta (through a correspondent), offered an article on the benefits of cultivating "l'orge à malter" and information on the impact of a new provincial piece of legislation on the functioning of local cooperatives, covered a revolution in Argentina, warned its readers of the progress of Communist troops in China, and provided a more reassuring assessment of the increasing maritime supremacy of the British Royal Navy, before moving on to the social notes from Victoriaville. There is a richness to this varied content but also some disorder in the way it is presented to readers. It certainly reflects the variety of roles played simultaneously by these newspapers in the Townships as well as their relatively limited resources and the need to fill their pages with whatever they could find at as small a cost as possible.

Still, in many ways, papers played a central role in connecting local, regional, national, and global news during those decades when they were the main source of media. In the years following World War II, things changed quickly with the increasing influence and circulation of metropolitan newspapers such as *La Presse* and *The Gazette* as well as with the increasing popularity of radio and the coming of television in the 1950s.

Notes

1 Among these are Roy and de Bonville (2000), Roy (2009), and Marquis (2013).

2 For a later example, see O'Neil (1961).

3 Among these studies are, for example, Mills (1947), Little (1992), Little (2012), Bussières (1997), and Di Mascio (2020).

4 Of course, Huntingdon is not part of the Eastern Townships *per se*, but Sellar's newspaper had powerful echoes in the Anglophone community of the Townships.

5 It is difficult to determine exactly how many periodicals were published due to the incomplete nature of the sources, the many openings and closing of the press enterprises, their frequent name changes, and finally because of the "decomposition" of newspaper names in collective memory and in sources, a concept explained by Louis O'Neil (1961).

6 The newspapers and their periods of activity are: the *Bedford Times* (1879–98), *La Tribune* (1910–), *L'Écho des Bois-Francs* (1894–1909), *Le Pionnier* (1866–1902), *Le Présent* (1912–14), *L'Union des Cantons de l'Est* (1866–), the *Magog News and Stanstead County Advocate* (1887–1935), the *Sherbrooke Daily Record* (1897–), *The Spokesman* (1928–61), and

the *Waterloo Advertiser and Bedford District Advocate* (1856–1909). Our sample was constituted by selecting, for each of these papers, one issue at intervals of approximatively thirty years, plus the first and last issue published by the paper during the studied period (when possible). Of course, there were significant variations for each paper depending on its longevity and availability. For example, there are very few issues of the *Bedford Times* available and the paper was relatively short lived. So, we analyzed all of them. For each paper, our sample varied between two and ten issues.

7 In 1882, for example, one can read in the pages of the *Bedford Times*: "Our patrons will find the TIMES office in Rice's block, up one flight of stairs. Our old quarters were too small and dark, hence the change" (*Bedford Times*, 6 January 1882, 3).

8 For example, one can think of the *Bulletin de Saint-Benoît* published by the Oblats of Saint-Benoît-du-Lac) (1931–53), of the *Revue des éleveurs de renards* (1934–71), or of *La Ferme* (1939–74).

9 See, for example, "Appel aux abonnés," *L'Écho des Bois-Francs*, 3 December 1910, 4; "Avis à nos abonnés," *L'Union des Cantons de l'Est*, 11 September 1930, 5.

10 Founded in 1866, the *Union* is subtitled "Journal Politique, Industriel, Littéraire et Agricole.

11 See, for example, "Farm and Garden," *Waterloo Advertiser and Bedford District Advocate*, 7 September 1900, 4; "Agriculture – Les cendres," *Le Pionnier*, 6 January 1887, 1; "Agriculture – Animaux nuisibles," *L'Union des Cantons de l'Est*, 7 September 1900, 4; "Farmers urged to pay a visit to soil train," *Sherbrooke Daily Record*, 5 September 1930, 4; "Compton exporte sa crème – Conditions des cultures," *La Tribune*, 5 September 1930, 3; "La récolte au Canada," *L'Écho des Bois-Francs*, 3 December 1910, 4; "Soil Improvement Train Stops Here at End of Present Month," *The Spokesman*, 9 September 1930, 1; "Record dans les ventes de grain," *La Tribune*, 5 September 1930, 1.

12 See, for example, "La famille," *L'Écho des Bois-Francs*, 3 December 1910, 2; "La Dépopulation des Campagnes," *Le Pionnier*, 24 June 1881, 2; "Mouvement Agricole – Et la Jeunesse Canadienne," *L'Écho des Bois-Francs*, 8 September 1894, 1; "Colonisation," *Le Pionnier*, 8 September 1871, 1; "Suggestions pour favoriser la colonisation," *Le Pionnier*, 24 June 1881, 1.

13 See, for example, "Fall Fairs," *Waterloo Advertiser and Bedford District Advocate*, 7 September 1900, 3; "Dates of fall fairs in Eastern Townships," *Sherbrooke Daily Record*, 5 September 1930, 2; "Fine weather favored fair at Scotstown," *Sherbrooke Daily Record*, 5 September 1930, 1; "Brome Fair Was Well Attended All Three Days," *The Spokesman*, 9 September 1930, 1.

14 See, for example, "Prospectus aux abonnés," *Le Pionnier*, 13 October 1866, 2. See also Beaulieu and Hamelin (1975, 88).

15 See, for example, "Lettres Parlementaires," *Le Pionnier*, 24 June 1881, 2.

16 See "Robinson Brothers & Stevens' Column," *Waterloo Advertiser and Bedford District Advocate*, 9 September 1870, 3. The "Colonne Carsley," "Carsley's Column," or sometimes "Carsley's Advertisement" can be found in many papers of the province in the last decades of the nineteenth century. Here are some examples: *La Patrie*, Montreal, 16 February 1885, 4; *La Minerve*, Montreal, 25 February 1885, 2; *L'Étendard*, Montreal, 2 March 1885, 4; *La Presse*, 24 March 1887, 3; *Le Sud*, 20 May 1890, 2; *The Montreal Daily Witness*, 18 May

1882, 1; *The Montreal Herald and Daily Commercial Gazette*, 6 June 1890, 4; *The Weekly Examiner*, 27 July 1888, 1; *The Morning Chronicle*, 13 October 1890, 3.

17 For the details of these journeys, see *L'Union des Cantons de l'Est*, 7 September 1900, 2; *L'Écho des Bois-Francs*, 8 September 1900, 2.

18 See, for example, "Horrible Meurtre à Monte-Bello," *L'Union des Cantons de l'Est*, 7 September 1900, 4; "Pendaison du meurtrier de 22 personnes," *La Tribune*, 5 September 1930, 3; "Triste aventure en Californie," *L'Écho des Bois-Francs*, 8 September 1900, 2; "And Still They Come," *Waterloo Advertiser and Bedford District Advocate*, 23 June 1922, 4.

19 See, for example, "City News," *Sherbrooke Daily Record*, September 1911, 4–5. "Social and Personal," *Sherbrooke Daily Record*, 5 September 1930, 6; "Social & Personal," *The Spokesman*, 9 September 1930, 1; "The Town's Gossip," *The Spokesman*, 4 September 1928, 2.

20 For some examples of this, see "Échos de Partout," *Le Pionnier*, 24 June 1881, 2; "Eastern Township News," *Waterloo Advertiser and Bedford District Advocate*, 7 September 1900, 3; "South Stukely," *Waterloo Advertiser and Bedford District Advocate*, 7 September 1900, 2; "Dans les Bois-Francs," *L'Écho des Bois-Francs*, 8 September 1900, 3; "Dans les Cantons de l'Est," *La Tribune*, 9 September 1910, 3–6; "Bedford District Local Happenings," *Sherbrooke Daily Record*, September 1911, 3; "St Francis District Local Happenings," *Sherbrooke Daily Record*, 8 September 1911, 2.

21 In the same issue, a journalist of the *Times* writes about the Saint-Jean *News*: "No other paper in the Eastern Townships can descend to its level in that line."

22 For example, the *Bedford Times* quoted articles gleaned in the *Burlington Hawkeye* (see *Bedford Times*, 6 January 1882, 2. There are also examples in many of the sampled newspapers of advertisements from American shops and businesses located in Vermont.

23 See, for example, "Nouvelles d'Europe," *L'Union*, 10 January 1867; "Bulletin de la semaine," *L'Union*, 8 September 1870; "Revue Européenne," *Le Pionnier*, 24 June 1881; "Latest European News!" *Magog News*, 14 September 1888; "Autour du Monde," *L'Écho*, 8 September 1900; "Telegraphic Dispatches Summarizing Canadian and World News," *Sherbrooke Daily Record*, 8 September 1911.

24 See, for example, "À Ottawa – Séances tumultueuses," "La récolte au Canada," Écho des Bois Francs, 3 December 1910, 1, 4; "Joussard – En Alberta," *L'Union des Cantons de l'Est*, 11 September 1930, 6.

25 See, for example, Écho des Bois Francs, 8 September 1900, 2; *Waterloo Advertiser*, 23 June 1922, 4.

26 For a good example of this, see *L'Union des Cantons de l'Est*, 8 September 1870, 2.

27 These stories appeared in, among others, *The Magog News and Stanstead County Advocate*, 14 September 1888, 2; *The Magog News and Stanstead County Advocate*, 18 September 1891, 2.

References

Beaulieu, André, and Jean Hamelin. 1973. *La presse Québécoise des origines à nos jours. Vol. 1, 1764–1859*. Quebec City: Presses de l'Université Laval.

– 1975. *La presse Québécoise des origines à nos jours. Vol. 2, 1860–1879*. Quebec City: Presses de l'Université Laval.

Bédard, Mylène. 2017. "Flattée et pourfendue: représentations de la figure de la lectrice dans *Le Pionnier* de Sherbrooke." *Voix et Images* 42 (3): 39–52.

Benazon, Michael, and Sylvie Côté. 2000. "Minnie Hallowell Bowen (1861–1942): The Papers of an Upper-Class Anglophone Woman from Sherbrooke." *Journal of Eastern Townships Studies* 17: 75–85.

Bernier, Stéphanie, and Pierre Hébert. 2018. "'Je cours mettre ceci dans la prochaine boîte, par une pluie battante qu'il fait …': d'une lettre à la poste au mouvement des Écrivains de l'Est (1927–1934)." *Mens. Revue d'histoire intellectuelle et Culturelle* 17 (1–2): 107–34.

Bussières, Jacinthe. 1997. "*La Tribune*, *Le Devoir* et les manifestations de Québec contre La conscription en 1918: la diffusion d'une idéologie par le traitement journalistique." *Journal of Eastern Townships Studies* 10: 5–17.

Buxton, William J., and Catherine McKercher. 1998. "Newspapers, Magazines and Journalism in Canada: Towards a Critical Historiography." *Acadiensis* 28 (1): 103–26.

Côté, Sylvie, and Gilles Dallaire. 1998. "Dossier: *The Record*." *Journal of Eastern Townships Studies* 12: 61–101.

Courville, Serge. 2002. *Immigration, colonisation et propagande. Du rêve américain au rêve colonial*. Montreal: Éditions MultiMondes.

De Bonville, Jean. 1988. *La presse québécoise de 1884 à 1914: genèse d'un média de masse*. Quebec City: Presses de l'Université Laval.

Di Mascio, Anthony. 2020. "The Dissentient School Problem in the Eastern Townships, 1841–1867." *Journal of Eastern Townships Studies* 48: 61–77.

Farfan, Matthew. 2019. "The First Newspapers." *Townships Heritage WebMagazine*. http://townshipsheritage.com/article/first-newspapers.

Hill, Robert. 1998. *Voice of the Vanishing Minority: Robert Sellar and the Huntingdon "Gleaner," 1863–1919*. Montreal and Kingston: McGill-Queen's University Press.

Kesteman, Jean-Pierre. 1977a. "Les premiers journaux du district de Saint-François (1823–1845)." *Revue d'histoire de l'Amérique française* 31 (2): 239–53.

– 1977b. "'Le progrès' (1874–1878): étude d'un journal de Sherbrooke." MA thesis (History), Université de Sherbrooke.

– 2006. "Ruralité et mondialisation dans les Cantons-de-l'Est du Québec: Le regard de l'historien." *Journal of Eastern Townships Studies* 29–30: 5–18.

Kesteman, Jean-Pierre, Peter Southam, and Diane Saint-Pierre. 1998. *Histoire des Cantons de l'Est*. Sainte-Foy: Institut québécois de recherche sur la culture.

La Tribune. 1937. "Historique des journaux de Sherbrooke." 31 July, 4.

Levasseur, Jean. 2004a. "Rémi Tremblay (1847–1926); la trépidante histoire d'un journaliste dans les Cantons de l'Est (part 1)." *Journal of Eastern Townships Studies* 24: 31–50.

– 2004b. "Rémi Tremblay (1847–1926); la trépidante histoire d'un journaliste dans les Cantons de l'Est (part 2)." *Journal of Eastern Townships Studies* 25: 23–43.

Little, J.I. 1992. "The Short Life of a Local Protest Movement: The Annexation Crisis of 1849–50 in the Eastern Townships." *Journal of the Canadian Historical Association / Revue de la Société historique du Canada* 3 (1): 45–67.

– 2012. "From Borderland to Bordered Land: Reaction in the Eastern Townships Press to the American Civil War and the Threat of Fenian Invasion." *Social History/ Histoire sociale* 14 (89): 1–24.

Mackintosh, Phillip Gordon. 2017. *Newspaper City: Toronto's Street Surfaces and the Liberal Press, 1860–1935*. Toronto: University of Toronto Press.
Marquis, Dominique. 2013. "L'histoire de la presse au Québec: état des lieux et pistes de recherche." *Médias 19* (blog). http://www.medias19.org/index.php?id=15556.
Mills, G.H. Stanley. 1947. "The Annexation Movement of 1849–50 as Seen through Lower Canadian Press." MA thesis (History), McGill University.
O'Neil, Louis. 1961. "Des recherches n'ont pu permettre de déterminer le nombre exact de journaux qu'il y a eu à Sherbrooke." *La Tribune*, 16 December, 19.
Potter, Simon J. 2003. *News and the British World: The Emergence of an Imperial Press System 1876–1922*. Oxford: Oxford University Press.
Roy, Fernande. 2009. "Recent Trends in Research on the History of the Press in Quebec." In *Communicating in Canada's Past: Essays in Media History*, edited by Gene Allen and Daniel J. Robinson, 257–70. Toronto: University of Toronto Press.
Roy, Fernande, and Jean De Bonville. 2000. "La recherche sur l'histoire de la presse québécoise. Bilan et perspectives." *Recherches sociographiques* 41 (1): 15–51.
Rutherford, Paul. 1982. *A Victorian Authority: The Daily Press in Late Nineteenth-Century Canada*. Toronto: University of Toronto Press.
Schudson, Michael. 1981. *Discovering the News: A Social History of American Newspapers*. New York: Basic Books.
Sévigny, Yves. 1994. "L'image du pharmacien et les pratiques pharmaceutiques dans la presse de Sherbrooke (1837–1908)." MA thesis (History), Université de Sherbrooke.
Sotiron, Minko. 1997. *From Politics to Profit: The Commercialization of Canadian Daily Newspapers, 1890–1920*. Montreal and Kingston: McGill-Queen's University Press.
St-Onge, Audrey, Jody Robinson, and Will Fabian. 2019. *Quebec's Eastern Townships: A Brief History of Its Peoples, Politics, and Economy*. Sherbrooke, QC: Eastern Townships Resource Centre.

11

"A duty to her Indian citizens": Bishop's University and Canada's "Indian Problem," 1845–1945

Louis-Georges Harvey

> If we cannot face our own traditions without illusion,
> then the remembrance of the victims will become a farce.
>
> JÜRGEN HABERMAS (1993)

ON 6 MAY 1938, students, faculty, and community members assembled in Convocation Hall at the University of Bishop's College in Lennoxville to hear a lecture on the work being accomplished in St George's Indian Residential School in Lytton, British Columbia. The university's principal, Dr A.H. McGreer, welcomed the Reverend Adam Lett back to the college, his *alma mater*, where he had earned a licentiate in sacred theology (LST) in 1920 (Masters 1950, 191), less than two years before being appointed principal of the residential school. Reverend Lett explained that his school was not a missionary school *per se* but actually the property of the federal government, although the principal and staff were chosen by the Anglican Church. Nevertheless, under his administration it had prospered with the construction of many new buildings and facilities. "Today, Lett boasted, the new building accommodates 170 Indian children with grades from primary to senior matriculation. One third of the boys' training is agricultural; they are even taught to build log houses" (*Sherbrooke Daily Record* 1938b). Lett illustrated his talk with slides of the school and the children as well as a colour film, which highlighted the school buildings with dramatic mountain landscapes in the background.[1] By all accounts, the talk was extremely well received. Over the next few days Lett revisited the campus, renewing old acquaintances, and preached a sermon in St Peter's Church in Sherbrooke on the following Sunday. Those in attendance at the service found his account of Indigenous conversions moving and inspiring (*Sherbrooke Daily Record* 1938c).

This visit and talk by a residential school principal at the University of Bishop's College was a noteworthy event for the Anglican and broader anglophone communities of Sherbrooke and Lennoxville. Under the title "Canada's duty to her Indian citizens," the *Sherbrooke Daily Record* article announcing the talk recognized that Indigenous Peoples had been dispossessed of their land but claimed that they had been amply compensated, both financially and through the concession of reservations. Still, it remained the nation's duty to educate the "Indians" in order to make them productive members of society and thus allow them to fully assume Canadian citizenship (*Sherbrooke Daily Record* 1938a). It was understood that this sense of duty was shared by members of the university community in attendance and the broader local, regional, and national communities. This broad consensus on the causes and nature of what settler elites had identified as the "Indian problem" – which was essentially the problem of the continued existence of Indigenous Peoples after their lands had been appropriated by the settler state (Barker, Rollo, and Lowman 2016, 153–5) – and on the urgent need to resolve the issue through the use of institutions such as residential schools, emphasizes the extent to which the Anglican community of the Eastern Townships supported and sought to participate in the national effort to eliminate Indigenous cultures. Indeed, by the late 1930s, the goal of "civilizing the Indians" by making them "Canadian" was considered both a sacred and patriotic duty.

The Reverend Adam Lett's visit and talk at Bishop's University in 1938 also raises the question of the institution's relationship to the "Indian question" and more particularly to the use of residential schools to "civilize" Indigenous Peoples. By the time of Lett's talk, the university's Faculty of Divinity had been educating priests and missionaries for more than eighty years, and some of these had become Anglican bishops and Church officials who administered residential schools operating within their dioceses and sat on national committees overseeing "Indian and Eskimo" education. As one of the country's oldest Anglican colleges, Bishop's was also part of an institutional and personal network which enabled the Church's founding and operation of forty-one residential schools.

In general terms, the role of Canadian institutions of higher learning in making possible the operation of the residential schools by training its staff and administrators, as well as legitimating the system by perpetuating key ideas and concepts central to settler colonialism, has not been thoroughly investigated by historians. In 2009, a graduate student at the University of Toronto initiated such a project and produced a first paper on the topic, but that paper, though widely circulated, has never been published (Dyer 2009). A few years later, Anthony Di Mascio suggested that we need to widen our examination beyond the scope of residential schools themselves to better understand the role of other institutions, but his call was not immediately taken up (Di Mascio 2013). As far as the Canadian Anglican Church is concerned, Eric Taylor Woods attempted to explain support for residential schools by focusing on a heroic missionary narrative that justified their existence and was used to silence critics of the system in the early twentieth century (2016).

This view has since been broadened, both by historians interested in the extensive national and international networks of the Anglican Church (which included the Bishop's University) and those who insisted on the broader role of settler colonialism. In reviewing the foundation of the University of Western Ontario and Huron College (by a former member of Bishop's divinity faculty), Nathalie Cross and Thomas Peace argue that the role of colleges and universities must be understood in terms of their place within what they term the "mesh of settler colonial institutions and discourse," which both imposed a consensus on residential schools and helped suppress any criticism of the system (2021). In doing this, they were adapting a model developed by Andrew John Woolford, which emphasizes the broader structures of settler colonialism and their relationship to the residential school systems in Canada and the United States. At the "macro" and "meso" level, universities and colleges played a role by fostering consensus on the nature of the "Indian problem" and developing moral and "scientific" arguments that supported the racist underpinnings of civilization policies that aimed at cultural elimination (2014, 2015). Moreover, the Anglican colleges directly participated in the training of clerics and Church leaders who would play pivotal roles in shaping and administering the system.

It is from this perspective that we propose to reexamine the settler educational tradition established at the University of Bishop's College[2] in the mid-nineteenth century with a view to documenting its participation in shaping and abetting the genocidal policies associated with the Canadian residential school system. In the decades which followed its foundation, the university defined itself within the broader Christian mission of the Anglican Church on a global, national, and local level. The goal of Christianizing and civilizing Indigenous people was central to that mission, a point driven home in campus activities, talks, and publications. As the Anglican residential schools were reorganized under Canadian control, Bishop's graduates played a key role in setting policy and propagandizing in favour of the schools. Others acted as administrators, teachers, and missionaries on the diocesan level, and graduates who became bishops served on national boards that determined the Church's policies on "Indian education." In the midst of this reorganization, students at Bishop's University endorsed the civilizing mission of the schools as a solution to Canada's "Indian problem," and actively participated in national campaigns in their support. Finally, in the first half of the twentieth century, Bishop's students assimilated and reproduced dominant discourses that enabled and supported the genocidal policies which sought to eliminate Indigenous Peoples in Canada.

Sources examined in support of this analysis include *The Mitre*, a student literary journal published at Bishop's University and which acted in some ways as a student newspaper on the campus from the 1890s onward, and the Bishop's University *Yearbook*, which was consulted for the period from the 1920s to the 1940s. Information for the Algoma diocese was retrieved from the Anglican Diocese of Algoma Archives, which form part of the digital archives of Algoma University. The same archive contains holdings concerning the Shingwauk Residential School. Documentation concerning the relevant committees of the Canadian Anglican Church was retrieved from the General Synod Archives of the Anglican Church of Canada. Finally, the digital archive of the National Centre for Truth and Reconciliation provided information on various residential schools and their administration at the diocesan level.

THE UNIVERSITY *of* BISHOP'S COLLEGE *and the* ANGLICAN CHURCH'S SACRED MISSION

In 1899, the principal, faculty, and students of the University of Bishop's College, together with prominent members of the local community, assembled to witness the granting of a DCL to John George Bourinot, clerk of the House of Commons and one of the most prominent Canadian intellectuals of his generation. The subject of Bourinot's talk on this occasion was to be "The Study of Political Science in Universities," but he began with a tribute to the institution granting him the honour and more particularly to its founder, Bishop George Jehoshaphat Mountain. Citing Mountain's *Songs of the Wilderness* (1846), a book of poetry and musings written during a visit to the James Bay area and published around the time of the college's founding, Bourinot emphasized his prominent place in "the front rank of missionary Bishops of the dominion" (Bourinot 1899).

Mountain had indeed directly linked his travels and missionary work to the foundation of the university, and an engraving of the newly founded Bishop's College adorned the book's first page, which stated that proceeds from its sale should go to support the institution. The book also included several illustrations representing the Indigenous Peoples of James Bay and their way of life, exotic images clearly aimed at eliciting interest and contributions from an English audience, as the book was published in London. In poems such as "The Indian's Grave," Mountain described Indigenous Peoples as destined to disappear leaving no trace of their presence on the land soon to be occupied by Christians (1846, 71–2). Some thirty years later, a graduate of the University of Bishop's College, Reverend Frederick George Scott, expressed the same sentiment in a more direct way in his poem "Wahonomin," framed as an Indigenous lamentation aimed at Queen Victoria and which ended with the lines "We perish with the pine tree and the bird; we bow our head in silence. We must die." Both works later appeared in William Lighthall's *Songs of the Great Dominion*, an anthology of British Canadian settler poetry published in 1889 and a curious amalgam of imperialist and nascent Canadian patriotism which highlighted the inevitable elimination of Indigenous nations as part of a historical narrative centred on the rise of a settler colony toward nationhood (Lighthall 1889, 51, 52–8). These poems illustrate how sacred, imperialistic, and sometimes patriotic discourses combined powerfully in the first decades of the university's existence to shape its role in weaving the institutional mesh of settler colonialism which was taking shape in late Victorian Canada. Constructed on the unceded territory of the Abenaki nation, the college's founding was made possible by gifts of lands alienated from the Indigenous inhabitants, as well as funds from the clergy reserves raised on the sale of such lands. Its mission was to train clergy to serve the settler population of rural Quebec and particularly the Eastern Townships, but its broader purpose was to establish new educational traditions and narratives on the shores of the Massawippi in support of a much larger project of colonization (Nicholl 1994, ch. 1).

Although it remained small, by 1899 the University of Bishop's College was more than simply a local institution. Bourinot recognized that it had become a seat of higher learning and was playing a role throughout the dominion (1899). The institution was also firmly connected to the empire through the ties of faculty and students born in the United Kingdom who had migrated to Canada, sometimes precisely to train for a missionary career. Although "missionary work" often signified service to settler populations in frontier areas, in Canada, as in other regions of the Empire, the role of converting and "civilizing" Indigenous populations was given a place of prominence. As the same F.G. Scott reminded troops about to embark to serve in the Boer War in 1898, successful imperial expansion meant that inevitably "the savage is brought under the yoke of civilization … and religion, education and commerce raise him almost to the level of a European" (Scott 1898). Anglicans embraced their role in effecting this change, creating what Woods describes as the "triumphant narrative" of the work of Anglican missionaries among Indigenous Peoples (2016, 55–7). This was a tradition which the university proudly embraced and which it presented to students as an ideal of Christian service.

From the 1890s onward, the mission to Indigenous Peoples was highlighted in a series of lectures on campus by missionaries and bishops administering regions with large Indigenous populations. It seems such lectures were common in Anglican colleges at this time, occurring also at Toronto's Trinity College in the 1890s (Dyer 2009, 35–7). At Bishop's University, one of the more notable lectures was given by Bishop Jervois Arthur Newnham on 26 November 1894. In what was described as an entertaining talk illustrated with the use of lantern slides, the bishop described his diocese of Moosonee as mostly populated by "10,000 Indians: Crees, Ojibways and Chippewas, and besides these Eskimos." His description of Indigenous Peoples was hardly flattering. Newnham considered them dirty and dishonest but willing to listen and learn from missionaries. As such their education was paramount, and he bemoaned the lack of support from the government which, while it collected taxes and duties in the region, did little to help the Church in its mission. The task of educating Indigenous Peoples was further complicated by what he saw as their itinerant lifestyle, which he contrasted to the situation of tribes in the Northwest settled on reservations. Most of the lecture though, dealt with the exploits of the missionaries who had travelled vast distances on snowshoes or by dog sled in order to reach isolated Indigenous populations (Newnham 1894). Talks such as Newnham's emphasized the heroic nature of the Church's mission in the north and the need for schools which could exercise a civilizing influence on Indigenous inhabitants and called on young men to take up the call of missionary work.

Such events were commonplace on the campus of Bishop's University in the 1890s and 1900s. Often they ranged more widely, recounting the challenges and sacrifices involved by those working in Africa, India, China, and Japan as told by visiting missionaries or in published accounts summarized by speakers. Many of them were more intimate than Newnham's lecture, and the talks were largely organized by the Bishop's College Missionary Union (BCMU), a student organization which was active from the 1890s to the 1920s. The union sought out speakers in the region as well as those from farther afield. In 1898, for example, the Reverend Buckland from Eastman spoke to students of his work among the Inuit "in the far north," which in this case was the region of Hudson Bay. Buckland gave the students an idea of the hardships involved in living in this area and again his lecture was illustrated by slides ("B.C. Missionary Notes" 1898). A decade later, in 1908, the union welcomed the Reverend W.H. Cassop, who had worked in the Northwest and spoke on the subject of "The Planting of the Church of England in Rupert's Land." In 1911, a lecture by the Reverend A.E. Burgett of Quebec, ranged widely covering missionary work in China, India, and Africa, before giving examples from work closer to home on the Labrador Coast and the Northwest ("Missionary Union" 1911–12). Guaranteeing the Christian character of the Northwest, both by providing churches for settlers and by converting and educating Indigenous Peoples, was considered an essential project and appeals were repeatedly made to students who might make the choice to become missionaries. Speaking to the union in 1912, the Reverend F.G. Scott "exhorted all who were interested in the spreading of the Gospel message to endeavour to realize and make use of this God-given opportunity for forwarding the cause in such a splendid field" ("The Missionary Union" 1911). These appeals and financial aid from British missionary societies encouraged many to train for service in the Northwest and by 1908 fourteen divinity students from the college were preparing for careers on the frontier (Sweeny 1994, 70).

The BCMU also participated in national networks such as the Church Students Missionary Society, which organized a conference in February of 1899 at Trinity College in Toronto. The two delegates sent to the conference returned to Lennoxville and presented a report of their activities during a public meeting. One delegate read the paper he had presented which dealt with Jesuit missions. Published sometime later in *The Mitre*, it dealt mostly with the martyrdom of the Jesuit fathers, dwelling on the ritual torture and cannibalism practised by their captors. In this way, the paper highlighted themes of missionary sacrifice as well as those of Indigenous barbarism. Students present at the meeting also resolved to form a "Mission Study Class,' which most of those present agreed to attend ("The Church Students' Missionary Association" 1897–98).

Although the union was less active during the war, it seems to have returned to a prominent and militant role in the years following the armistice, participating in national campaigns directly aimed at the promotion of residential schooling, perhaps as a result of Bishop's connection to the development of this system. In a flush of post-war enthusiasm at the possibilities for moral regeneration, an article published in 1920 noted "All students of the University are of course, thereby, members of the B. C. M. U. The object of the Union is to stir up interest in the hearts of those whose missionary zeal has never yet really been aroused, and also to deepen the sense of responsibility which all earnest Christians feel, as being incumbent upon them to spread the Gospel of Christ, not in only foreign lands, but in our own broad Dominion as well" ("BCMU" 1920).

REORGANIZING CANADA'S INDIAN RESIDENTIAL SCHOOLS: THE BISHOP'S CONNECTION

The accounts of the BCMU's activities certainly indicate that the heroic nature of the Anglican church's civilizing mission was at the forefront of campus life at the turn of the twentieth century. However, the Anglican Church in Canada and particularly its Indian residential schools received significant funding from English missionary societies, who often owned and operated the schools outright. These organizations were now signalling their intention of ending this support or at the very least severely curtailing it. While the costs of these operations were cited as a factor, by the turn of the century Canada now seemed less important as a field for missionary work focused on the conversion of heathens, with the focus of British missionary societies moving to other parts of the empire and the world, notably Africa and Asia. It seemed evident that missionary and educational endeavours had to be assumed by the Canadian Church and this led to the formation of the Missionary Society of the Church of England in Canada (MSCC) in 1902. The society was created to take charge of general missionary work of the church domestically and abroad and would eventually be given control over the administration of most residential schools operated by the Anglican Church (Truth and Reconciliation Commission of Canada 2016, 228–9; Woods 2016, 58–60). Its foundation was a critical step in the evolution of Anglican thinking on both missions and schools since it fully shifted responsibility over these fields to the Canadian context. This opened the door to significant criticism of the residential schools and the church's role in operating them, directly challenging the heroic narrative which served to justify them in the eyes of most Anglicans (Woods 2016, 61–3).

The foundation of the MSCC also provides a strong indication of Bishop's University's influence over the emerging structure of the Canadian Anglican church. Indeed, the Reverend Norman Tucker, appointed first general secretary of the MSCC was a prominent Bishop's College graduate, earning a BA and an MA in 1874 and 1887 respectively (Masters 1950, 166). As secretary general of the MSCC, Tucker was directly involved in fending off a serious challenge to the Anglican residential schools system mounted by Toronto lawyer Samuel Blake between

1906 and 1909. Blake, who also sat on the council of the MSCC, was convinced that Anglican residential schools had been a failure and were not attaining their goals despite their high costs of operation. He introduced critical resolutions on the matter to the MSCC council, of which he was a member, and also published a memorandum on the subject addressed directly to Tucker as secretary general. Blake also highlighted the findings of the Indian department's chief medical officer Dr Peter Bryce, who revealed the high mortality rates within the residential schools (Truth and Reconciliation Commission of Canada 2016, 229–30; Acres 2021), resulting in newspaper headlines proclaiming, "Indian Schools Deal Out Death" (*Daily Colonist* 1907). Blake now charged the schools with inefficiency and presenting a threat to the very students they sought to help, anonymously publishing a pamphlet on the subject titled *Don't You Hear the Red Man Calling?* (1908).

Although he was successful in introducing doubts into the MSCC council, Blake's position was attacked directly by residential school officials and the bishop of Calgary, J.W. Tims, who in his own pamphlet accused the school's critics of exaggeration and ignorance of their true situation (1908). This Canadian conflict was further played out in a pan-Anglican Congress held in London in June of 1908, as both sides tried to win over British administrators of the major missionary societies. Blake did not attend, but Tucker did, as representative of the MSCC, and the challenge to residential schools was eventually defeated. For Woods, this demonstrates that the sacred narrative had prevailed, but it was also a sign that Anglican networks had been skillfully manipulated to defuse the issue (Woods 2016, 66–7; Acres 2021).

Although Norman Tucker's role in this affair is nebulous, his position on the church's boarding and industrial schools had been very clearly outlined in his writings. Indeed, Tucker was one of the Church's leading propagandists on the subject of Indigenous education and he wrote several books and pamphlets on the subject destined for Canadian and British audiences. In *From Sea to Sea: The Dominion* (1908), which surveyed the church's activities across Canada, Tucker recognized that the existing system had been weakened by the withdrawal of English missionary societies and that this crisis threatened the work which had been accomplished. What was needed was "a comprehensive plan by which the work could be carried on" in order that "the weak and dependent Red Man (be) raised to the status of citizenship in the life of the Dominion" (20–1). The book was clearly designed to elicit financial support for schools and missions to Indigenous communities, and it was available at the time of the Pan-Anglican conference. In *Western Canada* (1907), published a year earlier with a view to influencing English public opinion, Tucker had singled out the Lytton school as a source of concern stating that "The weak point in the Indian work of this, as of nearly all our Canadian dioceses, is the lack of practical training to fit the Indian to become a self-reliant citizen" (79–80). However, in the same book Tucker cited the diocese of Caledonia in British Columbia as an example of the successful education of Indigenous Peoples through mission work and boarding schools. There, Tucker wrote, "For humble and consistent Christian lives, for peaceful and triumphant death-beds, for intelligent, self-reliant, and progressive citizenship, these converted savages and cannibals afford a complete vindication of the cause of Missions" (88). In short, Tucker did not reject residential schools as a technology of elimination but rather, remaining within this paradigm, he argued that more resources were required to accelerate the process and thus contribute to the rapid colonization of the West. In a 1905 address to the Canadian Council in Toronto, Tucker underscored the urgency of imprinting a Christian and largely British character on these new territories and concluded, "We are engaged in laying the foundations of a nation in the Dominion of Canada to-day! six millions in number now, to be sixty millions before the end of this century" (1905). An active propagandist for western expansion and educating Indigenous Peoples, Tucker acquired a national reputation and became arguably Bishop's University's most prominent graduate.

Tucker's defence of the church's residential schools was vindicated by the victory of the western bishops and their supporters, which preserved the MSCC's mandate to operate them. The church committed more firmly to this course and Tucker was still secretary of the MSCC when, led by Bishop Tims, it negotiated agreements with the federal government to obtain per capita grants for its schools and the transfer of selected schools directly to Indian Affairs, while ensuring that they would remain under the administration of Anglican clergymen. Unlike earlier draft agreements which would have closed residential schools, the 1910 agreement maintained them and funded their continued operation (Truth and Reconciliation Commission of Canada 2016, 235). Through this conflict over the fate of residential schools Tucker remained in close contact with Bishop's University, which had awarded him a DCL in 1903 (Masters 1950, 166). He returned to the college on several occasions and in 1909 he offered a series of lectures packaged as a course on missionary work aimed specifically at young men interested in work in the Northwest ("Divinity Notes" 1908–09). There is no evidence to suggest that the Blake resolutions or the debate they engendered had any impact on the college or its students. The issue seems never to have been discussed at any of the BCMU meetings and no mention was made of the findings on the death of Indigenous children in the church's schools. From the perspective of Woods's analysis, the heroic narrative seems to have remained intact at Bishop's throughout this crisis.

Tucker's position on the issue of residential schools and his important role in ensuring their survival through the establishment of a new consensus and the negotiation of stable funding points to the importance of evaluating the college's participation in creating a framework for the operation of the system through the broader lens of settler colonialism. Making the "Indian" into a citizen, to paraphrase Tucker, was essentially a policy of cultural elimination that relied heavily on consensus within the settler community over certain ideas related to race and territoriality. Beyond a set of ideas and beliefs, however, settler colonialism can be viewed as a structure, operating at several levels, with colleges and universities involved both in defining the "Indian problem" *per se* and training those responsible for designing and operating the school systems. The work of Cross and Peace (2021) and that of Acres (2021) illustrate quite convincingly the importance of networks within the church which brought potential missionaries, teachers, and administrators into contact with the schools but also helped to move information in the opposite direction, through parish-based campaigns and printed materials facilitating fundraising and the involvement of Anglicans at the parish or campus level. Tucker's lectures held at Bishop's on organizing support for missionary work on the parish level were a case in point of the type of networking effort that could provide broad-based and considerable support to the church's Indian missions and schools. The lectures were no doubt drawn from a short manual that he had written designed to help clergymen mobilize parishioners by raising their awareness of the importance of mission work and teaching them how they could contribute to its success (Tucker 1902).

Although Bishop's was a small institution, Tucker's prominent role in the resetting of the residential schools system during the first decade of the twentieth century speaks eloquently to its place in the institutional framework that both defined the "Indian problem" and trained those who implemented policies aimed at the cultural elimination of Indigenous Peoples. The point is further driven home when we consider the case of George Thorneloe (class of 1872, MA 1877) who became third Bishop of Algoma in 1896 and remained in office until 1927. Thorneloe had a strong connection to Bishop's, serving as an examiner for the university from 1884 to 1896 and sitting on its council from 1889 to 1896 (Masters 1950, 166; Huskins 2003). His appointment was hailed as a major recognition for the college, and *The Mitre* predicted that his tenure would have a beneficial effect on the missionary zeal of Bishop's students: "We congratulate the Diocese of Algoma upon securing Dr. Thorneloe for its Bishop, and we feel that his former intimate connection with Bishop's College will produce among the students present and to come a greater interest in church work in the one missionary diocese of Eastern Canada" ("Divinity Notes" 1896–97). During his tenure, Thorneloe maintained a close connection with his *alma mater*, returning on several occasions to address students or preach sermons. The connection to Bishop's was extended by the selection of Rocksborough R. Smith, formerly dean of Divinity at Bishop's, as successor to Thorneloe in 1927.

This relationship led to the recruitment of Bishop's graduates to act as deacons and archdeacons, priests, and missionaries in the Algoma diocese: James Boydell (1866) was commissary to Archbishop Thorneloe, and C.W. Balfour (1897) was archdeacon ("List of Graduates" 1917–18; Masters 1950, 173). Bishop's graduates also served in the principal churches in Sudbury, such as O.L. Jull (1914) ("List of Graduates" 1917–18) and Charles Eugene Bishop (1893) (Masters 1950, 171). From the late 1890s to the mid-1930s more than twenty graduates of the university established themselves as regular clergy in the Algoma diocese (Ruggle, n.d.). Many more spent summers or year-long missionary appointments in the diocese, and several of these were in Indigenous communities. Most of these shorter-term missions were mentioned in *The Mitre*. For example, the paper announced in 1914 that "Mr. H.F. Cocks was once again among the Indians, having charge of the mission of Shegwaring and Silver Water in the Diocese of Algoma" ("Divinity Notes" 1914–15, 10). One student, Cyril Goodier was recognized by the Department of Indian Affairs for the quality of his work. Of English birth, he acted as a missionary to the Indigenous community near Elk Lake from 1918 to 1921 before returning to Bishop's to pursue an LST ("Ordinations" 1923–24). While their involvement with the residential school system is poorly documented, we do know that clergy trained at Bishop's officiated at the funerals of children who died in the schools.[3] Thorneloe's attitude to the Indigenous inhabitants of his diocese was described as one of benevolent paternalism. Alluding to his frequent visits to bands around Lake Nipigon, his biographer, another Bishop's graduate and archdeacon of Algoma, C.W. Balfour, commented, "The Archbishop never seemed to forget that his best was due even to the lowliest" and went on to describe happy moments around the campfire and "baptisms of little brown papooses" (Balfour 1943). It was Thorneloe who signed agreements in 1910 enabling the Church to formally take possession of the land on which the Shingwauk Residential School was located. The following year he entered into an agreement with the federal government to operate the Shingwauk and Wawanosh homes (the names given the residential schools) "in a manner satisfactory to the Superintedent General" of the Department of Indian Affairs. In 1935, the land was transferred to the federal government in an agreement designed by Bishop Smith, but the Church retained control over operation of the schools ("Shingwauk IRS School Narrative" 2015).

Another prominent graduate was the bishop of Calgary from 1927 to 1943, Louis Ralph Sherman (class of 1909), who succeeded Bishop Tims, an outspoken proponent of residential schools. Sherman inherited responsibility for several residential schools in his diocese including Old Sun Residential School, St Cyprian Residential School, and St Paul Residential School. All three schools underwent important renovations and construction projects in the first years of Sherman's bishopric ("Old Sun IRS. School Narrative" 2004; "St Cyprian's IRS School Narrative" 2005; "St Paul's IRS School Narrative" 2009). Whatever the cordiality of their personal relations with the Indigenous Peoples they met during their ministries, these bishops sat on the MSCC's Indian and Eskimo Commission, which determined the church's policies on Indigenous education and more particularly controlled its residential schools. The bishops on the committee not only consistently supported the existing system of boarding and industrial schools but they also endorsed resolutions calling for the establishment of more such institutions in the mid-1920s ("Resolution. Board of Missions" 1924).

BISHOP'S STUDENTS *and* CANADA'S "INDIAN PROBLEM"

Through this period of transformation and institutionalization of the residential school system, divinity students at Bishop's University, including Adam Lett who was working towards his degree from 1914 to 1920, continued their missionary activities and actively addressed what they saw as the persistence of Canada's "Indian problem." This discussion was now framed in a discourse that reflected an emerging English Canadian patriotism, with the issue of civilizing the Indigenous population being treated as a serious national challenge. The best example of this attitude was the publication in 1915 of the lead article in *The Mitre* under the title "A Canadian Duty," by divinity student William C. Dunn (Dunn 1915). Reacting to a talk on campus by the Bishop of Ottawa dealing with mission work among Indigenous communities, Dunn felt obligated to address the issue he considered "of vital importance to the Canadian Church and people, and which should receive earnest and sympathetic interest from every true Christian." The text begins by acknowledging that Indigenous Peoples had been deprived of their land by white settlement but claims that they had been adequately and fairly compensated by grants of land and money. Despite these apparently fair arrangements, the "Indians" had not been able to integrate into Canadian life because "generally speaking their educational and mental standing is not of a sufficiently high standard to enable them to make the best use of the means which are theirs." It was thus the Church's duty to improve the lot of Indians by transforming them into productive Canadian citizens and this despite "the great gulf of racial temperament" that separated them from the settler population. There follows an enumeration of the characteristics of the Indigenous population, consisting mainly of a racist representation of them as careless and irresponsible, happy-go-lucky, and impassive. However, in Dunn's opinion, some of the worst faults of Indigenous Peoples were the result of contact with immoral white men "who degrade and demoralize them" (2–3).

In this context, it was "our manifest duty ... to protect our weaker brothers and sisters, who, though of a different race and colour, are children of the same heavenly Father." The church's response was through schools and mission work: "We have industrial and boarding schools, where the Indian children receive a practical and moral training as well as an education. Here the boys learn farming, carpentering, and other useful accomplishments; the girls are taught cooking, laundrying, and general domestic science. From these institutions they are sent home to the reserves in the hope that they may show to their fellows a better way of living. There are also day schools on the reserves where, as at the larger institutions, efforts are made to lead the children to better things." Of course, this work required the strongest missionary spirit: "Sometimes a missionary has to live alone among people who socially, morally and intellectually, are of a low grade and whose ideas are of a very different stamp to his. The successful worker must be gifted with unusual patience and sympathy, and great tenacity and courage" (3–4). This strong statement of support for the church's efforts in the education of Indigenous children was published in an issue of *The Mitre* co-edited by Adam Lett.[4]

Dunn's article appeared in a period when the church was trying the revitalize its schools and make another appeal to the faithful to support this effort. Although the war capitalized attention until the armistice in 1918, the drive to educate Indigenous Peoples was at the forefront of a postwar enthusiasm for moral regeneration. Spurred on by Bishop Tims of Calgary, and acting on the suggestions Tucker had made a decade earlier, the MSCC launched a nation-wide appeal to support the residential schools in 1918. To that end, they sent out 2.5 million pamphlets to parishes throughout the country initiating a campaign they called the Anglican Forward Movement (AFM). The pamphlets were distributed by more than 2,000 women's committees and hundreds of laymen gave presentations in support of the appeal. Clergymen were encouraged to read special prayers for the success of the movement during services. This hugely successful campaign raised more than $500,000 by 1921 and helped to ensure the survival of the schools. The literature produced in support of the campaign emphasized the heroic nature of Anglican missionary work in the past, "a history rich in heroism and unsurpassed in the priceless treasures of courage and example" (Woods 2016, 68–9).

The Anglican Forward Movement also swept over the Bishop's campus in 1919 and 1920. In a first phase the Missionary Union's support was aimed at the campaign to provide the material necessities of the missions and schools, but once that goal was attained, an article in *The Mitre* argued that the next campaign had to be for men willing to take up the important work supported by the AFM. In an impassioned plea "A divinity student" tied the missionary cause to a rising sense of Canadian nationhood and the occupation of the West by settler populations. Missionaries would be required to serve those populations but also to act as agents of civilization in the task of educating Indigenous Peoples to act as productive citizens of the new Canada. Moreover, in a passage lauding the rural setting of the college and its emphasis on athletics, the author argued that Bishop's men would be particularly suited to this evangelical mission in the West, which required energy and virility. "She will supply her quota of men to carry on the required work," he concluded (A Divinity Student 1919–20). An article on the same topic published the following year emphasized work among Indigenous communities in a renewed call for recruits: "Appeals for new workers for Missionary Dioceses are now before the Missionary Society. These include men for Baffin's Land, Mackenzie River, Yukon and other fields. The reorganization of Indian Schools, now being undertaken by the MSCC will require men and women of consecration and ability as principals, teachers, matrons, nurses and assistants. The Society will welcome inquiries from any source relative to taking up work in these important spheres" ("The Call of the World" 1920–21). It was in the flush of this enthusiasm that Adam Lett accepted his position at St George's school in December of 1921.

THE PREVALENCE *of* RACISM

Thomas Wolfe writes that "both genocide and settler colonialism have typically employed the organizing grammar of race" (2006), and in the first decades of the twentieth century, discourse on the "Indian problem" in Canada had gelled into what Woolford terms "a genocidal formulation" which enlisted "an array of institutions, organizations and actors in the project" (2014) of eliminating Indigenous Peoples. By the early 1920s, the heroic missionary narrative which supported residential schools had been linked to an appeal to Canadian patriotism just as new levels of financial support and compulsion were added to further reduce Indigenous agency. An appeal to Christian duty framed in a paternalistic discourse emphasized the apparent helplessness of Indigenous communities in the midst of the rapid transformations sweeping across Canadian society, driving home the urgency of immediate action to address the "Indian problem." Universities and colleges were among the settler institutions which helped define and inculcate this "genocidal frame of reference," and Bishop's University, through its training of Anglican clergy and of a growing population of Christian undergraduates participated in this crusade. Since all students at the university were required to take divinity courses, they were exposed to Christian ideals and beliefs related to race which reinforced support for the project of eliminating Indigenous Peoples. As such, racist representations of Indigenous Peoples abound in student publications produced at Bishop's University between the 1890s and 1940s.

The lack of documentation on curriculum makes it difficult to correlate attitudes on race with what was taught at the college, but certain articles published in *The Mitre* offer a glimpse of the state of knowledge disseminated in divinity and arts classes. For example, a review of Harold Hamilton's *An Inquiry into Christian Origins* (1912) dismissed Indigenous spiritual beliefs in North America as "purely magic," adding that magic is the "primitive science" ("The People of God" 1913). Savagery and primitivism were highlighted in Hamilton's book, which discussed the moral and spiritual consequences of "a primitive race being brought into contact with an advanced modern civilization." "Unless the savage was protected from them," Hamilton wrote, "he and his race fall victim to the opportunities of self-indulgence which the higher civilization brings with it" (Hamilton 1912, I, 113). This eurocentric view justified the elimination of Indigenous societies through Christian missionary activity by presenting it as a humanitarian crusade designed to protect "savages" and save their souls. Discussions of Indigenous spirituality usually revolved around such notions, and in a missionary study group held in 1918, primitive religions were held to be responsible for "superstition, polygamy, and the consequent degradation of women" in traditional Indigenous societies (Dunn 1917–18).

Reflecting the prevalence of a dominant discourse which racialized Indigenous bodies, less academically oriented student publications and activities can be classified into two categories: historical representations and contemporary observations. Historical representations focused largely on what were seen as markers of savagery and barbarism, dwelling on the brutality of Indigenous warfare, with numerous references to scalping ("The Call of the World" 1924–25). In 1901, Bishop's hosted a vaudeville show by a troupe which performed both in blackface, posing as African bushmen, and in red face, posing as "Indians in their war paint and brandishing their tomahawks" ("Grand Entertainment in Williams Theatre" 1901).

In historical fiction, Indigenous people appeared either as dim-witted followers of white characters or as dark and menacing figures. One story was constructed around the rescue of a white maiden from the clutches of a dark and threatening savage by two French Canadian voyageurs. The inevitable and dramatic death of the "savage," whose body plunged into the water after he was shot, was immediately followed by the author reverting to his own time, where on the river "instead of dangerous paths and bands of savages, a steamer plies her daily course" (A.H.B. 1899). If these threats were projected into the writer's own time, it was done out of derision. Still, a satirical text purporting to be the letter of a European writing to relatives at home of his fear of "savages" exploited the newly arrived student's belief that bloodthirsty Indians were still a threat in southern Quebec. Relieved to find that this was not the case, he assured his brother in a letter that he "had not been kidnapped by red Indians, to be afterwards roasted or boiled alive" ("Canada through French Eyes" 1907).

Accounts of contemporary contacts with Indigenous Peoples were frequent, although Indigenous communities in the immediate vicinity of the university were never mentioned. Bishop's maintained connections with various missions, particularly what was termed the "Labrador mission," which was actually located at Mutton Bay on the lower north shore of the St Lawrence. Missionaries and travellers sent out to this area often recounted their contacts with Indigenous people, whom they usually described as aloof and sullen. These young male travellers often focused on Indigenous women, sometimes represented as licentious young temptresses. One writer, John S. Ford, suggestively compared three young Indigenous women to "Flappers," warning that "one must use judgement" and "not approach too near," while remarking on their "attractive eyes, and features that were not in the least repulsive." Alternatively, the same writer used a more virginal image to describe the women he saw: "they reminded me of certain pictures I have seen of rather attractive squaws about to offer themselves to the rapid current of some great river as a sacrifice to the Evil Spirit" (Ford 1930–31, 16, 43). As Kim Anderson has noted, these stereotypical representations of Indigenous women were in fact deeply rooted in settler culture and served to reinforce gender roles assigned to white women. It was in this discourse that Indigenous women were "reinvented" as "easy," "deficient," or "drudges," portrayed as princesses or whores (Anderson 2013, 272–3). In writing of more mature Indigenous women, the same traveller and others focused rather on their capacity for work and their drudge-like existence.

In essence, these contacts reported by student travellers did nothing to challenge dominant stereotypes. As late as 1942, a divinity student wrote of his encounter with "four or five hundred of these uncivilized human beings," Indigenous

Peoples who had travelled south from James Bay overland because transportation links had been disrupted by the war. He described having to guard his property lest the Indians steal it, the apparent drudgery of Indigenous life, the disease environment, and the difficulty of communicating through an interpreter. Unable to understand their language, he assumed that Indigenous mothers did not know the surnames of the fathers of children they brought to be baptized. At the end of his account he concluded, "The time I spent among these Indians has helped me to realize the importance of missionary work, and to admire all who have sacrificed their lives for it" (Patterson 1942). For the most part, the settler gaze posed by divinity students presented Indigenous people as childlike and needy, requiring the paternalistic intervention of the missionary to raise them up, and these racist descriptions remained relatively unchanged between 1920 and 1945.

One new feature of discourse on Indigenous Peoples after 1920 is the emergence of a discussion of the Inuit, always termed "Eskimos" in the literature of the time. The Inuit were considered to still be in a primitive state because the majority of the population had yet to be Christianized. As such they were seen with a certain amount of dispassionate anthropological interest in the few articles that dealt with them. Still, they were considered prime targets for the activities of missionaries and many seemed to have considered that a mission to the Eskimo, with the harsh environment and the hardships this implied for the missionary would be particularly heroic and worthy (Annett 1934). Soon enough, the Inuit were also attributed the characteristics of primitivism, including cannibalism and the degraded nature of their women. Indeed, a series of racist cartoons representing Indigenous Peoples appeared in the Bishop's University yearbook between 1937 and 1942 on the title page of the section introducing the graduating divinity class. Two of the cartoons involved representations of Africans as cannibals who had boiled and eaten a missionary (*Bishop's '38* 1938, 32; *Bishop's '45* 1945, 25). One presented what were apparently Inuit women practically assaulting a hapless missionary with amorous intent in an Arctic setting depicting ice floes, open water, and penguins. The flustered missionary was armed with a scroll titled "civilization" sticking out of his pocket (*Bishop's '37* 1937, 32). The last of this series of cartoons appeared in 1946 and depicted a horrified missionary standing outside an igloo adorned with human bones and a skull, again suggesting cannibalism as a marker for barbarism (*Bishop's '46* 1946, 29). It is worth noting that these yearbooks included introductory letters of endorsement, from prominent politicians, businessmen, and the university's principal.

It should not be a surprise to find racist representations of Indigenous Peoples and cultures in a settler institution of the early twentieth century. At Bishop's, though, this discourse combined with patriotic appeals to develop the nation and Christian injunctions to help lift up the "Indians" by providing them with the benefits of civilization. Anglican networks created ample opportunities to put such ideas into practice through mission work or work in the Indian schools. Beyond that, generations of Anglican clergymen trained at the college participated in fundraising campaigns in support of the schools led notably by the women's auxiliaries. In emphasizing the urgent need to "civilize" Indigenous people and make them into productive Canadian citizens, the appeals of these clergymen to their parishioners no doubt disseminated and reinforced dominant ideas which solidified the national consensus around the mission of residential schools. Bishop's also trained generations of teachers who worked primarily in Quebec's English Protestant school boards, particularly in rural regions (Nicholl 1994). Like all other students in the university, these graduates had taken obligatory divinity classes over their first two years at the college, some of which reinforced dominant discourses on the need to eliminate Indigenous Peoples (Leivo 1995). It is largely beyond the scope of this study to document the impact of such discourses on graduates of the university or on their careers but there can be little doubt that their education at Bishop's contributed to solidifying the broader consensus in the settler population on the necessity of policies aimed at eliminating Indigenous Peoples.

CONCLUSION

In 1941, just a few years after he spoke at Bishop's, Reverend Adam Lett stepped down as principal of St George's Indian Residential School in Lytton, British Columbia. According to a family biographer, Lett's two decades as principal of St George's were marked by his incessant concern for the children under his care and his efforts to modernize and improve the school's facilities. Indeed, this short biography speaks eloquently of Lett's devotion to his work and the affection the children held for him, but one sentence betrays the reality behind this rosy account: "The pupils of this government school were brought in by police from all parts of B.C. where other churches had not been in contact" (Lett 1992). It seems the reality of life at St George's during Lett's tenure was much darker than this account suggests, as documents and the testimony of survivors recount cases of forced labour, abuse, and neglect which led to the death of dozens of children under Lett's care ("St George's IRS School Narrative" 2004, 1112).

Lett's long tenure as principal of St. George's school is beyond the scope of this study, and telling the story of conditions in the school rightly belongs to the victims and survivors whose voices are emerging as archival evidence is made available and testimony is gathered. However, the differing perspectives on the actions of a residential school administrator illustrate Woolford's point that the positive experiences of some participants or the apparently noble motivations of others tells us little about the implacable logic and genocidal intent of a system designed to make Canada's Indigenous population disappear either through assimilation or attrition. Colleges and universities played a part in shaping the beliefs that molded individuals who participated in this endeavour and they helped define the societal goals that created a need for the residential school system they worked within. In the case of Bishop's University, an institution founded with the intent of imprinting a largely British and Christian character on what was considered an inevitably dominant settler society, support for the project of eliminating Canada's Indigenous population included training teachers, missionaries, administrators, and bishops who actively played a role in setting up and operating Canada's residential school system. It is also clear that students at the university were taught to see the elimination of "the Indian" as a Christian, progressive, and humane solution to Canada's "Indian problem."

As a settler institution with close ties to Britain, Bishop's was part of a global movement which sought to universalize European Christian "civilization" while eliminating Indigenous Peoples and their cultures. By the first decade of the twentieth century, its students, professors, and graduates were at the centre of an ongoing discussion of the "Indian problem" and of the church's role in the residential school system, which was reorganized in 1910. This involvement grew out of the important place of missionary ideals in the training of Anglican clergy within the Faculty of Divinity, but those ideals were also ingrained in the university's very identity. Indeed, from its earliest years, speakers visiting the college, both lay and clerical, underlined the importance of mission work and that of civilizing Indigenous Peoples, stoking the missionary zeal of students committed to church and empire. Throughout these activities and particularly within the Faculty of Divinity, "civilizing" the "savage" was emphasized as the missionary's Christian duty and the ultimate solution to Canada's "Indian problem."

Moreover, racist representations of "the Indian" either as simple and lazy or as savage and bloodthirsty were common in the fiction, editorial writings, and cartoons undergraduates published in their literary magazine *The Mitre* and in the college's *Yearbook* throughout the period. In addition to the direct participation of graduates and faculty in shaping and administering the Church's Indigenous educational projects, the persistence of a colonizing and racist discourse within the university community both abetted and justified the operation of the residential school system, committing its members to a religious and national crusade dedicated to the obliteration of Indigenous cultures.

Woods has argued that once the Anglican Church was finally confronted with the record of the residential schools, it sought to cut itself off from that period of its history, only to have to face it again later in a more significant and meaningful manner (2016). Bishop's also engaged in an active form of forgetting its past as an Anglican college, undertaking the university's secularization and its formal rebranding as "Bishop's University" in 1958, and finally closing the Faculty of Divinity in 1970. This has no doubt helped it to ignore several less palatable episodes of its past, but the university's recent commitment to reconciliation calls for it to recover from this institutional amnesia. Indeed, although Bishop's has acknowledged its presence on unceded territory, its recent attempts at reconciliation with Indigenous neighbours and students is destined to failure if it does not heed Habermas's warning to actively "confront its traditions." The first stage of that will be to come to terms with its role in developing and supporting educational projects imposed on generations of Indigenous students which are only briefly outlined here, aspects of which were no doubt elaborated and discussed in Divinity House, which ironically is the very building the university has renovated to act as an Indigenous Gathering Space and Resource Centre.

Notes

1 Although no transcript of Lett's talk was published in the newspaper or in student publications, a manuscript containing a talk on the school given by Lett in July of 1938 and corresponding to the themes mentioned in the summaries of the talk at Bishop's was published in 2001 by the Lytton Museum and Archives (Lett 2001). As for the film, it was probably part of a documentary series shot by Vancouver filmmaker Alfred E. Booth. The Royal British Columbia Museum has made the clip available on YouTube (Royal BC Museum 2016).

2 From its founding in 1845, the institution was known as Bishop's College or the University of Bishop's College. The name "Bishop's University" seems to have been used more informally from the beginning of the twentieth century, although the university retained the formal appellation of University of Bishop's College until 1958, when the official name change took place (Nicholl 1994).

3 A partial record of students who died at the Shingwauk school was compiled by Reverend Alan Knight in 1997 and it includes some information on the clergy who officiated at their funerals. Among these we find Bishop Thorneloe, Charles Eugene Bishop, Henry Arthur Brooke, and Bishop Rocksborough Smith who all either graduated from or taught at Bishop's (Masters 1950, 170, 171; Knight 1997).

4 Lett's name appears as "associate Editor-Divinity" in *The Mitre*'s 1915–16 issue 2 (p. 12). Dunn and Lett seem also to have been very active in the BCMU. In 1917–18, Lett was vice-president of the union while Dunn served as secretary-treasurer. Among the members of the executive committee, one finds a young F.R. Scott. See *The Mitre* (1917–18), 1: 61.

References

Acres, William. 2021. "Samuel Hume Blake's Pan-Anglican Exertions: Stopping the Expansion of Residential and Industrial Schools for Canada's Indigenous Children, 1908." In *Trauma and Survival in the Contemporary Church: Historical Responses in the Anglican Tradition*, edited by Jonathan S. Lofft, and Thomas P. Power, 9–26. Newcastle upon Tyne, UK: Cambridge Scholars Publishing.

Anderson, Kim. 2013. "The Construction of a Negative Identity." In *Gender and Women's Studies: Critical Terrain*, edited by Margaret Hobbs and Carla Rice, 269–79 Toronto: Canadian Scholars.

Annett, K.H. 1934–35. "Neighbours to the North." *The Mitre* 5 (1934–35): 12–13.

Anonymous [Blake, Samuel]. 1908. *Don't You Hear the Red Man Calling?* Toronto: William Tyrrell.

Balfour, Charles Wilfred. 1943. "George Thorneloe." In *Leaders of the Canadian Church*, edited by Bertal Heeney. Toronto: Ryerson. http://anglicanhistory.org/canada/bheeney/3/5.html.

Barker, Adam J., Toby Rollo, and Emma Battell Lowman. 2016. "Settler Colonialism and the Consolidation of Canada in the Twentieth Century." In *The Routledge Handbook of the History of Settler Colonialism*, edited by Edward Cavanagh and Lorenzo Veracini, 153–68. London, UK: Routledge.

"BCMU" 1920. *The Mitre* 1 (1921): 46–7.

Bishop's '37. The Year Book of the University of Bishop's College. 1937. Lennoxville.

Bishop's '38. The Year Book of the University of Bishop's College. 1938. Lennoxville.

Bishop's '45. The Year Book of the University of Bishop's College. 1945. Lennoxville.

Bishop's '46. The Year Book of the University of Bishop's College. 1946. Lennoxville.

Bourinot, J.G. 1899. "The Study of Political Science in Universities." *The Mitre* 3 (1899): 39–42.

"The Call of the World." 1920–21. *The Mitre* 28, no. 2 (1920–21): 34–6.

Cavanagh, Edward, and Lorenzo Veracini. 2016. *The Routledge Handbook of the History of Settler Colonialism*. London, UK: Routledge.

"The Church Students' Missionary Association." 1897–98. *The Mitre* 5 (1897–98): 79–86, 90–1.

Cross, Natalie, and Thomas Peace. 2021. "'My Own Old English Friends': Networking Anglican Settler Colonialism at the Shingwauk Home, Huron College, and Western University." *Historical Studies in Education / Revue d'histoire de l'éducation* 33 (1): 22–49.

A Divinity Student. 1919–20. "The Position of Bishop's University in the New Anglican Forward Movement." *The Mitre* 1 (1919–20): 36–8.

Dunn, William. 1915–16. "A Canadian Duty." *The Mitre* 2 (1915–16): 2–4.

– 1917–18. "BCMU" *The Mitre* 1 (1917–18): 55.

Daily Colonist. 1907. "Indian Schools Deal Out Death." 16 November 1907.
Di Mascio, Anthony. 2013. "Beyond Church and State: Rethinking Who Knew What When about Residential Schooling in Canada." *First Peoples Child & Family Review* 7 (2): 85–96.
"Divinity Notes." 1896–97. *The Mitre* 4 (1896–97): 44–5.
– 1907–08. *The Mitre* 3 (1907–08): 101–2.
– 1908–09. *The Mitre* 4 (1908–09): 95–8.
– 1914–15. *The Mitre* 1 (1914–15): 9–11.
Dyer, Monica. 2009. "The University of Toronto and Aboriginal Residential Schools: A Silent Partner." Unpublished paper. University of Toronto. http://icdr.utoronto.ca/wp-content/uploads/2015/10/Heidi-Bohaker-The-University-of-Toronto-and-Aboriginal-Residential-Schools-A-Silent-Partner-4MB.pdf.
Ford, J.F.S. 1930–31. "The Indians of the Labrador Coast." *The Mitre* 1 (1930–31): 16, 43.
"Grand Entertainment in Williams Theatre." 1901–02. *The Mitre* 2 (1901–02): 58–9.
Habermas, Jürgen. 1993. "On the Public Use of History: The Official Self-Understanding of the Federal Republic Is Breaking Up." In *Forever in the Shadow of Hitler? Original Documents of the Historikerstreit, the Controversy Concerning the Singularity of the Holocaust*, translated by James Knowlton and Truett Cates, 162–70. Atlantic Highlands, NJ: Humanities Press. http://archive.org/details/foreverinshadowooopro m.
Hamilton, Harold Francis. 1912. *The People of God: An Inquiry into Christian Origins*. London: H. Frowde, Oxford University Press.
Huskins, Harry. 2003. "THORNELOE, GEORGE." In *Dictionary of Canadian Biography*, vol. 16. http://www.biographi.ca/en/bio/thorneloe_george_16E.html.
Knight, Alan. 1997. "Burials in Shingwauk Cemetery, Sault Ste Marie." Sault Ste Marie (ON). Shingwauk cemetery series. Algoma University. http://archives.algomau.ca/main/sites/default/files/2015-050_001_002.pdf.
Leivo, M.-L. 1995. *Educated in the Townships: The students of the University of Bishop's College, 1930–39*. MA Thesis, Simon Fraser University. https://summit.sfu.ca/item/6740.
Lett, Adam R. 2001. "St George's Church of England Residential School: Its Introduction and Development." *Lytton Museum and Archives* 2 (2): 1–3, 5.
Lett, Cecil. 1992. "Rev. Adam Lett 1880–1960." *Lake Dore WI Tweedsmuir Community History*, Federated Women's Insitutes of Ontario Digital Collections, 1: 113–15.
Lighthall, W.D. 1889. *Songs of the Great Dominion: Voices from the Forests and Waters, the Settlements and Cities of Canada*. London, UK: W. Scott.
"List of Graduates." 1917–18. *The Mitre* 4 (1917–18): 20–9.
Masters, D.C. 1950. *Bishop's University: The first hundred years*. Toronto: Clarke, Irwin.
Miller, James Rodger. 1996. *Shingwauk's Vision: A History of Native Residential Schools*. Toronto: University of Toronto Press.
Milloy, John Sheridan, and Mary Jane Logan McCallum. 2017. *"A National Crime": The Canadian Government and the Residential School System, 1879 to 1986*. Winnipeg: University of Manitoba Press.
"Missionary Union." 1911. *The Mitre* 5 (1911–12): 23–4.
"The Missionary Union." 1911. *The Mitre* 4 (1912): 26–7.

The Mitre. 1894–1950. Lennoxville: Bishop's University.

Mountain, George J. 1845. *The Journal of the Bishop of Montreal, during a Visit to the Church Missionary Society's North-West American Mission: To Which Is Added, by the Secretaries, an Appendix, Giving an Account of the Formation of the Mission and Its Progress to the Present Time*. London, UK: Seeley, Burnside, and Seeley.

– 1846. *Songs of the wilderness: Being a collection of poems, written in some different parts of the territory of the Hudson's Bay company, and in the wilds of Canada, on the route to that territory in the spring and summer of 1844; interspersed with some illustrative notes*. London, UK: F. & J. Rivington.

Newnham, Jervois. 1894. "Bishop Newnham's Addresses." *The Mitre* 2: 28–30.

Nicholl, Christopher. 1994. *Bishop's University, 1843–1970*. Montreal and Kingston: McGill-Queen's University Press.

"Old Sun IRS. School Narrative." 2004. National Centre for Truth and Reconciliation. archives.nctr.ca/uploads/r/National-Centre-for-Truth-and-Reconciliation-NCTR/c/c/9/cc96410eb0d6b176143892d575fe49a8abd2942237b8d9ba5e351cbd307a0fb6/OLD_SUN.pdf.

"Ordinations." 1923–24. *The Mitre* 1 (1923–24): 53.

Patterson, E. 1942–43. "A Day at an Indian Mission." *The Mitre* 2 (1942–43): 11.

"The People of God." 1913–14. *The Mitre* 4 (1913–14): 17–25.

Ravenhill, Alice. 2016. "Chapter Five." *The Ormsby Review*. 16 December. https://ormsbyreview.com/2016/12/15/chapter-five/.

"Resolution. Board of Missions." 1924. General Synod Archives. Anglican Church of Canada. http://archives.anglican.ca/en/permalink/official6643.

"Rocksborough Smith." 2021. *Wikipedia*. https://en.wikipedia.org/w/index.php?title=Rocksborough_Smith&oldid=1048710780.

Royal BC Museum. 2016. *St George's Indian Residential School, Lytton, ca. 1936*. https://www.youtube.com/watch?v=qg7sXeSyul8.

Scott, F.G. 1899. "Sermon by the Rev. F.G. Scott on the occasion of the Departure of the 2nd (special service) Battalion of the Royal Canadian Regiment for South Africa." *The Mitre* 2, (1899): 32–5.

Sherbrooke Daily Record. 1938a. "Canada's Duty to Her Indian Citizens," 5 May 1938.

– 1938b. "Reviewed Work of St George's Indian School," 7 May 1938.

– 1938c. "Inspiring Sermons at St Peter's Church," 9 May 1938.

Sherman, Louis Ralph, and Joan Weir. 1976. *Sherman: Reflections*. Toronto: Anglican Book Centre.

"Shingwauk IRS School Narrative." 2004. National Centre for Truth and Reconciliation. https://archives.nctr.ca/uploads/r/National-Centre-for-Truth-and-Reconciliation-NCTR/8/9/6/896bb5e56b74199be25c039f659c2e929a1613d8553859f45f08ee0dfac667a8/SHINGWAUK.pdf.

"St Cyprian's IRS School Narrative." 2005. National Centre for Truth and Reconciliation. https://archives.nctr.ca/uploads/r/National-Centre-for-Truth-and-Reconciliation-NCTR/2/b/5/2b58d70d568d83dd10ba07cbdf90ff35c7093c7bd86188a0cef9b9948cdadacc/ST_CYPRIAN.pdf.

"St George's IRS School Narrative." 2004. National Centre for Truth and Reconciliation. https://archives.nctr.ca/uploads/r/National-Centre-for-Truth-and-Reconciliation

-NCTR/1/7/2/172ce8cc81c2131290c16b46e37d2262e667220d05ca90694729620e694f7a9d/ST_GEORGE.pdf.

"St Paul's IRS School Narrative." 2009. National Centre for Truth and Reconciliation. https://archives.nctr.ca/uploads/r/National-Centre-for-Truth-and-Reconciliation-NCTR/f/7/d/f7d6b4c0c2656f5f66c042103df404827bbee1189b25ff1b64e0aceca9480cc0/ST_PAUL.pdf.

Sweeny, James T. 1994. "A History of the Faculty of Divinity, Bishop's University, 1843–1971." MA thesis, Bishop's University.

Tims, J.W. 1908. *The Call of the Red Man for Truth, Honesty, and Fair Play*. N.p.

Truth and Reconciliation Commission of Canada. 2016. *Canada's Residential Schools: The History, Part 1, Origins to 1939: The Final Report of the Truth and Reconciliation Commission of Canada, Volume I*. Kingston and Montreal: McGill-Queen's University Press. https://doi.org/10.2307/j.ctt19rm9v4.

Tucker, L. Norman. 1902. *Missionary Organization in the Parish*. N.p.

– 1905. *The Problem of the West: An Address*. Toronto: Canadian Council.

– 1907. *Western Canada*. The Musson Book Company.

– 1908. *From Sea to Sea the Dominion*. N.p.

– 1910. *Problem of the West: An Address*. Toronto: Canadian Council.

Wolfe, Patrick. 2006. "Settler Colonialism and the Elimination of the Native." *Journal of Genocide Research* 8 (4): 387–409.

Woods, Eric Taylor. 2016. *Cultural Sociology of Anglican Mission and the Indian Residential Schools in Canada*. New York: Palgrave Macmillan.

Woolford, Andrew. 2014. "Discipline, Territory and the Colonial Mesh." In *Colonial Genocide in Indigenous North America*, edited by Alexander Laban Hinton, Jeff Benvenuto, and Andrew Woolford, 29–48. Durham, NC: Duke University Press.

– 2015. *This Benevolent Experiment: Indigenous Boarding Schools, Genocide, and Redress in Canada and the United States*. Lincoln: University of Nebraska Press.

12

Fight Nights: The Sherbrooke Athletic Commission and the Boxing World, 1955–66

Andrew C. Holman

WEIGHING IN: A NEAR MISS *in* '66

On Tuesday, 8 March 1966, Sherbrooke newspapers presented their readers with a rare prospect. In a hastily called press conference with local media, Mayor Armand Nadeau and Olivier Routhier, the secretary of the Sherbrooke Athletic Commission (SAC), announced that American boxing promoter Dick Fine had contacted them, proposing the Sherbrooke Arena as a venue for the next World Boxing Association heavyweight title fight between controversial contender Muhammad Ali and champion Ernie Terrell. If the city wanted it, the promoter all but guaranteed, the match was theirs to host. A prominent figure in the boxing world, Fine had used Sherbrooke as a fight venue in the recent past and was impressed by its 4,000-seat arena. In *La Tribune*, Routhier translated Fine's message: "Dites oui, ce sera oui!" In a closed-door session on 7 March, Sherbrooke City Council promptly said yes, and spent the following day anxiously awaiting confirmation (*Tribune* 1966c; see also *Sherbrooke Daily Record* [hereafter SDR] 1966a).

On 9 March, the disappointing news came through. Fine couldn't seal the deal and the answer was no. Sherbrooke had been one of many cities in North America where the Ali–Terrell title fight had been shopped – first in the United States and then in Canada. It was pitched to and then rejected by New York, Chicago, Pittsburgh, Louisville, Lewiston (Maine), Las Vegas, and other places.

In New York, the state athletic commission refused to sanction the bout because of Terrell's alleged ties to organized crime. But elsewhere, it was his opponent's character that was the problem. Born Cassius Clay, Ali was an American Olympic gold medalist in 1960, a brilliant tactical fighter, a voluble self-promoter, and a Black rights advocate who in 1964 had joined the Nation of Islam and changed his name to Muhammad Ali (though the press everywhere, including Sherbrooke, continued to call him Clay).[1] He also openly opposed American aggression in Vietnam. When his draft status was changed by the United States government from 1Y (eligible for service in national emergency) to 1A (available for military service) in February 1966, Ali said he would refuse to serve in the US Army and if called up would, as a Muslim, claim conscientious objector status. The response was predictable. Other US cities that had once considered hosting the fight dropped out in response to Ali's "un-American" views, but Canadian venues remained interested: Montreal dallied briefly with the idea; so did Sorel, Verdun, Edmonton, London, and others before all deciding against making a pitch for it (Carroll 1966; *Tribune* 1966a, 1966b). On 8 March 1966, Toronto's Maple Leaf Gardens accepted the bout, but only after the Government of Ontario's minister of labour decided that there was nothing he could do legally to the stop the fight, and only after a member of the Gardens' board of governors, the irascible Conn Smythe, resigned in protest against Ali and any fighter who aimed to "evade conscription in their own country."[2] There was one more twist: no sooner had the Gardens accepted the match than Ernie Terrell pulled out, claiming that the prize money offered in the Gardens' contract was not enough. As a replacement, the promoter quickly signed George Chuvalo, a white Canadian journeyman whose bruising style and toughness made him an appealing contrast to Ali. The show went on. On 29 March 1966, the fifteen-round match ended in a victory by decision for Ali. In a way, it was also a symbolic "win" for the plucky Chuvalo and for Canada, as historian Bryan Palmer has written.[3]

Back in Sherbrooke, upon hearing the bad news that the match was to be held in Toronto, Mayor Nadeau was philosophical: "we did all we could. It would have been a good thing for Sherbrooke" (SDR 1966b). His stoicism may have papered over a division in his administration over the merits of hosting *this* particular fight, with *that* notorious fighter. But no one among them doubted that, if chosen, they could pull it off – because they had already done similar things. For more than a decade, between 1955 and 1966, the Sherbrooke Athletic Commission (with the support of the local council) promoted the city as a viable site for world-class professional boxing matches and had gained a reputation as one of the few Canadian places to do it well. By the early 1960s, Canada's once lively professional boxing scene had developed "bleak prospects," one analyst noted, injured by competition from televised fights broadcast from the US and sullied by reports of "gangster influence." Canada has "few boxing shows to speak about ... apart from Halifax and Sherbrooke, Que." (SDR 1960).

Among the boxing "shows" held in Sherbrooke in the 1950s and 1960s, two stood out. The first of these was held in September 1958, when light heavyweight Tommy "Hurricane" Jackson stepped into the ring to box New Yorker Johnny Vick in a ten-round bout. The second one was held in May 1963, when former welterweight and middleweight champion Sugar Ray Robinson took on challenger Maurice Rolbnet, knocking him out in the third round. But there were many others. For about a decade, these events put Sherbrooke and the SAC on the global boxing map and connected it to a broad and vibrant network of athletes, managers, fight promoters, local and state athletic commissions, and national boxing organizations across the continent.

The story of Sherbrooke's "Fight Nights" is complex. Though several themes emerge from the local and non-local press coverage of the bouts staged by the SAC, two of them are most important. First, Sherbrooke's golden years of boxing reveal a good deal about the bureaucracy of control, the challenge of regulating this professional sport in Canada and Quebec, and the temptation for smaller boxing sites and individual promoters to break the rules and occasionally step outside the web of control. Second, the portrayal of boxing in Sherbrooke's local media provides a window on a changing global discourse about Black masculinity in mid-twentieth century North America. Unlike earlier eras, Sherbrooke's biggest boxing spectacles in these years featured prominent Black boxers from the United States whose presence in a region populated largely by white settlers invited reflection on the changing meaning of Black masculinity symbolized and prescribed by professional boxers. Through these matches and the robust coverage of them in the local press, sports fans in the Eastern Townships were given ringside seats to a continent-wide culture shift in the construction of Black manliness, from an aging accommodationist model of the 1930s, '40s, and '50s toward a more militant, loud, and subversive version of the sort modelled by Ali in the 1960s and beyond.

SETTING *the* STAGE: BOXING BEFORE SHERBROOKE'S GOLDEN AGE

As in many other regions of Canada, boxing got its start in Quebec's Eastern Townships in the 1850s as a largely renegade pastime that followed male bachelor workplace subcultures in the region's resource development industries, along its railways, and in its military encampments. By the late Victorian era, boxing had developed a strange, split identity. Despite its place among the rougher sort, it came to be championed also by the respectable middle class (and especially physical educators in Canada's elite schools and universities) as "sparring," a useful and safe training activity for young men in an age when Muscular Christianity lauded a balance between the development of the bodies and the minds of prospective leaders in a new nation. With proper equipment and supervision and without regard for victories, records, or prizes, boxing "exhibitions" took their place in Canada's towns and cities in the 1870s, '80s, and '90s, alongside lacrosse and hockey as legitimate "gentlemen's" pursuits, means to build manliness and character (see Donnelly 1988–89; Putney 2001). But throughout those years, the earliest vein of boxing remained constant. As with other sports, boxing was in the nation's rougher places a way for "chancers" to make money. In working-class Canada, boxing became prizefighting, undertaken by both occasional athletes trying it on and, by the early twentieth century, a handful of accomplished professionals who travelled the country to find opponents, promoters to publicize their fights, paying spectators to watch, and gamblers willing to set stakes on the outcomes.[4]

Progressive reformers abhorred such organized and commercial violence and their loud protests prompted lawmakers to act. In Canada, prizefighting was criminalized by federal statute in 1881. An amendment to the law lifted that sanction in 1934, but in truth prizefighting was never penalized harshly or effectively and so the 1881 law itself provided no real deterrence. In some places, the regulatory slack was picked up by local authorities whose civic Progressive Era reformers saw prizefighting as one of the many social ills that must be stamped out by "Good Government." In Montreal, the city council passed municipal ordinances in 1887 and 1895 that prohibited prizefighting within city limits. But, as historian Gilles Janson has written, these regulations "ne diminue[nt] en rien la fréquence des rencontres. Les combats ont souvent lieu la nuit, à l'extérieur des limites de la ville, dans les granges ou les maisons abandonnées" (Janson 2003, 90).

In the Eastern Townships, legal amateur sparring exhibitions and illicit commercial prizefights coexisted uneasily in the first two decades of the twentieth century and local press reports show that both forms of the sport were followed enthusiastically. Among the former sort were short (four- or six-round) contests – no knockouts, decisions on points only – sponsored and legitimized by the simon-pure Sherbrooke Athletic Association or held at the Bishop's College School on special sports days that were open to the public for free (see SDR 1914a, 1914c, 1913c). Increasingly after 1910, commercial matches were advertised in the press and staged locally in a variety of Eastern Townships venues (including Sherbrooke's city hall, arena, and drill shed). Often, paying customers could watch local fighters take on those from away. One such bout in March 1911 featured an eighteen-round fight between Billy Bishop of Thetford Mines and Joe Harris of Leicester, England "for a purse of $50" (SDR 1911). The *Daily Record* seems to have had low regard for the law and published notices from boxing barnstormers who announced that they would be passing through the region and were willing to take on opponents "for a suitable purse." One of them going by the name "Young Sampson" arranged to box Bob Murray of East Angus, offering anyone who would take it a side bet of $200, so confident was he of victory (SDR 1914d; see also SDR 1912b, 1914b). Only occasionally did local authorities step in to scuttle these affairs. One well-attended boxing match held in May 1913 in Cowansville – outdoors, "between the Ottawa Hotel and Laflamme's Barber Shop" – was allowed to go five rounds before being stopped by the town constable (SDR 1913a). One month later, in a pique of conscience, perhaps, the *Daily Record* published the proceedings of the annual Methodist Conference of Canada meeting, reminding readers that prize fights were actually prohibited under the Criminal Code (SDR 1913b). The onset of the war in 1914 altered the sport's popular appeal. In this new context, prizefighting seemed a poor use of time and resources for a country at war; at the same time, sparring took on a critical purpose for young men training for military action – as one newspaper piece noted in 1915: "[i]n view of the war ... [boxing is] a good means to develop courage and strength" (SDR 1915a). Encamped in Sherbrooke throughout the war, the 5th Mounted Rifles hosted regular "tournaments" at the Sherbrooke armory and invited townspeople to witness the soldiers box in matches that the *Daily Record* called "clean, gentlemanly, and good humoured" and carried off in an "exceptionally scientific manner" (SDR 1915b; see also SDR 1915c).

After the war, amateur boxing continued as a form of physical training in Canadian schools and amateur athletic associations into the late twentieth century, and it remains today both a thriving form of recreation and, for elite athletes, a competitive Olympic pursuit. But prizefighting in Canada and Quebec took a more dynamic turn. Its popularity increased notably in Canada in the post-war years and its revived prominence pushed politicians to settle its shaky legal status. As with the liquor trade, Progressive reformers who once saw in prize-fighting a social ill to be outlawed pursued a different tack in the 1920s. If authorities couldn't prohibit it (and clearly, they couldn't), professional boxing must be regulated by government-appointed authorities to make it safe and profitable (through the sale of permits for events and a percentage of gate receipts).[5] This sort of thinking helped spawn the Ontario Athletic Commission in 1920 (Kidd 1995). Quebec took a different path to the same end. Wary of the "légalité douteuse" of professional boxing, Premier Louis-Alexandre Taschereau offloaded the responsibility: his government passed a law in March 1922 that permitted the province's municipalities to institute their own local athletic commissions to regulate and profit from the sport. Montreal and Quebec City established their athletic commissions almost immediately, in April 1922 (Janson 2003, 98–9; *Quebec Chronicle* 1922). After some delay, the Sherbrooke Athletic Commission was created in September 1929.[6]

Between 1922 and 1987, Quebec's local athletic commissions governed the sport of boxing in the province. In those seven decades, they promoted and policed it, sanctioning local fights, appointing ringside judges, maintaining updated lists of registered fighters, licensing promoters for local events, collecting permit fees and match revenues, advertising local bouts and encouraging local athletes, and enforcing the rulings of their fellow governing bodies across Canada (including the Canadian Boxing Federation [CBF], founded 1922) and the United States (including the National Boxing Association [NBA], founded 1921). Creatures of their local governments, commission members always included some elected municipal politicians, as well as medical officials and prominent sportsmen. Of the three, the Montreal commission did, by far, the steadiest and largest volume of boxing business throughout these years.[7] The work of the SAC was more intermittent: periods of steady activity were followed by years of near dormancy.

In the 1920s, Sherbrooke was distinguished, historian Gilles Janson writes, "particulièrement par le nombre and la qualité des boxeurs qui s'y produisent," such as featherweight Frank "Young" Lebrun ("la terreur des Cantons-de-l'Est") and Canadian lightweight champion René Loubier (Janson 2005, 156, 206, 209). But the timing of the SAC's founding was not auspicious. After an initial flurry of activity in 1929,[8] the Depression hit, and it was not until the mid-1930s that commercial boxing events were regularly staged in town. In those years, the SAC worked hand-in-glove with Albert Kouri, an enterprising local promoter and impresario who managed several Canadian fighters and recruited others from across the US and Canada to box for prize money in Sherbooke. One such event in September 1935 was a five-fight card that featured four athletes from Sherbrooke, three from Lewiston, Maine, and one from Boston (*Montreal Gazette* 1935). Kouri was an influential man. In April 1937, he charged one of his clients, Ottawa boxer Eddie Carroll, with breach of contract (for boxing in prizefights without Kouri's sanction and pocketing all of the returns) and the SAC didn't hesitate to flex its muscles on Kouri's behalf. It suspended Carroll in Sherbrooke. But it also successfully petitioned the Montreal Athletic Commission (MAC) and the Canadian Boxing Federation (CBF) to lift Carroll's licence to fight in Canada and the National Boxing Association to bar him from doing so in the US (*SDR* 1937a;

Montreal Gazette 1937; see also Fonds, Procès verbaux 1934–37, 290). By August, Kouri and Carroll had mended their rift. Kouri convinced the SAC, CBF, and NBA to reinstate the boxer – just in time for him to headline a five-fight boxing card held in the open air in Sherbrooke's exhibition grounds (*SDR* 1937b, 1937c). The burst in SAC activity was short lived. By the onset of World War II, local boxing was in decline. City council continued to appoint members to the SAC throughout the war but, as a columnist in the *Daily Record* remarked in 1941, "boxing and wrestling shows are so few and far between that Ald. A.C. Ross and his co-members have very little to do" (*SDR* 1941). Perhaps most telling was an incident in May 1945, a "fiasco," according to press reports, when a Montreal promoter staged an amateur card in Sherbrooke for the benefit of soldiers without ever submitting the program or the fighters' contracts to the SAC for approval. Sidestepped, the SAC had become almost irrelevant (*SDR* 1945). It remained that way for most of the next decade. When city council investigated the athletic commission's operations in 1955, the findings were dire: Ross, the former mayor, admitted that the full commission had not met since 1939 and had kept no proper records of its activity. Its bank account held $38. In response, the council revived it with several new appointees, but some, like the *Daily Record*'s Len O'Donnell, were skeptical: "We sincerely trust they will do more than their predecessors, which was nothing" (*SDR* 1955b).[9]

The new SAC did much more than that. Starting from a near standstill, it was the catalyst for a decade of frenetic activity (*Tribune* 1955a, 1957; Spafford 1957). Sherbrooke was a busy place in the 1950s and early '60s. The self-styled "Electrical City" had a robust postwar economy rooted in hydroelectric generation, textile manufactures, mining, and metal industries. Its population grew steadily, from 50,443 in 1951 to 80,711 in 1971, which matched almost exactly the national average annual rate of growth of 2.1 per cent. Demographically, the city was overwhelmingly white and francophone. People of colour (including Indigenous Canadians) made up a tiny slice of the population: less than 1.3 percent in 1961.[10] A majority French-speaking population since 1871, by 1962 almost 85 per cent claimed French as their mother tongue (Ministère 1962, 62). Despite that imbalance, a customary "bonne entente" bound the two language groups locally, as Frank Hamilton wrote in a rosy, pre–Quiet Revolution *Maclean's* article. Like its mayoralty and city council, "Sherbrooke's social, service and sports clubs are open to, and frequented by, any citizen irrespective of French or English ancestry. Proceedings are always conducted in both languages, with speakers talking in their native tongues last" (Hamilton 1951).

That spirit seems to have informed the local SAC during its revival. Among the five members of the revitalized commission were aldermen Everett Nicol, Gérard

Bérard, and Carl Camirand, prominent Quebec sportsman Ivan Dugré, and City Treasurer Routhier. (Alec Ross was the lone holdover; the SAC's nominal president since the 1930s, he stepped aside in favour of Nicol in 1956.) Bérard, Dugré, and Routhier drove the commission. Bérard presided over commission business from the late 1950s into the mid-1970s and served as its voice on council. The prominence of Dugré, an admired senior amateur hockey player and coach, lent the commission legitimacy in the broader sports community.[11] Bérard and Routhier, the commission's secretary treasurer, served as the links between the SAC and the boxing authorities across North America, connections they cultivated well. In 1962, Bérard was elected president of the CBF and Routhier became vice-president of that organization in 1975. By 1978, Routhier was serving on the World Boxing Association's Ethics Committee. But it was the work they did in the late 1950s and early 1960s that set the stage for Sherbrooke's golden era of boxing. In 1956, the group surveyed the constitutions and by-laws of their sister athletic commissions in Quebec and beyond (SDR 1956; *Tribune* 1956). The following year, they wrote their own new foundation documents, which the provincial assembly made law. Among the new rules was an important change: the SAC increased the percentage of revenue that the commission could draw from local professional bouts, to make the sport pay.

In this new context, Sherbrooke was now equipped legally and physically to join the ranks of other elite, global boxing venues. Working with ambitious local promoters, like Sherbrooke's Warren (Pee Wee) Berwick and Windsor Mills's Clément Robitaille, and American promoters, like New York's Al Bachman and Connecticut's Dick Fine, the SAC brought big-time professional boxing events to the Eastern Townships from the mid-1950s to the mid-1960s. These included five fights involving Canadian light heavyweight champion and Sherbrooke native Burke Emery in 1957, 1958, and 1960, as well as others that featured Canadian welterweight champion Armand Savoie in 1957 and Montreal middleweight Marcel Piau in 1957. And in December 1959, the SAC hosted a boxing exhibition performed by recent world heavyweight champion Floyd Patterson (*Tribune* 1959b, 1959c). Aside from these events, two others capture our attention for what they reveal about the question of control and the prevailing discourse about race in North America's "fight game."

ROUND ONE: JACKSON *vs* VICK, 1958. A QUESTION *of* CONTROL

Professional boxing in 1950s North America was a complex "alphabet soup" of acronyms, a patchwork of jurisdictions, some local and some state/provincial, all of them held together by umbrella confederations: the Canadian Boxing Federation and the National Boxing Association. The legitimacy of the sport depended upon athletic commissions' ability to control local boxing, and to prevent rogue promoters, managers, and fighters from operating outside of their sanction. It depended equally on cooperation among governing authorities. As a commercial venture and as a purportedly medically safe enterprise, pro boxing could not survive unless the myriad separate authorities respected each other's rulings. Like most boxing authorities, the SAC was committed to the cooperative principle (see for example *SDR* 1957a; *Tribune* 1959a). Among the very first items of SAC business in 1929 were applications to the Canadian Boxing Federation and the Montreal Athletic Commission for formal affiliation. By mid-century, the SAC was also formally affiliated with the New York State Athletic Commission (NYSAC) – one of the oldest and most powerful organizations in the sport. But the SAC's closest regulatory partner was the Montreal Athletic Commission, whose members kept close tabs on the SAC and made occasional visits to Sherbrooke to watch matches and to cement ties (*SDR* 1941b; Fonds, Procès verbaux 1926–33, 323 and 1937–38, 6).

Occasionally, the ties among boxing authorities could bind too tightly. Pitted against larger urban venues like New York, Chicago, Toronto, and Montreal, it was a challenge for smaller, less well-heeled authorities like Sherbrooke's Athletic Commission to attract big boxing cards. There were exceptions, of course, but the natural flow of things favoured the metropolises, where more money was concentrated along with larger fan bases and better communications infrastructure to promote prize fights. For the SAC, abiding by the system must have meant a resignation to settle for second-tier status and second-rung fighters. In September 1958, that conundrum came into sharp focus when the SAC held an event headlined by a prominent US boxer, Tommy "Hurricane" Jackson. The match demonstrated that Sherbrooke's SAC was willing to break the regulatory code to lift itself to prominence.

Never had the SAC hosted an event with a boxer of Jackson's calibre and notoriety. How the promoter, Pee Wee Berwick, went about arranging the scheduled ten-round bout between Jackson and New Jersey boxer Johnny Vick on 15 September 1958 is unknown, but it is clear that Jackson had few options.

A professional since 1951, the Georgia-born New Yorker had risen to as high as third in the world rankings as a heavyweight in 1956. He had an unorthodox style of fighting that included "pawing and slapping" opponents and stumbling about the ring. He was known for his stamina and his willingness to withstand (or inability to avoid) punishment. In July 1957, boxing aficionado and *New Yorker* magazine writer A.J. Liebling called Jackson "primitive," "a Negro … who is the most untalented but indefatigable contestant – it would be eccentric to call him a boxer – of his age" (Liebling 1957). His style led him to injury. Jackson was banned from boxing in 1957 in two American states (per NBA and CBF recommendations) on medical grounds, after absorbing, the *New York Times* said, "a couple of savage beatings," including one from future heavyweight champion Floyd Patterson (*New York Times* 1958).

It was in this circumstance, in 1958, when Berwick presented the SAC with a rare opportunity, though one that came with a prickly choice: observe the ban slapped on Jackson by their affiliates or look the other way and sanction a local boxing event that promised a star headliner and potentially sizeable payday. The commission chose the latter, and though it took some time for the news to make its rounds, the fallout was widespread. Dozens of newspapers across North America ran a UPI story claiming that by accepting the fight, SAC officials had transgressed the code that boxing's governing bodies were expected to honour.[12] Taken aback by the response, the SAC held its ground. The Hurricane would be examined by local medical officials in advance of the match to ensure his safety. "Unless Jackson is in A-1 shape," SAC secretary Routhier told the press, "he won't go in the ring" (*Boston Globe* 1958). One local newspaper went so far in its pre-match coverage as to paint Jackson's appearance as a statement of principle: a stand against a "system" that had treated him unfairly.

> Tonight the eyes of the boxing world are tuned on the city of Sherbrooke. This is the first time in the history of this city that so much interest from outside centres such as New York City, has been turned to this Eastern Townships city. They are waiting to see if a mistake has been made. Many are also pulling for one man to prove that he has been "done wrong." That man is Hurricane Jackson … He can hardly read or write, and the only trade he knows is boxing … What is at stake is his own ability to make a living in the ring. (Powell 1958b; see also Powell 1958a)

But there were considerations at play other than the fighter's health and livelihood, and collegiality among boxing organizations. As Routhier reportedly explained in a private telegram to CBF commissioner Gene Létourneau days before the fight, "ticket sales and promotions were far advanced … the fight must go on" (*Edmonton Journal* 1958). It did. Jackson won in a unanimous decision over the unranked Vick, a result witnessed by 1,600 spectators and reported in news stories across North America. In a daring move, Sherbrooke had staked its claim to a place on the global boxing map (Powell 1958c).[13]

It is surprising how few real consequences there were for the SAC in the wake of the Hurricane Jackson imbroglio, given the real power of the NYSAC, the NBA, and the CBF. Renowned sports columnist Red Fisher denounced Berwick and the SAC in his column in the *Montreal Star*, claiming that they were merely using a desperate Hurricane for local gain. And CBF commissioner Létourneau initially supported the NBA recommendation, before changing his tune and insisting only that the SAC hire a referee for the bout who would "stop the fight if it appears that Jackson is taking severe punishment" (*SDR* 1958). In the end, neither the CBF nor the NBA formally penalized the Sherbrooke commission, probably due to Létourneau's intervention. Even so, the SAC's willingness to go ahead sent a firm message to the millions of newspaper readers who would have read about the fight in syndicated reports – the SAC would keep its own counsel when it came to regulating boxing in Sherbrooke.

ROUND TWO: ROBINSON *vs* ROLBNET, 1963. A WINDOW *on* BLACK MASCULINITY

The Sherbrooke Athletic Commission's push for prominence in the late 1950s and early 1960s created a local stage for the discussion of race in North America. In a region populated largely by white settlers, the SAC's biggest bouts in these years involved relatively well-known African American boxers. Burke Emery's Sherbrooke fights in 1957 and 1958 were all against African American opponents (Gene Hamilton, Ricardo King [twice], and Jimmy Skinner) and his title-winning match in 1960 was against Gordie Baldwin, a Black fighter from Toronto. The presence and performances of Black boxers in Sherbrooke involved the region's sports followers in an unfolding cultural discourse about the Black athletic body and Black masculinity in the era of Civil Rights and Black Power. Confronting Blackness was an unavoidable part of the SAC's search for prominence and profit. In the 1950s and 1960s, most of the best boxers in the world were Black.

The place of Blackness in sport was a subject of controversy and clamour across North America in the middle decades of the twentieth century. Jackie Robinson's breaking of the colour barrier in major-league baseball in 1947 and Willie O'Ree's feat as the first Black National Hockey League player in 1958 were monumental achievements that opened doors for Black athletes in "white" games. Talented athletes, their notoriety came nonetheless from a specific narrative: the *first ones* to break a colour barrier, they were lauded as exceptions to a culturally imposed rule (see Nzindukiyimana and Wamsley 2021). Indeed, older sportsmen in Sherbrooke knew that storyline well. From 1946 to 1949, the Sherbrooke senior amateur hockey team featured an all-Black line, the "trio des noirs" – Herb Carnegie, Ossie Carnegie, and Manny McIntyre – who gained national notoriety for their singularity and talent (Harris 2003; Carnegie 2019; *Petit Journal* 1947).

The story of race in mid-twentieth-century boxing was different. The presence of African Americans in staged fights was nothing new in America. "The exhibition of the Black body, as a captive body, in the boxing ring within the United States," Harvey Young writes, "began with boxing lessons on southern plantations." From the late nineteenth century forward, Black boxers used the ring to challenge white supremacy outright (not merely qualify it). Black boxers undermined the myth of Black inferiority through their prowess in the plainest form of hypermasculine combat (Moore 2010; Gems 2014). Jack Johnson did that when he won the world heavyweight boxing championship in 1908 and famously defended it against "White Hope" Jim Jeffries in 1910. Joe Louis did, too, when after more than two decades of a restored colour line, he won the heavyweight crown in 1937 and held it for twelve years. Between 1949 and 1967, non-Black boxers held the world heavyweight title for a total of only five years. Black domination of the sport constituted, for many, a symbol of progress in addressing North America's intractable race problem.

By the 1950s, the critical question in the sport was not whether African American boxers could be world champions; it was, rather, what *kind* of champions they would be. Black champions (heavyweights, especially) held a powerful position in North American society, a sports "pulpit" from which they could model Black masculinity and shape the thinking of a new generation of young men. Wary of the sort of white backlash wrought by the brash, incendiary antics (public drinking, consorting with white women, reckless driving, showy displays of wealth, and brutal punishment of inferior opponents) of champion Jack Johnson (1908–15), Joe Louis (1937–49) was modelled as an anti-Johnson, a model of quiet dignity, composure, moral decency, patriotism, and deference to authority. Louis was held out as a version of Black masculinity that could both raise the pride of Black Americans and stand as one that white North Americans might accept. As heavyweight champion, Floyd Patterson (1956–62) continued in Louis's mould, routinely praised, one biographer noted, "for his gentlemanly, intelligent, modest character," a champion who would not rock the boat. Into that heritage walked

Cassius Clay, who turned professional in 1960 and defeated Sonny Liston to become heavyweight champion in 1964. Clay (later Ali) turned the Louis–Patterson Black Champion persona on its head. Arrogant, loud, humorous, playful, bombastic, he modelled the rebellious anti-establishment spirit of the 1960s. His demeanour angered both white and Black middle classes, as well as boxing oldtimers and the sport's fleet of journalists, a feeling that turned to hatred among many when he declared his Muslim faith and announced his opposition to the Vietnam War (see Remnick 1998; Eig 2017; Ezra 2016; Cople Jaher 1985).

Against this transitional backdrop, the Sherbrooke Athletic Commission licensed American promoter Dick Fine in 1963 to bring acclaimed former middleweight champion Sugar Ray Robinson to town to fight Moroccan Maurice Rolbnet in a bout scheduled for ten rounds. By 1963, Robinson had become boxing royalty, a lauded professional since 1940 who had won world championship belts in two different weight categories. He entered the ring with a record of 155 wins, twelve losses, and three draws. Though he was forty-two years old and in the gloaming of his career, having Sugar Ray as a headliner was a significant coup for the SAC. At the Sherbrooke Arena, 2,800 people watched him knockout Rolbnet in the third round (*SDR* 1963c). As a display of boxing talent, the match was forgettable,[14] but the discourse it generated gave Sherbrookers a glimpse of the culture war that was then gripping the American boxing world.

Robinson's Sherbrooke fight was a demonstration of an old order that was about to pass. Before the mid-1960s, Palmer writes, "African-American fighters remained locked into the paradigms of the past." They now dominated boxing's top ranks, but they continued to do so "in the structured and typecast roles that whites assigned, and profited from" (Palmer 2009, 121). The boxing apparatus in Sherbrooke was wholly white, from the promoter who secured the deal to the commissioners who licensed and staged it, the reporters who covered it, the ring announcer who introduced the fighters, the referee (the long-superannuated Young Lebrun) who officiated it, and the spectators under whose gaze these two Black boxers fought. Here, as elsewhere, Black male athletic bodies were subjects for white amusement. Racial hierarchy underpinned the discourse. In the press, African American fighters were often described specifically as "*colored* fighters" and "boxeurs *de couleurs*" (see, for example, *SDR* 1957b; *Tribune* 1955b). In Sherbrooke, one local sportswriter referred to Robinson and Rolbnet as "boys" (*SDR* 1963b). Their subjectivity was expressed perhaps most starkly in a photograph of the pre-fight weigh-in that ran in both the *Tribune* and the *Daily Record*, in which a SAC commissioner takes measurements of one semi-clad Black combatant while another commissioner looks on. Pre-fight weigh-ins were standard practice for all legitimate fights, to be sure, but the

Figure 12.1 Pre-fight weigh-in. Sugar Ray Robinson vs Maurice Rolbnet

selection of this particular photograph, with its stark racial juxtaposition, is telling. These exotic athletes were on display, and the newspapers used it to pump local curiosities about boxing and about the performance of Black masculinity in the ring.

Also in that photograph was none other than ex–heavyweight champ Joe Louis – by then a business partner of Fine's, who had travelled from Los Angeles to Sherbrooke the week before to talk up the fight and to promote Sugar Ray. Locally, the presence of Louis outside the ring was almost as significant a coup for the SAC as having Robinson inside of it. Like Patterson's visit in 1959, Louis's arrival in town was announced well in advance and local officials took full advantage, creating a busy schedule of public appearances for the ex-champ. Louis was kind and generous with his time. He signed the "Golden Book" at city hall, held a press conference soon after his arrival, and demonstrated his appreciable non-boxing skills in a round of golf at the Sherbrooke Country Club. He attended a SAC-hosted dinner and, led by SAC commissioner Dugré, was taken on a tour to the Collège Val-Estrie, the Séminaire Saint-Charles-Borromée, and the L'Orphelinat agricole Saint-Joseph de Waterville (*Tribune* 1963b, 1963a). There, ten miles south of the city, he addressed the boys, told them stories about boxing and encouraged them to study hard, answered every one of their questions and signed so many autographs that "the Bomber finished with writer's cramp … Although he spoke in English, they understood him well" (SDR 1963b). According to reports, Louis was in good humour all week and forthcoming when prodded by reporters' questions about Robinson and the "fight game" in general. Most telling, however, was the contrast in his responses to local reporters' questions about Robinson and about Clay: Sugar Ray, he declared, "'is without a doubt the best fighter pound for pound, of all time … [He has] a unique style' … Regarding Cassius Clay[,] Louis just put his finger to his mouth signifying he had nothing to say about him as he could do his own talking" (SDR 1963a). Louis's silence spoke volumes. It was, as race scholar Harvey Young observed of Louis in other contexts, "a brilliant performance of stillness" (Young 2010, 109). He had been champion long enough to understand well how professional boxing had commodified and essentialized the Black male body in America. A conservative man and an ex-veteran, his customary stoicism was part of his boxing tool kit, a way to win acceptably and stay champion. And he understood, and abhorred, what Clay (Ali) stood for (see Mead 1985, 292). Muhammad Ali never did set foot in Sherbrooke, Quebec. But in May of 1963 (as in March of 1966) his presence hovered there and elsewhere across North America, threatening boxing's old order, and challenging a version of Black masculinity that was now on the wane.

AFTERMATH: DRAWING CONCLUSIONS

By the late 1960s, professional boxing in Quebec (and in many places across North America) had begun to experience a sort of existential crisis. The sport had been catapulted into prominence in the post-World War II era by the emergence of Black champions, many of whom had comparatively long tenures at the top and who, following the lead of Joe Louis, had become accepted, indeed, embraced by a large segment of middle-class North America that crossed racial lines. Professional boxing became more mainstream in the 1940s, 1950s, and early 1960s; television and closed-circuit venues (for major title fights) exposed more consumers to the sport's terminology, tactics, personalities, and hype. And yet, even as its audience expanded, several factors worked to undermine its powerful appeal (see Lindsay 1995).

First, across North America, critics reasserted long-brewing concerns about the unsavoury connection between boxers, managers, and criminality. In the 1950s, repeated accusations were made that major matches were fixed and that big-city gangsters had controlled certain high-profile fighters, including Jake

LaMotta, Sonny Liston, and even Ray Robinson (Sussman 2019). When Ernie Terrell backed out of the 1966 title fight with Ali in Toronto, rumours circulated that he had been threatened and directed to do so by the Chicago mob, which couldn't profit once the fight moved to Canada. And to white North America, Ali's new management in 1966–67, Main Bout Inc., and its connection to the Nation of Islam, simply meant control of the sport by another type of corrupt "mob" (see Ezra 2016).

In addition, longstanding concerns about fighter safety reemerged more strongly in the 1960s and 1970s. News of the death of Cuban welterweight Benny "The Kid" Paret ten days after being knocked unconscious in a nationally televised fight in Madison Square Garden in March 1962 revived anxieties about the dangers of pro boxing and the ethics of money-driven staged combat, both internationally and locally. Soon after Paret's death, in April 1962, SAC and CBF president Gérard Bérard promised *La Tribune* that he would propose new safety reforms to the NBA on behalf of the CBF, though there is no record that they had any effect (*Tribune* 1962a). When, one year later, in October 1963, heavyweight Ernie Knox was killed in the ring in a Baltimore fight, *Sports Illustrated* responded, "This Death Might Kill Boxing" (Boyle 1963). But it didn't, and beyond the headlines about boxing deaths, the spectre of punch-drunk ex-fighters – those who survived the ring – served as human reminders of the real costs of legalized professional boxing. One article published in the *Sherbrooke Record* noted simply, "Fight Game in Limbo" (Soosar 1972).[15]

Finally, beginning in the 1960s, criticism of Quebec's peculiar form of regulation of the sport came into question. Journalists and others within the sport began to voice their view that the regulation of combat sports in the province was too spotty, inconsistent, and open to unscrupulous promoters and managers, who could easily evade oversight and sanction from local athletic commissions in Montreal, Quebec City, and Sherbrooke. In 1962, crafty New York promoter Al Bachman attempted to stage matches for boxer Robert Cléroux in "les petits centres provinciaux du Québec, là où il n'y a pas d'autorités de la boxe afilliées à la NBA" (*Tribune* 1962b). The NBA had suspended and blacklisted Cléroux for refusing to follow their directive to fight George Chuvalo. Cléroux fought anyway, unsanctioned – against Jim Cherokee in Granby in late September and against Lloyd Jones in Noranda one month later. CBF and WBA commissioner Létourneau lamented in an open letter to the editor of Quebec City's *Le Soleil* in 1969 "des lacunes déplorées dans la boxe" that were allowing boxing promoters to stage unregulated fights beyond the reach of legitimate local boxing commissions (*Soleil* 1969; see also *Tribune* 1962c, 1962d). What was needed was a province-wide regulatory authority over the sport, something akin to those already functioning in other states and provinces.

The Government of Quebec first broached the idea of province-wide regulation in 1970, but it took until the end of the decade before critics got their wish (*SDR* 1970). In 1980, the Parti Québécois government established a provincial Régie de la sécurité dans les sports, a product of Law 78, An Act Respecting Safety in Sport, which consolidated the sanctioning of professional combat sports and stipulated new rules that demanded the licensing of sparring partners, outlawed overweight fighters, and insisted on a minimum of thirty amateur bouts before a boxer could go pro (*Montreal Gazette* 1987). Opposition from promoters and fighters helped delay the implementation of the new law until 1987. In that year, along with its counterparts in Montreal and Quebec City, the SAC passed out of existence.

In truth, the SAC was dead well before the province assumed its authority. By the late 1960s, its fuel was spent, and though individual Sherbrookers like Bérard and Routhier continued their roles in national and international organizations, the local boxing scene and the local relevance of the SAC fell precipitously. Once a prominent civic credit and vector to the sports world beyond the region, the body quickly lost its magic and the people's trust. "Il y a à Sherbrooke une commission athlétique," one local editor wrote in 1973, "mais je ne suis pas pour l'instant en measure de vous fournir le nom du responsable …" (*Tribune* 1973a).[16] In 1979, when the minister of Leisure, Hunting, and Fishing, Lucien Lessard, introduced Bill 78 in the National Assembly, he quoted one-time 1970s SAC chairman Antonio Pinard, who described the situation starkly: "Je vois d'un bon oeil la disparition prochaine des commissions athlétiques de Montréal, de Québec et de Sherbrooke lorsque sera adoptée la loi sur la sécurité dans les sports. Toutefois, en ce qui concerne Sherbrooke, il faut préciser que c'est chose faite depuis un an parce qu'elle n'avait plus de raison d'être" (Assemblée nationale 1979).

In 1987, no one mourned the passing of the SAC (publicly, at least), but its quiet demise belied a more spectacular past. A generation earlier, between 1955 and 1966, the Sherbrooke Athletic Commission put that Eastern Townships city on the global map of professional boxing. For a brief time, the "sweet science" allowed local officials to participate in a powerful international sports regulatory network. They used that brief foothold in the sport to bring to their city the "Hurricane," "Sugar Ray," the "Brown Bomber" and, with them, the racial politics of boxing in its most contentious years.

Notes

1 A great many analyses of Ali's career and his place in American culture have been written; perhaps the best ones among them are Remnick (1998) and Eig (2017). From January 1966 until May 1967, Ali's career management was controlled by Main Bout Inc., a group associated with the Nation of Islam, after his contract with a consortium of white businessmen from his hometown of Louisville expired. On the role of Main Bout in brokering the Terrell (later Chuvalo) fight, see Ezra (2016).

2 "They put cash ahead of class," Smythe wrote to Gardens chairman John Bassett in his resignation telegram. "The Gardens was built for many things, but not garbage disposal" (*Vancouver Sun* 1966). See also *Tribune* (1966d).

3 "In courageous defeat, in going the distance with a larger-than-life United States, in standing to the end in a posture, however slouched, of resilient difference, Chuvalo seemed to speak for Canada in ways that Canadians understood" (Palmer 2009, 111).

4 On this division, see Wamsley and Whitson (1998, 420–1). In one 1912 article titled "To the Defence of the Boxers," the views of the *London Spectator* on this matter were presented to Townships readers (SDR 1912a).

5 On one province's postwar approach to regulating the liquor trade, see Malleck (2012). In the United States, prizefighting was first legalized in 1920, when New York State's Walker Law established the New York State Athletic Commission as a governing body. Soon thereafter, thirteen other states followed suit and, together in 1921, they established the National Boxing Association (which changed its name to the World Boxing Association in 1962). The NBA began to sanction "national" title fights and name "World Champions."

6 In June 1922, a "Mr E.W. Farwell and others" had proposed that an athletic commission be formed locally, but the city council refused to consider it. See *Tribune* (1922), SDR (1922, 1929).

7 The surviving Montreal Athletic Commission records attest this fact. See Fonds Commission athlétique de Montréal (1926–68). https://www.archivesquebec.com/montrealvm058.html.

8 The commission's first matters of business were to apply for affiliation with the Montreal Athletic Commission, "so that athletes registered under one commission could appear under the other without the necessity of a second inspection" and to issue a permit to the Tuque Rouge Snowshoe Club for a fight between Kid Durant and Lebrun, to be held in Sherbrooke's 54th Armory on 5 October (SDR 1929).

9 O'Donnell's sour tone may have stemmed from personal lament for the sport. He had been a member of the SAC in 1937, when boxing in Sherbrooke enjoyed its first spike of success. See SDR (1955a); *Tribune* (1955). There are no surviving business records from SAC deliberations and no evidence that, even in its later, more flourishing years, records of its meetings and decisions were kept. Author's email communication with Karine Savary, conservatrice, Musée d'histoire de Sherbrooke, 11 January 2022.

10 This figure represents those who declared their ethnic/racial origins as other than British, French, German, Italian, Jewish, or Polish. It is a little more than the figure of .94 per cent that constituted the total percentage of "Asiatic, Indian and Eskimo and 'Other'" and "not stated" for all of Quebec but smaller than the 3.2 per cent for those categories in the whole of Canada (Ministère 1962, 51).

11 Soon after his death from a heart attack at age fifty-eight, full-page tributes to Dugré appeared in both of Sherbrooke's dailies. See Messier (1972); *Tribune* (1972); *Sherbrooke Record* (1972).

12 The United Press International (UPI) version of the story was reprinted across the continent, in papers as far flung as the *McAllen* (TX) *Monitor*, the *Logan* (UT) *Herald-Journal*, and the *Deadwood* (SD) *Pioneer Times*.

13 The long article concluded: "Sherbrooke is really on the boxing map now." See also *Tribune* (1958).

14 Robinson's Sherbrooke fight is not mentioned in any of the numerous biographies and the one autography of his life. See, for example, Haygood (2009).

15 Indeed, Hurricane Jackson became a walking symbol of the costs of professional fighting. In 1964, still banned from boxing in New York and the United Kingdom, African American magazine *JET* featured a picture of him on his knees, working as a shoeshine in Brooklyn (*JET* 1964).

16 When, later the same year, it came to light in the local press that SAC members planned to travel to Puerto Rico to take part in the World Boxing Association's annual meeting, the press was suspicious of a junket at taxpayer's expense and called for a municipal inquiry (*Tribune* 1973b). In less than a decade the SAC had fallen off its perch.

References

Assemblée nationale du Québec. 1979. *Journal des Débats*, Quatrième session – 31st Legislature. 14 December 21 (81): 4551.

Boston Globe. 1958. "Jackson Fights Tonight Despite N.B.A. Opposition." 15 September, 27.

Boyle, Robert H. 1963. "This Death Might Kill Boxing." *Sports Illustrated*, 28 October. https://vault.si.com/vault/1963/10/28/this-death-might-kill-boxing. Accessed 4 June 2022.

Carnegie, Herb, with Bernice Carnegie. 2019. *A Fly in a Pail of Milk: The Herb Carnegie Story*. Toronto: ECW Press.

Carroll, Dink. 1966. "Playing the Field. No Political Pressure." *The Gazette* [Montreal], 7 March, 34.

Cople Jaher, Frederic. 1985. "White America Views Jack Johnson, Joe Louis, and Muhammad Ali." In *Sport in America: New Historical Perspectives*, edited by Donald Spivey, 45–92. Westport CT, Greenwood Press.

Donnelly, Peter. 1988–89. "On Boxing: Notes on the Past, Present and Future of a Sport in Transition." *Current Psychology* 7 (4): 331–46.

Edmonton Journal. 1958. "Quebec Explains Why Hurricane Must Fight." 13 September, 11.

Eig, Jonathan. 2017. *Ali: A Life*. Boston: Houghton Mifflin Harcourt.

Ezra, Michael. 2016. "Main Bout, Inc., Black Economic Power, and Professional Boxing: The Canceled Muhammad Ali–Ernie Terrell Fight." In *From Jack Johnson to LeBron James: Sports, Media, and the Color Line*, edited by Chris Lamb, 293–331. Lincoln: University of Nebraska Press.

Fonds Commission athlétique de Montréal Fonds. 1926–68. Montreal City Archives, Fonds VM058. https://www.archivesquebec.com/montrealvm058.html.

Gems, Gerald R. 2014. *Boxing: A Concise History of the Sweet Science*. Lanham, MD: Rowman & Littlefield.

Hamilton, Frank. 1951. "Sherbrooke. Where Two Live as Happily as One." *Maclean's*. 15 October. https://archive.macleans.ca/article/1951/10/15/sherbrooke-where-two-live-as-happily-as-one.

Harris, Cecil. 2003. *Breaking the Ice: The Black Experience in Professional Hockey*. Toronto: Insomniac Press.

Haygood, Wil. 2009. *Sweet Thunder: The Life and Times of Sugar Ray Robinson*. New York: Alfred A. Knopf.

Janson, Gilles. 2003. "La boxe au Québec (1822–1922): de l'illégalité à la légitimité." *Bulletin d'histoire politique* 11 (2): 87–104.

– 2005. *Un boxeur gentilhomme: Eugene Brosseau, 1895–1968*. Sillery, QC: Septentrion.

JET. 1964. "Back to the Bottom." Vol. 28, no. 2 (15 October): 21.

Kidd, Bruce. 1995. "'Making the pros pay' for Amateur Sports: The Ontario Athletic Commission, 1920–1947." *Ontario History* 87 (2): 105–27.

Liebling, A.J. 1957. "Big Fight at the Polo Grounds." *The Observer* [London], 28 July, 8.

Lindsay, Andrew John. 1995. "The Decline of Professional Boxing in Toronto, 1920–1993." MA thesis, University of Windsor.

Malleck, Dan. 2012. *Try to Control Yourself: The Regulation of Public Drinking in Post-Prohibition Ontario, 1927–44*. Vancouver: UBC Press.

Mead, Chris. 1985. *Joe Louis: Black Champion in White America*. New York: Charles Scribner's Sons.

Messier, Denis. 1972. "Le Québec pleure Ivan Dugré." *La Tribune*, 27 March, 9.

Ministère de l'Industrie et du Commerce. 1962. *Annuaire du Québec*. Quebec: Imprimeur de la Reine.

Montreal Gazette. 1935. "Costillo Is Victor." 23 September, 15.

– 1937. "Carroll Suspended. Ottawa Boxer Set Down by Sherbrooke Commission." 24 April, 17.

– 1987. "New Boxing Regulations Come under Fire." 28 August, B-15.

Moore, Louis. 2010. "Fine Specimens of Manhood: The Black Boxer's Body and the Avenue to Equality, Racial Advancement, and Manhood in the Nineteenth Century." *MELUS* 35 (4): 59–84.

New York Times. 1958. "Hurricane Jackson Bout Set." 12 September, 33.

Nzindukiyimana, Ornella, and Kevin Wamsley. 2021. "Black Canadian Sporting Histories in the 19th and 20th Centuries." In *Sport and Recreation in Canadian History*, edited by Carly Adams, 227–46. Champaign, IL: Human Kinetics.

Palmer, Bryan D. 2009. *Canada's 1960s: Ironies of Identity in a Rebellious Era*. Toronto: University of Toronto Press.

Petit Journal. 1947. "Des noirs brillent, maintenant, au hockey et il s'agit des frères Carnegie et de McIntyre." 12 January, 49.

Powell, Nick. 1958a. "Sherbrooke Boxing Fans Placed in Unique Position for Monday's Fights, Tommy Jackson to be on Trial Basis." *Sherbrooke Daily Record*, 12 September, 11.

– 1958b. "Stage Set for Much-Talked About Jackson-Vick Battle Here Tonight." *Sherbrooke Daily Record*, 15 September, 11.

– 1958c. "Hurricane Jackson Decisions Vick; Emery Scores Win Over Mercer." *Sherbrooke Daily Record*, 16 September, 22.

Putney, Clifford. 2001. *Muscular Christianity: Manhood and Sports in Protestant America, 1880–1920*. Cambridge, MA: Harvard University Press.
Quebec Chronicle. 1922. "City of Quebec, City Hall. By-Law No. 46. By-Law concerning Boxing Exhibitions, etc.," 1 May, 6.
Remnick, David. 1998. *King of the World: Muhammad Ali and the Rise of an American Hero*. New York: Vintage.
Sherbrooke Daily Record (SDR). 1911. "Boxing at Thetford Mines." 16 March, 6.
– 1912a. "To the Defence of the Boxers." 6 February, 6.
– 1912b. "Boxing. Sherbrooke Man Issues Challenge." 8 August, 6.
– 1913a. "Sports. Sporting Events at Cowansville." 31 May, 2.
– 1913b. "To Prohibit Prize Bouts." 11 June, 2.
– 1913c. "Bishop's College School Closing." 27 November, 6.
– 1914a. "Boxing and Wrestling." 14 January, 5.
– 1914b. "Boxing." 16 March, 7.
– 1914c. "Mackay vs Salina Burns." 14 April, 8.
– 1914d. "Young Sampson." 7 July, 5.
– 1915a. "E.T. Boxing Tournament." 6 January, 5.
– 1915b. "More Recruits to Mounted Rifles." 8 March, 1.
– 1915c. "Fine Boxing Exhibition." 19 April, 6.
– 1922. "Sherbrooke Athletic Commission." 19 September, 10.
– 1929. "Commission on Athletics Had First Meeting." 21 September, 24.
– 1937a. "Eddie Carroll Facing Threat of Suspension." 23 April, 8.
– 1937b. "Snappy Boxing Card Lined up for E.T. Fans." 6 August, 10.
– 1937c. "Eddie Carroll is Ready for Keen Contest." 11 August, 12.
– 1941a. "In the Sporting Vein by Allan Bryce." 29 May, 12.
– 1941b. "Rulings of Montreal Sports Body to Be Sanctioned Here." 29 May, 12.
– 1945. "Athletic Commission Disclaims Any Responsibility for Boxing Fiasco." 26 May, 10.
– 1955a. "Launch Investigation into Defunct Athletic Commission." 11 June, 3.
– 1955b. "Len O'Donnell's Sport Shots and Pot Shots." 11 June, 10.
– 1956. "Ald. Nicol President of Athletic Group." 27 April, 3.
– 1957a. "SAC Suspends Three Boxers." 27 July, 8.
– 1957b. "Marcel Piau to Enter Arena Ring as Underdog to Guder Thursday." 17 September, 12.
– 1958. "Sherbrooke Boxing Commission Claims Tommy Jackson Was Signed to Fight Before NBA Recommendation Came." 13 September, 14.
– 1960. "Canadian Boxing Scene Presents Bleak Prospects." 23 March, 10.
– 1963a. "Joe Louis Arrives in Sherbrooke." 1 May, 12.
– 1963b. "Len O'Donnell's Sport Shots and Pot Shots." 4 May, 10.
– 1963c. "Sugar Ray Registers KO in Third over Rolbnet." 6 May, 8.
– 1966a. "Would Welcome Clay and Terrell. Sherbrooke Joins Line Seeking Title Belt." 8 March, 1.
– 1966b. "Clay-Terrell Bout Gets Blessing from Ontario Minister for Staging." 9 March, 10.
– 1970. "Quebec to Regulate Boxing, Wrestling by '71." 13 August, 7.
Sherbrooke Record. 1972. "Sherbrooke Mourns Ivan Dugre." 29 March, 2.
Soleil. 1969. "Des lacunes déplorées dans la boxe." 21 January, 26.

Soosar, John. 1972. "Fight Game in Limbo." *Sherbrooke Record*, 20 December, 12.
Spafford, Warren. 1957. "Townships Topics." *Sherbrooke Daily Record*, 3 November, 3.
Sussman, Jeffrey. 2019. *Boxing and the Mob: The Notorious History of the Sweet Science*. Lanham, MD: Rowman & Littlefield.
Tribune. 1922. "Sherbrooke établira-t-elle une commission athlétique?" 20 June, 1.
– 1955a. "Le conseil de ville ressuscite l'ancienne commission athlétique." 16 June, 3.
– 1955b. "7 Combats de boxe, demain soir à Windsor – Piau opposé à Croxon." 23 June, 13.
– 1956. "Une commission athletique est créée dans notre ville." 17 July, 3.
– 1957. "La commission athletique locale veut promouvoir le sport de la boxe." 13 April, 10.
– 1958. "Jackson bat Vick – Burke Emery Vole la Vedette." 16 September, 14–15.
– 1959a. "La Commission athlétique de Sherbrooke ne croit pas s'être fait rouler par Al Bachman." 26 May, 13.
– 1959b. "Floyd Patterson, à Sherbrooke, Dimanche." 11 December, 8.
– 1959c. "Tournée Patterson à Sherbrooke." 14 December, 12.
– 1962a. "Le président de la Fédération de boxe ..." 13 April, 14.
– 1962b. "A lire sans rire!" 5 September, 16.
– 1962c. "Randonnée Sportive." 20 September, 13.
– 1962d. "Cléroux dans les petites villes." 11 October, 14.
– 1963a. "L'arrivée de Robinson retardée d'un jour." 2 May, 13.
– 1963b. "Excellent golfeur." 4 May, 12.
– 1966a. "Clay et Terrell mis à la porte du Forum." 4 March, 12.
– 1966b. "Verdun s'oppose au match Clay–Terrell." 5 March 1966, 14.
– 1966c. "Le combat a Sherbooke. Une réponse définitive doit être donnée aujourd'hui même." 8 March, 11.
– 1966d. "En protestation entre le combat Clay–Terrell, Conn Smythe démissionne comme directeur du Maple Leaf Gardens." 10 March, 13.
– 1972. "Le Québec pleure Ivan Dugré." 27 March, 9
– 1973a. "D'un banc à l'autre ..." 30 January, 14.
– 1973b. "La Commission athlétique refait surface à Porto Rico." 22 August, 3.
Vancouver Sun. 1966. "Conn Smythe Quits Gardens. 'Clay–Terrell' Fight Garbage." 9 March, 1.
Wamsley, Kevin B., and David Whitson. 1998. "Celebrating Masculinities: The Boxing Death of Luther McCarty." *Journal of Sport History* 25 (3): 419–31.
Young, Harvey. 2010. *Embodying Black Experience: Stillness, Critical Memory, and the Black Body*. Ann Arbor: University of Michigan Press.

13

Recent Transformations and Dynamics in the Eastern Townships' Religious Landscape: A Perspective from Sherbrooke

Claude Gélinas, Lorraine Derocher, and Camille Sasseville

SINCE THE 1960s, the Quebec religious landscape has undergone significant transformations. Christians who attend mainstream churches are appreciably fewer (Meunier and Wilkins-Laflamme 2011, 689–91, 696–7), but their religious fervour may persist, being expressed within charismatic movements, within independent or non-confessional churches, or through adherence to other religious traditions. For instance, we see a growing number of new religious groups and movements, often of a syncretic or esoteric nature.[1] To this must be added followers of Islam, Hinduism, Buddhism, and other major religious or spiritual traditions. The result is a religious landscape that is not only diverse but in constant transformation. To better document this new reality and make up for the lack of empirical knowledge regarding new religious groups and movements in the province, a vast ethnographic study was carried out from 2006 to 2015 by a team of researchers led by anthropologist Deirdre Meintel from the University of Montreal (Meintel 2022). In the course of this project, a census of places of worship and religious groups[2] in the Eastern Townships was carried out (Derocher 2007; Gélinas and Derocher 2012), including the production of twenty-five small-scale and six in-depth studies of specific groups.

Carried out in 2007, this census identified more than a hundred places of worship or religious groups within the limits of the city of Sherbrooke.[3] A large majority were traditional Christian churches, although many were experiencing disaffection. A more limited but growing number of syncretic and esoteric groups were identified, as well as groups influenced by Asian religious or spiritual traditions. All these had the particularity of being predominantly made up of members of the majority,[4] thus illustrating a departure from traditional religious practice and beliefs among a fringe of this population. Likewise, from a quantitative perspective and contrary to a widespread impression at the time – fueled by the religious accommodation "crisis" and in subsequent years by proponents of a regime of strict secularism, culminating in the adoption of Bill 21 (An Act Respecting the Laicity of the State) in 2019 – religious diversity was not mainly a consequence of immigration but of influences exerted on the Christian population by other religious and spiritual currents rendered more accessible through literature, the media, the Internet, travel, and growing cultural diversity. At the same time, only a few religious groups, all made up of Muslims, had a majority of immigrant followers. Hence the findings that newcomers tended to join religious groups predominantly made up of members of the majority instead of forming new ethnoreligious groups or churches, and that several religious groups in the Eastern Townships played an important role in the socioeconomic integration of immigrants (Gélinas and Vatz-Laaroussi 2012).

Almost fifteen years after this first census, we undertook to redo a similar exercise to document in the long term the religious dynamics of the Eastern Townships and the city of Sherbrooke in particular. By updating the number of local places of worship and religious groups, our objective was to ascertain the extent to which the abandonment of mainstream Christian churches and the growth of new religious groups persisted since 2007, while measuring the influence of immigrants on the city's religious landscape. After updating the data collected in our first survey to identify places of worship and religious groups still in existence or now absent, a tracking process was carried out in April and May 2021 using numerous digital tools[5] and field visualization to locate places of worship and religious groups established since 2007. Here, we compare in the first place the results from our two surveys and bring out the main changes or trends noticed in the various religious affiliations.

Based on these observations, we illustrate how phenomena of global reach such as immigration, the openness to the world offered by digital means of communication, and the decline of mainstream Christian churches are transforming the religious identity of the Eastern Townships, and that of the city of Sherbrooke more

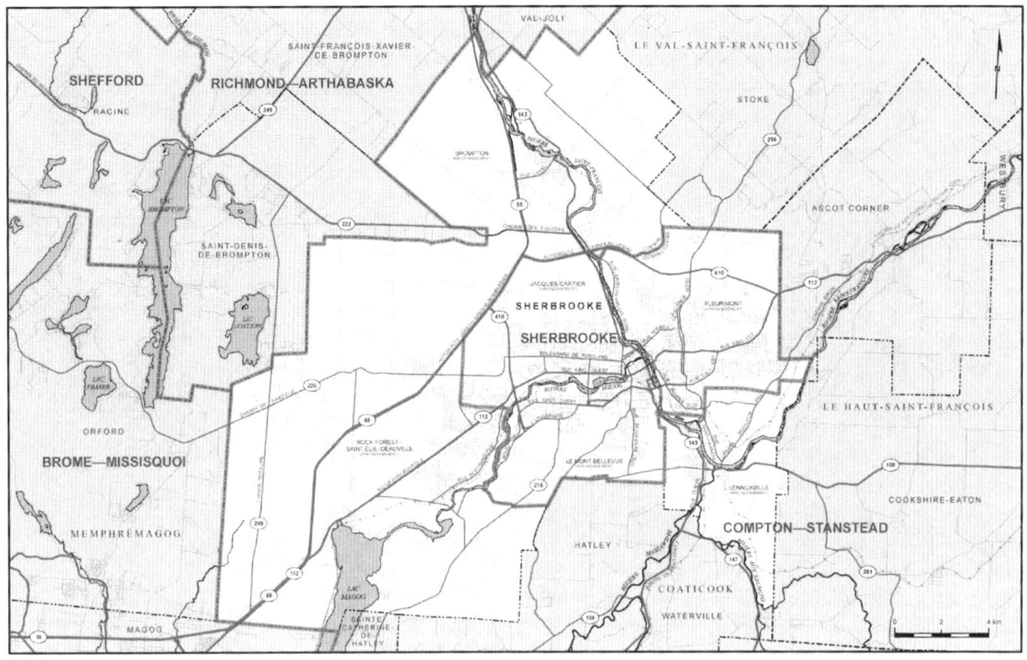

Figure 13.1 Territory covered by the 2021 survey of Sherbrooke religious groups

specifically. Although Catholic and Protestant presence remains predominant although experiencing some changes, a growing diversity of religious and spiritual affiliations is taking hold. At the same time, most religious groups in Sherbrooke, old and new, contribute to the wider phenomena of diversification and pluralism within contemporary Western societies, in part because they welcome and facilitate the social and cultural integration of their immigrant followers and because they constitute spaces which allow the latter to preserve part of their cultural and religious identity.

RESULTS *of the* 2021 SURVEY

In 2021, the population of Sherbrooke still identified itself mostly as Christian, although the traditional churches had seen their representation decrease since the 2001 federal census: the number of Catholics has fallen from 81.1 per cent to 53.9 per cent of the population, and Protestants affiliated to mainstream churches from 2.9 per cent to 1.2 per cent (table 13.1). Other Christian churches such as Pentecostal and Adventist, as well as Christian-inspired religious movements such

Table 13.1
Religious identities among the Sherbrooke population since 2001

	2001 (%)	2011 (%)	2021 (%)
Catholic	81.1	78.4	53.9
Liberal Protestant	2.9	1.9	1.2
(affiliated with the Anglican, Baptist, United Church, Presbyterian or Lutheran Churches)			
Pentecostal	0.2	0.2	0.3
Other Protestant	1.4	3.0	0.5
Orthodox Christian	0.5	0.6	0.6
Jewish	0.0	0.1	0.0
Muslim	0.8	1.7	3.7
Hindu	0.0	0.2	0.1
Sikh	0.0	0.0	0.0
Buddhist	0.1	0.2	0.2
Indigenous spirituality	0.0	0.0	0.0
Other religions	0.7	0.1	0.4
No religious affiliation	5.9	13.8	33.2

Sources: 2001: federal census; 2011: federal census and the National Household Survey, 2011 (Statistics Canada 2015), compiled by Sarah Wilkins-Laflamme; 2021: federal census.

Table 13.2
Number of places of worship and religious groups in Sherbrooke by religious categories, 2007, 2021

Religious categories	2007	2021	Difference
Catholic	47	34	- 13
Protestant	35	43	+ 8
Christian Orthodox	1	2	+ 1
Christian influence	6	6	–
Jewish	1	2	+ 1
Muslim	3	5	+ 2
Asian religions/spiritualities	10	17	+ 7
Syncretism and Esotericism	6	7	+ 1
Total	109	116	+7

as Jehovah's Witnesses and the Church of Jesus Christ of Latter-day Saints, have seen their overall representation cut in half. In contrast, Muslims now account for 3.7 per cent of the population, up from 0.8 per cent twenty years ago. Other religious traditions have remained relatively stable, while the number of "nones" has risen from 5.9 per cent in 2001 to an impressive 33.2 per cent in 2021, a category which is trending among the younger population across Quebec (Wilkins-Laflamme 2020, 278–9). Data from our own 2021 survey appear to reflect many of these larger trends (table 13.2), but they also allow us to identify certain changes specific to different religious affiliations.

Christian groups

At the time of our field research in 2007, eighty-nine (81.6 per cent) of the 109 religious groups in Sherbrooke were of Christian allegiance. Of this number, forty-seven were Catholic and thirty-five were Protestant. Of course, such predominance relates to the ethnoreligious history of the Eastern Townships, first populated mainly by Protestants from New England, until Catholics became the majority by the second half of the nineteenth century (Kesteman 1998, 264–5). However, this numerical importance of Christian groups masks a phenomenon of disaffection toward mainstream churches, particularly on the Catholic side where the number of places of worship has decreased from forty-three (twenty-seven churches, sixteen missionary residences) in 2007 to thirty (nineteen churches, eleven missionary residences) in 2021 according to our survey. This phenomenon was illustrated by the closure of eight church buildings (29.6 per cent of the Catholic church buildings listed in 2007) which were converted either into social housing, a cultural centre, an educational institution, or a business, while one was purchased by a group of Baptist Protestants. Such trends have prevailed across the Eastern Townships where thirty church buildings (predominantly Catholic) have been demolished or converted for other purposes between 2004 and 2013, the third highest rate in Quebec (Shaffer 2013); in 2020 alone, three of those on the immediate outskirts of the city of Sherbrooke were closed (Quirion 2021). These closures are mainly explained by insufficient financial resources to ensure the use and maintenance of the buildings but also by a decline in church attendance due to the aging of the population or a lack of interest in practice. In fact, since 2007 no new Catholic church has been inaugurated in Sherbrooke, where parish mergers have rather been observed. At the same time, several large residences housing missionary congregations were sold, while their occupants, ever fewer and often advanced in age, relocated to other places. For example, three congregations of nuns have jointly settled in a new residence better suited to their needs (Rondeau 2018). The old buildings have been transformed into health centres and real estate projects or bought by other religious groups, while the adjacent burials have been moved in some cases (Larochelle 2015).

Any parallel between such desertion of the Catholic institution and the state of beliefs would nevertheless be risky. In Sherbrooke, Catholicism continues to be lived and practised in different ways and in new spaces, whether through charismatic movements, new post-conciliar communities, Christian cafes, or various forms of social implication. This phenomenon is also apparent among young people, as evidenced for example by the popularity of the Famille Marie-Jeunesse community in the 2010s, which had about a hundred members dedicated, among other things, to missionary work, more specifically with young people in need. Smaller post-conciliar communities gathering in residential buildings for ritual and healing activities have also been counted in Sherbrooke, and it is likely that other less visible ones exist. As elsewhere in Quebec, this suggests that Catholicism seems to be existing more and more on the fringes of the traditional institution.

As for Protestants, the number of religious groups recorded in 2021 was forty-three, compared to thirty-five in 2007. However, this overall increase hides a decline among mainstream congregations – a phenomenon encountered throughout Quebec at least since the 1970s – due in large part to the demographic decline of the English-speaking population in the Sherbrooke area, the merger of churches, the aging of the population, and few gains among newcomers (Wilkins-Laflamme 2011, 58–9). This trend persisted after 2007 with the closure of St Peters Anglican Church – now occupied by a Catholic group – and of the Biblical Baptist Church of Rock Forest, which became too large a building for its community (Custeau 2021). As for the Anglican Church of the Advent, it is now shared with a Lutheran congregation. Conversely, the number of evangelical groups has increased considerably; of the fifteen Protestant groups founded since 2007, eleven are part of the evangelical movement. Mostly French speaking, these communities appear to be especially attractive to young people who meet there in large numbers.[6]

As for other Christian-inspired groups, Jehovah's Witnesses and the Church of Jesus Christ of Latter-day Saints remain present in the city of Sherbrooke as in 2007. Finally, the Saint Simeon Syriac Church now joins the Church of St-Ephrem as an Orthodox place of worship.[7]

Other religious and spiritual groups and services

The last decades have seen the emergence in Quebec of new forms of religiosity articulated around belief systems integrating elements from various religious or spiritual traditions, whether Christian, Theosophical, Celtic, Shamanic, Buddhist, or others, to which can be added scientific or pseudoscientific knowledge. Rarely having more than a few dozen members and being only or overwhelmingly made up of members of the majority, such groups usually reveal a flexible mode of organization, with little hierarchy and a rather informal leadership. In addition to relying on cosmologies, sacred texts or rituals that may include prayers, themes like the ideal of a universal society and conscience, holism, balance, concern for individual health and well-being are often promoted, just like practices such as vegetarianism and abstinence from tobacco, alcohol, and drugs. In general, followers are free to adhere to other belief systems, thus it is not uncommon for some to be practising Christians as well. The Baha'i community of Sherbrooke, which has some thirty members, is particularly representative in this regard. While it recognizes its founder as a messenger of God and holds prayer meetings in private residences or online, its goals include the improvement of health, the unity of humanity, and economic and racial justice.[8] Four of the six religious groups of this category identified in Sherbrooke in 2007 were still active in 2021, while three more were added, including a shamanism therapy centre and an esoteric shop offering various treatments and training.

Also in 2007, eleven religious groups or therapeutic services[9] inspired by Asian religions or spiritualities were located within the city limits of Sherbrooke, compared to seventeen in 2021. Mainly frequented by members of the majority and showing a flexible mode of operation, a lack of hierarchical relations, and a respectful attitude about individual spiritual paths, these groups are focused on supporting personal development. Doctrine is more about spirituality than religion, with an emphasis on promoting moral values such as truth, justice, peace, love, and non-violence from a universal perspective, and searching for spiritual well-being and physical health, even healing, hence an interest in alternative medicine and vegetarianism (Mossière and Meintel 2022). While most of the groups and services identified in 2007 were still present fifteen years later, a second Buddhist centre was added during that period, along with a multiplication of master teachers of Reiki, a holistic and energetic technique originating in Japan and enjoying increasing popularity.

Finally, this overall religious landscape is supplemented by five places of worship (three mosques, a community centre, and a prayer room) frequented by

Muslims, two more than in 2007, while after several decades without an institutional presence in Sherbrooke – the Agudath Achim synagogue was closed in 1983 – members of the Jewish community have inaugurated in 2010 a new community centre (Chabad Jewish Centre) and the Jewish students at Bishop's University have founded a religious club.

In sum, the data collected during our recent survey tend to confirm the challenges encountered by mainstream Christian churches in meeting the needs of their followers, whether in terms of practice, values, or concerns (Bibby and Archambault 2008, 169–72; Gélinas and Derocher 2012, 62). Many young people including members of the majority are still attracted to religion but prefer to join or found new groups that better meet their expectations, hence the popularity of certain new Christian communities and Evangelical Churches. Other individuals of Christian background will rather join syncretic or esoteric religious groups or turn to groups or services based on Asian religious or spiritual traditions. Moreover, these different affiliations are not mutually exclusive. All this corresponds to a current phenomenon well documented in the Western world and characterized by the individualization of religion, the prioritization of freely lived experience, the search for authentic social relationships in connection with a humanist and universal conscience, and the importance given to the practical dimension of the faith rather than the doctrine *per se*.

However, our recent survey undoubtedly provides only a partial reflection of the state of religion in Sherbrooke. As in 2007, the survey was limited to identifiable places of worship and religious groups in the public space. There are arguably several more anonymous places where religious and spiritual activities take place discreetly, whether they are rented spaces, community halls, or private residences. For instance, the Fraternité St-Pie X held gatherings in a garage before purchasing its current church building (Brochu 2017). In addition, several religious groups may share the same place of worship, while others may hold their meetings and activities outside, such as in parks or in the woods. Also, there are now informal places of convergence for followers of specific religious or spiritual currents, notably on social networks. These groups meet regularly or not, over a shorter or longer period, and usually operate without formality and established leadership; basically, they regularly bring together people interested in talking to each other or holding ceremonies online or face-to-face. In the Eastern Townships, such networks have been reported in connection with the attraction to Indigenous spiritualities (Petropavlovsky 2018, 37–8, 57–8). Finally, some people avoid publicly displaying their religious or spiritual beliefs and practices because of a taboo

Table 13.3
Presence of Sherbrooke religious groups on digital platforms and social networks, 2007 and 2021

	2007	2021
No. of groups	109	116
Email	58 (53.2 %)	76 (65.5 %)
Website	43 (39.4 %)	90 (77.5 %)
Facebook page		62 (53.4 %)
YouTube channel		21 (18.1 %)

surrounding religion in Quebec society or because of the negative representation of certain forms of religiosity (Meintel 2022).

Finally, a significant change noticed since 2007 is the widespread use of digital platforms and social media by religious groups and services (table 13.3). About fifteen years ago, slightly more than half of the active religious groups provided an email address for correspondence, and nearly 40 per cent had a website; in several cases, these were organizational sites not specific to the Sherbrooke branch. Now a large majority of religious groups and services have an email address, and even more have a website offering mostly locally anchored information. Meanwhile, more than half the groups and services now have a Facebook page, and more than 20 per cent of them, often on the evangelical side, also operate a YouTube channel. These platforms are mobilized to circulate information about the group, its doctrine, and its activities to which can be added the publication of training sessions, ceremonies, sermons, songs, music, testimonials, or opinions on current affairs. Websites are also becoming the primary vehicle through which donations are solicited or as a means to sell products and services. Digital platforms have also been widely used to maintain contact and regularly inform members about the health situation and sanitary policies during the COVID-19 pandemic. Also, ceremonies were broadcast live or recorded and uploaded on Facebook or YouTube, while Zoom and Teams were used to hold meetings, to allow pastoral teams to continue their work, and to offer help and support services online.

Such extended use of digital platforms seems to reflect a dynamic where religious groups now strive to reach out to the people, instead of the other way around, with notable success in some cases. For instance, religious groups whose Facebook page indicates the number of subscribers had an average of 726;[10] while most of them reached a few hundred subscribers, others attracted large numbers of followers: the a'Rahman mosque and the Kadampa Buddhist centre had 2,388 and 2,416 subscribers respectively, the Axe-21 Church had 3,723, and Famille Marie-Jeunesse had 3,888. The latter two tend to confirm the importance of digital platforms as sources of information and religious expression for young people (Gauthier and Perreault 2013, 7). However, while Facebook and YouTube may constitute effective platforms to reach and keep in touch with their followers far beyond local and national boundaries, most Facebook pages and YouTube channels operated by religious groups in Sherbrooke are strictly community oriented and offer religious and informative content first and foremost for local members. Nevertheless, groups that are part of larger religious organizations or networks may also share online material produced elsewhere in the world, allowing followers to access popular preachers and be informed of activities carried out by their co-religionists in other countries. But in general, this generic content does not reflect a concern to maintain close ties other than the idea of belonging to the same greater religious family.

EXTERNAL INFLUENCES *over the* SHERBROOKE RELIGIOUS LANDSCAPE

Between 2010 and 2019, the equivalent of about 700 immigrants a year settled in Sherbrooke, coming from different ethnocultural backgrounds,[11] an important number of which were refugees, given that than 40 per cent of newcomers in the Eastern Townships belong to this category as a result of government choices regarding the regionalization of immigration (Gouvernement du Québec 2022, 22). After opening its borders to refugees from Yugoslavia, Afghanistan, Bhutan, Iraq, Colombia, and humanitarian camps in Central Africa (Burundi, Rwanda), the Democratic Republic of the Congo, and the Central African Republic starting in the mid-1990s, in recent years the city has received a substantial number of Syrian refugees fleeing civil war. However, the overall diversity among immigrants' countries of origin is much wider; for the year 2019–20 alone, the Service d'aide aux Néo-Canadiens, based in Sherbrooke, came to support newcomers from sixty-eight different countries (SANC 2020, 11). The main countries of origin, according to the 2021 federal census, are shown in table 13.4.

In addition to permanent residents and refugees, a growing number of international students, nearly 2,600 per year on average from 2014 to 2019 (Gouvernement du Québec 2020, 45), attend all universities and colleges in Sherbrooke.

Among these people, many arrived with beliefs and religious or spiritual practices that they wished to express and preserve, thus exerting influence on the city's

Table 13.4
Main places of birth for the immigrant population living in Sherbrooke, 2021

Countries	No. of immigrants
France	1,825
Colombia	1,135
Afghanistan	1,085
Morocco	790
Bosnia-Herzegovina	615
Congo (Democratic Republic of)	535
United States	500
Algeria	495
Syria	280
Brazil	275

Source: Statistics Canada, Census Profile, 2021 Census of Population, Sherbrooke, Quebec, Selected places of birth for the immigrant population, https://www12.statcan.gc.ca/census-recensement/2021/dp-pd/prof/details/page.cfm?Lang=E&SearchText=Sherbrooke&DGUIDlist=2021A00032443&GENDERlist=1&STATISTIClist=1&HEADERlist=0.

religious landscape and dynamism. From the outset, religious groups composed mostly of migrants remain rare in Sherbrooke, especially those associated with a single ethnic community. Besides the relatively small number of newcomers who settle in the city, the fact that several of them, especially refugees, will eventually leave for other cities either to study, to find employment, or to join relatives partly explains this reality. Moreover, some immigrants belong to ethnoreligious groups or networks based outside the city and thus travel long distances to participate in religious and cultural activities; several members of the Jewish and Orthodox Christian communities go to Montreal to participate in worship, as did the Bhutanese refugees who did not have a temple in Sherbrooke. But most of all, many newcomers who arrive in Sherbrooke are looking for a church or religious community like the one they attended in their country of origin. However, given the small sizes of minority ethnocultural groups in Sherbrooke, immigrants often only have available to them membership in religious congregations in which they make up cultural minorities.

In 2007, only three places of worship frequented mostly by immigrants were identified, all associated with Islam. For instance, the mosque managed by the Association culturelle islamique de l'Estrie gathered hundreds of followers, among them several first-generation newcomers of Arabic-speaking origin, especially from northern Africa and Egypt, and other Muslims coming from various countries: Afghanistan, Saudi Arabia, Bangladesh, Benin, India, Indonesia, Iraq, Lebanon, Mali, Mauritania, Nigeria, Pakistan, Senegal, Somalia, Syria, Yugoslavia. Since then, two other Muslim places of worship have been added, a mosque (the third in the region) and a prayer room for students at Bishop's University. It should also be noted that for ideological or more practical reasons, some practising Muslims do not frequent these places of worship and choose to organize prayer and preaching sessions in private homes or other anonymous locations.

Meanwhile, the Serbian Orthodox Church now has a mission parish in Sherbrooke and its followers, most of whom are Serbs who arrived in Quebec as refugees, attend the new Saint Simeon church. As for the St Ephrem Syriac Orthodox Church, it has experienced a renaissance after years of neglect following the recent arrival of Syrian refugees (Elkouri 2015). Finally, half a dozen religious groups, mainly those of the Evangelical Churches, also gather mostly immigrants, a trend observed elsewhere in Quebec (Meintel 2020, 34). Some assemble Spanish-speaking newcomers and keep websites and Facebook pages that are unilingually Spanish or with translation into French or English. Thus, in a still modest but increasing way, newcomers contribute effectively to the emergence of new places of worship and new communities of practice in Sherbrooke.

Otherwise, immigrants who join religious groups predominantly made up of members of the majority also contribute to their vitality and sustainability.[12] This is particularly the case among Catholic churches where newcomers from Latin America are numerous and display a high rate of attendance. This forces the former to be creative in liturgies and pastoral activities to attract such followers and respond to their religious and cultural needs. Some offer ceremonies in Spanish as well as bilingual content on their YouTube channels,[13] while administrative committees formed by Spanish-speaking followers have been created to organize and supervise religious and social activities on an ethnocultural basis. For example, in 2018 the church Notre-Dame de la Présentation became the first bilingual parish – French and Spanish – of the Diocese of Sherbrooke (Nadeau 2015). The Adventist Church also has a Hispanic group that regularly holds its own spiritual and social activities. At the Syriac Orthodox Church of St Ephrem, it is mainly the arrival of numerous refugees in recent years that made it possible to preserve the place of worship (Elkouri 2015). Also, to be noted, twenty of the 116 religious groups identified in 2021 (17.2 per cent), including some Catholic churches, were under the leadership of a person born in a country other than Canada.

In sum, not only does immigration prove to be a source of change in the religious landscape of Sherbrooke but it contributes to making religious groups present in the city's intercultural spaces – some even publicly display their openness towards people of all nationalities[14] – where followers from various national and ethnic backgrounds come together. In some cases, this requires rethinking the offer of religious services, both structurally and in terms of dogma. However, such necessary adaptation to diversity extends far beyond the sole functioning of religious organizations; one may think of the field of funeral practices with the inauguration of a Muslim cemetery in Sherbrooke in 2021 and the incentive among funeral parlors to adapt to the specific needs of believers from various religious and spiritual traditions (Radio Canada 2017). Finally, such diversity characterizing religious groups in Sherbrooke is a reminder of another important role these latter continue to play regarding the welcoming and integration of newcomers.

RELIGIOUS GROUPS *as* VECTORS *of* DIVERSIFICATION *and* PLURALISM

Although immigration has several advantages for Quebec society, it also comes with challenges in terms of welcoming, supporting, and retaining newcomers, especially refugees. Measures and resources are displayed by the state, but an important part of the effort in assisting immigrants rests upon community organizations, ethnocultural associations, and religious groups. Sherbrooke is no exception in this regard, since many religious groups in the city play a significant role in offering moral and material support to newcomers, just as they did fifteen years ago (Gélinas and Vatz-Laaroussi 2012). In this way, they are contributing not only to the Quebec interculturalist project, which aims for the social inclusion and participation of newcomers, but more widely to the ongoing movement of cultural diversification throughout Western societies.

Upon arrival in Sherbrooke, some immigrants can count on the support of an ethnocultural or ethnoreligious network, including members of their own family already established in the city (Vatz-Laaroussi 2011). Muslim groups, for instance, participate in such networks; in addition to offering different forms of support (psychological, financial, academic, linguistic), they allow newcomers to integrate a primary social network and a reassuring community framework that also facilitates the preservation of their cultural and religious identity. By way of sponsorship – which requires offering financial guarantees and assisting refugees in learning French and finding work – the Syriac Orthodox Church has welcomed and helped a few hundred families over the past ten years. To this end, it keeps a list of available housing near the place of worship as well as a reserve of clothing, furniture, and other necessities to help families settle (Nadeau 2015; Roberge

2021). The new Serbian Orthodox Church, built from donations from Serbs who arrived in Sherbrooke since 1995, has a community hall used for festivities intended for the community, although it is sometimes open to the entire local population. Jehovah's Witnesses have been particularly active in welcoming and helping newcomers since Latino immigrants joined their ranks; their involvement in this area even influences the choice of Sherbrooke as a destination by newcomers (Radio Canada 2012). The Refugio de Paz Mennonite Church is also heavily involved in welcoming and supporting immigrants – again mainly those coming from Latin America – holding, among other things, integration activities for its members such as French lessons and intercultural meetings with other local organizations.

Mainstream Christian churches and congregations also play an active role in assisting newcomers. For instance, the parish of Notre-Dame-du-Perpétuel-Secours has set up a committee responsible for seeing to their welcoming of immigrants. The Précieux-Sang parish collaborates with the Soutien aux familles réfugiées et immigrantes de l'Estrie (SAFRIE) in helping with the children's homework, while the Sœurs servantes du Saint-Cœur de Marie are involved with the Service d'aide aux Néo-canadiens (SANC), just like the Sœurs Servites de Marie are invested in francization and literacy.

Religious groups also facilitate social integration since they usually constitute interethnic, intercultural, and sometimes even interfaith meeting. As such, they are conducive to raising awareness about the richness of diversity, while offering an environment where status relations do not operate as they might on the outside; despite their often-precarious initial socioeconomic situation, newcomers find themselves associating with other followers through a more egalitarian relationship, without their ethnic or "racial" difference necessarily coming into play. This proves helpful, subsequently, to a wider integration within Quebec society, especially since most religious groups also promote values based on respect for differences and openness to others, including in terms of religious and spiritual beliefs. Moreover, far from being closed in on themselves, most religious groups seek to facilitate and promote their members' interactions with society, whether by offering French or English language courses to newcomers, by getting involved at the community level (organizing neighbourhood parties, participating in volunteer organizations) or encouraging their followers to vote or act responsibly towards the environment (Gélinas, Meintel and Moisa 2022). Therefore, far from the popular image still largely conveyed of religion as an obstacle to integration, the action of religious groups is generally more conducive to bringing together citizens of different origins and cultures, while helping to make Quebec a more inclusive society.

CONCLUSION

The current state of religiosity in Sherbrooke seems to reflect overall trends documented in the wider Quebec population and elsewhere in the Western world. While Catholic and Protestant mainstream churches remain strongly represented, attendance in many of them is decreasing. At the same time, a growing number of groups and services of a religious or spiritual nature, and of various tendencies (charismatic, syncretic, esoteric, of Asian influence, or others), attracts a substantial portion of the mainstream churches' followers. Some of the latter completely abandon their church's beliefs and practices in favour of new modes of religiosity, while others remain faithful to them but access a wider range of available spiritual resources, according to their needs. All this without necessarily giving up their primary religious identity, which no doubt explains why identification to Catholicism remains high despite a concomitant abandonment of the practice.

Likewise, the significant and growing religious diversity prevailing in Sherbrooke and the Eastern Townships is not just the result of immigration and must not be reduced to the issue of ethnicity. Certainly, some newcomers bring with them beliefs and religious practices different from mainstream Christian traditions but the majority are already Christians on arrival, and some will even establish Christian churches eventually. Consequently, as it did in 2007, the effective diversity in terms of religious and spiritual ideologies in Sherbrooke and the Eastern Townships continues to emanate mainly from members of the majority who create and participate in new spheres of beliefs and practices, more in line with their current values and concerns.

Nevertheless, as a global phenomenon immigration exerts influence on the city's religious profile. While religious groups mostly made up of immigrants – whether monocultural or multicultural – remain rare, their number is increasing, mainly among Evangelical churches. As such, newcomers, and especially those from Africa and Latin America, contribute to the emergence of new communities of practice in Sherbrooke and, thus, to the transformation of the city's religious identity. Others, especially among the Spanish speaking community, contribute through their religious fervour to safeguarding part of Catholic heritage, while forcing the institution to rethink the way to meet its followers' needs. Other religious groups, including new ones founded by members of the majority owe part of their vitality to the presence and participation of immigrants of various ethnic and cultural backgrounds. But whether being made up predominantly of followers from the majority, multicultural, or mainly ethnic, most religious groups play an important role in the socialization and integration of immigrants within the broader Quebec society, while allowing them to preserve, by the same token, part of their cultural identity. As such, they also work to firmly anchor Sherbrooke and the Eastern Townships region in a larger trend of cultural and religious diversification within Western societies.

Finally, this overview shows how inadequate is the argument often heard in past years of a cleavage in Quebec society between a majority distancing itself from religion, both in public and private life, and immigrants carrying with them religious diversity, if not seeking to impose their beliefs and practices, and looking to live in closed and exclusive communities. As was the case fifteen years ago, the reality encountered in Sherbrooke and the Eastern Townships appears to be very different.

Notes

1 The terms *syncretic* and *esoteric* respectively refer to groups which combine in their doctrine different religious or spiritual traditions or are based on beliefs which fall within what is commonly referred to as occult sciences or the paranormal.

2 By religious groups, we mean any gathering of people sharing the same system of beliefs and meeting at the same location to engage in common activities of a religious or spiritual nature. These gatherings can be held in institutional places of worship such as churches, temples, or mosques but also in various places such as community halls, private residences, or even digital platforms.

3 This territory includes the former towns (now merged) of Rock Forest, Deauville, Saint-Élie-d'Orford, Fleurimont, Bromptonville, Lennoxville, Ascot, and part of the village of Stoke (figure 13.1).

4 By majority, we mean the population of French and English Canadian descent whose ancestors may or may not have originated from the city. According to the 2021 federal census, 86.4 per cent of the Sherbrooke population indicated having French as a mother tongue compared to 3.9 per cent having English: Statistics Canada. *Census Profile, 2021 Census of Population, Sherbrooke, Quebec*, https://www12.statcan.gc.ca/census-recensement/2021/dp-pd/prof/details/page.cfm?Lang=E&SearchText=Sherbrooke&DGUIDlist=2021A00032443&GENDERlist=1&STATISTIClist=1&HEADERlist=0.

5 The main websites consulted for the purpose of locating places of worship and religious groups in Sherbrooke are as follows: Inventaire des lieux de culte du Québec, https://www.lieuxdeculte.qc.ca/; Registre des entreprises, ministère du Travail, de l'Emploi et de la Solidarité sociale, http://www.registreentreprises.gouv.qc.ca; Centre de ressources et d'observation de l'innovation religieuse, https://croir.ulaval.ca; Regroupements étudiants, Université de Sherbrooke, https://www.usherbrooke.ca/etudiants/vie-etudiante/associations-etudiantes/regroupements-etudiants/; Places of worship, Bishop's University, https://www.ubishops.ca/future-current-students/student-campus-life/student-services/health-wellness/spiritual-care/places-of-worship/; Pages jaunes, https://www.pagesjaunes.ca/.

6 Although no specific data was gathered regarding the social profile of members among religious groups in our 2021 survey, at first glance the available information seems to indicate that some Evangelical groups are mostly made up of women. Data available for

five Evangelical groups in 2007 show women where systematically in larger proportion than men (Derocher 2007, 47, 52, 60, 68, 78).

7 Citizens of Sherbrooke, and more specifically members of the community of Russian language and culture, can also attend the monastery of the Transfiguration affiliated with the Russian Orthodox Church Outside Russia and located in Mansonville, about sixty kilometres east of the city (Romanova 2017, 25, 27).

8 Communauté bahá'ie de Sherbrooke, https://www.bahaisherbrooke.org.

9 In 2007 and 2021, we chose to identify professionals in Sherbrooke offering therapeutic services inspired by Asian religions or spiritualities. Although not considered religious groups according to the definition given above, their presence allows us to quantify to a certain extent the apparent growing interest in these beliefs within the local population, here on an individual basis.

10 We have ignored Facebook pages managed by international organizations.

11 In 2021, 88 per cent of immigrants established in the Eastern Townships resided in Sherbrooke (Gouvernement du Québec 2022, 38).

12 Although apparently still marginal in Sherbrooke, the reverse phenomenon also prevails as members of the majority have converted to Islam and attend Muslim places of worship as a minority.

13 Paroisse NDP Sherbrooke. YouTube channel, https://www.youtube.com/channel/UCGJi6KjbRKWBBHk7VAEoUkg.

14 Mission Rehoboth International Source de Vie, Website, https://www.svrehoboth.org/la-mission/objectifs.

References

Bibby, Reginald, and Angus Reid. 2016. *Canada's Catholics: Vitality and Hope in a New Era*. Ottawa: Novalis.

Bibby, Reginald, and Isabelle Archambault. 2008. "La religion à la carte au Québec: Un problème d'offre, de demande, ou des deux?" *Globe, Revue internationale d'études québécoises* 11 (1): 169–72.

Brochu, Tommy. 2017. "L'église Sainte-Jeanne-d'Arc redeviendra un lieu de culte." *La Tribune*, 12 December. https://www.latribune.ca/2017/12/12/leglise-sainte-jeanne-darc-redeviendra-un-lieu-de-culte-3f7dd73212e4ff5e225bc57aa3d8318e/. Accessed 10 February 2024.

Centre de ressources et d'observation de l'innovation religieuse. https://croir.ulaval.ca. Accessed 3 January 2022.

Communauté bahá'ie de Sherbrooke. n.d. https://www.bahaisherbrooke.org/. Accessed 15 January 2022.

Custeau, Jonathan. 2021. "Une église baptiste sera démolie dans Rock Forest." *La Tribune*, 22 January. https://www.latribune.ca/2021/01/22/une-eglise-baptiste-sera-demolie-dans-rock-forest-78d4dae5b877d1746b4c4ecae05009ec/. Accessed 10 February 2024.

Derocher, Lorraine. 2007. *Panorama des groupes religieux Estrie/Sherbrooke*. Sherbrooke: SoDRUS (unpublished report).

Elkouri, Rima. 2015. "Un Noël syrien à Sherbrooke." *La Presse*, 27 December. https://www.lapresse.ca/debats/chroniques/rima-elkouri/201512/24/01-4934372-un-noel-syrien-a-sherbrooke.php. Accessed 10 February 2024.

Gauthier, François, and Jean-Philippe Perreault. 2013. "Les héritiers du *baby-boom*. Jeunes et religion au Québec." *Social Compass* 60 (4): 527–43.

Gélinas, Claude, and Lorraine Derocher. 2012. "Profil de la diversité religieuse en Estrie." *Journal of Eastern Township Studies* 39: 55–72.

Gélinas, Claude, and Michèle Vatz-Laaroussi. 2012. "Les lieux de culte comme espaces d'intégration pour les nouveaux arrivants: l'exemple de l'Estrie." *Diversité urbaine* 12 (2): 35–51.

Gélinas, Claude, Deirdre Meintel, and Daniela Moisa. 2022. "La contribution des groupes religieux au vivre-ensemble." In *La pluralité religieuse au Québec*, edited by Deirdre Meintel, 79–99. Montreal: Presses de l'Université de Montréal.

Gouvernement du Québec. 2020. *2014–2019. L'immigration temporaire au Québec*. Quebec: ministère de l'Immigration, de la Francisation et de l'Intégration.

– 2022. *2021. Présence et portraits régionaux des personnes immigrantes admises au Québec de 2010 à 2019*. Quebec: ministère de l'Immigration, de la Francisation et de l'Intégration.

Inventaire des lieux de culte du Québec. https://www.lieuxdeculte.qc.ca/. Accessed 20 June 2021.

Kesteman, Jean-Pierre. 1998. *Histoire des Cantons de l'Est*. Sainte-Foy: Les éditions de l'IQRC/Les presses de l'Université Laval.

Larochelle, Luc. 2015. "Un pas vers la sortie." *La Tribune*, 18 October. https://www.latribune.ca/2015/10/18/un-pas-vers-la-sortie-910c80be425de0ec0d5e51c59c628eb6/. Accessed 10 February 2024.

Meintel, Deirdre. 2020. "Le religieux au Québec aujourd'hui: une étude de terrain." In *Étudier la religion au Québec: regards d'ici et d'ailleurs*, edited by David Koussens, Jean-François Laniel, and Jean-Philippe Perreault, 337–51. Quebec: Presses de l' Université Laval.

– ed. 2022. *La pluralité religieuse au Québec*. Montreal: Presses de l'Université de Montréal.

Meunier, É.-Martin, and Sarah Wilkins-Laflamme. 2011. "Sécularisation, catholicisme et transformation du régime de religiosité au Québec: Étude comparative avec le catholicisme au Canada (1968-2007)." *Recherches sociographiques* 52 (3): 683–729.

Mission Rehoboth International Source de Vie. https://www.svrehoboth.org/la-mission/objectifs. Accessed 8 June 2021.

Mossière, Géraldine, and Deirdre Meintel. 2022. "La mobilité et la diversité religieuse." In *La pluralité religieuse au Québec*, edited by Deirdre Meintel, 43–58. Montreal: Presses de l'Université de Montréal.

Nadeau, Jacynthe. 2015. "L'Église syriaque accueille une nouvelle famille syrienne." *La Tribune*, 5 December.

Pages jaunes. https://www.pagesjaunes.ca/. Accessed 15 June 2021.

Paroisse NDP Sherbrooke (YouTube channel). https://bit.ly/3fw7QiV. Accessed 14 January 2022.

Petropavlovsky, Marie-Noëlle. 2018. "Allumer le Huitième Feu? Analyse de la rencontre entre Autochtones et non Autochtones lors de cérémonies de guérison autochtones au Québec." PhD diss., Université de Montréal.

Places of worship, Bishop's University. https://www.ubishops.ca/future-current-students/student-campus-life/student-services/health-wellness/spiritual-care/places-of-worship/. Accessed 16 June 2021.

Quirion, René-Charles. 2021. "Quatre églises fermées en un an." *La Tribune*, 17 April. https://www.latribune.ca/2021/04/17/quatre-eglises-fermees-en-un-an-fe45e2c08ba6c586a5b15e753d374d53/. Accessed 10 February 2024.

Radio Canada. 2012. "Les Témoins de Jéhovah séduisent beaucoup d'immigrants catholiques." 15 July 2012. https://ici.radio-canada.ca/nouvelle/570112/sherbrooke-jehovah-immigrants. Accessed 18 June 2021.

– 2017. "Mieux accompagner les communautés culturelles dans leurs rituels funéraires." ICI *Radio-Canada Estrie*, 1 March 2017. http://ici.radio-canada.ca/nouvelle/1019561/mieux-accompagner-les-communautes-culturelles-dans-leurs-rituels-funeraires. Accessed 18 June 2021.

Registre des entreprises, ministère du Travail, de l'Emploi et de la Solidarité sociale. http://www.registreentreprises.gouv.qc.ca. Accessed 22 June 2021.

Regroupements étudiants, Université de Sherbrooke. https://www.usherbrooke.ca/etudiants/vie-etudiante/associations-etudiantes/regroupements-etudiants. Accessed 22 June 2021.

Roberge, Simon. 2021. "Sauver des centaines de familles." *La Tribune*, 17 September. https://www.latribune.ca/2021/09/18/sauver-des-centaines-de-familles-9d7c2d7b4d2b5b42e180efa19e6745ef/. Accessed 10 February 2024.

Romanova, Tatiana. 2017. "Le rôle de la culture dans l'intégration des immigrants russophones en Estrie." MA thesis, Université de Sherbrooke.

Rondeau, Jasmine. 2018. "Les sœurs Missionnaires quittent Lennoxville." *La Tribune*, 12 June. https://www.latribune.ca/2018/06/12/les-soeurs-missionnaires-quittent-lennoxville-dfa064fc9121a1783c34e75d495331e1/. Accessed 10 February 2024.

Service d'aide aux Néo-Canadiens (SANC). 2020. *Rapport annuel 2019–2020*. Sherbrooke.

Shaffer, Marie-Eve. 2013. "Une nouvelle vocation pour près de 300 églises du Québec." *Le Reflet du Lac* 8: 4

Statistics Canada. Census Profile, 2021 Census of Population, Sherbrooke, Quebec. Accessed 3 December 2023. https://www12.statcan.gc.ca/census-recensement/2021/dppd/prof/details/page.cfm?Lang=E&SearchText=Sherbrooke&DGUIDlist=2021A00032443&GENDERlist=1&STATISTIClist=1&HEADERlist=0.

Vatz-Laaroussi, Michèle. 2011. "Les immigrants à Sherbrooke: des familles en projet!" *La Tribune*, 3 December. https://www.latribune.ca/2011/12/03/les-immigrants-a-sherbrooke-des-familles-en-projet-8352f18e1f35a0be8b5d1cbca47ae9b0/. Accessed 10 February 2024.

Wilkins-Laflamme, Sarah. 2011. "Les églises unie et anglicane au Québec anglophone: enjeux contemporains." *Journal of Eastern Townships Studies* 36 (1): 55–68.

– 2015. "Une question de religion ou de culture? Convergences et divergences religieuses entre anglophones et francophones québécois depuis 1985." In *Catholicisme et cultures: regards croisés Québec-France*, edited by Solange Lefebvre, Céline Béraud, and É.-Martin Meunier, 115–41. Quebec: Presses de l'Université Laval.

– 2020. "De nouveaux enjeux pour la recherche sur le paysage religieux québécois." In *Étudier la religion au Québec: regards d'ici et d'ailleurs*, edited by David Koussens, Jean-François Laniel, and Jean-Philippe Perreault, 275–96. Quebec: Presses de l'Université Laval.

Part Four

The Eastern Townships as an Imagined Place and a Global Commodity

Three essays make up the final section of *Quebec's Eastern Townships and the World: A Region and Its Global Connections*. The chapters here consider how fiction writers, photographers, and artists have represented and used the Townships as a setting for narratives that connect the local with the global. "Quebec's New Regional Fiction and the Eastern Townships: Literary Landscapes of Deindustrialization" (chapter 14), by Ceri Morgan, surveys and analyzes contemporary novels and short stories "on and of the Townships." In it, she focuses on recent works by Liane Keightley, Denis Coupal, and Michèle Plomer, which are part of a growing body of literature removed from Montreal that addresses global issues such as deindustrialization. The collective focus of these writings, Morgan maintains, contradicts any effort to classify the Eastern Townships "as enclosed, static, and inward-looking." In chapter 15, "Postcards, Cultural Landscape Analysis, and the Eastern Townships in the Past 125 Years," Caroline Beaudoin traces the visual representation of the Eastern Townships to the broader world. Evaluating postcard imagery in the context of cultural landscape theory, Beaudoin maintains that postcards featuring the Townships' physical landscape, particularly in the early twentieth century, offered two diametrically opposed depictions to the international community: the first, a bucolic, idyllic, restorative environment; the second a resource to be exploited by industrial development with little regard for environmental sustainability. J. Debbie Mann's contribution, "Dimensions of Community in the Novels of Louise Penny" (chapter 16), the final contribution is this section, captures the meanings of place that emerge in the many novels of Louise Penny, whose work is set in and has become closely identified with the Eastern Townships. Mann examines how Penny's fictional Three Pines has been recreated and reflected in the literary imagination and how these renderings have been received and embraced by readers around the world.

14

Quebec's New Regional Fiction and the Eastern Townships: Literary Landscapes of Deindustrialization

Ceri Morgan

THE EASTERN TOWNSHIPS are increasingly present in Quebec fiction, often represented as "cottage country," "border territory," and "sites of crime," or murderscapes (Morgan 2017, 5). This chapter argues that we can read contemporary novels and short stories on and of the Townships as examples of what I term Quebec's "new regional fiction" – a growing body of literature set outside of Montreal. The apparent locatedness of this writing is complicated, however, by its aesthetics and/or themes, which serve to situate it within broader continental and transnational contexts. If "regions" (and places within regions) are to be understood as fluid nodes in networks of power and communication (see, e.g., Massey 2004), "regional fiction" is similarly open, potentially contested, and subject to change. This fiction will always be in dialogue, whether directly or indirectly, with works of literature and criticism from other regions and national or cultural centres. In what follows, I shall explore how select examples of Eastern Townships fiction engage with global issues notwithstanding their commitment to the local. Crucially, I argue that stories and novels by Liane Keightley, Denis Coupal, and Michèle Plomer comprise a deindustrialization literature of sorts: different from the literatures of industrial heartlands in the United States or the United Kingdom but, like them, offering reminders of alternative modes of working and living to those available in the present.

NEW REGIONAL FICTION

Since 2000, *hors-Montréal*, or the ROQ (rest of Quebec), has attracted renewed public, political, and creative interest. This is especially true of French-language fiction, which has seen an outpouring of novels and short stories set in regions like the Saguenay, the Gaspé, the North Shore, and Abitibi. Examples include Samuel Archibald's short story collection *Arvida* (2011), Virginie Blanchette-Doucet's *117 Nord* (2016), and Gabrielle Fiteau-Chiba's *Encabanée* (2018). This embracing of the "regions" marks a significant departure from trends in Quebec's French-language fiction of the previous forty to fifty years. As is well known, the Quiet Revolution helped to equate modernity and nationalist assertion principally with the urban, specifically Montreal. Not surprisingly, the city came to dominate the production of French-language fiction from the 1960s onwards (Nepveu and Marcotte 1988, 8). As the economic and cultural centre of the province and historic "home" to a concentration of anglo-Quebecers, Montreal is also a key setting within English-language fiction. This is true of the work of several authors identified with this literature's so-called heyday, such as Hugh MacLennan and Mavis Gallant, and those associated with its more recent "renaissance," namely Heather O'Neill, Neil Smith, Rawi Hage, Dimitri Nasrallah, and Anita Anand. It is also true of writers whose careers began in the intervening decades, like Mordecai Richler, Leonard Cohen, David Homel, and Gail Scott. Nevertheless, there are examples of English-language writing on and of the "regions," such as Nalini Warriar's *The Enemy Within* (2005), Jeffrey Moore's *The Extinction Club* (2010), and Louise Penny's murder mysteries.

There are doubtless various reasons for the literary turn to Quebec's "heartlands" (Morgan and Laforest 2011, 115–17). Once translated by a conference panel chair as "le Canada profond" – a phrase that suggests rurality – I use "heartlands" to suggest places that are bound up in, or prompt, particular emotions. In so doing, I play on the cultural connotations of "heart" suggested in slogans proclaiming fondness for a place or a thing. The reasons for the literary turn to the ROQ include attachments to place, nostalgia, and the emergence of what Daniel Chartier calls "hipster" writers (cited in Morgan 2017, 2). All the same, the growing body of regional fiction coincides with cultural and critical trends within and beyond Quebec. The twenty-first century has seen practitioners and theorists in North America, the UK, and elsewhere engage with non-metropolitan themes like second cities (Hodos 2011), suburbs (Delisle 2002; Hamel and Keil 2015), exurbs (Delvaux 2009; Farley and Symmons Roberts 2011; Keil and Addie 2016), and the rural (Woods 2004; Cloke et al. 2006; Fowler 2020; Sethi 2021). A key insight offered by this literature and scholarship is that spatial borders are, and always were, more porous than they seem(ed). As early as 1973, Raymond Williams argued that the framing of the rural and urban as separate and frequently opposing spheres in literature and other forms of cultural and social production is a conceit (Williams 1975 [1973], 1). Recent work in rural geographies draws attention to how communications and media technologies complicate spatial divides (Cloke 2006). Similarly, theorists of suburbs and exurbs flag the diversity within developments on the edges of cities (Fortin et Després 2011). A region may well shape political and socioeconomic realities via administrative bodies. It may mean something, too, to the people who live in or visit it, as well as to people who do not. It goes without saying that these meanings might vary widely. A region can also be an important imaginary and creative concept, a source of inspiration or of provocation, even if it does not coincide with political, administrative, or linguistic boundaries (Brathwaite 1984). The Eastern Townships are a case in point, since they do not align exactly with the administrative region of l'Estrie established in 1981, which does not include the municipalities of Granby-Bromont and Brome-Missisquoi.

If geographical regions are fluid and shifting, so too is regional literature, both in and beyond Quebec and Canada. This is underlined by Janice Fiamengo in her 2004 study of debates concerning English-language Canadian literature, or CanLit: "most critics use the term [regional literature], as I do here, with the understanding that its meanings are unstable and that, as a category, it is rarely absolute or exclusive" (2004, 244). Proposing that "in the simplest definition, regional literature portrays regional experience" (242), Fiamengo traces how "regional" is linked by some critics and practitioners to the geographical, whereas others connect it with the social as well as the spatial, and others still with a marginalized and/or contestatory position (242). Like Herb Wyile et al., who call into question an association in Canadian and US literary criticism between regionalism and "provincialism … a rural context, or … local-colour writing" (1998, xi), Fiamengo problematizes an identification of "regional" with rural or small-town settings, highlighting the fact that most Canadians actually live in cities. Nevertheless, she proposes that much "regional" literature defines itself against "the urban centers of culture and political power" represented by Toronto, Montreal, Vancouver, and Ottawa (256). In contrast, Keith D.M. Snell argues in a 2002 publication that the "regional novel" in the UK and Ireland actually tends to focus on the urban, more accurately a few key cities such as Glasgow, Dublin, and London, with nonurban settings only coming into play when associated with particular authors, such as the Brontës (1, 3).

In the twenty-five years since these contributions by Fiamengo, Wyile et al., and Snell, there has been an enormous increase in, and appetite for, writing on all kinds of places. Of particular note is English-language place-based creative non-fiction and nature writing, both subgenres growing exponentially in production and popularity over the last five years (e.g., Lindo 2011; Bradbury 2018; McAnulty 2020). David Cooper and Rachel Lichtenstein suggest that a "return to place" in (UK) English-language writing is prompted by multiple motivations, "from the anxiety regarding the meaning of place within the context of late-capitalist globalisation to the apocalyptic fear generated by the climate emergency" (2020, 1). In this way, a move away from Montreal-as-setting in much twenty-first-century French-language fiction in Quebec is remarkable in that it represents a sea change in the cultural production of the province. It also differs from trends in CanLit criticism, in which we see a focus on the urban after decades of looking at "wilderness" (Ivison and Edwards 2005). All the same, the embracing of Quebec's "heartlands" is part of a broader tendency in creative, and critical-creative, writing.

EASTERN TOWNSHIPS FICTION: PASTORAL, BORDER WRITING, MURDER MYSTERY

The Eastern Townships have long been associated with creative writing in English and French. Indeed, it is possible to write of the Eastern Townships novel, given the number of publications of this form over the last twenty years. As set out in the introduction to this chapter, previous work I have undertaken on Eastern Townships fiction in French and English identified three main subgenres: the Townships pastoral in which the region is represented as "cottage country" (Keightley 2007, 59); border fiction; and the murder mystery. Clearly, these subgenres can, and often do, overlap. Representations of the Townships as leisure idylls and pastoral playgrounds are found in novels in both of Quebec's majority languages, as in Mordecai Richler's *Joshua Then and Now* (1980) and Hélène Lapierre's *Les Barricades* (2014). In these texts, the Townships offer escape from the pressures of urban life in Montreal or comprise gathering points for social elites moving regularly between the region and the city. This routine movement between the Townships and Montreal can be interpreted as expanding the imaginative, if not administrative, boundaries of the city-region (Morgan 2022).

We see a similar undercutting of spatial boundaries in some fiction on and of the Townships, which casts this as border territory. Topographical features like rivers, mountains, caves, cathedrals, skyscrapers, power stations, and other "natural" or built constructions within urban and non-urban environments shape both conceptions and lived experiences of places.[1] For example, Gillian Roberts and David Stirrup refer to "the heavy presence" of the Canada–US border which, they suggest, can comprise "a state of mind" or a "scar" (2013, 11, 22). Not surprisingly, Eastern Townships novels and stories often feature the border with the United States. Works like William S. Messier's *Dixie* (2013), which adapts the conventions of the US southern gothic to a Quebec context, and Johanne Seymour's murder-mystery *Le Cri du cerf* (2005) insist on the porosity of the border regarding legal and illegal crossings of goods and bodies. Such texts draw attention – implicitly if not explicitly – to the region's positioning within national and international power relations,[2] as well as the arbitrary nature of a human-imposed boundary. In contrast to some examples of English-language Canadian literature, the country's border with the US is not used to shore up an identity defined in opposition to it (Langer 2014) but rather to raise questions around belonging, territory, and "ownership" in local, national, and continental contexts (Morgan 2021).

As is evident above, borders tend to be associated with criminality as well as institutions of the law. Crime is a key theme in the genre most associated with the Eastern Townships and l'Estrie, namely the murder mystery. This identification between genre and region is due in no small measure to Louise Penny's bestselling Inspector Gamache novels, set in the imaginary Townships village of Three Pines, and the fan culture surrounding them (see Mann 2020 and her chapter in this volume). Drawing on the work of Debbie Mann and others on the global reach of genre fiction, I have argued elsewhere that Townships murder mysteries undercut the notion of a stable region, even as they celebrate specific regional places and identities (Morgan 2021). In this way, Three Pines is a rendering of Knowlton that cannily calls to mind the English villages featured in canonical examples of the village cozy by Agatha Christie. The bleaker landscapes of Johanne Seymour's Inspector MacDougall quintet give us a vision of the region as shaped by various forms of noir (Morgan 2021). In this series, the area around Lac-Brome is reminiscent of woodlands in Denmark and Sweden, along with sparsely populated, dying villages in mid-Wales, as portrayed in television series like *Forbrydelsen/The Killing*, *Bron/The Bridge*, and *Hinterland/Y Gwyll*. The framing of the Townships' lakes and forests as noir settings also echoes fictional and screen portrayals of the Ozarks (e.g., Woodrell 2006; Granik 2010), recalling both regions' links with New France, and so further subverting any notion of the region – and nation – as fixed.

TRACING DEINDUSTRIALIZATION

There is a fourth tendency I have recently identified in Townships fiction. Whilst not really comprising a subgenre, in that the works concerned do not necessarily engage explicitly with the theme, some Townships novels and short story collections can be seen as tracing deindustrialization. A global phenomenon, deindustrialization can be compared to suburbanization as described by Pierre Hamel and Roger Keil (2016), in that it has both local and shared characteristics. Jean-Pierre Kesteman suggests that the period 1860–1913 represented a high-point regarding the size of the Townships' population and the region's embeddedness in industrial capitalism (2006, 11). During this time, the Townships exported wood, preserved goods, cheese, breeding cattle, and beef (Kesteman 2006, 10). Other industries included mining (copper, asbestos), the railway, and manufacturing, with textiles important in Coaticook and Magog (Toé 2016). Prompted by changes such as the end of protectionism (Kesteman 2006, 11), growth in textiles manufacturing in China, India, and Mexico, new technological developments overseas, and the outsourcing of labour (Toé 2016, 65–6), deindustrialization began in the region in the 1950s. Several small towns, like Coaticook, Waterloo, and Asbestos were fading by the early 2000s, as were many villages, with unemployment and youth exodus two key social impacts (Kesteman 2006, 13). In a similar vein, Guy Laperrière highlights how deindustrialization has removed many traces of the former textile and pulp-and-paper factories, and asbestos mines from the Eastern Townships, largely turning the region into a service economy (Laperrière 2009, 140). This shift makes its presence felt in some of the fiction of and on the region, even if this is a rather absent presence that seems, on first reading, to elide the Townships' industrial past.

Strictly speaking, Liane Keightley's *Seven Openings of the Head* (2007), Denis Coupal's *Blindshot* (2019), and Michèle Plomer's *Dragonville* (2011) do not constitute examples of what Phil O'Brien describes as "the deindustrial novel" (2018, 229) and Sherry Lee Linkon terms "deindustrialization literature" (2018, 9). Both scholars flag the importance of particular forms of labour in the texts they analyze, with O'Brien arguing that "work, or rather its absence … continues to be pressing and formative" in the novels he analyzes from the first decade of the twenty-first century (230). Linkon defines "deindustrialization literature" as produced by those immediately affected by deindustrialization and the subsequent generation, and as "focus[ing] on daily life as seen from working-class perspectives" (9). We do not necessarily get a focus on industrial labour and working-class identities in each of the examples of Townships fiction I am considering here. All the same, the short stories and novels can be interpreted as inscribing social and economic changes within and beyond the Townships, primarily through a critical rendering of the region as a "blank" canvas, reimagined as a "wilderness," commuter belt, or as a leisurescape for affluent retirees and part-time or occasional residents.

Work in postcolonial studies and sociology has taught us that "blank" or "empty" landscapes only appear such via viewing, conceptualizing, and representational practises that suppress forms of human and other-than-human life in support of colonialism, neocolonialism, and/or tourism (van Eeden 2011, Hulan 2002, Urry 1990). Townships fiction can invite postcolonial readings by mediating the violence of settler colonialism or slavery. I have considered elsewhere how Messier's *Dixie* alludes to histories of free and enslaved Blacks in the Townships in references to the Black cemetery at Saint-Armand (Morgan 2016). The focus of this present chapter, however, is the drawing out of the effects of socioeconomic change. I argue that the apparent emptiness of the settings in fiction by Keightley and Coupal can be seen as pointing to the deindustrialization that is directly explored in Plomer's novel, because it suggests the factory closures, depopulation, poverty, and social exclusion associated with this phenomenon.[3] The following discussion will focus on how the legacy of changes to work and sociability in the late twentieth century and twenty-first century shape the Eastern Townships of *Seven Openings of the Head*, *Blindshot*, and *Dragonville*.

Liane Keightley's *Seven Openings of the Head* reprises the popular association of Townships with "cottage country" (59) to subvert it, the "tiny lake" resembling "a large muddy puddle" (59), and the water "too cold" (67). All but one of the seven stories in Keightley's collection are set in an amalgamation of the Townships, although we rarely get a direct reference to an identifiable place. The stories deal with the minutiae of a range of social and intimate relationships among couples, friends, neighbours, and acquaintances. The nuances of these relationships are finely calibrated, from the complex and contradictory emotions a daughter feels towards the mother she is driving to a medical appointment, to the smell of a man's unwashed hair somehow confirming his partner's doubts about her future with him. What predominates throughout, however, is a sense of dislocation. There is an eeriness within the rural that is fostered by a lack of social density combined with a menacing, hostile, or simply indifferent other-than-human world. The opening story, "No One Tells You," is set in an "uncertain terrain of forest and back roads" (11). In the title story, the cold becomes dangerous when a character loses his hat whilst cross-country skiing at night, the wind blowing it away and making retrieval impossible (95). The final story features large, intimidating crows that "shriek" (105), according to protagonist Helen, as well as frogs "calling out for mates" (115) in a contrast to the avoidance or withholding of sex by her male partner.

The unsettling quality of the "wild," farm, or garden environments is intensified by references to scant numbers of unemployed or under-employed residents, cut off from each other. In "Ten-Cent Packs," an unnamed female protagonist stays in her grandmother's house for longer than she originally intends following the elderly woman's death. She interacts to a small degree with her neighbours, especially thirty-something Sender and his dog Milo, but otherwise she does little besides stockpile canned goods and plan winter menus even though it is summer (74). This is a story about loss and loneliness: not only has the narrator lost her grandmother but Sender has recently separated from his partner Mona, who announces via voicemail her intention to have Milo live with her. "Ten-Cent Packs" also deals with un- and underemployment, poverty, neglect, and isolation: before her death, the narrator's grandmother's room was "filthy" (76). Sender, whose house "smells faintly of urine" (71), watches daytime TV when he is not working, leaving Milo to run about unmonitored outside. The formerly amicable Mrs Goody takes to "frown[ing] severely" (80) at Sender, when he fails to build the birdhouse he promised to protect her errant budgie, who flew off to settle in a birch tree when its cage was being cleaned (77–8).

Themes of underemployment, social isolation, and boredom are also found in "Triton and Tex," which charts the demise of a couple's relationship following a burglary. Whilst Artie spends more and more time away from the house, playing bridge with friends, Helen feels increasingly out of place within it, finding her once-comforting domestic rituals prevented by inconveniences like the theft of the rocking chair in which she used to sit whilst waiting for the kettle to boil (104). She befriends an eccentric older male neighbour, Al, who, by somewhat unclear means, has the rocking chair in his home. Helen also takes to looking in the windows of other people's houses, ostensibly searching for her stolen belongings but also out of curiosity and a lack of more engaging pastimes She is surprised to find residents "asleep on their couches in the middle of the day, or sitting up and staring out at nothing" (118). A sense of drifting or rootlessness is furthered by descriptions of the trains from which the story gets its title. In contrast to the trains of the past, these have no markers identifying them with particular places in, or even beyond, Canada: "Helen turned to watch the train pass on the opposite side of the road. The names offered no indication of points of origin. The cars used to have *Alberta Wheat* or BC *Lumber* painted on them, giving her a feeling of size, the tracks stretching all the way across the country. But Helen hadn't seen those trains lately. Only these unidentifiable ones, that gave her the feeling that she had been left behind" (104). Representing a move to global, deterritorializing capital (Morgan 2022), the trains are not comforting, even if they contribute to the Townships' sound ecologies.[4] We learn that "a train blasted its whistle" (103), then "roared past" (103). Another causes the house "to shiver" (106). References to driving or other forms of travel between the Townships and elsewhere, notably Montreal, occur in five of the stories set in the region (e.g., 31, 109). In "No One Tells You," the incongruous appearance of a bungalow (15) – a form of vernacular architecture more usually associated with the suburb – both hints at a past where more employment was available locally and casts the Townships as part of the Montreal city-region (Morgan 2022). The Townships become a place to pass through or leave, an everyplace of postindustrial capitalism or rootless commuter country, even if their woodlands and farmlands have a distinctive beauty or charm (94, 35).

In an interview I undertook with her in 2014, Keightley attributed the tension within her collection to her feeling of being out of place in the Townships, where she spent her holidays as a child: "That area of the Eastern Townships [near Eastman] is very francophone. And so I feel doubly isolated. But I guess I've come to like that isolation … I speak French, but I'm not a francophone, right? … I guess I feel similarly there to how I feel in Montreal … Being an anglophone in Montreal is … a strange thing, because I feel like a stranger in my own home, a little bit."[5] However, her stories trace more than a personal and linguistic history. An emptying of the landscape caused by the removal of buildings, machinery, people, and associated smells, sounds, and sights appears to be a common characteristic of deindustrialisation – in the global south and north (Schindler et al. 2020). For example, research on Montreal's Pointe-Saint-Charles by Piyusha Chatterjee and Steven High highlights the contrast between the noisy, busy, and sociable district interviewees recalled from their youth, when most inhabitants worked at one of the local factories, mills, or railway yards with the "emptiness and silence of today" (2017, 185). A sense of "emptiness" permeates *Seven Openings of the Head,* since despite the collection's exploration of human relationships, the other-than-human tends to dominate. For example, in "No One Tells You," the non-committal Levy addresses his comments to the ever-present and unresponsive woods rather than his partner (11). In "Ten-Cent Packs," the protagonist finds her environment increasingly threatening, the "late-August mowers scream[ing] up and down the lawns" (73) and the corn she planted from old seed packets she discovered in a drawer smelling "like a throat that needs to be cleared" (76). Although planted in gardens, grass, corn, and apple trees resist domestication, mirroring the woods in following their own plans as to how, when, and where they grow or die back. Reflecting on cultural associations between plants and secrets, environmental philosopher Michael Marder suggests that plants are unknowable to human frames of understanding: "the plants' non-givenness has to do with the divergence of the time-scale of their lives from ours, not to mention the variance of their world and modes of accessing it from our own" (2013, 19). An eluding or resisting of human knowledge and containment prevents readers from romanticizing the rural and semi-rural environments of Keightley's stories in which humans often seem incidental.

If Keightley's collection sees the other-than-human take over a region in which humans feel adrift due to a lack of purpose, the "emptied" landscape of Denis Coupal's *Blindshot* is host to clashes between permanent and part-time, or occasional, residents drawn to a region almost all see as a source and/or symbol of wealth and leisure. *Blindshot* seems like a murder mystery on first reading, opening with financier Paul Carignan getting shot whilst retrieving wood for the fire in his luxurious home in the imaginary Townships county of Beaufort. It goes on to dramatize familial and community tensions. Paul and his wife, architect-engineer Catherine Martelle-Carignan, are divorcing at the time of his death. Jack and Noah, their two teenage sons, are staying at Valhalla, the family's country home designed by Catherine, along with their father and his new partner, Anne. The boys and their friend, Zeph, see a group of hunters, including county police chief Arthur Bernier and local troublemaker Jeffrey Lennox, set off on a drunken night-time hunt after Bernier's birthday party. Jack, in particular, becomes obsessed by the idea that one of the hunters must have killed his father, whose death remains unsolved a year after the event. He, Noah, and Zeph decide to pursue their own investigation, kidnapping and holding prisoner first one, then several of the hunters. Caught up in the various dynamics is Deputy Police Chief Tom Doran, nicknamed "Brooder" due to his taciturn and introverted personality.

Blindshot represents the Townships as both hillbilly homeland and luxury leisurescape, this apparently incongruous pairing being produced by particular socioeconomic structures. Like Seymour's Kate MacDougall series, which casts the Townships as a noirscape characterized by economic decline, poverty, addiction, and violence (Morgan 2021), Coupal's novel reprises elements of "hillbilly gothic" (Sheehan 2016, np) or "ruralité trash" (Arsenault 2012, 38), notably in the character of Lennox, a "chronic trespasser and free-wheeling, year-round game hunter" (32). A violent man, Lennox is land rich but cash poor, as suggested by the seasonal labour he undertakes and the cheap whisky he drinks. As member of both a rural property-owning class and socioeconomic quasi-underclass, Lennox is tolerated by his long-term Townshipper friends. Comprising a police chief, an accountant, and an artisanal gun-maker, Lennox's lower-middle-class and middle-class blue- and white-collar pals represent a midpoint between the very rich and the semi-poor. Many of them form an effectively self-governing body, working together to evade provincial and federal law or adapt these to their own ends (291).

Coupal's novel takes up themes we see in other examples of hillbilly and regional cultural production elsewhere in North America, such as the television series *Ozark* (2017–22), including clashes between an older, settled (and Settler) population, and newcomers or perceived incomers. At times, these clashes make their presence felt in the racist comments of some of the longstanding residents, like Lennox (246). *Blindshot* is careful, however, to stress the ethnic diversity of the region (46), undercutting popular conceptions of a monocultural regional Quebec that contrasts with an ethnically and linguistically diverse Montreal. At other times, altercations between longstanding and newer Townshippers take the form of experiential know-how pitted against city smarts, and a rural labouring class against an urban middle, or upper-middle, class. Towards the end, Lennox turns the tables on his captors, escaping his bonds and tying up the boys and Catherine before setting fire to Valhalla. He pronounces, "the Carignans are not really outdoorsmen. No, you guys are geeks. Private school nerds" (319). The family's lack of experiential knowledge gained by rural living is evident in the choice of a site for their enormous house. Valhalla lies on what Lennox describes as "the best hunting trail in the whole county" (318). The design of the house also highlights the (Martelle-)Carignans' relative ignorance of its rural setting, since it features a window wall that is imperceptible to birds. We learn from early in chapter 1 that "countless birds, of all kinds" (24) repeatedly fly into this window, becoming injured or dying as a result.

In this contested county, Doran is the only possible redeemer, although as befits a novel that plays with genre conventions, like a noir detective, he is not entirely law-abiding, since he ignores the council's refusal to grant him permits to convert the abandoned church in which he has made his home. Doran is both noir detective, used to navigating the mean streets of Boston and Montreal, and cowboy: physically attractive (146), introverted, moody, and barely in control of a simmering physical violence. In some respects, *Blindshot* reads like a critical western, reprising some of the tropes of this genre in order to critique or subvert them. In ways similar to noir fiction, the western mobilizes anxieties around social and cultural change. In its classical formulation, the western is a nostalgic genre, mourning particular constructions of implicitly white, implicitly cis, and heterosexual masculinity in the figure of an individualistic cowboy able to pit himself against an ostensibly "wild" nature (Morgan 1999). *Blindshot* critiques these tropes, particularly in relation to setting. If Beaufort County is "wild," this is because swathes of it are owned by a relatively small number of wealthy families, many of whom live most of the year in Montreal, western Canada, or the United States. For these second-home owners, the region is just "a vast, forested playground" (47). If, in Keightley's collection, the "emptiness" of the Townships is embodied/emspaced by sites of unhappy stasis, disconnected passage, and commuting, in *Blindshot*, low population density is a vital component of the leisurescape available to, and shaped by, very affluent occasional residents. This is due to these residents having bought up "considerable stretches of land" (47) on which to build their "elaborate, well-hidden estates" (47). Some of Beaufort's occasional residents, notably Catherine Martelle-Carignan and her children, are represented sympathetically. Overall, however, the novel critiques the absenteeism of newer landowners and their view of the region as a lifestyle-enhancing resource. This absenteeism is suggested in the "hands-off" or neglectful parenting performed by Zach's mother and father, who do not monitor their child's actions. More longstanding residents come under critique for their own extractive relationships to a region they see as something to control legally and financially via various political and economic strategies, some of which, such as the awarding of building contracts to a local asphalting company (126–7), are nepotistic. Like Penny's Three Pines, Beaufort is "off the radar" (127). However, in contrast to the idyllic village far removed from the tensions of urban life portrayed in the Inspector Gamache series, Beaufort is self-contained insofar as it is governed – and corruptly so – by a handful of local social elites.

Like many Townships novels, *Blindshot* casts the region as a murderscape and deathscape (spoiler alert: as the title suggests, the apparent murder was not premeditated). Whilst the theme of settler colonialism is not explored in depth, Coupal's novel refers to it in the description of the residents of Beaufort County. They include people whose "family lineages … could be traced back to the very beginnings of the European conquest, from the great battles with the Abenaki and Iroquois" (46). In this context, the trees so often found in Townships fiction – *Blindshot* refers to "the rich scents of the forest" (1), "the dark woods" (1), "dense woods" (10) and "the woods [that] raced by, not fast enough" (13) – act as witnesses to historical traumas. In the present-day, the investigation into Paul's apparent murder is carried out against a backdrop of a culture of killing, with deer and other animals hunted and displayed on walls as trophies by long-established residents (125–6).

By offering representations of the region as a "blank" screen primed – if not always successfully – for new, postindustrial forms of capitalism or the projection of tourist and leisure dreams, *Seven Openings of the Head* and *Blindshot* implicitly conjure histories of industrialization via their absence. This absence is suggested by social isolation, under-employment, and particular forms of housing and residence. In contrast, Michèle Plomer's *Dragonville* engages directly with deindustrialization, even if this is not the main theme. Plomer's novel alternates between Hong Kong in 1910 and a town on Lake Memphremagog in 2010, with the two narratives coming increasingly together as the text progresses. In the twenty-first century, Sylvie Mathews returns to her home in the Eastern Townships after several years of living in Shenzhen and Hong Kong where she was in a relationship with a Chinese man. She leases a shop on rue Principale, where she plans to sell luxury goods from China. Renovations on the shop undertaken by a former schoolmate, Jean, reveal Chinese characters and a dragon painted on the walls. Sylvie enlists the help of Ping Ping, a young Chinese Québécoise woman, and her little brother, Louis, to translate, learning that the writing repeats, "je t'aime" (135). Readers can assume that there is a link between this former laundry and the story taking place in 1910 Hong Kong. This last features Li, an impoverished but beautiful young man, who is sought by the police after killing a sailor who had been abusive to Li's mother, and Lung, a fantastical dragon able to assume any form. Lung rescues Li from further violence or capture, and nurses him to recovery at her luxury home. There, she takes the form of a woman, and the two become lovers. In Quebec, Sylvie's return to the Townships sees her under pressure to sell the family home on the lake front, empty since her mother was placed in a home due to her progressing dementia and where she later died. Originally owned by a wealthy Monsieur Allen, it was bequeathed to Sylvie's grandfather, whom Allen had brought over from Inverness to captain his beloved steamboat, *Mistress of the Lake*. The end of Plomer's novel has Li on a boat to Vancouver to escape capture by either the authorities or the triads to whom his mother, an opium addict, owed money, and Sylvie preparing to move back into Lake House.

Work is a feature of Plomer's novel, with much of the present-day narrative centring on Sylvie's new business venture and the renovations required to realize it. Other forms of work include selling real estate, owning and managing a motel, and serving in a restaurant. In contrast to *Seven Openings of the Head* and *Blindshot*, *Dragonville* makes direct references to Townships deindustrialization by invoking the history of textile production in the region. In this way, Sylvie reflects on the fact that the families of most of the children with whom she went to school were textile workers (35). The closure of the textile factories turned the town into a location of choice for affluent retirees or tourists. (34). Many heritage buildings had been, or were in the process of being, demolished and replaced by postmodern architecture. Unsympathetic to its setting, this architecture renders the town a global anyplace, or everyplace (Morgan 2017, 13). This is suggested by Sylvie's reflections on the condominium development near Lake House: "j'avais vu des quartiers identiques en banlieue de Montréal, en Floride et dans des banlieues cossues en Chine du Sud" (104). Worse, the condos are empty, despite all being sold. A conversation between Sylvie and Monsieur Théoret, the owner of the motel in which she takes a room on her return to the Townships, reveals economic decline in the town, as indicated by empty shops on the main street and homes abandoned by their former owners (24).

In a 2015 interview, Plomer critiqued the blocking of public access to the lake by property development companies.[6] *Dragonville* offers a reminder of the importance of sharing resources like blue spaces in the character of the affluent former lakeside resident who allowed other locals to cut across his land to the water (105). This reminder comprises an important counter to a loss of cultural and communal memory, represented in the dementia suffered by Sylvie's late mother. Like *Blindshot*, Plomer's novel acknowledges that racism exists in the present as well as in the past, as is evidenced in the derogatory comments made by the landlord from whom she rents her shop (159) and the motel owner's reminiscing about his youthful fears of the Chinese working in the laundry that, by a strange coincidence, occupies the same building as Sylvie's business (127–8). All the same, *Dragonville* can be said to mediate Laurajane Smith's and Gary Campbell's notion of "progressive" and "hopeful" nostalgia (2017, 613). This avoids a reactionary looking-back, seeking instead to build solidarities through dialogue about the past, present, and future. The novel's blend of fantasy and realism contributes to this hopefulness, taking us to a past-perhaps-one-day, like Derrida's hopeful ghost who disrupts chronological time with a warning that can prompt action that leads to a more positive future (1993, see also Morgan 2018).

CONCLUSION

Deindustrialization is a key feature of Townships history, albeit one that is not particularly present in tourist and promotional literature on the region. Referring to Linkon's work, O'Brien suggests that deindustrialization gives rise to "an inheritance of loss" (239). Creative writing can conjure backstories or broader contexts via the unsaid – sometimes, but not always, through formal techniques like fragmentation and nonlinear narratives. These techniques prompt reading strategies that look for meanings beyond the words on the page. Whilst the fiction explored in this chapter is not particularly experimental, comprising forms of realism (Keightley, Coupal) or a blend of realism and fantasy (Plomer), its mediation of themes around the other-than-human, land access, and land ownership invokes histories of loss. *Seven Openings of the Head*, *Blindshot*, and *Dragonville* offer potential counters to this "inheritance" (O'Brien 2018, 239), gesturing towards more communal modes of being by drawing attention to the social and spatial fragmentation generated by landscapes and homes emptied of workers, factories, and full-time residents. These texts celebrate as well as critique the Townships, highlighting the other-than-human in the forms of plants, animals, mountains, and lakes and giving readers a rich and complex material and imaginary geography in which ethnolinguistic diversity is an everyday, and longstanding, reality. In so doing, they engage with themes and forms with a global reach. Undercutting a conceptualization of the region as enclosed, static, and inward-looking, these stories and novels demonstrate that: (i) in a globalized world, places still have their own identities and meanings, (ii) places' identities and meanings are actively shaped by communities, even if these communities are not harmonious, (iii) places have identities, meanings, and agencies (Marland 2013) besides those attributed to them or understood by humans, and (iv) deindustrialization literature can take many forms and come out of rural or exurban, as well as urban, contexts. In exploring recent examples of Townships fiction, this chapter demonstrates that whilst this literature can be seen as "regional" in its celebration of a particular geographical space, this space, just like any other, should be understood as contingent, fluid, and always connected with national and international elsewheres.

ACKNOWLEDGMENTS

Research for this chapter was supported by an Arts and Humanities Research Council (AHRC) Leadership Fellowship. Project title: "Heartlands/*Pays du coeur*: Geohumanities and Québec's 'regional' fiction," grant number [AH/T006250/1]. I am grateful to Rebecca (Becky) Yearling and Steve Hewitt for reading and commenting on an earlier draft of this chapter.

Notes

1 All spaces on earth are impacted by human intervention. See, for example, Emma Marris, "Why the Myth of 'Wilderness' Harms Both Nature and Humanity," *New Scientist*, 1 December 2021, https://www.newscientist.com/article/mg25233634-400-why-the-myth-of-wilderness-harms-both-nature-and-humanity/. Accessed 28 June 2022.

2 In her work on English-language Canadian fiction, Gillian Roberts proposes that we think of the Canada–US border as "the primary site of examining Canada's overlapping relationships to colonialism, postcolonialism, and neocolonialism" (2015, 19).

3 The economic difficulties and social exclusion of many members of Quebec's English-speaking communities, particularly those outside Montreal, is highlighted in Toula Drimonis's review of Guy Rex Rodgers's documentary, *What We Choose to Remember* (2022). See https://cultmtl.com/2022/05/anglos-in-quebec-a-new-documentary-portrays-a-reality-far-from-the-pampered-elite-anglo-montreal-myth-what-we-choose-to-remember-guy-rex-rodgers/. Accessed 24 June 2022.

4 A group interview I undertook with Michèle Plomer, Anne Brigitte Renaud, and Hélène Guy confirmed this. Parc national du Mont-Orford, 3 May 2015.

5 Liane Keightley, interview, Centre for Oral History and Digital Storytelling, Concordia University, Montreal, 14 August 2014.

6 Group interview, parc national du Mont-Orford, 3 May 2015.

References

Archibald, S. 2011. *Arvida*. Montreal: Le Quartanier.

Arsenault, M. 2012. "Ruralité trash." *Liberté* 53 (3): 38–47.

Blanchette-Doucet, V. 2016. *117 Nord*. Montreal: Boréal.

Bradbury, K. 2018. *The Bumblebee Flies Anyway: A Year of Gardening and (Wild)life*. London: Bloomsbury Wildlife.

Brathwaite, E.K. 1984. *History of the Voice: The Development of Nation Language in Anglophone Caribbean Poetry*. London: New Beacon.

Chatterjee, P., and S. High. 2017. "The Deindustrialization of Our Senses: Residual and Dominant Soundscapes in Montreal's Point Saint-Charles District." In *Telling Environmental Histories: Intersections of Memory, Narrative and Environment*, edited by K. Holmes and H. Goodall, 179–210. New York: Palgrave-Macmillan.

Cloke, P. 2006. "Conceptualizing Rurality." In *The Handbook of Rural Studies*, edited by P. Cloke, T. Marsden, and P. Mooney, 18–28. London: Sage.

Cooper, D., and R. Lichtenstein. 2020. "What Is Place Writing?" https://www.mmu.ac.uk/media/mmuacuk/content/documents/english/What-is-Place-Writing-June-2020.pdf. Accessed 26 April 2022.

Coupal, D. 2019. *Blindshot*. Montreal: LLP.

Davey, F. 1998. "Toward the Ends of Regionalism." In *A Sense of Place: Re-Evaluating Regionalism in Canadian and American Writing*, edited by C. Riegel, H. Wyile, K. Overbye, and D. Perkins, 1–17. Edmonton: University of Alberta Press.

Delisle, M. 2002. *Dée*. Montreal: Leméac.

Delvaux, M. 2009. *Rose amer*. Montreal: Héliotrope.

Derrida, J. 1993. *Spectres de Marx: L'État de la dette, le travail du deuil et la nouvelle Internationale*. Paris: Galilée.

Drimonis, T. 2022. "The Quebec Anglo: A New Documentary Portrays a Reality Far From the "Pampered Elite" Myth." *Cult Mtl*, 22 May. https://cultmtl.com/2022/05/anglos-in-quebec-a-new-documentary-portrays-a-reality-far-from-the-pampered-elite-anglo-montreal-myth-what-we-choose-to-remember-guy-rex-rodgers/. Accessed 24 June 2022.

Dubuque, Bill, and Mark Williams, dirs. *Ozark*. 2017–22; Beverly Hills, CA: MRC Television.

Farley, P., and M. Symmons Roberts. 2011. *Edgelands: Journeys into England's True Wilderness*. London: Jonathan Cape.

Fiamengo, J. 2004. "Regionalism and Urbanism." In *The Cambridge Companion to Canadian Literature*, edited by E.-M. Kröller, 241–62. Cambridge, UK: Cambridge University Press.
Fiteau-Chiba, G. 2018. *Encabanée*. Montreal: XYZ.
Fortin, A., and C. Després. 2011. "Étalement urbain et développement durable: enjeux et défis." In *La Banlieue s'étale*, edited by Andrée Fortin, Carole Després, and Geneviève Vachon, 13–34. Quebec: Éditions Nota bene.
Granik, Debra, dir. *Winter's Bone*. 2010; Los Angeles: Anonymous Content.
Hamel, P., and R. Keil. 2015. *Suburban Governance: A Global View*. Toronto: University of Toronto Press.
– 2016. "Governance in an Emerging Suburban World." *Cadernos Metrópole* 18 (37): 647–70.
Hodos, J. 2011. *Second Cities: Globalization and Local Politics in Manchester and Philadelphia*. Philadelphia: Temple University Press.
Hulan, R. 2002. *Northern Experience and the Myths of Canadian Culture*. Montreal and Kingston: McGill-Queen's University Press.
Ivison, D., and J.D. Edwards. 2005. "Introduction: Writing Canadian Cities." In *Downtown Canada: Writing Canadian Cities*, edited by J.D. Edwards, and D. Ivison, 3–13. Toronto: University of Toronto Press.
Keightley, L. 2007. *Seven Openings of the Head*. Montreal: Conundrum Press.
Keil, R., and J-P. Addie. 2015. "'It's Not Going to Be Surburban, It's Going to Be All Urban': Assembling Post-suburbia in the Toronto and Chicago Regions." *International Journal of Urban and Regional Research* 39 (5): 892–911.
Kesteman, J.-P. 2006. "Ruralité et mondialisation dans les Cantons-de-l'Est du Québec. Le regard de l'historien." *Journal of Eastern Townships Studies* 29/30: 5–20.
Langer, B. 2014. "Coca-Colonials Write Back: Localizing the Global in Canadian Crime Fiction." In *Detecting Canada: Essays on Canadian Crime Fiction, Television and Film*, edited by J. Sloniowski, M. Rose. Waterloo: Wilfrid Laurier University Press, Kindle Edition.
Laperrière, G. 2009. *Les Cantons-de-l'Est*. Quebec: Presses de l'Université Laval.
Lapierre, H. 2014. *Les Barricades*. Montreal: Québec/Amérique.
Lindo, D. 2011. *The Urban Birder*. London: New Holland.
Linkon, S.L. 2018. *The Half-Life of Deindustrialization: Working-Class Writing about Economic Restructuring*. Ann Arbor: University of Michigan Press.
Mann, J.D. 2020. "The World(s) of Three Pines: Creating Community in the Novels of Louise Penny." *Journal of Eastern Township Studies* 48: 13–25.
Marder, M. 2013. "Of Plants, and Other Secrets." *Societies* 3 (1): 16–23.
Marland, P. 2013. "Ecocriticism." *Literature Compass* 10 (11): 846–68.
Marris, E. 2021. "Why the Myth of 'Wilderness' Harms Both Nature and Humanity." *New Scientist*, 1 December. https://www.newscientist.com/article/mg25233634-400-why-the-myth-of-wilderness-harms-both-nature-and-humanity/. Accessed 28 June 2022.
Massey, D. 2004. "Geographies of Responsibility." *Geografiska Annaler: Series B, Human Geography* 86 (1): 5–18.
McAnulty, D. 2020. *Diary of a Young Naturalist*. Beaminster, UK: Little Toller.
Messier, W. 2013. *Dixie*. Montreal: Marchand de feuilles.

Moore, J. 2010. *The Extinction Club*. London, Toronto: Quercus, Hamish Hamilton.
Morgan, C. 1999. "It's the End of the World as We Know It: Quebec's Remembered Landscapes." *British Journal of Canadian Studies* 14 (1): 52–62.
– 2016. "Walking Studies, the Eastern Townships, and William S. Messier's Dixie." *Nottingham French Studies* 55 (2): 224–38.
– 2017. *Writing, Talking and Walking Québec's Eastern Townships*. London: The British Library.
– 2018. "Sonic Spectres: Word Ghosts in Madeleine Thien's *Dogs at the Perimeter* and the Digital Map Project, 'Fictional Montreal/Montréal fictif." *London Journal of Canadian Studies*, 14 November. https://uclpress.scienceopen.com/hosted-document?doi=10.14324/111.444.ljcs.2018v33.004.
– 2021. "Québec's New Regional Fiction: Louise Penny and Johanne Seymour." *British Journal of Canadian Studies* 33 (2): 225–40
– 2022. "Mobilities in Montreal Fiction." In *Routledge Companion to Literary Urban Studies*, edited by L. Ameel et al., 299–312. London: Routledge.
Morgan, C. and D. Laforest. 2011. "Introduction." *British Journal of Canadian Studies* 24 (2): 115–17.
Nepveu, P., and G. Marcotte. 1992. "Introduction: Montréal, sa littérature." In *Montréal imaginaire: ville et littérature*, edited by P. Nepveu and G. Marcotte, 7–12. Saint-Laurent, QC: Fides.
O'Brien, P. 2018. "The Deindustrial Novel: Twenty-First-Century British Fiction and the Working Class." In *Working-Class Writing: Theory and Practice*, edited by B. Clarke and N. Hubble, 229–46. London: Palgrave.
Penny, L. 2005. *Still Life*. London: Headline.
Plomer, M. 2011–13. *Dragonville*. Montreal: Marchand de feuilles.
Richler, M. 1980. *Joshua Then and Now*. Toronto: McClelland and Stewart.
Roberts, G. 2015. *Discrepant Parallels: Cultural Implications of the Canada–US Border*. Montreal and Kingston: McGill-Queen's University Press.
Roberts, G., and D. Stirrup. 2013. "Introduction: Culture at the 49th Parallel: Nationalism, Indigeneity, and the Hemispheric." In *Parallel Encounters: Culture at the Canada–US Border*, edited by G. Roberts and D. Stirrup, 1–24. Waterloo, ON: Wilfrid Laurier University Press.
Rosenfeldt, Hans, dir. *Bron/The Bridge*. 2011–18; Copenhagen: Nimbus Film.
Schindler, S., et al. 2020. "Deindustrialization in Cities of the Global South." *Area Development and Policy* 5 (3): 283–304.
Seymour, J. 2005. *Le Cri du cerf*. Outremont: Libre expression.
Smith, L., and G. Campbell. 2017. "'Nostalgia for the Future': Memory, Nostalgia, and the Politics of Class." *International Journal of Heritage Studies* 23 (7): 612–27.
Snell, K.D.M. 2016 [2002]. *The Bibliography of Regional Fiction in Britain and Ireland, 1800–2000*. London: Routledge [Abingdon: Ashgate].
Sveistrup, Søren, dir. *Forbrydelsen/The Killing*. 2007–12; Copenhagen: DR.
Talfan, Ed, dir. *Hinterland/Y Gwyll*. 2013–16. Cardiff, Wales: Fiction Factory Films.
Toé, F.T. 2016. "Trame historique du textile à Coaticook (1971 à nos jours)." *Journal of Eastern Townships Studies* 46: 59–74.

Urry, J. 1990. *The Tourist Gaze: Leisure and Travel in Contemporary Societies.* London: Sage.
Van Eeden, J. 2011. "Surveying the 'Empty Land' in Selected South African Landscape Postcards." *International Journal of Tourism Research* 13: 600–12.
Warriar, N. 2005. *The Enemy Within.* Toronto: Tsar.
Williams, R. 1975 [1973]. *The Country and the City.* Oxford: Oxford University Press.
Woodrell, D. 2006. *Winter's Bone.* London: Sceptre.
Wyile, H. et al. 1998. "Introduction: Regionalism Revisited." In *A Sense of Place: Re-Evaluating Regionalism in Canadian and American Writing,* edited by C. Riegel, H. Wyile, K. Overbye, and D. Perkins, ix–xiv. Edmonton: University of Alberta Press.

15

Postcards, Cultural Landscape Analysis, and the Eastern Townships in the Past 125 Years

Caroline Beaudoin

IN 1885 THE FIRST ILLUSTRATED POSTAL CARDS appeared in Germany in the form of "Grüss aus" or "Greetings from" various places; colour print lithograph cards also appeared throughout Europe between 1885 and 1889. In Canada, private illustrated postcards did not begin circulating until 1898, although private postcards without illustrations were introduced in January 1895. Picture postcards are either "printed cards" or "real photos" (figure 15.1). Illustrated images were initially reproduced from engravings, drawings, or paintings up until 1901, at which point photographs prevailed as the predominant pictorial medium.

During the first decade of the twentieth century, German-issued cards dominated most postcard markets, with one scholar describing how during this era "hundreds of companies in Germany were producing billions of cards each year" (Woody 1998, 32). Although the postcards were printed in Germany, many of them were ordered by retailers and distributors from around the world and were often based on photographs taken by regional or local photographers. The billions of postcards that circulated during the first decades of the twentieth century are a testament to that era's worldwide achievement in mobilizing people and things on an unprecedented scale, with, arguably, unparalleled efficiency. Postcards back then were regularly delivered the day after being posted, and many even arrived

Figure 15.1 *Lake Memphremagog Newport Vt.*, c.1920. View looking north toward the Eastern Townships, QC

on the same day that they were mailed. The postcards' newly shortened messages were often no more elaborate or personal than any one of today's briefest tweets or texts. During the Edwardian period (1901–10), as remains true today, rapid changes in technology, globalization, communication systems, and social issues "dominated conversations and newspaper articles; then as now, cultures of mass consumption stamped their mark on the time; then as now, the feeling of living in an accelerating world … was overwhelming" (Gillen 2013, 489).

When studying the landscape imagery on postcards, an analysis of those images stands to gain much from cultural landscapist perspectives which draw on Henri Lefebvre's theories on everyday life in the modern world, as well as J.B. Jackson's understanding of landscape as a material and visual culture agent. Jackson, a scholar of history and literature, founded cultural landscape studies in America during the mid-twentieth century in order to reverse the nation's "visual illiteracy," which he attributed to people's inability "to consciously notice their everyday environments" (quoted in Groth and Bressi 1997, 1). Jackson's insistence on "seeing" vernacular landscapes aligns well with Lefebvre's recognition of ordinary life, as each seeks to advance an awareness of the socio-cultural ambiguities and dichotomies embedded within routine practices of labour and leisure – practices that characterize modernity's everydayness. As the founder of cultural landscape studies, one of Jackson's priorities was to awaken an appreciation for the ordinary visual and material experiences people encountered on a daily basis.

An everyday landscape is an interdisciplinary and material landscape that differs from the art historical and aesthetic fields' understanding of landscape, which have traditionally privileged the scenery's visual qualities measured against standards of taste related to picturesque, beautiful, romantic, or sublime ideals. Jackson argued that because the word *landscape*'s etymology is a human construct it "is not a natural feature of the environment but a *synthetic* space, a man-made system of spaces superimposed on the face of the land" (quoted in Groth and Bressi, 8). Geographer Denis Cosgrove reinforced that the term landscape was conceptually ambiguous and difficult to define, given that in order for a landscape to materialize it must first be seen. He insisted that "from a cultural perspective, the pictorial dimension of landscape has frequently been charged with duplicity" (Cosgrove 2006, 51) citing, for example, how the re-presentation often contains a hidden agenda to reinforce particular cultural values or myths. He questioned the curious and persistent nature of "landscape's capacity to 'naturalize' social or environmental inequities through an aesthetic of visual harmony" (Cosgrove 2006, 51). Cosgrove further refers to landscape as a "hegemonic tool" that evolved into a "landscape idea" which references the pictorial and spatial way of "connecting the individual to the community" (Cosgrove 2006, 51).

Accordingly, this study of postcards focusing on the Eastern Townships in the early twentieth century considers visual culture as a part of larger cultural processes and is consistent with Jay David Bolter and Richard Grusin's argument that no single media event, in this case postcards, "seems to do its cultural work in isolation from other media, any more that it works in isolation from other social and economic forces" (Bolter and Grusin 1999, 15). Postcards may now be understood and analyzed as one of the most widely circulated forms of imagery that have performed diverse socio-cultural functions. Any examination of the modern era's communication practices through the exchange of picture postcards contributes to a deeper understanding of the power of images and how that power stems from their ability to communicate in addition to the range of emotions they elicit.

One of the postcard's fascinating aspects is how, through its diverse "pictured" scope, it often operates according to all three of Bolter and Grusin's media categories: immediacy, hypermediacy, and remediation. Figure 15.1, a postcard identified as *Lake Memphremagog Newport, Vt.*, exemplifies the theory of immediacy, which strives to remove visible traces of the medium or by invoking other strategies to facilitate the viewer's entrance into the image. As a viewer looking upon such a landscape, it is easy to situate oneself on an imagined balcony or ledge pictured in

Figure 15.2 *Loading Our Catch*, Knowlton, QC, 1943

figure 15.1, in order to absorb and wander through the picturesque scenery, while the typeset printed on the image simultaneously reminds the viewer that it is obviously a remediated photograph.

The centuries-old three-part picturesque tradition is further reinforced by the image's horizon line which is strategically placed where the middle ground and background converge, and clearly, although organically, delineated from the foreground, just as the linear perspective draws the viewer's eyes to a vanishing point designated by the convex mountain range. In this picture the perspectival vanishing point is further reinforced by an emphasis on atmospheric perspective as colour saturation progressively fades into the distance. The elements are also carefully and deliberately framed in order to optimize variety in shapes and textures, thereby further enhancing the picturesque qualities of the landscape. Water, mountains, architecture, trees, clouds, and paths offer viewers a vivid, natural and constructed ensemble of elements to view.

Figure 15.2, *Loading Our Catch*, is an excellent example that embraces the concept of hypermediacy as an image that takes pleasure in and insists upon the medium. The image features four well-dressed men as they busy themselves with strapping a larger-than-life fish to the roof of a car in this playfully surreal, collaged, photographed, then printed picture postcard. Figure 15.3, *Typical Canadian Winter Scene*, also offers a good example of remediation – repurposing images and

Figure 15.3
Returning from Church: Typical Canadian Winter Scene, c.1904

texts. The stamps, postmarks, and inscriptions often added to postcards, however, further emphasize notions of hypermediacy, all of which are present on this particular card's recto interface. In this instance the black and white image is a reproduced artwork signed at the bottom right by Canadian painter, illustrator, and cartoonist Henri Julien (1852–1908) entitled *Returning From Church: Typical Canadian Winter Scene*; this postcard conforms to the hypermediacy concept due to the remediated picture and the other markings including typeset printed text, handwritten numbers and signature, postage stamp, and the circular ink stamped postal details. During his lifetime, Julien was a well-regarded Canadian artist recognized for his black and white paintings of rural Quebec. The snow-covered street is animatedly populated by small groups of people and horse-drawn carioles all travelling in the same direction away from the church, presumably returning home following an evening mass. The postcard, in turn, incorporates printed text and pictorial framing, thereby deliberately showcasing how the remediated image published by Montreal's Illustrated Postcard Co. entitled "Typical Canadian Winter Scene" was a reproduction of an original work signed by Julien.

Bolter and Grusin have insisted that what is new about "new media" not only "comes from the particular ways in which they refashion older media" but also from "the ways in which older media refashion themselves to answer the challenges of new media" (Bolter and Grusin 1999, 15). Visual culture, Leibovics notes, has "broadened the study of visual artifacts, including postcards, from images *per se* to the more densely woven context of their production and reception" (quoted in Prochaska and Mendelson 2010, xii). Interdisciplinary studies and theories of remediation have opened a Pandora's box of possibilities and complexities for scholars. The picture postcard's growing momentum as a pictorial artifact (commencing in the late nineteenth-century) was part of a significant cultural shift whereby images were liberated from their traditional and insular confines that included private mansions and galleries, elite clubs, museums, and illustrated books – and were catapulted into mainstream circulation for sale and display on ordinary street corners, busy train stations, and local shops that ranged from drugstores to shoemakers. Within the broader category of picture postcards, those that represent landscapes and places are key; one scholar, Naomi Schor, notes that "topographicals or view cards [are] the largest and most popular category of postcards representing familiar places" (quoted in Prochaska and Mendelson 2010, 8). J.B. Jackson has advocated that all landscapes retain some sense of familiarity, despite having various elements that may appear foreign or other, due to his understanding of landscape as, ultimately, a community's "visible manifestation [which] is simply the by-product of people working and living" (Jackson 1984, 12). As a material and visual cultural legacy, postcards are at once public and personal, intimate and formal, purposive and whimsical, and can seem uncannily familiar as they are re-read and re-viewed, in many cases more than a century after they were originally posted. Artist Timothy Van Laar has addressed the complicity between postcards and familiarity, explaining that

> Postcards use the traditions and conventions of art to do work in addition to best exemplifying a place ... we either recognize the place because it clearly represents something or some kind of thing with which we are familiar, or we recognize the worthiness of the image, and therefore the place, because we are familiar with its artistic conventions of beauty and the like. (quoted in Prochaska and Mendelson 2010, 196)

Postcards contributed significantly to reversing the modern world's visual illiteracy, well before Jackson introduced the concept of cultural landscape studies to America during the mid-twentieth century and far beyond the United States to reach a global audience. Postcards provide a greater understanding of the landscape as a territory that harbours a collection of identities, in accordance with Jackson's insistence on how "no landscape can be exclusively devoted to the fostering of only one identity" (Jackson 1984, 12). Picture postcards, as image-objects, can thus be understood as remediated visual cultural artefacts that often call upon pre-existing representational conventions, strategies, and traditions – most notably established through painting, drawing, and photography – in order to illicit a reaction or communicate an ideal or message. Within the context of this study, the concept of remediation refers to the modes in which postcards refashion older or traditional modes of pictorial representations such as printing, photography, painting, and illustrating.

This chapter's focus – a cultural landscape analysis of postcards featuring the Eastern Townships in the early twentieth century – argues and illustrates that two dominant yet visually opposed perspectives simultaneously thrived. Indeed, these respective groupings of print imagery convey starkly different visual representations relating to the realities the Townships physically encapsulated. The first, decidedly bucolic and engaging, portray the Townships as a destination environment for restorative enjoyment and human pleasure. Such postcard imagery conveys a landscape in which humans have an admiration for, and who have successfully blended with, their physical surroundings. The use of postcards certainly played a central role in first promoting and later documenting the development of tourism in the Eastern Townships. Luxurious hotels, steamships, and eventually highways (which still serve travellers today) are all portrayed as attractive pathways to allow urban society to enter into and personally engage with the natural variety and beauty of the Eastern Townships landscapes. The second collective grouping of images – printed and circulating at the same time – suggests a decidedly different perspective on the physical terrain of the Eastern Townships, a perspective that focuses on industrial advances and commercial usage which features, most notably, railways and mines.

POSTCARDS: TRAVEL, TOURISM, *and* TECHNOLOGICAL ADVANCEMENTS *in the* TOWNSHIPS

Just as Cornelius Van Horne and his partners were developing a Canadian westward-oriented tourist industry, local and regional investors in the Eastern Townships were similarly endeavouring to establish tracks and stations in their communities in order to secure their personal business interests and potential for future development. During the second half of the nineteenth century, towns, and villages in the Townships, as elsewhere, either prospered or vanished depending on their proximity to a railway and a station. According to one scholar "in addition

Figure 15.4
Perkins Landing, Que. Lake Memphremagog, 1908

to the convivial atmosphere aboard its steamers and in its resort hotels, selling features for Lake Memphremagog, were its fresh air, clear cool water, and relative freedom from black flies and mosquitoes" (Little 2009, 739). From this historical point forward the circulation of people and things became a routine part of burgeoning modern economies. Within this economic context travel can be understood as "a commodity, a service performed, transportation purchased in the form of a ticket" (Schivelbusch 1979, 186).

When examining landscape, travel, and postcards together a greater understanding of how the commoditization of place pointed to a new cultural experience which took form as an industry based on tourism. Within this tourist paradigm the destination or place itself became a new type of commodity. Postcards can be understood as important players in the industrial conquest of space for their efficient and quick means of communicating but also due to the extensive circulation of images that represented particular places. Touristic postcards articulate a particularly specific kind of relationship to place. For example, a postcard identified as *Perkins Landing, Que. Lake Memphremagog* (figure 15.4) represents the landscape

Figure 15.5 *Livingston's Pharmacy, The Wharf on Lake Memphremagog, Newport, Vt.*, c.1906

from a tourist's point of view, one of the docks along the lake's shoreline that extends from Newport, Vermont, to Magog, Quebec. The postcard was mailed in 1908 by Gordon who sent the following short message to Maude in Roxbury, Massachusetts: "Am on the 1st trip of the 'Lady'. This is one of our stops, mailed while in Canada."

This particular card reinforces how postcards enabled individuals to share even minute details of their personal experiences, despite distances, without requiring a telegraph office to do so or the time needed to compose a conventional letter. Accordingly, as Gillen and Hall note, "the early 20th-century postcard mobility meant an incredible change in the way people communicated and imagined the world. Although most people could not travel, they were nevertheless affected by those who did" (quoted in Konstantinos and Mavrič 2013, 21). The postcard facilitated Maude's experience of imagining herself next to Gordon, admiring the landscape from the dock at Perkins Landing and, depending on what other cards Gordon may have sent her, she may have also had the opportunity to picture the experience of travelling across Lake Memphremagog aboard the steamer *Lady of the Lake* (figure 15.5) as he mentions.

The paddle wheel steamer was the property of Montreal's shipping magnate Sir Hugh Allan. The *Lady* was a grand iron steamship that measured 167 feet in length and could comfortably accommodate more than 650 passengers, travellers, and vacationers between Magog and Newport as it stopped at villages and various landings along the way (Farfan, n.d.a). It was launched on Magog's Lake Memphremagog in 1867 amidst a spectacular celebration, therefore Gordon's reference to the *Lady*'s first trip in his 1908 message to Maude must have referred to that particular season's first voyage. The boat sailed from Newport twice a day stopping at the Owl's Head Mountain House Hotel (shown in the photograph identified here as figure 15.6), Perkins Wharf, and Georgeville from Tuesday to Sunday. On Mondays, the boat made a single round trip that crossed the full length of the lake. An 1891 timetable issued for "The Fine Iron Steamer" noted how on Mondays the boat arrived in Newport at 3:45 p.m., in season to connect with the express train for Montreal via the Canadian Pacific Railway. The advertisement emphasized how the boat sailed among many beautiful residences "making a trip of 75 miles, affording ever-changing views of Lake and Mountain Scenery." The ad also promoted the boat's first-class restaurant that served "nice warm meals at all hours" and "offered fine cigars, confectionary, and views of the lake on sale at its news stand" (Nelson and Malloy 2003, 89.)

Figure 15.6, *View of Mountain House Hotel and Lady of the Lake on Lake Memphremagog*, is a panoramic photograph of a beautiful, romantic landscape. It is a representation of a place that fully naturalizes the steamer and hotel's harmonious integration into the natural environment. The view conveys a refreshingly docile and pleasant setting where human-made assets (boat, docks, and buildings) are subordinate to nature and all the pleasures and resources that nature promises in summer: an abundant supply of fresh fish, game, and produce, clean water to bathe in, refreshingly cool canopies of shade beneath the trees, and an extensive amount of forested space to leisurely explore. The *Lady* was subsequently purchased by the Connecticut and Passumpsic Rivers Railroad in 1885 and continued to provide its excursion tours to the railway's passengers staying at select hotels such as the Memphremagog House, a luxury hotel in Newport, Vermont, shown on the left in figure 15.7.

Figure 15.7 features a photograph of Lake Memphremagog's southern shore. It was taken before 7 May 1907 – the day Memphremagog House (upper left corner) was destroyed by fire. The hotel is the most imposing structure in this landscape, situated at left in the background at the water's edge, easily accessible by boat or bridge. The hotel was built in 1838, although it underwent progressive expansions over the decades until it was eventually purchased by the Passumpsic Railroad in 1861. The railway company incorporated a train station and ticket office into the hotel's basement (Nelson and Malloy 2003, 32).

Figure 15.6 Owl's Head Mountain House on Lake Memphremagog, QC, c.1887

Figure 15.7 Newport, VT, c.1906: Memphremagog House

This landscape is compelling due to its serenity, balance of light and dark, and assortment of varying textures. In it, nature has been domesticated: the hillside encompasses a community, and the lake works as a holding boom for logs. The diagonal fence cutting across the foreground adds dynamism to the composition which without it would be less engaging. In this image, the built and natural environments appear as equal and compatible partners in a subtle and harmonious way that further emphasizes the domesticity of the landscape. What is particularly fascinating about this representation is how two of the region's most important industries, lumber and tourism, are naturalized within the landscape and successfully it masks the exploitation of nature. The logs floating in their pen in the foreground enrich the image and reinforce a sense of prosperity, as does the large, distinct white hotel that commands the tip of the point where the town meets the port. *The Lady of the Lake* was eventually purchased by the Canadian Pacific Railway, which had the boat's schedule synchronized with its train arrivals and departures in Newport and Magog (Farfan, n.d.b). The paddle-wheeler remained in service until 1915, later being towed from Newport to Magog in 1917 where, shortly thereafter, it was dismantled for parts. Historian Matthew Farfan emphasized how "the decline of train travel, big hotels, excursion tours, and the rise of the automobile, ensured that a large steamer like the *Lady* would not remain profitable – at least not on a lake the size of Memphremagog" (Farfan, n.d.b). Nonetheless, *The Lady of the Lake* reinforces how industrialization's steam engine technology contributed to revolutionizing perceptions of the landscape by enhancing its accessibility and promoting it as a commercial resource.

At a glance, the image in figure 15.8 suggests how Lillian's regards to Angelina in St-Malo would arrive by train, passing through Sherbrooke's CPR station as featured in red print on the card. This particular postcard, however, is interesting on several other levels as well. For instance, the Canadian Pacific Railway Company typically favoured more imposing and dynamic images than the one shown here to represent its corporate image to the public and to its competitors. This image of the company's Sherbrooke station is not a conventionally picturesque or otherwise pleasing view to look upon nor does it suggest how vital the station was in the heart of a busy urban Eastern Townships centre, such as Sherbrooke was during that period. It represents a rather industrial and mundane space that on the one hand suits the casual and ordinary content of Lillian's message, reinforcing the everydayness of this particularly routine postcard. Additionally, the train, dirt road, and railway pictured on the card visually convey the underlying theme of connectivity between places and people that is the very impetus for Lillian's message. These transportation networks offer the physical means to connect her

Figure 15.8 *C.P.R. Station, Sherbrooke, P.Q.*, 1907

(Sherbrooke) to Angelina (St-Malo), while the postcard becomes an emblem of that spatial link. On the other hand, the image's emphasis on industrial and technological iconography that features locomotives, hydroelectric poles and lines, and public or commercial architecture is incongruous with the intimate nature of the message that performs as a personal and domestic space. The casual bilingualism of the message further suggests that both the sender and recipient are familiar with colloquial English and French. In an article by Konstantinos and Mavrič, the authors argue that although "literacy was still limited at the time, postcards were seen as a medium for which one did not need to possess perfect language skills. Writing down a few words, or simply saying 'greetings' was enough, and the front image would compensate for the lack of words" (Konstantinos and Mavrič 2013, 32). The postcard presented in figure 15.8 reinforces how quickly and accessible an ordinary greeting, kiss, or simple "Bonjour" was made due to technological innovations, thus enabling people to stay in touch more regularly and easily.

As many pictorial and textual examples reveal, train schedules were often the subject of postcard communications during an era when railroads spread across continents covering greater distances at record-breaking rates. For example, in figure 15.9, the sender wrote on the recto that it was 2:20 p.m., and the individual was "waiting on my train." The message on the card's verso includes a precise account of the times and reasons why they decided to leave so abruptly. The image on the postcard features the new steel bridge that linked Melbourne to Richmond, attesting to the towns' enhanced prosperity and use of new technology which was made possible by the heightened railway traffic Richmond experienced during that industrial era. Despite the standardization of time to a twenty-four-hour clock, however, the variety of local time zones regularly "caused confusion with scheduling, accidents, and passenger irritation. No one could easily determine when a train

Figure 15.9 *Pont St François – St Francis Bridge, Richmond and Melbourne,* Sherbrooke, QC, 1907

would arrive at a particular station, and worse, trains crashed because of shared lines" (Sawchuk 2001, 157).

St. Francis bridge from Richmond and Melbourne P.Q. (figure 15.9) reinforces the postcard's significance as visual and material mediators of technology, mobility, and communications. Both the images and texts appearing on these cards represent cultural signifiers that embodied an era's perception of progress and prosperity, as well as space and time. When looking at the printed photograph of the St Francis bridge in figure 15.9, we can appreciate the sense of immediacy, the foreground's close-up details, and the distant features that are particularly compelling in the then relatively new medium. As a viewer, it is easy to situate oneself within the landscape, standing on the embankment right next to the photographer. Heins Buddemeier found that the nineteenth-century public initially became fascinated "not by the taking of a picture of any specific object, but by the way in which any random object could be made to appear on the photographic plate. This was something of such unheard-of novelty that the photographer was delighted by each and every shot he took" (quoted in Schivelbusch 1979, 65). He enthusiastically further described "how intensely the first photographs were scrutinized, and what people were mostly looking for. For instance … tiny, until then unnoticed details are stressed continuously: paving stones, scattered leaves, the shape of a branch, the traces of rain on the wall" (quoted in Schivelbusch 1979, 65). This commentary seems particularly relevant to the postcards' miniature scenes which are held in the hand, tilted one way and the other, then peered at closely. Viewing the St Francis Bridge postcard, one is struck by the dark and detailed plant stalks bending organically towards the river in the foreground and the extent to which they contrast with the carefully engineered and calculated regularity of the bridge's diagonally criss-crossing manufactured metal trusses that cut across

Figure 15.10 *Main Street, Magog, Que.*, c.1910

the middle ground. Beneath and beyond the bridge, tiny white buildings highlight the distant shoreline, offering evidence of settlement and community. This particular image gives every indication that the prevalent enthusiasm for photographed minutia and details of random objects were regularly carried forward into the picture postcard era, undoubtedly contributing to the postcard industry's unprecedented social mania enabled by new technology.

When examining the image presented on the postcard of *Main Street, Magog, Que.* (figure 15.10), the viewer becomes aware of that close relationship between space and traveller that Wolfgang Schivelbusch references. This particular picture contains several traditional methods of moving through space, other than by train, including by foot, horse-drawn open carriage, hard top and open top automobile, and bicycle. Other than by foot, they all represent a mechanized means of travelling through the landscape which offers each traveller a mediated relationship between themselves and the publicly travelled space. The streetscape is a vibrant and active ordinary space in which the business and pleasure of early twentieth century everyday life unfolds. The streetlights, hydro lines, and cement sidewalks that line Main Street in figure 15.10 are all modern products of the era's growing industries and evolving technologies that altered, to varying degrees, people's experience of circumventing the landscape. Some, however, found that the train, on

Figure 15.11 *Lansdowne Market. - Sherbrooke (Canada)*, c.1905

the other hand, had disrupted the close relationship between traveller and space, and one source described the experience as being on "a projectile, and traveling on it, as being shot through the landscape – thus losing control of one's senses" (Schivelbusch 1979, 58).

The postcard of Lansdowne Market (figure 15.11) represents a place located in Sherbrooke QC at the turn of the twentieth century that reflects several themes relating to postcards. Going to market during that era was very much a social experience and an event that brought people together, from varying distances, for the purpose of commodity exchange. The human figures pictured in this image are either on the move or gathered together closely in conversation; this marketplace was a commercial site that necessitated mobility and facilitated communication, in essence a cultural production similar to the postcard's. The market was where people and products circulated within a produced space; one that can be understood as a practical site or a destination created for consumption. Although the image does not represent a landscape of nature, it is very much a commercial and everyday landscape. The human traffic at the marketplace is generated in the context of a leisurely experience that is driven by a consumption-based behaviour directed towards commodities and the social experience itself. Symbols of technology are embedded in the image's materiality and represented in its iconography through its photographic reproduction of a place, the printed image and typeset, its architecture, the hydroelectric poles, and the railway tracks in the foreground. Lansdowne Market, like the postcard it is pictured on, is a commodified social space that mediates communication, production/consumption exchange, and mobility within a cultural landscape context.

INDUSTRIAL MODERNITY *and the* DARKER SIDE *of* LANDSCAPE

The Eastern Townships' landscape as pictured and conveyed in early twentieth century postcard images from the Asbestos region contrast significantly to the tourist-oriented themes and subjects, as they represent physically decimated sites that feature monumental dumps and heaps of material waste representing the remnants of industrial activity focused on the extraction of ore. As each pit grew deeper over the years, the ravaged landscape was increasingly disfigured by mountains of tailings. The miners' labour steadily transformed their local surroundings; each day they added 90 per cent of what they extracted from the ground to the piles (Keys to History, n.d.). By the late 1960s, more than 30 million tons of fibrous minerals had been extracted; it is estimated that by that time there had been approximately 270,000,000 tons of tailings excavated from the ground and dumped into mountainous deposits in the region.[1] The tailings, resulting from asbestos mining, also called mine dumps or refuse, represented a significant negative and material impact on the local landscape underscoring the extent of environmental waste generated. The traces of manual labour left in the form of steel tracks laid, wooden towers erected, and ravished open-faced dug and blasted mines featured in the sepia-toned postcard above entitled "Johnsons Asbestos Works" (figure 15.12), leave no doubt as to the role human activities had in transforming some vast natural spaces within the Eastern Townships into harsh industrial wastelands.

Examined together, the two postcards – one photographed by Gilchrist Studio (figure 15.13) and another produced by the Illustrated Post Card Company of Montreal (figure 15.14) – convey a very similar message; industrial mining practices approach and regard the natural environment as a labour-intensive resource well suited for commercial exploitation. The fibrous thread, or asbestos, that was scraped from the green coloured stones was incombustible, rendering it a highly valued resource to mine. Additionally, the growing railroad industry "was among the first to make extensive use of asbestos and asbestos-containing products. The

Figure 15.12 *Johnson's Asbestos Works, Thetford Mines, Que.*

Figure 15.13 *Kings Asbestos Co., Thetford Mines. P.Q.*, c.1907

Figure 15.14
Mines de Thetford Mines. La Descente dans les "Pits" à 800 pieds de profondeur du niveau de la Ville, c.1906

demand for the product increased as railroad engineers began to use asbestos materials to line refrigeration units, boxcars and cabooses; it was especially useful for insulating pipes, boilers and fireboxes in the steam locomotives of that era" (Habashi 2011). As railway tracks inched their way throughout the region during the late nineteenth and into the early twentieth century, the demand for asbestos rose steadily, as did the mountainous tailing piles extracted by the miners on a daily basis. Accordingly, "by 1943, the Jeffrey Mine encompassed 115 acres of land, and local workers were extracting 6,000 tons of rock and mineral daily. Despite these impressive figures, JM was unable to expand the mine quickly enough to meet industrial demand when the United States went to war in 1941" (Van Horssen 2016, 46). Van Horssen also noted how "over their history, the people of Asbestos developed a sense of ownership of the Jeffrey Mine and a balanced system of land use, which they never hesitated to defend. The local population also developed a sense of trust in the land, and it was difficult for them to accept that it was dangerous: after all, this was their home" (Van Horssen 2016, 184). What becomes

Figure 15.15 *Pont sur la rivière Magog, Wolfe Street Bridge and Dam, Sherbrooke, Que.*

evident looking at these postcards today is the extent to which the local working class and their collective manual labour contributed to physically reshaping the landscape we inhabit today.

The postcards presented in this study address their ability to operate communicatively through both image and text, even when the messages conveyed through the two mediums are unrelated. They reinforce how the material landscape of the Eastern Townships, as a subject of scholarly inquiry, moves well beyond its visual and aesthetic qualities into the much broader domain of everyday life. As the mining images compellingly illustrate, landscapes can represent much more than harmonious and soothing sites for recreation, leisure, pleasure, or escape. Not all landscapes are carefully designed, cultivated, nurtured, admired, prized, or prioritized for their exoticism, beauty, or mystery. Landscapes of labour were pictured in abundance, with just a very few examples included here which represent different areas and industries within the Eastern Townships such as mining (figures 15.12–15.14), dams for hydro-powered factories (figure 15.15), and rail-

Figure 15.16 *Great Northern Lumber Company's Mill, Scotstown, Que.*

ways and lumber companies (figure 15.16). The Thetford Mines postcards present landscapes that feature natural environments which have been dramatically transformed by industrial activity. These landscapes appear harsh and hazardous, while others represented on these postcards were clearly conceived to be used promotionally by competing companies in the region.

CONCLUSION

Postcards during the early twentieth century played a central role in promoting and showcasing the development and advancement of tourism, communication, and industrialization within the Eastern Townships, as they did elsewhere around the globe's prospering regions during the modern era. According to one scholar addressing the rise and interest in tourism initiatives during the late nineteenth century "industry and tourism were linked by a 'a common language and common pursuit of progressive economic growth.' This was not a localized phenomenon … the picturesque had transformed into 'a way of defining cities, nations, and regions'" (Little 2009, 739). It is evident that early postcards were not used solely by tourists and travellers, nor were they necessarily produced exclusively for, or indeed by, those growing industries. Postcards may thus be viewed as historical media which contribute to documenting the beginning of countries breaking down vast distances and or isolation, and people's passion to collect images and communicate via them in addition to text. The insight postcards have added to the advancement of visual studies is increasingly recognized amongst scholars from various disciplines. As objects that encapsulate modern interests on multiple levels, postcards popularized the collecting and trading of images and became highly distributed pop culture commodities. As David Prochaska and Jordana Mendelson have emphasized, "postcards form a constitutive part of the way in which the business of art, commerce, history, and identity is negotiated on a daily basis" (Prochaska and Mendelson 2010, xi).

The modern era's trend of stripping the natural environment of its resources and/or reconfiguring the landscape for profit spared very few regions around the globe. While many postcards featuring landscape representations of the Eastern Townships region clearly advanced a physically inviting if not idyllic environment attractive for rest, relaxation, and tourism, others reviewed in this chapter offer compelling evidence of an alternate modern reality, one that was motivated by commercially driven interests that present very different visions of the territory's landscape. Such visual images of the Townships have captured a critical period in history, presenting inconsistent and seemingly irreconcilable realities to the outside world – realities, that operated co-terminously in the first part of the twentieth century. Postcards brought landscape representations into mass and public circulation on an unprecedented scale which contributed to those representations' universal appeal. This study's exploration of postcards – visual cultural images that are communicative, set into circulation, and often re-circulated – which focused on moments within the landscape of the Eastern Townships, illustrates and reinforces their ability to capture, convey, and transmit multiple physical representations of the region, at times offering deeply contrasting messages, to the larger international community.

Note

1 Asbestos mining closed in 2012.

References

Bolter, Jay David, and Richard Grusin. 1999. *Remediation: Understanding New Media.* Massachusetts: MIT Press.

Carlson, Allen. 2009. *Nature & Landscape: An Introduction to Environmental Aesthetics.* New York: Columbia University Press.

Cosgrove, Dennis. 2006. "Modernity, Community and the Landscape Idea." *Journal of Material Culture* 11 (1–2): 49–66.

Davis, Allen F. 2002. *Postcards from Vermont: A Social History, 1905–1945*. Hanover, NH: University of New England Press.

Farfan, Matthew. n.d.a. "Steamers of Lake Memphramagog, Part 1." *Township Heritage Magazine*. http://townshipsheritage.com/article/steamers-lake-memphremagog-part-1. Accessed 15 June 2013.

– n.d.b. "Steamers of Lake Memphramagog, Part 2." *Township Heritage Magazine*. http://townshipsheritage.com/article/steamers-lake-memphremagog-part-2. Accessed 15 September 2022.

Fond Magella Bureau. n.d. Bibliothèque et archives nationales du Québec (BANQ), P547. http://pistard.banq.qc.ca/unite_chercheurs/description_fonds?p_anqsid=20140127131254149 6&p_centre=03Q&p_classe=P&p_fonds=547&p_numunide=1568.

Geary, Christraud M., and Virginia-Lee Webb, eds. 1998. *Delivering Views: Distant Cultures in Early Postcards*. Washington, DC: Smithsonian Institution Press.

Gillen, Julia. 2013. "Writing Edwardian Postcards." *Journal of Sociolinguistics* 17 (4): 488–521.

Groth, Paul, and Todd W. Bressi. 1997. *Understanding Ordinary Landscapes*. New Haven: Yale University Press.

Gudis, Catherine. 2004. *Buyways: Billboards, Automobiles, and the American Landscape*. New York: Routledge.

Habashi, F. 2011. "Historical Metallurgy: History of Asbestos." CIM Magazine. November. http://www.cim.org/en/Publications-and-Technical-Resources/Publications/CIM-Magazine/November-2011/history/historical-metallurgy.aspx. Accessed 25 May 2020.

Jackson, J.B. 1984. *Discovering the Vernacular Landscape*. New Haven: Yale University Press.

Jessup, Lynda. 2001. *Antimodernism and Artistic Experience: Policing the Boundaries of Modernity*. Toronto: University of Toronto Press.

– 2002. "The Group of Seven and the Tourist Landscape in Western Canada, or The More Things Change …" *Journal of Canadian Studies* 37, no. 1 (March): 144–79.

Kern, Stephen. 1983. *The Culture of Time and Space 1880–1918*. Cambridge, MA: Harvard University Press.

"Keys to History." n.d. "White Gold Pioneers: Asbestos Mining. McCord Museum." Online exhibit. Image 29 of 32. http://www.mccnew.mcgill.ca/scripts/viewobject.php?section=162&Lang=1&tourID=VQ_P3_11_EN&seqNumber=28&carrousel=true. Accessed 7 June 2016.

Konstantinos Andriotis, and Mišela Mavrič. 2013. "Postcard Mobility: Going Beyond Image and Text." *Annals of Tourism Research* 40 (January): 18–39.

Little, J.I. 2009. "Scenic Tourism on the Northeastern Borderland: Lake Memphremagog's Steamboat Excursions and Resort Hotels, 1850–1900." *Journal of Historical Geography* 35 (4): 716–42.

MacCannell, Dean. 1976. *The Tourist: A New Theory of the Leisure Class*. New York: Schocken.

McKay, M.J. 2011. *Picturing the Land: Narrating Territories in Canadian Landscape Art, 1500 to 1950*. Montreal and Kingston: McGill-Queen's University Press.

Mitchell, W.J.T., ed. 2002. *Landscape and Power*. 2nd ed. Chicago: University of Chicago Press.

Nelson, Bea Aldrich, and Barbara Kaiser Malloy. 2003. *Images of America around Lake Memphremagog*. Charleston: Arcadia Publishing.

O'Brian, John, and Peter White, eds. 2007. *Beyond Wilderness: The Group of Seven, Canadian Identity, and Contemporary Art*. Montreal and Kingston: McGill-Queen's University Press.

Prochaska, David, and Jordana Mendelson. 2010. *Postcards: Ephemeral Histories of Modernity*. University Park: Pennsylvania State University Press.

Reid, Dennis. 1979. *"Our own country Canada": being an account of the national aspirations of the principal landscape artists in Montreal and Toronto, 1860–1890*. Ottawa: National Gallery of Canada.

Sawchuk, Kim. 2001. "Modernity, Nostalgia, and the Standardization of Time." In *Antimodernism and Artistic Experience: Policing the Boundaries of Modernity*, edited by Lynda Lee Jessup, 155–64. Toronto: University of Toronto Press.

Schivelbusch, Wolfgang. 1979. *The Railway Journey: Trains and Travel in the 19th Century*. Oxford, UK: Basil Blackwell.

Stevens, Gerald. 1958. *Frederick Simpson Coburn, R.C.A.* Toronto: Ryerson Press.

Van Horssen, Jessica. 2016. *A Town Called Asbestos: Environmental Contamination, Health, and Resilience in a Resource Community*. Vancouver: UBC Press, 2016.

Woody, Howard. 1998. "International Postcards." In *Delivering Views: Distant Cultures in Early Postcards*, edited by C.M. Geary and V. Webb, 15–46. Washington, DC: Smithsonian Institution Press, 1998.

16

Dimensions of Community in the Novels of Louise Penny

J. Debbie Mann

LOUISE PENNY is the author of seventeen English-language detective novels to date in which the imaginary Eastern Townships village of Three Pines serves as the primary setting for murder investigations led by Armand Gamache of the Sûreté du Quebec. Beginning with *Still Life*, published in 2005, her novels portray linguistic and cultural cohabitation, both in bucolic Three Pines and in urban Quebec locations. According to Penny, the books, "while clearly crime fiction, are not primarily about death. They're about duality, about choices, about belonging and friendship, and community" (Penny, n.d.c).

In this chapter, I argue that the dualities of inside/outside or centre/border are key to the construction of Penny's fictional universe and that her exploration of the notion of community goes beyond the levels of plot and theme to become an embedded structural element of the Gamache novels. This approach reflects Penny's use of the literary/artistic device of *mise en abyme*, the placing of a small copy of an image inside a larger one. I hold that *mise en abyme* describes the way the centrality of community is communicated through the structure of Penny's novels.

Mise en abyme provides an insight into the triple role of the Eastern Townships as the location where Penny writes, the inspiration for her fictional community, and as the setting for her novels in which she depicts fictional acts of artistic creation that mirror her own. Just as the Eastern Townships is a borderland and a social contact zone for different languages and cultures, this chapter delineates the ways in which Louise Penny's oeuvre functions as a literary space in which "the border" is a place that unites rather than divides. A shifting and permeable interface that can exist on the material, abstract, or virtual levels, the geographical borderland position of the Eastern Townships, where Penny lives and writes, serves as a structuring principle of the narrative space of Three Pines, creating a *mise en abyme* fictional world composed of multiple communities. One of these communities, brought into being through the shared endeavour of artistic creation, is the source of poetic, pictorial, and musical works that provide a virtual space of communion both inside and outside the diegetic universe.

Thanks to the international success of Louise Penny's literary creation, the Gamache series novels featuring the fictional village of Three Pines, the Eastern Townships region has become known to a global readership. While the "local" audience (taken in the larger North American context of both Canada and the United States) of her work represents the greatest number of copies sold, Penny's popularity is well-established in Europe, with the United Kingdom, Germany, Sweden, the Czech Republic, and Italy rounding out the list of countries with the highest number of sales.[1] Readers also interact with the author and discover more about the Eastern Townships and her life there by means of Penny's official twenty-one-page website, www.louisepenny.com/louise.htm. Between January and April 2022, monthly traffic averaged 32,500 visits and the countries represented are indicative of the wide-ranging reach of Penny's writing.[2] The online community created around her Three Pines characters and their Eastern Townships setting extends far beyond the "local," with Canada coming in second in terms of traffic by country at 345,009 hits. The largest number of hits originating from outside of Canada came from the United States (994,781) followed by Great Britain with 56,458. The remainder, totalling 183,964, originated from locations not only in Europe (104,109) but also from as far away as Australia (32,034), New Zealand (6,298), Asia (Indonesia [1,478], India [2,696], China [269]), and the Middle East (Israel [3,625], Iran [408]).[3] Thus, thanks to the permeability of geographic and cultural boundaries in the print publishing and online environments, the Eastern Townships locale of Louise Penny's fiction both gains an identity beyond its local borders and serves as a centre of gravity, becoming a virtual meeting place for an international literary audience.

Reflecting the concepts of borderland, movement, and centre, this study takes as a starting point the relationship between the fictional Three Pines village and the Eastern Townships communities that inspired it. It begins by exploring how readers seeking the imaginary locale manage to find it. Tourists travel to the Eastern Townships to visit the real places that Louise Penny has portrayed in her books and to experience firsthand the local culture she describes. In the virtual online world, a global readership recreates on an emotional level the warmth and comfort of the relationships depicted among the Three Pines residents.

Next, the study examines the progression of the Three Pines crime fiction series. Over the course of Louise Penny's first seventeen novels, an outward movement is traceable in the widening scope of the geographic settings and social issues that are described. At the same time, attention turns inward as the personal and professional emotional trauma that Penny's protagonist Armand Gamache has experienced is increasingly foregrounded.

In the third section, the focus remains on the notion of inward–outward movement, but emphasis shifts to the blurring of borders between art and life for both characters and readers in search of a safe place in the fictional Eastern Townships. The circle motif, especially overlapping or concentric circles, prevalent in Penny's fiction, reflects the hybrid nature of the Gamache series books as both illustrations of the healing power of community and as works of crime fiction. In addition to functioning as a thematic element, the circles suggest the structural device *mise en abyme* that serves as a principle of analysis for delineating the space in which the creation of community takes place in Louise Penny's novels.

The last portion of the study focuses on *mise en abyme* and its application to the interpretation of visual arts and literary texts. Instances of reflection and embedding in Penny's works are examined in order to delineate the ways in which the author uses *mise en abyme* as a structuring device. Just as the imaginary Three Pines village is a reproduction of the real Eastern Townships where Penny lives and writes, the works of her visual and verbal artist characters, especially Clara and Ruth, mirror their own fictional world and serve as a means of revealing what lies at its centre. Following a discussion of the ways in which meaning is passed across narrative and visual frames, the study concludes with an exploration of the notion of the centre in Penny's fictional universe and proposes that rather than being an *abyme* or "abyss," it is a space in which the creation and expression of community are represented.

The semicircle of the adjoining bistro, bookstore, bakery, and general store, like an embrace, embodies the Three Pines community's values of kindness, safety, and mutual aid (Penny 2007, 2). First among these is the responsibility to help others, as Myrna explains to Gamache, when he inquires about why she and other villagers made the choice to hide and defend visitors who were in danger. In response to his question, the retired psychologist and bookstore owner replies, "Because my life and this village would lose all meaning, if we turned our backs" (Penny 2014, 146). Somewhat like the remote and cloistered monastery of Saint-Gilbert-Entre-les-Loups, which serves as the setting for Penny's eighth novel, *The Beautiful Mystery,* in the hidden community of Three Pines residents learn to accept each other and to work cooperatively for the welfare of all. Neighbours gather in the bistro located at the heart of Three Pines, "a place where kindness trumped cleverness," and find not only delicious food but especially conversation and companionship (Penny 2007, 2, 112). In this village, endowed with "a rare ability to heal," the pine trees had been a code for sanctuary for Loyalists crossing the Canadian border from the United States to flee a revolution in which they did not believe (Penny 2013a, 117).

Today, thanks to the international success of Louise Penny's Gamache series, which has sold more than thirteen million copies and been translated into thirty-one languages to date, visitors from all over the world make their way to the Eastern Townships.[4] The description of Three Pines as a place "[t]hat did, and did not, exist" (Penny 2016, 87) underlines the paradox that an imaginary village, hidden and remote even in Louise Penny's fictional world, has created a "closet tourism industry" that brings fans to the Eastern Townships to explore the real places mentioned in her novels (Pennington 2020, B11). Danielle Viau's "Three Pines Tours," inaugurated in 2018, have become very popular, especially with tourists from the United States who make up 96 per cent of her clientele. In 2019, participants came from twenty-six states as well as from overseas, including visitors from as far away as Australia, Belgium, England, and Peru "to discover the charming villages and beautiful sights of the Eastern Townships that have inspired Louise Penny to write such great novels for us" (Pennington 2020, B11; "Three Pines Tours," n.d.).[5]

For those making the journey on their own, a Three Pines inspirational map is available at www.easterntownships.org, providing a driving route which stretches from North Hatley as far west as Ange-Gardien.[6] Brome Lake Books in Knowlton, owned by Penny's close friends Danny McAuley and Lucy Hoblyn, provides printable PDF *Three Pines Inspirations* and *The World of Three Pines* maps on its website and is a source of "all things Louise Penny," including items as varied as Mélange Gamache blend coffee, mugs from which to drink it, T-shirts, pins, and videos, as well as Penny's novels.[7] Thus, although visitors do not actually find the fictional village, the Three Pines memorabilia they can take home with them, either to recall good memories or to give as souvenir gifts, continues to "sell" the Eastern Townships and brings "celebrity status" to the region thanks to its most famous resident (Pennington 2020, B11).

For readers of the Gamache series, a trip to the Eastern Townships provides the opportunity to experience Three Pines "come alive." Three Pines Tours invites participants to "unearth the canvas where Armand, Clara, Myrna, Ruth, Gabri, Olivier, and Reine-Marie come to life in the printed word" ("Three Pines Tours," n.d.). Penny's novels mirror real Eastern Townships locations, culture, and environment and thus, the "quiet, pretty, forgotten little village of Three Pines" is a location where one can "get across the border easily" (Penny 2017, 358), not only the geographic boundary between Canada and the United States but also, and especially, the shifting, porous border between art and life.

Penny has said in interviews that she is sometimes asked "Where is Three Pines?" and she explains, "Three Pines is my ideal village … every now and then I just feel the need for a safe place, whether it's a physical place or a place I go to in my head. When I was creating these books, I thought, 'That's what I want. I want a safe place, a place I will enjoy visiting' … I think of Three Pines as a state of mind … I think of Three Pines as the place I live in when I choose to be kind" (Penny 2013b). The picturesque hamlet with its close-knit harmonious society and decent, caring inhabitants is an ideal place that would naturally attract visitors and potential residents. The global reach of Penny's Gamache series can be explained by the fact that the Three Pines values and sense of community inscribed in the novels are universal in scope, transcending borders and differences of language and culture. Through her books, she offers readers "a companion for difficult times" and the same kind of emotional refuge that she found in writing while her husband waged a losing battle with dementia (Penny 2017, 389).[8] However, the comfort both readers and the author find in the Three Pines novels is not derived solely from a solitary reading or writing experience.

Although readers of the mystery series cannot actually find Three Pines in the Eastern Townships, they can partake in life there thanks to the virtual communities centred on the Three Pines mysteries that create a space for recreation and also for the re-creation of the types of relationships that make the village seem so idyllic.[9] Like her character Marie Valois in *A Great Reckoning* (2016), Louise Penny is a mapmaker, helping others find the Three Pines sense of community, even if they cannot visit the actual village, and drawing them to the Eastern Townships as they seek out the ambiance, culture, and landscapes found in the novels. Her oeuvre, like Valois's drawing, is "both a map and a work of art" showing "a small corner of Quebec … [j]ust villages and homes." It is meant to transport us there, just as Valois's map to Three Pines was meant to bring her sons home (38).

In *A Great Reckoning*, the four Sûreté Academy cadets with a connection to the murdered professor Serge Leduc and who Gamache takes to Three Pines in order to keep them safe are confronted with the paradox of the "invisible" village, not on any map, but which is for them a very real place. If it isn't on the map it doesn't exist, they are told, to which they respond, "But of course it does, we're staying there" (242). Louise Penny's readers, especially those who partake in the sense of community created in the online virtual bistro or through communication on discussion boards or blogs, have followed the emotional map to the "real" Three Pines, where linguistic, cultural, and geographical borders are porous. Just as in the village bistro, "[w]here secrets were exchanged and yearnings admitted … a place where both grandmother and granddaughter would feel at home" (Penny 2019, 276), they experience the shared core (Penny 2009, 203), what one cannot see when visiting the actual Eastern Townships settings but which, nevertheless, constitutes the essence of Louise Penny's art.

It must be noted, however, that as idyllic as Penny's fictional village is, murder finds its way there even if readers and admirers of the Gamache series cannot. According to the author, the books, "while clearly crime fiction, are not primarily about death" (Penny, n.d.c). They constitute a sort of "literary genre hybrid" in which ethical questions and the examination of how moral decisions are made are as significant as the criminal investigation carried out by Penny's detectives (Romano 2021). As the series progresses, it is possible to trace a change in focus, with the first five novels (*Still Life* [2005], *A Fatal Grace* [2006], *The Cruelest Month* [2007], *A Rule Against Murder* [2008], *The Brutal Telling* [2009]) dealing primarily with a local killing, while in the five that follow (*Bury Your Dead* [2010], *A Trick of the Light* [2011], *The Beautiful Mystery* [2012], *How the Light Gets In* [2013], *The Long Way Home* [2014]), long-standing issues of corruption in the Sûreté are foregrounded. In books eleven through seventeen (*The Nature of the Beast* [2015], *A Great Reckoning* [2016], *Glass Houses* [2017], *Kingdom of the Blind* [2018], *A Better Man* [2019], *All the Devils Are Here* [2020], *The Madness of Crowds* [2021]), the scope widens, with geopolitics, global societal problems such as illegal drugs and domestic violence, corporate crime, and even the effects of the COVID-19 pandemic becoming central to the plot lines.

A geographic turning point can be found in Penny's sixth novel, *Bury Your Dead*, in which the setting of the story expands from Three Pines, its surrounding villages, and Montreal to include Quebec City. This outward movement continues in *The Beautiful Mystery*, set in the remote, fictional Benedictine monastery of Saint-Gilbert-Entre-les-Loups, inspired by the real Abbaye St-Benoît-du-Lac, overlooking Lake Memphremagog. *The Long Way Home*, Penny's tenth novel, takes the reader to Baie-Saint-Paul in the Charlevoix region and beyond, to Anticosti Island in the region of Côte Nord, and as far as Tabaquen on the lower North Shore, near the boundary with Labrador. This novel differs from those that precede and follow it in two ways. Unlike Penny's other books, in *The Long Way*

Home, the murder does not occur until very near the end of the story. Instead, the book focuses on two searches. The first takes Gamache, his colleague and son-in-law Jean-Guy Beauvoir, Myrna, and Clara on a road trip from the Eastern Townships outward to distant regions of Quebec, looking for Clara's husband Peter. The second leads Gamache and Clara to undertake an inward, emotional journey in which they confront past trauma and seek a way forward. In addition, while an exploration of the process of artistic creation constitutes an important aspect of all of Penny's novels, in *The Long Way Home* the act of painting receives particular attention.

A thematic turning point, present in *How the Light Gets In* and further developed in *The Nature of the Beast* and the novels that follow, represents another kind of outward movement. In addition to the characteristic elements of Louise Penny's fiction – criminal investigation, the centrality of community, issues of morality, and reflections on the production and meaning of works of art – the scope of her later novels is enlarged to encompass a more marked opening to the outside world and a treatment of wider societal problems. In *How the Light Gets In*, the creation of a satellite link from Three Pines, where telecommunications options typically were limited to the telephone and dial-up connection to the Internet, coincides with the arrival in the village of violence linked to Gamache's struggle to rid the Sûreté of corruption. The local, double murder plot in *The Nature of the Beast* is linked to a discovery with startling geopolitical implications, the existence of a weapon of mass destruction, a supergun, pointing south at the United States and situated in the woods a half kilometre from Three Pines (Penny 2015, 67, 103, 110). Like this "mystery with global scope and consequences" (2), the three novels that follow, *A Great Reckoning*, *Glass Houses*, and *Kingdom of the Blind*, deal with an issue that is international in nature, the cross-border illicit drug trade, as well as the resulting drug-related criminal activity. In Penny's next three novels, *A Better Man*, *All the Devils Are Here*, and *The Madness of Crowds*, the focus shifts to other social issues that readers from around the world may recognize from newspaper headlines, including police brutality, domestic violence, corporate corruption, and debates over access to health care.

As the series progresses, this turn outward is accompanied by a movement in the opposite direction, an increasing emphasis on introspection in Armand Gamache's character. Over the course of the seventeen novels to date, the reader follows Gamache's career as chief of Homicide, head of the Sûreté academy, and chief superintendent of the Surêté and gains insights into his family roles as husband, father, and grandfather. Gamache's relationship with Jean-Guy Beauvoir, his second-in-command and, later, son-in-law, strengthens, dissolves, then deepens as the two men confront challenges stemming from perversions of justice and power struggles within the Sûreté. Gamache's childhood loss of his parents is explored more explicitly in later novels, with Stephen Horowitz and World War II refugee Zora, who served as his surrogate father and grandmother, becoming central to plot events in *All the Devils Are Here*. The books provide a detailed professional profile of Gamache both as a leader in the Sûreté and as a detective, highlighting his courage and integrity. Gamache's perseverance in challenging the dishonest and unethical regimes of Pierre Arnot and Sylvain Francoeur, his predecessors as chief superintendent, led to a profound change in the Sûreté, in which there was "a before and after ... 'Before' was a time of fear. Of distrust. Of enemies disguised as allies. It was a time of vast and rampant brutality. Of senior officers sanctioning beatings and even murders. Gamache had led the resistance, at huge personal risk, and had eventually agreed to become Chief Superintendent himself" (Penny 2019, 23). As an investigator, Gamache is described as an explorer, "[t]he one who went where others refused to go, or couldn't go. Or were too afraid to go. Into the wilderness. Gamache found the chasms, the caves, and the beasts that hid in them" (Penny 2009, 125).

However, even though Gamache's record of solving crimes using this approach is stellar, he is not immune from error. His mistake while leading a raid in an abandoned factory, resulting in the death of several of his agents, is first recounted in Penny's 2010 novel *Bury Your Dead*. The factory episode, relived repeatedly by Gamache in flashbacks, permeates more than half of the series and reappears in multiple contexts. Jean-Guy Beauvoir, like Gamache, is wounded both physically and psychologically by this experience, and for each of them, "[n]othing had been the same since" (Penny 2013a, 47). They both bear the burden of survival and suffer in different ways, Beauvoir falling victim to an addiction to prescription painkillers and Gamache haunted by the voice of agent Paul Morin whose life he had failed to save.

In addition to providing insights into his character and his conscience, Gamache's recurring memories of the disastrous Sûreté operation create a strong emotional connection with the reader. Especially in the fragments of recalled dialogue, interspersed in *Bury Your Dead*, the reader is brought into Gamache's head and into his heart as he struggles with the loss of the young man he had vowed to protect. The threshold between the spatiotemporal world of the Quebec City murder that Gamache is investigating and that of the isolated factory where Morin was killed is very porous. Fragments of conversations and images of violence constantly resurface in Gamache's thoughts and appear in the narrative of *Bury Your Dead* and in subsequent novels in which Gamache is reliving this past experience almost as much as he is inhabiting the present moment. His assurance to Morin, "Don't worry, son. It will be all right," and Morin's response, "Yes sir, I believe you," is a leitmotif that brings to the forefront Gamache's sense of guilt (Penny 2010, 235). Recurring and unmediated excerpts of Morin's conversations with Gamache such as "And then at Christmas, we visit both Suzanne's family and my own. We go to hers for *réveillon* and mine for Mass on Christmas morning" and "My family wanted me to become a priest, you know … I never seriously considered it … I'd fallen in love with Suzanne when she was six and I was seven. I figured that was God's plan" (37, 129–30) take the reader directly into Gamache's mind, through "the door he kept closed, deep in his memory" (Penny 2017, 90), where it is possible to identify with him on an emotional level that transcends language, culture, and even analytical thought.

The permeability of borders – narrative, geographic, and especially of that between art and life – is a central motif in Louise Penny's oeuvre. The very founding of the village of Three Pines by United Empire Loyalists crossing the boundary separating the United States and Canada attests to the physical fact that "[t]he border was porous. Always had been" (Penny 2017, 312). The "[t]housands of miles of forest," full of "holes that had never been plugged" (261, 357) that allow drugs and money to flow back and forth between the two countries become the setting, in *Glass Houses*, for Gamache's pursuit of cartel kingpins who have chosen Three Pines as their crossing point. Called upon to explain the circumstances under which he killed one of the drug lords, he admits, "It's difficult to tell in the forest exactly where the border is … But I believe I crossed the line, yes" (366). Porous or shifting artistic borders allow other characters to "cross the line" as well, mirroring the experience of Louise Penny and her readers searching for solace and a "safe place" and finding it in fictional Three Pines.

For Clara, the painter, and Olivier, the B&B owner, mentally crossing the border into an imaginary world – a Christmas display window for Clara (Penny 2006, 10, 21) and for Olivier, the fairy tale books he read as a child (42) – brings comfort and security. Both find in Three Pines the very place to which they had longed to escape when the world was harsh. Conversely, for art critic Dominica Oddly visiting the village in *A Better Man*, the border is crossed in the opposite direction as she is almost able to see "the stone and brick and clapboard homes, the church on the hill and forest behind, turning into a watercolor before her eyes" (Penny 2019, 275). In the fictional universe, the permeable border between life and art is also revealed in the plot of *The Brutal Telling*, and, to a lesser extent, that of *Bury Your Dead*, which revolve around carvings and a tale told by Olivier to the Hermit who lives in a cabin in the woods near Three Pines. In a play of mirrors, the tale Olivier recounts to the Hermit reflects a betrayal of trust of which they are both guilty. Likewise, in the carvings the Hermit makes, inspired by Olivier's story, one finds a visual reproduction of Olivier's words (Penny 2009, 337, 347, 353).

The blurring of the boundaries between art and life extends even to those who learn only thirdhand of Olivier's narration and the Hermit's role as a listener. When other characters see the fourth carving in the series the Hermit created to illustrate Olivier's story, they "feel like part of the work" (323). As a writer, Louise Penny seeks to offer a similar experience to her readers. During her 1 December 2018 visit to St Louis, Missouri, Penny stated that in her novels she wants "the fourth wall to come down," using the stage metaphor to refer to her intent that while reading, "you're not just watching, you're there, walking, eating, etc." (Penny 2018a). Foregrounding the existence of the real Eastern Townships communities that inspire the depiction of Three Pines, in the Barnes and Noble exclusive edition of *Kingdom of the Blind*, a nine-page section focuses on the villages of Sutton and Knowlton, including essays by the co-owners of the businesses that inspire Myrna's bookstore and Sarah's Boulangerie, thus bringing down the wall that separates the fictional universe from the extra-fictional one (Penny 2018b). The reader is introduced to the smells, sounds, sights, and tastes of Sutton's La Rumeur Affamée bakery and to the spirit of solidarity that led thirty-five residents of Knowlton, including Louise Penny, to carry boxes and shelves to help the owners of Brome Lake Books move their shop to a different building. According to co-owner Danny McAuley, "It was a very Three Pines day" ("The Real Places," n.d.).

This porosity of the borders between the real communities of Sutton and Knowlton and the no-less-real sense of community in Penny's novels suggests that in both the fictional and the extra-fictional settings, while challenges and even horror exist, they can be faced more effectively as a group. When the harsh reality of the "outside" world encroaches for the Three Pines characters beginning in *The Brutal Telling* and continuing through *Kingdom of the Blind*, revealing the problems of drugs, gangs, and homelessness which exist as close by as Montreal, the supportive reality of community provides a counterbalance. Whether the community exists online, is located in the Eastern Townships villages of Knowlton and Sutton, or is depicted in the fictional setting of Three Pines, when the walls come down, an intimate and safe space emerges and provides a refuge.

In the Three Pines universe, the shape of that space is a series of concentric circles. As well as being a thematic element suggesting community, this "world within a world" motif can be explored through the lens of the literary/artistic device of *mise en abyme*. Unlike juxtaposition, in which boundaries may exist to impede or restrict movement across lines of demarcation, the borders between "inside" and "outside" in Louise Penny's work are permeable and permit passages in both directions. In a geographic sense, the location of the village of Three Pines within the real-world setting of the Eastern Townships provides a first example of the "theme of the circular" (Dällenbach 1989, 135).[10] In the fictional world, within the border of "the forest ringing the village" (Penny 2017, 345), one finds "the stone and clapboard and brick cottages, radiating in circles from the village green" (Penny 2014, 121). Inside "the small circle of light that was Three Pines" (Penny 2013a, 111), other circular motifs repeat the larger pattern, creating a sort of "mirror-imagery" (Dällenbach 1989, 121).[11]

The contexts in which these smaller circles are found reflect the hybrid nature of Louise Penny's novels as both illustrations of the comforting and healing power of community and works of crime fiction. Among the circles that overlap thematically and echo each other in the imaginary hamlet are those formed by a yellow ribbon of crime scene tape (Penny 2008, 101), the incident room conference table that recalls the shape of village itself (Penny 2009, 45) and, indicative not of crime but of mutual aid and the exorcism of destructive emotions, the smudging ritual and prayer stick ceremonies conducted by the women of the village after the loss of life due to murder (Penny 2011, 112–13). The clearest depiction of the sense of community that defines Three Pines is to be found in the wooden arms of the Adirondack chairs belonging to Armand Gamache and his wife Reine-Marie, passed down from a recently deceased resident of the village, "stained with rings from years, decades, of drinks taken in the quiet garden. Emilie's rings had been added to, and overlaid, by the Gamache's morning mugs and afternoon *apéritifs*. Peaceful lives intertwined" (Penny 2014, 16).

When the circles become overlapping and, especially, concentric, like those on the Adirondack chairs, rather than being simply a descriptive or thematic element, they suggest the structural device *mise en abyme*, which serves as a basis for further exploration of the dimensions of community in Louise Penny's Gamache series. The analysis of how this concept functions as a structuring element leads to a consideration of what lies at the centre, specifically, the nature of the *abyme* or abyss. It also prompts an examination of how *mise en abyme* constitutes a principle of interpretation which is key to understanding the space in which the creation of community takes place in Penny's novels.[12]

Louise Penny's oeuvre reveals a complex, multi-levelled composition that also includes the extradiegetic (i.e., outside the narrative) world of the Eastern Townships in which the author lives and that serves as her inspiration. Writing in that real world, Penny creates, at the diegetic, or story level, the world of Three

Pines, a reflection of the Eastern Townships. Similarly, in the fictional Three Pines world, artists, especially Clara, create works, at the metadiegetic or embedded representation level, mirroring the fictional world in which they themselves exist (see Genette 1972, 238). Thus, the *mise en abyme* functions on two levels and we find in Penny's novels an expression of the "mirror of a mirror" effect described by literary scholar Lucien Dällenbach (1989, 59).[13]

Perhaps the best example of the re-creation of diegetic (story-level) Three Pines on the metadiegetic level is to be found in Clara's portraits of Three Pines residents displayed in the bistro after the cancellation of her solo show in Montreal due to the violent events depicted near the end of *Glass Houses*. The exhibition of the portraits in that location serves as one way to exorcise the horror of the gun battle and resulting injuries and physical damage that had taken place in the bistro by recreating the sense of community that that place had always represented for the village. However, the visual depiction of Three Pines residents in a place where those residents regularly gather is only the first level of *mise en abyme* within the story world. In these artistic works within the story world – visual representations of the main characters who live in that world - there is a further reflection within each portrait of another Three Pines inhabitant or frequent visitor, for "in each of their eyes, a loved one was perfectly reflected" (Penny 2017, 385). Therefore, the play of mirrors is double, thanks to the two artistic miniatures, leading inward from the story (diegetic) level to the metadiegetic (portrait) and meta-metadiegetic (portrait within a portrait) levels: both reflect the world of Three Pines back into that same world.

Thanks to Clara's talent for capturing the hidden essence of her subjects, what is invisible on the surface is revealed in her paintings. As a portraitist, "Clara Morrow didn't actually paint faces" but rather, "she painted emotions, feelings, hidden, disguised, locked and guarded behind a pleasant façade" (Penny 2014, 29). An artist who "painted people's souls" (Penny 2009, 64), "a sort of alchemist" who "could render emotions, even memories, into paint" (Penny 2017, 176), she has the ability to see "things visible and those not" (Penny 2007, 64). If Clara succeeds in capturing intimacy in her portrait of the triad of elderly village women depicted in *The Three Graces*, the poet Ruth, on the other hand, produces works that reflect, in miniature, the pain she and others go to great lengths to conceal. As visual and verbal artists, they both "try to make the invisible visible" (Dällenbach 1989, 75)[14] or, in the mirror-imagery terms of French novelist/essayist Michel Butor, to create works which, as Dällenbach says, make it possible "to focus on, and thus to grasp, the invisible" (121).[15] Like the local artists, Penny's detective Armand Gamache also seeks to find hidden feelings. "Just as Clara put together the elements of a painting, as Ruth the elements of a poem, Gamache pieced together the elements of a case. And like a painting or a poem, at the heart of his cases there was a strong emotion" (Penny 2014, 111). Like the reflexive properties of *mise en abyme* that reproduce certain aspects of the text or visual image that help to shed light on its underlying meaning, the artistic creations produced by Clara and Ruth and the investigative work carried out by Gamache are revelatory in nature.

The hidden emotions collected by Gamache in the course of his police work and those which are made visible by Clara and Ruth through their art find an echo in the story of the corruption and concealed rancour warping the highest levels of the Sûreté. Embedded within the "public mystery" of the murder investigations undertaken by Gamache and his team is the search for the source of the internal criminal activity that has been responsible for the deaths of many innocent Quebecers. Following the delineation proposed by German theorist Werner Wolf, who uses the terminology *mise en cadre* to designate the framing level while *mise en abyme* refers to the embedded element (2010, 64–5), it is possible to see in the Gamache novels a series of inset variations on the murder investigations that form the main plot lines of the books. Like the framing murder investigations, the "inside" Sûreté mysteries raise questions about whom it is possible to trust and show the violent result of years of hidden anger, ambition, and jealousy. The undercover, internal inquiry enriches the series by providing insights into how Gamache handles moral issues and ethical choices as well as showing him navigating among colleagues who are current or former friends or allies, such as Isabelle Lacoste, Jean-Guy Beauvoir, or Michel Brébeuf, and those who reveal themselves as enemies, such as Sylvain Francoeur and Pierre Arnot.

The Arnot case, involving brutality by Sûreté agents against young Cree men and women as well as greed and dishonesty on the part of Arnot himself, the former head of the organization, is, for a long time, at the centre of the private mystery Gamache seeks to solve. However, after Arnot's guilt has been established and he has been brought to justice, Gamache realizes that this is not the end of his personal mission to bring back integrity and professionalism to the Sûreté. Gamache discovers that inside the Arnot case there is another, even better-hidden source of rot, leading not just to Francoeur, the current leader, but all the way up to the premier of Quebec. Raising questions about unwarranted use of lethal force and problems in the justice system with which many readers are familiar based on their local headlines and news reports of police brutality, the "backstory" insets represent an example of larger global issues which are telescoped, by *mise en abyme*, into concentric circles inside a story framework that is anchored in Quebec and often situated in an Eastern Townships setting.

Similarly, but in the opposite sense, it is possible to identify examples of embedding of smaller elements carrying revelatory significance within a larger Three Pines/Eastern Townships frame. One of these is to be found in *Still Life*, Penny's first novel, in which Jane Neal, the murder victim, paints a stylized version of a scene from the closing parade of the county fair. In her *Fair Day* canvas, Jane had not only provided her own miniaturized vision of the members of her extended community but had also incorporated a detail that led to the identification of her killer. The Three Pines inhabitants, as well as investigators Gamache and Beauvoir, join forces, working from both sides of the border between art (the clue in Jane's representation) and life (the Three Pines story world) to bring the murderer to justice.

Later in the Gamache series, in *The Nature of the Beast*, an embedded, smaller-scale element of artistic expression, this time a play, also constitutes a personal interpretation of the Three Pines world. As in the previous example, there is a telescoping effect by which elements of the outer frame, the Three Pines diegetic or story world, are reproduced in the metadiegetic theatrical representation that calls attention to an essential point. In this case, that significant aspect is the underlying need that led all of the residents who adopted Three Pines as their home to settle there. The play *She Sat Down and Wept*, at the centre of the resolution of all three plot lines (the mystery of the supergun located just outside Three Pines, the killing of the village child Laurent, and the haunting, evil presence of mass murderer John Fleming), also provides an insight into the residents of the larger diegetic world. They are depicted *en abyme*, in the metadiegetic play, as characters in search of a lifeboat, a second chance. As villagers Myrna, Reine-Marie, Ruth, Clara, and Gabri read the play aloud in order to help Gamache and Beauvoir in their investigation, the rendering they provide brings into focus their own experience of having recognized their second chance in moving to Three Pines and is a reminder of the very permeable border between art and life in Penny's metafictional, fictional, and extra-fictional universes.

Ruth, who as a poet "ground up good people and turned them into poetry" (Penny 2008, 142), is herself depicted as an embittered Mary, the mother of Jesus, in Clara's portrait entitled *Still Life* (Penny 2011, 26). Like the village women who served as the model for *The Three Graces* canvas, she is both a character in the diegetic Three Pines world and a painting, and when she attends Clara's solo exhibition at the Montreal Musée d'Art Contemporain, where the work is displayed, it is "as though the painting had come alive" (27). The presence of the "real" Ruth in proximity to Clara's artistic rendering (Penny 2018b, 235, 379) suggests transposition or the crossing of boundaries that exist in *mise en abyme*, since normally, the levels of framing or reflection depict separate worlds, so distinct that the characters cannot intervene in what is taking place on the other side of the frame or narrative border. A glimmer of hope barely discernable in her "thunderous" expression (Penny 2011, 314), Clara's Mary looks directly out at those who inhabit the Three Pines world in which the cantankerous and surly poet Ruth lives. In her turn, Ruth keeps the hope of her muse and beloved duck Rosa's return buried deep within her heart, detectable and inspirational only to those who are able to see beyond her irascible exterior.

The passing of meaning across the frame, a vacillation between "within and without" (Dällenbach 1989, 37)[16] and the resulting blurring of the art–life border, can be seen most clearly in the references to the St Thomas Church stained-glass window that recur throughout the Gamache series. The young soldiers depicted there are all children of Three Pines killed on a World War I battlefield. One of them is carrying a map on which the location of the village is shown. As revealed in *A Great Reckoning*, it is an orienteering map made by his mother and given to him so that he might be able to find his way home. The three pine trees pictured on the map within the window frame, in the soldier's metadiegetic world, are a miniature version of those located near the church, on the village green. As the residents of Three Pines gather to celebrate the christening of Armand and Reine-Marie Gamache's grandson, Honoré Beauvoir, Gamache realizes that the soldier is not, as everyone had always assumed, pointing at something in his own world, on the battlefield. Instead, observes Gamache, "He's not pointing into his world. He's pointing into ours" (Penny 2016, 378). The direction the young soldier is indicating is the rose window of the church, showing the four cardinal points, like a compass. His action depicted in the stained-glass window brings about change in the diegetic universe. His metadiegetic intervention, the directional indication he provides, holds the key to finding the grave of his mother Marie Valois, who worked as a mapmaker under the pseudonym Antony Turcotte.

This reaching out of the frame, from one world into another, coincides with poetics scholar Viveca Füredy's assertion that textual boundaries are not impenetrable (1989, 758). Marie-Laure Ryan has further developed one of Füredy's concepts of boundary transgression, calling it "rhetorical metalepsis," a concept explained by Marcus Snow as opening "a small window that allows a quick glance across levels" and as "a process of carrying over of meaning from one place to another" (Snow 2016, 72, 13). However, if the *mise en abyme* device allows the transfer of meaning across framing boundaries and between levels, an essential question remaining to be explored concerns if and how that meaning is expressed in the centre, the *abyme* toward which the reduplications converge. In Louise Penny's novels, the concept of "centre" can be applied to Three Pines which is depicted as a point of convergence, since "the four roads radiating off the village green formed a sort of sundial ... the roads were a compass. Each one corresponding exactly to north, south, east, and west. With Three Pines in the center" (Penny 2021, 343). Within the village, "[t]he homes formed a circle, and in its center was the village green. And in the center of that were the pine trees that soared over the community" (Penny 2014, 8). Emblematic of the village, the trees represent the companionship, communication, and creativity that are the basis of the sense of community in Three Pines.

For the residents, the village is a space in which connections can flourish, especially for the artists Clara and Ruth who do not paint and write in isolation but rather are dependent on others for the creation of their works. Three Pines neighbours are the object of Ruth's observations, serving as inspiration for her poems, just as for Clara, they are the subjects that she paints. They represent, as well, a source of support, encouragement, and constructive commentary as the works are being created. In the same way, Louise Penny does not create in solitude, for the Eastern Townships where she lives also provide inspiration and emotional support. There, on the extradiegetic level, she "found the sense of community she had been looking for" (Pennington 2020). As an artist, Penny has said that writing about Three Pines was her refuge because she found comfort in the fictional diegetic world she had created (Groen 2021). Thus, for Penny as for her characters, artistic creation itself is both a result and an embodiment of community.

The works that the Three Pines artists, especially Clara, produce are at the "centre," in terms of *mise en abyme*, of the Three Pines story world, and, by extension, of the surrounding extradiegetic universe of the Eastern Townships setting that serves as Penny's inspiration. The essential question that remains is the exploration of what lies at the centre of those embedded metadiegetic representations which mirror or transpose elements of the larger frame(s). In the visual arts, the internal duplication of images creates receding repetitions which eventually converge into a blind spot. However, in Louise Penny's fiction, *mise en abyme* functions as the literary and artistic motif that reveals the space, not an abyss signifying absence but rather an opening allowing connection, where the creation of community takes place. According to Ruth and Clara in *The Long Way Home*, at the centre of the centre (i.e., the artistic work) one finds emotion (Penny 2014, 109). When Gamache inquires, "Does a painting begin with a lump in the throat? A sense of wrong? A homesickness, a lovesickness?" Ruth responds, "The best ones do, yes. We express ourselves differently. Some choose words, some notes, some paint, but it all comes from the same place" (152–3). Later in the novel she explains, "Fear lives in the head. And courage lives in the heart. The job is to get from one to the other," which prompts Gamache to conclude, "And between the two is the lump in the throat" (277). It is in that "between" space, on the deepest metadiegetic level, where the essence of Three Pines exists.

When Clara, the diegetic version of the author herself, paints, she tries "to leave a little space, a kind of crack" (Penny 2006, 174). Likewise, for the monks of *The Beautiful Mystery* whose art is the Gregorian chant, the silences are equally as important as the notes. There is space between the words and space between the notes (Penny 2012, 117). When their musical creation takes shape, "[t]he holes became whole. The damage repaired" (280). Just as boundaries can serve to create a new space between two elements, in Louise Penny's fictional universe, it is in the centre, a *creux* or "hollow," that community is represented and defined. This sense of community is found in a virtual space of communion which brings together those from inside and outside the diegetic universe. Like a borderland, it functions as a meeting place on the level of emotions and of healing. For the characters that find the village on the story level as well as the readers who arrive there by way of Louise Penny's novels, the universality of the emotions that lie at the heart of the *mise en abyme* in Penny's fictional world allows that space, like Three Pines, to function as a place not to "hide … from the woes of the world" but rather as one that can "help heal the wounds" (Penny 2015, 6). Far from being an abyss of absence, it is a place of "compearance," in philosopher Jean-Luc Nancy's terminology. Nancy explains, "It [compearance] consists in the appearance of the *between*," that is "as you *and* I" (between us), a formula in which the *and* does not imply juxtaposition but exposition, i.e., "you shares me." According to Nancy, in juxtaposition we are almost forced to see the lack of connection whereas exposition gives the sense of opening to an outside and thus implies a kind of joining (1991, 29).[17]

In Penny's seventeenth novel, *The Madness of Crowds* (2021), a visitor to Three Pines, Haniya Daoud, observes the villagers, friends, and families in the bistro and notes, "There were small cracks between them. She knew that because she could see the light" (273). Daoud herself provides the subject for Clara's most recent canvas, a departure from her usual style. On the surface, a landscape, but also an orienteering map, and for those who "stopped trying to see it with their eyes," a portrait of Daoud "whose face was scored. But not scarred. The deep lines were the route home" (431). The hollows are wounds, but in them, Clara shows that there is space for healing and for finding both a way in and a way out. As torture survivor Daoud is en route back to her homeland in Sudan, she carries with her the gift of Three Pines – a photo accompanied by a message of hope signed by the inhabitants with whom the bond of shared emotion had allowed her to find a sense of belonging.

Likewise, in Louise Penny's artistic production, the concentric circles that surround a centre in which the open space signifies a meeting place rather than an abyss both radiate out and pull in. Her fictional world, with its permeable borders between inside and outside and the movement that takes place across those lines of demarcation mirrors the position of the Eastern Townships, where Penny herself has found a sense of belonging, as a centre, a bridge, and, especially, a site of creativity and connections.

Notes

1 Information conveyed by Lise Desrosiers (Louise Penny's assistant), e-mail message to author, 11 May 2022.

2 The number of visits per month is as follows: January 2022, 40,267; February 2022, 32,219; March 2022, 30,300; April 2022, 27,193. Ibid.

3 The European countries represented (in descending order of number of hits) are Germany (17,756), France (17,128), Ireland (13,988), Italy (10,143), Switzerland (8,030), Sweden (7,421), Russian Federation (6,002), the Netherlands (5,087), Spain (4,882), Denmark (3,741), Romania (3,369), Finland (3,042), Poland (1,794), and Ukraine (1,726). The total number of hits indicated in the text also includes 29,242 for locations listed in the category of "Others" and 3,805 for which the place of origin could not be determined. Ibid.

4 Ibid.

5 The tour includes stops at locations such as the Benedictine monastery of St-Benoît-du-Lac and the Manoir Hovey, which have served as inspiration for the settings of Penny's novels *The Beautiful Mystery* and *A Rule against Murder*, as well as visits to Penny's adopted village of Knowlton and to the town of Sutton, with a stop at La Rumeur Affamée bakery, which readers of her novels, such as *The Cruelest Month*, know as Sarah's Boulangerie. Travac Tours, based in Ottawa, also offers an Eastern Townships three-day itinerary, entitled "On the Trail of Louise Penny," http://www.travactours.com/quebec-on-the-trail-of-louise-penny/#itinerary.

6 Patricia Prijatel, a Louise Penny fan who visited the Eastern Townships with her husband in late May 2019, found that the Knowlton B&B where they had booked accommodations provided them a Louise Penny map of the area even before they were fully checked in because according to one of the owners, "most of our visitors come because of her" (Prijatel 2019).

7 See https://www.bromelakebooks.ca/contact.

8 In the words of Azita Rassi, a literary translator based in Malaysia and Louise Penny enthusiast, "Whenever there is something I have been grieving or feel anxious for, I take a trip to Three Pines and the warmth of their love and friendship offers haven … Reading the books is therapeutic" (Groen 2021).

9 On her Facebook page (Penny, n.d.a), which had 136,000 followers in May 2022, Louise Penny regularly posts glimpses of her daily life and maintains a line of communication with her readers. Even more personal in nature and broader in scope is Penny's monthly newsletter (Penny, n.d.b) to which fans of the Gamache series can subscribe. Through the newsletter, which had 68,000 subscribers as of May 2022, readers can follow the stages

of creation of the novel Penny is currently writing, rejoice in the success of her latest work, receive her expressions of gratitude, and, especially, share in the joys and sorrows of the author's personal journey. Fans of Three Pines who wish to gather in the village bistro can do so, online ("The Bistro" 2022), in order to share their own stories as well as to discuss the story lines and character development of the village inhabitants. In this virtual meeting place, the close-knit sense of community that makes Three Pines such an enticing locale is created not just among inhabitants of the same tiny village, but among readers from different countries and cultures. The support and understanding that the fictional characters show for each other is mirrored in the exchanges that take place in the virtual bistro, which represent for the participants a real, if not real-world, source of companionship and acceptance. In the fictional Three Pines bistro, bonds are created not only through conversation but also through food. It is inevitable, therefore, that food would be a way to bring together the virtual community of Penny's readers. Two of them started a blog entitled *The Night Is a Strawberry, Cooking Our Way to Three Pines* (n.d.) and they explain, "Reading may seem like a solitary pleasure, but we do not believe it is so. As we read, we intimately interact with writers, the worlds they create, and our own inner selves as well as the real world that surrounds us." As the bloggers work through the books, recreating the meals that are described, they use the culinary experience as a way to reflect on the novels, to communicate their thoughts with other readers, and to share recipes that transport them to Three Pines. In anticipation of the publication of *The Nature of the Beast* in August 2015, the publisher, Minotaur Books, created "The Nature of the Feast" (n.d.), a bi-weekly "reveal" of a recipe from one of the previous books accompanied by a cookbook-quality photo and a space for discussion of the dish and, especially, the novel from which it comes. Readers from as far away as Australia compare and exchange recipes, refer to their family traditions, and share personal stories, just as the characters do in Three Pines. As a lead-up to the publication of Penny's 2017 novel *Glass Houses*, every two weeks, Minotaur opened a discussion forum around a creative work of cultural significance from each of the Inspector Gamache novels ("The Real Places," n.d.). The publisher highlighted in a virtual visit format some of the real places, including locations in Sutton, Williamsburg, and Knowlton, that inspire the author as she produces the Inspector Gamache novels. Including essays, photos, and a discussion forum, "The Real Places" archive provides a chance to discover Eastern Townships sites that are key to the series or to relate personal experiences and memories linked to these locales.

10 In the original French, "thématisation du circulaire" (ibid., 173).

11 In the original French, "métaphore spéculaire" (ibid., 156).

12 The term *mise en abyme* was first coined by Claude-Édmonde Magny in 1950, following on André Gide's 1893 use of heraldic terminology in his diary referring to self-reflexive repetition in literature and in the visual arts. After Magny, other French critics in the 1970s both nuanced and extended the scope of the discussion. In "Un Héritage d'André Gide," Bruce Morrissette defined the aim of *mise en abyme* as an inner play of mirrors, heightening and reinforcing the theme by multiplying its perspectives (1971, 131). In *Le Nouveau Roman*, Jean Ricardou observed that through repetition each *mise en abyme* serves to multiply that which it imitates, or, if one prefers, underlines it by restating it (1973, 50).

The most extensive exploration of *mise en abyme* is Lucien Dällenbach's 1977 study *Le récit spéculaire: essai sur la mise en abyme*, translated by Jeremy Whiteley and Emma

Hughes as *The Mirror in the Text* (1989). Dällenbach gives particular attention to the action of reflection, defining the term *mise en abyme* as "any aspect enclosed within a work that shows a similarity with the work that contains it" (1989, 8; in the original French, "est mise en abyme toute enclave entretenant une relation de similitude avec l'œuvre qui la contient"; 1977, 18). Dällenbach focuses on the mirror metaphor and of the four observations that underlie his definition, two are particularly useful for the examination of Louise Penny's novels. According to Dällenbach, "the *mise en abyme*, as a means by which the work turns back on itself, appears to be a kind of reflexion" and "its essential property is that it brings out the meaning and form of the work" (1989, 8; in the original French, "Organe de retour de l'œuvre sur elle-même, la mise en abyme apparaît comme une modalité de la réflexion" and "Sa propriété essentielle consiste à faire saillir l'intelligibilité et la structure formelle de l'œuvre"; 1977, 16). Dällenbach's concept of reflection and the applicability of this interpretation of *mise en abyme* to both literature and visual arts makes it an especially pertinent critical framework for analyzing Penny's fiction in which painting plays a central role. In addition, the notion of embedding in a frame, as expressed by Werner Wolf (2010) and that of transposition or the carrying over across boundaries, as theorized by Viveca Füredy (1989), will also provide valuable insights into the functioning of *mise en abyme* in the Gamache series.

Taken in a literary sense, according to Brian McHale, a North American contributor to *mise en abyme* scholarship, "[*m*]*ise-en-abyme* involves the paradoxical reproduction … within the fictional world of the fictional world itself" (1992, 155). The examples taken from Louise Penny's oeuvre correspond to McHale's three criteria of *mise en abyme* as (1) a nested or embedded representation which is placed at a narrative level lower than that of the primary diegetic narrative world, (2) which has a resemblance to some element at the level of the primary diegetic world, and (3) reproduces or duplicates the primary representation as a whole (McHale 1987, 124).

13 In the original French, "ce miroir d'un miroir" (Dällenbach 1977, 81).

14 In the original French, "rendre l'invisible visible" (ibid., 100).

15 In the original French, "métaphore spéculaire" and "à donner un point de vue sur l'invisible" (ibid., 156).

16 In the original French, "entre son dedans et son dehors" (ibid., 53).

17 In the original French, "Elle consiste dans la parution de l'*entre* comme tel: toi *et* moi (l'entre nous), formule dans laquelle le *et* n'a pas valeur de juxtaposition, mais d'exposition … *toi partage moi*" (Nancy 2004, 74).

References

"The Bistro." 2022. Louise Penny's Inspector Gamache Series. Gamache Series Open Discussion, Minotaur Books. https://www.gamacheseries.com/the-bistro/. Accessed 29 May 2023.

Brome Lake Books. n.d. https://www.bromelakebooks.ca/contact. Accessed 29 May 2023.

Dällenbach, Lucien. 1977. *Le récit spéculaire: essai sur la mise en abyme*. Paris: Éditions du Seuil.

– 1989. *The Mirror in the Text*. Translated by Jeremy Whiteley with Emma Hughes. Chicago: University of Chicago Press.

Füredy, Viveca. 1989. "A Structural Model of Phenomena with Embedding in Literature and Other Arts." *Poetics Today* 10 (4): 745–69.
Genette, Gérard. 1972. *Figures III*. Paris: Éditions du Seuil.
Groen, Danielle. 2021. "Why Readers Love Quebec Crime Writer Louise Penny." *Chatelaine*, 24 August. https://www.chatelaine.com/living/louise-penny-books/. Accessed 29 May 2023.
McHale, Brian. 1992. *Constructing Postmodernism*. London: Routledge.
– 1987. *Postmodernist Fiction*. London: Routledge.
Morrissette, Bruce. 1971. "Un Héritage d'André Gide: la Duplication Intérieure." *Comparative Literature Studies* 8 (2): 125–42.
Nancy, Jean-Luc. 2004. *La Communauté désœuvrée*. Paris: C. Bourgois.
– 1991. *The Inoperative Community*. Translated by Peter Connor, Lisa Garbus, Michael Holland, and Simona Sawhney. Minneapolis: University of Minnesota Press.
"The Nature of The Beast: Apple and Avocado Salsa with Honey-Lime Dressing." n.d. The Nature of the Feast Archive, Minotaur Books. https://www.gamacheseries.com/the-nature-of-the-beast-apple-avocado-salsa/. Accessed 29 May 2023.
The Night Is a Strawberry: Cooking Our Way to Three Pines. n.d. Weblog. https://thenightisastrawberry.blogspot.com/. Accessed 29 May 2023.
Pennington, Gail. 2020. "The Real 'Three Pines.'" *St Louis Post-Dispatch*, 30 August B11.
– 2020. "There Is No Mystery about the Charm of the Real 'Three Pines.'" *St Louis Post-Dispatch*, 29 August. https://www.stltoday.com/travel/there-is-no-mystery-about-the-charm-of-the-real-three-pines/article_6a9636a8-2d5f-5a3e-9580-666ef733ee56.html.
Penny, Louise. n.d.a. Louise Penny Facebook page. https://www.facebook.com/louisepennyauthor. Accessed 29 May 2023.
– n.d.b. Newsletters Archive. https://www.louisepenny.com/newsletters.htm. Accessed 29 May 2023.
– n.d.c. Louise Penny Official Site http://www.louisepenny.com/.
– 2005. *Still Life*. New York: Minotaur Books.
– 2006. *A Fatal Grace*. New York: Minotaur Books.
– 2007. *The Cruelest Month*. New York: Minotaur Books.
– 2008. *A Rule against Murder*. New York: Minotaur Books.
– 2009. *The Brutal Telling*. New York: Minotaur Books.
– 2010. *Bury Your Dead*. New York: Minotaur Books.
– 2011. *A Trick of the Light*. New York: Minotaur Books.
– 2012. *The Beautiful Mystery*. New York: Minotaur Books.
– 2013a. *How the Light Gets In*. New York: Minotaur Books.
– 2013b. "Louise Penny with Margaret Cannon." 17 September. Video, 1:06:26. https://www.youtube.com/watch?v=2_vsfEr_pSg. Accessed 29 May 2023.
– 2014. *The Long Way Home*. New York: Minotaur Books.
– 2015. *The Nature of the Beast*. New York: Minotaur Books.
– 2016. *A Great Reckoning*. New York: Minotaur Books.
– 2017. *Glass Houses*. New York: Minotaur Books.
– 2018a. "In Conversation about *Kingdom of the Blind*." Talk sponsored by the St Louis County Library Foundation, St Louis, MO, 1 December.
– 2018b. *Kingdom of the Blind*. New York: Minotaur Books.
– 2019. *A Better Man*. New York: Minotaur Books.

– 2020. *All the Devils Are Here*. New York: Minotaur Books.
– 2021. *The Madness of Crowds*. New York: Minotaur Books.
Prijatel, Patricia. 2019. "How My Louise Penny Tour Helped Soothe My Anxious Spirit." *Psychology Today*, 26 June. https://www.psychologytoday.com/us/blog/all-is-well/201906/how-my-louise-penny-tour-helped-soothe-my-anxious-spirit. Accessed 29 May 2023.
"The Real Places of Three Pines: The Long Way Home." n.d. https://www.gamacheseries.com/the-long-way-home-real-place/. Accessed 29 May 2023.
Ricardou, Jean. 1973. *Le Nouveau Roman*. Paris: Éditions du Seuil.
Romano, Aja. 2021. "One Good Thing: These Dark Detective Novels Are Really about Ethics and Hope." *Vox*, 20 June. https://www.vox.com/22533094/inspector-gamache-louise-penny-cozy-series-mystery-novels. Accessed 29 May 2023.
Snow, Marcus. 2016. "Into the Abyss: A Study of the *mise en abyme*." PhD diss., London Metropolitan University. https://repository.londonmet.ac.uk/1106/1/SnowMarcus_IntoTheAbyss.pdf.
"Three Pines Tours." n.d. Three Pines Tours Official Site. https://www.threepinestours.com/. Accessed 29 May 2023.
Wolf, Werner. 2010. "*Mise en cadre*: A Neglected Counterpart to *Mise en abyme*." In *Post-classical Narratology: Approaches and Analyses*, edited by J. Alber and M. Fludernik, 58–82. Columbus: Ohio State University Press.

– CONTRIBUTORS –

DARREN BARDATI is a full professor and the founding director of the Sustainable Agriculture and Food Systems (SAFS) program at Bishop's University, where he has been employed since 1996. His research interests revolve around agroecology and sustainable foods systems, adaptation to climate change, and water management.

GORDON S. BARKER was educated at McGill University (BA economics, BA honours in history) and the College of William and Mary in Virginia (MA and PhD in history). He has been teaching at Bishop's University since 2006. A specialist in African American, revolutionary-era and civil war–era history, he has published two major books, chapters in peer-reviewed volumes, and articles and reviews in leading scholarly journals. He recently contributed an article titled "Reconsidering the Underground Railroad in Canada West" for the United States National Park Service and Dickinson College Underground Railroad Online Handbook, which can be accessed at https://housedivided.dickinson.edu/sites/ugrr/regional-essays/reconsidering-the-underground-railroad-in-canada-west-barker/.

CAROLINE BEAUDOIN is currently the editorial assistant to the chair of IEEE's CEB and ACC conferences. She is also a bilingual assessment reviewer for Development Dimensions International, a multinational human resources and leadership company that specializes in development consultancy. Her current research interests focus on material and visual cultural studies of Quebec's Eastern Townships.

HAROLD BÉRUBÉ is a full professor at the Université de Sherbrooke. He is interested in the political and cultural history of North American cities and their inhabitants. In 2019, he published *Unité, autonomie, démocratie. Une histoire de l'Union des municipalités du Québec* (1919–2019) (Boréal), in which he examines the history of Quebec's main municipal association and its role as mediator between municipalities, the Quebec provincial government, and municipal transnational networks. His current research project focuses on the role of the press in the urban ecosystem.

PHILIPPE CHARLAND (PhD geography, McGill University, 2005) is a professor of Abenaki language at Kiuna Institution and a lecturer in Abenaki language at the Université de Sherbrooke and Bishop's University. He has also taught Abenaki language for several years in the Abenaki reserves of Odanak and Wôlinak, and in Montreal. His research interests include toponymy, geography, history, and linguistic issues related to the Aboriginal peoples of the Northeast but more specifically in relation to the Abenaki. He has worked on various projects related to language, including a French–Abenaki dictionary and a grammar of the Abenaki language. He is a member of the Office de la langue abénakise.

LORRAINE DEROCHER is an adjunct professor in the Faculty of Law, Centre d'études du religieux contemporain at the Université de Sherbrooke in Quebec, and a researcher at the Centre for Research on Children and Families at McGill University. Her work focuses on the protection of minors in isolated communities and in sectarian groups. The author of four books and several articles, she also works as an expert consultant and trainer for youth protection agencies and professionals.

ANTHONY DI MASCIO is a professor in the School of Education at Bishop's University. His research examines the historical forces that have shaped mass schooling. He is the author of the award-winning book *The Idea of Popular Schooling in Upper Canada: Print Culture, Public Discourse, and the Demand for Education* (McGill-Queen's University Press, 2012).

HENRI DION is writing a master's thesis on the roles and particularities of the local daily press in the city of Sherbrooke, Quebec, in the first half of the twentieth century. In 2023, he co-organized the conference "Perspectives croisées en histoire de la presse," in which he presented findings on the Eastern Townships' regional press around 1910. Besides the North American press, his interests also include local and regional history, urban development, and architecture. In recent years, he participated in a number of related research projects, and worked with local museums.

CLAUDE GÉLINAS is an anthropologist and full professor in the Department of Philosophy and Applied Ethics at the Université de Sherbrooke in Quebec. His current research focuses on Indigenous religious rights in Canada and religious diversity in Quebec.

CHERYL GOSSELIN is a professor in the Sociology Department at Bishop's University, where she has taught for thirty-three years. She has been involved with the Eastern Townships Resource Centre as a researcher, board member, and president; currently she is the ETRC's secretary treasurer. She is also very active in the Eastern Townships English-speaking community as a researcher as well as board member of the Townshippers' Association. Her research focuses on the English-speaking population of the region and throughout Quebec, the settlement of newcomers to the Townships, identity negotiation between the French-speaking majority and Quebec's linguistic minority demographic, as well as attachment to place among immigrants and Anglophone Quebecers who are often framed as "other" by the dominant francophone majority.

LOUIS-GEORGES HARVEY, emeritus professor of history at Bishop's University, specializes in the history of Canadian and Québécois political culture and political discourse. His recent publications include *Une lecture impériale de la résistance de 1837 et de sa répression: le rapport Ogden*, with Yvan Lamonde (Quebec: Presses de l'Université Laval, 2023), and "Louis-Joseph Papineau et le petit écran: Le demi-dieu (1961) de Louis-Georges Carrier," *Cahiers des Dix* (2022).

ANDREW C. HOLMAN is professor of history and director of the Canadian Studies Program at Bridgewater State University in Massachusetts. He is author or editor of eight books, including *A Hotly Contested Affair: Hockey in Canada. The National Game in Documents* (Champlain Society, 2020).

JANE JENSON is *professeure émérite* of political science at the Université de Montréal. In retirement, she turned to research on the social history of Canton d'Orford and the Eastern Townships more generally. Her work on the political economy of nineteenth-century Orford has appeared in *Histoire sociale/Social History* and that about soldiers from the Townships who fought in the American Civil War was published in the *Canadian Historical Review* and *Histoire sociale/Social History*. In 2023, she was awarded the prix Léon-Gérin, which is a Prix du Québec, and in 2022 the Innis-Gérin Medal from the Royal Society of Canada. Both awards recognize an outstanding career in the social sciences.

CHRISTOPHER KIRKEY is director of the Center for the Study of Canada and Institute on Quebec Studies at State University of New York at Plattsburgh. A scholar of comparative foreign policy and international relations theory, he has been a professor at Bridgewater State University (1993–2001), Columbia

University (2002–12), and SUNY Plattsburgh (2002–present). His most recent work is (with Richard Nimijean) *The Construction of Canadian Identity from Abroad* (Palgrave Macmillan, 2022). He has published books and book chapters with a variety of publishers including Oxford University Press, Routledge, Palgrave Macmillan, University of Ottawa Press, University of Toronto Press, and McGill-Queen's University Press. He has guest-edited issues in and contributed articles to several journals, including *Canadian Journal of Political Science, International Journal, Canadian Foreign Policy Journal, Armed Forces & Society, American Review of Canadian Studies, British Journal of Canadian Studies, Journal of Canadian Studies, International Journal of Canadian Studies, London Journal of Canadian Studies, Quebec Studies,* and the *Journal of Eastern Townships Studies.* He served as president for the Association for Canadian Studies in the United States, and the Middle Atlantic and New England Council for Canadian Studies.

JACK LITTLE is a professor emeritus in the History Department of Simon Fraser University. His most recent book is *Reading the Diaries of Henry Trent: The Everyday Life of a Canadian Englishman, 1842–1898* (McGill-Queen's University Press, 2021).

RODERICK MACLEOD is a course lecturer at McGill University in Montreal. Among his recent publications are *Montreal: The History of a North American City* (co-edited with Dany Fougères, McGill-Queen's University Press, 2018) and "The High Ground: Mansions, Mythology and the Mountain," in *Crossing Boundaries and Constructing Linkages: The History of Montreal's Square Mile in National and International Context,* edited by Elizabeth Kirkland, Don Nerbas, and Dimitry Anastakis (forthcoming, University of Toronto Press, 2024).

J. DEBBIE MANN is professor emerita of French in the Department of Foreign Languages and Literature at Southern Illinois University Edwardsville. Her current research focuses on Québécois literature and popular culture. Her publications include articles on works by Jacques Poulin and Louis Hémon and, most recently, the novels of Louise Penny (*Journal of Eastern Township Studies,* 48, 2020).

JEAN L. MANORE is dean of humanities and professor of history, Bishop's University. Her research interests focus on First Nations/settler relations in Canada, with a particular interest in treaty and Aboriginal rights. Her recent studies have included an examination of decolonization efforts within universities and the re-assertion of Abenaki history within the transnational area of the Canada–US border.

CERI MORGAN is professor of place-writing and geohumanities in the School of Humanities at Keele University in the United Kingdom. Her most recent publication is "Québec's New Regional Fiction: Louise Penny and Johanne Seymour," *British Journal of Canadian Studies* (2021).

MARY ANNE POUTANEN teaches interdisciplinary studies in the Quebec Studies Program at McGill University and at the McGill Institute for the Study of Canada and part-time in the Department of History at Concordia University, where she is an affiliate professor. She is a long-standing member of the Montreal History Group and co-director of the axis "Immigration, Daily Life, and Religion" at the Centre for Interdisciplinary Research on Montreal at McGill. She has received awards for her book *Beyond Brutal Passions: Prostitution in Early Nineteenth-Century Montreal* and for a co-authored monograph with Roderick MacLeod, *A Meeting of the People: School Boards and Protestant Communities in Quebec, 1801–1998*. Her current SSHRC- and FRQSC-funded research focuses on women who kept public houses and retailed groceries and alcohol in mid-nineteenth-century Montreal. Her next project, with Liz Kirkland, will study female domestic servants in Montreal, 1870–1920.

CAMILLE SASSEVILLE is a graduate of the Université de Sherbrooke with a degree in applied communications and a master's degree in intercultural mediation.

– INDEX –

Page numbers followed by (f) refer to illustrations; page numbers followed by (t) refer to tables.